EIGHTH EDITION

A Short History of Western Civilization

Volume Two: Since 1600

RICHARD E. SULLIVAN
Michigan State University

DENNIS SHERMAN
John Jay College of Criminal Justice
City University of New York

JOHN B. HARRISON
Late Professor Emeritus of History
Michigan State University

McGraw-Hill, Inc.

New York   St. Louis   San Francisco   Auckland   Bogotá
Caracas   Lisbon   London   Madrid   Mexico City   Milan
Montreal   New Delhi   San Juan   Singapore   Sydney   Tokyo   Toronto

to Mary, Vivian, and Pat

The present overwhelms our forgotten selves;
but we are what we were,
with only a frosting of changes
—D.S.

A Short History of Western Civilization
Volume Two: Since 1600

 This book is printed on recycled, acid-free paper containing 10% postconsumer waste.

2 3 4 5 6 7 8 9 0   DOH DOH   9 0 9 8 7 6 5 4

ISBN 0-07-026900-9

This book was set in Palatino by Ruttle, Shaw & Wetherill, Inc.
The editors were Pamela Gordon and Larry Goldberg;
the production supervisor was Richard A. Ausburn.
The cover was designed by Katherine Hulse.
The photo researcher was Elsa Peterson.
R. R. Donnelley & Sons Company was printer and binder.

Credits
COVER: John O'Connor, "St. Pancras Hotel and Station from Pentonville Road," 1884, Museum of London. *PART OPENING PHOTOS: Part Five,* Alinari/Art Resource; *Part Six,* The Granger Collection; *Part Seven,* NASA. *MAPS: Map 40.1:* From *Civilizations of the West: The Human Adventure* by Richard L. Greaves, Robert Zaller, and Jennifer Tolbert Roberts. Copyright © 1992 by HarperCollins Publishers. Reprinted by permission. *Map 59.1, left:* From Perry, Marvin, Myrna Chase, James R. Jacob, Margaret C. Jacob, and Theodore H. Von Laue, *Western Civilization: Ideas, Politics and Society,* Fourth Edition. Copyright © 1992 by Houghton Mifflin Company. Used with permission. *Map 59.1, top right:* Copyright Carto Ltd. Used by permission of Carpress International Press Agency, Brussels. *Map 59.3:* From *Facts On File.* Copyright © 1992 by Facts On File. Reprinted with permission by Facts On File, Inc., New York.

Library of Congress Cataloging-in-Publication Data

Sullivan, Richard Eugene, (date).
   A short history of Western civilization / Richard E. Sullivan,
Dennis Sherman, John B. Harrison.—8th ed.
      p.   cm.
   Rev. ed. of: A short history of Western civilization / John B.
Harrison. 7th ed. c1990.
   Includes bibliographical references and indexes.
   Contents: v. 1. To 1778—v. 2. Since 1600.
   ISBN 0-07-026899-1—ISBN 0-07-026900-9.
   1. Civilization, Western—History.   I. Sherman, Dennis.
II. Harrison, John Baugham.   III. Harrison, John Baugham. Short
history of Western civilization.   IV. Title.
CB245.S9415   1994
909'.09812—dc20   93-42015

ABOUT THE AUTHORS

Richard E. Sullivan was born and raised near Doniphan, Nebraska. He received a B. A. degree from the University of Nebraska in 1942, and an M.A. degree and a Ph.D. degree from the University of Illinois in 1947 and 1949 respectively. His doctorate was earned in the field of medieval history. He has taught history at Northeast Missouri State Teachers' College (1949–1954) and at Michigan State University (1954 until his retirement in 1989). While at Michigan State University he has served as chairman of the Department of History (1967–1970), Dean of the College of Arts and Letters (1970–1979), and Associate Provost (1984–1987). Professor Sullivan held a Fulbright Research Fellowship and a John Simon Guggenheim Fellowship to Belgium in 1961–1962. He is a Fellow in the Medieval Academy of America. He is the author of *The Coronation of Charlemagne* (1959), *Heirs of the Roman Empire* (1960); *Aix-La-Chapelle in the Age of Charlemagne* (1963), *Speaking for Clio* (1991), and *Christian Missionary Activity in the Early Middle Ages* (forthcoming). His articles have appeared in many scholarly journals.

Dennis Sherman is Professor of History at John Jay College of Criminal Justice, the City University of New York. He received his B.A. (1962) and J.D. (1965) from the University of California at Berkeley and his Ph.D. (1970) from the University of Michigan. He was Visiting Professor at the University of Paris (1978–1979, and 1985). He received the Ford Foundation Prize Fellowship (1968–1969, 1969–1970), a fellowship from the Council for Research on Economic History (1971–1972), and fellowships from the National Endowment for the Humanities (1973–1976). His publications include *Western Civilization: Images and Interpretations* (1991), *World Civilizations: Sources, Images, and Interpretations* (co-author), a series of introductions in the Garland Library of War and Peace, several articles and reviews on nineteenth-century French economic and social history in American and European journals, and short fiction in literary journals.

John B. Harrison was born in Lawrenceville, Virginia, and grew up in Rich Square, North Carolina. He received his B.A. and M.A. at the University of North Carolina, and his Ph.D. at the University of Wisconsin. He also studied at the Sorbonne. He taught history at Lees Junior College, Jackson, Kentucky, the University of Wisconsin extension, Ohio Northern University, and Michigan State University, where he was Professor Emeritus of History. He was Visiting Professor at the University of North Carolina, 1963–1964. Professor Harrison was a member of the American Historical Association and the Society for French Historical Studies. During seven trips to Europe he visited twenty-one countries. He had also traveled in the Far and the Middle East, Africa, and Latin America. He is the author of *This Age of Global Strife* (1952), and of a number of articles and book reviews.

CONTENTS

PREFACE

[*Publisher's Note: In order to provide an alternative to the hardcover edition,* A Short History of Western Civilization *is being made available in a three-volume paperbound edition. Volume One includes Chapters 1–36; Volume Two, Chapters 31–59; and* Renaissance to the Present *volume, Chapters 25–59. The page numbering and cross-references in these chapters remain the same as in the hardcover text.*]

In this eighth edition of *A Short History of Western Civilization*, we have attempted to achieve the right mix of continuity and change. Those features that made the seventh and previous editions so successful have been retained. We have kept our account brief enough so it offers readers a realistic opportunity to absorb a meaningful overview of the essentials of the history of Western civilization. The scope of the book is not limited to European history; brief treatments of other parts of the world, such as the United States, and non-Western civilizations as they have come to interact with the Western world, are included to put Western civilization into a broader context. Introductory and retrospective essays at the beginning and end of each of the units of the book provide a broad summarizing perspective on major historical eras. Primary documents introduce readers to the sources historians use to investigate a subject. The interpretative essays featuring points on which historians disagree are designed to encourage readers to develop a healthy skepticism toward accepted generalizations about the past and to learn to ask questions about the meaning of historical investigation. The large number of maps and illustrations highlights and complements the written text. The suggested reading lists offer alternatives for deeper study of topics. The student and instructor's guides are available to assist in making full use of this book.

Several important changes have been made in this edition to improve the quality and appeal of the book. There has been an additional infusion of social history and women's history into the text, continuing the changes already made in this direction in the seventh and sixth editions. The addition of this material reflects a growing consensus in modern scholarship that such matters need greater attention in order to portray past human experience fully and accurately. Several parts of the book have been reorganized to better integrate our understanding of the past. There have been extensive revisions of the text to include the most recent historical scholarship, and in some cases new sections have been written. A number of illustrations are new to this edition. Most of the maps have been revised and clarified. Seven "Historians' Sources" sections have been created for this edition, providing a balance to the "Where Historians Disagree" essays and the introductory "History and the Historian" essay. A new chapter covering the extraordinarily important developments of the past few years has been written. The suggested readings have been completely revised and updated.

As in previous editions, our goal is to produce a high-quality, clearly written, useful, and flexible account of Western civilization. We are indebted to numerous teachers and students who have aided us in this effort. We hope this book can serve as the basis for an effective survey of the history of Western civilization, a subject that remains essential for any understanding of who we are and what of significance is happening in the present.

We would like to thank the following reviewers: Janet Cornelius, Danville Area Community College; Kenneth E. Cutler, Indiana University; John C. Moore, Hofstra University; James Parry, Seattle University; and Carl Pohlhammer, Monterey Peninsula College.

RICHARD E. SULLIVAN
DENNIS SHERMAN

HISTORY AND THE HISTORIAN

This book seeks to expand and enrich our readers' connections with the past. Before each of you becomes engaged in that adventure, we ask you to reflect for a moment on some of the challenges involved in discovering, understanding, and retelling what has already happened.

Why should we turn our faces from the present and the future to explore what has already happened? Despite the inclination of many in our time to take seriously Henry Ford's pronouncement that "History is bunk," most of us find looking backward irresistible, as did our forebears. Many have found and still find the past inherently interesting, chiefly because a venture into that realm offers us an opportunity to relive in our minds all kinds of experiences otherwise closed to us by limitations imposed by the cultural environment in which we live. Others have been and still are convinced that learning about the past has an important social function. It can inform us about who and what we are as human beings. It can shed light on contemporary conditions, either by providing an understanding of how things came to be what they are or by supplying analogies that help us to comprehend our situation and formulate solutions to issues that face our society. Societies have especially prized history as an instrument for socializing their members (particularly their young), that is, for teaching them how and how not to behave and to think in ways that are appropriate to the cultural milieu in which they find themselves. As you begin your venture into the past, we urge each of you to reflect on why you are making the journey. Whatever your answer, it will make a difference in what you find and how you interpret your discoveries.

Also, we urge each of you to be mindful that the past is a unique territory. It involves an infinite number of "happenings," each of which is finished and therefore cannot be experienced directly. We can gain access to these already completed events only by reconstructing them in our minds and putting those constructs into words.

Thus, there is always a distance between what actually happened in the past and what those who try to reconstruct the past can discover and make understandable. As a consequence, the exploration of the past goes on continuously, and its reconstruction incessantly changes as those who explore it discover more information and bring new perspectives to bear on their interpretations of their findings.

Although any person is capable of reconstructing the past and often does so with respect to his or her personal or family past, most societies have entrusted that task of discovering the past to specialists, called historians. Most of them agree that there is a basic methodology suited to the task of reconstructing what happened. A first step involves formulating a question about past happenings. For example, this book was shaped by the question of what happened in the past that made the present world what it is. Or, on a smaller scale, suppose you asked yourself what happened to you between the ages of six and eight that relates to what you are now. The range of such questions is obviously infinite; as a result, historical inquiry is richly and unpredictably varied. In many ways the vitality of inquiry about the past depends on the imagination and ingenuity of historians in formulating problems they wish to study.

Once having defined a "subject," the historian starts searching for empirical, verifiable evidence that might provide an answer to his or her question. In the case of your interest in your earlier years, you might begin to look for letters and diaries, school records, picture albums, old clothing in the attic, toys in the basement, oral accounts of those who knew you then, and anything else possibly connected with your activities during that period in your life. What you would be looking for are "traces" left behind that provide evidence that something happened in the past involving you. These traces are what historians call primary sources, which are pieces of evidence produced by human beings who were directly involved in the past activity under investigation or by those in a position to know what happened. Primary sources exist in many forms. Most important are written documents in which observers of past events recorded what they thought happened; this book contains some examples of primary documents. But other kinds of primary sources can help historians find out what happened, including buildings, artworks, maps, pottery, tools, clothing, and oral traditions. Primary sources seldom speak to the historian in clear terms. Historians must subject them to rigorous criticism in order to assess their value as witnesses to what actually happened and to extract information from them that has a bearing on what the historian wants to know. In addition to primary sources, historians must also take into account and critically evaluate what are called secondary sources, which consist of the works of other historians who have examined the same general subject and the same segment of time. You will find examples of how secondary sources are used in the "Where Historians Disagree" sections of this book.

The search for, criticism of, and extraction of data from sources by no means finishes the historian's work. In our hypothetical cases involving your earlier years, when you had gathered and evaluated all the sources you could find, you would still not be able to say what had happened to you; all you would have is a collection of raw data. You, like all historians, would have to put your data together into some form that would approximate the realities in which you were involved then. This is a formidable task. In oversimplified terms it involves a series of choices: what sources deserve the greatest weight; what data are not relevant; how the sources relate to one another; how to organize the data contained in the sources in a way that would convey a meaningful and believable account of what happened; what literary devices to use in order to permit others to experience vicariously and to understand what happened. The process of converting data into history can never be totally objective, for historians inevitably decide these issues in terms of their own perspective and their own values. For this reason, many prefer to call the reconstruction of the past an art rather than a science.

In a rough way historians tend to reflect one of two perspectives in organizing their data to provide a comprehensible reconstruction of past reality. Some, representing a humanistic orientation, see the past in terms of unique actions and events that provide insights into the human situation in a particular setting. These historians tend to present the past as a narrative, telling a story that unfolds in a chronological order with each succeeding episode having its own significance but somehow related to and conditioned by what went before. If you were to choose this model in reconstructing your early life, you would proceed day by day, focusing attention on unique events in your experience that had a particular meaning to you then and something to do with what happened to you the next day or month or year. Other historians, reflecting a social science orientation, look for generalized patterns emerging from the record of the past. They tend to focus on repetitive commonalities rather than on the uniqueness of each happening, on thematic rather than chronological arrangement of evidence, on analysis rather than description, and on causal relationship linking data rather than linear connections. Sometimes they even seek to extract from their reading of the past generalized statements about human behavior that suggest how the future may unfold. Your own history written in this mode might highlight common occurrences in your life, an analysis of the relative weight of different experiences in making you what you are now, and what your experiences tell about what might happen to other children in the future. Quite clearly, each perspective produces a different history. Perhaps a combination of the two allows the fullest and most meaningful reconstruction of the past. We have tried to achieve that end in our reconstruction of the past.

Given the vastness and the complexity of the past, historians have been forced to adopt strategies that allow them to segment the past into manageable entities. One means to this end is to divide the past into discrete segments of time, each of which has common features that allow it to be treated as an entity. Another is to treat the past in terms of major topics around which data can be clustered to create meaning. Still another way of segmenting the past is to focus on geographical areas. As each of you proceeds through this book, you will become aware that we have employed all of these strategies as a means of making the past more understandable. Be aware that these are artificial devices, imposed on the record by historians. Choices have been made in defining periodization schemes, significant topics, and geographical partitions. Obviously, those choices have an important bearing on how the past is reconstructed. We urge each of you to be alert to the uses we have made of these conventions and to think about what the consequences might have been had other periodization systems, topical approaches, and geographical divisions been chosen.

Historical research and writing are decisively affected by judgments made by historians as to what facet of human activity is most important in shaping the destinies of individuals and collectives in the past. For example, in reconstructing your personal history, you might conclude that private reading was more significant to you than formal schooling or that your family's economic status was more important in shaping your life than its political affiliation. Such choices would obviously affect how you reconstructed your past. In viewing the past from a broader perspective, historians are influenced by similar considerations. Some argue that political factors are crucial in forming societies, while others insist that economic conditions are decisive. Such formulations have produced several widely recognized categories or branches of history: political history, economic history, social history, intellectual history, religious history, and cultural history. The marks of this compartmentalization of past events will be evident in this book, calling on each of you to think about what facet of human activity was most crucial in determining the course of events at any particular stage in human development. Perhaps the supreme challenge for historians is achieving a synthesis that will produce a version of the past embracing all aspects of human activity. In presenting our reconstruction of the past we have sought to meet that challenge, and we urge each of you to try to grasp the whole picture that undergirds the diverse activities into which the human experience can be categorized.

Each passing generation brings changes in approaches to the past that provide particular stimulation to the historical consciousness and a special thrust to historical inquiry. In recent years three broad developments have been particularly influential. We have tried to integrate some of the results of these developments into our reconstruction of the past.

First, there has been a broadening of the approach to social history. Social historians increasingly emphasize looking at the past "from the bottom up" by studying the everyday experiences and attitudes of "ordinary" people, including especially subordinated groups, rather than concentrating on political leaders, elite groups, and "high culture" produced by great thinkers, writers, and artists. To recount the history of these heretofore "silent" people and to assess its significance in the total picture of the past, social historians have had to ask new questions and to make innovative use of sources often overlooked by traditional historians. Their efforts have greatly expanded the stage that we call the past, increased the number of actors on that stage, and changed the theme of the drama played out there in ways that have radically altered our understanding of the dynamic forces that gave shape to the past.

The second development has been the emergence of what is often termed "the new history" (although, like many elements of social history, its roots go back several decades). The new history has been shaped by the marriage of history and the social sciences. By applying the techniques and concepts formulated by demographers, psychologists, anthropologists, geographers, physiologists, linguists, and biologists derived from their study of the present, historians have been able to open immense new vistas on the past pertaining to matters of vital importance to the human condition. Just to cite a few examples, we are learning much more about past birth and death rates, marriage patterns, fertility rates, family size, child rearing, sexuality, death, disease, environmental conditions, patterns of popular belief, the impact of technology, ethnic stereotypes, insanity, and criminality. Many historians practicing the new history rely on comparative and statistical analyses of quantitative data to expand their knowledge of what happened in the past, a methodological technique that has been greatly facilitated by the use of computers. The result of the new history is unmistakable: the past looks different than it once did.

A third development has been the growing interest in women's history. Traditionally history was written from a male perspective and was focused primarily on the thoughts and behavior of men. Women's history attempts to correct this neglect of women in history and the distortions that inevitably result. It focuses on women's experiences and on the roles women played in a variety of developments in the past. It seeks to discern and clarify what has been unique and distinctive in the past experiences of women. And it tries to alert us to gender bias in the way historical questions are posed, evidence is evaluated, and history is written. Once again, the past has been enlarged and a different view of what mattered has taken shape.

Perhaps all of these considerations relative to reconstructing the past lead to one final and all-important point: Establishing a relationship with the past presents a real challenge to our intellectual faculties. Access to the past is possible only to those willing to perform a diverse range of mental activities: posing questions about what is essential in human existence; searching out evidence; evaluating the worth of that evidence;

making judgments about the relative weight of different kinds of data; establishing causal relationships; organizing information into intelligible patterns; interpreting the meaning of newly acquired knowledge; communicating new knowledge and insight to others in ways that are intelligible and relevant to their situation. All of these are essential mental powers that each of us must exercise if we are to live usefully in the present. It follows, then, that the greatest value to come from the effort to connect with the past stems from the way that enterprise stretches our minds and hones our intellectual powers along lines that equip us to respond more effectively to challenges that face us and our society now and in the future. We hope that your venture into the past that we have reconstructed in the pages that follow turns out to be a great intellectual experience. Indeed, the writing of this book was that for us, not the least because we had to stretch our minds in order to cope with new evidence about what happened, changing views about how to judge things past, and new questions about what really matters in the human experience.

INTRODUCTION

To discover the roots of modern Western civilization, we must go back nearly six thousand years to the river valleys of the southwest Asia and northeast Africa. Subsequent peoples constantly reshaped and enriched the basic ingredients of civilized life established there and spread them over a large part of the globe, including Europe. A brief overview of those complex developments may be helpful in providing a context for the segment of the history of Western civilization that will be covered in detail in this volume.

THE ANCIENT NEAR EAST, 4000–300 B.C.

Over an immensely long prehistoric period the human species slowly developed the unique physical and mental faculties and the basic cultural equipment that made possible the first higher civilizations in the unique environment of the river valleys of the Near East. About 4000 B.C. some of these prehistoric groups who had already perfected the basic techniques of agriculture found ways to control the floodwaters of the Tigris-Euphrates and Nile rivers and to take advantage of the rich soil watered by these rivers. Their feat involved not only the technical skills required to create and maintain complex irrigation systems but also, more importantly, the organization of large numbers of people into institutional patterns that promoted planning, disciplined cooperation, and specialization of labor. These organizational structures triggered the leap forward from the limited Stone Age cultures to higher civilizations. In both Mesopotamia and Egypt, the focal points of the new order were urban centers directed by powerful rulers whose authority was sanctioned primarily by religion. In order to exercise their authority over their subjects, Mesopotamian priest-kings and Egyptian pharoahs developed highly sophisticated institutions: bureaucracies, armies, systems of taxation and record keeping, law codes, courts. In the hands of a governing elite these instrumentalities served chiefly to plan and direct the activities of agricultural laborers, merchants, and artisans whose efforts combined to produce the material wealth that sustained higher civilizations.

The successful mastery of the river valley environment and the material wealth that resulted stimulated a wide range of cultural activities that characterized higher civilization in Mesopotamia and Egypt. Writing developed to serve not only the practical ends of political and economic life but also as a means of expressing ideas about the human condition. Those ideas were shaped mainly by religious systems based on a belief in powerful nature deities that were thought to control both natural processes and human destiny. In order to praise and please them, huge temples were constructed and elaborately decorated, sculpture was perfected to portray them and the earthly rulers who served them, myths were recorded to explain their origins and activities, and data about natural phenomena were collected to help predict their behavior. The result was a splendid art, literature, and science that enriched Mesopotamian and Egyptian life and provided models of civilized existence for future generations living far beyond the two great river valley systems.

The maturation of these first civilizations occurred over a long perod of time—from about 4000 to about 1750 B.C.—and these ancient centers remained vital long after the latter date. However, between about 1750 and 800 B.C. a new chapter of ancient history unfolded, characterized by the spread of the wonders wrought by the Mesopotamians and the Egyptians beyond the narrow confines of the river valleys to embrace a wide sweep of southwest Asia and northeast Africa and to involve new peoples in the benefits and the burdens of sustaining civilized life. Several factors were involved in this process of diffusion and assimilation: the outward thrust of the original creators of higher civilization; imitation of the superior ways of the river valley civilizations by peoples long settled on their fringes; and the intrusion into the Near Eastern scene of new peoples who created new centers of political power directed by leaders anxious to share the benefits of civilized life. During the early part of this period, between about 1750 and 1200 B.C., the agents of diffusion were numerous: the Kassites, who asserted influence over peoples living east and north of the Tigris-Euphrates Valley; the Egyptians, who thrust outward into Libya, Nubia, and Syria-Palestine; the Hittites, who spread their civilization to Asia Minor; and the Minoans, who developed a brilliant civilization on the island of Crete that asserted a powerful influence over the entire Aegean world, including the Greek peninsula. After about 1200 B.C. these major agents of diffusion suffered an eclipse, but other peoples—such as the Phoenicians, the Arameans, and the Hebrews—continued the process until about 800 B.C.

Of all the peoples prominent during the era of diffusion, the Hebrews deserve special attention, chiefly because of their religious system, which set them apart in their own time, provided the point of departure for such other religions as Christianity and Islam, and has persisted to the present. Originating as a loosely knit group of nomadic tribes, the Hebrews moved into the mainstream of Near Eastern history as a result of a series of encounters with the more advanced Mesopotamians, Egyptians, and Canaanites from whom they slowly became acclimated to the ways of higher civilization. Their early history culminated with the establishment in Palestine of an independent kingdom that under the leadership of kings Saul, David, and Solomon (ca. 1020–930 B.C.) was among the major states of the contemporary world. However, that moment of political greatness was brief; a combination of internal quarrels and the armed might of more powerful neighbors eventually obliterated the independent Hebrew state, leaving behind only a unique religious community held together by shared beliefs that had been shaped through centuries of Hebrew triumph and tribulation. That religion centered on belief in a single all-powerful, righteous god existing outside of nature and time who had entered into a covenant with the Hebrews. By the terms of that covenant the He-

brews became a "chosen people," destined to be the instruments through which the divine plan for humanity was to be realized within the framework of history. But to be worthy of that special role had a price: The covenant obligated the Hebrews to obey God's law. That law not only required the observance of ritual practices under the direction of priestly leaders but also involved moral responsibilities. It stressed the obligation of each individual to treat others with righteousness and justice, and it imposed on the Hebrew community and its leaders a collective responsibility to act justly and mercifully toward all of its members. With its emphasis on a universe ordered by a single, transcendant, just, and merciful deity and on behavior shaped to conform to the purposes for which such a God had created human beings, ancient Judaism opened new vistas that challenged the human spirit to create a social and moral order defined in terms that transcended the norms governing the lives and values of most other early Near Eastern societies.

The long period of diffusion of the basic elements of Mesopotamian and Egyptian civilization across extensive area of western Asia and northeastern Africa eventually provided large numbers of people with common technical skills and equipment, interdependent economic interests, shared cultural values, and similar religious beliefs and practices. Advancing cultural homogeneity invited attempts at political unification, and adventuresome leaders were at hand to respond to that opportunity. The result was the creation of extensive empires whose histories dominated the Near East from about 800 to 300 B.C. The most successful of the empire builders were first the Assyrians and then the Persians, both of whose empires were created by military conquest. The rulers of these empires strove to create political and social structures that would promote peace, order, and harmony among various peoples of different ethnic, religious, and cultural backgrounds. Their efforts helped to bring ancient Near Eastern civilization to its peak, and many of the achievements of these cosmopolitan societies, especially those of the Persian Empire, were passed along to other peoples yet to establish their place in history.

Yet, for all the majesty and power of these empires, they proved fragile, as was demonstrated by the ease with which Alexander the Great and his Greek-Macedonian armies toppled the Persian Empire. Alexander's victories showed that the ancient Near Eastern world, despite its remarkable accomplishments, was losing its vitality and that other peoples were ready to take the lead in shaping Western destiny. However, these newcomers were to benefit in untold ways from earlier achievements in government, economic life, social organization, art, literature, science, and religion.

GRECO-ROMAN CIVILIZATION, 1200 B.C.–A.D. 500

While the civilizational patterns of the ancient Near East were reaching maturity in the huge Persian Empire, a new civilization was developing to the west, one destined to find its ultimate locus in the Mediterranean basin and its chief creative agents in the Greeks and the Romans.

This new civilization originated in the lands washed by the Aegean Sea—the Greek peninsula, the western coast of Asia Minor, and the islands that dotted the Aegean. Beginning about 2000 B.C., these people—the Greeks—were affected by powerful influences from the more advanced civilizations of the Near East, resulting in a chapter in Greek history called the Mycenaean Age, during which there were many signs that the Greek world would be folded into the increasingly homogeneous cultural patterns of the Near East. However, around 1200 B.C. forces beyond their control cut the Greeks off from these contacts. In subsequent centuries the Greeks developed their own unique pattern of life and began to spread it around the Mediterranean as colonizers and traders. Central to that development was a particular institution that provided the framework within which Greek civilization evolved: the *polis*, or city-state. Over time several hundred independent city-states emerged in the Aegean basin. Although there was infinite variety in their structure, certain features were common to all. Each city-state was small in area and population. In each *polis*, group life focused on an urban center where there were concentrated political, economic, religious, and cultural activities that bore directly on the lives of the city-state's rural and urban inhabitants. Direct, active participation in the affairs of these intimate communities increasingly became a precious aspect of the life of each citizen. One unique feature was the development of mechanisms that involved citizens (only males were citizens) in making the ultimate political decisions which determined the course of collective life; thus, some degree of direct democracy was a common feature of the ancient Greek *polis*. Involvement in public affairs nourished a fierce patriotism among the citizens of each *polis* which made them eager to expend their talents in the services of the larger community.

As the many small, independent, inward-oriented city-states developed in the crowded and resource-poor Aegean world, a challenge emerged to test the Greek system: the problem of intercity relationships. In the early stages of Greek development intercity rivalry was muted by the economic safety valve provided by overseas colonization and by Panhellenic ties based on a common language and shared religious practices and cultural values. Indeed, at a crucial point in Greek history early in the fifth century B.C., several major city-states joined forces to repel a Persian attack that threatened to absorb the Greek world into the Persian Empire. But eventually rivalry among the proud communities, each claiming the absolute right of self-determination, gained the upper hand to dominate Greek history during the fifth and early fourth centuries B.C. A key factor fueling this rivalry was the imperialist ambition of Athens, the most democratic and creative of all the city-states. The mounting fear of Athenian domination ultimately led to the Peloponnesian Wars (431–404 B.C.), which pitted two great alliances of city-states, respectively led by Athens and Sparta, against each other in a destructive struggle that depleted the material resources of the participants, weakened the institutional fabric of the *polis*, and diminished the morale that sustained civic life. Despite Athens' ultimate defeat, the senseless rivalry continued. These struggles so weakened the Greeks that they were unable to resist conquest by the Macedonians, who, after a decisive victory in 338 B.C., imposed a peace that constricted the traditional independence of the *polis*.

Before the world of the city-states succumbed

to conquest, however, the Greeks had made their mark in another way. They shaped a view of the universe and of the place of humans in it that stood in sharp contrast with the values undergirding Near Eastern civilization. As expressed in a brilliant art, literature, philosophy, and science, the Greek cultural achievement was intensely humanistic, placing human beings on center stage. It stressed harmony between humans and nature, coexisting in an ordered universe that operated according to laws implicit in its very nature. It exalted the power of reason, which enabled humans to understand the natural world, solve problems through their own intelligence, and fashion ways of conducting their lives that allowed them to be good. It emphasized restraint and balance in human conduct as keys to happiness. It celebrated a spirit of inquiry that pushed men and women to learn more about themselves and their world. Inspired by these concepts, Greek thinkers, artists, and writers greatly expanded their knowledge and understanding of humanity and the natural world, all of which they shared with their fellow citizens in the environment provided by the *polis*. The quest to realize the Greek vision of human potential has inspired thought and action in the Western world since the Golden Age of the fifth century B.C.

The conquest of the Greek city-states by the Macedonians opened a new chapter in the history of Greco-Roman civilization called the Hellenistic Age, whose history extended from the early fourth to the late first century B.C. The essential feature of this era was the geographic extension of Greek civilization. The Greeks themselves had begun to spread their pattern of life and culture in the Mediterranean basin as early as the eighth and seventh centuries B.C., chiefly through colonizing efforts that planted Greek city-states in southern Italy, southern France, and around the Black Sea. Led by Alexander the Great (ruled 336–323 B.C.), Greeks and Macedonians joined forces to conquer the Persian Empire and establish Greek political, economic, and cultural domination over a large segment of the ancient Near East. Large numbers of Greeks migrated to the conquered lands to reinforce Greek domination. The political history of the Hellenistic age centered on three large kingdoms into which Alexander's empire was divided—the An-

tigonid, Ptolemaic, and Seleucid kingdoms—in each of which prevailed a system of monarchy reflecting both Greek and Near Eastern concepts and practices of government. Within these kingdoms, city-states, many newly founded on the model of the ancient Greek *polis*, played an important role as cultural and economic centers, thus sustaining urban life as a focal point of human activity. The Hellenistic age saw the spread of Greek cultural models and concepts over much of the Near East. As time passed, Greek and Near Eastern cultural styles and values intermingled to enrich each other. Out of this amalgam emerged new cultural achievements, especially in science and philosophy. While the Greek pattern of thought and expression tended to dominate cultural life, Near Eastern religious concepts increasingly asserted a powerful influence on thought and conduct.

Even as Greek influences spread eastward and changed society and culture over most of the Near East, the ground was being prepared for the transmission of Greek culture westward and for the unification of the Mediterranean world into a single political and cultural community. The agents of this development were the Romans, whose history began in a tiny village on the Tiber River in west-central Italy. Having been introduced to the ways of higher civilization by the Etruscans, who dominated Rome during the seventh and sixth centuries B.C., the Romans in 509 B.C. rejected Etruscan overlordship and established the Roman Republic, an event which in their eyes marked the beginning of Rome's independent history. They slowly forged an effective internal political structure dominated by a narrow circle of partician aristocrats but permitting plebeian citizens sufficient involvement in political affairs to make them loyal supporters of the Republic. Between 509 and 265 B.C. the well-led and loyal Roman citizen body conquered most of Italy and effectively organized its population, providing the Roman state with the human and material resources needed to establish ascendancy over the entire Mediterranean basin. Beginning in 265 B.C., the Romans proceeded step by step to conquer the major powers of the Mediterranean area: first the maritime empire of Carthage, embracing North Africa, Sicily, and Spain; then the Hellenistic kingdoms in the East; and finally the small principalities of Gaul. By the end of the first century B.C., the Romans were the unchallenged masters of the lands and peoples ringing the Mediterranean Sea.

However, these successes had a cost: Expansion engendered complex problems that, between 133 and 31 B.C., created an internal crisis so severe that it brought the republican political order to an end. In essence, the republican constitution, shaped originally to govern a small city-state, was unable to resolve the problems associated with the governance of a vast empire and to cope with the internal political, economic, and social dislocations caused by the creation of that empire. The resultant tensions engendered civil strife, which expressed itself first in bitter partisan struggles among factions seeking to control the republic and then in deadly rivalry among ambitious individuals willing to use force to gain power without regard for traditional political processes. The gradual erosion of republican institutions paved the way for the formation of a political system called the Roman Empire, which constituted Rome's greatest achievement.

The architect of the new order was Augustus (ruled 31 B.C.–A.D. 14), a product of the bloody power struggles of the late republic who acted decisively to end civil strife. He fashioned a political order that concentrated power in the hands of a single ruler—called the *princeps,* or emperor—while still respecting the rights of the Senate and citizen body as the source of his power. During the first and second centuries A.D., that system was steadily perfected as the prime instrument bringing peace across the huge Roman Empire. The authority of the emperor, exercised through a professional army and a well-regulated bureaucracy and guided by a sophisticated legal system, was the decisive factor in establishing the Roman peace. A succession of gifted emperors effectively enlisted the talents of the Roman aristocracy in the service of the imperial government and encouraged local city-state governments dominated by provincial aristocrats to play a significant role in shaping local affairs, thereby sustaining a Greek institution as a focus of civic life. This harmonious arrangement resulted in one of the most stable and effective political systems ever devised.

The Roman peace and its accompanying economic prosperity promoted the spread of a common culture across the Mediterranean world. In its form and content that culture was essentially Greek, for from as early as the third century B.C. the Romans became ardent admirers, imitators, and disseminators of Greek culture. Not only did they appropriate its basic elements, they also managed to capture its essential spirit in their own language and cultural creations, especially literature, engineering, and law. Their efforts not only kept Greek culture alive but also propagated it over a large area in the west, which had until then hardly been touched by higher civilization.

Greco-Roman civilization reached its apogee in the second century A.D. Beginning late in that century, forces of change began to affect it in ways that pointed toward transformation and decline. In contrast to the peaceful second century, the third century was marked by almost incessant civil war. Although outwardly caused by elements in the army that sought to control the government for the benefit of the soldiery, these destructive struggles were products of fundamental flaws within the structure of the Roman imperial order: a constitution that provided no effective system of succession to the imperial office and no clear definition of the limits on the emperor's power; a defense system that could not cope with the mounting threats by foreign enemies; an economic system incapable of sufficient expansion to cover the expenditure of a profligate society; a social system that encouraged a narrow elite to oppress those upon whose labor their dominant position depended; and cultural values that increasingly failed to satisfy the universal yearning for security in an age of anxiety.

During this critical century, subtle changes in Greco-Roman civilization began to occur. The emperors became increasingly autocratic, and the imperial government, chiefly in the interests of strengthening the military establishment, moved inexorably toward greater regimentation of both society and economic production. As the central government increases its powers, the role of the once-vital local city-state governments was progressively constricted. Urban life began to decay, and agriculture became more crucial; as a result, the economic base of imperial society began to shrink. New elites—landowners, army leaders, bureaucrats—asserted greater control over society at the expense of the traditional aristocracy and the peasants, artisans, and shop-keepers. Perhaps most ominous of all was the widespread loss of faith in the humanistic, rational values of traditional Greco-Roman civilization and the increasing quest for meaning through identification with the Divine.

The spiritual searching of this troubled age manifested itself in many ways, but one development was especially significant for the future: the emergence of Christianity. This new religion originated as an offshoot of Judaism at a moment when the Jewish community was agitated by differing expectations concerning the fulfillment of God's promise to his Chosen People, who had long suffered at the hands of oppressors, the last of whom were the Romans. Although the exact import of the message proclaimed by the living Jesus has been differently interpreted, there can be no doubt that not long after his death his followers accepted him as the Messiah made flesh by God to sacrifice his life for humanity's sin and to herald the imminent coming of a new kingdom where believers would enter a new state marked by mutual love and moral purity. That message won an ever-growing following during the first, second, and third centuries A.D. After some of the early disciples of Jesus made a special effort to universalize his message, Christianity's appeal was especially strong among the non-Jewish population of the Roman Empire. As the movement grew, it gradually became disassociated from Judaism to constitute a separate religion. To its basic religious message the Christian movement added other elements that promoted its success: a solid organization; a persuasive articulation of its basic teaching that was greatly enriched by the adaptation of Greco-Roman philosophical concepts and literary forms to Christian uses; an appealing set of ritual practices; and a social consciousness that emphasized charity and concern for society's unfortunates. By A.D. 300 these factors combined to create a vital community within the Roman state whose members no longer gave their full allegiance to the Greco-Roman version of civilized life.

The crisis of the third century A.D. eventually evoked a response aimed at restoring Roman society. The crucial elements of that reform were shaped by two able emperors, Diocletian (A.D. 284–305) and Constantine (A.D. 306–337), who sought to reconstruct society chiefly by political

means aimed at strengthening central authority. In seeking to vest total power in their own hands, they reorganized the machinery of government so as to place direct control over political life in the hands of the emperors and an expanded bureaucracy. They enlarged the military establishment and focused its mission on defense of the fragile frontiers. To pay for all of this, the emperors took steps to regiment the work force so as to maximize the production of goods and services and to ensure their availability to the state. Finally, they sought to channel the religious forces increasingly capturing the public mind into support of the state, a decision that led to Constantine's legalization of Christianity and the adoption of policies pointing toward the Christianizing of the entire Roman Empire.

The vast reorganization of imperial society by Diocletian and Constantine appeared to have saved the empire. The fourth century A.D. was marked by internal peace, economic and social stability, intellectual and artistic vitality (chiefly in the service of Christianity), and considerable progress toward religious unity under the banner of Christianity. Yet there were ominous signs of deep-seated troubles. The cost of the autocratic government and military forces bore heavily on the population, causing many to evade their civic responsibilities. The reluctance of citizens to meet military obligations forced the imperial government to rely increasingly on non-Roman recruits, whose commitment to Roman institutions and values was limited. The quality of service offered by the bloated bureaucracy deteriorated, giving rise to corruption and oppression. The economy stagnated even further. The administrative reorganization effected by Diocletian and Constantine encouraged regional divisions within the empire that threatened political unity. Finally, although eventually made the legal religion of the empire, Christianity failed to unify the populace in support of the state. The sudden transition from a religious movement awaiting the coming of a new kind of kingdom to the official religion of the Roman Empire sent tremendous shocks through the Christian world that divided that community on a wide range of difficult issues: how to discipline the hordes of new converts; how to attain holiness; how to adjust to the demands of an opressive political regime that shared few of the values central to

Christian teaching; what constituted right belief; how to react to Greco-Roman cultural values. In formulating responses to these issues the Christian movement was itself transformed down lines that increasingly diminished the importance of sustaining many key elements of Greco-Roman civilization.

All of these signs of deteriorating imperial strength were ominous, for as the fourth century drew to a close a crisis was in the making that involved Rome's relationship with the turbulent Germanic world of central Europe. The Romans and the Germans had long faced each other across a fixed frontier. Each represented a distinctive pattern of life, for the Germans had over many centuries developed unique political, social, economic, and religious institutions that differed markedly from those of their southern neighbors. These two worlds were by no means isolated from each other. Prior to A.D. 400, many Germans had entered the Roman Empire to serve as soldiers, farmers, and servants, and Roman products and techniques had crossed the imperial frontiers into the Germanic world. The Germans knew of Greco-Roman civilization, admired it, and were eager to share its fruits. Nor did the Romans hold any deep-seated animosity toward the Germans; they were not averse to Romanizing the Germans as long as they could control the process. This depended on maintaining their frontier defenses. During the third and fourth centuries, the Germanic pressure on the frontier steadily increased, due chiefly to changes in Germanic society that produced larger political groupings, an organized warrior aristocracy, and the need for more agricultural land.

During the last years of the fourth century Rome's frontier defenses finally broke down, leading to what has variously been called the "barbarian invasions" or the "German migrations." The phenomenon was marked by the movement of several Germanic nations across the old frontiers and their settlement on Roman soil, primarily in the western part of the empire. Although the number of the "invaders" or "migrants" was small in relation to the Roman population, the imperial government was unable either to stop the intruders or to control them once they had entered the empire. As a result, the newcomers were able to establish a number of independent kingdoms that by the end of the fifth century had embraced most of the western territories of the empire: Italy, Gaul, Spain, North Africa, England. As these Germanic kingdoms took shape, the Roman imperial government gradually disappeared in the west—a significant sign that a turning point in history had arrived. The disappearance of that government and the political disturbances accompanying the advent of the new Germanic kingdoms hastened trends already in progress in late antiquity: a reversion to an agricultural economy, a contraction of trade, a decline in urban life, the social ascendancy of great landowners, and a stagnation of traditional cultural activities. However, important elements of the old order survived to assert a civilizing influence on the Germanic masters. Especially significant was the energetic Christian establishment, which during the fifth century expanded its role in political and social life and established a virtual monopoly on intellectual and artistic activities.

While giving due weight to the impact of the Germanic migrations as a decisive event in marking the end of Greco-Roman civilization, it is crucial to remember that the eastern part of the old Roman Empire escaped the fate of the west. There the established patterns persisted with considerable vigor. However, the invasions reduced contacts between east and west, thus ending the political, religious, and cultural unity of the Mediterranean world. In that changed environment the surviving eastern Roman Empire began to experience subtle changes destined to make it different from the empire from which it had emerged.

Taken together, the events unfolding across the Mediterranean world during the fifth century leave no doubt that an old order had ended. The complex techniques devised by the Greeks and Romans to unify the diverse peoples of the Mediterranean world into a single political community animated by a shared value system given expression in one of the most creative and sustained literary, artistic, and intellectual effort recorded in all history combined to mark a high point in human achievement. For all its glories and its splendors Greco-Roman civilization was ultimately unable to cope with the new peoples who ruptured political unity and the new concepts of human destiny which overturned its most cherished values. In fact, its most influential leaders surrendered to these new forces. In that sense Greco-Roman civilization came to an end about A.D. 500, by which time the political unity of the Mediterranean world had ended and Christian religious values had replaced the humanistic, rationalistic values of classical civilization. However, to speak of the fall of Greco-Roman civilization is to utter only a partial truth. That civilization left behind models of civilized existence that served to shape human activity over a wide sweep of territory around the Mediterranean Sea far beyond A.D. 500. Greco-Roman civilization had changed the course of history. Its legacy must occupy the attention of all who would understand the development of civilization during the next millenium and a half.

THE EARLY MIDDLE AGES, 500–1000: TOWARD A NEW ORDER

The events of the fifth century produced such extensive disarray that the peoples living around the Mediterranean Sea were faced with the challenge of reconstructing the basic patterns governing their existence. Despite considerable confusion, they met this challenge with remarkable creativity. As a result of their efforts, three new cultural communities emerged between 500 and 1000: Byzantine, Islamic, and Latin western European. In each of these communities the shaping of new institutions and values was powerfully affected by vestiges of Greco-Roman civilization; thus, in a sense, each was an heir of the Roman Empire. However, in each emerging civilization new peoples and religious forces played a crucial role in transforming the remnants of classical civilization into new and distinctive patterns.

Byzantine civilization began as a direct continuation of the Roman imperial order in the eastern provinces of the old Roman Empire, which had escaped the impact of the Germanic migrations. For a time the rulers of this remnant of old Rome nourished the fiction that, as successors of the Roman emperors, they were masters of the old Roman Empire in its entirety. The emperor Justinian (527–565) even undertook a major military campaign to recapture the western provinces from their Germanic masters. However, his effort made it clear that the eastern

emperors could not assert effective control over most of the German-dominated west. In reality, the very survival of the reduced empire depended on the ability of its rulers to defend their territories against attackers from the east and north. Most of Byzantine history from Justinian's reign to 1100 centered on a struggle to fend off a variety of such attackers, who nevertheless pared away substantial territories, ultimately reducing the direct sphere of Byzantine influence to Asia Minor, the Balkan peninsula, and southern Italy. While the territory controlled directly by "new" Rome was shrinking, the Byzantines expanded their cultural and religious sphere of influence into the Slavic world of eastern Europe and Russia. That success, accomplished chiefly through diplomatic and missionary activity, played an important role in absorbing the Slavs into the mainstream of civilization.

The ability of the Byzantine Empire to survive and even to flourish despite the constant onslaught of external foes stemmed chiefly from the vitality of its institutions, which, increasingly across the early Middle Ages, developed unique characteristics that distinguished Byzantium from other cultural worlds. The pillar of Byzantine society was its strong government, directed by an emperor who claimed to be God's agent and who exercised absolute power through a dedicated clergy, a skilled bureaucracy, and a loyal army and navy. A strong, carefully directed economy featuring a productive agricultural system, a wide-reaching trading system, and skilled artisanry provided a solid material base for Byzantine society. Especially vital to Byzantine civilization was its Christian religious establishment, which developed distinctive organizational, doctrinal, and liturgical features that set it apart from other segments of the Christian world. Particularly characteristic of the Greek Orthodox church was its close alliance with the state, a tie that reinforced the authority of the emperors and made obedience to the state a Christian duty. The Byzantine world gradually shaped its own unique artistic, literary, and intellectual patterns, rooted in ancient Greek culture but also deeply colored by Christian concepts and values.

The Islamic cultural world was created by a people "new" on the scene as shapers of history: the nomadic inhabitants of the Arabian Desert.

Previously divided and impoverished, the Arabs were suddenly united in the early decades of the seventh century under the banner of a new religion, Islam, founded by Muhammad (ca. 570–632). Claiming to be the last in a long succession of prophets (including the Hebrew prophets and Jesus), Muhammad proclaimed that he was the recipient of the final revelation of Allah, the single, all-powerful god of the universe. Calling on the Arabs to abandon their false gods, to submit to Allah, and to regulate their lives according to Allah's commands, Muhammad was able before his death to unite a large segment of the Arab world into a dynamic religious community inspired by a mission to spread its faith to the entire world.

During the century following Muhammad's death the adherents of Islam, called Moslems, performed one of the great military feats of history: They drove eastward out of their desert homeland to engulf the Persian Empire and push beyond it into India and to the borders of China. Simultaneously, they struck westward to seize substantial territories once part of the Greco-Roman world: Syria, Palestine, Egypt, north Africa, Spain. These conquests shaped a vast empire that immediately became a major force in world affairs. In the wake of their victories the Arab leaders of Islam fashioned a centralized government under a leader, called the caliph, whose authority was defined chiefly in religious terms. The caliph was a deputy of Allah, charged with interpreting and applying Allah's law as it was revealed by the Prophet and written down in the Koran, the sacred book of Islam. This religiously based political regime managed to maintain a unified Islamic state until the tenth century, but after that the Moslem Empire began to fragment into rival caliphates, each led by a caliph who claimed to be the true upholder of Allah's law.

Although the political bonds holding together the followers of Islam were fragile, other factors combined to give unity to the Islamic world. The initial political unification achieved by Muhammad's Arab followers stimulated the expansion of trade that created economic linkages over a vast territory and made the prosperity of diverse regions dependent on maintaining those ties. More important was the force of Islam as a bond of unity. Within a relatively short time the new religion proclaimed by Muhammad was widely accepted; most of the new converts came from the ranks of Jews, Christians, and Zoroastrians who not only gained certain political, social, and economic advantages from accepting the religion of their conquerors but who also found the new religion appealing on its own terms. Most of the converts were non-Arabs, so that Islam soon lost its original ethnic orientation. A long succession of experts in law, theology, and philosophy constantly reinterpreted the Koran in ways that made its message relevant to peoples of diverse cultural, ethnic, and religious backgrounds. As a consequence, Islam was soon capable of appealing to peoples never embraced in the Moslem Empire, especially in southeast Asia and sub-Saharan Africa. All of these forces combined to provide a set of beliefs, a way of worshiping, and a code of conduct shared by a vast population. Another powerful bond of unity was a unique Islamic culture shaped within the matrix of Islamic religion. That culture represented a synthesis of elements derived from earlier cultures—Greco-Roman, Persian, Indian, Jewish, Germanic—which were drawn together, reshaped, and interconnected to fit the precepts of Islamic religion and articulated in Arabic, the language of the Koran. Although the genius of Islamic culture was reflected in a unique art and literature, its most notable achievements were in science and philosophy, which were destined to be influential down through history and far beyond the borders of the Moslem Empire.

The third new culture to arise in the immediate postclassical period was that of Latin western Europe. The setting within which that cultural community was shaped was provided by the several Germanic kingdoms established on Roman soil during the fifth century. In 500 neither the boundaries nor the governments of these kingdoms were clearly established. As a result, at least down to about 750, the western European world suffered from political instability. During this era several of these kingdoms disappeared; by 750 only the Frankish, Anglo-Saxon, and Lombard kingdoms remained. With the exception of the Anglo-Saxon kingdoms, the leaders of most of the early Germanic kingdoms tried and failed to imitate Roman patterns of government. Amid the political turmoil accompanying this experimentation, certain distinctively western European political institutions began to take shape:

a form of monarchy allowing rulers only limited powers; private political authority vested in the hands of a warrior-landowner nobility; a system of personal dependency subordinating the weak to the powerful; a customary law defining a wide range of interpersonal relationships. All of these political institutions reflected a mixture of Roman and Germanic elements that gave the emerging political order a distinctive quality. During the period extending from 500 to 750 the west suffered a progressive impoverishment, marked by the decline of urban-based commerce and industry and the emergence of an agricultural system geared to local self-sufficiency. Reflecting the predominance of agriculture and rural life, the structure of society became simpler, embracing only two classes: a land-owning, power-wielding nobility and a peasantry whose status was defined in terms of dependence on the powerful and attachment to the soil controlled by the nobility.

Amid the political disorder and the economic recession of the period from 500 to 750 religious forces played a vital role in giving shape to the new order in Europe. Maintaining some of the momentum that had allowed Christianity to become dominant in the Greco-Roman world of late antiquity, the Christian establishment in the west was well positioned to exploit the Greco-Roman heritage for guidance and models in reconstituting society. Its clerical leaders enlarged the Christian community, chiefly through its efforts to convert Germans and the rural population, thereby creating at least one common bond in an otherwise fragmented world. Those same leaders extended and solidified the organizational structures through which the religious lives of the faithful were directed, thereby establishing some degree of order in an otherwise chaotic world. They greatly increased the wealth available to the Christian community, providing a means of alleviating misery and promoting cultural activities. They expanded the role of the clergy in political, economic, and social life, thereby allowing them to shape the values that governed the ordinary affairs of the world. In a sense, all of these activities put a strong religious stamp on the new society emerging in Latin western Europe.

The greatest challenge to the religious establishment in the early medieval west was to sustain the spiritual dimensions of Christianity. The violence and ignorance that surrounded life posed monumental challenges in that respect. Complicating the problem was the fact that the above-noted successes enjoyed by religious leaders tended to involve them in enterprises that rewarded them with power and wealth and that diverted them from spiritual concerns. Although the period from 500 to 750 was not a notable era in terms of the enrichment of religious sensibilities, it was an age when some religious leaders sought ways of deepening spirituality and in so doing shaped institutions, ideas, and practices that spoke to the spiritual poverty of their world. It was an age during which idealized "athletes of Christ," holy men and women who by their individual efforts to imitate Jesus, won the admiration of both the powerful and the simple in the Christian community as vessels through which divine favors could be gained and as models of how Christian life should be lived. This model of spiritual excellence found its institutional setting in western monasticism, especially those establishments guided by rules formulated in Ireland and by Benedict of Nursia. These "schools for the service of God" produced cadres of specially prepared Christians who served as models of Christian perfection and who engaged in a wide range of activities that provided living examples of religious excellence. Of crucial importance for the future was the expanding influence of the bishops of Rome—the popes—who were increasingly seen as the source of spiritual guidance and the arbiters of right belief for all Christians in the Latin west.

The struggle to sustain spiritual life was abetted by Christian leaders who sensed the importance of maintaining contact with the religious, intellectual, and artistic traditions out of which Christianity had grown. Their efforts helped to sustain the rudiments of cultural life, especially the maintenance of Latin literacy, which allowed access to classical and patristic literature as guides to spiritual life. Crucial to this cultural enterprise were monastic schools where Latin was taught, books were copied and collected, ancient texts were commented on in search of their meaning, and original writings in history, theology, and poetry were nourished. In their efforts to provide suitable places of worship, religious leaders devoted part of their resources to the patronage of the arts. At least in rudimentary form, the Latin west was shaping its own unique cultural life, rooted in an earlier Latin-Christian tradition but bearing its own unique stamp.

By 750 the reshaping of society had progressed far enough to permit an upsurge of activity that gave western Europeans an expanded awareness of their distinctive pattern of life and made their society more visible in a larger world. The central force behind this revival was a new dynasty of Frankish kings, the Carolingians, who with the support of the clergy and some of the nobility, dominated the western European scene between 750 and 900. After seizing the Frankish throne in 751 with the blessing of the papacy, a succession of Carolingian rulers greatly enlarged and consolidated the Frankish kingdom, strengthened its internal political institutions, promoted a vigorous renaissance in education, literary and artistic activity, and theological inquiry, and instituted religious reforms guided by norms established by a conscious effort to recover the Christian traditions defined in earlier ages. A major consequence of the royal effort in these enterprises was the addition of new dimensions to the concept of royal power and the role of public authority in collective life. Crucial support to the renewal of society was provided by the clergy, especially by the papacy, which with Carolingian support was able to establish a papal state in central Italy, thus freeing the popes from domination by the Byzantine emperors. The culmination of the Carolingian renewal came in 800, when Charlemagne was crowned emperor by the pope, renewing in the west an exalted title and concept of governance that Byzantium had monopolized since the late fifth century.

In the long run, the Carolingian rulers and their allies were unable to sustain the effort to unify the west, to improve its governance system, and to uplift spiritual and cultural life. Their reforming effort did little to expand the material base supporting society or to minimize the forces of localism that had become deeply rooted in society since the collapse of the Roman political system. After 843 the unified empire was divided into several small kingdoms, chiefly to serve dynastic interests. In quest of support the several members of the Carolingian family ruling over each of these kingdoms greatly weakened the central government by ceding lands and political privileges to ambitious aristocrats and religious officials. The fragmentation of the Frankish state and of public authority was hastened by attacks by hostile outsiders: Moslems, Magyars, Vikings. By 900 the Carolingian Empire was divided beyond repair into several smaller kingdoms whose rulers exercised little power but whose boundaries prefigured the future political map of western Europe.

As the Carolingian Empire disintegrated, a new pattern of social organization and control took center stage to provide the basis for the eventual reestablishment of order and prosperity. At the heart of this system were economic and social arrangements involving lordship and dependency. These arrangements were based on practices that had roots extending back to the late Roman and early Germanic societies. By the tenth century a relatively few powerful and enterprising individuals exploited these deeply rooted practices to establish the right to command those whom they could compel into dependence. The establishment of lordship almost always involved the usurpation of powers exercised by public authorities. As a consequence, lordship led to the localization and privatization of political power. Successful lordship was based on the ability of power wielders to command the obedience and the service of dependents. Dependency took two distinct forms: noble and servile.

Those who were linked to a lord in noble dependency served primarily to provide him with the armed forces needed to enforce his authority. The bonds between the lord and his warrior dependents were defined by a system that later historians called feudalism. Under this system a lord accepted as his vassal a qualified free individual who willingly pledged under oath to obey and serve him in a military capacity. In return the lord pledged to protect his vassal and to grant him the use of something of value called a fief (usually land and an office) from which could be derived an income sufficient to support the vassal. Implicit in the practices that created a circle of vassals around a lord was a rudimentary form of government that regulated relationships among the members of the noble caste, whose monopoly on military power allowed them to dominate society. Although each such community was made up of a limited number of people and provided numerous opportunities for conflict with other such communities, each had considerable potential to maintain order and provide security at the local level. The system of lordship based on services provided by noble dependents required another kind of dependency. Both lords and their noble dependents relied upon the exploitation of land to provide the material resources needed to sustain their political and social dominance. To achieve that end, lords and their noble vassals imposed a system of servile dependence, sometimes called the seigneurial system, on the nonnoble population. In essence, that system placed agricultural laborers in a condition of serfdom which bound them to a seigneur's land under terms that required them to devote part of their labor to tilling his fields and to pay various kinds of dues. In return the serf received hereditary possession of a tenancy consisting of a simple dwelling, a plot of land sufficient to sustain his household, and rights to a share of the produce of forests and pasture lands associated with agricultural production. As the seigneurial system evolved, it grouped servile dependents into self-sufficient communities, called manors, that featured cooperative efforts on the part of the peasantry to exploit the seigneur's land. Each agricultural community developed its own customs to regulate peasant life and define peasant relationships with the seigneur. Taken together, the institutional patterns involved in noble and servile dependency worked to create small, closely knit, stable political and economic collectivities that had a potential for growth.

Although sometimes characterized as a "dark age," the complex developments unfolding between 500 and 1000 marked a decisive era in history. The challenges posed by the disintegration of Greco-Roman civilization unleashed a new range of creative forces and brought new peoples into a prominent place in the historical setting, especially the Germans, Arabs, and Slavs. The emergence of three new civilizations as heirs of the classical world created a cultural configuration around the Mediterranean basin whose contours are still visible. The coexistence of these three new civilizations created a new source of dynamism in the form of interactions among them that played a decisive role in determining the future of each.

THE CENTRAL AND LATER MIDDLE AGES, 1000–1500: THE RESURGENCE OF EUROPE

By about 1000 the new cultural patterns shaped in the Byzantine, Islamic, and Latin western European worlds during the early Middle Ages were solidly in place, allowing each to play a significant role during the centuries to come. From the perspective of the history of Western civilization the next five centuries were highlighted by a remarkable surge of activity in the western European world, which previously had been much less developed than the Byzantine and Islamic worlds. The medieval resurgence of western Europe, which was most marked between 1000 and 1300, not only gave a new shape to that society but also elevated it to a central place in the world setting.

Two developments provided the prime impetus for the achievements of this period: greatly increased material wealth and the revival of urban life. These changes came up from the bottom of society—from toiling peasants, peddler merchants, simple artisans, and modest seigneurs. Pressured by steady population growth, these working people increased agricultural production by clearing and colonizing new lands, improving agricultural technology, and developing more effective management techniques. Commerce and industry grew steadily to create new sources of wealth and flourishing urban centers. For the first time, western Europeans developed a thriving international trade, penetrating the richer, more advanced Byzantine and Moslem economies. Vigorous local exchange, linking the rural world to the growing urban centers, added a vital dimension to the total economy. Enterprising merchants developed a variety of business techniques that facilitated the exchange of goods and the investment of wealth in new ventures. Skilled artisans steadily increased the volume, quality and variety of manufactured products as a further stimulant to exchange. Economic growth resulted in more diverse and complex social structures. The warrior nobility continued to dominate society, but as a consequence of greater affluence and changing intellectual and religious currents, its members evolved a more refined code of conduct based on concepts of chivalry. Especially notable was the appearance of a new social group, the bourgeoisie, which consisted of urban dwellers who succeeded in establishing a distinctive place for themselves in the social order, an effort that resulted in new institutional patterns which had an important impact on political, economic, religious, and cultural life.

While western Europe's working people were producing more wealth and shaping new social structures, its kings and nobles were building more effective political structures. Most notable was the shaping of large kingdoms in which central governments represented by monarchs developed the means of asserting greater authority over local interests and formulating policies that gave common direction to the activities of large numbers of people. Each of the major states prominent in this period—the Holy Roman Empire, England, France, Castile, Aragon, Portugal—had its own institutional forms. But in each one kings drew on a variety of sources to define a unique kind of lordship that gave them the power to command their dependent subjects. Each fashioned instruments of central and local government that allowed the king to exercise his lordship: armies, taxation systems, law, courts. At the heart of the consolidation process was the ability of royal governments to reduce private jurisdictions that had been fashioned by nobles, the ecclesiastical establishment, and town corporations. As a result of that effort, medieval monarchical government was characterized by a delicate balance between common interests and privileged status; the maintenance of the "rights" claimed by each component found expression in basic laws aimed at defining the extent and limits of royal authority and in representative institutions through which members of privileged groups could protect their rights. In the final analysis the balance struck between royal power and special privilege allowed considerable room for royal government to play a role in providing security, justice, and material well-being for all who shared membership in the kingdom that was unprecedented in the western European world of the early Middle Ages.

The economic growth and political consolidation of western Europe provided the material and human resources that made possible a remarkable geographical expansion of the European sphere of influence at the expense of the

Byzantine, Moslem, Slavic, and Scandinavian worlds. Expansion took many forms. Missionaries converted and brought into the sphere of western Christendom large numbers of western Slavs and Scandinavians. Noble and peasant colonists occupied extensive lands in central Europe, Spain, southern Italy, and Sicily. Enterprising merchants, especially from Italy and the Baltic and North sea areas, established their presence in the Byzantine and Moslem empires and gained control over large areas of the Mediterranean Sea. Western European military forces captured most of Spain from the Moslems, southern Italy and Sicily from the Byzantines and Moslems, and—most dramatically—an outpost in Syria and Palestine, this last as a consequence of the Crusades. Of course, western European institutions and ideas were transported to these areas, which had previously been untouched by European influence. This medieval expansion marked an important initial step toward establishing the western European domination of the world.

The creative energies of western European society also manifested themselves in a powerful religious "reformation" that not only reshaped the organization and governance of the Christian community but also established powerful bonds uniting western Europe's population. The reform movement was fueled by a growing awareness of the moral laxity afflicting Christian society, defects that became especially visible as a result of the entanglement of religious leaders in the system of lordship and dependence of the tenth and eleventh centuries. The reform movement took two complementary directions: a drive to free the religious establishment from lay control and to strengthen it as an independent community capable of determining its own destiny; and an effort to probe the spiritual and moral meaning of Christianity more profoundly.

The first kind of reform was spearheaded by the papacy. The papal reform movement assumed its basic thrust during the investiture struggle that began in the middle of the eleventh century. Drawing on a variety of ancient traditions, the papal reformers began to insist that the community of the faithful—the Church—was the primary earthly community created by God under his vicar, the pope, to amend human behavior in ways that would assure the salvation of souls according to God's plan. To restore their version of the Church to its ordained place in the world, the papal reformers initiated a move to free the religious establishment from the control exercised over its property, personnel, and operations by secular lords and to shape institutional patterns within the Christian community that would allow it to assert its preordained directive role in society. Their program involved ecclesiastical leaders in a long struggle with kings and nobles that resulted in a greatly extended sphere of independence for religious leaders in controlling religious property and offices and in disciplining the personnel identified with the religious establishment. A key factor in this success was the creation of a powerful organization directed by Rome which knit together the various levels of the clerical hierarchy into a corporate entity capable of imposing a unified body of belief and a standard code of behavior on the entire Christian community. By the thirteenth century the Church, so constituted, was able to assert a decisive influence over the political, economic, and social life of western Europe.

The reform efforts of the popes and the clerical hierarchy of bishops and priests always sought to focus attention on improving the spiritual and moral lives of the Christian flock. These endeavors focused primarily on rediscovering and imposing traditional patterns of belief and discipline on the faithful. The second form of medieval religious reform sought to transcend this mode of spiritual and moral renewal, to seek new levels of spiritual meaning in the Christian message, and to define new patterns of behavior defining holiness. That quest found its most vital voice in the monastic world and among the laity rather than in the hierarchy. The era extending from about 1000 to 1300 was marked by repeated efforts to redefine monastic life in ways that would mold a more perfect form of Christian life. Each of these experiments produced a new monastic order that in turn exercised a powerful influence on Christian life. Each such "reform" had its unique characteristics and emphases, but all stressed the need for perfect Christians to involve themselves more directly in the world scene as warriors against sin and injustice. Another common thread was an emphasis on the individual's ability to work actively for God's grace as opposed to waiting passively for eventual salva-

tion. Various popular religious movements added yeast for the spiritual concerns of this questing age, usually stressing poverty, charity, and simplicity of worship as keys to winning God's favors. Because they were often critical of the clerical hierarchy's increasing wealth, power, and inflexible insistence on conformity in belief and practice, some of these popular movements were condemned as heretical and forcibly suppressed, often with the assistance of secular rulers.

The vast changes occurring in economic, social, political, and religious life combined to stimulate a vigorous outburst of cultural activity that played an important role in defining the unique identity of western European society and in establishing its preeminence in the setting of a larger world. Many of the cultural artifacts shaped by the medieval revival of thought and expression played a significant role in giving shape to modern European cultural history. Cultural activity in this age proceeded on two levels defined chiefly in terms of language: Latin and vernacular languages.

The world of Latin culture was the preserve of an elite who had mastered what had become a "foreign" language. That culture was nourished in a constantly evolving educational system (culminating in the establishment of the first universities) which in the process of sustaining Latin literacy emphasized expanding and intensifying contacts with the intellectual and literary products of classical Roman and Christian patristic culture. This learned world utilized its efforts primarily in the service of the religious establishment and the state. Perhaps its most impressive product was a huge body of theological writings inspired by a quest to define what constituted right belief in a Christian society. A major challenge surrounding that effort involved reconciling the Christian revelation set forth in Scripture with human knowledge, which was greatly expanded by the recovery in the west of Greek and Islamic philosophy and science. In the process of achieving that reconciliation medieval scholars devised a methodology called scholasticism, which emphasized the use of logical reasoning to resolve the contradictions between divine and human knowledge. The learned world also produced other cultural monuments: a unified code of religious (canon) law; a massive body of commentary on Roman law; a systematic body of political theory; an increasing accumulation of knowledge about the natural world derived from both classical and Islamic sources and the observation of natural phenomena; and a diverse body of Latin belles letters, including history, political polemics, poetry, and letters. While all these facets of Latin culture reflected the strong imprint of classical and patristic Latin learning, they were given vitality by the ability of scholars and writers to relate their derived learning to contemporary political and religious concerns.

Perhaps the unique cultural achievement of this age was the development of a literature written in the several languages which previously had only been spoken. This vernacular literature was produced chiefly for the amusement and edification of the nobility, most of whom had been illiterate prior to this period, but it also touched the lives of other social groups. Vernacular literature took many forms: epics recounting the deeds of warrior heroes; troubadour lyrics voicing the joys and pains of love; romances combining adventure and love to exalt the chivalric lifestyle increasingly dominant in the courtly circles of noble society; *fabiaux* treating the humor of everyday life and satirizing the foibles of men and women; religious dramas; saints' lives; history. While never entirely disassociated from learned culture and the values it represented, vernacular literature gave special emphasis to the human, earthly dimensions of existence.

While medieval literate culture tended to create two distinct cultural spheres, the visual arts struck a more universal note. Inspired chiefly by the demands of Christian worship and by religious values, the era produced two notable architectural styles, first Romanesque and then Gothic, which found expression in churches, both great and small, that served as the focal point for human activity in cities and villages across all of western Europe. The adornment of these distinctive structures stimulated a variety of other arts: sculpture, painting, metalwork, woodwork, manuscript illumination, textiles, glasswork. The basic features of Romanesque and Gothic art left their imprint on the building and decoration of castles, palaces, and town halls.

The creative energies that worked so powerfully to reshape western European society between 1000 and 1300 began to flag early in the fourteenth century. The next two centuries, characterized by considerable tension and dislocation, provided the setting for the transition to modern Europe. In a fundamental way, the difficulties of the fourteenth and fifteenth centuries stemmed from new problems and new aspirations growing out of the earlier achievements of medieval western Europe. The changing situation required adjustments in the basic patterns of life, a process that produced a variety of stresses.

A major source of difficulty in the late Middle Ages stemmed from economic contraction and the consequent social dislocations. The prolonged economic growth of the central Middle Ages came to an end after about 1300, and economic production began to decline. In part this development resulted from a demographic disaster—repeated outbreaks throughout all of western Europe of a deadly bubonic plague which drastically reduced the population, disrupted the labor supply, altered demand patterns, and disturbed conventional production techniques. The economic situation was exacerbated by the unavailability of new lands to put under cultivation and by developments beyond western Europe that limited commercial expansion, both of which had been important factors in stoking economic expansion in the preceding centuries. Limitations inherent in the medieval agricultural system and in the localized, guild-dominated trading and manufacturing establishments restricted, at least in the short run, the ability to respond to the forces producing economic depression. The economic decline severely disturbed established social relationships and put important elements of the nobility, the peasantry, and the urban tradesmen and artisans under stress. The resultant tensions spawned social discontent, armed competition among noble factions, and peasant and urban violence.

The political system prevailing in western Europe likewise encountered difficulties. As we have seen, the medieval state system was based on a sharing of power between central governments directed by kings and privileged groups on the basis of well-defined mutual rights and obligations. That system eventually proved incapable of coping with such problems as disputed successions, large-scale national wars, and complex economic and social problems affecting whole populations. The intrinsic limitations of medieval monarchy in the face of new problems led to a declining respect for royal dynasties, disaffection with traditional political processes, and self-seeking by privileged groups, especially the nobility. All over western Europe, kingdoms suffered from civil war, disregard for law, expansion of privileges for the few, and oppression of the many. At one time or another during the fourteenth and fifteenth centuries, it seemed that every medieval kingdom might disappear, as did indeed one of the most powerful medieval political entities, the Holy Roman Empire, which embraced Germany and most of Italy. This political instability was aggravated by vigorous assaults from the Mongols and the Ottoman Turks which overpowered western Europe's eastern outposts, destroyed the Byzantine Empire, and left the west open to new attacks.

Considerable ferment in the world of religion added to the tensions in western Europe. The powerful ecclesiastical establishment, which had earlier given cohesion and direction to society, encountered increasing difficulties in asserting its leadership role. Its teaching and its system of governance were subjected to merciless criticism and open defiance, and its leaders failed to devise new ways of responding to these assaults. Part of the difficulty stemmed from a failure of leadership at the apex of the ecclesiastical structure, the papacy. Papal claims to "fullness of power" were effectively challenged by secular rulers, especially the kings of France, as early as 1300. The clash between the papacy and France led to the relocation of the papal court from Rome to Avignon, where—in the eyes of many—the popes became agents of the French monarchy rather than vicars of Christ serving all Christendom. Efforts to deal with what was called the "Babylonian captivity" of the papacy led to the Great Schism, during which two and even three popes claimed headship of the Christian community, a situation that spread confusion and discontent throughout the ranks of the faithful. Important lay and ecclesiastical leaders promoted the conciliar movement, which challenged the idea of papal supremacy over religious life by claiming that a representative body of Christians should exercise supreme authority in reli-

gious affairs. Amid these challenges, the beleaguered popes gave more attention to increasing papal resources and expanding papal legal jurisdiction than to handling pastoral problems. The result was an ever more onerous system of financial exactions managed by an ever more corrupt ecclesiastical bureaucracy, which produced bitter criticism, resistance, and open defiance of papal authority. Ineffectively guided from above, the lower clergy became increasingly venal and negligent of pastoral care. Even the monastic world, once a major source of spiritual renewal, was afflicted by decadence.

Accompanying the disarray in the ecclesiastical governance system—and partly caused by that disarray—was a widespread outcropping of new religious movements. Many of them reflected a search for religious fulfillment outside the formal, rigid patterns of religious life sanctioned by official theology and canon law. This searching took many forms: mysticism, which sought direct, personal contact with God; the founding of brotherhoods and sisterhoods of laypeople, based on the sharing of wealth and simple devotional practices; attacks by intellectuals on papal claims to supremacy and on the sacramental system; a search for spiritual meaning through a return to Scripture; apocalyptic cults aimed at preparing for the approaching end of the world; emotional rituals focused on the expiation of sin and death; witch-hunts; savage anti-Semitism. For the most part, religious officials disregarded these movements or suppressed them as heretical, thereby demonstrating an insensitivity to felt religious needs and to the inadequacies of the conventional system. All of these phenomena pointed to the need for a major reformation of religious life.

Subtle shifts in the intellectual world added to the turmoil in religious life. The efforts of the scholastic theologians and philosophers to reconcile, through reason, Christian revelation and human knowledge into one consistent, complete order of truth increasingly appeared sterile to many thinkers. Some of the dissatisfied devised arguments demonstrating that religious knowledge and human knowledge were separate, irreconcilable spheres that required different approaches. Others increasingly challenged the authorities upon which scholastics had depended as their sources for human knowledge.

Instead they insisted that the realm of human knowledge must depend on sense perceptions gained from observation of individual objects existing in the natural world; in this way, the philosophical groundwork for modern sciences was laid. Still other intellectuals turned to the Greek and Roman classics where they discovered not only new stimuli to intellectual activity but also a value system that clashed with the medieval worldview. The secular views initially reflected in the medieval vernacular culture found increasing favor in both noble and bourgeois circles.

Taken together, the diverse trends affecting late medieval society pointed to the emergence of a new order. In fact, by the late fifteenth century, the stresses of the late Middle Ages had begun to abate and signs of recovery were appearing. Included were the restoration of royal authority on new bases; renewed population growth; the stabilization of the agricultural system; new techniques for the accumulation of capital, which permitted the establishment of large-scale trading and manufacturing enterprises; new technological advances; tentative explorations by sea of new frontiers; fresh approaches to knowledge and expression; and new religious insights. All of these newly emerging patterns of civilization were rooted in the medieval civilization of western Europe. No catastrophic break such as that which had marked the transition from the Greco-Roman to the medieval era would herald the advent of the "modern" European world.

THE BEGINNING OF EARLY MODERN TIMES: THE FIFTEENTH AND SIXTEENTH CENTURIES

During the fourteenth and fifteenth centuries various tensions and a weakening of social institutions marked the transformation of the medieval world. During the fifteenth and sixteenth centuries the institutions and developments that would characterize early modern times grew out of the changing medieval system.

The first challenge to the medieval system came in the cities of northern Italy during the fourteenth and fifteenth centuries. There the ideas, values, and culture of the Renaissance arose. Although rooted in the medieval world, scholars, writers, and artists began looking back to classical Greece and Rome for models instead of accepting medieval scholastic authority. Cultural leaders focused more on individual human beings living in a concrete, material, Christian world rather than on medieval theology. The social and cultural elite were becoming more self-centered, proud, versatile, and materialist. These Renaissance qualities produced new, vibrant literature and art, making northern Italy the cultural center of the West.

During the fifteenth and sixteenth centuries the Renaissance spread from Italy to northern Europe, particularly to the courts of princes and kings and to university towns. There the Renaissance took on a more piously religious character as northern humanists tried to reconcile Christian and classical cultures.

In place of the declining feudal monarchies and empires arose the national or territorial state, which became the dominant political institution of the early modern era. The rise of the national states ended the independence of numerous feudal lords by bringing them under the authority of national monarchs. Talented monarchs such as Ferdinand and Isabella in Spain, Louis XI in France, and Henry VII in England increased their own power and established foundations for the continued growth of national monarchical power. Those areas that did not unify into national states, such as in Germany and Italy, suffered from political weakness.

National monarchs encouraged Europeans to expand into the non-Western world. Voyages of "discovery" soon led to commercial trade, spreading Christianity, and political control. During the fifteenth and early sixteenth centuries, Portugal and Spain led in this expansion of Europe. England, France, and the Netherlands soon followed. By the end of the sixteenth century, large parts of the rest of the world, particularly in the Western Hemisphere, southern Asia, and coastal Africa had come under European economic and political domination.

The expansion of Europe was also stimulated by new economic developments. Europe's medieval economy, characterized by subsistence agriculture, monopolistic guilds, and localism, slowly gave way to capitalistic practices and institutions. Increasing population and rising prices spurred commerce and created social turmoil, with poorer peasants suffering the most. The old landlord aristocracy was now threatened by newcomers into the class and by a new middle class of aggressive entrepreneurs, merchants, bankers, and lawyers. It is true that the bourgeoisie sought most of all to enter the ranks of the nobility and did so whenever possible, and that the nobility held the upper hand politically and socially for two or three more centuries. But by 1600 class lines had become more fluid.

The fifteenth and sixteenth centuries were marked by a deepening concern for religious matters. During the 1500s the western Christian Church, which had monopolized religious life and strongly influenced the intellectual, political, and economic life of Europe during the Middle Ages, was split asunder by the Reformation. Great religious leaders such as Martin Luther and John Calvin broke from the Roman church and laid the foundations for the various Protestant churches. Much of northern Europe became Protestant. This advance of Protestantism stimulated reform efforts already under way within the Roman Catholic church. Catholic doctrine was forcefully affirmed at the Council of Trent, and new religious orders such as the Jesuits reinvigorated the Church.

The religious struggles of the Reformation combined with political forces to give rise to the Wars of Religion. From the middle of the sixteenth to the middle of the seventeenth centuries, much of Europe was struck by war and political turmoil that was connected to religious issues. The most devastating of these wars was the Thirty Years' War, which broke out in Germany in 1618 and was not concluded until 1648 with the Peace of Westphalia.

PART FIVE

EARLY MODERN TIMES: THE SEVENTEENTH AND EIGHTEENTH CENTURIES

The fifteenth, sixteenth, and first half of the seventeenth centuries were a period of change and upheaval. The Renaissance, the Reformation and the Wars of Religion, the rise of the new monarchs, the commercial revolution, and the expansion of Europe marked the period as substantially different from the preceding Middle Ages and as the beginnings of early modern times.

The mid-seventeenth century to the last decades of the eighteenth century was marked by relative stability. Most people remained tied to agriculture and their small villages, which were only starting to evolve as the tentacles of central governments and economic change reached them. However, Europe's medieval economy increasingly gave way to commercial capitalism, and during the eighteenth century the agricultural revolution and the spread of cottage industry foreshadowed the greater changes that were to come. The landed aristocracy generally retained its power but was forced to absorb new members into its ranks and face growing challenges from middle-class merchants and entrepreneurs. Most religious affiliations remained as determined during the course of the Reformation and Wars of Religion. The dominant cultural trends—the baroque and the classical styles—continued to reflect the tastes of the elite classes. Central governments generally increased their power, usually in the form of royal absolutism, but in some areas kings lost the struggle for greater power.

Finally, the scientific revolution and the Enlightenment of the seventeenth and eighteenth centuries initially affected only a relative few. But these two developments would eventually help undermine the traditional order of early modern Europe and provide a foundation for the modern society of the nineteenth and twentieth centuries.

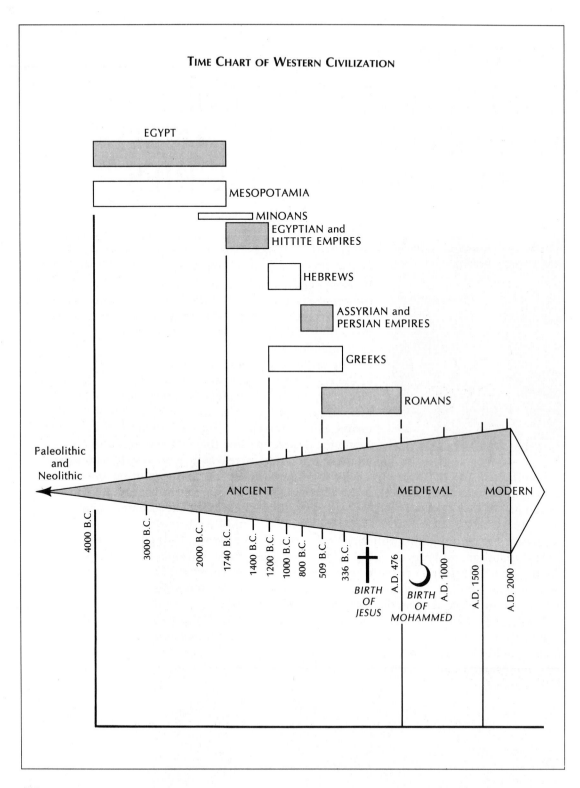

Time Chart of Western Civilization

EGYPT

MESOPOTAMIA

MINOANS

EGYPTIAN and HITTITE EMPIRES

HEBREWS

ASSYRIAN and PERSIAN EMPIRES

GREEKS

ROMANS

Paleolithic and Neolithic

ANCIENT   MEDIEVAL   MODERN

4000 B.C.

3000 B.C.

2000 B.C.

1740 B.C.

1400 B.C.

1200 B.C.

1000 B.C.

800 B.C.

509 B.C.

336 B.C.

BIRTH OF JESUS

A.D. 476

BIRTH OF MOHAMMED

A.D. 1000

A.D. 1500

A.D. 2000

CHAPTER 31

Society, Faith, and Culture in the Seventeenth and Eighteenth Centuries

FIGURE 31.1 **Thomas Gainsborough,** *Miss Catherine Tatton* Although the middle class was growing during the early modern era, the culture of the period was still dominated by the aristocracy. This portrait of an aristocratic lady by Thomas Gainsborough (1727–1788) reflects the luxury and tastes of the eighteenth-century aristocracy, which commissioned many such paintings. (Scala/Art Resource)

For most people the structure of society, the way of life, and the relevant social institutions changed only slowly throughout most of the seventeenth and early eighteenth centuries. More rapid change occurred thereafter, but it was usually concentrated in certain areas and classes. Despite the continued rise of the bourgeoisie and considerable political change, the aristocracy remained socially dominant and governments headed by kings generally continued to centralize their power. Religious faith remained of great importance to most people, but after the middle of the seventeenth century new religious movements such as pietism were no longer the revolutionary force they had been during the previous century. The literature and arts of the period reflected the spirit of royal absolutism and the values of the aristocracy, with their exaltation of kings, princes, and nobility and also their concern for order and form.

1. SOCIETY

Population Growth

One of the greatest sources of change in Western society has been population growth. As we have seen (see pp. 377–380), European population grew substantially during the sixteenth century, putting pressure on economic life, adding to social turmoil, and creating changes in the quality of life for different classes of people. This population growth leveled out during the first two decades of the seventeenth century. On the whole, during the seventeenth century Europe's population was able only to maintain itself or grow slightly. In some areas population declined markedly. The typical enemies of population growth were poverty, disease, famine, and war. Most people lived close to the subsistence level. Any disturbance—a poor harvest, a natural catastrophe, a war—quickly used up their meager reserves of food and opened the door to hunger, declining health, disease, and famine. The Thirty Years' War was particularly devastating, leading to a decline in the German population of some 40 percent during the first half of the seventeenth century. The relatively late age of marriage—late twenties for men, mid-twenties for women—also helped keep down the number of births in a society in which life expectancy was short and only about half of the babies born would reach maturity.

During the eighteenth century, particularly after the 1730s, the European population grew sharply—from approximately 110 million in 1700 to 190 million in 1800. Although the causes are unclear, it seems that an increasing birthrate and declining death rate were achieved by earlier marriages, better and more regular nutrition, fewer plagues, and less devastating wars. Agricultural and commercial prosperity, along with continuing improvements in transportation facilities, diminished the periodic famines in many areas. In particular, historians credit the introduction of the potato from the New World and its widespread cultivation in eighteenth-century Europe with crucially increasing supplies of nutritious food. More effective urban sanitation and increased use of quarantines probably improved health. Medical practices were not one of the causes of population growth. Certainly some progress was made in medical knowledge and there were a few better hospitals in eighteenth-century Europe than before. But with the exception of developing smallpox inoculation, which was little used outside England until the nineteenth century, eighteenth-century doctors, hospitals, and medicines probably caused more deaths than they prevented.

There was an ironic price to pay for this eighteenth-century increase in population. Greater competition for food drove prices up while that same competition for jobs usually drove wages down. At the same time that more people were able to survive, more experienced hunger and poverty. The poor were forced to wander and migrate more than ever.

Social Structure

Seventeenth- and eighteenth-century people viewed their society as divided—into different occupational groups and classes—and hierarchically ordered—the different groups and classes ranked from high to low status by birth, office, wealth, or education. Mobility between these ranked orders of society was viewed as the exception. People considered the social order to be relatively rigid and correct. In fact, however, mobility and change occurred. Wealth, education,

FIGURE 31.2 **Louis le Nain, *The Cart*, 1641** In contrast to most seventeenth-century artists, le Nain shows the life of the French peasantry. This farmyard scene (notice the mixture of ages), so typical of the countryside, contrasts sharply with the life of the aristocracy. (The Louvre, Paris)

and new opportunities for governmental service opened avenues for middle-class merchants, bankers, and professionals as well as the gentry to move into the ranks of the aristocracy. Nevertheless, social mobility was never the option for many, as it would become during the nineteenth and twentieth centuries.

As in previous centuries, the aristocracy enjoyed the highest status and the greatest number of privileges. Their position was defined not by wealth but by title and blood. Some were fabulously rich, but others were relatively impoverished. However, an aristocrat was expected to have enough wealth to fulfill costly political, social, and military functions. Usually that wealth derived from the lands they owned, and most of it was protected by numerous exemptions from taxes.

Below the aristocrats were the clergy and commoners. In these groups there were ordered ranks as well. In the cities the wealthiest merchants, particularly those from "old families," were on top. They enjoyed some of the distinctions of rank and power that aristocrats had, and some were granted aristoratic status. Below them were guild members, followed by artisans and unskilled workers. In the countryside the ownership of land usually determined status. The

wealthiest landowners, often called the gentry, performed many of the functions of the landed aristocracy. Below them, landowning peasants enjoyed some position, leaving the landless peasants toward the bottom—though even they were in a higher position than those who were still serfs and bound to their masters.

Within this social structure, it was the group rather than the individual that was supposed to be of primary importance. First came the family and the household, then the local community, finally the larger social order with its various orders and hierarchies. In our sense of the term, national identity was still of secondary importance for most people.

Rural Life

Seventeenth- and eighteenth-century Europeans lived predominantly in rural settings. In western Europe approximately 80 percent still lived in the countryside; in the less urbanized eastern Europe the percentage was even higher. In rural areas life was centered on the traditional village (see Figure 31.2). Most villages were small, ranging in size from a few families to little over a hundred families. There life was communally oriented: villagers knew each other, strangers stood out, and almost all effective authority was local. Community pressures limited what we today would consider the rights of dissent and privacy. The local church or manor served as a center of communal activities. Still relatively isolated, villages had to be self-sufficient. When bad harvests occurred, as they did on a regular basis, help from outside was rarely available.

Most people were relatively poor, living in small, crowded structures. Inside there few furnishings or possessions. At one end was a stone hearth for light, cooking, and heat, but shortages of fuel (wood and peat) meant people suffered from the cold. Bread and grain products made up most of their meals, though in various areas meat, vegetables, fruits, and dairy products supplemented their diets. If they owned or had rights to land, they could raise their own food. Even this was of little help when the crops failed.

During this period the traditional pattern of rural life was slowly being altered. The traditional village was experiencing intrusion from the outside, change in its age-old pattern of life, and loss of people to the growing cities. The political isolation of the village was being broken by the increased presence of officials from the growing central governments, by the growing absence of the local nobility (who were attracted to the courts and capital cities), and by the decline of communal political institutions. Above all, economic life was being changed by the agricultural revolution and the spread of cottage industry—both of these facilitated by improving means of transportation.

The Agricultural Revolution At the beginning of the seventeenth century, crops and animals were raised in western Europe much as they had been since the Middle Ages. Most fields were open and divided into various strips of land. Crops were rotated and land allowed to lie fallow (unplanted) one out of every two or three years to keep the soil fertile. Large strips of land were set aside as "commons"—open areas where villagers grazed their animals and gathered food and hay. Decisions about crops, animals, and land use were usually determined by tradition and the practices of the community.

During the seventeenth and eighteenth centuries, changes in agricultural production initiated in Holland spread to England and then to other areas of western Europe. These changes were so important that they have been called an agricultural revolution. New crops such as potatoes, turnips, and clover were introduced. New methods of rotating crops, such as from grains to tubers (potatoes and turnips) to hay (grasses for animal fodder), were developed. Fertilization of the soil was increased by using manure from larger animal herds. These changes enabled farmers to eliminate fallow land. In addition, Dutch innovators developed methods of draining wetlands so that new crops and methods could easily be introduced. They also experimented with breeding to create new strains of more productive cattle.

In the early eighteenth century, the new crops and methods spread to England. Charles "Turnip" Townsend experimented with crop rotation and the use of turnips and clover. His contemporary and compatriot, Jethro Tull, advocated the use of a seed drill, which made planting more efficient and productive. Another Englishman, Robert Bakewell, improved the existing types of sheep and cattle by selective breeding.

These changes were sometimes connected to the enclosure of open fields and commons, particularly in England. The consolidation and enclosure of scattered strips and farms allowed larger landowners the freedom to apply new agricultural methods. Enclosures had been used in Great Britain since the sixteenth century, but the profits that could be made in commercial agriculture employing new crops and methods stimulated numerous landlords to seek enclosures during the eighteenth century. After 1750 Parliament authorized a wave of enclosures that transformed the British countryside. While these enclosures hastened the agricultural revolution, they left large numbers of rural poor unable to survive as small farmers. Many of them were forced into the ranks of rural or urban workers.

Cottage Industry During the seventeenth and eighteenth centuries, "cottage industry," or the "putting-out system," expanded greatly in rural areas. According to this system, a merchant-capitalist provided raw materials (usually for production of textiles such as wool or linen) and sometimes equipment (such as a handloom or spinning wheel) to peasants. Peasants, working in their cottages, turned these raw materials into

Figure 31.3 Cottage Industry Most cottage industry was in textiles. Here the various members of a rural household in Ireland work together, beating and combing flax into linen, which will be spun and woven. (The Mansell Collection)

finished products—spinning and weaving wool into cloth (see Figure 31.3). The merchant periodically returned, paid for the peasants' labor by the piece, and distributed the finished products to distant markets. The pay was low, lower than that offered in cities, but it was enough to help large numbers of peasants and rural workers to survive. The growth of cottage industry during the eighteenth century, particularly in Great Britain and parts of France and Germany, helps explain how so many people could remain in rural areas.

Urban Life

Cities grew during the seventeenth and eighteenth centuries, but unevenly. Until the middle of the eighteenth century, most of the growth was in the capital and port cities, particularly in northern and western Europe. These cities swelled with the growth of central governments and commerce. After the 1750s new cities arose and small cities grew, reflecting the general population growth and new concentrations of agricultural and industrial activity, particularly in Great Britain.

This urban growth meant greater prosperity for some, but a large percentage of the urban masses were not beneficiaries. They continued to live precariously at little more than a subsistence level. The poorest were the hardest hit by the surplus of labor, inflation, and disasters such as war, disease, and failed harvests. In bad times, food riots were common. As traditional ways of aiding the poor—through the Church or private charity—were overwhelmed, cities tried to control begging and enact various sorts of poor relief. Legislation, such as the English Poor Laws, required the impoverished to work on public projects or in workhouses and provided some training, but laws such as these were often not carried out or were used more to control and discipline the poor than to help them.

However, there were more kinds of food, more goods, and more opportunities in cities. Artisans and skilled workers lived relatively comfortable lives. Those who found regular unskilled jobs as haulers or domestic servants were probably better off than the rural poor. Many worked or supplemented their income on small plots of land within or just outside the city; some cities owned large tracts of land and hired people to farm them.

Those who benefited most from improvements in the standard of living were the middle and aristocratic classes, particularly those taking advantage of the opportunities in commerce and industry and in the expanding governmental bureaucracies. A growing class of urban professionals attended institutions of higher education. In an expanding number of colleges they joined young aristocrats sent by families who felt that more education and culture were appropriate to members of the aristocracy. The middle classes continued to use their wealth to enter the aristocracy through the purchase of titles and offices, the acquisition of large estates, and judicious marriages.

The Family

The family, so central to social life and the socialization of future generations, is usually one of our most conservative institutions, evolving only gradually over time. This pattern of subtle, slow change held true for most of the seventeenth and eighteenth centuries.

The family functioned as both a social and an economic unit. In this household economy (or family economy), everyone who could worked for the good of the household. Husband, wife, children, servants, and apprentices were part of this unit of production and consumption. Even those who earned wages elsewhere usually sent part of their earnings back to the family. Children were often sent away to other households when they could earn more outside their own family.

Child rearing and attitudes toward children were strikingly different from those of today. Children were generally not at the center of family life nor of primary concern. Girls were less valued than boys, reflecting women's subordination to men. Infanticide, though illegal, was not unknown, abandonment was a common practice, and what we would consider neglect was more often the rule than the exception. Much of this behavior may be explained by the high rate of infant mortality (some 30 to 50 percent of children died within the first five years of life), the generally precarious state of the household economy, and simple poverty. Certainly the lack of birth control may have played a role: Modern methods were unknown, the unreliable method of withdrawal was discouraged or condemned, and abortion was dangerous. Parents usually had to view those children who survived not only as family members but as assets or liabilities in the survival of the family. With life so precarious for their children, any great emotional involvement with them was risky.

It was once thought that most people lived in extended families—more than one married couple and their children in the same household; however, most historians now agree that as a rule people lived in a nuclear family household consisting of one couple and their children. Nevertheless, the typical family household during the sixteenth, seventeenth, and most of the eighteenth centuries was a much more populated, public place than the household of a modern nineteenth- or twentieth-century nuclear family. At various times a variety of relatives lived in or moved through the household, as did domestics and laborers. The household was far more open to members of the community and pressures from the community at large. The father, older children, other relatives, and community adults in general participated with the mother in raising and socializing young children.

Marriages continued to be entered into for primarily economic and social reasons. The land, wealth, skills, and position one held were the most important considerations in contemplating marriage; sentiment, particularly being in love, played a secondary role. Children were the expected product of a successful marriage. Typically, a married woman gave birth to more than five children, though the odds were that many of those would fail to reach adulthood or even get beyond the first few years of childhood. Marriages whether happy or not, were expected to last. Divorce, though permitted in Protestant communities, was in most cases difficult if not impossible. Separation was more accepted, but death, which often struck people at a relatively young age, was usually the only way out of an unsuccessful marriage.

Within the middle and upper classes, a significant change came during the second half of the eighteenth century. Sentiment became more important as a motivation for marriage; economic and social considerations, while still important, were not quite as dominant as before. Premarital sex and sex outside of marriage were on the increase, as evidenced by the growing number of births registered within a few months of marriage and by the rising rates of illegitimacy. People were marrying at an earlier age and moving around more. Child rearing and homemaking were being turned into a woman's profession in middle-class households. Along with the rising likelihood that most babies born would survive came a changing perception of children as more special, precious, and loved—not miniature adults to be used, as they had more often been perceived in the sixteenth and seventeenth centuries. Indeed, what was happening during the second half of the eighteenth century was a slow transformation to the modern family, which would come into bloom with the spread of industry and the dominance of the middle class during the nineteenth century.

Women

Women, while continuing to play a subordinate role to men, were central to the economic well-being of the family among the lower classes. Their work started when they were children, helping with the lighter tasks of farming or cottage industry. In her early teens, a girl often left home to work as a servant, trying to gain skills and money for her future marriage and the establishment of a new household. As a married woman, she could expect to spend much of her time pregnant (five or more pregnancies were not unusual) and involved with child care. But her tasks as childbearer and child rearer were no more important than her other economic and social functions. In addition to the standard household chores, women were expected to work as much as possible. Women participated in the collecting and threshing of grain, took primary responsibility for gardening, raised poultry, supervised and processed dairy production, and shared in the manufacture of household items and products for commerce (particularly spinning) as the putting-out system spread. When women worked in wage-earning occupations, it was generally at less pay and in lower-status positions than men. The line between acceptable "women's work" and "men's work" widened as the emphasis on women's domestic responsibilities grew. Within the household women were legally subordinate to their husbands and generally expected to be subject to his authority. Outside a household, women were particularly vulnerable. They lacked many legal rights and were denied most alternatives for independent employment. There were some occupations open to women, such as glove making, spinning yarn, midwifery, and nursing, but the status and pay of these occupations were often diminished because of their association with women.

Middle- and upper-class women had fewer opportunities for participation in economic life. Respectable careers open to unmarried middle-class women were limited to those of governess or lady-in-waiting. Once married, the middle-class woman was at the center of the family, but for any real economic independence she had to wait for the death of her husband. More than lower-class women, middle-class women were increasingly seen as responsible for upholding standards and supervising the help within the home. Most aristocratic women were similarly limited in the economic roles they played, but they could turn to influential social and cultural roles (see Chapter 36). Some, such as Queen Christina in seventeenth-century Sweden, Maria Theresa in eighteenth-century Austria, and Catherine the Great in eighteenth-century Russia, became rulers. Others, such as Maria de Médicis in seventeenth-century France, became surrogate rulers or royal regents. More often, they held privileged positions in royal courts and served as unofficial advisers. As courtiers women could gain position, wealth, and prestigage for themselves and their families.

2. FAITH: THE GROWTH OF PIETISM

After the end of the Wars of Religion in the mid–seventeenth century, a relative status quo existed between Catholicism and Protestantism. While hostility still existed among the believers of different Christian faiths, it no longer broke out into the violence and revolution characteristic of the Reformation era. Religious life remained centered in the local parish. In his church, the priest or pastor conducted services and supervised various charitable and educational activities. Although most people retained an allegiance to the established Catholic or Protestant churches, some new religious movements did arise during the seventeenth and eighteenth centuries. The most important were a number of pietistic sects which stressed the importance of active faith in leading a religious life.

In Germany Philipp Spener (1635–1705) and Count Zinzendorf (1700–1760) became leaders of pietist movements of considerable dimensions. Spener, a Lutheran pastor, recoiled from the formal officiousness that his church had fallen into after the heated religious strife of the sixteenth and early seventeenth centuries. He minimized dogma and external forms in favor of inner piety and holy living. His largely Lutheran following included some of the leading intellects of Germany. Count Zinzendorf, a well-to-do Saxon nobleman, undertook to restore the Bohemian Brethren, the persecuted and scattered followers of the early-fifteenth-century reformer Jan Huss. He called his group the Moravian Brethren. The Moravians, too, shunned intricate dogma and formal ritual. They set up model communities based on brotherly love, frugal living, hard work, and inner piety.

In Lutheran Sweden, Emanuel Swedenborg (1688–1772), a distinguished scientist, inventor, and public servant, founded a movement somewhat like the Moravian Brethren, based on his visions, which he took to be direct revelations of God. Swedenborg wrote several learned theological works stressing inner and outward piety and individual communion with God.

England, however, was the seat of the most widespread and influential pietistic movements of the seventeenth and eighteenth centuries. The first was the Society of Friends, or Quakers, as they were generally called, founded by George Fox (1624–1691). Fox, a man of great energy and stubborn independence, detested formalism in religion as well as in society and government. He believed that true Christianity is an individual matter—a matter of plain, pious living and of private communion with God under the guidance of a divine "inner light." Opposed to war, rank, and intolerance, the Quakers refused military service, the use of titles, and the taking of oaths. In these respects the Quakers were different from most of the other pietists. They were considered dangerous to the established order and were severely persecuted.

A more moderate and popular pietist movement was Methodism. The prime mover in Methodism was John Wesley (1703–1791). John Wesley and his brother, Charles, became converted to a more fervent, evangelical type of Christianity. When the Anglican churches closed their doors to John Wesley, he preached emotional sermons to huge throngs in the streets and fields. George Whitefield, the most eloquent of all the early Methodists, electrified tens of thousands in England and America and converted many to pietistic Christianity. The real founder of Methodism in the American colonies was Francis Asbury (1745–1816), who in many respects duplicated the work of John Wesley in England. In both England and America the Methodists grew rapidly in numbers, mostly among the middle and lower classes.

The various pietist groups were definitely not political revolutionaries. They were intensely interested in social reform—in education, health and sanitation, temperance, penal reform, and abolition of the slave trade. But they hoped to achieve these reforms by private charity rather than political action. They tended to accommodate themselves to the political status quo in the belief that spiritual and social conditions could be improved within that framework of government.

3. CULTURE

The cultural styles of the seventeenth and eighteenth centuries reflected the dominance of royal and aristocratic tastes—particularly in the baroque, classical, and rococo styles. The main exceptions were in the Dutch Netherlands and eighteenth-century England, where paintings and literature often reflected the tastes of the ascending middle class. Bridging the middle and upper classes were the scientific revolution and the Enlightenment, two intellectual and cultural developments of great importance that will be examined on their own in Chapters 35 and 36.

Literature

The reign of Louis XIV (1643–1715) was the golden age of French literature. The elegance, the sense of order, and the formalism of the court of the Grand Monarch were all reflected in the literature of the period, sometimes called the Augustan or classical period of French literature. It was in the field of drama that the French writers attained their greatest success. Corneille wrote elegant tragedies in the style of and often on the same subjects as the ancient Greek tragedies. The struggles of human beings against themselves and against the universe furnish the dramatic conflicts. Corneille's craftsmanship and style are handsomely polished, though often exalted and exaggerated.

Even more exquisitely polished were the perfectly rhymed and metered couplets of Racine's tragedies: *Andromaque* relates the tragic story of Hector's wife after the death of her husband at the hands of Achilles and the ensuing fall of Troy. *Phèdre* is about the wife of the legendary Greek king Theseus who falls in love with her stepson. This story had also been the subject of plays by Euripides, Sophocles, and Seneca.

One of the greatest of all the French dramatists was Molière. In his charming and profound comedies—such as *Tartuffe, Le Misanthrope,* and *Les Femmes Savantes (The Learned Ladies)*—Molière devastatingly portrays and satirizes the false, the stupid, and the pompous: egotists, pedants, social climbers, false priests, quack physicians. The tragic conflicts and personality types of Corneille, Racine, and Molière are universal and eternal.

Perhaps the most popular novel of the period was *Grand Cyrus,* a historical romance by Madeleine de Scudéry. The fact that this book was published under the name of her brother Georges indicates some of the difficulties women faced in cultural pursuits.

Other major French writers of the age of Louis XIV were Blaise Pascal, the scientist and mathematician who also wrote the marvelously styled *Provincial Letters* against the Jesuits and the deeply reflective *Pensées (Thoughts);* Madame de Sévigné, who wrote almost two thousand letters to her daughter, each a work of art; and the duke of Saint-Simon, who spent the latter part of his life writing forty volumes of *Mémoires.* Madame de Sévigné and the duke of Saint-Simon, both of whom were eyewitnesses at the court of Louis XIV, constitute two of the most important sources we have for the history and life of that period.

The common denominator among all these writers is their emphasis on and mastery of elegant and graceful form. In this emphasis they reflect the spirit of royal absolutism at its height. However, form is valued not merely for its own sake but as an artistic clothing for subtle and critical thought. French literature in the late seventeenth century overshadowed that of all other countries of Europe, much as did French military and political influence. The lucid, graceful French language became the fashionable language of most of the royal courts and courtiers on the European continent.

French literature in the eighteenth century continued for the most part in the classical vein. Voltaire wrote dramas and poems carefully tailored to the dictates of classical formalism. His prose works exalted logic and the ideals of Greece and Rome. Only Rousseau among the major eighteenth-century French writers departed from the classical spirit to anticipate the romanticism of a later era.

Next to France, England produced the most important literature in the seventeenth and early eighteenth centuries, and like the French, the English authors generally wrote in the classical vein. The giant of English letters in the mid–seventeenth century was John Milton (1608–1674). This learned Puritan was steeped in the literature of ancient Greece and Rome. His exquisite lyrics *L'Allegro* and *Il Penseroso* and incomparable elegy *Lycidas* are thickly strewn with references to classical mythology. The conscientious Milton contributed much of his great talent and energy to public affairs. During the Puritan Revolution he went blind while working as a pamphleteer for the Puritan cause and secretary for Oliver Cromwell. The chief literary product of this period of his life is *Areopagitica,* probably the noblest defense of freedom of the press ever penned. Milton's masterpiece is *Paradise Lost,* written in his blindness and after the restoration of the Stuart kings had ruined his public career. *Paradise Lost* is a poem of epic proportions based on the Genesis account of the rebellion of Satan against God and the temptation and fall of human beings. This majestic theme is treated in stately blank verse of formal elegance. Even in this deeply religious work, Holy Writ is interwoven with classical pagan myth.

The two greatest poets to succeed Milton were John Dryden in the late seventeenth century and Alexander Pope in the early eighteenth century. Both were satirists, both displayed a massive knowledge of Greek and Roman lore, and both wrote chiefly in the formal rhymed couplets typical of the classical period. In the precision of their form, as in the sharpness of their satire, their appeal was to reason rather than to emotion.

The eighteenth century in English literature was an age of great prose. Following the upheavals of the seventeenth century, the Puritan and Glorious revolutions, it was a time of political and religious bitterness and bickering. In pungent and incisive prose Jonathan Swift, in his *Gulliver's Travels* and political essays, and Richard Sheridan, in his numerous dramas, pilloried the fops, pedants, bigots, and frauds of the day, much as Molière had done a century earlier across the Channel. It was in the eighteenth century that the English novel was born. More than other literary forms, it was aimed at and reflected the tastes of England's rising middle class. Samuel Richardson, in *Clarissa Harlowe,* and Henry Fielding, in *Tom Jones,* used this medium to analyze human personality, emotions, and psychology, just as Corneille and Racine had used the poetic drama in France for the same purpose.

In the eighteenth century several writers—

Robert Burns in Great Britain, Rousseau in France, Schiller and Goethe in Germany—anticipated romanticism (see Chapter 41). But the prevailing spirit in eighteenth- as in seventeenth-century literature was classical. Precision, formalism, and ofttimes elegance marked the style. Ancient Greece and Rome furnished the models. The appeal was generally to reason. The royal monarchs and their courts had little to fear from this literature. They could derive comfort from its formal order and laugh with the rest of the world at its satire, which was aimed at humankind in general rather than at the ruling regimes.

Painting and Architecture

If the literature of the seventeenth and eighteenth centuries did not offend the absolutist kings and their aristocratic courtiers, the visual arts of the period usually glorified them (see Color Plate 17). The dominant style of painting and architecture during the seventeenth century was baroque, which used elaborate swirling forms and colors to achieve dramatic, emotional effects. The baroque style was originally associated with the Roman Catholic Reformation and reflected the resurgence of a revitalized Roman Catholic church led by the militant Jesuits. Later its massive and ornamental elegance reflected the wealth and power of the absolutist monarchs and their courts, then at the peak of their affluence.

The most popular of the baroque painters of the early seventeenth century was the Fleming Peter Paul Rubens (1577–1640). After studying the work of the Italian High Renaissance masters, Rubens returned to Antwerp and painted more than two thousand pictures, many of them huge canvases. He operated what amounted to a painting factory, employing dozens of artists who painted in the details designed and sketched by the master. Rubens, a devout Roman Catholic, first painted religious subjects (see Color Plate 14). His later subjects were pagan mythology, court life, and especially voluptuous nude women—all painted in the most brilliant and sensuous colors (see Figure 31.4).

Spain boasted two of the greatest seventeenth-century painters: El Greco and Velásquez. El Greco, whose real name was Domenikos Theotokopoulos, was a native of the Greek island of Crete (hence "The Greek"). After studying the

FIGURE 31.4 Peter Paul Rubens, *Henry IV Receiving the Portrait of Marie de Médicis,* 1621–1625 Rubens was commissioned by Marie de Médicis, widow of King Henry IV of France, to paint this allegorical scene showing Henri IV considering a proposed marriage to Marie de Médicis. The swirling lines, dramatic perspective, rich color, and opulence are typically baroque. (The Louvre, Paris)

Italian Renaissance masters, he settled down in Toledo and developed a style of his own. By deliberate distortion and exaggeration he achieved sensational effects. *View of Toledo, St. Jerome in His Study,* and *Christ at Gethsemane* illustrate his genius. El Greco's favorite subject was the reinvigorated Church of the Roman Catholic Reformation. Considered by his contemporaries to be a madman, he is now regarded as the forerunner of several schools of nineteenth- and twentieth-century painting. Velásquez was a painter of great versatility. Although much of his earlier work was of a religious nature, he also painted genre subjects (depicting the life of the common people) and later portraits. He is considered one of the greatest of portrait painters. As official court painter, he exalted and glorified the Spanish royalty and ruling classes at a time when they had really passed their peak in world affairs.

During the second half of the seventeenth and then the eighteenth century, classicism, with its greater emphasis on control and restraint, gained favor. Good examples of classicism are in the works of the French artists Nicolas Poussin and Claude Lorraine (see Color Plate 15). Poussin spent most of his life in Italy studying the Renaissance masters. Although his biblical and mythological scenes are more vibrant and pulsating than the Italian Renaissance paintings that inspired them, they are much more serene, subtle, and controlled than the works of Rubens and El Greco.

In eighteenth-century Great Britain, Joshua Reynolds, Thomas Gainsborough, George Romney, and Sir Thomas Lawrence vied with one another for commissions to paint the portraits of royalty and aristocracy. The results were plumes, jewels, buckles, silks, brocades, and laces in dripping profusion (see Figure 31.1).

FIGURE 31.5 The Baroque Style This photo is of the interior of the basilica St. Andrea della Valle, which was built in the latter part of the seventeenth century. It well illustrates the elaborate, gaudy splendor of the baroque style, the hallmark of the age of royal absolutism and affluence. In this case the royal monarch was the pope, ruler of a Church reinvigorated by the Roman Catholic Reformation. (Alinari/Scala/Art Resource)

In the Dutch Netherlands painting did not reflect royal and aristocratic tastes. Here in the busy ports and marketplaces commerce was king, and the great Dutch painters of the seventeenth century, notably Frans Hals, Jan Vermeer, and Rembrandt van Rijn, portrayed the bourgeoisie and common people (see Color Plate 16). Rembrandt is universally recognized as one of the greatest artistic geniuses of all time. As a portrayer of character he has never been surpassed. His mastery of light and shade (*chiaroscuro*) made it seem as if the very souls of his subjects were illumined. *Syndics of the Cloth Guild*, *The Night Watch*, and *The Anatomy Lesson of Dr. Tulp* (see p. 443) are among his most pow-

erful portrait studies. These three paintings also vividly depict the commercial prosperity, the festive urban life, and the growing interest in natural science in the seventeenth-century Dutch Netherlands.

Baroque architecture, like baroque painting, was an elaboration and ornamentation of the Renaissance and a product of the Roman Catholic Reformation (see Figure 31.5). In the late sixteenth, the seventeenth, and the eighteenth centuries Jesuit churches sprang up all over the Roman Catholic world. The most important and one of the best examples of the baroque style is the Jesuit parent church, Il Gesù, in Rome. Also, like the painting, baroque architecture was later used to represent the gaudy splendor of the seventeenth- and eighteenth-century absolute monarchs and their courts.

Towering over all other monuments of baroque architecture, much as St. Peter's towered over all other Renaissance structures, was the Versailles Palace of Louis XIV (see Figure 32.1). The exterior of Versailles is designed in long, horizontal, classic lines. The interior is lavishly decorated with richly colored marbles, mosaics, inlaid woods, gilt, silver, silk, velvet, and brocade. The salons and halls are lighted with ceiling-to-floor windows and mirrors and crystal chandeliers holding thousands of candles. The palace faces hundreds of acres of groves, walks, pools, terraces, fountains, statues, flower beds, and clipped shrubs—all laid out in formal geometric patterns. So dazzling was this symbol of royal absolutism that many European monarchs attempted to copy it. The most successful attempt was Maria Theresa's Schönbrunn Palace in Vienna.

In England Sir Christopher Wren was the greatest architect of the baroque period. The great fire that destroyed most of the heart of London in 1666 provided Wren with an opportunity to build numerous baroque structures. His masterpiece is St. Paul's Cathedral, with its lofty dome and columns.

In the eighteenth century, architecture tended to become less massive, relying heavily on multiple curves and lacy shell-like ornamentation. This style is usually referred to as rococo. One of the best examples of the rococo style is Frederick the Great's Sans Souci Palace at Potsdam. The rococo style, like the baroque, represented an age of royal and aristocratic affluence.

Music

The classical spirit pervaded the music of the seventeenth and eighteenth centuries as it did the literature and the visual arts; and like the literature and the visual arts, the music was an outgrowth of Renaissance developments.[1] The piano and the violin family of instruments, whose fore-

bears appeared in the sixteenth century, developed rapidly in the seventeenth. In the late seventeenth and early eighteenth centuries, three Italian families, the Amati, the Guarneri, and the Stradivari, fashioned the finest violins ever made. The seventeenth century was also marked by the rise of the opera. Alessandro Scarlatti in Italy, Jean-Baptiste Lully in France, and Henry Purcell in England popularized this grandiose combination of music and drama. The eighteenth was the great century of classical music—the age of Bach, Handel, Haydn, and Mozart.

Johann Sebastian Bach (1685–1750) was a member of a German family long distinguished in music. Noted in his own lifetime chiefly as an organist, he composed a vast array of great music for organ, harpsichord, and clavichord (forerunner of the piano), orchestra, and chorus, much of which has been lost. Most of Bach's compositions were religiously inspired, and he holds the same position in Protestant music that the sixteenth-century Palestrina does in the music of the Roman Catholic church. Bach was not widely appreciated in his own day. It was not until Felix Mendelssohn "discovered" him in the nineteenth century that he became widely known.

George Frederick Handel (1685–1759) was born in central Germany in the same year as Bach and not many miles distant. He studied Italian opera in Germany and Italy and wrote forty-six operas himself. He became court musician of the elector of Hanover. Later he made his home in England, as did the elector, who became King George I of England. Handel wrote an enormous quantity of music, both instrumental and vocal. All of it is marked by dignity, formal elegance, and melodious harmony—fitting for and appreciated in an age of royal splendor. His best-known work is the majestic oratorio *The Messiah*, heard every Christmas season.

Franz Joseph Haydn (1732–1809), unlike Handel, was primarily interested in instrumental music; he was the chief originator of the symphony. During his long career in Vienna, which he helped to make the music capital of the world, he wrote more than a hundred symphonies in addition to scores of compositions of other forms of music, particularly chamber music. It was in his hands that orchestral music really came into its own. All his work is in the formal, classical style. He became a friend and an important source of inspiration for the younger Mozart.

---

[1] Some music historians designate the music of the seventeenth and early eighteenth centuries, including that of Bach and Handel, as baroque, which was a forerunner of classical.

FIGURE 31.6 Pieter Brueghel the Younger, *Flemish Country Festival* This early-seventeenth-century painting shows one of the many typical festivals that took place during the year. Often such festivals were occasioned by religious holidays and celebrations. Here the lines between religion, social life, and popular culture blur as villagers gather and celebrate. (Galleria Sabauda, Turin/Art Resource)

Wolfgang Amadeus Mozart (1756–1791) is regarded by many students as the greatest musical genius of all time. Born in Salzburg, he spent most of his adult life in Vienna. Mozart began composing at the age of five (possibly four), and gave public concerts on the harpsichord at the age of six. At twelve he wrote an opera. Before his untimely death at the age of thirty-five, he wrote more than six hundred compositions in all the known musical forms. Symphonies, chamber music, and piano sonatas and concertos were his favorite forms. His best-known operas are *The Marriage of Figaro, Don Giovanni,* and *The Magic Flute.* In the masterful hands of Mozart the classical style reached the peak of its perfection. Never had music been so clear, melodic, elegant, and graceful.

Popular Culture

The formal literature and the baroque art of the seventeenth and eighteenth centuries reflected the concerns and tastes of the elite classes. However, the lower classes were not without cultural outlets that fit their lives and were available to them.

Numerous festivals and public ceremonies occurred throughout the year (see Figure 31.6). Some reflected the seasons, which were of particular importance to societies so dependent on agriculture, while others reflected events on the Christian calendar, such as Christmas and Easter. Traditional weddings involved a community procession and festivities as well as a religious ceremony. Music, dancing, feasts, game, and play were part of these festivals and community events.

Sports also brought communities together and were often violent. The most popular involved animals, such as cockfighting and dogfighting. Others, such as soccer and cricket, became more organized, sometimes drawing large crowds.

Literacy was growing, thanks to the printing press, the demands of business, and more primary schools. Some 40 to 60 percent of the population in England and France could read by the end of the eighteenth century, and this was reflected in the growth of popular literature. Stirring religious tracts as well as romances of chivalric valor were widely circulated.

Finally, the line between elite and popular culture was not very sharp. Members of all classes could be found at village festivals and sporting events. The middle and upper classes read some of the same popular literature enjoyed by the lower classes, while the lower classes had some access to the plays, art, and architecture that reflected elite tastes.

SUGGESTED READING

General

F. Braudel, *The Structures of Everyday Life: The Limits of the Possible* (1982). A massive, highly respected social history.

H. Kamen, *European Society, 1500–1700* (1985). A solid survey.

I. Woloch, *Eighteenth Century Europe, Tradition and Progress, 1715–1789* (1982). Emphasizes social history and popular culture.

Society

P. Ariés, *Centuries of Childhood: A Social History of Family Life* (1962). A path-breaking work.

J. V. Beckett, *The Aristocracy in England* (1986). A good recent study.

J. Blum, *The End of the Old Order in Rural Europe* (1978). Excellent comparative study.

M. W. Flinn, *The European Demographic System, 1500–1820* (1981). A recent survey.

A. Fraser, *The Weaker Vessel: Woman's Lot in Seventeenth-Century England* (1985). Portraits of seventeenth-century women.

P. Laslett, *The World We Have Lost* (1965). A classic study of English society during the period.

E. Shorter, *The Making of the Modern Family* (1975). Interpretive, controversial, and well written.

L. Stone, *The Family, Sex and Marriage in England, 1500–1800* (1977). A sophisticated interpretation.

L. Tilly and J. Scott, *Women, Work and Family* (1978). A highly respected work.

J. de Vries, *European Urbanization, 1500–1800* (1984). Broad recent survey.

Faith

A. Armstrong, *The Church of England, the Methodists, and Society 1700–1850* (1973). A broad survey.

G. R. Cragg, *The Church and the Age of Reason* (1961). A solid survey.

Culture

A. Adam, *Grandeur and Illusion: French Literature and Society 1600–1715* (1972). A thorough survey of French literature and its relation to seventeenth-century society.

P. Burke, *Popular Culture in Early Modern Europe* (1978). Focuses on ordinary people.

J. Held, *Seventeenth and Eighteenth Century Art: Baroque Painting, Sculpture, Architecture* (1971). A useful general survey.

C. Palisca, *Baroque Music* (1968). Excellent survey.

C. Rosen, *The Classical Style: Haydn, Mozart, Beethoven* (1972). Excellent study.

I. Watt, *The Rise of the Novel: Studies of Defoe, Richardson, and Fielding* (1957). A good introduction.

CHAPTER 32

Royal Absolutism in Western and Eastern Europe

FIGURE 32.1 Pierre Patel the Elder, *Versailles*, 1668 This painting shows Louis XIV's palace and grounds at Versailles in 1668. The scale and order of Versailles reflected the grandeur of the French monarchy at its height. Other European monarchs modeled their palaces after Versailles in an attempt to increase their own prestige. (Lauros-Giraudon/Art Resource)

During the seventeenth and eighteenth centuries, several monarchs in western and eastern Europe increased the power of their central governments and elevated themselves as holders of that power. These monarchs often justified their absolute powers as a divine right and surrounded themselves with advisers and admirers who supported royal absolutism. While in some countries the trend was away from monarchical power, royal absolutism became the dominant political development of this period.

1. ABSOLUTISM IN WESTERN EUROPE: FRANCE

France was the most powerful nation in western Europe throughout most of the seventeenth and eighteenth centuries. Under Louis XIV royal absolutism not only reached its peak in France but also served as a model that other monarchs sought to emulate.

While French monarchs had been gaining power for their central government and themselves since the fifteenth century (see pp. 362–363), the immediate roots of royal absolutism in France go back to the reign of Henry IV (1589–1610).

The Roots of French Absolutism

When Henry IV became king of France in 1589, his country was torn by several decades of bitter religious war. Respect for law and order had broken down. The feudal nobility had in many cases reasserted its own authority. The finances of the central government were in chaos. Roads and bridges were in disrepair. French prestige abroad was at a low ebb; even the city of Paris was garrisoned by the Spanish troops of Philip II.

Henry of Navarre, the first of the Bourbon dynasty to rule France, set out to change all this. The new king, in his prime at the age of thirty-six, was debonair and witty, courageous, generous, and optimistic. His slogan "A chicken in the pot of every peasant for Sunday dinner" was more than an idle phrase; it is little wonder that *Henri Quatre* became the most popular monarch in French history. The romantic Henry had in the duke of Sully an able, methodical administrator to serve and steady him. The most urgent task

was to restore the authority of the central government. This Henry set out to do by vigorously suppressing brigandage and enforcing the law. The lesser nobility was brought to heel directly and quickly. The powerful nobility was dealt with more gingerly, but by the end of Henry's reign real headway had been made toward reducing the nobles to obedience to the central government.

Henry and Sully launched a comprehensive program of economic reconstruction. Agriculture and commerce benefited from the increased security of life and property, from the repair of roads, bridges, and harbors, and from the freeing of internal and external commerce from many obstructions and tariff barriers. Marshes were drained for farming. Better breeding methods were introduced. Peasants' livestock and implements were protected against seizure for debt or taxes. New industries producing glass, porcelain, lace, tapestries, and fine leather and textiles were subsidized and protected by the state. Silk culture, which brought vast wealth to France, was introduced. Sully's efficient administration of expenditures resulted in a budget surplus for the first time in many years.

Henry defused the religious turmoil that had weakened France by granting religious toleration to the Huguenot minority. A *politique*, Henry abjured Protestantism in order to gain acceptance as king of an overwhelmingly Roman Catholic nation. The Edict of Nantes, which Henry IV issued in 1598, granted the Huguenots not only complete freedom of conscience and limited public worship but also civil and political equality. Moreover, they were given military control of some two hundred fortified cities and towns as a guarantee against future oppression.

Having laid the foundations for royal supremacy, economic health, and religious toleration, Henry IV in the last years of his reign devoted an increasing amount of attention to foreign affairs. His goal was to make France first secure and then supreme in Europe by weakening the power of the Spanish and Austrian Hapsburgs. In 1610 he readied his armies for a campaign, but just as he was preparing to join them he was assassinated by a fanatic.

After fourteen years of retrogression under Henry IV's Italian wife, Marie de Médicis, and their young and inept son Louis XIII (1610–1643),

Cardinal Richelieu gained active control over the government of France. Although technically a mere servant of the fickle Louis XIII, the masterful cardinal made himself so indispensable that for eighteen years (1624–1642) he held firm control over French affairs. Handsome, arrogant, and calculating, Richelieu was a true Machiavellian. His twofold policy, from which he never veered, was similar to that of Henry IV—to make the royal power supreme in France and France supreme in Europe.

Believing the high nobility and the Huguenots to be the chief threats to royal absolutism, Richelieu crushed them both. With the royal army at his disposal, he boldly destroyed the castles of nobles who remained defiant, disbanded their private armies, and hanged a number of the most recalcitrant. The special military and political privileges that the Huguenots enjoyed under the Edict of Nantes were considered by Richelieu to be intolerable, giving them the status of a state within a state. After a bloody two-year struggle, he stripped the Huguenots of these privileges, although he left their religious and civil liberties intact.

In order to dilute local political influence, which in some provinces was still strong, the dynamic minister divided France into some thirty administrative districts called *généralités,* each of which was placed under the control of an *intendant,*[1] who was an agent of the crown. These *intendants* were chosen from the ranks of the bourgeoisie and were shifted around frequently lest they become too sympathetic with the people over whom they ruled. The royal will was thus further extended throughout France.

Although Richelieu was a cardinal in the Roman Catholic church, he did not hesitate to plunge France into the Thirty Years' War in Germany on the side of the Protestants. His purpose, of course, was to weaken the Hapsburgs, chief rivals of the French Bourbons for European supremacy. When Richelieu died in 1642, he had gone far toward bringing to fruition Henry IV's policies of royal supremacy in France and French supremacy in Europe. Richelieu, however, did

not share Henry IV's concern for the common people. Their lot became harder under the imperious and ruthless cardinal, at whose death they rejoiced.

Richelieu was succeeded by his protégé, Cardinal Mazarin. Louis XIII's death in 1643, one year after that of his great minister, left the throne to Louis XIV (1643–1715), a child of five. Mazarin played the same role in the early reign of Louis XIV that Richelieu had played during most of the reign of Louis XIII. From the death of Richelieu in 1642 until his own death in 1661, Mazarin vigorously pursued the policies of his predecessor. The Thirty Years' War was brought to a successful conclusion. Between 1648 and 1652, he put down the *Fronde*—a series of uprisings by disgruntled nobility and townspeople. All who challenged the crown's authority were crushed. When Marazin died in 1661, he passed along to young Louis XIV a royal power that was unprecedented and a national state that was easily the first power of Europe.

Louis XIV and His Government

Louis XIV was twenty-three years old when, in 1661, he stepped forth as the principal actor on the world's gaudiest stage. Young Louis was well fitted for the part. He had a sound body and a regal bearing. His lack of intellectual brilliance and deep learning were more than offset by a large store of common sense, a sharp memory, a sense of responsibility, and a capacity for hard, tedious work. From his Spanish mother, from Mazarin, and from his tutors he had gained the conviction that he was God's appointed deputy for France. In Bishop Bossuet he had the most famous of all theorists and exponents of royal absolutism. Bossuet in numerous writings argued that absolute monarchy is the normal, the most efficient, and the divinely ordained form of government. He contended that, furthermore, the royal monarch, the image of God and directly inspired by God, is above human reproach and accountable to God alone. These ideas as acted out by Louis gained and held the ascendancy throughout the continent of Europe during the late seventeenth and most of the eighteenth centuries.

Absolute though he might consider himself (the words *"L'état, c'est moi"* ["I am the state"]

---

[1]The *intendants* had existed before Richelieu's time, but he greatly increased their power and functions.

are often attributed to him), Louis could not possibly perform all the functions of government personally. Actually, the great bulk of the decisions and details of government were handled by a series of councils and bureaus and were administered locally by the *intendants*. Distrusting nobles, Louis appointed members of the middle class to the important offices of his government. As supervised by the industrious Louis XIV, however, the administrative machinery worked smoothly and efficiently. In fact, it was the envy of his fellow monarchs and probably constituted his most constructive achievement. There was no semblance of popular participation in government. The role of the people was to serve and obey; in return, they enjoyed reflected glory and received such benefits as the monarch might be willing and able to bestow on them.

In line with Louis XIV's concept of divine right absolutism, he believed that he should have a palace worthy of God's chief deputy on earth. Hating tumultuous Paris, congested and crowded with vulgar tradespeople, he selected Versailles, eleven miles southwest of the city, to be the new seat of government. There as many as thirty-five thousand workmen toiled for thirty years, turning the marshes and sandy wastes into the world's most splendid court (see Figure 32.1). Around his court Louis XIV gathered the great nobles of France and turned them into court butterflies (see Figure 32.2). He subsidized and brought to Versailles the leading French artists and literacy figures. But this great monument to royal absolutism was not beloved by all. The balls, parades, hunts, and social ritual were not sufficient to absorb the energy of the vivacious and ambitious nobility of France. The court seethed with gossip, scandal, and intrigue. Nor did the hard-toiling, heavily taxed French masses, who were supposed to enjoy the reflected glory of the monarch, always appreciate such extravagant glamour. Indeed, there were increasing expressions of discontent.

Colbert and the French Economy

Louis XIV was fortunate to have at his command during the first half of his reign a prodigious financial manager. Jean-Baptiste Colbert (1619–1683) was an inordinately ambitious social climber who realized that, because of his bourgeois origin, his only means of advancement was through indispensable service to the king. An engine of efficiency, he toiled endlessly, supervising the countless details of the French economy.

Under Colbert, mercantilism reached its peak. French industries were protected by prohibitive tariffs, while exports and new industries were subsidized. Raw materials, however, were strictly husbanded. Imperial and commercial activities in India and North America were vigorously promoted. To protect this growing empire and the commerce it generated, a large navy was built. But Colbert did not stop with these traditional mercantilist practices. In order to gain a worldwide reputation for the uniformly high quality of French products, all manufacturing was subjected to the most minute regulation and supervision. So many threads of such and such quality and color must go into every inch of this textile and that lace. A veritable army of inspectors enforced the regulations. This extreme policy of mercantilism, the economic adjunct to royal absolutism, has come to be called Colbertism. It achieved its immediate end so far as quality and reputation were concerned, but it stifled initiative and retarded future industrial development. That Colbert was able to balance the budget and achieve general economic prosperity in the face of Louis XIV's lavish expenditures, including the building of Versailles, was a remarkable feat. It is well, however, that Colbert died in 1683, for Louis' wars of aggression eventually wrecked most of the great minister's work. Much of Europe copied Colbert's policies and techniques during the latter part of the seventeenth and most of the eighteenth centuries.

Absolutism and Religion

It was virtually inevitable that Louis XIV's concepts of divine right monarchy would have religious repercussions. First, they ran counter to the papal claims of authority over the French clergy. Numerous conflicts between the king and pope resulted in a statement of Gallican Liberties, which greatly freed the French church from Roman domination. Second, Louis' absolutism ran afoul of the Jansenists, an influential group within France's Catholic church that emphasized predestination, inner piety, and the ascetic life.

FIGURE 32.2 Charles Lebrun, *Chancellor Seguier* Chancellor Seguier, a patron of the seventeenth-century French artist Lebrun, is shown here as an ambitious courtier to Louis XIV. In formal robes, this member of France's new nobility (*noblesse de robe*) is attended by pages as if he were a monarch. (The Louvre, Paris)

Eventually the Jesuits persuaded the pope to declare Jansenism heretical and aroused Louis XIV against the Jansenists. He outlawed the sect and destroyed its buildings. Finally, Louis XIV moved against the Huguenots—France's Protestants. In 1685 he revoked the Edict of Nantes and the Protestant religion was outlawed. Although Huguenots were forbidden to emigrate, many—probably a quarter million—succeeded in doing so, taking much of their wealth and all their economic knowledge and skills with them to Protestant areas of Europe and America.

Louis XIV's Wars of Aggression

The Sun King was not content to rule the world's most powerful nation. He wanted to expand France's borders. Louis' war minister, the marquis of Louvois, organized France's huge military establishment on a scientific and business-like basis, replete with supply depots and hospitals. He introduced strict discipline, uniforms, and marching drills. Sébastien de Vauban was one of the great designers of fortifications and of siege operations. It was a common saying that a city defended by Vauban was safe and that a city besieged by Vauban was doomed. Henri-Jules Condé was an able and dashing military leader and the viscount of Turenne a masterly planner of campaigns and battles.

During the last four decades of his seventy-two-year reign Louis XIV fought four wars of aggression, at times unifying most of the other military powers of western Europe against him. By the end of the Dutch War in 1678, Louis XIV had gained some valuable territories. But the tide turned. His final struggle, the War of the Spanish Succession, lasted eleven years (1702–1713) and resulted in a series of defeats. Beaten and exhausted, Louis XIV was forced to accept the Treaty of Utrecht (1713). He was left with little more than he had started with some fifty years earlier.

Louis XIV lived only two years after the signing of the Treaty of Utrecht. He had long outlived his popularity. As the body of the grandest of all the absolute monarchs was drawn through the streets of Paris, some of his abused people cursed in the taverns as the coffin passed.

The Decline of French Absolutism

The French monarchy never again achieved the power it had wielded under Louis XIV. Certainly France remained a first-rank power with a large army, a centralized bureaucracy, and a growing economy. But between 1715 and 1789 the monarchy slowly declined.

Expensive wars and unreformed taxation policies left the treasury depleted after Louis XIV's death. The clergy and nobility retained most of their immunity from taxation despite the efforts of several ministers to break those privileges. The debt grew, and the monarchy was weakened by its inability to reform its finances to lessen the burden of that debt.

Underlying these political and financial problems was a resurgence of the aristocracy. In the decades between 1715 and 1789 the monarchy was faced by an increasingly assertive aristocracy anxious to recapture some of its old political power. Ambitious aristocrats thwarted the kings' efforts to reform taxes. They set themselves up as centers of aristocratic opposition to the monarchy, above all through their control of the *parlements* (law courts).

Thus, by the middle decades of the eighteenth century, the French monarchy had clearly declined from its heights under Louis XIV. When problems came to a head in the 1780s, the king was unable to handle them and the monarchy was toppled by a great revolution.

2. ABSOLUTISM IN EASTERN EUROPE

At the beginning of the seventeenth century eastern Europe exhibited certain characteristics that set it in sharp contrast to western Europe. Economically, the states east of the Elbe River were less commercially developed than those in western Europe. Estate agriculture (large landed estates owned by lords and worked by their serfs) remained the rule. Socially, the landed aristocracy dominated these areas to a greater extent than in western Europe. Indeed, this aristocracy had generally succeeded in reversing the medieval trends toward greater freedom for the peasantry and the growth of towns. During the fifteenth, sixteenth, and seventeenth centuries serfdom was reimposed with greater severity than ever, and the landed aristocracy won in its struggle with competing urban centers. Politically, many areas lacked the strong central government found in the western European states.

The most significant political developments in central and eastern Europe during the seventeenth and eighteenth centuries were the rise of Prussia, the centralization of Austria, and the expansion of Russia, three states that developed strong national governments and powerful monarchies. At the opening of the seventeenth century, the two chief powers in central and eastern Europe were the Ottoman and Hapsburg empires. Although the Islamic Ottoman Turks had been restrained by Hapsburg military power in the sixteenth century on both land and sea, they were about to renew their effort to conquer Christian Europe. The Austrian Hapsburgs, in addition to disputing the control of southeastern Europe with the Turks, dominated the Holy Roman Empire, which included all the German states. In northeastern Europe, Sweden, Prussia, Poland, and Russia competed for hegemony. Among all these powers, Prussia and Russia had hitherto been the least conspicuous in world affairs. During the seventeenth and eighteenth centuries, Prussia and Russia would become major powers and assume an active role in international politics.

The Hohenzollerns and the Hapsburgs

The political history of Prussia is in large measure the history of Hohenzollern family rulers. In 1415 the Hohenzollerns became rulers of Brandenburg (1415), a bleak and thinly populated little province within the Holy Roman Empire. In the centuries that followed until they were finally overthrown at the end of the World War I in 1918, they followed a threefold policy: militarism and territorial aggrandizement, paternal despotism, and centralized bureaucracy. The first to take major steps toward making Brandenburg an important power was Frederick William (1640–1688), the Great Elector. One of the ablest of all the Hohenzollerns, he acquired several new territories at the end of the Thirty Years' War. He centralized and administered the governments of his scattered territories with energy and skill. He won in his struggles with the Estates, the representative assemblies of the realm, gaining the crucial power to collect taxes and eliminating the Estates as a functioning institution. He established and strengthened his standing army. He managed an important compromise with the landed aristocracy, allowing them complete control over their serfs but committing them to his government as members of his bureaucracy and his military officer corps. He protected the native industries, improved communications, and aided agriculture. In a most intolerant age he followed a policy of religious toleration. When Louis XIV revoked the Edict of Nantes in 1685, Frederick William welcomed thousands of industrious Huguenots to Brandenburg. At the death of the Great Elector in 1688, Brandenburg was on the road to becoming a great power.

The next Hohenzollern, Frederick I (1688–1713), acquired the title of king for the dynasty. The Hapsburg Holy Roman emperor in 1701 granted Frederick the title in return for aid against Louis XIV in the War of the Spanish Succession. Frederick I chose Prussia rather than Brandenburg for the name of his kingdom, since Prussia was outside the Holy Roman Empire and a free sovereign state. Hence Brandenburg became Prussia.

From 1713 to 1740 Prussia was ruled by a vigorous militaristic autocrat, Frederick William I (since he was the first Frederick William to be king). Unquestioned absolutism, machinelike centralized bureaucratic administration, and, above all, militarism were his obsessions. He built the Prussian army into the most efficient and one of the largest fighting forces in Europe. And yet Frederick William was so efficient and miserly that he was also able to pass along to his talented son, Frederick II, a well-filled treasury.

In the same year (1740) that Frederick II became King of Prussia, Maria Theresa became archduchess of the Austrian Hapsburg dominions. During the second half of the seventeenth century the Austrian Hapsburgs had successfully carried out a policy of centralizing their power in those lands they directly controlled (rather than the Holy Roman Empire) and expanding to the east. The monarchy improved its administration, established a powerful standing army, gained at least a fragile allegiance of the nobility, and acquired territories at the expense of the Ottoman empire and Poland.

In 1740 Frederick II challenged Maria Theresa's authority by marching his troops into Silesia, one of the richest of the Hapsburg provinces. This Machiavellian act by the young Prussian king plunged most of the major European states into a series of wars for the mastery of central Europe. The War of the Austrian Succession lasted for eight years (1740–1748). Maria Theresa successfully repelled the Bavarians, Saxons, French, and Spaniards, but she was unable to dislodge Frederick II from Silesia. Frederick, on his part, cynically deserted his allies as soon as he had achieved his own purposes.

The Hapsburgs, however, had no intention of being thus despoiled of one of their fairest provinces by the upstart Hohenzollerns. Proud rulers over territories many times the size and population of Prussia and for centuries emperors of the Holy Roman Empire, they viewed the Hohenzollerns with condescension. Maria Theresa's able diplomat, Count Kaunitz, was soon at work lining up allies.

Frederick was not one to wait for his enemies

FIGURE 32.3 Frederick II Before His Troops During the seventeenth and eighteenth centuries, the rulers of Brandenburg-Prussia used their armies to build up the state, making it one of the major powers of eastern and central Europe. Here, Frederick II of Prussia is shown in a characteristic military pose, exemplifying the strong alliance of the monarchy and army. (The Mansell Collection, London)

to strike first. As soon as he became aware of their designs, he opened hostilities by overrunning Saxony (see Figure 32.3). Thus began the Seven Years' War (1756–1763). Frederick, with his slender resources, soon found himself at bay; the four greatest military powers on the continent of Europe were closing in on him from all directions. After tenaciously holding his enemies off for six years, defeat appeared to be near. Then in 1762 the Russian Tsarina Elizabeth, one of his bitterest enemies, died and was succeeded by the ineffective Peter III, who was an ardent admirer of Frederick II and who put Russia's forces at the disposal of Prussia. Although Peter III was soon murdered by a group of his own officers and court nobility and Russia withdrew from the war, the remaining allies had no further stomach for the fight. The Peace of Hubertusburg in 1763 left things as they had been at the beginning of the war, with Prussia retaining the controversial Silesia. In the same year the Treaty of Paris brought to a close the colonial struggle between Great Britain and France in India and North America, leaving Great Britain master of both.

Having so narrowly escaped destruction, Frederick the Great spent the remaining twenty-three years of his life reconstructing his war-ravaged territories. He encouraged agriculture, subsidized and protected industry, and invited immigrants into his well-governed territories. At no time, though, did he neglect his war machine. In 1772 he joined Austria and Russia in the first partition of Poland. Frederick took West Prussia, thus joining East Prussia with the main body of the Prussian state. When Frederick II died in 1786, Prussia had been raised to the status of a great power, sharing the leadership of central Europe equally with Austria. During his reign Prussia's size and population had more than doubled, and its military exploits pointed to a spectacular future (see Map 32.1).

Russia and the Romanovs

While Prussia was becoming a great power in central Europe, Russia was rising to prominence to the east. The first of the grand dukes of Muscovy under whom Russia took on the shape of a modern national state was Ivan III (1462–1505). In 1480 Ivan III defeated the rapidly declining Mongols and limited their power in Russia to the southeastern area. Ivan greatly extended his sway to both the north and the west by military conquest. After his marriage to Sophia Palaeologus, heiress to the now-defunct Byzantine (Eastern Roman) Empire, Ivan declared himself successor to the Eastern Roman Caesars—hence the title "tsar." When he died, the foundations of a Russian national state had been laid (see Map 32.2).

Ivan IV (1533–1584), "the Terrible," added both to the authority of the Russian tsars and to the territories over which they ruled. He destroyed the remaining power of the Mongols in southeastern Russia and annexed most of their territory. It was during Ivan IV's reign that Russia's conquest of Siberia was begun. Half a century later the Russian flag was planted on the shores of the Pacific.

The twenty-nine years following the death of Ivan IV are known as the Time of Troubles (1584–1613). Weak rulers and disputed successions resulted in such anarchy that the Poles were able

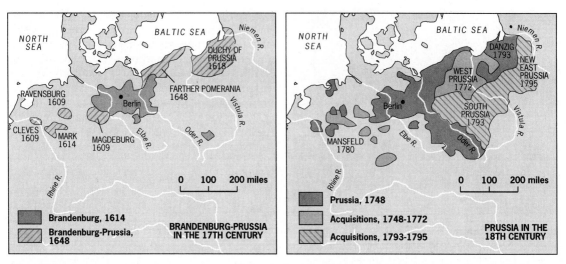

Map 32.1 **THE GROWTH OF PRUSSIA, 1614–1807** These maps show the growth of Brandenburg-Prussia during the seventeenth and eighteenth centuries. The maps reveal the lack of connections among many of Brandenburg-Prussia's lands; one of Prussia's long-term goals in the eighteenth and nineteenth centuries was to connect those territories it already controlled as well as to expand its holdings.

to capture Moscow and hold it briefly. To end the political chaos, a group of leading nobles in 1613 chose Michael Romanov as tsar.

The early decades of the Romanov dynasty, which was to rule Russia until the Revolution of 1917, were not easy. There were great popular discontent and numerous uprisings between the late 1640s and the early 1670s as the lower classes rebelled against the nobles and the central government, who were making serfdom even more onerous and life for townspeople more difficult. The discontent reached a climax with the revolts led by Stenka Razin in the late 1660s and early 1670s. Razin was finally caught and executed, thus ending that series of threats. During this same period problems within the Russian Orthodox church broke out as many, known as the Old Believers, rejected liturgical changes initiated by the patriarch of Moscow. The effect of this controversy was to drive the Church into greater dependence on the secular government. Nevertheless, by the final decades of the seventeenth century the Romanov tsars had managed to overcome these problems, improve the central administration, and extend their authority. They

gradually established commercial and cultural contacts with the West. Increasing numbers of traders, artisans, and adventurers from central and western Europe, particularly Germany, came to Russia to seek their fortunes. Thus the stage was set for Russia to become more fully involved in European affairs. This involvement became especially important during the reign of Peter the Great.

Peter I (1689–1725) was an unusually large, vigorous, and ambitious individual. At the age of seventeen he seized the reins of government from his elder sister. For the next thirty-six years he devoted his boundless energy to the twofold policy of strengthening his own authority and his military forces and of gaining access to the west on the Baltic and Black seas.

Peter concluded that one of the best ways to increase his own political and military power was to copy Western practices. He traveled in western Europe and learned much about Western customs and techniques, which he proceeded to introduce into Russia. After crushing a revolt of his bodyguard with a ruthlessness that cowed all potential troublemakers, he adopted the bu-

Map 32.2 THE GROWTH OF RUSSIA IN THE WEST These maps show the steady expansion of Russia to the west and south, acquiring access on the Baltic and Black seas under Peter the Great and extending its territories further in the course of the eighteenth century.

reaucratic system of western European monarchs in both central and local government to make his authority more absolute. Western technicians were brought to Russia in large numbers, and new industries were subsidized and protected by mercantilist policies. Western, particularly French, social customs were introduced to the upper and middle classes of Russian society. Women were brought out of seclusion, and the long beards and flowing Oriental robes of the men were banned. These reforms hardly touched the peasant masses, who were increasingly tied down in a system of serfdom bordering on slavery—a process that had been going on in Russia throughout the sixteenth and seventeenth centuries. When the patriarch of the Russian Ortho-

dox church opposed the tsar's authority and some of his Westernizing policies, Peter abolished the patriarchate. Henceforth, the Orthodox church was a powerful instrument of the Russian government. But Peter the Great's chief concern was always his military establishment. He built a navy and patterned his conscript army after that of Prussia. By the end of his reign, Russia had one of the major fighting forces of Europe.

When Peter became tsar, Russia had no warm-water access to the west. Sweden held the coveted shores of the Baltic Sea, and the Ottoman Turks occupied the territory north of the Black Sea. Peter's efforts to dislodge the Ottoman Turks were not very successful, but after an extended, costly war with Sweden, in which Peter lost the early battles to his adversary, Charles XII, Peter's efforts were rewarded. By the Treaty of Nystad in 1721, Russia received the Swedish Baltic provinces of Livonia, Estonia, Ingria, and Karelia. On the Neva River near the Baltic, Peter built a new, modern capital, St. Petersburg, facing the west. At his death in 1725, Russia was a great and growing power ready to play a major role in European affairs.

Peter the Great was followed by a succession of weak or mediocre rulers. After an interval of thirty-seven years, Catherine the Great (1762–1796) ascended the Russian throne. Catherine was an obscure princess from one of the little German states. She had been married for political reasons to young Peter III, grandson of Peter the Great, while he was still heir to the Russian crown. After he became tsar, Peter III quickly alienated all classes of his subjects. Less than a year after her husband became tsar, Catherine conspired with a group of aristocratic army officers, who murdered Peter and declared Catherine tsarina of Russia.

The Machiavellian tsarina prided herself on being an enlightened despot, as was fashionable in the late eighteenth century, but few of her enlightened ideas were translated into political or social deeds. Some apparent reforming efforts ended when Russian serfs rose in one of the greatest insurrections in history. In 1773, under the able leadership of a Don Cossack, Pugachev, hundreds of thousands of serfs marched against their masters. The rebellion was put down with difficulty. The cruel repression left Russian serfs almost as slaves to the privileged nobility.

Catherine the Great followed an aggressive foreign policy. Peter the Great had reached the Baltic by despoiling the Swedes. Catherine reached the Black Sea, the Balkan peninsula, and the heart of Europe by defeating the Turks and destroying Poland. When she finally died in 1796, Russia was a nation ominous in size and power and a major factor in European and world affairs.

Poland, Sweden, and the Ottoman Empire

By the end of the eighteenth century, Prussia and Russia were rising, major powers in Europe. Poland, Sweden, and the Ottoman Empire did not fare so well.

Poland, at the opening of the eighteenth century, was the third largest country in Europe, exceeded in size only by Russia and Sweden. In the sixteenth and seventeenth centuries it had appeared that Poland would become a major power. Taking advantage of Russia's Time of Troubles (1584–1613), the Poles had captured Moscow. In the latter part of the century they had saved Vienna from the Turks.

Actually, however, the Polish nation was far from strong. Sprawling over a large area between Russia and the German states, it enjoyed no natural boundaries either to the east or to the west. The eastern half of its territory was inhabited by Russian-speaking people. The northern provinces were peopled largely by Latvians, Lithuanians, and Germans. There were also many Germans in the west. Religious cleavages followed the language lines.

Moreover, there was no strong middle class to vitalize Poland's economy. In the late Middle Ages a sizable overland commerce between the Black and Baltic seas had flowed across Poland. But with the shifting of commercial routes and centers to the west in the early sixteenth century, Poland's commerce had withered. Furthermore, the Polish nobility, jealous of its own power and fearful of an alliance between the bourgeoisie and the king, deliberately penalized commerce with severe restrictions. The great mass of the people were serfs, tilling the soil of the powerful nobility.

In the face of so many divisive forces, only a strong central government could have made Poland into a stable national state. But here lay Poland's greatest weakness. The kingship was elective, and the great nobles who held the elective power saw to it that no strong king ever came to the throne. During the eighteenth century the kings were all foreigners or puppets of foreign powers. The legislative Diet was completely monopolized by the nobility. So that each noble's rights were safeguarded, unanimity was required for the passage of every measure. This system guaranteed virtual political anarchy. National spirit was weak. The all-powerful nobles were far more concerned for their own private interests than for the well-being of the nation.

It would have been surprising had such a power vacuum as eighteenth-century Poland not invited the aggression of its ambitious neighbors.

In 1772 Catherine the Great and Frederick the Great bargained to take slices of Polish territory. The somewhat less greedy Maria Theresa of Austria, fearful of being outdistanced by Russia and Prussia, joined them. This aggression at long last stirred the Poles to action. Sweeping reforms were passed, improving the condition of the peasants and the bourgeoisie and giving the king and the Diet power to act effectively. But it was too late. They were no match for the professional armies of Russia, Prussia, and Austria, who in 1795 divided the remainder of Poland among themselves.

Poland was not the only victim in eastern Europe of the powerful Russian, Prussian, and Austrian armies. Sweden and the Ottoman Empire also declined, both relatively and actually. Sweden had become the dominant military power in northern and eastern Europe under Gustavus Adolphus in the early seventeenth century. At the opening of the eighteenth century Sweden was second only to Russia in size among the nations of Europe, holding large areas east and south of the Baltic in addition to the homeland. However, its population and resources were too small to hold such far-flung territories, which were coveted by the ambitious and growing Prussia and Russia, for very long. Charles XII made a spectacular effort to hold them, but in the end he lost all his trans-Baltic territories except Finland, and he dissipated Sweden's strength in doing so. Sweden has never been a major power since.

The Ottoman Turks, after reaching the gates of Vienna early in the sixteenth century and again late in the seventeenth century, weakened rapidly. The Treaty of Karlowitz in 1699 limited their power in Europe to the Balkan peninsula and a strip of territory north of the Black Sea. Their two serious defeats at the hands of Catherine the Great marked the beginning of the breakup of the Ottoman Empire.

By the end of the eighteenth century, the three dominant powers in central and eastern Europe were the relatively static Austrian Hapsburg Empire and the two rapidly rising states—Prussia and Russia (see Map 32.3). Each of these states, like France in western Europe, had developed strong central governments with standing armies, large bureaucracies, and organized systems of taxation under the monarch's control.

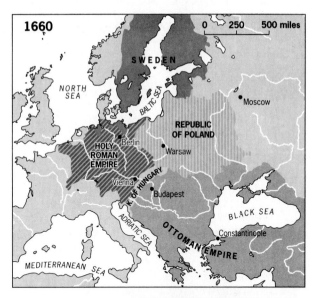

Map 32.3 EASTERN EUROPE, SIXTEENTH–EIGHTEENTH CENTURIES Between the sixteenth and eighteenth centuries, political power in central and eastern Europe shifted fundamentally. The first map shows Sweden, the Holy Roman Empire, Poland, and the Ottoman Empire in the sixteenth and early seventeenth centuries. The second map shows that by the end of the eighteenth century, these powers except for Sweden had all but been replaced by Prussia, the Russian Empire, and the Austrian Empire, and Sweden's holdings had been diminished by Russian Expansion.

SUGGESTED READING

General

P. Anderson, *Lineages of the Absolutist State* (1974). A good Marxist analysis.

R. N. Hatton, *Europe in the Age of Louis XIV* (1979). A well-illustrated survey.

D. McKay and H. Scott, *The Rise of the Great Powers, 1648–1815* (1983). A good survey.

D. Pennington, *Europe in the Seventeenth Century* (1989). A recent introduction.

Absolutism in Western Europe

W. Beik, *Absolutism and Society in Seventeenth-Century France* (1985). A well-written interpretation of French absolutism.

W. F. Church, ed., *Louis XIV in Historical Thought* (1978). Conflicting interpretations of Louis XIV.

P. Goubert, *Louis XIV and Twenty Million Frenchmen* (1970). A respected study of French society and politics.

H. Rowen, *The King's State: Proprietary Dynasticism in Early Modern France* (1980). Analyzes the theory of Louis XIV's rule.

V. L. Tapié, *France in the Age of Louis XIII and Richelieu* (1974). A good survey.

A. Trout, *Jean-Baptiste Colbert* (1978). Analyzes his economic policies.

Absolutism in Eastern Europe

P. Coles, *The Ottoman Impact on Europe, 1350–1699* (1968). A well-written study.

N. Davies, *God's Playground: A History of England,* Vol. 1; *The Origins to 1795.* (1981). A full introduction.

P. Dukes, *The Making of Russian Absolutism: 1613–1801* (1982). A solid survey.

R. J. Evans, *The Making of the Hapsburg Empire, 1550–1770* (1979). A solid, recent account.

H. Holborn, *A History of Modern Germany 1648–1840* (1966). The best on the subject.

H. C. Johnson, *Frederick the Great and His Officials* (1975). Focuses on Prussian administration.

H. W. Koch, *A History of Prussia* (1978). A good analysis of the rise of Prussia.

I. de Madariaga, *Russia in the Age of Catherine the Great* (1981). Highly regarded recent study.

M. Roberts, *Sweden's Age of Greatness* (1973). A good summary of Sweden during this period.

CHAPTER 33

The Challenge to Absolutism: England and the United Netherlands

FIGURE 33.1 **The English Cabinet** This scene shows Robert Walpole, who served as prime minister of England from 1721 to 1742, presiding over a session of the cabinet. Walpole and the other cabinet members shown here were all members of Parliament and belonged to the majority party in that body. In sessions such as this they decided upon the major policies to be followed by the government; their control of Parliament allowed them to enact their decisions. Thus, the cabinet became the effective executive power in Great Britain, a position that it still holds today. The emergence of the cabinet system was one of the major outcomes of the bitter political struggle in seventeenth-century England. (The Bettmann Archive)

While royal absolutism dominated the political scene in France and elsewhere on the Continent, England and the United Netherlands moved toward a form of government that placed limitations on the authority of the executive and the power of the state. In these two nations a constitutional system was emerging that gave a representative body the authority to define the law and sought to create a balance between the power of the state and the rights and liberties of citizens of the state. The constitutional changes made in England and the United Netherlands during the seventeenth century strongly influenced later struggles against absolutism in many parts of the world.

1. EARLY STUART ATTEMPTS AT ABSOLUTISM

The absolutism shaped by the Tudors (see Chapters 27, 29 and 30) was subjected to serious challenges during the seventeenth century. "Good Queen Bess" died in 1603 without a direct heir. She was succeeded by a distant cousin, James Stuart (1603–1625), king of Scotland. He was an avowed absolutist, but he was woefully ignorant of the delicate workings of the Tudor political system and not suited by temperament for the hard work or gifted with the political adroitness needed to keep that system going. His political ineptitude contributed to a progressive breakdown of the Tudor system and to a polarization of political forces.

But not all the troubles of James I's reign were the makings of a king known in his own days as "the wisest fool in Christendom." New problems were facing England that threatened the general satisfaction most people had felt toward Tudor governance. Major economic changes were in process, creating new opportunities for highly profitable investments in agriculture, manufacturing, and trade. Those who benefited most from these changes, the lesser nobility (the gentry) and merchants, were increasingly insistent on having a voice in shaping royal policies affecting their economic interests and on limiting arbitrary royal interference that curbed their freedom of action. These same changes were adversely affecting other groups, especially rural tenants and laborers, thereby fostering popular discontent. A major realignment of power was taking shape in Europe, marked by the ascendancy of France. This development encouraged the English rulers to seek closer ties with their traditional enemy, Spain, a course that many still basking in the glories of the victory over the Armada viewed as unpatriotic.

The very structure of the Tudor political system lacked key elements required for effective absolutism. Too much depended on the personal qualities of the monarch and a narrow circle of royal advisers. England lacked a well-developed bureaucracy and a well-organized military force to support the ruler's absolute authority. The central government had limited control over local government, which was dominated by the local gentry, the members of which were jealous of their offices and protective of their local interests. The traditional system of common law served to limit arbitrary acts by the royal government. Most serious of all were the limited financial resources of the Crown. It could not manage on the traditional sources of revenue from royal lands, customs duties, and feudal dues. Additional income could be derived only from taxes, which Parliament had long since established its right to approve. If absolutism were to continue, significant political reforms aimed at increasing the power of the monarch would be required. Such changes posed a threat to powerfully entrenched interests in England.

Another increasingly acute source of tension involved religious issues. Many people, including an important segment of the gentry and the merchants, were not satisfied with the Anglican settlement carried out during Elizabeth's reign (see Chapter 30). The major dissenters were the Puritans, who wanted reforms that would make the established religion more "Protestant": simpler ritual, more emphasis on Scripture, less episcopal control over local churches. There also remained many Roman Catholics who hoped to undo the Reformation; their presence was a cause of constant concern for all Protestants.

During James I's reign these issues found their focus in Parliament, especially in the House of Commons, a body that theoretically represented the entire English populace but was actually dominated by the country gentry, merchants, and lawyers. The king was forced to summon Parliament because of the increasing need for funds. Although Parliament usually provided some financial aid, its members constantly raised issues that challenged royal policy. They criticized James I's royal advisers for corruption, favoritism, and incompetence. They questioned his unwavering support of Anglicanism and his lenient policy toward the Catholics. They condemned the alliance he made with Spain early in his reign and his failure to support the Protestant cause when the Thirty Years' War began in 1618. James responded by repeatedly dismissing Parliament. He then tried to utilize other means of raising money, but these efforts were challenged in the courts as contrary to custom and therefore illegal. The king answered by dismissing judges, which led to more parliamentary criticism. Throughout this long series of clashes, Parliament proved itself to be an undisciplined, intemperate body. But its confrontations with the king heightened the fear that the royal government was bent on extending its prerogatives to the point where customary political processes, traditional rights, and the law would be subverted, opening the way to tyranny.

Under James' successor, Charles I (1625–1649), the conflict deepened into civil war. Charles was no less stubborn than James in his insistence on royal supremacy and in his refusal to bend before the claims of Parliament and the courts. The king's major problem continued to be a need for funds, a need made more desperate by a blundering foreign policy that resulted in costly but unsuccessful military ventures in France and Spain. To Charles' requests for additional taxes Parliament responded by continuing to challenge royal policy on a variety of issues. Increasingly, the leaders of Parliament began to make specific their definition of what they meant by royal violation of the traditional system and the law. Their views found particularly forceful expression in the Petition of Rights submitted to the king in 1628. This bold document demanded that the king desist from various illegal acts: imposing martial law in peacetime, levying taxes without Parliament's approval, imprisoning citizens without trial, and quartering soldiers with private citizens. Desperate for money, Charles accepted the Petition of Rights, thereby admitting that he had acted illegally. But when Parliament in its next session, in 1629, insisted that the king respect the petition's provisions on taxation, Charles dismissed it over the bitter protests of its leaders.

For the next eleven years Charles ruled without Parliament. To do so, he was forced to rely on a variety of means of raising funds that pushed royal authority to the limits of legality. Ultimately, it was Charles' religious policy that forced him once again to confront his enemies on their own ground—in Parliament. With Charles' support, his chief religious adviser, William Laud, archbishop of Canterbury, initiated a vigorous "reform" aimed at giving greater emphasis in the Church of England to elaborate rituals, episcopal authority over local churches, and the doctrine of free will. To the Puritans Laud's reforms were detestable, the very opposite of the most fundamental precepts of Calvinistic Protestantism. Many fled to the New World in search of a setting where they would have the freedom to institute real Protestantism. Laud's policies even alarmed some Anglicans, who sensed that England was on a course that would lead it back to Roman Catholicism. But it was the absolute refusal of the Scotch Presbyterians to accept the "beauty of holiness," as Charles called Laud's reforms, that precipitated a crisis. In 1639 they revolted and invaded northern England, creating a military crisis that forced Charles to summon Parliament into session in 1640 in order to raise money to resist the Scottish threat to the kingdom.

The first Parliament of 1640, called the Short Parliament, was dismissed after three weeks because it again challenged royal authority. But the Scots continued to press, and Charles was forced to capitulate. He summoned the Long Parliament, so called because it was to sit for twenty years. With an amazing show of unity Parliament proceeded to legislate the end of Stuart absolutism. It forced Charles to sacrifice his chief ministers, including Laud. It abolished the hated extraordinary courts, including the Star Chamber and the Court of High Commission, which had long been tools used by the Crown to avoid the common law. An act was passed requiring a meeting of Parliament every three years and curbing the power of the king to dismiss Parliament. Severe limitations were placed on the king's power to tax without parliamentary approval. To all of this Charles acceded, chiefly because he needed money to fight the Scots.

Up to this point Parliament had succeeded brilliantly in legislating what amounted to a bloodless revolution that established limited monarchy. But the parliamentary forces then began to divide over the question of how to use Parliament's power. In general, its leadership was forced into directions that caused alarm in many quarters and drove many back toward support of the king, who gave every sign that he would resist being a limited monarch. Suspicion of his intentions caused parliamentary leaders to remove control of the administration and the army from his hands and to impose taxes that seemed as burdensome as those imposed by Charles earlier. Religious opinion in Parliament moved in the direction of ending Anglicanism "root and branch" in favor of some form of Presbyterianism. This mounting extremism caused many influential leaders to believe that Parliament was setting a course that would upset the established order. The division in the parliamentary ranks emboldened Charles to try to restore his control; he went so far in early 1642 as to attempt to arrest the leaders of Parliament. This action was a call to arms, pitting against one another elements of a ruling class that had lost its community of interest, an interest that had long focused on the monarch.

2. CIVIL WAR, COMMONWEALTH, AND PROTECTORATE, 1642–1660

The opening of armed strife divided England along lines that defy easy definition. The opposing forces did not represent clear-cut economic interests or social classes. A considerable following, soon known as the Cavaliers, rallied around Charles, who represented himself as the champion of the established order against the political and religious radicals in Parliament. The backbone of the Cavalier forces came from the great noble families and their clientele among the country gentry living in the more economically backward areas of northern and western England. Although the opposition, called the Roundheads, also had noble supporters, it drew its main strength from lawyers, the gentry of the south and east, and the commercial interests; many from these elements were Puritans. This core was soon reinforced by advocates of radical political and economic changes favoring the poor and oppressed. In the intricate matter of choosing sides there figured complex personal factors—family ties, friendships, personal loyalties—much after the fashion of the American Civil War.

The first phase of the civil war lasted through 1646. While neither side was prepared militarily, for a time the Cavaliers seemed to have the upper hand. But the Roundheads had forces working in their favor: support by the navy, domination of the richest part of England, control over the regular administrative system and Parliament, the power to vote taxation. In 1643 the Roundhead cause was bolstered by an alliance with the Scots. But ultimately the outcome of the struggle was determined by the success of the Roundheads in creating an effective army. The chief architect of the victorious army was a simple farmer with strong Puritan convictions, Oliver Cromwell. He organized a cavalry regiment of disciplined, deeply religious recruits who proved more than a match for the Cavalier forces they faced. His system was soon applied to the entire Roundhead force to create the New Model Army, made up of highly motivated troops paid and equipped in a businesslike fashion. It quickly proved itself superior to the Cavalier army, so that by 1646 the Cavalier army was crushed and Charles was forced to surrender.

However, with victory within their grasp, the Roundheads were unable to work out an acceptable settlement. Moderate leaders in the Roundhead camp wished to establish a limited monarchy and a Presbyterian religious order. Charles remained unwilling to accept such a settlement and raised fears of a renewal of the civil war by fleeing his captors and allying himself with the Scots. More ominous was the increasing prominence of Roundhead leaders who demanded a more radical religious reform favoring the independence of local churches and freedom of conscience. These religious Independents were supported by various political radicals, most notably the Levellers, who advocated the end of monarchy, democratic elections, and the redistribution of wealth. These religious and political radicals dominated the New Model Army, where discontent was fed by the fact that pay was considerably in arrears. Fearful that the radicals would seize complete control, the moderate

Roundheads ordered the army demobilized. They turned back to the king, who suddenly expressed considerable enthusiasm for parliamentary control over the monarchy as well as for Presbyterianism. The Independents, led by Cromwell, would not be denied. They destroyed the hope of Charles and his Scottish army in a single battle in 1648 and, along with it, the cause of the Cavaliers and the moderate Roundheads. Backed by the New Model Army, Cromwell acted decisively to ensure the position of the Independents. He purged the Long Parliament of all members not dedicated to his cause and gave the so-called Rump Parliament chief authority in the land. It immediately legislated out of existence the Anglican church, the House of Lords, and the monarchy. And at Cromwell's urging it decreed the execution of the king in 1649 on the grounds that he was "a tyrant, traitor, and murderer."

For eleven years after Charles I's death Cromwell and his Independents sought to rule England without a king. Always in a minority and dependent on the army, the Cromwellians experimented with various forms of government but ultimately failed to establish an acceptable order. They first sought to create a republican form of government called the Commonwealth. A one-house Parliament was made the supreme authority, with a state council of forty-one members charged with conducting the daily affairs of government. Under Cromwell's guidance this government pursued several positive policies. Considerable toleration was extended to all Protestants, a policy that required curbing political and religious extremists in the army. Effective, albeit severe measures were taken to subdue the rebellious Irish and Scots. An aggressive foreign policy, aimed at promoting English commercial and colonial interests, was undertaken. Navigation acts were passed to ensure that trade within England's emerging empire would be monopolized by England. None of these policies, however, helped to popularize the Commonwealth. The Cromwellians could not shed their image as regicides, Puritan extremists, and political radicals (see Figure 33.2). Resistance to the Commonwealth grew steadily. Cromwell ultimately blamed the failure of the Commonwealth on what he considered the self-serving leaders of Parliament, causing him to take steps to curb its

Oliver seeking God while the K. is murthered by his order.

FIGURE 33.2 A Satire on Cromwell The deep religious fervor of the Puritans and the taint of regicide that lingered throughout the Commonwealth and the Protectorate are satirized here as Oliver Cromwell is shown at prayer while Charles I is being executed. (NYPL Picture Collection)

power and to act without it—a course that convinced many that Cromwell was no less a tyrant than his royal predecessors.

In pursuit of what he called a "healing and settling" course for England, Cromwell tried one more experiment, called the Protectorate. A written constitution was drawn up that entrusted power to a lord protector (Cromwell), who was advised by a Council of State and guided by a one-house Parliament elected by property holders. From the beginning the lord protector and Parliament clashed on most issues, largely because the elected Parliament represented political and religious positions that ran contrary to the convictions of those who alone could assure Cromwell's continued dominance, the "godly" men of the New Model Army. To sustain his power Cromwell was forced to impose a virtual military dictatorship that aroused resistance across a wide spectrum of opinion and bred conspiracies that constantly threatened public order. More and more people began to see the restoration of monarchy as an alternative to Cromwell's regime. In fact, in 1657 Parliament asked Cromwell to become king, an honor he declined; but he did agree to remain lord protector for life. Thus, when he died in 1658, the wheel had come nearly full circle: A man who had led his soldiers to the abolition of monarchy had himself become king without title.

Cromwell was succeeded as lord protector by his son Richard, but this weak figure was soon swept aside by forces favoring the restoration of monarchy. By 1660 elements in the New Model Army joined with people of property and commerce to end the Protectorate. The Long Parliament voted to dissolve itself. A new Parliament was elected and in 1660 invited Charles Stuart, the son of Charles I, to return from exile and assume the crown.

3. THE RESTORATION, 1660–1688

The Restoration that brought the Stuarts back to the throne also saw the reestablishment of both houses of Parliament, the Anglican church, the traditional courts of law, and the old system of local government. However, what seemed outwardly to be a return to the system that had prevailed before the execution of Charles I by no means resolved the basic problems that had divided England since 1603, particularly those involving the relationship between king and Parliament and the religious establishment. Nor did it negate the advancing claims of England's gentry and merchants to a decisive voice in political decision making. Between 1660 and 1688 political tensions continued, although at a less violent level than had been the case in the preceding two decades.

The reign of Charles II (1660–1685) began in a climate of forgiving compromise. The king and Parliament joined in repealing all the acts of the Commonwealth and the Protectorate. Only a few Cromwellians were punished for their part in killing Charles I. Confiscated properties were returned to their original owners. The king was assured of a sizable income on a regular basis, but he was deprived of many ancient rights that had allowed his predecessors to exact taxes without approval of Parliament. Not only was control of taxation reserved to Parliament, but the Triennial Act was passed to ensure that it would meet every three years whether or not the king so wished. However, this settlement did not get to the basic political issue: Where did ultimate authority rest? Even more disconcerting was the religious settlement embodied in a series of parliamentary acts passed in 1661 and 1662 and known as the Clarendon Code after Charles II's chief adviser, the earl of Clarendon. These acts not only reestablished the Anglican church but also made it illegal for nonconformist Protestants, including Independents and Presbyterians, to meet for religious purposes, to conduct services in their own way under the leadership of their own preachers, and to hold local political offices. In brief, the Clarendon Code promised to nonconformists (that is, non-Anglicans) little better than criminal status.

Dissatisfaction stemming from these issues once again surfaced in Parliament. The discontent was intensified by a series of disasters that befell England during the early years of Charles' reign. He involved England in a war with the Dutch that led to a humiliating defeat. In 1665 a plague struck England, followed the next year by a fire that destroyed most of London. Many God-fearing English felt that these misfortunes were divine retribution for the immorality of the royal court, where the model of profligacy was set by the king himself. Parliament reacted to public wrath over religious issues by forcing Clarendon out of office in 1667 and to a failed foreign policy by becoming stingier in approving taxes. Charles paid little heed to the growing opposition, choosing instead to pursue two policies he personally favored: an alliance with France and religious tolerance in England that would permit Roman Catholics to worship freely. In 1670 he signed a secret treaty with Louis XIV by which he agreed, in return for a subsidy, to join France in a war on the Dutch and to promote the Catholic cause in England; when the terms of this treaty became known, anti-Catholic and anti-French sentiment reached fever pitch. In 1672 Charles issued a Declaration of Indulgence, which set aside the laws restricting the practice of Roman Catholicism. An outraged Parliament forced the king to withdraw the Declaration of Indulgence and passed the Test Act (1673), which excluded Catholics from all public offices. And when Charles joined France in another unsuccessful war against the Dutch in 1672–1674, Parliament forced him to seek peace by refusing financial support.

As his reign progressed, Charles showed considerable ingenuity in neutralizing his opponents in Parliament. Increased tax returns resulting from an improving economy coupled with Louis XIV's subsidies minimized Parliament's ability to pressure the Crown by denying taxation. More significantly, Charles skillfully built a political following—an embryonic "party"—devoted to a strong monarchy and Anglicanism. Its members, scornfully dubbed "Tories" (a term used to designate Irish bandits) by the opposition, could often control Parliament in support of the king. An opposing "party," committed to parliamentary supremacy and religious tolerance for all Protestants, was also formed; its members were called "Whigs" (after a term used to designate Scottish horse thieves and murderers). Charles' successes led many to feel that absolutism was returning to England. But one obstacle kept Charles from totally controlling English political life: a rising fear that the king was determined to restore Catholicism.

James II (1685–1688) inherited a strong position from his brother, based in large part on the Tory majority in Parliament, a sound financial position, and the legitimacy of his claim to the throne. But he soon dissipated this strength by his open avowal of Catholicism and attempts to improve the position of Catholics in England, which neither the Tories nor the Whigs would tolerate. When in 1688 a son was born to James and his Catholic wife and baptized in the Catholic faith, ensuring that the Stuart dynasty would be perpetuated by a Catholic successor, Tory and Whig leaders invited James' Protestant daughter, Mary, and her husband, William of Orange, the stadholder of several provinces in the Dutch Netherlands, to assume England's throne. When William invaded England in late 1688, the great

majority of the people rallied to his side; James II fled to France. For a second time, the unhappy Stuarts had been forced off England's throne, but this time the revolution was bloodless.

4. THE GLORIOUS REVOLUTION AND ITS CONSEQUENCES

Unlike the execution of Charles I, the flight of James II did not lead to radical political experimentation. Instead, what the English call a Glorious Revolution was carried through in the form of several fundamental legal enactments that established the basis for England's future constitutional system.

Immediately after the triumph of William and Mary, Parliament declared the throne vacant by reason of James' abdication. It then voted to grant the crown to William III and Mary as co-rulers, thereby establishing Parliament's control of the throne. A Bill of Rights was passed in 1689 that set forth clear limits on royal power. This fundamental charter assured the members of Parliament of the right of free speech and immunity from prosecution for statements made in debate. It forbade a variety of acts that had long been the basis of royal absolutism: taxing without the consent of Parliament, suspending laws passed by Parliament, maintaining a standing army in peacetime, requiring excessive bail, depriving citizens of the right to trial in the regular courts, interfering with jurors, and denying people the right to petition the king. The Bill of Rights implied that government was based on a contract between ruler and ruled, a concept of government increasingly attractive among "enlightened" leaders in western Europe. This theory of government was set forth with special force by John Locke in his *Two Treatises on Civil Government*, published in 1690 (see pp. 464, 468, 473). Locke argued that a government was the product of a contract entered into by rational people in order to establish an authority capable of protecting rights that belonged to all humans by the laws of nature: the rights of life, liberty, and property. Any government that violated these natural rights broke the contract that had brought it into existence; in this event its subjects had a right to correct or even overthrow it. To settle the long-standing religious issue, a Toleration Act was passed that allowed religious freedom to Puritans and Independents but not to non-Protestants. Finally, the Act of Settlement was enacted in 1701 to ensure that none but Protestants could inherit the throne.

The initial settlement marking the Glorious Revolution certainly resolved some fundamental issues that had troubled England for nearly a century. However, there still remained problems to be addressed. Under William's leadership England's foreign policy underwent a basic reorientation which called on the nation to commit its resources to a long, burdensome but eventually successful series of wars in many parts of the globe to prevent France from establishing world dominance (see Chapters 32 and 34). Closer to home the Irish problem was resolved to England's advantage. Early in his reign William led an army into this unhappy land, where discontent had long festered and which now became a center of Stuart intrigue—funded by the French—aimed at recovering the English throne. Having established control by force, William instituted a policy aimed at the suppression of Roman Catholicism and at reducing Ireland to colonial status, a policy that provided expanded opportunity for English landlords to uproot Irish Catholic landowners and take possession of their property. Scotland enjoyed an easier fate in the face of increasing English power. Early in his reign William began negotiations with the Scots that finally bore fruit after his death. In 1707 Parliament passed the Act of Union, which joined the two kingdoms into a single nation henceforth known as the United Kingdom of Great Britain. The settlement gave the Scots a liberal number of seats in Parliament and guaranteed their Presbyterian religious establishment.

A major consequence of the Glorious Revolution was Parliament's increasing involvement in the conduct of affairs of state. Partly this expanded role was a consequence of the fundamental principle established by the settlement of 1688–1689: the need for parliamentary approval of important political decisions. No less important was the royal need for additional funds. Chiefly as a result of the burdens of global war, annual government expenditures had increased threefold between the reign of Charles II and that of William and Mary. To meet these expenditures, the monarchs had to call Parliament nearly every year. These frequent sessions of Parliament required that the royal government pay special attention to the election process in order to gain sufficient votes from qualified voters—chiefly property owners—to secure a majority in Parliament that was willing to support royal policy. Because Parliament was increasingly important, party strife between Whigs and Tories became a decisive feature of political life. Party leaders played an ever-larger role in counseling the rulers and overseeing public affairs. This ever-increasing identification of Parliament with the management of the nation's affairs probably did more than the noble principles of the Bill of Rights to secure parliamentary control of public life.

These developments raised a major constitutional issue: How should the Crown and Parliament interact so that the monarchy could discharge its executive functions in a way acceptable to Parliament? Certainly, the Glorious Revolution in no sense sought to deprive the Crown of the responsibility for administering affairs of state; but just as certainly, that settlement made the traditional executive system inadequate. For centuries English monarchs had relied on powerful ministers of their own choice and responsible to them alone to assist them in conducting government affairs and shaping policy. In the face of the new reality posed by the supremacy of Parliament, that system was no longer workable. The need for a new mechanism of interconnecting Crown and Parliament became especially obvious during the reigns of the first members of the Hanoverian dynasty, George I (1714–1727) and George II (1727–1760), both of whom spoke English poorly and were more interested in affairs in Germany than in England.

The answer was the *cabinet system,* under which royal ministers were increasingly chosen from members of the House of Commons on the basis of their ability to secure parliamentary approval to carry on the affairs of state in the name of the monarch. Since the Commons tended to divide into parties, it was only prudent for the rulers to seek the leaders of the majority party in the House of Commons for appointment as ministers responsible for exercising executive functions. Those chosen to constitute the cabinet of ministers slowly learned to accept mutual responsibility for the formulation and execution of policy and to assert their collective influence in ensuring that their party followers in Parliament supported their program. If the cabinet failed to command a majority in the House of Commons, its members had to surrender their positions as ministers in favor of a new cabinet that did have a parliamentary majority. One member of the cabinet, eventually called the *prime minister,* came to be recognized as the leader and spokesperson of the whole group; a major qualification for this designation was leadership of the majority party in the Commons.

Although Queen Anne (1702–1714) relied heavily on John Churchill, duke of Marlborough, to conduct her government, the key figure in shaping the cabinet system was Robert Walpole (see Figure 33.1). A longtime member of the Commons, he became George I's chief minister in 1721, primarily because of his leadership of the dominant Whig party in the Commons. From then until 1742 he virtually ran England by surrounding himself with fellow ministers who could control votes in Parliament and who would follow his leadership. Walpole proved to be a master at dispensing patronage and manipulating elections as a means of sustaining a Whig majority in Parliament and maintaining discipline among his Whig followers. Not until he lost control of the Commons over a foreign policy issue was he forced to relinquish his position as prime minister. However, the king had little choice but to appoint another prime minister and cabinet that could command a majority in Parliament. Henceforth to the present, the executive functions of government in Great Britain would be carried out in the name of the monarch by a circle of party leaders who could command a majority in the House of Commons but who were likewise required to render account to that body for their conduct of public affairs.

The Glorious Revolution marked a turning point in Great Britain's history. Two great decisions had been reached. First, royal absolutism had been repudiated in favor of a limited monarchy in which ultimate authority was entrusted to an elected Parliament. Second, religious uniformity had given way to religious toleration for all Protestants. The resolution of these issues restored Great Britain's internal stability and provided a basis for its rapid advance to the status of world power. However, the "revolution" had its limitations. The right to vote in parliamentary elections and eligibility for election to a seat in the House of Commons were limited to a narrow circle of men of wealth, chiefly landowners and merchants. The apportionment of seats in the House of Commons had less to do with ensuring that each seat represented the same number of people than with guaranteeing "safe" seats to prominent families. The Glorious Revolution was a victory for a narrow oligarchy of entrepreneurial landowners and merchants who had successfully taken advantage of changing economic conditions to establish themselves as the wealthiest segment of the English population. Until the nineteenth century these "gentlemen" dominated Great Britain in a fashion that served their collective interests.

5. THE UNITED NETHERLANDS

Absolutism was also successfully challenged during the seventeenth century by the Dutch. Their success led to the creation of a new nation in which prevailed a political and social environment that allowed the Dutch to forge themselves a leadership role in European commerce, banking, and intellectual and artistic life. That new nation emerged from the Dutch refusal to accept the absolutist system that Philip II of Spain attempted to force on them (see Chapter 31). Although Philip II was able to impose Spanish rule over the ten southern provinces of the Netherlands (now Belgium; see Map 33.1), the seven northern provinces resisted and by 1609 had established effective independence as the United Provinces of the Netherlands; their independence was officially recognized by the Treaty of Westphalia in 1648.

The new state adopted a republican form of government. Each province, ruled by an elected executive (called the *stadholder*) and a provincial representative assembly, retained extensive control over local affairs. Although most of the stadholders came from the landed aristocracy, especially from the House of Orange, a powerful family that had played a crucial role in the struggle for independence, the provincial governments over which they presided were dominated by commercial and financial leaders who resisted the establishment of a strong central government. The only truly national political institution was the Estates General, made up of delegates from each province who acted only on instructions from the provincial governments. It en-

Map 33.1 THE UNITED PROVINCES, 1609 This map illustrates how small a territory the Dutch Republic occupied in its golden age—no larger than a corner of England. Yet through the cities of this small area flowed much of the commerce of the seventeenth and eighteenth centuries. With that commerce came a flow of money that made such cities as Amsterdam the financial centers of the world.

overseas colonies to reap a rich reward. When Spain temporarily annexed Portugal in 1580, the Dutch seized most of Portugal's lucrative holdings in the East Indies. The Dutch East India Company, set up in 1602 to develop trade with the East Indies, returned huge profits to its stockholders during the entire seventeenth century. The Dutch also established a flourishing colony in North America. In addition, Dutch traders took advantage of their favorable geographical position to gain a near-monopoly on the carrying trade of Europe. A large proportion of Europe's ships were built in Dutch shipyards.

The extensive trading activities of the Dutch produced a huge flow of wealth into the hands of Dutch merchants. This capital allowed them to become Europe's leading moneylenders, serving princes, merchants, and landowners willing to pay for the use of Dutch capital. The financial activities of the Dutch were institutionalized in the Bank of Amsterdam, set up in 1609. It became a model for national banks later established elsewhere in western Europe. Its location in Amsterdam reflected the fact that that city had become the world's chief commercial and financial center.

The wealth and freedom of Dutch society generated a vigorous cultural outburst. Some of the chief intellectuals in Europe found refuge in the United Provinces, including the philosophers René Descartes from France, John Locke from England, and Baruch Spinoza, a Jewish refugee from Portugal. Among the notable Dutch intellectuals was Hugo Grotius, whose *On the Law of War and Peace* was the first great treatise on international law and has remained a classic on the subject ever since. Freedom of the press enabled the United Provinces to become the leading European center of book publishing. This was also the golden age of Dutch painters. While baroque painters in other countries were glorifying royalty and nobility, Jan Vermeer, Franz Hals, and, above all, Rembrandt van Rijn were celebrating the spirit of Dutch society by dignifying—sometimes glamorizing—the middle and lower classes (see Figure 33.3). Dutch scientists played an important role in advancing the scientific revolution, including the invention of the telescope and the microscope. All of these activities gave the Dutch an important role in western European intellectual and artistic life.

joyed limited powers and asserted very little direction over national affairs. The citizens of the Dutch Netherlands enjoyed considerable freedom to pursue their personal and collective interests. Particularly noteworthy was religious freedom. The Reformed church, strongly Calvinist in doctrine and practice, was established by law, but other religious groups, including Roman Catholics and Jews, were tolerated, a fact that attracted religious refugees from other European nations.

The Dutch Netherlands, a nation of only about a million, made its chief mark on the seventeenth-century world in commerce and finance. That success was based on the seafaring skills of its people and the entrepreneurship of its vigorous bourgeoisie. Those talents, developed over many centuries, allowed the Dutch to become world leaders in commerce. Experienced Dutch sailors plundered Spanish commerce and

As the seventeenth century drew to a close,

FIGURE 33.3 Rembrandt van Rijn, *Syndics of the Cloth Guild* In the Dutch Netherlands of the seventeenth century, commerce was king. Under the leadership of such men as are shown here, the tiny Dutch Netherlands attained a first-rank position in the world of science, philosophy, and trade. Rembrandt, one of the greatest portrait painters of all time, was probably also the greatest of the baroque painters. (Fotocommissie Rijksmuseum, Amsterdam)

the Dutch preeminence in commerce and banking began to decline, especially in the face of England's sea power and France's land might. But that decline could not efface the notable contributions of the Dutch to seventeenth-century western European civilization, a contribution due at least in part to the freedom enjoyed by Dutch citizens to assert their talents as they chose.

SUGGESTED READING

General Treatments

Barry Coward, *The Stuart Age. A History of England 1603–1714* (1980). A fine overview of Stuart England.

Derek Hirst, *Authority and Conflict: England, 1603–1658* (1986).

J. R. Jones, *Country and Court, England, 1658–1714* (1978). Taken together, these two volumes give a balanced treatment of the period.

Christopher Hill, *A Century of Revolution, 1603–1714*, 2nd ed. (1991). A provocative study from a Marxist perspective.

C. G. A. Clay, *Economic Expansion and Social Change: England, 1500–1700,* 2 vols. (1984). An excellent synthesis, rich in details.

From Civil War to Glorious Revolution

Robert Ashton, *The English Civil War: Conservatism and Revolution, 1603–1649,* 2nd ed. (1989). Good on issues.

Ann Hughes, *The Causes of the English Civil War* (1991). A challenging overview of the causes of the Civil War.

G. E. Aylmer, *Rebellion or Revolution? England, 1640–1660* (1986). A balanced treatment of the civil war and the era of Cromwell.

Ronald Hutton, *The British Republic, 1649–1660* (1990). Excellent on the political affairs of Cromwell's age.

Christopher Hill, *The World Turned Upside Down: Radical Ideas During the English Revolution* (1972). An important work on radicalism.

Patrick Morrah, *Restoration England* (1979). A good social history.

John Miller, *The Glorious Revolution* (1983). A brief, thoughtful description and assessment of the Glorious Revolution.

Lois G. Schwoerer, ed., *The Revolution of 1688–1689: Changing Perspectives* (1992). Presents various views on the nature and significance of the Glorious Revolution.

P. Laslett, *The World We Have Lost,* 2nd ed. (1971). A brilliant evocation of the English society of about 1700.

The Dutch Netherlands

Charles Wilson, *The Dutch Republic and the Civilisation of the Seventeenth Century* (1968).

K. H. D. Haley, *The Dutch in the Seventeenth Century* (1972). Either of these two titles will provide a good overview of Dutch society in its most glorious age.

Jonathan I. Israel, *Dutch Primacy in World Trade, 1585–1740* (1989). An excellent description of Dutch economic activity in a world setting.

Simon Schama, *The Embarrassment of Riches. An Interpretation of Dutch Culture in the Golden Age* (1988). A brilliant portrayal of social life.

Biographies

Pauline Gregg, *King Charles I* (1981).

Antonia Fraser, *Cromwell. The Lord Protector* (1973).

Barry Coward, *Cromwell* (1991).

Antonia Fraser, *Royal Charles: Charles II and the Restoration* (1979).

S. B. Baxter, *William III and the Defense of European Liberty* (1966).

CHAPTER 34

Overseas Colonization and the Competition for Empire

FIGURE 34.1 The Taking of Quebec, 1759 This eighteenth-century engraving shows British forces capturing Quebec from the French in 1759. This victory was a major turning point in the eighteenth-century competition for world empire. (Library of Congress)

During the seventeenth and eighteenth centuries the European nations intensified their competition for overseas possessions and commerce. They were spurred on in large part not only by the riches that flowed to Europe from these possessions but also by a conviction that overseas possessions enhanced the power of nations. Whereas Spain and Portugal had led the way beyond the Atlantic frontier during the sixteenth century, England, France, and the United Netherlands threw themselves vigorously into colonization and commercial expansion during the seventeenth and eighteenth centuries and soon outstripped their older rivals. As large as the world beyond western Europe was, the competition for it led to struggles among the leading European powers which decisively affected the power relationships among the competing nations. And while Europeans colonized, traded, and competed around the globe, European civilization spread with them, impacting with varying results on the native populations encountered by the Europeans. The seventeenth and eighteenth centuries marked a turning point in the establishment of western European domination over much of the world. No less significantly, European expansion laid the basis for a global economy.

1. THE NEW WORLD: THE ENGLISH, THE FRENCH, AND THE DUTCH

One of the areas attracting the English, French, and Dutch was the New World, where all three established colonies during the seventeenth century and soon became embroiled in bitter rivalry for dominance. Spain and Portugal still retained their vast empires in Central and South America and during the seventeenth and eighteenth centuries continued to earn rich returns from their enterprises. Having exhausted the easy hauls of gold and silver, the Spanish and Portuguese turned their energies toward creating large plantations worked by oppressed natives and imported African slaves to produce agricultural products marketable in western Europe. Their presence in South and Central America forced the attention of the English, French, and Dutch toward North America and the Caribbean area.

The English were the most successful colonizers in North America. Although some settlers left England to escape political and religious oppression, most were lured by the prospect of cheap land. Colonizing ventures were organized by joint stock companies chartered by the government or by individuals granted huge tracts of land for the purpose of colonization. Between 1607, when the first English colony was planted at Jamestown, Virginia (see Figure 34.2), and 1733, when the last colony was founded in Georgia, England established control of the Atlantic seaboard from Maine to the Spanish colony in Florida. In the thirteen colonies a stable order soon emerged that had a growing potential to supply England with not only raw materials and agricultural products but also markets for manufactured goods. Before long settlers were pushing westward from England's coastal colonies in search of new lands to occupy. English explorers and traders penetrated into the Hudson Bay area in Canada and claimed for England a huge territory, where a profitable fur trade soon developed. Flourishing English colonies were established in the West Indies, especially in Barbados, Jamaica, and Bermuda. In this area the English concentrated on developing profitable sugar plantations, utilizing African slaves as a labor supply.

France also undertook to colonize in the New World, although not as successfully as England. The first French colony in the New World was established by Samuel de Champlain at Quebec on the St. Lawrence River in 1608. Champlain later explored and claimed for France the entire St. Lawrence Valley from the Atlantic to the Great Lakes. Toward the end of the seventeenth century, during the reign of Louis XIV, the French extended their holdings in North America by exploring and claiming a huge territory called Louisiana, stretching down the Mississippi Basin from the Great Lakes to the Gulf of Mexico. The French also established prosperous colonies in the West Indies, especially on Martinique and Guadeloupe, where sugar production was the major economic activity. Except for the West Indies, settlers were slow to come to France's vast, rich lands in the New World, in part because of governmental policy. France closed its empire to non-Catholics, thus excluding an element so important in populating England's colonies—the religiously dissatisfied. By

FIGURE 34.2 The New World Frontier This representation of the first settlement at Jamestown, Virginia, suggests something of the drastic changes that affected those who left European society—symbolized by the great ship standing at anchor—to face the wilds of the New World. (Culver Pictures)

adopting a policy of land allocation that favored the aristocracy, the French government made it difficult for commoners to obtain land overseas. The opportunities for profit offered by the fur trade also discouraged agricultural settlement. When England seized France's American empire in 1763, perhaps no more than eighty thousand settlers lived in New France, compared with the 2 million inhabitants of the English colonies. But that sparse population left its imprint, especially in the form of Roman Catholicism, the French language, and social practices established by settlers in the St. Lawrence Valley and southern Louisiana—marks that persist to the present.

The Dutch also became involved in the colonization of North America. In 1621 the Dutch West India Company was chartered to undertake colonizing and commerce in the New World. In 1624 a Dutch colony was planted on Manhattan Island, a location especially attractive because of its potential as a center from which trade could be controlled. Soon other Dutch communities were established in the valleys of the Hudson, Connecticut, and Delaware rivers. However, the Dutch did not push their colonizing effort very

seriously. Their interest was chiefly in trading, which led them to concentrate their energies on the more profitable East Indies. In 1664 the English seized New Netherland, ending Dutch colonization in North America.

2. EUROPEAN PENETRATION OF THE FAR EAST AND AFRICA

During the sixteenth century, Portugal was the dominant European power in the Far East. In the seventeenth century, however, the Dutch, English, and French aggressively entered into the area (see Map 34.1). The Dutch were the first. In 1602 all the competing Dutch companies interested in Far Eastern trade were joined into a single Dutch East India Company, to which the Dutch government gave almost complete freedom of action. The company soon drove the Portuguese out of the East Indies and established a trading empire that embraced Sumatra, Java, Borneo, the Moluccas, the Celebes, the Malay peninsula, and Ceylon. The English tried to seize a share of this rich area, but they were rebuffed

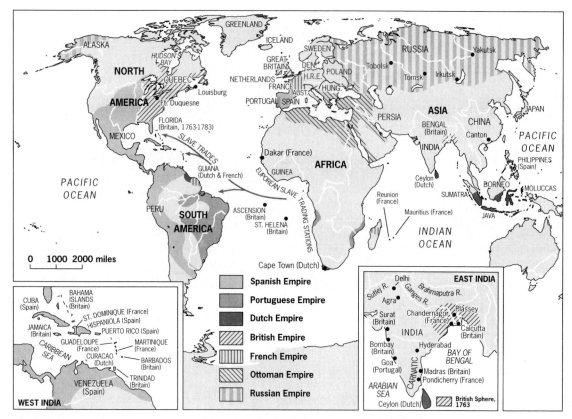

Map 34.1 OVERSEAS POSSESSIONS, 1763. This map shows the extent to which the major European powers had established control over the world by the middle of the eighteenth century. It especially points up the success of England in the quest for overseas possessions. The rich trade flowing between Europe and the overseas possessions had become a vital factor in the economies of these nations. Increasing its overseas possessions and trade was of vital importance to every European state.

by the Dutch as early as 1623. To safeguard the sea route to the Indies, the Dutch established a colony at the Cape of Good Hope in South Africa. Its growth was slow, but the Dutch influence was eventually strong enough to influence the history of South Africa to the present. The Dutch East India Company's interests in the East Indies were represented by a governor-general with headquarters in Java, who in turn set up several other fortified governmental centers throughout the island empire. For years after, the Dutch continued to profit from their holdings in the Indies. They demonstrated remarkable skill in utilizing the native agricultural economy to produce commodities such as spices that were in great demand in western Europe. Consequently, their presence disturbed the existing patterns of life in the area very little. The Dutch also made attempts to penetrate China and Japan but enjoyed only limited success, chiefly because neither the Chinese nor the Japanese welcomed Europeans or their products.

Although shut out of the East Indies by the Dutch, the English soon carved out their own niche in the Far East. An English East India Company was chartered in 1600 and given a monopoly on English trade in the East. This company concentrated chiefly on India, slowly forcing the

FIGURE 34.3 A Refuge in a Foreign World. This drawing shows a European factory, or trading settlement, built in seventeenth-century India. Within the confines of such structures were warehouses, places of residence, market facilities, and even a church. The structure illustrates how the Europeans isolated themselves from the native population in the Far East. (The Bettmann Archive)

Portuguese to let English traders into that rich land. The company founded its own "factories" (trading posts) at key locations—Surat, Madras, Bombay, and Calcutta (see Figure 34.3). For a long time the East India Company was content to exploit the trading opportunities available in these cities; the merchants interfered little with Indian affairs and had little influence on Indian society. Eventually, however, they had to contend with another European rival in India. In 1664, the French organized their own East India Company, which soon established an outpost at Pondicherry. From this center the French company built up an expanding sphere of influence

in India and a prosperous trade that returned large profits.

During the seventeenth and eighteenth centuries, western Europeans made significant inroads into sub-Saharan Africa. Again the Portuguese had been the early leaders, but they were eventually joined by others. It was the establishment of the plantation system in the New World that sparked Europeans' new interest in Africa. The plantations needed labor; African slaves could provide that commodity. Portuguese, Dutch, English, French, and North American traders and adventurers, acting with the support of their governments, established a series of trading posts along the West African coast stretching from modern Senegal to Angola chiefly for the purpose of purchasing slaves to be transported to the New World. The lure of these markets for human beings soon asserted a sinister effect on the native African population far inland from the slave coast.

3. THE IMPACT OF EUROPEAN EXPANSION: NATIVE AMERICANS

The increasing presence of European colonists and traders around the globe during the seventeenth and eighteenth centuries had a significant effect on the native populations of the areas to which Europeans went. In many ways these encounters between Europeans and natives set a pattern that was to impose a bitter heritage on the modern world.

Of all the non-Europeans who felt the impact of the Europeans, the native Americans—American Indians—were perhaps most immediately and drastically affected. Their long-established patterns of life, ranging from the sophisticated civilizations of the Incas in Peru and the Aztecs and Maya in Mexico and Central America to the pastoral and hunting cultures of the North American Indians, were irreparably disrupted by the onslaught of the intruders.

We have already described the destructive impact of the Spanish and Portuguese *conquistadores* on the Aztec, Maya, and Inca civilizations. During the seventeenth and eighteenth centuries, the dislocation continued. The Spanish and the Portuguese had put into place an administrative system that allowed them to dominate political, economic, and social conditions with little regard for the established patterns of native life. Since their fundamental concern was their own enrichment, they viewed the Indians chiefly as laborers on the expanding plantation system and in the mining enterprises from which huge profits could be gleaned. To add to the disruption of native social and economic life, the European masters imported large numbers of black slaves from Africa. Despite their dominance and their disdain for the native Americans, the Europeans in Latin America were never numerous enough to destroy the native American cultures com-

pletely. With passing time their blood and their culture intermingled with those of the native Americans. As a result, significant elements of native American culture were assimilated into the dominant European pattern of life, especially in family structure, agricultural techniques, art motifs, and even religion. Although the ancient Indian civilizations of Central and South America were disrupted forever, enough Indian culture survived to give Latin American society a special hybrid character that has survived to this day.

The Indians of North America suffered a different, and perhaps crueler, fate. In general, the interactions between French settlers and the Indians were not particularly disruptive to Indian society, chiefly because the French were few in number and usually more concerned with trade than land occupation. The English settlers pursued a more ruthless course. From the beginning they were chiefly interested in occupying and exploiting the land, an intention that in the final analysis demanded the displacement of the natives. Although English-Indian relationships were occasionally marked by friendliness and mutual assistance, the English colonial establishment almost from the beginning asserted inexorable pressures on the Indians. As a consequence, the Indians began to disappear from "new" America; their demise was often accompanied by conniving and brutality on the part of the settlers, who began to perceive themselves as the real "Americans." In an effort to protect their land, the Indians fought back savagely. In their struggle for survival they inevitably became embroiled in the mounting rivalry between the English and French for control of North America, a course that made them even more vulnerable. Their resistance nourished a feeling among the colonists that the native Americans were inferior savages whose extermination would best serve everyone's interests. The British government struggled from afar to establish an Indian policy aimed at respecting Indians' rights to their lands and dealing with them honorably in resolving conflicts. But the land-hungry settlers paid little heed and proceeded with the grim business of displacing or exterminating the Indians in the vast Indian stronghold lying between the Appalachians and the Mississippi. The resultant dislocations completely undermined the foundations of native American culture and condemned the Indians to a long-standing inferior status.

4. THE IMPACT OF EUROPEAN EXPANSION: THE FAR EAST

In contrast with the dislocation of native life that marked the coming of the Europeans to the New World, Europeans' impact on the peoples of the Far East was far less disruptive. Few Europeans went to that part of the world; those who did were seeking trading opportunities rather than land upon which to settle. The newcomers isolated themselves in trading depots located in seaboard cities in India and the East Indies, where their contacts with and influence on the natives were slight.

When the Europeans first became involved in India, they encountered a strong state led by other foreigners, the Islamic Moguls, a branch of the Mongol horde of Tamerlane, who early in the sixteenth century had conquered and imposed unity on India. Mogul rule brought prosperity to India's upper classes and created a brilliant chapter in India's already rich cultural history. As the seventeenth century progressed, however, Mogul power began to decline. Political power increasingly fell into the hands of native Indian princes, a development that proceeded rapidly during the eighteenth century. Because this situation aided both the English and the French in establishing their commercial interests in India, the intruders encouraged political localism. Thus, their presence had an impact on the political structure of India but in no sense a determining influence until much later.

Indian society retained both its cohesion and its unique identity despite the presence of the foreigners, be they Islamic Asiatics or Christian Europeans. India's long-established primary social institutions—the family, the village, and the caste system—exercised a decisive role in shaping the lives of most Indians, who were little affected by those who wielded political power. Undergirding these ancient social institutions was a conservative mentality rooted in the religious beliefs and practices embodied in Hinduism and sustained by Hindu priests, called Brah-

mins, who played a powerful role in directing Indian life. Indians were inclined to accept their situation in the present world because they believed that each individual's lot represented a necessary step in the progression toward ultimate fulfillment in another world. Progress, competition for wealth, and the search for new things did not hold the same attraction for Indians as for Europeans. Indians were not impressed by European civilization. They were convinced that they had reflected as deeply on human problems as the foreigners had and had arrived at superior answers. Indians could point to a remarkable art and literature as proof of the vitality of their way of life. Little the Europeans could offer to India seemed able to improve on Indian institutions and values. The outsiders found that a few hundred soldiers and a few cannon could not shake the Indians' confidence in their village and family life, their caste system, their religion, and their culture. Moreover, the continued existence of the basic pattern of Indian civilization in no way impeded the Europeans from reaping huge profits from their commercial enterprise in India. Only slowly and almost imperceptibly did the European way of life make any significant impression on India. And as time passed, Europeans developed a deep respect for some aspects of Indian civilization.

The Dutch presence in the East Indian world likewise had little influence on native society. In fact, the Dutch found it in their interests to sustain the existing order because it lent itself easily to commercial arrangements favorable to the outsiders.

The other major cultural centers in the Far East—China and Japan—were also little affected by the intrusion of Europeans during the period from 1500 to 1800. Again, this was a consequence of the vitality of the native civilizations. In China the Manchu dynasty established a strong political regime during the seventeenth century that brought internal peace, prosperity, and a revitalization of Chinese social, religious, and cultural life along traditional patterns. Chinese civilization came to be greatly admired in Europe in the eighteenth century. However, the Manchus carefully controlled the activities of Western traders—called "Ocean Devils" by the Chinese—with the consequence that European influences were barely felt in China. Japan also enjoyed internal stability under the rule of the Tokugawa shoguns, who in the early seventeenth century established firm control over Japan's ancient feudal system and encouraged a close adherence to ancient social, cultural, and religious customs and values. The new rulers soon adopted a policy of excluding all Europeans from access to Japan, a policy of isolationism that continued until the nineteenth century and that ensured that European influences would be minimal.

5. THE IMPACT OF EUROPEAN EXPANSION: SUB-SAHARAN AFRICA

European expansion into sub-Saharan Africa during the seventeenth and eighteenth centuries had a decisive effect on the societies existing in that vast territory. The centuries prior to 1500 had witnessed the formation of several prosperous states across a wide belt of territory south of the Sahara from the Atlantic to the Indian oceans and then far southward along the east coast of Africa. These states—Ghana, Mali, Songhay, the kingdoms of Hausaland, and the Swahili city-states on the east coast of Africa—were strongly influenced by the Islamic religion, culture, and technology from North Africa. However, in all of them the imprint of much older native African cultures was also strongly felt, producing an amazingly cosmopolitan culture, especially in the cities that dominated these states. The remarkable affluence of these states depended on a vigorous trans-Saharan and Indian Ocean trade that carried gold, ivory, slaves, and many other products northward to the Islamic and European worlds and eastward to India. In fact, many of these states had been brought into existence by enterprising native chieftains who organized extensive realms so as to control more effectively the trading ventures that brought such great riches. Because their existence depended so heavily on trade and because the techniques their rulers borrowed to assert their power had little impact on the great bulk of the native population, these states tended to be unstable. Nonetheless, their creation and their active intercourse with outside cultures marked an important stage in the development of sub-Saharan Africa and its involvement with the larger world. Farther to the south, beyond the sphere of Islamic influence, the native population continued its agricultural existence according to ancient customs, as yet little touched by developments to the north.

These developments in pre-1500 sub-Saharan Africa created a situation that made Africa particularly susceptible to the onslaught of the western Europeans, chiefly because the destinies of so many African states were tied directly to trade with the outside world. Coming by sea to the Atlantic coastal areas of sub-Saharan Africa, the Europeans very quickly caused a redirection of trade routes. Whereas the traditional trade routes plied by African traders had been oriented northward toward the Mediterranean world and eastward toward the Indian Ocean, attention now shifted toward the Atlantic coasts of Africa that gave access to western Europe and the expanding European empires in the New World and the Far East. The European newcomers made little effort to settle in sub-Saharan Africa, chiefly because they could get what they wanted by doing little more than establishing a few trading posts on the Atlantic shores of Africa. What they wanted were the valuable raw materials of Africa, especially gold, and then before long the Africans themselves—as slaves to perform the arduous labor of creating a rich agricultural establishment in the New World. Throughout the seventeenth and eighteenth centuries massive numbers of black Africans—perhaps as many as 11 or 12 million—were uprooted from their native soil, sold into the hands of English, French, Dutch, Portuguese, Spanish, and American slave traders, packed into ships that transported them under inhuman conditions to the New World, and auctioned off to white masters to toil as chattels on the plantations and in the mines of the New World. This traffic in human beings and the cheap labor it supplied resulted in huge profits that became a major source of capital formation in the western European world. In a real sense, the slave trade and slave labor underpinned the rising level of prosperity enjoyed by many people in both Europe and the New World who were not directly involved in either trading or exploiting slaves.

As the Europeans opened slave stations along the coasts of sub-Saharan Africa, significant new political alignments arose in Africa. African kingdoms along or with access to the West African coast flourished as a result of their domination of the trade flowing from inland Africa into the hands of European traders. Among the most prominent of these kingdoms were Oyo, Benin, Asante, Kongo, and Ngola. Often the ruling elements of these kingdoms became prime agents in supplying slaves to the Europeans, leading them to intervene among inland tribes to find slaves to sell. Native chiefs living inland likewise became caught up in the slave trade. Armed with guns supplied by Europeans, the native tribes began to wage war on one another as a means of procuring slaves. The Europeans asserted subtle influences on the coastal states in order to enhance their own trading interests, thus promoting a slow deterioration of the capability of the Africans to control their own destiny. As the demand for slaves increased and the prices commanded by the African slave suppliers rose, European traders moved farther and farther south along the west coast of Africa to turn the attention of more and more native Africans toward serving European trading interests, especially slavery, with the same disruptive consequences. On the east coast of Africa the European presence was equally disruptive. Here the Portuguese effort to seize control of the trade in gold and copper that flowed from central Africa through the Swahili city-states toward Persia and India brought about a decline of those cities and the brilliant civilization they supported. Only deep in the central part of Africa did the native population remain relatively free of the impact of European intrusion.

On the whole, the development of sub-Saharan Africa was seriously impeded by the encounter of its peoples with the western Europeans during the seventeenth and eighteenth centuries. Africa's human resources were depleted, its natural resources plundered, and its political and social structures disrupted. The Europeans gave little in return, especially when compared with what the Moslems of North Africa had contributed to the enrichment of sub-Saharan Africa prior to 1500. Despite the traumatic consequences of European expansion in this era, the Africans retained many elements of their native tradition, which would reemerge later as a significant aspect of their liberation from European domination. And those who were uprooted from Africa took elements of their native culture with them that helped sustain their miserable lives as slaves and that eventually asserted an influence on the civilization of the New World.

6. THE STRUGGLE FOR OVERSEAS EMPIRE

In spite of the vast lands available in the New World and rich trading opportunities to exploit in the highly civilized East and sub-Saharan Africa, the aggressive European nations could not keep out of one another's way in their overseas expansion. As a consequence, their rivalry became global, and the outcome of their struggles began to determine the destinies of peoples only remotely involved in the affairs of Europe.

During the seventeenth and eighteenth centuries the competition for empire was rooted in two interrelated factors: the essential importance of overseas trade to the expanding economies of the major European nations and the policy of mercantilism practiced by most European powers.

The growing importance of overseas commerce not only to national economies but also to people's daily lives was abundantly clear. New products from abroad—among others, spices, sugar, tobacco, cotton, silk, and tea—were in high demand; some of them even became necessities. So also were some manufactured goods from the Far East, especially cotton textiles and chinaware. Colonists needed the products of European manufacturers. The desire of traders to transport these goods stimulated shipbuilding. The distribution of products from colonial and commercial outposts created new opportunities for merchants. The funding of overseas trading and colonizing ventures stimulated the development of banking and credit. The profits garnered from overseas trading activities not only improved the standard of living of those who earned the profits but also became a prime source of capital for investment in western European agriculture, manufacturing, and commerce. Even governments relied on the gains from overseas trade to provide taxes and loans. In short, Europe's economy had been given a new and vital dimension by its global involvement. Control of that economy was vital to the well-being of each European nation, even to the point of fighting others for a share of the lucrative overseas trade.

The realities of seventeenth- and eighteenth-century economic life found expression in the widely accepted economic policy of mercantilism, which accentuated the importance of overseas trade and colonies to every nation. Mercantilist policy was based on the conviction that the economic well-being of a nation depended on governmental management of exchange operations in a way that would produce a favorable balance of gold and silver coming into the economy. Colonies were viewed as a source of cheap food and raw materials and an outlet for manufactured goods that would return a profit to the mother country. Such a view made the accession and careful management of colonies crucial to each nation that aspired to be rich, and thus powerful. Especially important was the need for each nation to monopolize trade with its own colonies, which placed a premium on developing naval power and regulating economic life in the colonies. Likewise, mercantilism dictated that each nation make every effort to restrict the colonizing ventures of rival nations and to deprive them of their colonial possessions whenever possible. Adherence to mercantilist policy meant that every conflict among the major European nations in the seventeenth and eighteenth centuries was extended to their colonies and that every major peace settlement included a redistribution of overseas possessions.

The competition for the fruits of overseas empires began in the sixteenth century with the English and Dutch assaults on Spanish and Portuguese trading activities and overseas holdings. Initially the Dutch won the advantage, but by the middle of the seventeenth century England began to play a more aggressive role in the competition for empire and trade, a development that was one of the major outcomes of the seventeenth-century political upheaval that put control of the English state into the hands of the country gentry and the merchants. As early as 1651 England passed its first Navigation Act, which provided that all goods coming to and from England and its overseas possessions must be carried in English ships. This policy posed a challenge to the commercial interest of the Dutch, who were especially successful in providing shipping services to other nations. It also encouraged the growth of the English merchant fleet and the navy, which had been badly neglected during the early Stuart period. On three different occasions between 1651 and 1688, England engaged the Dutch in warfare. As a result, Dutch commercial ascendancy began to be undermined while England's commercial power grew. Indicative of the shifting balance was the seizure of the Dutch North American colonies by the English.

Toward the end of the seventeenth century both the English and the Dutch began to see that France was their chief threat, for France too became increasingly committed to expanding its colonial and commercial power. The result was an Anglo-Dutch alliance made by William of Orange when he became king of England in 1689. No longer the major sea power in Europe, the Dutch were increasingly content to keep their already established holdings in the East Indies, to continue their declining but still profitable carrying trade, and to reap great profits as the chief bankers and moneylenders of Europe.

From 1689 to 1763 England and France fought each other regularly in Europe (see Chapter 32 for the European aspect of these wars), and each engagement had its repercussions abroad (see Map 34.1). Several times during the War of the League of Augsburg (1688–1697), English and French forces engaged in North America, where the war was called King William's War. Neither in Europe nor in America was the action decisive, and no changes were made in the holdings of either combatant. England had more success during the War of the Spanish Succession (1702–1713). In North America, where the struggle was called Queen Anne's War, England captured Acadia (Nova Scotia) and received recognition of its claims to Newfoundland and Hudson Bay. From France's ally, Spain, England received Gibraltar and Minorca, ensuring access to the Mediterranean. Spain also granted to England the right to supply Spain's colonies with slaves (the *asiento*) as well as the privilege of sending one ship a year to the Spanish colonies in America. These concessions ended Spain's long effort to close its empire to outsiders and gave England the advantage over other nations in exploiting the trading opportunities provided by the Spanish overseas holdings.

From 1713 to 1740 England and France remained at peace. During this calm neither nation was idle in overseas matters. France, realizing the weakness of its position, was especially active in North America. It tried to protect its holdings from English sea power by building a strong fort at Louisburg at the mouth of the St. Lawrence. The French also began to construct and garrison a series of forts to make its hold on the vast territories it claimed along the St. Lawrence valley through the Great Lakes region and down the Mississippi Valley more secure. England concentrated its efforts on widening the commercial breach it had made in Spain's empire in 1713. However, English colonists in North America were steadily advancing westward beyond the Appalachians toward a confrontation with the French for control of the Ohio Valley, where a powerful coalition of native American nations, the Iroquois Confederacy, still held the balance of power. A new European war in 1740, the War of the Austrian Succession, led to a sharp conflict between England and France in both America (King George's War) and India. At the end of the war in 1748 each power restored its spoils to the other, England giving up Louisburg and France restoring Madras.

An eight-year truce ensued in Europe, each side preparing desperately for the struggle that everyone knew would soon reopen. In North America, the French renewed their effort to build a barrier against the westward expansion of the English colonies, focusing their attention now on the Ohio Valley. The inevitable clash came in 1755, when a British attempt to oust the French from Fort Duquesne, at the present site of Pittsburgh, was defeated. The battle in America was clearly joined; one power must destroy the other. In India a no less dramatic struggle was shaping. Although the French had entered the scene in India later than the English, by 1740 they had created a position of some strength. Between 1740 and 1756 the French and British each sought to take advantage of the deepening political crisis in India that resulted from the decline of Mogul power to wring from native Indian princes and political factions concessions that strengthened its own position. Competition became so vicious that soon an undeclared war was on.

Thus, at the opening of the Seven Years' War (called the French and Indian War in America) in 1756, France and England were pitted against each other on three continents. In that war England, led by William Pitt, threw its chief efforts into the colonial war and won a smashing victory. In North America the French, with considerable support from their native American allies, held their own until 1757. After that the superior British forces, supported by the navy, overpowered the French outposts one by one. The decisive blow came in 1759, when the British captured Quebec, opening all Canada to the British (see Figure 34.1). British naval units captured the chief French holdings in the West Indies. In India, Robert Clive, a resourceful agent of the East India Company, won a decisive victory for the British at the battle of Plassey in 1757 and enlarged England's sphere of influence by conquering several native Indian states.

The Seven Years' War ended in 1763 with the Treaty of Paris. France surrendered Canada and all Louisiana east of the Mississippi (except New Orleans) to England. Spain, which had been an ally of France, ceded Florida to England. By a special treaty France compensated Spain for this loss by giving Spain the rest of Louisiana (west of the Mississippi). All French possessions in the West Indies except Guadeloupe and Martinique also fell to England. France's empire in India likewise went to Britain. The French were permitted to enjoy trading privileges in India and to keep Pondicherry, but Britain controlled the chief centers of trade, ending any hope of a French recovery of power there. The Treaty of Paris closed an era in European expansion. Although the Dutch and Spanish still had extensive holdings abroad, Great Britain had fought its way to supremacy in colonial and commercial affairs. The English could now turn to the exploitation of that empire.

Since Columbus' voyage the Europeans had wrought an important change around the world. Energetic colonizers had planted European civilization on the soil of the New World. Enterprising merchants had begun to tap the wealth of a considerable part of the Far East and sub-Saharan Africa, creating for the first time a global economy in which the level of prosperity in European nations was directly related to their access to the labor and products of peoples all over the earth. European patterns of civilization had begun to alter the lives of peoples who had developed their own cultures long before the Europeans came. For good or bad, the Europeanization of the world had begun. And from then on, European history never ceased to have a global scope.

SUGGESTED READING

European Expansion

J. H. Parry, *Trade and Dominion: The European Overseas Empires in the Eighteenth Century* (1971).

Holden Furber, *Rival Empires of Trade in the Orient, 1600–1800* (1976).

Either of these studies will provide an excellent account of the building of commercial empires.

Alan K. Smith, *Creating a World Economy: Merchant Capital, Colonialism, and World Trade, 1400–1825* (1991). Treats the major factors involved in the emergence of a global economy.

The Impact of European Expansion

Bernard Bailyn, *The Peopling of British North America: An Introduction* (1986).

W. J. Eccles, *France in America*, rev. ed. (1990).

These two works will help the reader understand the occupation of North America by Europeans.

Gary B. Nash, *Red, White, and Black. Peoples of Early America*, 2nd ed. (1982). An interesting study of interactions among different peoples in colonial America.

Wilcomb E. Washburn, *The Indian in America* (1975). A good survey.

Karen Ordahl Kupperman, *Settling with the Indians: The Meeting of English and Indian Cultures in America, 1580–1640* (1980).

James Axtell, *The Invasion Within: The Contest of Cultures in Colonial North America* (1985).

Two excellent studies of the impact of European civilization on native American life.

Richard White, *The Middle Ground: Indians, Empires, and the Republics in the Great Lakes Region, 1615–1815* (1991). A brilliant analysis of what happened to Indians caught between European rivals for power in North America.

James Lockhart and Stuart B. Schwartz, *Early Latin America: A History of Colonial Spanish America and Brazil* (1983).

Mark A. Burkholder, *Colonial Latin America* (1990).

Either of these two excellent surveys will provide information on the fate of Indian civilizations in Latin America.

Stanley Wolpert, *A New History of India*, 4th ed. (1992). The appropriate parts of this work will provide a good introduction to Indian society at the time of the European intrusion.

Roland Oliver and Anthony Atmore, *The African Middle Ages, 1400–1800* (1981). A clear treatment of a complex subject.

James A. Rawley, *The Transatlantic Slave Trade: A History* (1981). A balanced account.

Patrick Manning, *Slavery and African Life: Occidental, Oriental and African Slave Trades* (1990). Excellent on the impact of slave trade on African culture.

Imperial Rivalry

W. L. Dorn, *Competition for Empire, 1740–1763*, rev. ed. (1963). A classic work.

CHAPTER 35
The Scientific Revolution

FIGURE 35.1 Isaac Newton Isaac Newton (1642–1727) became the leading figure of the Scientific Revolution, employing the new methods of science and drawing together discoveries in astronomy and physics to create a systematic explanation of the physical laws of the universe. This portrait suggests his youthful vigor and keenness. He was still in his twenties when he developed some of his greatest theories. (The Bettmann Archive)

Until the seventeenth century even the most learned scholars of Europe agreed with the standard medieval understanding of the physical nature of the earth and the universe. This medieval understanding was based on the views of the fourth-century B.C. Greek Aristotle, as modified by Ptolemy and medieval Christian scholars. According to this Christian medieval understanding the earth was stationary and in the center of the universe. Around it moved the planets, the sun, the stars, and the heavens in an ascending series of spheres. This universe was finite and focused on the earthly center of God's concern. "Scientific" investigation generally took the form of making deductions from accepted, authoritative medieval assumptions about the physical universe. The questions asked were usually the more philosophical or theological ones of ultimate causes for an event—guesses as to why something had occurred.

During the seventeenth century a relatively small number of scholars undermined this medieval understanding of nature and replaced it with a modern scientific view. According to this new scientific view, the earth was a moving body and no longer at the center of the universe. Rather, it, along with the planets, moved around the sun in an infinite universe of other similar bodies. Scientific investigations generally took the form of observing, measuring, experimenting, and coming to reasoned conclusions through the use of sophisticated mathematics. Medieval assumptions about the physical universe were viewed with a skeptical eye. The questions asked were usually the more concrete, pragmatic ones of *how* an event had occurred rather than the ultimate reasons for *why* such an event had occurred. The new scientific synthesis was one of a mechanistic universe of forces acting according to mathematically expressible laws and open to human reason and investigation.

Until the eighteenth century the impact of this modern scientific view, known as the Scientific Revolution, was limited. Nevertheless, it was an intellectual revolution of great significance, for with it Western civilization was making a turn from its medieval assumptions and embarking in a direction unique among the cultures of the world. Science would grow to become one of the main factors distinguishing the West and accounting for its power and dynamism.

1. CAUSES AND SPREAD

There were several causes for the development and spread of the Scientific Revolution, some of which extend back to the late Middle Ages and Renaissance. Medieval universities had been growing for some time and included the study of philosophy and other subjects that would be central to the Scientific Revolution, including astronomy, physics, and mathematics. Certainly the emphasis and the greatest prestige were accorded to theology and nonscientific study in these medieval universities, but nevertheless there were places on the faculty for many of the central figures of the Scientific Revolution, such as Galileo and Newton.

The Renaissance involved a search for classical writings. The discovery of Greek authorities who contradicted Aristotle and the growth of Neoplatonism as an alternative to Aristotelian thought in Renaissance Italy encouraged scholars to question medieval scientific assumptions. The Renaissance stimulated interest in analyzing and describing physical reality, a key concern of the Scientific Revolution. The Renaissance was also an age of commercial and geographic expansion in the West, which created a demand for new instruments and precise measurements, particularly for navigation on open seas. This demand encouraged scientific research, especially in astronomy and mathematics. In turn, the better instruments developed during the Renaissance helped scholars make accurate measurements, something crucial for the new science. During this same period, the printing press was invented, which facilitated the dissemination of the new science, even if initially to only a select few.

The Reformation played a mixed role in the Scientific Revolution. Generally, both Catholics and Protestants criticized the scientific discoveries that so threatened the medieval Christian view of the universe. During the sixteenth century there was perhaps more room within the Catholic church for scientific research than among Protestants, but by the middle of the seventeenth century this was clearly not the case. By then the Counter-Reformation Catholic church had turned into an enemy of much of the new science, while Protestants began to accept it. This was particularly so in England, where the Puritans encouraged the new science and where it took hold most firmly.

During the seventeenth century, governments supported science, in part hoping that scientific inquiry would yield discoveries that would increase the power and prosperity of the state. With governmental support scientific academies were established and played a significant role in the advancement of science. The earliest and most important of these were the Royal Society in England, chartered in 1662 by Charles II, and the Académie des Sciences in France, founded by Colbert four years later. These organizations and others patterned after them furnished laboratories, granted subsidies, brought scientists together to exchange ideas, published their findings, and encouraged scientific achievement generally. They also helped make scientists a more socially acceptable group and contributed to the creation of a new set of values supportive of the new science.

Finally, religious and psychological factors played an important, if difficult to evaluate, role in the development and spread of the Scientific Revolution. Many of the new scientists had strong, though not always traditional, religious motives for their work, particularly a desire to gain insight into the perfection of God's universe.

2. ASTRONOMY AND PHYSICS: FROM COPERNICUS TO NEWTON

The first branches of modern natural science to attract systematic attention were astronomy and physics. Discoveries in these fields would dramatically alter the perception of nature and the earth's place in the universe.

Nicolaus Copernicus

The first steps were taken in the sixteenth century by Nicolaus Copernicus (1473–1543), a Polish clergyman interested in astronomy, astrology, mathematics, and church law. Like so many other northern European scholars in the fifteenth century, he crossed the Alps to study in an Italian university. There he was influenced by the rediscovery of Greek scholarship, particularly Platonic and Pythagorean thought, that differed

from the accepted, mathematically complex Aristotelian-Ptolemaic tradition. This rediscovered Greek thought emphasized the importance of a hidden, simpler, mathematically harmonious reality underlying appearances. With a religious, mystical passion, Copernicus sought a simpler mathematical formulation for how the universe operated. This search convinced him that the earth was not the center of the universe but rather that the sun was the center. Moreover, the earth was not stationary but moved in perfect divine circles around the sun, as did other bodies in the universe. This change from an earth-centered (geocentric) to a sun-centered (heliocentric) universe has come to be known as the Copernican revolution (see Figures 35.2 and 35.3).

Copernicus worked on his heliocentric model of the universe for almost twenty-five years, but, fearing the ridicule of the laity and the ire of the clergy, he did not have it published until 1543, the year of his death. Few knew of his views and even fewer accepted them. Nevertheless, their significance and their threat to the Christian conception of the universe would be recognized and condemned by both Catholic and Protestant authorities, who would denounce the Copernican system as illogical, unbiblical, and unsettling to the Christian faith. Nevertheless, his views would stimulate other scholars investigating the physical nature of the universe.

Tycho Brahe

After Copernicus, the most important astronomer of the sixteenth century was a Danish aristocrat, Tycho Brahe (1546–1601). He persuaded the king of Denmark to support him, and he built the most advanced astronomy laboratory in Europe. There he gathered unusually accurate, detailed information about the planets and stars, even though the telescope had not yet been invented. Particularly important were his discoveries of a new star in 1572 and a comet in 1577, both of which undermined the Aristotelian assumptions about a sky of fixed, unalterable stars moving in crystalline spheres. He did not share Copernicus' belief in a heliocentric universe, nor did he grasp the sophisticated mathematics of the day. He believed that the earth remained the stationary center of the universe, as argued by Aristotle and Ptolemy, but he concluded that the

FIGURE 35.2 The Medieval View of the Universe
This woodcut (1559) shows the traditional Ptolemaic conception of the universe. At the center is the earth, surrounded by ascending spheres of air, fire, the sun, the planets, the stars ("firmament"), the crystalline ring, and the "primum mobile." (The British Museum)

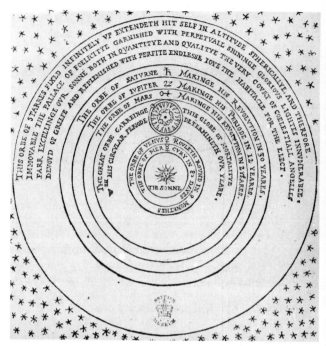

FIGURE 35.3 The Copernican Conception of the Universe (Woodcut, 1576) At the center is the sun, surrounded by the circling planets (one of which is the earth), all bounded by an infinity of stars and the heavens. One of the central developments of the Scientific Revolution was the replacement of the Ptolemaic geocentric by the Copernican heliocentric conception of the universe. (The British Museum)

other planets revolved around the sun, which itself moved around the earth and moon. However, the astronomical observations he gathered would be used by other scholars who became convinced that the earth moved around the sun.

Johann Kepler

Tycho Brahe's assistant, Johann Kepler (1571–1630), built upon Brahe's observations while returning to the Copernican heliocentric theory. A German Lutheran from an aristocratic family, Kepler believed there was an underlying mathematical harmony of mystical significance to the physical universe. He sought such a mathematical harmony that would fit with Brahe's observations. His most important findings were the three laws of planetary motion, proposed between 1609 and 1619: first, that the planets moved in ellipses around the sun; second, that their velocity varied according to their distance from the sun; and third, that there was a physical relationship between the moving planets that could be expressed mathematically. He thus further undermined the Aristotelian universe accepted by medieval thought and provided support for the Copernican revolution. Moreover, he extended the Copernican revolution in ways that would be fully realized by Galileo and Newton.

Galileo Galilei

The Italian astronomer, physicist, and mathematician Galileo Galilei (1564–1642) believed, like Copernicus and Kepler, that there was a hidden harmony to nature. He felt that this harmony could be discovered through experimentation and mathematics. He investigated motion through controlled experiments and demonstrated that motion could be described mathematically. He showed that bodies once set into motion will tend to stay in motion and described the speed of falling bodies mathematically. He thus undermined Aristotelian physics and established rules for experimental physics.

Galileo then moved on to astronomy, using a telescope he built in 1609. The telescope revealed to Galileo that the moon had a rough surface not unlike the earth's, that Jupiter had moons, and that the sun had spots. He confirmed the Copernican hypothesis and provided support for the view that other heavenly bodies were like the earth and imperfect. By implication, this finding meant that the natural universe was ordered and uniform, without the hierarchical distinctions of the accepted medieval view.

Galileo aggressively published and defended his views against detractors, most notably in *Dialogue on the Two Chief Systems of the World,* published in Italian in 1632. This text brought him into conflict with conservative forces in the Catholic church, which condemned his theories at an inquisition in 1633, forcing him to recant.

Isaac Newton

The uphill trail blazed by Copernicus, Brahe, Kepler, and Galileo was continued on to a lofty peak by Isaac Newton (1642–1727) (see Figure 35.1). As a student at Cambridge University, he distinguished himself enough in mathematics to be chosen to stay on as professor after his graduation. Starting in his early twenties, Newton came forth with some of the most important discoveries in the history of science—or indeed of the human intellect. He developed calculus and investigated the nature of light. He formulated and described mathematically three laws of motion: inertia, acceleration, and action/reaction. He is probably best known for the laws of universal attraction, or gravitation. The concept matured and was refined in Newton's mind over a period of years. As it finally appeared in 1687 in his *Principia (The Mathematical Principles of Natural Knowledge),* the law is stated with marvelous simplicity and precision: "Every particle of matter in the universe attracts every other particle

with a force varying inversely as the square of the distance between them and directly proportional to the product of their masses." This law, so simply expressed, applied equally to the movement of a planet and a berry falling from a bush. The secret of the physical universe appeared to have been solved—a universe of perfect stability and precision.

What Newton had done was to synthesize the new findings in astronomy and physics into a systematic explanation of physical laws that were true for earth as well as for the heavens. This Newtonian universe was uniform, mathematically describable, held together by explainable forces, atomic in nature. The universe was essentially matter in motion.

Like most other figures of the Scientific Revolution, Newton was profoundly religious; he believed in God and a God-centered universe, as well as alchemy. By the later years of the seventeenth century and the beginning of the eighteenth century, the new science was becoming more acceptable than it had been for Newton's predecessors, as is illustrated by his career. He became a member of Parliament and served for many years as director of the Royal Mint. He was knighted by Queen Anne. His acceptance, as contrasted with the ridicule and persecution suffered by Copernicus and Galileo, indicates the progress that had been made by the scientific community between the sixteenth and the eighteenth centuries.

3. SCIENTIFIC METHODOLOGY

The scientists who made discoveries in astronomy and physics succeeded in undermining the medieval view of the universe as stable, fixed, and finite, with the earth at its center. They replaced it with a view of the universe as moving and infinite, with the earth merely one of millions of bodies, all subject to the laws of nature. In the process they were also developing and using new methods of discovery, of ascertaining how things worked, and of determining the truth. Indeed, at the heart of the Scientific Revolution was the new methodology of science. According to this new methodology, earlier methods of ascertaining the truth, which primarily involved referring to traditional authorities such as Aristotle, Ptolemy, and the Church and making deductions from their propositions, were unacceptable. The new methodology emphasized systematic skepticism, experimentation, and reasoning based on observed facts and mathematical laws. The two most important philosophers of this new scientific methodology were Francis Bacon and René Descartes.

Francis Bacon

Francis Bacon (1561–1626) was a politician and was once lord chancellor of England under James I. He had a passionate interest in the new science. He rejected reliance on ancient authorities and advocated that scientists should engage in the collection of data without holding preconceived notions. From that information, scientific conclusions could be reached through inductive reasoning—drawing general conclusions on the basis of many particular concrete observations. He thus became a proponent of the empirical method, which was already being used by some of the new scientists. In addition, he argued that true scientific knowledge would be useful knowledge, as opposed to medieval Scholasticism, which he attacked as too abstract. He had faith that scientific discoveries would be applied to commerce and industry and generally improve the human condition by giving human being great power over their environment. He thus became an outstanding propagandist for the new science as well as a proponent of the empirical method (see Figure 35.4). He did not, however, have a good understanding of mathematics and the role it could play in the new science. Descartes did.

FIGURE 35.4 Title Page of Bacon's *Novum Organum* This title page from Francis Bacon's *Novum Organum* (*New Instrument*), published in 1620, shows a ship of discovery sailing out into the unknown. Below is the quotation "Many shall venture forth and science shall be increased." (The Bettmann Archive)

René Descartes

René Descartes (1596–1650) was born in France and received training in Scholastic philosophy and mathematics. He spent his most productive years as a mathematician, physicist, and metaphysical philosopher in Holland. In 1619 Descartes perceived connections between geometry and algebra that led him to discover analytic geometry, an important tool for scientists. He expressed his philosophy and scientific methodology in his *Discourse on Method* (1637), a landmark in the rise of the scientific spirit. It was an eloquent defense of the value of abstract reasoning.

He would question all authority no matter how venerable—be it Aristotle or the Bible. He tried to remove systematically all assumptions about knowledge to the point where he was left with one experiential fact—that he was thinking. "I think, therefore I am" he believed to be a safe starting point. From this starting point he followed a rigorous process of deductive reasoning to come to a variety of conclusions, including the existence of God and the reality of the physical world. He argued that the universe could be divided into two kinds of reality: mind, or subjective thinking and experiencing, and body, or objective physical substance. According to this philosophy, known as "Cartesian dualism," the objective physical universe could be understood in terms of extension and motion. "Give me extension and motion," said Descartes, "and I will create the universe." Only the mind was exempt from mechanical laws.

Descartes, like Bacon, rejected Scholastic philosophy as not useful (although his deductive method had similarities to the reasoning used in Scholastic thought). He emphasized the power of the rigorous, reasoning individual mind to discover truths about nature and turn them to human needs. Unlike Bacon, he emphasized mathematical reasoning, not empirical investigation. By challenging all established authority, by accepting as truth only what could be known by reason, and by assuming a purely mechanical, physical universe, Descartes was in dispute with medieval thought and established an influential philosophy and methodology for the new science.

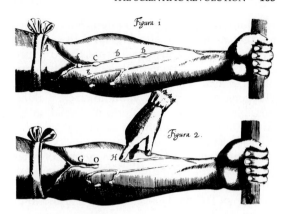

FIGURE 35.5 Modern Anatomy This illustration from an anatomy book published in 1639 by William Harvey shows the circulation of blood. Harvey's empirical, descriptive approach was typical of the new science. (Art Resource)

4. OTHER DISCIPLINES

The individuals who made the great discoveries of the Scientific Revolution all used, to varying degrees, the new scientific methodologies promoted by Bacon and Descartes during the first half of the seventeenth century. Clearly astronomy and physics led the way, but important discoveries were made in other sciences as well.

In the sixteenth century Vesalius, a Fleming living in Italy, wrote the first comprehensive textbook on the structure of the human body to be based on careful observation. Because he dissected many human bodies in order to make his observations, he ran into serious opposition from clerical authorities. In disgust he gave up his scientific studies and became the personal physician of Emperor Charles V. In the seventeenth century William Harvey, an Englishman who also studied in Italy, discovered the major principles of the circulatory system, thus making it possible for surgeons to operate on the human body with somewhat less fatal consequences than had previously been the case (see Figure 35.5). Vesalius and Harvey are regarded as the founders of the science of anatomy.

In the seventeenth century, an Irish nobleman, Robert Boyle, laid the foundations for modern chemistry by attacking many assumptions inherited from the ancients and by beginning the systematic search for the basic physical elements. He relied on the experimental method and argued that all matter was composed of atoms. He discovered a law of gases that still bears his name.

The language in which science is expressed is mathematics. In the early seventeenth century a Scotsman, Sir John Napier, invented logarithms, by which the process of multiplying and dividing huge numbers is greatly simplified. Shortly afterward the system was applied to the slide rule. About the same time, René Descartes adopted the symbols now used in algebra and devised analytic geometry, a method of combining and interchanging algebra and geometry. In the latter part of the seventeenth century Newton and the German Wilhelm Leibnitz, working independently, invented calculus, upon which many of the most intricate processes of advanced science and engineering are dependent.

During the seventeenth century some of the basic scientific instruments were invented. Both the telescope and the microscope were products of the Dutch Netherlands. However, it was Galileo who first used the telescope in systematic astronomical observations. Antoni van Leeuwenhoek, a Dutchman, was the chief pioneer in the use of the microscope. He discovered bacteria two hundred years before Pasteur learned how to combat them; he also observed the cellular structure of plant and animal tissue, the structure of the blood, and its circulation through the capillary system. Another Dutchman, Christiaan Huygens, invented the pendulum clock, making possible the precise measurement of small intervals of time for the first time in history.

The methods and discoveries of the Scientific Revolution spread to disciplines outside of what are usually considered the sciences. A good example is political theory, with the seminal thought of Thomas Hobbes (1588–1679) and John Locke (1632–1704).

Hobbes gained contact with the new sciences from several quarters. As a young man he served as a secretary to Francis Bacon. While traveling on the continent, he came into contact with Descartes and Galileo. He studied the writings of William Harvey. Hobbes acquired an expertise in both geometry and optics. Toward the middle of his life Hobbes became involved in the political events of his times and turned his attention to political theory. Dismayed by the civil strife raging during the civil war in England, Hobbes developed a political theory justifying absolutism in the name of law and order. In his *Leviathan* (1651), Hobbes started from a very few principles about human nature and rigorously deduced explanations for the founding and proper functioning of the state. He argued that human beings are most concerned with the preservation of their own lives, the avoidance of pain and pursuit of pleasure, and striving for power to protect themselves and get what they want. In the hypothetical state of nature, people are in a continual competitive struggle with one another. Self-interest and reason eventually lead people to exit the state of nature by way of a social contract among themselves. This social contract creates and grants massive powers to a sovereign, who uses those powers as necessary to keep the peace. Hobbes, like other seventeenth-century scientists, assumed a mechanistic, materialistic universe. His reasoning was much like Descartes'—rigorous, mathematical, and deductive. In the end, Hobbes concluded that absolutism was in accordance with natural law, though his method of reasoning pleased neither kings nor aristocrats.

Locke was also heavily influenced by the new seventeenth-century science. He acquired a medical education at college, read the works of leading scientific thinkers such as Francis Bacon and Isaac Newton, and was a friend of Robert Boyle. Like Hobbes, Locke was involved in some of the political events of his times. Locke also started with human beings in a state of nature, made some basic assumptions about the human condition, and traced the exit from the state of nature by way of a social contract. Yet Locke came to some significantly different conclusions. Assuming that human beings were not quite so self-centered and that things in the state of nature were not so bad, Locke argued that the sovereign had far fewer powers than Hobbes had claimed and that individuals retained the right to revolt under certain circumstances. Applying reasoning similar to that of seventeenth-century scientists, Locke concluded that British constitutionalism was in accordance with natural law.

Thus both Hobbes and Locke extended the Scientific Revolution to new fields. While their conclusions differed, they set a new standard for political theory, becoming two of the most influential political theorists of modern times.

5. IMPACT

By the end of the seventeenth century, the Aristotelian medieval world view had been broken and replaced by the Copernican-Newtonian worldview. The methodology of modern science was established. Scientists had created the foundations for the modern sciences of astronomy, physics, mathematics, chemistry, and anatomy, and study in other disciplines was under way.

Although the new scientists' work had gained some acceptance, their ideas were still known to only a few. Only a small group of people actually participated in this revolution in science. Most were men. Certainly some women overcame barriers and did participate. Margaret Cavendish (1623–1673) wrote works on natural philosophy and the scientific method. Maria Sibylla Merian (1647–1717) became a leading entomologist. Other women participated in scientific research. But men were reluctant to recognize them, and women were generally excluded from scientific societies. Moreover, the findings of the new sciences were not used to liberate women from traditional assumptions or roles, but rather to reaffirm notions of women's inferiority.

The impact of science on the masses remained minimal during the seventeenth century. Some members of the wealthy elite supported and were influenced by the new sciences, seeing potential benefits from them. But even they were few in number. It was not until the Enlightenment of the eighteenth century that the ideas of the Scientific Revolution spread widely and were applied in new ways.

SUGGESTED READING

General

J. Ben-David, *The Scientist's Role in Society* (1971). A sophisticated social interpretation.

A. R. Hall, *The Revolution in Science, 1500–1750* (1983). Full of detail.

M. Jacob, *The Cultural Meaning of the Scientific Revolution* (1988). A strong interpretation.

L. Schiebinger, *The Mind Has No Sex? Women in the Origins of Modern Science* (1989). An informative recent study.

A. G. R. Smith, *Science and Society in the Sixteenth and Seventeenth Centuries* (1972).

Astronomy and Physics

S. Drake, *Galileo* (1980). A brief study.

F. Manuel, *A Portrait of Isaac Newton* (1968). Uses a psychoanalytic perspective.

E. Rosen, *Copernicus and the Scientific Revolution* (1984). A good recent study.

R. S. Westfall, *Never at Rest: A Biography of Isaac Newton* (1981). An excellent biography.

Scientific Methodology

T. S. Kuhn, *The Structure of Scientific Revolutions* (1962). An important, influential interpretation of the Scientific Revolution.

Other Disciplines

P. Laslett, *Locke's Two Treatises of Government* (1970). Includes an introductory analysis with the texts.

C. B. MacPherson, *The Political Theory of Possessive Individualism: Hobbes to Locke* (1962). A controversial Marxist interpretation.

Sources

M. B. Hall, ed., *Nature and Nature's Laws: Documents of the Scientific Revolution* (1970). A good collection.

CHAPTER 36
The Enlightenment

FIGURE 36.1 *Madame Geoffrin's Salon,* **1755** Meetings in aristocratic Parisian salons such as this were typical of the Enlightenment. Here thinkers, artists, musicians, writers, and aristocrats exchanged views and helped spread the philosophy of the Enlightenment. (Giraudon/Art Resource)

As a period of intellectual history, the eighteenth century is usually referred to as the Enlightenment, or the Age of Reason. The Enlightenment was initiated toward the end of the seventeenth century by a number of intellectuals who attempted to popularize the ideas of the Scientific Revolution. During the eighteenth century this popularization continued, and new attempts were made to apply the methods of natural sciences to human behavior and social institutions. Western thinkers were speculating on the broader meaning of science—its ethical, political, social, and economic implications. They subjected almost everything to the critical standard of reason. In doing so, Enlightenment thinkers rejected the assumptions of their medieval and Renaissance predecessors, who had looked to the Christian or classical past for guidance. Enlightenment thinkers argued for reform and change. They felt that people were ready to shrug off the shackles of tradition and custom and participate in the progress of civilization; to these optimistic intellectuals, people were ready to become enlightened.

The Enlightenment was limited in some respects. During the eighteenth century the Enlightenment was centered in western Europe. Moreover, Enlightenment thought spread primarily to only the elite of the urban aristocracy and middle classes. Nevertheless, the ideas and attitudes developed during the Enlightenment would come to dominate most parts of Western civilization over the next two centuries.

1. ENLIGHTENMENT CONCEPTS

Although Enlightenment thinkers differed widely among themselves, they shared a belief in certain broad concepts that together make up the philosophy of the Enlightenment. The three most important concepts were reason, nature, and change and progress.

Enlightenment thinkers argued that all assumptions should be subjected to critical and empirical reasoning. Traditional institutions or customs should not be accepted because they have been long-lasting but rather should be examined critically and held up to the standard of reason. True knowledge is gained empirically. All we know and all we can ever know is what we perceive through our senses and interpret with our reason. There are no such things as innate ideas or revealed truth.

Enlightenment thinkers believed that nature is ordered, functions reasonably, and constitutes a standard for judgment. Nature is governed by a few simple and unchangeable laws. Those who think they can change one of these laws—who think they can, by praying, for instance, bring down rain on parched crops and perchance a neighbor's unroofed house—are dupes of their own egotism. Nature does not act capriciously. Proper empirical analysis will show that nature functions in line with the laws of reason. Nature is good and beautiful in its simplicity. Human beings have corrupted it with their complex political, social, and religious restrictions. A move to nature is a move toward wholesome vigor and freedom.

Most Enlightenment thinkers felt that change and progress work hand in hand as human beings work to perfect themselves and their society. Change should not be viewed with distrust as a deterioration from a previously superior, more perfect state of things. Change, when dictated by reason and in line with nature, liberates individuals and should be pursued. Such change contributes to individual and social progress on earth. Human beings are naturally rational and good, but the proponents of mystic religions have distorted human thinking and prevented proper progress by preaching false doctrines of original sin and divine moral laws. Rid people's minds of these religious hindrances, and they can and will build a more perfect society for themselves.

The concepts of reason, nature, and change and progress worked together in the minds of Enlightenment thinkers and generally formed a structure for their more specific ideas. Enlightenment thinkers used reason and nature to criticize institutions and customs of the past that still dominated their eighteenth-century society. Reason and nature further guided these thinkers as they determined what changes should take place. They felt that as individuals and societies made appropriate changes, human life would become more informed by reason and more compatible with nature. They believed that human beings were on the verge of enlightenment—of great progress—if people would simply open their eyes and become mature, reasoning adults. This progress would take the form of people leading increasingly happier, freer, more moral lives.

2. THE *PHILOSOPHES*

Enlightenment ideas were put forth by a variety of intellectuals who in France came to be known as the *philosophes* (see p. 470). *Philosophes* is French for "philosophers," and in a sense these thinkers were rightly considered philosophers, for the questions they dealt with were philosophical: How do we discover truth? How should life be lived? What is the nature of God? But on the whole the term has a meaning different from the usual meaning of "philosopher." The *philosophes* were intellectuals, often not formally trained or associated with a university. They were usually more literary than scientific. They generally extended, applied, popularized, or propagandized ideas of others rather than originating those ideas themselves. The *philosophes* were more likely to write plays, satires, histories, novels, encyclopedia entries, and short pamphlets or simply participate in verbal exchanges at select gatherings than to write formal philosophical books.

It was the *philosophes* who developed the philosophy of the Enlightenment and spread it to much of the educated elite in western Europe and the American colonies. Although the sources for their philosophy can be traced to the Scientific Revolution in general, the *philosophes* were most influenced by their understanding of Newton, Locke, and English institutions.

The *philosophes* saw Isaac Newton as the great synthesizer of the Scientific Revolution who rightly described the universe as ordered, mechanical, material, and only originally set into motion by God, who since then has remained relatively inactive. Newton's synthesis showed to the *philosophes* that reason and nature were compatible: Nature functioned logically and discernably, and what was natural was also reasonable. Newton exemplified the value of reasoning based on concrete experience. The *philosophes* felt

that his empirical methodology was the correct path to discovering truth.

John Locke (1632–1704) agreed with Newton but went further. This English thinker would not exempt even the mind from the mechanical laws of the material universe. In his *Essay Concerning Human Understanding* (1690), Locke pictured the human brain at birth as a blank sheet of paper on which nothing would ever be written except by sense perception and reason. What human beings become depends on their experiences—on the information received through the senses. Schools and social institutions can therefore play a great role in molding the individual from childhood to adulthood. Human beings were thus by nature far more malleable than had been assumed. This empirical psychology of Locke rejected the notion that human beings were born with innate ideas or that revelation was a reliable source of truth. Locke also enunciated liberal and reformist political ideas in his *Second Treatise on Civil Government* (1690), which influenced the *philosophes*. On the whole Locke's empiricism, psychology, and politics were appealing to the *philosophes*.

England, not coincidentally the country of Newton and Locke, became an admired model for many of the *philosophes*. They tended to idealize it, but England did seem to allow greater individual freedom, tolerate more religious differences, and evidence greater political reform than other countries, especially France. England seemed to have gone furthest in freeing itself from traditional institutions and accepting the new science of the seventeenth century. Moreover, England's approach seemed to work, for England was experiencing relative political stability and prosperity. The *philosophes* wanted to see in their own countries much of what England already seemed to have.

Many *philosophes* reflected the influence of Newton, Locke, and English institutions, but perhaps the most representative in his views was Voltaire (1694–1778) (see Figure 36.2). Of all the leading figures of the Enlightenment, he was the most influential. Voltaire, the son of a Paris lawyer, became the idol of the French intelligentsia while still in his early twenties. His versatile mind was sparkling; his wit was mordant. An outspoken critic, he soon ran afoul of both church

FIGURE 36.2 Frederick the Great with Voltaire Voltaire, seated, talks with Frederick the Great. This picture reveals the image of the great Enlightenment thinker at work with books, papers, and pen and with the international stature sufficient to gain the ear of enlightened despots such as Frederick. Yet Frederick's enlightenment may have been more form than substance. (Bibliothéque Nationale, Paris)

FIGURE 36.3 The Encyclopedia This engraving from one of the many technical articles in the *Encyclopedia* shows workers preparing type for printing, with details of materials used in the process. It reveals the optimistic faith in the ease and practicality of learning that was typical of Enlightenment thought. (French Embassy Press and Information Division)

and state authorities. First he was imprisoned in the Bastille; later he was exiled to England. There he encountered the ideas of Newton and Locke and came to admire English parliamentary government and tolerance. In *Letters on the English* (1733), *Elements of the Philosophy of Newton* (1738), and other writings, he popularized the ideas of Newton and Locke, extolled the virtues of English society, and indirectly criticized French society. Slipping back into France, he was hidden for a time and protected by a wealthy woman who became his mistress. Voltaire's facile mind and pen were never idle. He wrote poetry, drama, history, essays, letters, and scientific treatises—ninety volumes in all. The special targets of his cynical wit were the Catholic church and Christian institutions. Few people in history have dominated their age intellectually as did Voltaire.

The work that best summarizes the philosophy of the Enlightenment is the *Encyclopedia*. The *Encyclopedia* was a collaborative effort by many of the *philosophes* under the editorship of Denis Diderot (1713–1774) and Jean le Rond d'Alembert (1717–1783). This gigantic work undertook to explore the whole world of knowledge from the perspective of the *philosophes*. Its articles on subjects ranging from music to machinery expressed the critical, rationalistic, and empiricist views of the *philosophes* (see Figure 36.3). The practicality of science and knowledge in general was emphasized. One of the work's main messages was that almost anything could be discovered, understood, or clarified through reason. An

The *Philosophes*

Enlightenment thinkers often referred to themselves as "philosophes," which is technically the French word for philosophers. The term had a special meaning bound up with the spirit of the Enlightenment. This is dealt with directly in the following selection, "The Philosopher," from the Encyclopedia. *It has traditionally been assumed that Diderot is the author of "The Philosopher," but it may have been written by another person, perhaps Du Marsais. In any case, it is an authoritative treatment of the topic according to Enlightenment precepts.*

Other men make up their minds to act without thinking, nor are they conscious of the causes which move them, not even knowing that such exist. The philosopher, on the contrary, distinguishes the causes to what extent he may, often anticipates them, and knowingly surrenders himself to them. In this manner he avoids objects that may cause him sensations that are not conducive to his well being or his rational existence, and seeks those which may excite in him affections agreeable with the state in which he finds himself. Reason is in the estimation of the philosopher what grace is to the Christian. Grace determines the Christian's action; reason the philosopher's.

Other men are carried away by their passions, so that the acts which they produce do not proceed from reflection. These are the men who move in darkness; while the philosopher, even in his passions, moves only after reflection. He marches at night, but a torch goes on ahead.

The philosopher forms his principles upon an infinity of individual observations. The people adopt the principle without a thought of the observations which have produced it, believing that the maxim . . . so to speak, of itself; but the philosopher takes the maxim at its source, he examines its origin, he knows its real value, and

SOURCE: Merrick Whitcomb, ed., "French Philosophers of the Eighteenth Century," in *Translations and Reprints from the Original Sources of European History*, Vol. VI, No. 1 (Philadelphia: University of Pennsylvania Press, 1898), pp. 21–23.

only makes use of it, if it seems to him satisfactory.

Truth is not for the philosopher a mistress who vitiates his imagination, and whom he believes to find everywhere. He contents himself with being able to discover it wherever he may chance to find it. He does not confound it with its semblance; but takes for true that which is true, for false that which is false, for doubtful that which is doubtful, and for probable that which is only probable. He does more—and this is the great perfection of philosophy; that when he has no real grounds for passing judgment, he knows how to remain undetermined.

The world is full of persons of understanding, even of much understanding, who always pass judgment. They are guessing always, because it is guessing to pass judgment without knowing when one has proper grounds for judgment. They misjudge the capacity of the human mind; they believe it is possible to know everything, and so they are ashamed not to be prepared to pass judgment, and they imagine that understanding consists in passing judgment. The philosopher believes that it consists in judging well: he is better pleased with himself when he has suspended the faculty of determining, than if he had determined before having acquired proper grounds for his decision. . . .

The philosophic spirit is then a spirit of observation and of exactness, which refers everything to its true principles; but it is not the understanding alone which the philosopher cultivates; he carries further his attention and his labors.

Our philosopher does not believe himself an exile in the world; he does not believe himself in the enemy's country; he wishes to enjoy, like a wise economist, the goods that nature offers him; he wishes to find his pleasure with others; and in order to find it, it is necessary to assist in producing it; so he seeks to harmonize with those with whom chance or his choice has determined he shall live; and he finds at the same time that which suits him: he is an honest man who wishes to please and render himself useful.

underlying current was criticism of the irrational and of whatever stood in the way of the Enlightenment, whether it was religious intolerance or traditional social institutions. The first volume appeared in 1751. Its threat to the status quo was recognized by governmental and church authorities, who censored it, halted its publication, and harassed its editors. Thanks in great part to the persistence of Diderot, who fought the authorities and dealt with a difficult group of contributing authors, the project was completed with the publication of the final volume in 1772. The *Encyclopedia* sold well and played an important role in the penetration of Enlightenment ideas outside the major cities and courts.

By this time the Enlightenment was evolving to a different stage. The *philosophes* were becoming more quarrelsome among themselves. This disagreement reflected a greater acceptance of the fundamental philosophy of the Enlightenment, for the debates tended to center on how far Enlightenment concepts could be extended. Some *philosophes*, such as Baron d'Holbach (1723–1789), verged on atheism in attacks on organized religion. Others, such as Marie-Jean de Condorcet (1743–1794), were so optimistic that they almost made a religion out of progress itself. Enlightenment thinkers were also tending to specialize. Some laid the foundations for the development of the social sciences during the nineteenth century. For example, Cesare Beccaria (1738–1794) contributed works on modern criminology and penology, and Adam Smith (1723–1790) wrote what would be the fundamental text of classical economics. Finally, some Enlightenment thinkers took more challenging positions, often contradicting some of the ideas of the Enlightenment itself and providing a transition to the succeeding intellectual traditions. The most important example of these thinkers is Jean-Jacques Rousseau (1712–1778).

One of the most original thinkers and writers of all time, Rousseau crusaded for a return to nature—beautiful, pure, simple nature. The message struck home in a society weary of arbitrary and often corrupt governmental bureaucracy and an oppressively artificial and elaborate code of social etiquette. Rousseau was lionized. Great ladies, including the queen of France, began playing milkmaid. In his novel *La Nouvelle Hé-*

loïse, Rousseau extolled the beauties of free love and uninhibited emotion. In *Émile* he expounded the "natural" way of rearing and educating children. He would let children do what they like and teach them "practical" knowledge. Rousseau shared much with other *philosophes*, even contributing to the *Encyclopedia*, but after the 1750s he broke from them for personal as well as intellectual reasons. In *The Origin of Inequality among Men* (1753), Rousseau argued that civilization was not necessarily a progressive boon to humanity, that human beings had lost much since their exit from the state of nature. In *The Social Contract*, Rousseau became one of the few *philosophes* to make a fundamental contribution to political theory. Rousseau generally placed greater faith in emotion, feeling, and intuition than in reason. In this he was a forerunner of the romantic spirit and expounded its principles long before that movement reached its peak.

The *philosophes* had a self-conscious sense of a spirit of enlightenment. They felt that they were leading a mission of liberation, that by striking the match of reason the darkness of the past would be dispelled and humanity would quickly and easily liberate itself. By becoming thus enlightened, humanity could move from childhood to adulthood. They attacked war and the military values of the traditional aristocracy. They rejected artificial social distinctions. They lauded most forms of freedom, including freedom of the press, speech, and religious belief. They supported the application of science to economic activity, a view appealing to the middle class and liberal aristocracy. They believed that their eighteenth-century civilization was ready for enlightenment and the great progress that would result. Yet the optimism of most of the *philosophes* was not wild-eyed; indeed, there was an underlying current of pessimism in the works of thinkers such as Diderot, the marquis de Sade, Rousseau, and even Voltaire.

In characterizing the *philosophes*, historians have disagreed. Some view the *philosophes* as shallow, self-concerned dilettantes who had few deep or original ideas and who were afraid of real reform. Most historians, however, argue that the *philosophes* were thoughtful, sincere thinkers who performed an important service by laying the intellectual foundations of modern society.

3. WOMEN AND THE SOCIAL CONTEXT

There were several centers of Enlightenment thought in the cities and courts of Europe, particularly western Europe, but the heart of the Enlightenment was in Paris. Gatherings were regularly held in the salons of several wealthy Parisian patrons, usually women of the aristocracy or upper middle class such as Madame du Deffaud or Madame Geoffrin (see Figure 36.1). There the *philosophes* met with one another and members of the international upper middle class and aristocratic elite. They debated the ideas of the Enlightenment in an environment lush with art, music, and wealth. These gatherings facilitated the spread of Enlightenment ideas among social and intellectual elites and added much to the social respectability of intellectuals.

As patrons and as intellectual contributors to these gatherings, women played an important role in the Enlightenment. Women such as Madame Geoffrin provided essential financial support to several *philosophes,* particularly for the *Encyclopedia*. Other women corresponded by letter with leading intellectual, political, and social figures throughout Europe, using letter writing as an art just as conversation was an art in the salons. The salons were open to women with the right intellectual or social qualifications. The *philosophes* tended to support improving the education and position of women. The Enlightenment emphasis on individualism theoretically and in the long run led toward accepting the idea of political and social equality between men and women. Nevertheless, it cannot be said that the *philosophes* advocated equal rights for women in a modern sense nor that they challenged fundamental assumptions about the subordinate public roles appropriate for women. One of the few people to argue for real change in the condition of women in the eighteenth century was Mary Wollstonecraft (1759–1797). In 1792 she published *Vindication of the Rights of Women,* but generally her plea for equal rights for all human beings fell on deaf ears.

Meetings in Paris salons were paralleled by smaller meetings in other French and foreign cities as well as by less organized meetings in coffeehouses and the homes of the liberal aristocracy. Enlightenment ideas were read and discussed in local academies, Freemason lodges, societies, libraries, and clubs.

4. ENLIGHTENMENT AND RELIGION

The Enlightenment was profoundly secular in character, but religion played an important role. Very few Enlightenment thinkers were either atheists or traditional Christians. Most were skeptics influenced by the arguments of Pierre Bayle (1647–1706). Many believed in some form of deism. They believed that this wonderful mechanism called the universe could not have come into being by accident. Some infinite Divine Being must have created it and set it in motion. However, the finite mind of human beings cannot comprehend the infinite. Therefore, God is unknowable. Furthermore, God, having set his perfect mechanical laws into motion, will never tamper with them or interfere in human affairs. God is impersonal.

It is readily apparent that the beliefs of the *philosophes* were in conflict with the doctrines of the Christian churches—Roman Catholic, Protestant, and Orthodox alike. Christian theologians argued that God remained active in the universe, that God's ways are revealed through religious literature and institutions, and that faith constitutes a valid alternative to reason. Enlightenment thinkers and Christian leaders were soon engaged in debate, spending much time and effort attacking each other. In countries such as France and Italy, where clerics were strongly entrenched in government, they censored the writings of the *philosophes* and sought to interrupt their work. In the long run, however, the ideas of the Enlightenment spread, and the Church probably lost more than it gained by so ardently attacking the *philosophes* and their ideas.

In general the Enlightenment promoted toleration toward religious minorities, whether Christian or otherwise. For example, Enlightenment thinkers such as Locke in England and Baron de Montesquieu in France were among several who attacked discrimination against Jews. While the century did not witness an end to anti-Semitism, monarchs and political leaders influenced by the Enlightenment lessened some dictates against Jews in Austria, France, Prussia, and Portugal.

5. POLITICAL AND ECONOMIC ASPECTS OF THE ENLIGHTENMENT

Enlightenment thinkers devoted much thought to matters of government. If human beings are by nature rational and good, then surely, if given the opportunity, they can devise for themselves efficient and benevolent political institutions. Corrupt tyrannies were no longer tolerable. Of the numerous "enlightened" thinkers in the field of political science, three stand out above the others in influence: Locke, Montesquieu, and Rousseau.

Locke's most eloquent plea was for the natural rights of human beings, which are life, liberty, and property. He theorizes, in his *Two Treatises on Civil Government,* that to safeguard these rights individuals voluntarily contract to surrender a certain amount of their sovereignty to government. The powers of the government, however, whether it be monarchical or popular, are strictly limited. No government may violate the individual's right to life, liberty, and property. If it does, the people who set it up can and should overthrow it. These ideas were fundamental in the thinking of the makers of both the French and the American revolutions. Jefferson wrote many of Locke's ideas into the Declaration of Independence, frequently using his exact words. They likewise appear in the U.S. Constitution and in numerous French declarations of liberty.

Baron de Montesquieu (1689–1755) was less a theorizer than a discerning student of history and shrewd analyst of political systems. His masterpiece is *The Spirit of the Laws.* Although a great admirer of the English government after the Glorious Revolution, Montesquieu came to the conclusion that different types of government are best suited to various conditions. For instance, absolute monarchy is best for countries of vast area, limited monarchy for countries of moderate size like France, and republics for small states like Venice or ancient Athens. Not only did he approve of Locke's doctrine of limited sover-

eignty, but he specified how it can best be secured—by a separation of powers and a system of checks and balances. The powers and functions of government should be equally divided among king, lords, and commons, each one being checked by the other two. This theory was probably Montesquieu's greatest practical contribution to the science of government. The principle was incorporated into the U.S. Constitution—kings, lords, and commons becoming the executive, judicial, and legislative branches of government.

Rousseau offered a more radical political theory. This morbid, erratic genius based the conclusions in his *Social Contract* and his *Second Discourse* upon pure imagination. People in the state of noble savagery were free, equal, and happy. It was only when some began marking off plots of ground, saying "this is mine," that inequality began. In order to restore their lost freedom and happiness, people entered into a compact, each with all the others, surrendering their individual liberty to the whole. Since sovereignty is indivisible, the general will is all-powerful. Although Rousseau never made it clear just how the general will would actually operate in practice, he apparently assumed that the individual would be free by virtue of being part of the general will. Rousseau had great influence on the leaders of the second and more radical phase of the French Revolution.

Some of the eighteenth-century planners of the better life through reason turned their thoughts to economics. Since the late fifteenth century, mercantilism had been the dominant economic theory and practice in western Europe. This system of regulated nationalistic economy reached its peak in the seventeenth century. Only the Dutch Netherlands held out for free trade. But if, according to the fundamental assumptions of the Enlightenment, the universe is run by a few simple mechanical laws, why should there not be a similar natural order in the field of economics? A group of French Physiocrats, led by François Quesnay, personal physician to Louis XV, began to teach that economics has its own set of natural laws, that the most basic of these laws is that of supply and demand, and that these laws operate best when commerce is freed from government regulation. This doctrine came to be known as *laissez-faire* (or free trade and enterprise).

The chief developer of the theory of laissez-faire was Adam Smith, a Scottish professor of philosophy who associated with the Physiocrats while sojourning in France. His *Wealth of Nations,* published in 1776, has remained the bible of laissez-faire economics ever since. The ideas of the French Physiocrats and Adam Smith strongly influenced the leaders of the American and French revolutions.

6. ENLIGHTENED DESPOTISM

While critical and combative, the *philosophes* were not political or social revolutionaries. They hoped for fairly painless change from above rather than a revolutionary transfer of power to the still-unenlightened masses. Many followed Voltaire in believing that enlightened despotism was the form of government that offered the greatest chances for enactment of enlightened reforms. By the middle of the eighteenth century several monarchs found these views attractive, styled themselves as enlightened monarchs, and attempted to enact reforms that at least appeared to fit with Enlightenment thought. These monarchs have been distinguished from their predecessors and termed "enlightened despots." To what extent this is a valid characterization of their rule remains to be seen.

The most sensational of the enlightened despots was Frederick the Great of Prussia (1740–1786). Frederick had from boyhood loved music, poetry, and philosophy. At the end of the Seven Years' War (1756–1763), the second of his two wars of aggression, he settled down as a model enlightened despot and attempted to apply the laws of reason to statecraft. Frederick was an avid reader of the French philosophers. He even invited Voltaire to visit him at Potsdam, but Prussia was not big enough to hold two such egos at once. The two quarreled and, after several years, parted.

Frederick made much of religious toleration. However, he continued to penalize the Jews and never ceased to ridicule Christians of all denominations. He was a strong advocate of public education, although he spent very little on it in comparison with what he spent on his army. The centralized Prussian bureaucracy became the most efficient government in Europe. True to the prevailing thought of the Enlightenment, however, he had no faith in popular self-government. Nor did he make a move to free the serfs or end the feudal system in Prussia. Probably the most lasting of Frederick's contributions to Prussia were his codification of the law and improvements in the administration of justice. In the field of economics, Frederick was a mercantilist, although he did share the Physiocrats' appreciation of the importance of agriculture.

The most sincere of all the enlightened despots was Joseph II of Austria (1780–1790). Unfortunately, he lacked the practical sagacity of Frederick the Great. His well-meaning but ill-conceived efforts to centralize the administration of the far-flung Hapsburg territories, to replace the numerous languages of his subjects with German, to secularize the strongly entrenched Roman Catholic church, and to free the serfs in a society still based on feudalism all backfired.

Other monarchs, such as those of Sweden, Sardinia, Spain, and Portugal, attempted or enacted reforms that could be seen as enlightened. Even in Russia, Catherine the Great made apparent efforts at enlightened reforms, but ultimately she did not put most of those reforms into practice.

Significantly, France alone of the great powers on the Continent failed to produce an even faintly enlightened despot. Upon attaining the French throne in 1774, the well-meaning Louis XVI appointed the Physiocrat Turgot as minister of finance. Turgot, a friend of Voltaire, initiated a program of sweeping reforms that might have forestalled the French Revolution. However, within two years' time the powerfully entrenched vested interests persuaded the weak-willed king to dismiss him.

Whether there was a phenomenon of enlightened despotism occurring during the eighteenth century, remains a debated question among historians. If there was, it was usually a matter more of form than of content. Several eighteenth-century monarchs acted in certain enlightened ways, believed themselves to be enlightened, admired some of the *philosophes,* and were admired in return. Several supported culture, favored a less religious and more rational justification for their rule, and consulted with *philosophes*. Yet most of their "enlightenment" was superficial. Many of the reforms they made were simply an update in the long process of making the central government more effective and powerful. Few tried to enact fundamental social, political, or economic reforms dictated by Enlightenment thought, and even those who tried, such as Joseph II, generally failed to effect those reforms.

7. CONCLUSION

Enlightenment thinkers applied and popularized a secular, rational, reformist way of thinking that undermined the intellectual foundations of traditional society. Their ideas threatened the Church more than any other institution, and one of the legacies of the Enlightenment was a widening gap between religiously influenced ideas and accepted scholarly thought. These thinkers, probably unknowingly, laid the intellectual foundations for the revolutions that swept Europe and America from the last quarter of the eighteenth century to the mid–nineteenth century. Moreover, their way of thinking and the ideas that arose from it would form the intellectual core of the liberal middle-class ideology that was ascendant during the nineteenth century and is still strong in the twentieth century.

SUGGESTED READING

General

C. Becker, *The Heavenly City of the Eighteenth-Century Philosophers* (1932). An influential, thought-provoking classic.

P. Gay, *The Enlightenment: An Interpretation.* Vol. I: *The Rise of Modern Paganism.* Vol. II: *The Science of Freedom* (1969). Detailed treatment by a leading authority.

N. Hampson, *The Enlightenment* (1982). A highly respected survey.

The Philosophes

T. Bestermann, *Voltaire* (1969). A solid biography.

A. M. Wilson, *Diderot* (1972). An excellent biography.

The Social, Political, and Economic Context

L. Krieger, *Kings and Philosophers, 1689–1789* (1970). A broad survey making connections between thought and politics.

H. Payne, *The Philosophes and the People* (1976). Focuses on the gap between the *philosophes* and the people.

P. Quennell, ed., *Affairs of the Mind: The Salon in Europe and America from the 18th to the 20th Century* (1980). Emphasizes the role of women.

S. I. Spencer, ed., *French Women and the Age of Enlightenment* (1984). Covers important aspects of the topic.

Enlightened Despotism

H. Scott, *Enlightened Despotism* (1990). A good recent analysis.

E. Wangermann, *The Austrian Achievement, 1700–1800* (1973). A good study of enlightened monarchs.

Sources

L. G. Crocker, ed., *The Age of Enlightenment* (1969). A good anthology.

P. Gay, ed., *The Enlightenment: A Comprehensive Anthology* (1973). A good selection of documents.

RETROSPECT

The most noteworthy exceptions to royal absolutism in western Europe were found in England and the Dutch Netherlands, where constitutionalism prevailed. In England royal absolutism had reached its peak during the sixteenth century under the vigorous and politically crafty Tudor rulers. The Stuart kings, who came to the throne in 1603 when Elizabeth I died childless, were full of fine absolutist theories but were unable to carry them out smoothly. They soon found themselves in a running fight, mostly over money matters and power, with Parliament, a stronghold of the landed and commercial interests. In a showdown—the Puritan Revolution—the parliamentary forces, under the able leadership of Oliver Cromwell, triumphed. Before the century had ended, one Stuart king had been executed, another invited to the throne on terms, and a third driven out of the country. During the course of the seventeenth and eighteenth centuries England's parliamentary and cabinet system gradually took shape. Constitutionalism had prevailed over royal absolutism. The landed and commercial interests now in control of the English government, however, were no less aggressive in foreign and colonial affairs than the royal monarchs had been.

The Dutch Netherlands, while rather different, also developed a political system emphasizing constitutionalism rather than royal absolutism. Lacking the military resources and potential of their larger neighbors, France and England, the Dutch nevertheless achieved a phenomenal commercial and financial dominance of the Western world. Their economic exploits were accompanied by a preeminence in the fields of painting and philosophy. The Dutch lived under a republican form of government and enjoyed a degree of individual freedom that could not be matched in Europe.

While Prussia, Russia, and Austria were struggling for the mastery of central and eastern Europe, the French, English, and Dutch were competing for dominance in North America and Asia. In this contest the English emerged victorious in North America and India and the Dutch in the East Indies. The English found it relatively easy to drive the Indians out of eastern North America and colonize the continent with Europeans. In Asia the English and the Dutch defeated the natives but were unable to Europeanize these people who had such firmly established societies, cultures, and religions.

Finally, the seventeenth and eighteenth centuries spawned two developments that would eventually undermine the intellectual foundations of the traditional Christian Western society: the Scientific Revolution and the Enlightenment. The Scientific Revolution challenged the traditional, theological, earth-centered conception of the universe and offered a new perception of the universe as infinite, moving, and lawful, with the earth merely one of many bodies. Truth would no longer be based on custom, faith, or authority but rather on rigorous reasoning founded on observed facts and mathematical laws. In the process of this Scientific Revolution, the foundations of the modern natural sciences were laid. The Enlightenment popularized and extended the Scientific Revolution. The main Enlightenment thinkers—the *philosophes*—used reason to criticize traditional customs and institutions. They optimistically believed that people could easily become enlightened and thereby progress to a new level of maturity. Their ideas would play an important role in the revolutions of the late eighteenth and the nineteenth centuries and would form a basis for the liberal ideology that would rise to dominance during the nineteenth and twentieth centuries.

Yet even these intellectual developments properly belong to the seventeenth and eighteenth centuries. They stressed order and power, which were so important to the period. They reflected the dynamic between royal absolutism and constitutionalism—particularly in the Enlightenment admiration for English political institutions and enlightened despotism. They remained limited to a small elite, just as the glamour, affluence, and power of the period remained limited almost entirely to the royalty, the aristocracy, and the small upper middle class. The lower classes, whose labor and blood made so much regal and military splendor possible, received few benefits and were unaware of the fundamental intellectual developments that were occurring. From the late eighteenth century on, much would change.

PART SIX

REVOLUTION, INDUSTRIALIZATION, AND NATIONALISM, 1776–1914

During the last quarter of the eighteenth century political and economic revolutions were initiated that would transform Western civilization. So massive were the changes stemming from these revolutions that historians usually mark this period as the beginning of modern times.

The first political revolution occurred in America, where in 1776 the British colonies revolted and declared their independence as the United States. The American Revolution was followed by the French Revolution of 1789, which was of considerably greater significance, for it represented an almost complete overthrow of traditional institutions in a powerful country in the heart of Europe. During the succeeding two decades, the ideas and reforms of the French Revolution spread throughout Europe. New uprisings and revolutions, generally inspired by some of the same goals as the French Revolution, occurred in several areas during the 1820s, 1830s, and 1840s.

The more subtle but even more historically significant revolution of this period was economic: the Industrial Revolution. Starting in Great Britain, the Industrial Revolution spread to continental Europe and other areas of the world over the course of the nineteenth century. As economic activity shifted from the farm to the factory, cities grew, classes changed, and society itself was transformed.

These political and economic revolutions were in great part responsible for the growth of a number of ideologies—sets of ideas and beliefs that moved people, groups, and governments to demand action in important, compelling ways throughout the nineteenth and early twentieth centuries. Liberalism, conservatism, and socialism became very influential, but perhaps the most powerful was nationalism, which became a potent force for national unification, international competition, and imperialism.

CHAPTER 37
The American Revolution

FIGURE 37.1 **"In Order to Form a More Perfect Union"** This painting by Junius Brutus Stearns depicts the Constitutional Convention in session in Philadelphia in 1787 with George Washington presiding. At times the proceedings of the Convention were less sedate and reflective than this scene portrays; nonetheless, it catches the sense of high purpose the delegates believed they were serving in seeking to strengthen the new nation. (The Granger Collection)

The age of revolutions opened in a somewhat unexpected setting—in the British colonies in North America. There, by force of arms, the American colonists rejected British rule and established the new nation of the United States of America. Historians are not agreed on whether the course followed by the Americans represented merely a war of independence or a revolution in the fundamental sense of changing traditional society. However, to many contemporaries both in America and in Europe something fundamental happened in America between 1776 and 1800 that heralded the beginning of a new era in western European history. Placed in a global setting, the American Revolution was a major event in shaping the modern world.

1. AMERICAN COLONIAL SOCIETY

The American Revolution was a complex movement, but behind it lay one fundamental fact: During the century and a half prior to 1776, American society had become different from that prevailing in Europe. Its uniqueness was due chiefly to the fact that European immigrants and their offspring had to adapt traditional European patterns of life in order to survive in a new environment. As a consequence, many colonists came to think of themselves as a separate people. That perception, coupled with Great Britain's effort to bend colonial society to British purposes without taking into account the changes that had occurred across the Atlantic, led the colonials to act in the name of independence and nationhood.

By 1776 an obvious sign of the vitality of British colonial society was its large population, which had reached about 2.5 million. During the eighteenth century population had grown faster in America than in Europe. The growth was in large part due to emigration from Europe and Africa; by 1776 African Americans constituted 20 percent of the population. Americans of European descent were also reproducing more rapidly than was the case in Europe, largely because of a longer life expectancy resulting from a healthier environment and the fact that earlier marriages were made possible in a setting where it was easier to establish a new household than it was in Europe.

The rapidly growing population had created a bustling economy in the American wilderness. Its backbone was a diverse agricultural establishment, ranging from small, independently owned family farms in New England and the Middle Atlantic colonies to great plantations worked by slaves in the southern colonies. The American soil and climate permitted a variety of crops: grain, tobacco, cotton, rice, indigo, vegetables, fruits, livestock. After the first hard years of the seventeenth century the colonists were more than able to feed themselves; some of their crops, especially tobacco, also found markets in Europe. And off to the west lay areas of rich, unexploited land to attract the growing population.

The colonies had not neglected commerce and industry. In the face of formidable obstacles, colonial merchants, especially in New England and the Middle Atlantic colonies, slowly developed commercial exchanges within America and then extended their activities to Great Britain, the West Indies, and continental Europe. The bulk of the international trade involved colonial raw materials, which were exchanged for European manufactured goods, sugar and rum from the West Indies, and above all slaves from Africa. By 1776 the colonists were producing considerable amounts of manufactured goods, sometimes in defiance of British mercantilist regulations. An important by-product of commercial and manufacturing activity was the emergence of small but vigorous cities. The American colonists were by no means economically self-sufficient, but neither were they totally dependent on Great Britain and Europe. American entrepreneurs were increasingly intent on expanding their economic interests and minimizing external constraints.

By 1776 American society was becoming stratified into a class structure that bore an outward resemblance to the society of Great Britain. Although there were significant contrasts marking the social order from region to region in America, everywhere an aristocracy of wealth made up of merchants, plantation owners, and successful professionals dominated many aspects of life and grew increasingly conscious of its status. A large, enterprising group of free farmers, shopkeepers, and artisans ranked below the aristocracy. Still lower on the social scale were the numerous tenant farmers and laborers—a group that was increasing in size and economic deprivation. Finally, there were African slaves, who were legally considered to be property without any rights and subject to whatever treatment their masters chose to impose on them; the lot of African Americans was made even worse by the assumption among European Americans that they were inferior creatures. However, social stratification in America was neither as rigidly defined nor as inflexible as the class structure in Europe. The chief forces that sanctioned aristocratic status in Europe—birth, royal favor, tradition, unique lifestyle—simply did not exist in America. Few European aristocrats emigrated to America; the family trees of most American aristocrats had shallow roots. America had no peasant class condemned to semidependent status by ancient custom defining their relationships with landlords; although many emigrants originally went to America as indentured servants bound by contract to serve a master, most of them gained their freedom by fulfilling their contracts and became independent farmers. Since aristocratic status depended chiefly on wealth gained in America through farming or commercial activity, it was possible for a capable, enterprising, and lucky individual of low status to advance to aristocratic status by amassing a fortune. The frontier also offered an escape for those threatened with being made dependent. Colonial conditions thus loosened the bonds of aristocratic society and provided a measure of freedom for people of lesser status and modest means—except for African slaves.

Early American society was patriarchal in structure, dominated by males whose authority as heads of the basic social unit, the family, allowed them to dominate women and children. That system was sustained by English law, which prevailed everywhere in the colonies, and by a social code that stressed the virtue of submission of women and children to male authority. The system made women legally subject to their husbands and barred them from participation in almost all aspects of public life. In the typical household, whether on a farm or in a city, women were expected to carry out an array of tasks generally viewed as "women's work": preparing food, making clothing, tending animals, caring for a garden, raising children. Particularly harsh was the treatment of slave women. Although slaves were permitted to maintain nuclear family units, the traffic in slaves often disrupted these households, leaving slave women with the burden of caring for their children alone. In response to such uncertainties extended family networks developed in the slave population. Slave women were frequently sexually abused by their masters. In the upper classes, women of wealthy families enjoyed considerable comfort and leisure but little independence. The cities offered some opportunity for single women and widows to lead a more independent life as nurses, teachers, or shopkeepers. But on the whole colonial women had almost no opportunity to assert their talents beyond the confines of the household.

Religious life in colonial America assumed forms that slowly eroded the role that religion had long played in Europe as a buttress of the established order. Generally, the founders of each colony attempted to define a single religious establishment for that colony, usually based on a European model. One such establishment was the Puritan order that emerged in New England. Based on Calvinist theology and on the principles of local control of each congregation by those who believed themselves to be saved, simple ceremonies involving Scripture reading and preaching, and austere moral codes, the Puritan congregations exercised a powerful influence on the manners and morals of New England society. However, the Puritans were never able to exclude from their society those who would not conform to their religious system and eventually were forced to tolerate dissenters. Elsewhere an effort was made to implant Anglicanism as practiced in Great Britain. A variety of factors combined to make the Anglican church in America different from that in Great Britain. No Anglican bishoprics developed in America, and there was a shortage of educated clergymen trained to sustain the elaborate Anglican services. As a consequence, a hierarchically directed Anglican system capable of imposing uniform doctrines and rituals failed to develop. The Anglican establishment moved in the direction of a congregational system that allowed considerable latitude to local leaders and considerable toleration of differences. To some extent the other structured religions established in colonial America, especially Lutheranism and Roman Catholicism, found it difficult to maintain uniformity and conformity to traditional practices. Successive waves of immigrants from various parts of Europe constantly brought new religious sects to America. The influence of the traditional religious establishments was further challenged from the 1730s onward by a powerful revival movement called the Great Awakening, whose proponents emphasized a personal relationship with the Divine rather than authoritarian direction as the key to salvation. Appealing powerfully to those of precarious economic means and to women, this new piety created a variety of new religious congregations at the expense of older establishments. Still another stream of religious diversity began to emerge in slave society, where religious practices that mixed Christianity with African usages began to take shape as a fundamental element of African-American life. Religious diversity, toleration, and freedom came to be accepted in America to a degree unknown in Europe.

Prior to 1776 the colonists distinguished themselves only modestly in cultural activities. They did establish lower schools and colleges in an attempt to prepare people for careers. Newspapers and book publishers appeared in many areas. The rudiments of a distinct architectural style emerged. But in the main American cultural life depended on western Europe. Perhaps the most notable cultural development of the colonial era was the ability of some colonists to keep abreast of Europe's chief intellectual and cultural movements, especially those associated with the Enlightenment and science, from which were derived ideas that asserted a powerful influence over the colonial mentality at the time of the founding of the new nation.

Especially significant in setting the stage for the rebellion in America were developments involving the way the American colonies were governed. In theory the colonies were part of Great Britain, over which the British monarch and Parliament ruled through the same mechanisms that prevailed in Britain. In practice each colony slowly developed its own local government, which operated with only limited direction by the royal government in Britain. Each colony had a governor, usually appointed by the monarch, who represented the authority of the Crown and who provided a channel through which the concerns of the colonists were conveyed to the British government. Each colony (except Pennsylvania) had a two-house legisla-

ture, the lower house elected by male property owners and the upper house appointed by the king or the colonial governor. The property qualifications were such that a much larger proportion of male colonials was eligible to vote than was the case in Britain; as a consequence, colonial legislatures reflected a broader spectrum of society than did the British Parliament. The powers of colonial legislatures were never clearly defined, but in general they had extensive authority to control local affairs and to levy taxes. The governors had nearly absolute power of veto over the legislatures, but they were not usually in a position to exercise that power because they depended on legislatures for their salaries and operating funds. The colonists developed a system of courts patterned after the British court system, and they enjoyed the legal rights of British subjects as incorporated in English common law. Although the Americans recognized that the British government had authority over them, their system of local government encouraged them to feel that they had a right to decide their own political destiny. One hundred fifty years of experience in self-government created a breach wider than the Atlantic between Great Britain and its American colonies.

Although by 1776 there were large differences between the American and British societies, these differences did not preordain an American effort to establish independence. Most colonists still felt that they were British and were still attached to a European tradition. What eventually aroused American resistance to British rule was a conviction that the British were denying their American subjects the right to sustain the tradition they shared. That perception drew much of its substance from the fact that American society had become different, causing the Americans to view tradition in a different way than did their masters across the Atlantic.

2. THE AMERICAN REVOLUTION: FROM SALUTARY NEGLECT TO WAR

For a long time the unique society emerging in America was little understood in Great Britain. In conformity with mercantilist thought, the British authorities viewed America as a source of scarce raw products and a market for manufactured goods. This view was legislated by the Navigation Acts of the mid–seventeenth century, which implied that Britain would act politically and economically to shape the colonial economy to serve its own interests. It was assumed that the colonists would benefit by conforming to British direction. However, until the mid–eighteenth century the British government was lax in enforcing its mercantilist policies. Entrenched commercial interests in England resisted government interference in private enterprises that profited greatly from colonial trade. The British Crown failed to develop an administrative system in England to supervise the colonies. England was badly served by its officials in America, most of whom owed their offices to political favors or bribery rather than competence. In the meantime, the colonists grew accustomed to doing what they wished economically and politically.

With the end of the Seven Years' War in 1763, Britain began to change its policy in the direction of tightening control over its colonial empire. The vast lands won from the French needed some kind of administration that would ensure their utilization in ways that served British interests as well as deal with the Indian population, whose frustrations were expressed with frightening emphasis by a general Indian uprising in 1763, led by the Ottawa chief, Pontiac. Great Britain was faced with a huge debt, which from a British perspective had been incurred in part to save the Americans from the French and the Indians; it was time for the colonials to share that burden. Britain's rapidly growing population and the increasing importance of manufacturing to its economy had produced a mounting need for imported foodstuffs and for larger markets for manufactured goods. All of these considerations prompted legislation, such as the Grenville (1764–1765) and Townshend (1767) acts, which were designed to increase revenues, control the distribution of lands annexed from the French, and tighten administration in America.

The colonists were hardly in a mood to bend before British interests after so long enjoying the "salutary neglect" of earlier years. They felt they had made sufficient contributions to the British victories in the wars of the first half of the eighteenth century to relieve them of further responsibility. They resented what they felt was treatment as inferiors by the British forces sent to drive the French and Indians out of land that they increasingly believed belonged to them as the real "Americans." The American population was growing even faster than that of Great Britain, creating powerful pressures to expand the American economy and to move westward into the territories won from the French. The growing demand for manufactured goods created an unfavorable balance of trade, which increasingly made many Americans debtors to England. To correct this situation, the Americans needed to increase their native manufacturing and expand their markets in Europe, both of which ran counter to British mercantilist policy. A depression following the Seven Years' War sharpened the growing tension.

The Americans reacted to Britain's changing policy with fiery speeches, boycotts of British goods, protest meetings (such as the Stamp Act Congress of 1765), and occasional riots. They complained that they were being taxed without representation in Parliament and that their own legislatures, long the chief source of governing regulations, were being disregarded. Although the British reaction to the American resistance was inconsistent, the British government pressed on in its effort to tighten its hold on America. It increased its military presence in America and ordered royal officials to seize American property in ways that paid little heed to British law. Between 1768 and 1774 sterner measures, such as the Tea Act, the "Intolerable Acts," and the Quebec Act, were imposed to bring the colonials under tighter control. Resistance in America spread, reflected by the meeting of the First Continental Congress in 1774. And it was fed by growing ideological radicalism, which focused on the British violation of fundamental rights as justification for demanding independence and self-government.

In Great Britain some leaders realized the danger and even sympathized with the principles upon which the protests of the colonists were based. But those sharing these concerns could neither muster support for conciliatory actions that would reassure the considerable segment of the colonial population still not ready to break with Britain nor bring about a fundamental change of policy that would take into account the realities surrounding the relationships with the colonists, whose interests no longer coincided with those of the mother country. The British leaders agreed on only one thing: that it was an act of rebellion and a perversion of the British constitution to claim that British subjects had a right to disobey laws passed by Parliament, as indeed Americans were doing with increasing frequency. This attitude prompted an increase in the British armed forces in America, an action that appeard to reinforce King George III's words: "Blows must decide whether they are to be subject to the Country or Independent."

Indeed, it came to blows. Armed hostilities opened in April 1775, when American militiamen challenged British forces in skirmishes at Lexington and Concord. In May 1775 the Second Continental Congress assembled. Although some of its members still held out for attempts at reconciliation with England, those ready to break with Great Britain prevailed, giving emphasis to their position by appointing George Washington as commander of America's armies. The hour had come to settle the long-debated issues on the field of battle.

When the war began, Britain's larger population and superior resources seemed to doom the cause of the poor, disorganized rebels. In fact, the British government took the rebellion lightly; one royal official characterized the rebels as a "rude rabble without a plan." But such a view proved erroneous. It did not take into account Britain's ineffective military leadership, its distance from the war zone, and the determination of the rebels. For almost a year after the encounters at Lexington and Concord, the main British forces were pinned down in Boston by an American militia drawn chiefly from New England. The Second Continental Congress proceeded with its plans for raising money, recruiting and supplying a military force, and seeking allies. A variety of actions was taken to transfer power from British officials into the hands of American authorities. Most significant of all, once the shooting started, opinion in America moved rapidly toward acceptance of the idea of independence.

Popular sentiment in favor of independence crystallized in 1776, when several colonies instructed their delegations to the Second Continental Congress to break with Britain. On July 4, 1776, Congress issued the Declaration of Independence, crafted chiefly by Thomas Jefferson. Its magnificent preamble, which leaned heavily on the political philosophy of John Locke and European disciples of the Enlightenment, justified rebellion on the grounds of "self-evident" truths that bestowed on all people certain natural rights that must be protected by governments which derive their power from the consent of the governed. The Declaration set forth a long list of ways in which the British government had violated these "inalienable" rights. It therefore had no claim to the allegiance of its subjects, who were entitled to form a new contract to ensure those rights. For many, the Declaration of Independence elevated the struggle above mere revolt; it became a struggle for an "enlightened" polity. The principles enunciated in the Declaration would inspire later generations to act in the name of rights so fundamental that they were beyond the authority of any government.

However, Americans were far from united behind the cause of independence. Many—perhaps 20 percent—opposed independence and the war. Some of these loyalists—contemptuously dubbed "Torries" by Americans who called themselves "Patriots"—fled to Canada and Great Britain; those who remained were a source of concern to American leaders and a target of British efforts to promote dissension. Many Americans were essentially neutral; only under duress did these neutrals contribute to the war effort. Some African-American slaves saw the war as an opportunity to shed their shackles and enjoy the liberty of which the Patriots spoke so much. Loyalists and British alike tried to exploit this hope; the fear of slave revolts dampened enthusiasm for the war in the southern colonies. Even among the patriots there was perpetual disagreement on how to conduct the struggle for independence. The fact that the Americans did sustain their cause in the face of these divisions was remarkable. In part, success was due to the leadership provided by men like George Washington, John Adams, Thomas Jefferson, and Benjamin Franklin, all of whom demonstrated considerable talents for leading armies, organizing resources, rallying popular support, and negotiating with foreign powers.

The war itself unfolded indecisively during 1776 and 1777 (see Map 37.1). While there were

Map 37.1 REVOLUTIONARY WAR CAMPAIGNS This map portrays at least in broad outline the central strategy involved in the revolutionary war. With their main strength concentrated in New York City, where they could be reinforced by sea, the British tried to cripple the Americans first by attempting to seize control of the Hudson Valley and then by an extended campaign to win the South. The Americans countered both of these moves successfully while containing the main British forces in New York, New Jersey, and eastern Pennsylvania.

victories and defeats on both sides, the British seemed to be gaining the upper hand, especially when they undertook a major campaign in the Hudson Valley aimed at isolating New England from the other colonies. However, that bungled campaign ended in October 1777 with the surrender of a major British force at Saratoga. This victory not only raised the flagging American spirits but also was decisive in persuading a hesitant France to commit itself to the American cause. In 1778 a formal alliance was concluded, and France began to supply needed money, ships, and troops. Subsequently, other European powers showed increasing friendliness toward America; Spain and the Dutch eventually declared war on Britain, and several other nations threatened to do likewise. Britain now had a world conflict on its hands; the pressure on America was considerably relieved.

After 1777 the military activity spread over a large area. The British concentrated their main force in New York City, where it could be reinforced by sea. In a series of hotly contested engagements in New York, New Jersey, and eastern Pennsylvania the Americans managed to contain the British forces and avoid a decisive defeat in the crucial Middle Atlantic area. The British undertook a major offensive in the South in 1780 and 1781. Their campaign ended in a stunning defeat at Yorktown, Virginia, in October 1781. This was the last major battle of the war. By 1781 Britain was anxious to end a costly war that was threatening its position around the world. Prolonged negotiations involving not only Britain and America but also France and Spain finally ended with the Treaty of Paris in 1783. By its terms Britain recognized American independence and ceded to the Americans all territories east of the Mississippi from Canada to Spanish Florida. The new nation had won a magnificent victory.

3. THE AMERICAN REVOLUTION AND SOCIAL CHANGE

While the Americans were winning their war of independence against a somewhat inept mother country, a variety of developments occurred within American society that resulted in a political and social order sufficiently different from traditional society to make it unique in the contemporary world. Although many changes were pragmatic responses to the realities stemming from independence and war, the thrust toward restructuring society and government found inspiration in the concept of republicanism. Rooted in a tradition that reached back to ancient Greece and Rome, republicanism visualized the ideal society as one composed of independent property owners living as equals in small communities under a government exercising only limited power and controlled by its constituents. In such a society the natural virtue of people would constrain anyone from infringing on the rights of others and would allow all to pursue their individual interests according to their individual talents. It was the success the Americans achieved in moving toward the republican ideal that caught the attention of a world standing on the brink of other, more drastic revolutions.

The first important efforts at reordering society on republican principles were made within the several states (as the colonies were called after July 4, 1776). New governments, reflecting a mixture of elements draw from British political practices, colonial political experience, and theoretical concepts derived from Enlightenment thought, were formed in all the states. The framers of these governments were concerned above all else with protecting the people's liberties from tyrannical governments. Nearly every state drew up a written constitution that carefully defined the structure and functions of government. Elaborate bills of rights, stressing individual rights, were included in the constitutions. Since sovereignty rested with the people, all official positions were filled by elections and the right to vote was extended. Two-house legislatures were established in most states, the lower houses being controlled by property-holding male voters and the upper houses being selected by members of the lower chambers. Systems of representation were devised to ensure that each elected representative spoke for roughly the same number of voters. Legislatures were given wide-ranging powers that ensured their control over public affairs and especially over executive officials, who were universally suspected of being the chief instigators of tyranny. Independent judiciaries were almost universally adopted. The concept of separation of powers was thereby incorporated into the new state governments, signifying a strong conviction that the powers of government must be limited by constitutional safeguards. Taken as a whole, the state constitutions framed between 1776 and 1780 inaugurated a degree of popular control over government unknown in the contemporary world, although none of them was completely democratic.

The Revolution brought about changes in other areas of life as significant as those altering the political structures. Several states took steps to disestablish state-supported churches, to institute religious toleration, and in general to separate political and religious life. Many states passed new land laws that tended to make it easier to gain ownership of property. Especially significant was the abolition of primogeniture, a system of inheritance which provided that the eldest son receive all his father's land. Slavery was abolished in some northern states, in part at least because this institution seemed out of place in a society dedicated to the principles set forth in the Declaration of Independence. However, slavery survived the American Revolution in the southern and border states, perhaps reinforced by arguments devised by its defenders to counter those who claimed that bondage was inappropriate in a society founded on the principle that all were created equal. Efforts were made to expand educational opportunities and to take more adequate care of society's unfortunates. In the name of republicanism people spurned the old social customs that called for deference to aristocrats and replaced them with behavior patterns that reflected greater egalitarianism. Even the lot of women improved somewhat, although on the whole few changes were made in the legal constraints that kept women subject to men. In writing to her husband, John, in 1776 Abigail Adams chided him to "remember the ladies" in his schemes to increase liberty in America. Women came to be credited with playing a major role in building the virtues on which a republican society must rest. And expanding opportunities for occupations outside the household began to emerge for women. All these liberalizing movements pointed toward even greater freedom in the future.

Quite accidentally, the Revolution had an important leveling effect in terms of the distribution of wealth. Inflation, caused by the efforts of the Americans to pay for the war with paper money, wiped out fortunes, aided debtors, and allowed new fortunes to be built. Many established merchants suffered heavy losses from the disturbance of exchange patterns that had existed before independence, but new opportunities in trade and industry emerged once America was free from the British commercial system. Small farmers flourished during the war, bolstered by easy money and high prices. Under these varied pressures, the prerevolutionary social order did not survive intact. Again, a greater degree of social mobility, equality, and personal freedom emerged to characterize life in the new nation.

4. LAUNCHING THE NEW NATION

Once independence had been declared, the American leaders were faced with creating a central government. Formidable barriers challenged them in that task. Any movement toward a national political system had to take into account the forces working to liberalize society and the widespread republican distrust of large-scale government. The existence of thirteen separate states insistent on independence of action created a welter of contradictory interests. But there were forces working in favor of national union: the need for cooperation in a war for survival; the dangers inherent in a world of large, ambitious nations; and the sense of a shared experience in creating a new society in the American wilderness. In the end these forces drove sensible leaders toward forming a national government despite the formidable obstacles.

The first attempt at forming a national government was carried out by the Second Continent Congress. Dominated by men who had a deep distrust for strong government over which the populace had no control, the Congress shaped the Articles of Confederation, finally approved by all of the states in 1781. The Articles established a loose union of thirteen nearly independent states headed by a central government that could not compel the states to do anything but could only encourage them to cooperate. Despite the fact that this government had guided the new nation to victory over the British and made provisions for handling terri-

tories won from Great Britain, the inadequacies of the confederation, the self-serving actions of state governments, and a rising tide of social discontent eventually generated sentiment in favor of a stronger national government. As a result, in May 1787 a constitutional convention was summoned to consider revising the Articles of Confederation.

The convention immediately decided to scrap the Articles and write a new constitution (see Figure 37.1). Once this task was undertaken, the delegates found themselves in broad agreement on many crucial issues. They agreed that a republican form of government based on a written constitution enumerating the powers of the central government was necessary, that there must be popular control over the central government, that there must be a separation of powers with built-in checks among the various branches of government, that the states must enjoy jurisdiction in matters specifically reserved for them, and that the central government must have authority to deal independently with matters affecting the national interest. Working from these premises, the delegates forged a constitution outlining the basic framework for a new government. A two-house legislature, an elected president, and a national judiciary were established. Each branch was assigned specific functions, and an elaborate system of internal checks was devised to constrain each branch from exercising too much power. The powers of the national government were specifically enumerated, while other powers were reserved to the states. However, specific provisions were made allowing the central government to coerce the states in those matters over which it had jurisdiction. This principle of federalism was a unique feature of the new government. A major roadblock centering on the fears of smaller states was overcome by a compromise providing equal representation of each state in one branch of the legislature, the Senate, and representation in proportion to population in the other, the House of Representatives. To ensure a degree of flexibility, provisions were made for amending the Constitution.

By 1789 a sufficient number of states had approved the new constitution to allow the new government to begin operations with George Washington as president and with a Congress controlled by Federalists, that is, those who supported the Constitution and a strong national government. During the next decade the new government proved its worth. Congress enacted legislation that filled in vital details not provided in the Constitution: a Bill of Rights forbidding infringement on the basic rights of individuals; a federal court system; and administrative departments to assist the president in discharging his responsibilities. Taxes were levied and collected, public credit was established, and new states were added to the nation as a part of the process of utilizing the vast territory ceded by Britain in 1783. As president, Washington conducted himself in a way that gave the office dignity and allayed deep-seated fears of executive tyranny. Under the guidance of his cabinet, especially Alexander Hamilton as secretary of the treasury

and Thomas Jefferson as secretary of state, policies were formulated that helped to restore prosperity and to steer the fledgling nation along a path of neutrality in the stormy international scene agitated by the French Revolution.

Despite the successes of the new government under Washington and his successor, John Adams, there was mounting discontent with the Federalists who dominated it (see Figure 37.2). This party made it increasingly clear, especially through the policies promoted by Alexander Hamilton, that it intended to make the central government as strong as possible and to bind the wealthy to the cause of strong central government by favoring their economic interests. This direction aroused opposition not only from those who felt their economic interests threatened but

FIGURE 37.2 Congressional Debate This cartoon shows a "discussion" in the House of Representatives in 1798 between a Vermont Republican (with the tongs) and a Connecticut Federalist (with the cane). It reflects the intensity of party strife just prior to the key election of 1800. (New York Public Library Picture Collection)

also from those who were philosophically suspicious of strong government, those who were committed to human equality, and those who were confident of the political wisdom of the common people—ideas powerfully reinforced by the French Revolution. This opposition began to rally around Thomas Jefferson to form a new party, called the Republicans (not to be confused with the present Republican party, founded in 1854). The emergence of political parties added an element to the new political system that the makers of the Constitution had not foreseen. In a close and bitter election in 1800, Jefferson and the Republicans won the presidency in what has been called "the Revolution of 1800." Perhaps it would be more accurate to say that this election completed the revolution begun twenty-five years earlier. It provided final proof of the workability of the new government by demonstrating that the voters controlled the state and that they did not have to rebel to force a government to be responsive to the wishes of a majority.

Between 1775 and 1800 the Americans had put on an impressive display for a changing world. By force of arms they had rid themselves of a political regime they perceived to be tyrannical. To replace it, they had fashioned, by a rational process, thirteen state governments and a national government capable of effective governance but restricted from abusing the rights of citizens. These governments proved sensitive to popular control and made the exercise of popular sovereignty a fact. Liberal, enlightened people everywhere saw their ideals become a reality in America. Here was inspiration and guidance for those elsewhere who aspired to change society. Many believed, as the German poet Goethe put it, "America, thou hast it better/Than has our Continent, the old one." The age of revolutions had been launched in practice as well as in theory.

SUGGESTED READING

Colonial Society

Daniel J. Boorstin, *The Americans: The Colonial Experience* (1958). A challenging portrait.

James A. Henretta and Gregory H. Nobles, *Evolution and Revolution. American Society, 1600–1820* (1987). A stimulating treatment of many aspects of colonial society.

Jack P. Greene, *Pursuits of Happiness: The Social Development of Early Modern British Colonies and the Formation of American Culture* (1988). A challenging analysis of the social and cultural development of England and its colonies.

Edwin J. Perkins, *The Economy of Colonial America*, 2nd ed. (1988). A brief but effective description of the colonial economy.

Donald R. Wright, *African Americans in the Colonial Era: From African Origins Through the American Revolution* (1990). A brief but insightful overview.

Patricia U. Bonomi, *Under the Cope of Heaven: Religion, Society, and Politics in Colonial America* (1986). A broad survey stressing the vitality of colonial religious life.

Mary Beth Norton, *Liberty's Daughters: The Revolutionary Experience of American Women* (1980). A fine study.

The Revolutionary Era

Edmund S. Morgan, *The Birth of the Republic, 1763–1789*, rev. ed. (1977). A brief account of major events.

Bernard Bailyn, *The Ideological Origins of the American Revolution*, enl. ed. (1992). A brilliant study.

Marc Egnal, *A Mighty Empire. The Origins of the American Revolution* (1988). A challenging treatment stressing the role played by upper-class factions in the struggle against Great Britain.

Pauline Maier, *From Resistance to Revolution: Colonial Radicals and the Development of American Opposition to Britain, 1765–1776* (1991). An excellent analysis of changes in opinion leading to the Revolution.

Robert Middlekauff, *The Glorious Cause: The American Revolution, 1763–1789* (1982). A full narrative account.

Jeremy Black, *War for America. The Fight for Independence, 1775–1783* (1991). A good military history.

Merrill Jensen, *The American Revolution Within America* (1974). Stresses the impact of the Revolution on American society.

The New Nation

John C. Miller, *Toward a More Perfect Union: The American Republic, 1783–1815* (1970). A good narrative account of the first years of the new nation.

Richard B. Morris, *The Forging of the Union, 1781–1789* (1987). A superb analysis of the path toward the Constitution.

Gordon S. Wood, *The Creation of the American Republic, 1776–1787* (1969). Especially good on the growth of republican thought.

Richard B. Bernstein with Kym S. Rice, *Are We to Be a Nation? The Making of the Constitution* (1987). An exciting account of the Constitutional Convention.

CHAPTER 38

The French Revolution, 1789–1799

FIGURE 38.1 Jacques-Louis David, *The Tennis Court Oath*, June 20, 1789 This painting by the sympathetic artist Jacques-Louis David glorifies a crucial step in the French Revolution when the leaders of the newly formed National Assembly swore to draw up a constitution for France. In the center representatives of the three estates—clergy, nobility, and commoners—join in a cooperative gesture. (French Embassy Press and Information Division)

In 1789 the French monarchy was brought to its knees by one of the greatest and most far-reaching upheavals in the history of Western civilization—the French Revolution. During the following ten years revolutionaries eliminated the centuries-old French monarchy, overturned the social system of France's old regime, and transformed France's religious institutions. Underlying these changes was the spirit of the Revolution, best summarized by its slogan: *Liberté, Égalité, Fraternité* ("Liberty, Equality, Fraternity").

The Revolution was so fundamental, so dynamic, and so threatening that it could not be contained within France. The news alone of what was happening in France spread fear among those hoping to maintain the status quo and stirred the hopes of those longing for change. Then by force of arms the French carried the ideas and institutions of the Revolution beyond France's borders. For France, and for much of Western civilization, the Revolution was a watershed that would mark the beginning of the modern world.

1. THE LAST DAYS OF THE OLD REGIME IN FRANCE

France at the succession of Louis XVI, though somewhat weakened by the defeats and failures of Louis XV, was still the richest and most influential nation in continental Europe. During the course of the eighteenth century, France's commerce and prosperity had steadily increased. Half of all the specie in Europe was to be found in France. The French enjoyed a relatively high standard of living. It is not, therefore, to desperation born of poverty that one must look as an explanation for the French Revolution but rather to frustration caused by existing institutions—social, religious, political, economic—that had failed to adjust to changing conditions.

French society on the eve of the French Revolution was divided into three distinct orders, or *estates*. The first estate was the clergy, numbering approximately one hundred thousand out of a total population of some 24 million. The Catholic church in France owned over 10 percent of the land—the best land—and from its lands and tithes and fees enjoyed an income probably half as large as that of the government itself. It controlled all educational institutions and censored the press. It monopolized public worship and continued to harass all other religious groups at a time when the spirit of religious tolerance was rising throughout most of the Western world. The clergy itself was sharply divided. The upper clergy—the bishops and the abbots—were rich and powerful. They were drawn exclusively from the ranks of the aristocracy and were generally looked upon by most of the lower clergy and the common people as parasites. The lower clergy—the priests and the monks—came from the lower classes. The income of the priests was modest. They shared the lives of the people they served and were generally popular, but they had almost no influence on church policy.

The second estate was the nobility, numbering approximately four hundred thousand. The nobility owned over 20 percent of the land of France but was exempt from all direct taxation. The richest of them lived at Versailles as absentee landlords, where they hunted, intrigued, made love, and read the books of the *philosophes* of the Enlightenment. They were reputed to possess the best manners and the worst morals of any class in Europe. The most haughty of the nobility—the most jealous of their rights—were the newcomers, the *noblesse de la robe* (nobility of the gown). They were former rich bourgeois who had purchased judgeships in one of the high law courts. They led the newly reassertive eighteenth-century French aristocracy that had, since the death of Louis XIV in 1715, recouped some of their power and influence at the expense of the king and the bourgeoisie. By the second half of the eighteenth century, almost all high governmental posts were held by the nobility. This nobility was emboldened to challenge the authority of the monarchy when it sought reform and to assert ancient rights and privileges that had fallen out of use against those below them.

The third estate was composed of commoners—the bourgeoisie, the proletariat, and the peasantry—and comprised about 96 percent of the total population. Of all the social and economic groups in France in 1789, the bourgeoisie were probably the most frustrated. They were business and professional people—bankers, merchants, shopkeepers, and lawyers—who had grown into a middle class between the nobility and the peasantry. By the late eighteenth century France's upper bourgeoisie had gone as far as their wits and energy could take them. Some had become richer by far than most of the nobility—only to find the highest levels of government and society closed to them. Others, less wealthy but well educated and ambitious, resented the second-class status assigned to them by the nobility. Perhaps most frustrated were young lawyers and administrators who lacked social, economic, and political positions to match their talents and expectations.

The urban populace was a mixture of groups—wage earners, servants of the rich, artisans, and the unemployed. There was enough distress among them to create tensions—tensions that would increase with the maladjustments caused by the Revolution. During the course of the eighteenth century, the price of bread had risen three times as fast as wages. Paris was the only city in France with an urban populace large enough to make its influence strongly felt. There it included about three hundred thousand citizens (about half the total population of the city)—enough to play a significant role in a revolution.

In 1789 at least 90 percent of the French people were peasants, tillers of the soil. Although they were probably better off than most peasants elsewhere in Europe (they owned at least 30 percent of the land, and serfdom had virtually disappeared), they were on the whole discontented. Most peasant-owned land was subject to feudal dues. Probably a majority of the peasants owned no land at all but were sharecroppers who gave up 50 percent of their produce to the lord in addition to the feudal dues (the fees paid by the peasant for use of the lord's mill, oven, wine press, and breeding stock, death taxes, inheritance taxes, and sale-of-property taxes). Not only were peasants forbidden to hunt; they could not even protect their crops from the lord's hunting parties—nor, for that matter, from the game itself. Although French peasants no longer had to donate their labor to the lord, they were still required to furnish so many days' labor for roads and public works. On them fell nearly all the direct taxes levied by the national government.

Altogether, peasants gave up much of their income in taxes to their landlords, the Church, and the state.

The life of the peasantry too had evolved only slowly since the Middle Ages. Peasants generally lived in little rural villages, their houses close together. Each house usually consisted of one room with a dirt floor, thatched roof, and neither chimney nor glass windows. Livestock frequently lived under the same roof. The peasants' daily diet was made up almost entirely of dark bread and wine; meat was reserved for special occasions. Entertainment centered around the Church. On Sundays and holy days, of which there were many, the peasants' attire and attitudes were festive and gay. Ambitious young French peasants, unlike the peasants in most other parts of Europe, did have opportunities for advancement. Many engaged in cottage industry. A peasant could buy some land, become a priest or the lord's steward, a blacksmith or an innkeeper, or seek a new life in the city. Only relatively few, of course, would succeed.

The government of France was arbitrary. Usually the king's decree was, in effect, law. The Estates General, the French counterpart of the British Parliament, had not met for nearly two centuries. Justice was capricious and corrupt. There were 237 different codes of law to confuse litigants. There were no juries as in Great Britain. The king could arrest and imprison at will (although Louis XV and Louis XVI seldom did). The judges of the thirteen superior courts, called *parlements*, purchased or inherited their titles and were all members of the nobility. It was therefore impossible for a commoner to obtain justice in a case against the nobility. The arbitrariness and inherent injustice of this system, which had long been taken for granted, clashed with the widely circulated ideas of the Enlightenment.

2. THE BREAKDOWN OF THE OLD REGIME

In the decades preceding the Revolution the monarchy was beginning to weaken. Aristocrats in institutions such as the *parlements* (law courts) were challenging the king. The central government was losing control over political debate.

Louis XV (1715–1774) was not a popular or skilled king, and the costly French defeat in the Seven Years' War (1756–1763) only made matters worse. By the 1780s, the monarch's political authority was being seriously undermined.

It was a conflict over finance that set into motion a series of events that culminated in the breakdown of the monarchy and the Old Regime in France. Louis XVI had inherited a large and constantly growing national debt. It was not excessive for a nation as rich as France; Great Britain and the Netherlands had higher per capita debts. But when combined with the exemption of the nobility and the clergy and much of the bourgeoisie from direct taxation and the extravagant cost of maintaining the military establishment and servicing the national debt (most of which had been incurred by past wars), it spelled eventual bankruptcy. Furthermore, France lacked an adequate banking system and was still burdened with the corrupt system of tax collection (called tax farming) that allowed much revenue to be diverted from the treasury into the pockets of private collectors.

Upon assuming the throne, Louis XVI appointed the Physiocrat Turgot, a friend of Voltaire, as minister of finance. Turgot initiated a series of sweeping reforms designed to clean up the mess. However, those with vested interests in the old system brought about his dismissal at the end of two years, and his reform measures were rescinded. A succession of ministers then tried all kinds of palliatives, such as borrowing, pump-priming expenditures, and better bookkeeping, but to no avail. By 1786 the debt was 3 billion livres,[1] and the annual deficit had reached 125 million. Bankers refused to lend the government more money. In a desperate effort to save his regime, Louis called an Assembly of Notables in 1787 and attempted to persuade the nobles and the clergy to consent to be taxed. But the privileged orders refused and demanded, instead, a meeting of the Estates General, thinking that they could control it and thereby assert their

own interests. Pressured by a virtual revolt of his own nobility, the king gave in.

3. THE TRIUMPH OF THE THIRD ESTATE

During the early months of 1789 elections were held for members of the Estates General. All France was agog with excitement. Hundreds of pamphlets appeared, and there was widespread public debate. By tradition, each of the three estates, the clergy, the nobility, and the commoners, elected their own representatives. All males who had reached the age of twenty-five and paid taxes were permitted to vote. Since the third estate, which included the bourgeoisie, the peasantry, and the urban populace, comprised more than nine-tenths of the total population, it was given as many seats as the other two combined. However, by tradition the three estates sat separately and each group had one vote.

By April 1789 the delegates began to arrive at Versailles. Goodwill prevailed. Violent revolution was far from anyone's mind. The delegates came armed only with *cahiers*, the lists of grievances that had been called for by the king. Of the six hundred representatives of the third estate, not one was a peasant. Except for a handful of liberal clergy and nobles who were elected to the third estate, they were all bourgeois. Nearly all the members of the third estate, as well as many members of the two privileged estates, were acquainted with the philosophy of the Enlightenment. They held inflated hopes of quickly solving long lists of problems that had been growing for years.

The first formal session was held on May 5. Immediately a sharp debate began over the method of voting. The two privileged estates demanded that, according to custom, the three estates meet separately and vote by order—that is, each estate cast one vote. This procedure would mean that all attacks on privilege and inequality would be defeated by a vote of two to one. The third estate demanded that the three estates meet jointly and that voting be by head. Thus all measures for fundamental reform would pass, for not only did the third estate have as many members as the other two combined, but a number of lib-

---

[1] The livre was technically worth about twenty cents, but its purchasing power in the eighteenth century was much greater than that of the late-twentieth-century American dollar.

HISTORIANS' SOURCES

Signs of Revolution in France

To some sensitive observers of the time, the signs of revolution were at hand during the late 1780s. One of these observers was Arthur Young (1741–1820), a British farmer and diarist best known for his writings on agricultural subjects. Between 1787 and 1789 he traveled extensively throughout France, keeping a diary of his experiences. In the following selection from that diary, Young notes deep dissatisfaction among the French.

PARIS, OCTOBER 17, 1787

One opinion pervaded the whole company, that they are on the eve of some great revolution in the government: that every thing points to it: the confusion in the finances great; with a *deficit* impossible to provide for without the states-general of the kingdom, yet no ideas formed of what would be the consequence of their meeting: no minister existing, or to be looked to in or out of power, with such decisive talents as to promise any other remedy than palliative ones: a prince on the throne, with excellent dispositions, but without the resources of a mind that could govern in such a moment without ministers: a court buried in pleasure and dissipation. . . .

Pressured by discontent and financial problems, Louis XVI called for a meeting of the Estates General in 1789. In anticipation of the meeting of the Estates General, the king requested and received cahiers, lists of grievances drawn up by local groups of each of the three Estates. These cahiers have provided historians with an unusually rich source of materials revealing what was bothering people just before the outbreak of the Revolution in 1789. The following

SOURCES: Arthur Young, *Arthur Young's Travels in France During the Years 1787, 1788, 1789*, 4th ed., ed. Miss Betham-Edwards (London: Bell, 1892), pp. 97–98; "Cahier of the Grievances, Complaints, and Protests of the Electoral District of Carcassonne . . ." from James Harvey Robinson, ed., *Readings in European History*, Vol. II (Boston: Ginn, 1904), pp. 399–400.

is an excerpt from a cahier *from the Third Estate in Carcassonne.*

8. Among these rights the following should be especially noted: the nation should hereafter be subject only to such laws and taxes as it shall itself freely ratify.

9. The meetings of the Estates General of the kingdom should be fixed for definite periods, and the subsidies judged necessary for the support of the state and the public service should be noted for no longer a period than to the close of the year in which the next meeting of the Estates General is to occur.

10. In order to assure to the third estate the influence to which it is entitled in view of the number of its members, the amount of its contributions to the public treasury, and the manifold interests which it has to defend or promote in the national assemblies, its votes in the assembly should be taken and counted by head.

11. No order, corporation, or individual citizen may lay claim to any pecuniary exemptions. . . . All taxes should be assessed on the same system throughout the nation.

12. The due exacted from commoners holding fiefs should be abolished, and also the general or particular regulations which exclude members of the third estate from certain positions, offices, and ranks which have hitherto been bestowed on nobles either for life or hereditarily. A law should be passed declaring members of the third estate qualified to fill all such offices for which they are judged to be personally fitted.

13. Since individual liberty is intimately associated with national liberty, his Majesty is hereby petitioned not to permit that it be hereafter interfered with by arbitrary order for imprisonment. . . .

14. Freedom should be granted also to the press, which should however be subjected, by means of strict regulations, to the principles of religion, morality, and public decency. . . .

eral clergy and noblemen sympathized with the cause of reform. Both sides realized that the outcome of this issue would be decisive.

On June 17, after six weeks of fruitless haggling, the third estate, bolstered by the support of a few priests from the first estate, declared itself to be the National Assembly of France and invited the other two estates to join it in the enactment of legislation. Three days later, on June 20, when the members of the third estate arrived at their meeting hall, they found it locked. Adjourning to a nearby building used as an indoor tennis court, they took the "Tennis Court Oath," vowing never to disband until France had a constitution (see Figure 38.1). It was the third estate's first act of defiance. On June 23 the king met with the three estates in a royal session at which he offered many liberal reforms but commanded the estates once and for all to meet separately and vote by order. The king, his ministers, and members of the first two estates filed out, but the representatives of the third estate defiantly remained seated. When the royal master of ceremonies returned to remind them of the king's orders, Count Mirabeau, a liberal nobleman elected by the third estate, jumped to his feet and shouted, "Go and tell those who sent you that we are here by the will of the people and will not leave this place except at the point of the bayonet!" When the startled courtier repeated these words to his master, Louis XVI, with characteristic weakness, replied, "They mean to stay. Well, damn it, let them stay." A few days later he reversed himself and ordered the three estates to meet jointly and vote by head. The third estate had thus won the first round.

The monarchy might have still been able to reassert control had not the new National Assembly received unexpected support from two sources, the Parisian populace and the French peasantry. Both had been suffering from unusually poor economic conditions initiated by poor harvests. Revolutionary events raised expectations in these hard times, making both groups unusually volatile. The first important disturbances came in Paris. In early July alarming news began to arrive that the king was calling the professional troops of the frontier garrison to Versailles. It appeared that he was at last preparing to use force. At this critical juncture, the Parisians

countered the threat of force with force. On July 14 a riotous crowd searching for arms marched on and destroyed the Bastille, a gloomy old fortress prison in a working-class quarter that symbolized the arbitrary tyranny of the old regime (see Figure 38.2). (July 14 has long been celebrated as the French national holiday.) This show of force stayed the king's hand.

At the same time the forces of order were faced with uprisings in the countryside. During July and August peasants revolted against their lords throughout France, burning tax rolls, attacking manors, reoccupying enclosed lands, and generally rejecting the burdens of feudalism. These revolts were further inflamed by what has come to be known as the Great Fear—unfounded rumors that brigand bands, perhaps raised by nobles, were creating havoc everywhere. A panic swept the countryside. Many nobles fled from France (the *émigrés*). For all practical purposes, feudalism came to an end. The legal end of feudalism came on August 4 during a night session of the National Assembly, when, in an effort to make the best of a bad situation, one nobleman after another stood up and renounced his feudal rights and privileges.

These defeats suffered by the forces of order enabled the third estate in the National Assembly to take further actions. The most important of these actions occurred on August 26, when the National Assembly proclaimed the Declaration of Rights of Man and the Citizen. This document, which followed the English Bill of Rights by an even hundred years and preceded the American Bill of Rights by two years, was replete with the phrases of the philosophers of the Enlightenment. "Men are born and remain free and equal in rights." The natural rights were declared to be "liberty, property, security, and resistance to oppression." Liberty of opinion "even in religion," freedom of the press, and freedom from arbitrary arrest were all proclaimed. But despite the important role women had played in the Revolution, it was only men who were named as gaining these new rights (see Figure 38.3).

The forces of privilege and reaction, however, still had to be brought to terms. The king not only refused to sign the August decrees but began once more to assemble troops around Versailles and Paris. In answer to this new threat of

FIGURE 38.2 The Storming of the Bastille The storming of the Bastille represented the first act of crowd violence of the French Revolution. Actually, the crowd of Parisians was merely looking for arms to defend itself against rumored attack by the forces of the king. However, the Bastille was believed to have held hundreds of political prisoners and was a symbol of all that was oppressive under the Old Regime. Its fall symbolized a direct blow for freedom and stayed the hand of the king, who was contemplating suppressing the defiant third estate. (Culver Pictures)

force, on October 5 and 6 a huge mob of Parisian women marched eleven miles to Versailles, surrounded the palace, and with the help of the bourgeois National Guard forced the king to accompany them to the city, where he became a virtual prisoner of the populace. As the carriage bearing the royal family rolled toward Paris, the surrounding crowd shouted jubilantly, "We have the baker, the baker's wife, and the little cook boy! Now we shall have bread!" A few days later the National Assembly moved its sessions to Paris, where it increasingly came under the influence of the radical populace of the great city. The third estate had triumphed.

4. MAKING FRANCE A CONSTITUTIONAL MONARCHY

The National Assembly could now at last settle down to the task of transforming French institutions. During the next two years the Assembly passed a series of sweeping reforms that may be conveniently classified as follows.

Judicial

The *parlements* and the manorial and ecclesiastical courts with their arbitrary procedures and overlapping jurisdictions were swept away. An

FIGURE 38.3 Women in the Revolution This contemporary print shows the crowd of Parisian women who marched out to the king's palace in Versailles and forced him to return with them to Paris, where he would be more under the control of the populace. These women were recognized as revolutionary heroines. (Historical Pictures/Stock Montage)

orderly system of lower and higher courts was established. The administration of justice was decentralized and democratized. Judges were to be elected for six-year terms. Torture was abolished. In criminal cases juries were to be used for the first time in French history.

Economic

In accordance with the doctrine of laissez-faire, guilds, labor unions, and trading associations were abolished. All occupations were declared open to all classes. Feudal obligations, including labor on the public roads, had already come to an end on the night of August 4. Internal tolls and customs were abolished.

Financial

The complex, unequal taxes, both direct and indirect, were swept away. They were replaced by a tax on land and a tax on the profits of trade and industry. Both were uniform and no one was exempt. Tax farming was at long last abolished. Expenditures were henceforth to be authorized only by the national legislature. To meet the pressing financial needs of the government, the National Assembly issued paper money called *assignats* to the value of 400 million livres. To back up this paper money, the property of the Roman Catholic church, valued at approximately that amount, was confiscated.

Religious

The seizure of its property was the first step toward the nationalization of the Church. Monasticism was abolished. The clergy was to be elected by the people (including non–Roman Catholics) and their salaries paid by the state. The bishops were reduced in number, wealth, and power. They were no longer to be invested by the pope. These measures were incorporated in the Civil Constitution of the Clergy, to which all members of the clergy were required to take an oath of allegiance in order to perform their functions and draw their salaries. The pope, whose control over the organization and the clergy of the French church would have been broken, declared the Civil Constitution of the Clergy to be founded upon heretical principles and ordered the clergy to refuse to take the oath of allegiance. A majority of the clergy, including nearly all the bishops, followed the pope's command. The defection of the "nonjuring clergy" and of thousands of their devoted parishioners was the first serious split in the ranks of the revolutionists.

Political

Under the new constitution, which was completed in 1791, the judicial, legislative, and executive powers of the central government were separated. Lawmaking was given to the single-chamber Legislative Assembly of 745 members elected for two-year terms. Voting, however, was limited to males at least twenty-five years of age who paid taxes equivalent to three days' wages. It is estimated that some 4 million adult males ("active" citizens) could meet these qualifications and that some 2 million remained "passive" citizens. Actually to sit in the Legislative Assembly required the payment of taxes amounting to fifty-four livres. Only some seventy thousand Frenchmen could meet this qualification, and the weight of power fell to the bourgeoisie. The king was granted a suspensive veto over all but financial and constitutional measures, but three successive legislatures could pass a bill over the king's veto. The conduct of foreign relations was left in the hands of the king, but he could not declare war or make treaties without the consent of the Legislative Assembly. The king's expenditures were limited to a sum voted by the legislative body. France was greatly decentralized. For purposes of local government and administration, the country was divided into eighty-three departments, each of which was administered by a small elected assembly. The execution of the national laws was placed almost entirely in the hands of the local authorities.

In October 1791 the National Assembly, having completed its work, gave way to the Legislative Assembly, which had recently been elected under the new constitution. Within a brief span of two years and with very little bloodshed, France had been made over. The monarchy had been limited and made subject to a written constitution. The Roman Catholic church had been subordinated to the state. Feudalism had come to an end. Individual rights and liberties and legal equality for men, if not women, had been defined and established.

5. FOREIGN WAR AND THE FAILURE OF THE MODERATE REGIME

The new government so optimistically launched lasted less than a year. The chief gainers in the French Revolution thus far had been the bourgeoisie and the peasants. The bourgeoisie had gained political control over the country as well as greater social mobility. Most adult male peasants, who constituted the bulk of the French male population, could now vote, and all of the peasantry was at least free from feudal obligations. To the many peasant landowners who owned their land before the Revolution were now added others who had seized the lands of émigré nobles or had purchased confiscated church lands. Most of the bourgeoisie and the landowning peasants were satisfied and wished to see the Revolution stop where it was, lest they lose their sacred property and their political dominance.

However, other groups were quite dissatisfied. The royal family, the aristocracy, most of the clergy, and the army officers yearned for the restoration of their privileges. And many of Paris's urban populace, both men and women, wanted to see the Revolution continued in a more radical way. They had gained little except theoretical rights and legal equality. Owning no property, they could not vote. Yet they had supplied much of the physical force that had saved the third estate and made the moderate reforms possible.

Leadership for these disgruntled groups was found among radical members of the bourgeoisie, who came to favor overthrow of the monarchy and extension of the Revolution. These radicals, although a definite minority, were well organized and ably led. They came together in numerous clubs, which were formed to debate and plan political matters. The most important was the Jacobin Club. Although the Jacobins were and remained predominantly intellectual bourgeoisie and were moderate at first, they gradually became the most radical group in France. Three Jacobin leaders came to tower over all others. Jean-Paul Marat, Swiss by birth, was an inordinately ambitious and frustrated physician and scientist turned popular journalist (see Color Plate 18). His was the gift of rabble-rousing journalism. He incessantly demanded the beheading of all those leaders who opposed the further extension of the Revolution. Georges-Jacques Danton, a former lawyer in the king's council, was a thundering orator of great energy and ability. Maximilien de Robespierre was also a lawyer. This determined idealist was influenced by Rousseau and bent upon the creation of a virtuous republic.

Events soon played into the hands of the radicals. The kings of Austria and Prussia, fearful of the spread of revolutionary ideas to their own lands and urged on by the French émigrés, began to make threatening moves and to issue meddlesome warnings to the French revolutionaries. In France the reactionaries believed that a successful war would enhance the prestige and power of the throne and that a defeat would result in the restoration of the Old Regime. Most of the radicals believed that war would expose the inefficiency and disloyalty of the king and bring about his downfall. When, therefore, in April 1792 Louis XVI appeared before the Legislative Assembly to request a declaration of war against Austria and Prussia, only seven negative votes were cast. Thus lightly was begun a series of wars that was to last twenty-three years and embroil most of the Western world.

The French armies, almost leaderless since nearly all the high-ranking officers were members of the nobility and had either fled or been deposed, were badly defeated. As the Austrian and Prussian armies advanced toward Paris, there was panic in the city. The king, who had already forfeited his credibility when he attempted to flee the country in June 1791, was now rightly suspected of being in treasonable communication with the enemy. A huge Parisian crowd of men and women advanced on the king's palace. The royal family fled for its life to the Legislative Assembly. The interior of the palace was wrecked, and several hundred of the Swiss Guards were slain. The Legislative Assembly suspended and imprisoned Louis XVI and called elections for a national convention to draw up a new constitution to take the place of the one that had just failed.

6. THE TRIUMPH OF THE RADICALS AND THE REIGN OF TERROR

The elections to the constitutional convention took place in an atmosphere of panic and violence. During the interim between the overthrow of the limited monarchy and the meeting of the convention, Danton assumed emergency leadership of the nation. Feverishly he superintended the gathering of recruits and rushed them to the front. As the recruits were preparing to leave Paris, rumors spread that their wives and children would be murdered by the reactionary clergy and nobles. Violent elements began murdering members of the nonjuring clergy and reactionary nobles who were being held in the prisons of Paris. During the first three weeks of September 1792 more than a thousand such victims were massacred. In the elections of the National Convention, held amid this hysteria, the radicals won a sweeping victory. Most of the conservative elements fearfully stayed away from the polls.

In the National Convention a long-simmering struggle between different Jacobin factions came to a head. The Girondins, so called because many of their leaders came from the vicinity of Bordeaux in the department of the Gironde, had once been the dominant and most radical faction of the Legislative Assembly—the Left.[2] In the National Convention the Girondins found themselves on the Right. The new Left was made up of the Jacobin followers of Marat, Danton, and Robespierre, mostly from the city of Paris. They came to be called the Mountain, since they occupied the highest seats in the convention hall. This radical convention, elected for the purpose of drawing up a new constitution, was to rule France for the next three years (1792–1795).

The first act of the National Convention was to declare France a republic. The next move was to dispose of the king. After a close trial he was found guilty of treasonable communication with the enemy and sent to the guillotine—an instrument adopted by the revolutionists for the more mechanical and humane beheading of the condemned (see Figure 38.4). The execution of Louis XVI, accompanied by proclamations of world revolution by the evangelical Jacobins, sent a shudder of horror through the royal courts of Europe. Furthermore, the hastily recruited French revolutionary armies, which had checked the Austrians and Prussians at Valmy in September 1792, had taken the offensive and overrun the Austrian Netherlands.

Austria and Prussia were now joined by Great Britain, the Dutch Netherlands, Spain, Portugal, Sardinia, and Naples in a great coalition

---

[2] The present political connotation of the terms *right* and *left* derives from this period. In the revolutionary assemblies the conservatives sat quite by chance on the speaker's right, the liberals and radicals on his left.

FIGURE 38.4 **Execution of Louis XVI** In January 1793 Louis XVI was executed by guillotine in a public square before troops and a large crowd of citizens. Here the scene is portrayed as a triumph of the Revolution. (The Bettmann Archive)

bent upon the destruction of the French Revolution and the restoration of the Old Regime. The French armies were unable to stand up to such an array of armed might. But the defeats and invasions were not the worst disasters to confront the revolutionary government. The peasants of the Vendée region in western France, who had been stirred up by the nonjuring clergy, rebelled against the radical government. The rebellion spread until some sixty of the eighty-three departments were involved. Major provincial cities such as Bordeaux, Lyons, and Marseilles were in revolt. Toulon, the chief French naval base on the Mediterranean, invited the British fleet in. Inside the convention itself many of the moderate Girondins were sympathetic to the rebels.

Faced with what seemed to be inevitable disaster to their radical cause and indeed to the Revolution itself, the leaders of the Mountain decided on drastic action. For support they turned to the Paris Commune, as the city government

was called, which was controlled by radicals, and the *sans-culottes*—the common laborers, small shopkeepers, and artisans who wore trousers rather than the aristocratic knee breeches (or *culottes*). The men and women of this urban populace had already played an important role in the Revolution by opposing the old forces of order and supporting the leaders of the third estate at crucial times, such as in the storming of the Bastille. By 1793 they wanted to carry the Revolution further, and for the next two years their wishes and actions would have considerable weight in France. Economically, they favored price controls to keep the cost of bread down and other governmental intervention in the economy to narrow the gap between rich and poor; they envisioned a society of small shopkeepers, artisans, and small farmers as ideal. Politically, they were antimonarchical and strongly republican, indeed favoring as much direct democracy as possible. While leaders of the Mountain did not fully agree with the *sans-culottes*, they were willing to work with them. On June 2, 1793, the National Convention, now dominated by the Mountain and surrounded by a threatening Paris crowd urged on by *sans-culottes* leaders, voted the expulsion and arrest of twenty-nine Girondin leaders. Having thus silenced all opposition within the convention, the leaders of the Mountain and their followers inaugurated a "reign of terror" against their political enemies. Their goals were to unite France and to save and extend the Revolution.

The National Convention delegated unlimited powers to a Committee of Public Safety, composed of twelve men working in secret. The most influential member of this all-powerful committee was Robespierre. At its call was the Committee of General Security, a national police force. A Revolutionary Tribunal was set up to try, condemn, and execute suspects without the usual legal procedure and as quickly as possible. Members of the National Convention were sent out in pairs to carry the Terror to every nook and cranny of France. Although tens of thousands of persons, possibly half a million, were imprisoned during the Reign of Terror, only some twenty-five thousand are believed to have been executed. This drastic policy was remarkably successful. The disaffected elements were quickly silenced and the rebellions quelled. The defense of the republic was entrusted to Lazare Carnot. A *levée en masse* (general call-up) was ordered. All men, women, and children were called to the colors. The able-bodied young men were rapidly trained and rushed to the front. Everyone else contributed to the war effort on the home front. This common activity for defense of country produced a high state of morale—the first mass national patriotism in history. Able new officers were found. The armies of the coalition were defeated on every front and hurled back beyond the frontiers.

While Robespierre and his associates were saving the Revolution, they were also busy extending it to more radical ground. Robespierre was determined to make France a utopian republic where virtue and fraternity would reign supreme. During the emergency of 1793 a maximum price was placed upon the necessities of life for the protection of consumers, particularly the *sans-culottes*. Efforts were made to control inflation by forcing people to accept the badly in-

flated *assignats* at their face value. New measures made it easier for peasants to acquire land. The metric system was adopted; the Louvre Palace was turned into an art gallery; the national library and national archives were founded; a law (never implemented) provided for a comprehensive national system of public education. Women adopted the flowing robes and hairstyles of ancient Greece. Silk knee breeches, the symbol of aristocracy, gave way to trousers. Titles of all kinds were discarded and "Citizen" and "Citizeness" substituted. Even the calendar was revolutionized. The months were made equal and named after the seasons. Weeks were made ten days long, with one day of rest (thereby eliminating Sunday, a day of traditional Christian importance). The Year 1 was dated from September 22, 1792, the date of the declaration of the republic. However the Jacobins took no radical steps for women. Rather, they rejected women's participation in politics and outlawed women's associations.

Meanwhile, discontent with Robespierre and his policies was increasing. The defeat of the invading armies of the coalition and the suppression of the internal rebellion appeared to most people to remove the justification for the Terror, yet the Terror was intensified. Robespierre felt that the republic of virtue for which he yearned had eluded him. When Danton counseled moderation, Robespierre sent even him and his most prominent followers to the guillotine. No one, not even the members of the National Convention, felt safe any longer. Finally, in July 1794, the Convention found the courage and the leadership to overthrow Robespierre and send him to his own guillotine.

7. REACTION AND THE RISE OF NAPOLEON

Since Robespierre was overthrown on July 27, which was 9 Thermidor by the revolutionary calendar, the reaction that followed is known as the Thermidorian Reaction. The propertied bourgeoisie, who quickly gained control of things, had been frightened and angered by the restrictive measures of Robespierre's regime. All such measures still in force were repealed. The Terror was brought to an end and the chief terrorists executed. Armed bands of bourgeois hirelings went around for some time beating or killing Jacobins. Many individuals, weary of discipline and restraint, reveled in an outburst of licentious living. In 1795 the National Convention finally got around to the task for which it had been elected three years earlier: the drawing up of a new constitution. The resulting constitution reflected conservative reaction. Only property owners could vote for members of the legislative bodies. Executive functions were placed into the hands of five directors, who were chosen for five-year terms by the two legislative bodies. In October 1795 the National Convention turned over its powers to the Directory, the name that was given to the new government.

The Directory (1795–1799) was staffed by men of reasonable competence, but they were unable to restore tranquility. Though peace had already been made with Spain and Prussia, war with Great Britain, Austria, and Sardinia dragged on. Government finances were chaotic, and brigandage was rife. More and more people longed for a strongman who could bring peace abroad and order at home. Napoleon proved to be the man, and the story of his rise to power will be told in the next chapter. When in November 1799 Napoleon overthrew the Directory and made himself dictator, the French Revolution had run full cycle from absolute Bourbon monarchy to absolute Napoleonic dictatorship.

SUGGESTED READING

General

F. Furet, *Interpreting the French Revolution* (1981). An influential new interpretation.

L. Hunt, *Politics, Culture, and Class in the French Revolution* (1984). Analyzes the creation of a new political culture in the Revolution.

R. R. Palmer, *The Age of the Democratic Revolution*, 2 vols. (1959, 1964). Places the French Revolution in a broader transatlantic context.

S. Schama. *Citizens: A Chronicle of the French Revolution.* (1989). A vivid, revisionary account.

D. Sutherland, *France, 1789–1815: Revolution and Counter-Revolution* (1986). Stresses connections between social and political conflict.

The Old Regime and the First Phase of the Revolution

W. Doyle, *Origins of the French Revolution* (1988). Encompasses recent research.

G. Lefèbvre, *The Coming of the French Revolution* (1947). By one of France's leading authorities, it covers the first phase of the Revolution.

M. Vovelle, *The Fall of the French Monarchy* (1984). Emphasizes the social aspects of the Revolution, especially the role of the popular classes.

Second Phase

T. Blanning, *The Origins of the French Revolutionary Wars* (1986). A good study of the revolutionary wars.

N. Hampson, *The Terror in the French Revolution* (1981). Effectively covers the radical stage of the Revolution.

M. Lyons, *France under the Directory* (1975). A good brief treatment.

R. R. Palmer, *Twelve Who Ruled: The Committee of Public Safety During the Terror* (1970). Best book on the Reign of Terror.

A. Soboul, *The Parisian Sans-Culottes and the French Revolution 1793–1794* (1964). The most highly respected analysis of the *sans-culottes*.

Sources

J. H. Steward, *A Documentary Survey of the French Revolution* (1951). Excellent, broad collection of documents.

CHAPTER 39

The Era of Napoleon, 1799–1815

FIGURE 39.1 **Jacques-Louis David,** *Napoleon's Coronation* This painting by David was intended to glorify Napoleon at the height of his powers. Having just crowned himself emperor with a laurel wreath (alluding back to Roman emperors) in an 1804 ceremony presided over by Pope Pius VII (on his right), Napoleon prepares to crown Josephine as empress. (Alinari/Art Resource)

No individual in modern times has enjoyed a more meteoric career than Napoleon Bonaparte, the modern counterpart of Alexander the Great and Julius Caesar. He was essentially a product of the Enlightenment and the French Revolution. He rose to power in France quickly, both undoing and securing changes initiated during the French Revolution. As he extended his rule throughout Europe by military conquest, he spread revolutionary forces of change to other lands.

1. NAPOLEON'S RISE TO POWER

Napoleon was born on the French island of Corsica in 1769. At the age of nine he was sent to a military school in France. An unusually self-reliant individual, he studied history, geography, and mathematics. At sixteen he received his commission as second lieutenant of artillery. During several years of boring garrison duty he stuffed his photographic mind with history, the classics, and the philosophy of the Enlightenment.

The French Revolution provided unprecedented opportunities for soldiers of talent to rise in the officer corps. Most of the prerevolutionary army officers were nobles and had fled the country or been deposed. Moreover, the expanded size of the army created a new demand for skilled officers. Napoleon took advantage of his opportunities. In 1793 he gained attention in the recapture of Toulon. In 1795 Napoleon was again called upon, this time by the National Convention, which was threatened by a Parisian crowd. Using artillery—his famous "whiff of grapeshot"—Napoleon quickly dispersed the crowd and became the hero of the Convention. He used his new prominence to secure command of the French army still fighting in northern Italy. Napoleon's dynamism and skill quickly galvanized the lethargic French forces, who defeated the Austrians and Sardinians and forced them to sue for peace. He personally negotiated a favorable peace with Austria and sent back glowing reports of his exploits.

Napoleon then turned toward France's most formidable opponent, the British. The British navy was too powerful for France to dare an invasion of the British mainland. Napoleon concluded that an expedition to Egypt would be a telling blow to British commerce with its colonies and to the British Empire in general. Moreover, it might prove to be an unexpected thrust and thus an easy victory, something to contribute to Napoleon's image as a daring, heroic conqueror. Militarily, the expedition was a failure; Admiral Nelson (1758–1805) decisively defeated the French fleet at the Battle of the Nile on August 1, 1798. Yet Napoleon avoided personal disaster by slipping back to France with a few chosen followers and cleverly managing the reports that arrived from Egypt.

Meanwhile, matters were turning worse for France's government, the Directory. The expedition to Egypt prompted Great Britain, Austria, and Russia to join in a second coalition against France. By 1799 French armies had suffered defeats and France was threatened with invasion. Internally, support for the Directory was weakening as the economic situation worsened and as political factions vied for power. One of the conservative factions, led by Abbé Sieyès (who was already one of the directors), concluded that the Revolution had gone too far. The members of this faction wanted to return to a more authoritarian form of government which would respect the changes initiated during the first, moderate phase of the Revolution in 1789. This situation provided Napoleon with another opportunity. Sieyès and others conspired with Napoleon to overthrow the Directory in a coup d'état. This coup occurred on 18 Brumaire (November 9, 1799). Napoleon was only thirty.

2. THE CONSULATE—PEACE AND REFORM, 1799–1804

Having seized power by conspiracy and force, Napoleon had a constitution drawn up to conceal what amounted to a military dictatorship under the cloak of parliamentary forms. He gave himself the title of first consul with the power to appoint key civilian and military personnel, declare war and make treaties, and initiate all legislation through a hand-picked Council of State. Two other consuls without any significant powers served as camouflage. Two legislative bodies were selected from a list of candidates elected by all adult French males. But since they could not propose new laws, their power was very limited. Thus the voters were led to believe that they were participating in the government, whereas in reality their voice was but faintly heard. Local government was again brought under the strict control of the central government by placing each of France's eighty-three departments under the control of a powerful agent of the central government called a *prefect*.

Napoleon lost no time in making a treaty (1800) with the United States, bringing to an end a two-year undeclared naval war that had grown out of French seizures of American vessels and the pro-British, anti-French policies of John Adams' administration. Slipping over the Alps with a French army, Napoleon crushed the Austrian army in northern Italy in the battle of Marengo, knocking Austria out of the Second Coalition. Tsar Paul of Russia was cajoled with flattery and promises into making peace. Even Great Britain was persuaded to sign the Peace of Amiens in 1802. Shortly thereafter Napoleon cut his losses in North America and sold Louisiana to the United States.

Napoleon next proceeded to gain social support for his rule and create new permanent institutions. He approved the end of feudal privileges and the transfers of property, thereby winning favor with the peasantry. By affirming property rights as inviolable and formal equality before the law for adult males, he gained support from the middle class. He also welcomed back all but the most reactionary émigrés, most of whom had been part of France's old aristocracy. He deterred opposing groups by creating a secret police force under Joseph Fouché and suppressing political organizations. For those who displayed loyalty and achieved the most, he created the prestigious Legion of Honor.

Some of these measures were institutionalized in Napoleon's most important reform, the creation of the Civil Code of 1804 (the Napoleonic Code), which would later be copied by many other nations. The Civil Code, along with other codes of criminal and commercial law, reduced the dozens of different legal codes in existence. In general they affirmed the reforms sought in the beginning stages of the French Revolution while rejecting the more radical measures

enacted after 1792. But for women, the code was a clear defeat. Rather than granting them legal or political equality, it gave authority over the family to men and left married women legally and economically dependent on their husbands.

Napoleon was keenly aware of the political and social importance of religion. "Always treat the pope," he counseled his diplomats, "as if he had 200,000 men." He himself was a deist and a cynical moral relativist, believing that God was "always on the side with the most cannon." One of his first steps was to make peace with the pope and end the ten-year struggle between the French revolutionary governments and the Roman Catholic church. After arduous negotiations, the first consul and the pope signed the Concordat of 1801, which was to govern the relations between the French state and the Catholic church until the beginning of the twentieth century. The Catholic religion was declared to be the religion of the majority of the French people, but freedom for other religions was also to be protected. The state was to appoint bishops, but only the pope could invest them in their offices. The bishops were to appoint and discipline the lower clergy, thus restoring the traditional episcopal principle of the Church. The salaries of the clergy were to be paid by the state, and the clergy were to take an oath of allegiance to the state. The pope accepted the permanent loss of church property seized by the National Assembly. While the Catholic clergy was never pleased with the Concordat (indeed, Pope Pius VII eventually renounced it), it ended the religious cleavage that had harassed France since the early days of the Revolution.

Napoleon initiated several other institutional reforms. He established the Bank of France to handle government funds and issue paper money. He brought order and efficiency to government finances. He created a long-lasting system of secondary schools tied to the University of France. He established several professional and technical schools.

The first five years of Napoleon's rule were spectacularly successful. Law and order at home and peace abroad had been attained. Financial stability, equal and efficient justice, religious tranquillity, and the foundations of an effective educational system had all been achieved. Public morale was high. However, Napoleon was not satisfied with his accomplishments. He yearned for more glory. In 1804 he crowned himself emperor of the French and sought further fields to conquer (see Figure 39.1).

3. THE EMPIRE—WAR AND CONQUEST

Great Britain, France's inveterate foe, had become increasingly alarmed at Napoleon's growing strength. Napoleon had not only continued to build up his military forces but had also taken advantage of the Peace of Amiens to further his commercial and imperial schemes at Great Britain's expense. Before the end of 1803 the British government declared war and the next year joined with Austria and Russia to form a third coalition against France. This was what Napoleon expected and wanted. He soon appeared at the English Channel at the head of a force sufficient to conquer the British Isles, if only the twenty-four-mile water barrier could be crossed. In the Channel, however, lay the world's mightiest fleet, commanded by the greatest of all Britain's admirals, Lord Nelson. Meanwhile, Napoleon was watching the movements of the Austrians and Russians and readying his own army. When the time was ripe, he suddenly marched his army eastward, surrounded an exposed Austrian army at Ulm in southwest Germany, and forced it to surrender. But the day after Ulm, Nelson sighted the combined French and Spanish fleets off Cape Trafalgar on the southwest point of Spain and annihilated them (October 21, 1805). Although Nelson was killed early in the battle, his victory saved Great Britain from the menace of a Napoleonic invasion and limited the scope of the French emperor's conquests to the continent of Europe.

On land, however, Napoleon seemed invincible. Moving his army eastward from Ulm, he met and crushed the oncoming combined forces of Austria and Russia at Austerlitz. Austria immediately sued for peace, and the demoralized Russians retreated toward their home country. At this juncture Prussia declared war on Napoleon. The time was inopportune, and the Prussian army was no match for Napoleon. At Jena and Auerstädt Napoleon overwhelmed and virtually destroyed the Prussian forces (1806). Two weeks later the French were in Berlin. Hearing that the Russian troops were re-forming in Poland, Napoleon moved eastward to meet them. After being held to a draw by the Russians in a blinding snowstorm at Eylau, he defeated them decisively a few months later in the great battle of Friedland (1807). Tsar Alexander I now sued for peace. Although the Treaties of Tilsit (July 1807) were technically between equals, they actually left Napoleon master of the European continent and Alexander I only a junior partner. Russia was given a free hand to deal with Turkey in eastern Europe but was not permitted to take Constantinople, the prize the Russians most desired. In return for a dominant hand in eastern Europe, Alexander promised to join Napoleon against Great Britain and to force Sweden to do so. Tilsit recognized the changes that Napoleon had already made in central and western Europe and left him free to make any others he wished.

Between 1806 and 1808 Napoleon remade the map of Europe. The puppet Duchy of Warsaw was created out of part of Prussia's (and later, part of Austria's) Polish territory. Prussia's territory west of the Elbe was made a part of the kingdom of Westphalia, over which Napoleon's youngest brother, Jerome, was made king. Prussia was thus virtually halved in size. The Holy Roman Empire was at long last abolished and its hundreds of little principalities greatly consolidated. A strip of German territory along the North Sea was annexed outright to France. The rest of German territory west of the Elbe was brought into the Confederation of the Rhine, with Napoleon as protector. Napoleon's younger brother Louis was made king of Holland; but when Louis began to favor the interests of his Dutch subjects over those of the French Empire, Napoleon deposed him and annexed his territory to France. The Italian peninsula was brought under French dominance. The coastal areas along the northeastern Adriatic Sea were detached from Austria and annexed to France. In 1808 Napoleon overthrew the weak Spanish royal house and made his elder brother, Joseph, king of Spain. Shortly before, the Portuguese royal family had fled to Brazil at the approach of a French army. Denmark (including Norway) became Napoleon's most faithful ally.

Thus, by 1808, most of Europe was under French control or French influence (see Map 39.1). No other conqueror has so dominated Europe. In all those territories under direct French control, Napoleon's "enlightened" institutions and administrative efficiency were introduced. The rest of Europe, impressed with the effectiveness of the French revolutionary ideas and institutions, adopted many of them voluntarily.

4. DECLINE AND FALL OF THE EMPIRE

A number of factors contributed to the decline and fall of the Napoleonic empire. One of the most obvious was British sea power. Because of it, Great Britain alone of the European powers was able to withstand the Napoleonic military onslaught. After Trafalgar had dashed Napoleon's hopes of invading the British Isles, he sought the destruction of "perfidious Albion" by economic pressure. In order to wreck the economy of the "nation of shopkeepers," he attempted to blockade the entire continent of Europe against British shipping. All British goods were confiscated. French privateers were set upon British merchant ships. These measures, known as "the Continental System," did cause Great Britain distress. However, with control of the sea, Great Britain was able to apply a more effective counterblockade against the Napoleon-dominated Continent. The Continental System created an ever-increasing resentment against Napoleon's rule in France's satellite states.

Another factor that undermined the Napoleonic empire was the rise of a national spirit among the subject peoples. The mass spirit of intense patriotism or nationalism, which had had its origin in France during the *levée en masse* of 1793, spread to the rest of Europe in the wake of Napoleon's conquering armies. The first people to rebel openly against the French yoke were the proud Spaniards. Hardly had Napoleon's brother Joseph been placed on the Spanish throne when his unwilling subjects rose up and chased him out of Madrid. The superior French

armies, even when led by Napoleon himself, were ineffective against the hit-and-run guerrilla tactics invented by the Spaniards. The British government, observing Napoleon's predicament in Spain, sent an army under Arthur Wellesley, the future duke of Wellington, to exploit the situation. Spain became a running abscess that drained away much of Napoleon's military strength. Meanwhile, Prussia, after the humiliation of Jena, had begun a rejuvenation under the leadership of Baron von Stein. Partly in secret and partly in the open, the Prussians modernized their army and their civil institutions and prepared for the day of liberation. In 1809 Austria declared war on Napoleon in a premature effort to free itself from subservience to the French emperor. Although Austria was once more defeated, the heroic valor with which the Austrian armies fought served notice of the rising spirit of national pride and resistance. Napoleon could no longer enjoy the advantage of commanding soldiers fired with the heady wine of nationalism against lethargic professional armies.

The beginning of the end was a disastrous campaign against Russia in 1812. With their own interests pulling them apart, the alliance between Alexander I and Napoleon became strained. Napoleon, against the advice of his closest associates, decided to invade Russia. Amassing an army of six hundred thousand, the mightiest army ever assembled up to that time, he plunged into the vastness of Russia. Many of his troops, however, were unwilling conscripts from the puppet states. The Russian army retreated into the interior of the huge country, following a scorched-earth policy and drawing Napoleon ever farther from his base of supplies. Finally, after the bloody battle of Borodino about seventy-five miles from Moscow, Napoleon's hosts entered the city. But Alexander I refused to make peace. A fire destroyed much of Moscow, leaving the invaders without shelter in the face of approaching winter. Napoleon began his retreat too late. The Russian winter caught his forces burdened down with loot. Tens of thousands froze or starved. Russian cossacks, riding out of the blizzards, cut down or captured other thousands. Of the six hundred thousand men who marched into Russia, no more than one hundred thousand returned.

Map 39.1 EUROPE, 1810 This map shows the Napoleonic empire at its height. Generally, French revolutionary and Napoleonic institutions spread most in those areas closest to France and under its direct control. Napoleon's empire was weakened when he tried to extend his control to Europe's geographic extremes—Spain and Russia.

WHERE HISTORIANS DISAGREE

Who Was Napoleon?

Few individuals in history have inspired such passionate debate as Napoleon. In part, this controversy is a result of his meteoric rise to the heights of power and his string of military conquests. And in part, it is a consequence of the charismatic quality of his leadership. He combined personal dynamism and charm, which created faith in masses of followers and enabled him to dominate many of those with whom he came into contact. The debate is also related to difficulties separating the myth of Napoleon from the reality of Napoleon. Finally, all sides of the debate can find some support in the varied, contradictory legacy of Napoleon's intentions and deeds. Therefore it is not surprising that historians have bitterly disagreed over how to characterize Napoleon.

Many historians argue that Napoleon was fundamentally a dictator. They point to the methods he used to acquire power—the fame associated with military prowess, the coup d'état, and the plebiscite that seemed to affirm his power democratically without offering a real choice—as methods typical of modern dictators. They also point to his actions after acquiring power—crowning himself emperor, eliminating freedom of speech and press, removing the substance from representative institutions, initiating a systematic crackdown on political opponents, and creating a secret police—as characteristic of military dictatorships.

Other historians see him as a preserver of the Revolution. They stress his familiarity with Enlightenment ideas and his early support of the French Revolution. They point out that Napoleon did affirm the end of feudalism, the overthrow of the old aristocracy, the establishment of equality before the law for men, and the rights of property. They also argue that his most important service may have been in spreading the ideas and institutions of the Revolution beyond France's borders—in particular, the rejection of aristocratic privilege and the spread of the Napoleonic Code. In short, Napoleon affirmed the fundamental reforms of the early French Revolution, institutionalized them, and then helped spread them elsewhere in Europe.

Still other historians argue that Napoleon is best viewed as the last in a line of eighteenth-century enlightened despots. They point out that like other enlightened despots, such as Frederick the Great of Prussia and Joseph II of Austria, Napoleon was most interested in maximizing the political and military power of the state. Like them, he saw that to do so required centralizing and rationalizing the government, improving finances, codifying laws, and supporting the armed forces. He shared their tendency to make religious concerns secondary to political unity and to gain support through the creation of educational institutions. Thus, from an eighteenth-century perspective, Napoleon is recognizable as an enlightened despot.

Many historians argue that individual leaders, even those as extraordinary as Napoleon, do not decisively affect history's mainstream. More important are the forces, circumstances, and people that surround them. Other historians maintain that individuals, above all the rare charismatic leaders such as Napoleon, can have significant historical consequences.

Which of these interpretations best fits the historical record depends greatly on the perspective of the viewer and on what aspects of Napoleon's personality and rule are emphasized. At the same time, how much can be attributed to the actions of any historical figure must be kept in mind in deciding exactly who was Napoleon.

Napoleon dashed back to France to raise fresh conscripts, but the flower of French manhood was gone. One nation after another rose up to join the Russians in a war of liberation. At Leipzig in central Germany, in October 1813, Napoleon was at last decisively defeated. The next year the allies entered Paris and exiled Napoleon to the island of Elba, off the coast of Italy. When the allies began to squabble over the peace settlement, Napoleon escaped back to France and raised another army, but he was finally defeated in June 1815 by the duke of Wellington and the Prussians under Marshal Blücher at Waterloo in Belgium. This time he was imprisoned on the island of St. Helena in the South Atlantic, where six years later he died.

5. OVERSEAS EFFECTS: LATIN AMERICA

One vast area outside Europe upon which the impact of the revolution of Napoleon was strong and immediate was Latin America. During the eighteenth century, discontent with colonial rule had been steadily mounting in the Spanish and Portuguese colonial empires in North and South America. As in the thirteen English colonies in North America, the resentment was directed primarily against economic and political restrictions. As the native-born "Creoles" had come to outnumber the Spanish- and Portuguese-born settlers, the ties of loyalty to the mother countries had become more and more tenuous. The liberal writings of the French and British philosophers of the Enlightenment were smuggled into Latin America and made their converts, particularly among young intellectuals. These liberal Latin Americans could not help being impressed by the successful revolt of the English colonies to the north and the setting up of a liberal New World republic. The French Revolution had an even more profound influence on them. When, therefore, Napoleon overthrew Ferdinand VII of Spain and placed his own brother, Joseph Bonaparte, on the Spanish throne, the colonies' sentiments of loyalty for the mother country, which were already weak, became confused.

By 1810 the colonies were in open revolt. As with the English colonists three decades earlier, the cause of the Latin American revolutionists

FIGURE 39.2 **Simon Bolívar** Here, in heroic pose, Simon Bolívar is shown leading the struggle to liberate South America from Spanish rule. The painting is modeled on a well-known work by David showing Napoleon leading his troops across the alps. (The Granger Collection)

seemed hopeless. In addition to the regular Spanish troops, they had to struggle against most of the wealthy Spanish settlers and the local Roman Catholic hierarchy. Eventually two brilliant young leaders, Simón Bolívar and José San Martín, emerged to overcome the seemingly impossible obstacles and to lead the South American revolutionists to success (see Figure 39.2). By 1822 the independence of Spanish South America was won. In the same year the issue was decided in Spain's Central American colonies and in Mexico, which then included the southwest quarter of what is now the United States. In all the former Spanish colonies, republics were established, although a long period of troubled apprenticeship preceded the establishment of effective popular governments. Real stability has continued to be a problem for the Central and South American nations.

In the huge Portuguese colony of Brazil, the independence movement was delayed by the flight of the Portuguese royal family to Brazil in 1807. However, the return of the king to Portugal six years after Napoleon's fall and the efforts of the Portuguese government to reimpose colonial status on Brazil quickly fanned the embers of revolt into flame. In 1822 the Portuguese king's son, Pedro, whom he had left behind as regent, yielded to native pressure and declared himself king of independent Brazil. In all of free Latin America the Napoleonic Code was adopted as the basis of civil law, and the impact of the Enlightenment on political institutions was clearly visible.

6. THE SIGNIFICANCE OF THE FRENCH REVOLUTION AND NAPOLEON

The French Revolution and its Napoleonic sequel had a profound effect on the course of history. Like Pandora when she lifted the lid of that fateful box, they let loose forces and ideas that have influenced and shaken the world ever since, especially the revolutionary ideals of *Liberty, Equality, Fraternity*. Originally conceived in the eighteenth century by the philosophers of the Enlightenment, they were born materially in the American and French revolutions and spread by Napoleon.

In the era of the French Revolution, the ideal of *liberty* meant freedom from arbitrary authority—political, religious, economic, or social. It meant freedom of speech, press, conscience, assembly, person, and profession and the sacredness of property. During the moderate first phase of the French Revolution, a great deal of progress toward these goals was made; in the tumultuous, bloody second phase, a good deal was lost. Under Napoleon's rule there was no political liberty. However, he claimed that the efficiency, prosperity, and honor of his regime more than made up for the lack of popular government, for which, he believed, the world was not yet ready.

Equality meant essentially equality under the law and equality of opportunity for gain and advancement. In general, it did not apply to women, even though women had played important roles during the Revolution and had hoped

for gains that never came. It was only during the brief dominance of Robespierre that even partial social equality of all male citizens became a goal. Napoleon's law codes were a great boon to the more moderate kind of equality among men. The codes left women devoid of political rights and legally dependent on men.

Fraternity manifested itself in the mass movements (sometimes violent) for reform, in the comradeship in the conscripted armies, and above all in the new popular and dynamic spirit of nationalism. These forces, released by the American and French revolutions, spread first to the rest of Europe, then to Latin America, and eventually to the rest of the world. Much of the history of the world since the era of the French Revolution has revolved around these forces.

In another sense, the French Revolution and the Napoleonic era constituted a decisive political watershed marking the beginnings of modern times. The French Revolution opened the road to constitutional government and democratic institutions. Although there would be numerous reversals, constitutional governments and democratic institutions would generally flourish over the course of the succeeding two centuries and come to characterize politically modern times. The administrative bureaucracy and legal codes established during the Napoleonic era would be imitated and also come to characterize modern political systems.

Finally, the French Revolution and the Napoleonic era provided two images that would invite study and imitation throughout the nineteenth and twentieth centuries. The first image was that of the successful popular revolution. While the French Revolution was not the first revolution, it was the one that occurred in the heart of Western civilization and toppled not only the government but the major institutions of traditional society. This revolution would inspire revolutionaries and warn those representing the status quo for decades to come. The second image was that of Napoleon as a nationalistic, charismatic leader who could suddenly grasp power and exert his will with great effect. During the nineteenth and twentieth centuries, this powerful image would inspire individuals who envisioned themselves as potential Napoleons and people who yearned for easy, decisive solutions to deeply felt problems.

SUGGESTED READING

General

P. Geyl, *Napoleon, For and Against* (1949). A good study of changing interpretations of Napoleon.

J. C. Herold, *The Age of Napoleon* (1983). An entertaining, well-written survey.

R. Jones, *Napoleon. Man and Myth* (1977). A fine treatment.

G. Lefèbvre, *Napoleon*, 2 vols. (1969). A scholarly treatment by a leading authority.

F. Markham, *Napoleon* (1966). An excellent biography.

France

L. Bergeron, *France under Napoleon* (1981). A good analysis.

R. B. Holtman, *The Napoleonic Revolution* (1967). Good on domestic policy and propaganda.

The Empire

D. Chandler, *The Campaigns of Napoleon* (1966). Focuses on military history.

O. Connelly, *Napoleon's Satellite Kingdoms* (1965). A good study of Napoleonic rule in Europe.

F. Markham, *Napoleon and the Awakening of Europe* (1965). A good study of Napoleon's influence outside of France.

W. S. Robertson, *The Rise of the Spanish-American Republics* (1965). A good brief account.

J. Tulard, *Napoleon: The Myth of the Savior* (1984). A biography that also covers the empire well.

CHAPTER 40
The Industrial Revolution

FIGURE 40.1 François Bonhomme, *Workshop with Mechanical Sieves*, 1859 This realistic painting of a factory interior in France shows the mixture of raw material (zinc ore), machines, and division of labor that epitomized the Industrial Revolution. Men, women, and children work together in this dismal environment; but the men have the more skilled jobs (a foreman sits in the rear to the left), while the women and children are assigned to the less skilled jobs (sorting and splitting chunks of ore). (Conservatoire Nationale des Arts et Métiers)

The term *Industrial Revolution* refers to the vast economic and social changes initiated in Great Britain during the last few decades of the eighteenth century and spreading to the Continent and other parts of the world during the nineteenth and twentieth centuries. It involved a shift from production by individuals alone or in small groups using hand tools powered by muscles, wind, and water to production by organized groups of people in factories using machinery powered by steam. These changes in the methods of production resulted in sustained economic growth. In the process of industrializing, nations experienced rapid population growth and a general shift from a rural society based on agriculture to an urban society based on manufacturing. Along with the French Revolution, the Industrial Revolution set into motion changes that would transform almost all aspects of life in the West during the nineteenth and twentieth centuries.

1. THE COURSE OF THE INDUSTRIAL REVOLUTION

The Industrial Revolution began in Great Britain for several reasons. Demand for the production of goods in Great Britain was growing rapidly during the eighteenth century, thanks to relatively widespread domestic prosperity, a growing population, and abundant markets within Britain's large colonial empire. Great Britain was well positioned to meet this growing demand for goods. It had an abundance of conveniently located raw materials, such as coal and iron. Investment capital amassed from merchants and landowners was available to enterprising entrepreneurs through family connections, partnership arrangements, and banks. Thanks to their leading role in the eighteenth-century agricultural revolution, Britain's farmers could more efficiently produce food for urban populations (see pp. 408–409). A large, mobile force of both skilled and unskilled workers provided industrial entrepreneurs with a cheap supply of labor. The hindrances to commerce and industry so common in other countries were not present to the same degree in Great Britain. British transportation facilities were good, there were fewer governmental restrictions on commerce, and wealthy citizens did not disdain involvement in commerce and industry. Britain's government had been stable since 1689 and was strongly influenced by capitalistic landowners, merchants, and bankers.

British inventors and entrepreneurs responded to these conditions by developing new machines, sources of power, transportation facilities, and factories. These new developments increased production and trade tremendously and made Great Britain an early leader in the Industrial Revolution. By the middle of the nineteenth century, Great Britain was the first industrialized society. It was urbanized, covered with railway lines and canals, and dotted with factories. It produced far greater quantities of textiles, metals, and machines than any other country.

During the eighteenth century, nations on the Continent lacked this combination of circumstances so conducive to British industrialization. In addition, between 1789 and 1815 the Continent suffered from the economic, social, and political turmoil of the French revolutionary and Napoleonic periods. After 1815, and particularly after 1830, the Industrial Revolution spread, first to Belgium, shortly thereafter to France, parts of Germany, and the United States, and later to other areas of Europe (see Map 40.1). At first Continental entrepreneurs copied British inventions and imported skilled British laborers and technicians. Governments recognized the British lead and became more directly involved in promoting industrialization by supporting the construction of railways, subsidizing certain industries, and erecting protective tariffs for domestic industries. By the end of the nineteenth century, countries that had once lagged far behind Great Britain were competing successfully for industrial markets.

2. TECHNOLOGY AND TRANSPORTATION

Probably the most dramatic change the Industrial Revolution brought about was the continual creation of new technology and transportation facilities (see Figure 40.2). A virtual explosion of inventions increased productivity and mechanized productions, above all in textiles, mining, and metallurgy. The steam engine provided a vast new source of reliable power. New roads,

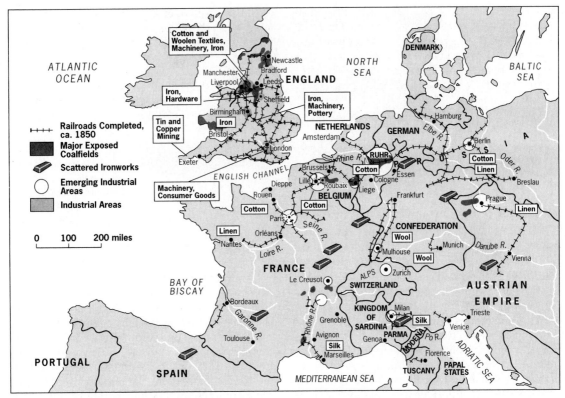

Map 40.1 THE INDUSTRIAL REVOLUTION IN EUROPE, 1850 This map reveals the spread of industrialization in Europe in 1850 by indicating the location of railroads, coalfields, and ironworks and showing which areas of Europe were becoming industrial centers.

canals, and especially railroads provided regular, inexpensive means of transportation for people and materials.

The cotton textile industry was the first to become mechanized. In 1733 John Kay invented the flying shuttle, which doubled the speed at which cloth could be woven. In 1764 James Hargreaves hitched eight spindles to his wife's spinning wheel instead of one. The result was the far more efficient spinning jenny (named after his daughter Jenny). The number of spindles was soon multiplied. Five years later, Richard Arkwright patented the water frame, a system of rollers driven by water power, which spun a much finer and firmer thread than the jenny. In 1779 Samuel Crompton, combining the principles of the spinning jenny and the water frame, produced the hybrid spinning mule—a great im-

provement over both. In 1785 Edmund Cartwright invented the power loom.

The mechanization of both spinning and weaving greatly increased demand for cotton. In 1793 a young American, Eli Whitney, invented the cotton gin, which helped meet this demand. Removing the seeds from cotton fiber by hand was a tedious process; one person could separate only five or six pounds a day. Cotton was therefore grown only in small patches. Whitney's gin not only made possible an adequate supply of cotton for Britain's mills but also brought into existence the huge cotton plantations worked by black slaves in the American South.

Meanwhile, better sources of power were being developed. In 1769 James Watt significantly improved on earlier inefficient steam engines and invented the first steam engine that

FIGURE 40.2 Railroad, Ship, and Factories
This nineteenth-century print shows the outward signs of the Industrial Revolution: railroads, steamships on canals, and smoke-belching factories. (The Bettmann Archive)

could be used to drive machinery. The power that could be generated by the steam engine was almost unlimited.

Constant improvements were made in the mining of coal and the production of iron, crucial for heavy industrialization. As large quantities of relatively inexpensive coal and iron became available, still better machines were produced and a sufficient supply of fuel was available to drive them.

An integral part of the Industrial Revolution was the improvement of transportation and communications. Without both, sufficient quantities of raw materials to feed the hungry machines and adequate markets to absorb the finished products would not have been available. Moreover, the massive population shifts accompanying industrialization would have been much more difficult.

The last decades of the eighteenth century and the first decades of the nineteenth were a time of road and canal building in Great Britain, France, and the United States. Around the turn of the century Thomas Telford and John McAdam in Great Britain pioneered in the construction of well-drained and -surfaced roads. In Great Britain canals were particularly useful for transporting coal. In the United States the completion of the Erie Canal in 1825 opened up the Great Lakes region to lucrative world communications and ensured the primacy of New York City as the chief port and metropolis of the United States.

A more dramatic revolution in transportation came with the application of the steam engine to locomotion. In 1807 Robert Fulton demonstrated the practicability of the steamship by steaming his *Clermont* the one hundred fifty miles up the Hudson from New York to Albany in thirty-two hours. In 1825 George Stephenson in Great Britain convincingly demonstrated the usefulness of the locomotive by hauling a train of thirty-four cars twenty-five miles at twelve miles an hour. By the middle of the nineteenth century, railway lines covered Great Britain and were spreading rapidly on the Continent and in North America. The railroad transported people and material, opened up areas to commerce and urban growth, constituted a major source of demand for industrial products such as coal and iron, and symbolized the spread of the new industrialized society.

3. THE FACTORY SYSTEM

Many of the components of the Industrial Revolution were brought together by the development of the factory system (see Figure 40.1). Industrial capitalists invested considerable funds in machines, buildings, and raw materials. They trained workers to do specific jobs in conjunction with artificially powered machines, which increasingly determined the pace and nature of the work. Industrial capitalists organized the process of producing goods into a series of steps and specialized tasks. Their new factories pumped out unprecedented quantities of manufactured goods.

Before the factory system was instituted, goods were produced either by craft guilds or under the domestic, or "putting out," system (see Chapter 31). Under this system workers did as much or as little work as they wished without supervision. The operations were necessarily small in scale, much time was lost distributing the raw materials from cottage to cottage and collecting the finished products, and uniformity of quality was virtually impossible to attain.

The spread of the factory system spelled the end of the domestic system of manufacturing. The rise of the factory system resulted in a tremendous growth of productivity in manufacturing and a seemingly fantastic increase of manufactured goods. Artisans, although not immediately displaced, found it increasingly difficult to compete with factories that were producing similar products much more rapidly and inexpensively. As the factory system took hold, hastily and cheaply built living quarters for workers and their families were crowded around factories. This factory system was the origin of the modern mill town and industrial city. It also contributed to the dramatic urbanization of industrial societies in the nineteenth century and fundamental changes among social classes in these societies.

4. SOCIAL CHANGES

Population Growth and Urbanization

A large variety of far-reaching social changes are related to the Industrial Revolution. The broadest changes were demographic. Population increased dramatically. In Great Britain population grew from about 9 million in 1780 to almost 21 million in 1850. European population as a whole rose from about 188 million in 1800 to 266 million in 1850. The exact causes of this explosion of population are difficult to pinpoint, but it was probably a result of a declining death rate (thanks to a decline in epidemics and an increase of food supplies) and a rise in the birthrate (caused by earlier departure from home, earlier marriage, and earlier childbearing in an increasingly mobile population).

A more direct result of industrialization was the shift of population from rural to urban areas and the growth in size and number of cities. In England and Wales in 1800 about 17 percent of the population lived in cities of over twenty thousand inhabitants. By 1850 the figure grew to about 35 percent. London alone grew from less than 1 million inhabitants in 1800 to over 2.5 million by 1850. Smaller cities and towns were also growing, so that by midcentury half of Britain's population lived in urban areas. This pattern was being repeated in other areas of Europe as they industrialized. Most of the urban growth was fueled by internal migration. These new emigrants crowded together in cities, often in neighborhoods where there were people from their own rural regions. Many would maintain ties to their old rural communities, temporarily returning when work was scarce. Not all came to work in factories; a large number of men were employed in the building trades, and many women came to work as domestics.

The consequences of this rapid urbanization were all too apparent. Already overcrowded, devoid of mass transportation facilities, and equipped at best with vastly inadequate sanitation facilities, the cities became more densely packed and unhealthy each year. In bad times they became centers of unemployment as much as they were markets for jobs in good times. In this urban environment women had to manage with less pay than men; meager pay or loss of a job forced a growing number of women into prostitution. Urban crowding and poverty provided fertile ground for the growth of crime. The creation of modern urban police forces in London and Paris was more a symptom of the growing crime rate than a solution to it.

At the same time, the cities had a vibrancy and an image of opportunity that continued to attract people; often the alternatives available in the countryside were even less appealing hovels and rural slums.

Social Classes

Even before the Industrial Revolution, the French Revolution had altered many people's perceptions of the social order. Industrialization added economic and social foundations to this new understanding of society. People viewed themselves less as part of a rigid, ranked, ordered society and more as part of a flexible society of a few classes with mobility between classes being both possible and proper. Class membership was not a formal designation but a description of the amount of money, the type of work, the style of life, and the beliefs of people. Nevertheless, this does not mean that society had in reality become egalitarian. As in previous centuries, there remained sharp differences between different classes of people.

The two classes most firmly tied to the traditional rural society, the aristocracy and the peasantry, were doomed by the Industrial Revolution. Over the nineteenth century they would decline in number, wealth, position, and influence. Yet the extent and speed of this decline should not be overestimated. It was not until the second half of the nineteenth century that urban dwellers outnumbered rural populations in even the most industrialized nations; in some countries, such as France, the small farm was more the rule than the exception. Moreover, the aristocracy remained influential even in industrializing nations, commanding considerable wealth and prestige. Aristocrats still dominated many localities, staffed the upper levels of government, and controlled certain professions such as the diplomatic and military officer corps.

The middle classes as a whole and the industrial bourgeoisie in particular grew in number and profited from the Industrial Revolution. Those who benefited most were the large factory owners, bankers, and merchants, who amassed great fortunes and rose toward the top of society. The smaller factory owners, professionals, shopkeepers, and "white-collar" workers who made up the various ranks of the middle class also benefited. They gained their wealth by mental rather than physical labor and by the investment or manipulation of capital. This middle class tended to favor liberal reforms and believe in certain values such as hard work, thrift, careers open to talent, and prudence. Over time they outdistanced their two main competitors: the aristocracy, which remained dependent on the traditional society and rural economy, and the artisans, who were increasingly unable to compete with factory production. Though still a minority (even in the largest cities such as Paris they constituted no more than 25 percent of the population), the middle classes gained in prestige, political power, and cultural influence thanks to their growing wealth and numbers. During the second half of the nineteenth century they would gain dominance over much of Western society.

The urban working classes changed, grew, and suffered during the Industrial Revolution. Many of these workers were domestics, and this class grew still larger as the middle classes gained the wealth to hire them. Artisans remained a large class throughout the nineteenth century. On the whole they commanded better pay than the less skilled factory workers, and their products were demanded by wealthier purchasers. However, new factories increasingly displaced the artisans, and they often reacted radically, sometimes violently, to the changes brought about by industrialization. They tended to join radical political organizations, lead in union-organizing activities and strikes, and be the most active elements of violent and revolutionary protests. After midcentury this class would decline in size.

The industrial proletariat was the newest class. Demand by new factories swelled the ranks of the factory workers. Large numbers of surplus agricultural workers and displaced artisans were absorbed into factory work along with part of the overall increase in population. It was this industrial proletariat that most visibly grew with industrialization and stood in most striking contrast to the industrial bourgeoisie.

Factory workers were ruthlessly exploited by factory owners, particularly during the early stages of the Industrial Revolution. Wages for a workweek of six or seven days at twelve to sixteen hours per day were kept to a subsistence level. Unmarried women and orphaned children were more cheaply and easily exploited than men and were thus employed in the new factories. Contracts were made with orphanages for the employment of children. Young children were marched off before daybreak to work all day in the factories. If they fell behind the pace set by the machines, they were beaten (see Figure 40.3). Sometimes they were chained to their machines.

After the first few decades of the Industrial Revolution, a pattern of hiring whole families to work in the new factories emerged. Although this system meant that the amount of wages nec-

FIGURE 40.3 Child Labor This woodcut, dated 1853, portrays the supervisor of an English cotton factory whipping a young boy. Incidents similar to this were not uncommon during the first phase of the Industrial Revolution. Such conditions spurred speculation on ways to control industrial capitalism. (New York Public Library)

essary for subsistence was kept to a minimum, it at least allowed the working-class family to stay together. By the middle of the nineteenth century the practice of hiring families and children was declining, but life for the industrial working class remained oppressive. The factories and mines were dark, dirty, and dangerous. The dwellings of the workers were likely to be hovels clustered around smoky, noisy mills or mine entrances.

The workers were frequently compelled to spend their wages at company stores, paying monopoly prices arbitrarily set by the owners. Work lost its dignity. The factory workers were disciplined to the clock and the machine. The dull, monotonous, robotlike repetition of a single operation on a machine brought workers none of the satisfaction and pride of skilled craftsmanship.

Many historians and social scientists argue that statistics show that the early factory workers received higher wages and enjoyed a better standard of living than they had ever had as agricultural or urban workers. Clearly, industrial workers were reaping material benefits from the Industrial Revolution after 1850, but in the years before 1850 workers may have lost more than they gained. Certainly the life of the agricultural laborer or artisan should not be romanticized: The conditions of work and life among the agricultural and urban poor had always been hard. But industrial work involved vast changes that were extraordinarily painful. The longer hours, greater insecurity, limits on freedom, and more frequent unemployment of the uprooted slum-dwelling factory worker of the early nineteenth century do not appear in statistics of wages and prices (see Figure 40.4). The overall picture of the industrial proletariat during the first half of the nineteenth century is dismal and can justly be characterized as a new kind of slavery—slavery to the machine and the machine owner.

One of the industrial proletariat's first reactions was violence. Throughout the winter of 1811–1812, when the pressure of the Napoleonic war and the blockade against British commerce was added to the maladjustments of the Industrial Revolution, a wave of personal violence and machine smashing swept (the Luddite riots) through Great Britain. Parliament, composed entirely of members of the property-holding classes, quickly made industrial sabotage a capital offense and suppressed violence with a heavy hand. Several dozens of offenders were hanged. However, sporadic outbreaks of violence continued for several years. This story was repeated in other countries as the Industrial Revolution spread. In the United States in the middle decades of the nineteenth century, violence broke out among the Irish immigrants working in the anthracite coal mines of eastern Pennsylvania. The exploited miners formed secret terror

societies called Molly Maguires. For a number of years they intimidated, even murdered, unpopular bosses and uncooperative nonmembers. They were eventually ferreted out by civil authorities and ruthlessly suppressed.

More peaceful efforts of the industrial proletariat to bring group pressure to bear on their employers by organizing unions also met with defeat at first. In 1799 and 1800 the British Parliament passed the Combination Acts, which outlawed all labor combinations organized for the purpose of securing better wages, hours, or working conditions. In 1824 trade unions were legalized in Great Britain, but their activities were still severely restricted. In other countries strikes and union activities were outlawed. In some cases, as in the United States, the owners themselves organized for the purpose of breaking up labor unions. Private detectives and police were set upon labor leaders, who were beaten, fired, and blacklisted. It was not until the second half of the nineteenth century that labor unions were able to make consistent headway in major struggles with employers.

Nevertheless, factory workers and other elements of the working classes managed to assert themselves in various ways even during the first half of the nineteenth century. Many local working-class organizations were established and survived. A few larger organizations, such as the Grand National Union in Britain, had at least a temporary life. Strikes, whether legal or illegal, were numerous and widespread if not always well organized. There were even significant working-class political movements in this early period, the most important of which was Chartism in Great Britain. Chartism, organized by the London Working Men's Association, arose in the 1830s and 1840s. Chartists agitated for various political and economic reforms and at times

FIGURE 40.4 Gustave Doré, *A London Slum* This woodcut by Doré portrays the squalor of an overcrowded London slum in the early nineteenth century. (Prints Division, New York Public Library, Astor, Lenox, and Tilden Foundations)

seemed to be a powerful, organized, even revolutionary threat in England. Although the movement broke up by midcentury without having achieved its goals, it did reveal some of the potential political strength of an organized working class.

The Family and New Social Institutions

Industrialization had a strong impact on social institutions during the nineteenth century. Some of the most subtle but significant and long-lasting changes took place in the family, particularly the middle-class family.

During the nineteenth century, what many historians and sociologists call the "modern family" predominated in the West, particularly in western Europe and the United States, and above all within the middle classes. Compared with the family of early modern times, this modern family was more tied together by emotional bonds, more child-centered, and more private. Within the middle-class modern family, which increasingly served as an accepted standard for all families, there was a growing division of roles and labor between the sexes. Ideally the middle-class man was authoritative, competent, and controlled. His wife was supposed to be deferential, emotional, and even frail—almost on a pedestal as a showpiece of success and propriety (see p. 524). Men increasingly specialized in the competitive world of work outside the home, while women specialized in domestic management. Proper middle-class women were excluded from almost all paid occupations, with the exception of such jobs as governess or elementary-school teacher, which were directly connected to the domestic role. Home was idealized as a "haven in a heartless world" of ruthless industrial capitalism to which the husband returned after work. The wife was to provide the emotional support for the husband, who supplied the money to support the household. The wife was to make sure the house was clean, the meals were served. In addition to being in charge of any domestic servants (a requirement for any middle-class home), she was supposed to be the all-caring mother. She was likely to have fewer children—two or three rather than five or six of an earlier era. At the same time, those that were born were more

likely to survive. Her children were at the center of the family, and their childhood was extended longer than ever before. The middle-class child was not viewed as an economic asset but as a fulfilling "product" of a good home.

Outside the middle class, patterns differed. In aristocratic families, the wider social and political connections remained important and still played a major role in the selection of marriage partners. In peasants' and artisans' families, the household economy was still a reality. In industrial working-class families, women were more likely wage laborers, though for less pay and in lower-status positions than men. Often women were able to find employment when men could find none, which weakened the traditional roles within the family. The stresses on the working-class family were so great that many broke apart, leaving a growing number of women to work and manage a household on their own.

Other social changes exacerbated by industrialization, such as poor housing, lack of public transportation, horrible sanitation, child labor, and periodic unemployment, did not go unnoticed. Many within the wealthier classes remained most comfortable supporting charitable institutions and self-help organizations, which proliferated during the nineteenth century. They tended to view the suffering of the poor as inevitable or as a matter of morals—something the poor brought upon themselves. Others saw the suffering as something caused by society, a social problem. Demands for social reforms by government intervention grew. Many of these demands came not simply from enlightened observers but from fear. Epidemics periodically swept cities. Popular unrest and crime seemed to explode during periods of economic decline. While it was the poor who were usually the victims, these social problems threatened all. In 1833 Britain outlawed the employment of children under nine years of age and restricted the hours of employment of older children. Public health organizations, sanitary codes, and housing regulations spread after the 1830s and 1840s. Governments took on greater responsibility for primary and secondary education. By midcentury, governments in industrializing areas had passed several laws to restrict child labor and control a few of the worst social conditions accompanying indus-

Elizabeth Poole Sandford: Woman in Her Social and Domestic Character

Industrialization had its effects on middle-class women. As the wealth and position of these women rose in a changing economic environment, previous models of behavior no longer applied. A variety of books and manuals appeared to counsel middle-class women on their proper role and behavior. The following is an excerpt from one of these, Woman in Her Social and Domestic Character *(1842), written by Elizabeth Poole Sandford.*

The changes wrought by Time are many. It influences the opinions of men as familiarity does their feelings; it has a tendency to do away with superstition, and to reduce every thing to its real worth.

It is thus that the sentiment for woman has undergone a change. The romantic passion which once almost deified her is on the decline; and it is by intrinsic qualities that she must now inspire respect. She is no longer the queen of song and the star of chivalry. But if there is less of enthusiasm entertained for her, the sentiment is more rational, and, perhaps, equally sincere; for it is in relation to happiness that she is chiefly appreciated.

And in this respect it is, we must confess, that she is most useful and most important. Domestic life is the chief source of her influence; and the greatest debt society can owe to her is domestic comfort: for happiness is almost an element of virtue; and nothing conduces more to improve the character of men than domestic peace. A woman may make a man's home delightful, and may thus increase his motives for virtuous exertion. She may refine and tranquillize his mind,—may turn away his anger or allay his grief. Her smile may be the happy influence to gladden his heart, and to disperse the cloud that gathers on his brow. And in proportion to her endeavors to make those around her happy, she will be esteemed and loved. She will secure by her excellence that interest and regard which she might formerly claim as the privilege of her sex, and will really merit the deference which was then conceded to her as a matter of course. . . .

Perhaps one of the first secrets of her influence is adaptation to the tastes, and sympathy in the feelings, of those around her. This holds true in lesser as well as in graver points. It is in the former, indeed, that the absence of interest in a companion is frequently most disappointing. Where want of congeniality impairs domestic comfort, the fault is generally chargeable on the female side. It is for woman, not for man, to make the sacrifice, especially in indifferent matters. She must, in a certain degree, be plastic herself if she would mould others. . . .

Nothing is so likely to conciliate the affections of the other sex as a feeling that woman looks to them for support and guidance. In proportion as men are themselves superior, they are accessible to this appeal. On the contrary, they never feel interested in one who seems disposed rather to offer than to ask assistance. There is, indeed, something unfeminine in independence. It is contrary to nature, and therefore it offends. We do not like to see a woman affecting tremors, but still less do we like to see her acting the amazon. A really sensible woman feels her dependence. She does what she can; but she is conscious of inferiority, and therefore grateful for support. She knows that she is the weaker vessel, and that as such she should receive honor. In this view, her weakness is an attraction, not a blemish.

In every thing, therefore, that women attempt, they should show their consciousness of dependence. If they are learners, let them evince a teachable spirit; if they give an opinion, let them do it in an unassuming manner. There is something so unpleasant in female self-sufficiency that it not unfrequently deters instead of persuading, and prevents the adoption of advice which the judgment even approves.

SOURCE: Mrs. John Sandford (Elizabeth Poole Sandford), *Woman in Her Social and Domestic Character* (Boston: Otis, Broaders and Co., 1842), pp. 5–7, 15–16.

trialization. But many of these laws were not effectively enforced until the second half of the century. Moreover, it was not until after 1850 that governmental programs such as urban planning, public sanitation (sewers and piped water), and urban transportation (horse-drawn and electric streetcars) had a real impact.

5. NEW ECONOMIC AND SOCIAL THOUGHT

Like the French Revolution, the Industrial Revolution and the social changes related to it were accompanied by new theories and doctrines. The increasingly dominant set of ideas, values, and beliefs—or ideology—was liberalism. Most middle-class liberals applauded both the Industrial and French revolutions while rejecting some of their "excesses" (see Chapter 43). Economic liberalism was more directly related to the economic and social changes accompanying industrialization. Socialism was another newer and more critical line of thought. Like economic liberalism, socialism directly related to industrialization, but not from the perspective of the middle class. Over the course of the nineteenth century, socialist ideology would grow and become the main alternative to economic liberalism.

Economic Liberalism

The growing middle classes, who were prospering from the Industrial Revolution, found intellectual support and justification for their interests in the doctrine of economic liberalism. This doctrine was best stated by the Scottish philosopher Adam Smith in his classic *Wealth of Nations* (1776). The essence of Smith's theory is that economics, like the physical world, has its own natural laws. The most basic of the economic laws is that of supply and demand. When left to operate alone, these laws will keep the economy in balance and, in the long run, work to the benefit of all. If the sanctity of property and contracts is respected, competition and free enterprise will provide incentive and keep prices down. Government regulations and collective bargaining only impede the workings of the natural laws of economics and destroy incentive. Government

should therefore follow a policy of laissez-faire, limiting its activities in the economic field to enforcement of order and contracts, public education and health, national defense, and in rare instances the encouragement of necessary industries that private enterprise does not find profitable. Here was a theory ready-made for the industrial capitalists, who already held all the trump cards.

A strong boost was given to laissez-faire thinking by a young Anglican clergyman, Thomas Malthus, who in 1789 published his *Essay on Population*. Malthus argued that since population increases by a geometric ratio whereas the food supply increases by only an arithmetic ratio, it is a basic natural law that population will outstrip the food supply. This alleged law has two important implications. One is that nothing can be done to improve the lot of the masses. If their condition is temporarily bettered, they will immediately produce children in such numbers that the food supply will be outstripped and starvation will threaten all. Only poverty and privation hold them in check. The second implication is that the rich are not to blame for the misery of the poor; the poor are themselves responsible because of their incontinence. These ideas were so soothing to so many of the book-buying upper classes that Malthus quickly attained fame and wealth.

David Ricardo supplied further support for policies of economic liberalism. Having made a fortune in stock market speculation while still a young man, Ricardo purchased a seat in Parliament and spent the rest of his life thinking and writing on economics. In *The Principles of Political Economy and Taxation* (1817), he propounded the law of rent and the iron law of wages. Rent is determined by the difference in productivity of land. Take off all restrictions and subsidies, and the poorest land will go out of cultivation, reducing the rent on the more productive lands proportionately. He argued for this idea so forcefully that it played an important part in the repeal of England's Corn Laws, which had maintained the price of grain at an artificially high level. Lower grain prices meant lower bread prices, which enabled industrial capitalists to pay lower subsistence wages to their workers. More important in economic thinking was Ricardo's iron law of wages, according to which the natural wage is the subsistence level and the market wage tends to conform to it. Raise the market wage, and workers will multiply so rapidly that soon the law of supply and demand will bring the market wage down below the subsistence level. Then the workers will die off from malnutrition and disease and slow down their reproduction rate. Eventually, they will become so scarce as to be able to bid the market wage up above the natural wage. Always, though, the pull is toward the subsistence level. This theory again was music to the ears of the industrial capitalists.

These economic liberals, being some of the earliest thinkers to analyze the economics of industrial capitalism, are often called the classical economists. Their ideas were popularized in Great Britain and spread to the Continent. There they were modified and expounded by men such as Jean-Baptiste Say and Frédéric Bastiat.

A related stream of economic liberalism was initiated by the British Utilitarian philosopher Jeremy Bentham as early as 1789, in his *Principles of Morals and Legislation*. Bentham was an eighteenth-century materialistic rationalist who lived on until 1832, bridging the eighteenth and nineteenth centuries with his life and thought. The Utilitarians believed that the useful is the good and that the chief purpose of government and society is to achieve "the greatest good to the greatest number." But since every individual is the best judge of his or her own best interests, the surest way to achieve general happiness is allow individuals to follow their own enlightened self-interest. Individualism, then, is the best safeguard of the general welfare. At the same time Bentham himself and several of his followers saw the necessity for the state to act for the common welfare. Utilitarians became active during the middle decades of the nineteenth century in promoting legislation and creating governmental bureaucracies to handle some of the economic abuses and social problems connected with the Industrial Revolution.

Over the nineteenth century, economic liberalism evolved as industrial capitalists proved unwilling to adhere to laissez-faire when it did not suit their interests, as the economic and social inequities of industrialism became too abhorrent to humanitarian sensibilities, and as perceptive criticisms of economic liberalism became persuasive. The most influential thinker to lead in this

evolution of economic liberalism was John Stuart Mill (1806–1873). Mill, a child prodigy, was brought up to be a good Benthamite. However, he was too sensitive and humanitarian to remain in the hard materialist camp of the Utilitarians. Moreover, living a generation after Smith, Malthus, Ricardo, and Bentham, he was able to see some of the social effects of the Industrial Revolution. Although Mill in no way rejected private property and free enterprise, he believed that in the industrial age restrictions must be instituted by the state for the protection of the poor. Although production is bound by the laws of supply and demand, the distribution of goods is not. Public utilities such as railroads, gas, and waterworks are natural monopolies and should be owned by the state. The state should provide free compulsory education for all and regulate child labor. He favored income and inheritance taxes as economic equalizers. Mill's chief work on economics, *Principles of Political Economy*, was published in 1848. Mill was also the first influential philosopher in modern times to advocate equal rights for women. His *Subjection of Women*, which appeared in 1869, came to be considered the classic statement on the subject of women's rights. In his later years he considered himself a moderate socialist. More than other nineteenth-century liberals, many of his views fit those of twentieth-century liberalism.

Utopian Socialism

During the first phase of the Industrial Revolution the economies of the industrialized countries belonged to the bourgeoisie in thought as well as in deed. The theories of the economic liberals enjoyed ascendancy. The hard-pressed proletariat, though increasingly disconcerted, did not formulate new economic theories. However, as early as the opening of the nineteenth century, a number of intellectuals from the upper classes began to question the fundamentals of the existing system, such as private property and private enterprise for profit. They stressed the need for economic planning and wanted to base society on cooperation and community rather than competitive individualism. The ideas of these intellectuals were speculative and had limited impact, particularly when compared with those of Marx and other hard-headed socialists of the later nineteenth century. A number of these early, speculative intellectuals came to be called Utopian Socialists.

One of the first Utopian Socialists was the French nobleman Henri de Saint-Simon (1760–1825). He and his followers believed that society should be reorganized on a "Christian" basis, that all should work, and that the inheritance of private property should be abolished. His ideal society would be run according to the formula "from each according to his capacity, to each according to his deserts." Women would be elevated from their unequal social positions. Saint-Simon would reward superior artists, scientists, engineers, and businesspeople according to their merits. But he laid down no plan of action for achieving his ideal society.

Charles Fourier (1772–1837), a Frenchman of middle-class origin, advocated doing away with economic competition, the source of so much evil. In his utopian society, agriculture and industry would be carried on by voluntary cooperatives whose members would pool their resources and live in communal apartment houses. Housework and child care would be a communal responsibility. Women, like men, would have rights to work and to their own money. Distribution of goods and profits would be based on a mathematical formula: workers, five-twelfths; capitalists, four-twelfths; management, three-twelfths. Although Fourier's elaborate plans included many impractical ideas, some of his ideas found their way into practice.

A step forward in socialist thinking was taken by Louis Blanc (1811–1882), another middle-class Frenchman. Louis Blanc wanted to abolish the evils of selfish competitive capitalism by setting up a system of social workshops. The government would lend money to voluntary workers' cooperatives, which would establish and run the workshops. Distribution of the proceeds would be according to the formula "from each according to his ability, to each according to his need," the formula later adopted by Karl Marx.

A different kind of Utopian was Robert Owen (1771–1858). Born in Wales, Owen quickly made an industrial fortune in Manchester and bought large cotton mills in New Lanark, Scotland. Early in the nineteenth century he set out to make New Lanark a model socialist utopia. Wages were raised, hours shortened, working conditions improved, child labor abolished, educational and recreational facilities provided, sickness and old-age insurance established. Owen spent the rest of his life and fortune drawing plans for and setting up model socialist communities. Several were established in America, notably New Harmony, Indiana. All were short-lived; nor was Owen's benevolent example followed by other industrialists.

The Utopian Socialists were all strongly influenced by the materialistic rationalism of the eighteenth-century Enlightenment. They recognized some of the deeper significance of the Industrial Revolution and the alternatives it presented. They attacked the unbridled pursuit of profits in an unregulated economy. They attempted to show how a well-organized community or state could eliminate the misery of industrial capitalism and create a society of happy people. They opposed existing organized religion, although Saint-Simon believed that his ideal society should be dominated by a new social Christianity—a brand of Christianity that had never yet been tried. Most of the Utopian Socialists had little influence on their own times. They did, however, start a trend of economic and social thought that was to become influential. During the second half of the nineteenth century a more virile type of socialism would arise. For the most part, this later socialism would be organized and revolutionary and bear the stamp of Karl Marx.

Marxian Socialism

During the second half of the nineteenth century a stronger type of socialism was formed—a type whose foundations were established in the social and intellectual atmosphere of the 1840s. For the most part, this socialism would be organized and revolutionary and bear the stamp of its founder, Karl Marx (1818–1883).

Marx was born into a German middle-class family. His father was a Jewish lawyer who had converted to Christianity. A brilliant student, Karl Marx attained his doctorate in philosophy and history, but he was denied an academic position because of his radical views. After embarking on a career in journalism, he was exiled from Germany and later from France because of his radical ideas. He spent the last thirty-four years of his life in London working on his ideas and trying to build organizations to put them into action. Marx collaborated with his friend Friedrich Engels, son of a wealthy German manufacturer, in writing *The Communist Manifesto* (1848). This work, along with the later *Das Kapital* (the first volume of which appeared in 1867), contains the fundamentals of Marxism. Marx built his ideology on a basis of German philosophy (Hegelian idealism), French social thought (what he referred to as the Utopian Socialists), and British economics (particularly the economic liberalism of David Ricardo). The most salient points of Marx's ideology are summarized next.

Economic Interpretation of History Although people and history are complex, material economic considerations are most important. Economic interests and motivations underlie the most critical actions of human beings, just as the dominant characteristic of a historical epoch is its prevailing system of economic production. Societies are formed around the means of production, around the principal ways that human beings make a living. The political, religious, and cultural systems that develop must conform to the necessities of the economic and social systems, which form around the economic realities of life.

Class Struggle Societies are broadly divided into the haves and the have-nots. The haves are the owners of the means of economic production; the have-nots are the exploited laborers for these haves. The haves and have-nots are opposing classes with opposing interests. Above all, the haves are interested in maintaining a fundamental status quo, while the have-nots have much to gain from fundamental change. Thus, "the history of all hitherto existing society is the history of class struggle": in ancient times freeman versus slave; in medieval times landlord versus serf; in modern times capitalist versus proletarian. The bourgeoisie (the capitalists), having overcome the aristocracy (the feudal landlords) in a revolutionary struggle (such as the French Revolution), will in time be displaced by the proletariat (the industrial working class) in a new revolutionary struggle.

Surplus Value In the capitalistic industrial economy, the law of surplus value prevails. According to this law, workers, who are paid only subsistence wages, create, by their work, value in excess of their wages. This excess, surplus value, is the illegitimate source of profit for the capitalist.

Inevitable Destruction of Capitalism Capitalists are locked into a competitive struggle with one another. This struggle forces them to continually introduce new, costly machines while keeping wages to a minimum. Larger factories must be built, fewer and fewer capitalists succeed in the competitive struggle, and greater and greater quantities of goods are produced in a system running out of control. Correspondingly, the capitalist system is characterized by alternating periods of prosperity and depression. Under capitalism, then, the law of surplus value plus the increasingly more frequent and deep periods of depression will finally produce such misery that the working class will revolt, seize the means of production from the capitalists, destroy the capitalist system, and ultimately establish a classless socialist society.

Internationalism Workers in all countries have more in common with one another than they have with capitalists of their own country. Therefore workers should unite across national boundaries in their struggle against the common enemy—the capitalist bourgeoisie.

When *The Communist Manifesto* first appeared in 1848, it had little impact on the already developing revolutionary events of that year. It reflected, however, the intellectual and social turmoil being produced by the Industrial Revolution. In the following decades, Marxian socialism would grow to become a major theoretical and ideological force in the West (see Chapter 45).

6. THE ARRIVAL OF INDUSTRIAL SOCIETY

The industrialization of Western societies during the nineteenth century was of tremendous significance. Indeed, industrialization has become a measure of whether a society is considered "modern" or "traditional." Industrialization carried in its wake fundamental changes in literally all aspects of life, from the concrete reality of an individual's everyday life to the arrangement of classes in society. Conflict wrought by these changes was inevitable and widespread, whether in an intellectual realm, at the work site, or on the barricades. Generally, it was the industrial bourgeoisie that emerged victorious in these struggles, establishing its control over the economies and governments of the industrialized countries. It is the story of these struggles, combined with the political changes stemming from the French Revolution, that constitutes much of the meat of nineteenth-century history.

SUGGESTED READING

Economic Aspects

P. Deane, *The First Industrial Revolution* (1975). A balanced brief analysis.

E. L. Jones, *The European Miracle* (1987). Compares economic development in Europe and Asia.

D. S. Landes, *The Unbound Prometheus: Technological Change and Industrial Development in Western Europe from 1750 to the Present* (1969). A thorough, insightful description and analysis of the developing technology of the Industrial Revolution.

P. Mathias, *The First Industrial Nation* (1983). A useful survey of British industrialization.

S. Pollard, *Peaceful Conquest: The Industrialization of Europe* (1981). A general survey with a regional perspective.

Social Changes

R. Bridenthal and C. Koonz, eds., *Becoming Visible: Women in European History* (1976). Contains chapters on the significance of the Industrial Revolution for women.

C. Morazé, *The Triumph of the Middle Classes* (1968). A sympathetic survey.

P. N. Stearns, *European Society in Upheaval* (1967). A general survey of social classes and social history during the nineteenth century.

A. Sutcliffe, *Towards the Planned City: Germany, Britain, the United States and France, 1780–1914* (1981). Covers urbanization well.

P. Taylor, ed., *The Industrial Revolution: Triumph or Disaster?* (1970). Samples a variety of views on the benefits and burdens of industrialization.

E. P. Thompson, *The Making of the English Working Class* (1963). Challenging interpretation stressing the culture and activities of the working class.

L. Tilly and J. Scott, *Women, Work and Family* (1978). A highly respected work.

E. A. Wrigley, *Population and History* (1969). Introduction to demographic changes during the Industrial Revolution.

Economic and Social Thought

R. Heilbroner, *The Worldly Philosophers* (1972). A well-written history of economists and their ideas.

A. S. Lindemann, *A History of European Socialism* (1984). A good modern treatment.

F. Manuel, *The Prophets of Paris* (1962). A study of the French Utopian Socialists.

D. McLellan, *Karl Marx: His Life and Thought* (1977). An excellent biography and introduction.

CHAPTER 41

Romanticism in Philosophy, Literature, and the Arts

FIGURE 41.1 Karl Friedrich Schinkel, *Medieval Town on a River,* 1815 This painting by the German romantic artist Schinkel contains many of the key elements of romanticism: glorification of nature, religious mysticism, adoration of the medieval, and concern with the emotional. With these characteristics, romanticism stood in contrast to many of the industrial, secular, and rationalistic trends of the period. (Neue Pinakothek, Munich)

Thought and art generally reflect the societies in which they arise—sometimes in support of the dominant historical trends of an era, sometimes in reaction to those trends. In the final decades of the eighteenth century, romanticism began to replace classicism as the prevailing cultural style in the West. During the first half of the nineteenth century romanticism became the dominant spirit in thought and art. It had competitors and would decline in the second half of the nineteenth century, but it remains popular to this day. What was romanticism, and how was it connected to the societies in which it flourished?

1. THE NATURE OF ROMANTICISM

The romantic spirit had many facets, but essentially it was a reaction against the rationalism and formalism of the classic spirit that had been so powerful in the eighteenth century. Whereas classicism extolled reason and perfection of form, romanticism appealed to the emotions, to feeling, and to freedom and spontaneity of expression. Whereas the classicist was interested in the natural order and the laws of human beings and the universe, the romanticist loved to sing of woods and lakes and lovers' lanes and to dream of faraway or imaginary times and places.

Romanticism was associated with and was in part a product of the French Revolution and Napoleon. Many classicists had been interested in peacefully reforming society in accordance with the natural law. They did not anticipate the violent upheaval that came, although many of the radical revolutionary leaders and Napoleon believed themselves to be in the tradition of classical Greece and Rome. It was the romanticists, breaking sharply with past forms and traditions and with bold abandon trying the new, who reflected the revolutionary spirit. This does not mean that all romanticists were political radicals or even liberals. Some, like Shelley and Heine, were. Others, like Edmund Burke and Sir Walter Scott, were conservatives representing a reaction against the excesses of the Revolution.

Nationalism was another facet of romanticism. Whether liberal or conservative, the romanticist was likely to be an ardent nationalist. The romantic poet Lord Byron lost his life fighting for Greek national independence against the Turks. The dreamer and orator Giuseppe Mazzini was called the soul of Italian nationalism. He spent most of his adult life in exile because of his labors for a free and united Italy. Johann Gottfried von Herder, as early as the eighteenth century, had pleaded eloquently for a German national culture. The fraternity and freedom so common to the national movements before 1850, no less than pride in real or imagined national achievements, gave outlet to the emotions of the romanticist.

Romanticism also represented a reaction against the rationalistic deism of the eighteenth century and a return to mystic religion. In literature and art, romantics stressed the emotion of Christianity and the presence of God in nature. Romantic theologians such as Friedrich Schleiermacher (1768–1834) emphasized that the important part of religion was emotional—the feeling of dependence on an infinite God—not religious dogma or institutions. The revival of religion as part of the romanticism of the early nineteenth century brought about a renewed interest in the Middle Ages. The classicists had drawn their inspiration from pagan Greece and Rome. Now in the early nineteenth century the Knights of the Round Table and Siegfried and Brunhild came back into style once more. No more perfect example of the romantic spirit can be cited than the novels and verse of Sir Walter Scott, whose subject matter was primarily medieval. Gothic architecture enjoyed a revival. The "Dark Ages" were transformed into the "Age of Faith."

Finally, the interest in the Middle Ages and in nationalism reflected another aspect of romanticism: its passionate concern with history. History, written by people such as Thomas B. Macaulay (1800–1859) in Great Britain and Jules Michelet (1798–1874) in France, was literary, exciting, and dramatic—a story of heroic individuals, national struggles, and great accomplishments. It became a subject of great interest among scholars as well as the reading public.

2. THE PHILOSOPHY OF IDEALISM

Any discussion of romantic thought should begin with Jean-Jacques Rousseau (1712–1778), even though this French genius lived during the heyday of rationalistic classicism and before romanticism came into full flower. Rousseau, like most of his fellow philosophers of the Enlightenment such as Voltaire, Diderot, and Montesquieu, was a deist, believing in the mechanical universe of natural laws. However, he differed sharply with them over the place of reason. Far from believing that a person can know only what is perceived through the five senses and interpreted by reason, Rousseau stressed feeling, instinct, and emotions. He also anticipated the romantic movement in his inordinate love of nature. He would stretch himself out on the ground, dig his fingers and toes into the dirt, kiss the earth, and weep for joy. This emotional genius was a true romanticist in his revolt against the rules of formal society. Free love, undisciplined childhood and education, the noble savage—all were features of Rousseau's revolt. His influence on later generations was enormous.

It seems a far cry from the rough genius of Rousseau to the exquisitely ordered thought of Immanuel Kant (1724–1804), but the German philosopher was admittedly indebted to Rousseau. Kant, who was partly of Scottish ancestry, was a native of Königsberg in East Prussia. A frail and insignificant-looking man who never traveled more than fifty miles from the place of his birth, he slowly developed into one of the most powerful and influential thinkers of modern times. He was often in difficulty with the Prussian government because of his liberal and unorthodox views. Kant started out as a scientist and always respected the methods of natural science. He was also steeped in the philosophy of the Enlightenment. However, he was not satisfied with the conclusions of the eighteenth-century materialistic rationalists, and eventually he thought on beyond them. Kant came to believe that there are in reality not one but two worlds—the physical realm and the spiritual realm, or the realm of ultimate reality. The first he called the realm of phenomena; the second the realm of noumena. In the physical realm of phenomena the approach to truth of Descartes, Locke, and Voltaire—sense perception and reason—suffices. But in the spiritual realm of noumena, these methods fail. Ultimate spiritual truth may be attained only by faith, conviction, and feeling. Truths in the realm of the noumena, such as the existence of God, the immortality of the soul, or the existence of good and evil, cannot be proved by reason. And yet we are justified in believing them because they reinforce our moral sense of right and wrong. His principal work, *Critique of Pure Reason*, was a metaphysical answer of the highest intellectual order to the philosophers of the Enlightenment. These ideas came to be called the philosophy of idealism. Kant and his early-nineteenth-century followers represented a sharp reversal in the philosophical trend toward rationalism and materialism, which in a sense began in the thirteenth century with the efforts of Albertus Magnus and Thomas Aquinas to rationalize Christian doctrines.

The most influential of Kant's disciples was Georg Wilhelm Hegel (1770–1831). Hegel's chief interest was the philosophy of history. Like his master, he rejected the mechanistic amoral universe of the Enlightenment. He believed, rather, that a benevolent but impersonal God created and runs the universe, making human society better by a process of purposeful evolution. This evolution is achieved by a dialectical system of thesis, antithesis, and synthesis. Any given system or civilization (thesis) is challenged by its opposite (antithesis). From the struggle emerges a new system containing the best elements of both (synthesis). This synthesis then becomes a new thesis, which when it has served its purpose is challenged by a new antithesis, and so on. Hegel believed that every historical epoch is dominated by a *zeitgeist* (spirit of the time). The zeitgeist of the nineteenth century was German civilization, whose greatest contribution was freedom through disciplined order. Hegel exalted the state. Only in and through the state, he felt, can the individual find meaning and be free. Hegel's influence on romanticism and on the early nineteenth century in general was substantial.

3. ROMANTIC LITERATURE

The spirit of romanticism can be made to come alive in no better way than by a study of the British romantic poets. A number of British writers began to break with classicism during the course of the eighteenth century. The best-known and probably most representative of these writers was Robert Burns (1759–1796). Born in a humble clay cottage, the Scottish poet lived an undisciplined life as if he had been reared in accordance with Rousseau's *Émile*. Burns idealized nature and the rustic rural life with which he was intimately acquainted. In spontaneous verse written in his native Scottish dialect, he wrote an ode to a field mouse, "Wee, sleekit, cow'rin', tim'rous beastie," which he had turned up with his plow. In "The Cotter's Saturday Night" we are given a charming and sympathetic picture of village life among the poor of Scotland. "Auld Lang Syne" is sung with nostalgia every New Year's Eve by millions throughout the English-speaking world. "John Anderson, My Jo," a touching tribute to love in old age, could never have been written by Racine or Alexander Pope.

The romantic spirit, early reflected in the poetry of Robert Burns, reached maturity with William Wordsworth (1770–1850) and Samuel Taylor Coleridge (1772–1834). The two were warm friends. Both were closely associated with the beautiful lake country of northwest England, Wordsworth by birth and Coleridge by adoption. Together they took a trip to Germany, where they fell under the influence of Kant. Both, as young men, were ardent social reformers. The two collaborated on *Lyrical Ballads,* which appeared in 1798. *Lyrical Ballads* contains some of the best work of these gifted poets, such as Wordsworth's "Lines Composed a Few Miles above Tintern Abbey" (see Figure 41.2) and Coleridge's "Rime of the Ancient Mariner." Both men were masters of versification and poetic expression. They were also lovers and students of nature, and both of them, particularly Wordsworth, sensed a brooding, mystical presence of the divine. Wordsworth's "Intimations of Immortality" is sublime in its spiritual depth and insight. In their ardent love of nature, their introspective concern for the individual, their preoccupation with the spiritual rather than the material, and their greater attention to substance than to form, Wordsworth and Coleridge broke distinctly with the spirit of classicism.

Once the vogue of romanticism was dignified and popularized in Great Britain by Wordsworth and Coleridge, a host of romantic writers appeared. A younger trio of poetic geniuses of the highest order, Lord Byron, Percy Bysshe Shelley, and John Keats (all of whom lived briefly and died between the years 1788 and 1824), are well

FIGURE 41.2 J. M. W. Turner, *Tintern Abbey* Tintern Abbey, a twelfth-century Gothic ruin in Wales, was the object of both literary and artistic romanticism. Here Turner, the leading English romantic artist, evokes the power of nature, religion, and the medieval past. (The British Museum)

known and loved. All three gave spontaneous and unrestrained vent to their emotions. Byron and Shelley combined an exquisite esthetic sense with irrepressible revolutionary zeal, defying the forms and customs of society. Keats was a gentler soul, who after a lifelong quest for the beautiful died at the age of twenty-five.

Meanwhile, Sir Walter Scott in novel and verse was devoting his longer life (1771–1832) to glorifying the Middle Ages and his native Scotland. Scott, unlike Byron and Shelley but like Wordsworth and Coleridge in their mature and mellow later years, was conservative in his attitude toward public affairs.

On the other side of the Atlantic, Henry

Wadsworth Longfellow, James Fenimore Cooper, and Washington Irving were founding an American national literature. In their subject matter, their style, and their attitudes, they reflected the European romantic spirit. Many other American writers in the early nineteenth century also wrote in the romantic vein. Ralph Waldo Emerson (1803–1882) was considered a religious radical and skeptic in his day. He gave up his Puritan (by then Unitarian) pastorate at Boston's Old North Church because of his heterodoxy. However, in his essays and poems it was the romantic philosophy of Kantian idealism, not the rationalism of the Enlightenment, that he introduced into America. Edgar Allan Poe (1809–1849), short story writer, literary critic, and romantic poet of a high order, was in a sense an American Shelley, though less ethereal and more morbid. Henry David Thoreau (1817–1862) took Rousseau's back-to-nature idea more seriously than did its author. Rousseau, for all his passion for nature, would never have withdrawn from society for two years to live by Walden Pond in introspective solitude. Emerson, Poe, and Thoreau were all individualists to the point of being mild social revolutionaries. Thoreau preached civil disobedience and allowed himself to be put in jail rather than pay taxes for what he considered to be unworthy causes. The sensitive Poe, enduring oblivion and poverty, turned to drink and an early grave. Emerson weathered a storm of hostility from organized religion and society for his nonconformist views.

Romanticism came to German literature in the latter half of the eighteenth century, partly under the influence of the early British romanticists and partly as a result of the conscious effort of the Germans, led by Herder, to free themselves from bondage to French classical culture. Foremost among all German writers is Johann Wolfgang von Goethe (1749–1832). Like Shakespeare, Leonardo da Vinci, and Beethoven, Goethe is a genius of such proportions that he cannot be confined to any single cultural school or movement. However, insofar as it is possible to classify him, he belongs more nearly to the romantic tradition than to any other, both in time and in spirit. His prodigious energies were devoted essentially to a lifelong (eighty-three years) search for the secrets of happiness and wisdom. His encyclopedic mind delved fruitfully into literature, philosophy, science, and public affairs. His novels, lyrics, essays, scientific and philosophical treatises, and dramas fill 132 volumes. No writer except Shakespeare has had so many of his lyrics set to music. Goethe's masterpiece is *Faust*, a philosophical drama written in exquisite verse. It is about a medieval scholar who, dissatisfied with the fruits of knowledge, sells his soul to the Devil in return for earthly pleasure and wisdom. Goethe explores the depths of human experience and aspiration. *Faust* was sixty years in the making. In his medieval interests, his fresh, emotional spontaneity, his love of nature and of individual personality, and his courageous, robust, pioneering spirit, Goethe was a romanticist.

Goethe's friend and protégé, Friedrich Schiller (1759–1805), was more popular in his own day than the master himself. Schiller drew heavily on the Middle Ages and on nationalism (at a time when national aspirations were associated with freedom) for his dramas, histories, and lyrics. *William Tell*, a drama based upon the Swiss struggle for freedom from Hapsburg tyranny, is probably Schiller's best-known work. Neither Goethe nor Schiller can be considered a German nationalist in the narrow sense; both were universal in their interests and their appeal.

Heinrich Heine (1797–1856) was considered to be Goethe's successor as a writer of German lyrics, though not of Goethe's stature. Most of Heine's voluminous writing was in the field of romantic lyrical poetry. One of his most representative works was an ode to the Silesian weavers who rose up against the hardships caused by the Industrial Revolution, which was just coming to Germany, and were shot down by Prussian troops. Because of the hostility of the various German governments in the age of Metternich to his radical political ideas, Heine exiled himself from Germany. The last twenty-five years of his life were spent in Paris. Many of his later lyrics show a touch of the light gaiety of the French.

Literary romanticism flowered later in France than England or Germany. François-René de Chateaubriand (1768–1848), a disillusioned nobleman who began writing during the reign of Napoleon I, was one of the first French writers of influence to react against the rationalism of the Enlightenment. His *Genius of Christianity* is a return to mystic religion. He also dreamed and wrote of glorified Indians in faraway tropical

America. At almost the same time, Madame de Staël (1766–1817) analyzed and helped popularize romanticism. Alexander Dumas the elder (1802–1870) continues to delight young and old alike with his romantic and melodramatic *Three Musketeers* and *Count of Monte Cristo,* painting the haunting afterglow of medieval chivalry. George Sand (1804–1876), an unconventional woman and gifted author, wrote numerous popular novels filled with romantic passion and idealism. Victor Hugo (1802–1885) in his long and tumultuous life wrote a vast quantity of exquisite lyrics, dramas, essays, and fiction in the romantic tradition. His *Hunchback of Notre Dame* is medieval in setting. In *Les Misérables* he immortalizes and idealizes the masses of underprivileged humanity, preaching redemption and purification not by planned social reform but through suffering. Jules Michelet crossed historical and literary lines in his seventeen-volume *History of France.* He tells the thrilling story of France's long and glorious achievements, usually with skillful historical craftsmanship and always with matchless grace.

The first great figure in Russian literature was the romantic poet Alexander Pushkin (1799–1837). The chief inspiration for his great lyrics, dramas, histories, novels, essays, and tales came from French and British writers, particularly Byron. Because of his revolutionary radicalism (of the French variety), he was for a while exiled to southern Russia by the Russian government. Later he became a Russian nationalist and took many of his themes from Russian history. His tragic drama *Boris Godunov* (patterned after Shakespeare) is considered to be his masterpiece.

4. THE ROMANTIC SPIRIT IN THE ARTS

Words fail to convey the messages and meanings expressed in the visual and musical arts. This is particularly true of art, whose appeal is primarily to the emotions.

The leading painters glorified nature, religion, and nationalism (see Figure 41.1). John Constable (1776–1837) in Great Britain, Camille Corot (1796–1875) in France, and George Inness the elder (1825–1894) in the United States painted landscapes fit to have illustrated the moods of

Wordsworth or Thoreau (see Color Plate 19 and Figure 41.2). Their idealizations of nature and the rural life would have delighted Rousseau and Burns. J. M. W. Turner (1775–1851) in England caught the romantic mood in his eerie, misty impressions of seascapes and mythological subjects (see Color Plate 20). Jean-François Millet (1814–1875) idealized both the French rural life (*The Sower* and *The Gleaners*) and mystic religion (*The Angelus*) (see Figure 41.3). His compatriot Eugène Delacroix (1798–1863) depicted on canvas Byron's *Prisoner of Chillon.* On great murals in the Louvre, the library of the Chamber of Deputies, and the Hôtel de Ville he portrayed glorious scenes from history (see Color Plate 21).

In the field of architecture the romantic movement was less pronounced. Its chief manifestation was a revived interest in the Gothic style. The French, after several centuries of apathy about if not scorn for anything associated with medievalism, suddenly showed a renewed interest in their magnificent Gothic monuments. The Houses of Parliament, constructed in London in the early nineteenth century when England was rapidly becoming industrialized, were built in the Gothic style.

The romantic spirit was caught and expressed by a host of great musicians. They went beyond the controlled classical music, trying to translate emotions into sound. First and foremost was Beethoven (1770–1827), who was not only one of the greatest of classic composers but also the first of the romanticists. His earlier work was in the spirit of his idol, Mozart. In maturity his originality overflowed the bounds of classic forms, becoming freer, more individualistic, and emotional. Beethoven lived through the upheavals of the French Revolution and Napoleon, and his keen interest in these dramatic events is reflected in his music. His Symphony no. 3 (*Eroica*) was dedicated to Napoleon, whom Beethoven at first regarded as the embodiment of the democratic ideals of the French Revolution. His Fifth and Seventh symphonies were inspired by the German nationalistic upsurge, which helped to overthrow Napoleon. Carl Maria von Weber (1786–1826), Franz Schubert (1797–1828), Felix Mendelssohn (1809–1847), and Robert Schumann (1810–1856) carried on in the spirit of the great Beethoven.

These gifted and youthful Germans ex-

FIGURE 41.3 Jean-François Millet, *The Angelus* The spirit of romanticism that dominated art during the first half of the nineteenth century was marked by a religious revival and by an admiration for the simple, rural life, which Millet effectively captures in painting. (Giraudon)

pressed in their melodic music the same spontaneous and emotional spirit that their contemporaries Byron, Shelley, and Keats were expressing in English verse. A German by adoption was the colorful Hungarian-born Franz Liszt (1811–1886) (see Figure 41.4). Liszt is believed to be the greatest concert pianist of his time. His glamorous personality and sensational, emotional compositions greatly popularized romantic music. Although Liszt was an international

figure, his Hungarian folk music was characteristic of the growing national sentiment of the time. He befriended the youthful Richard Wagner, who later married one of Liszt's illegitimate daughters.

The romantic spirit is nowhere better illustrated than in the work of the Polish-French pianist-composer Frédéric Chopin (1810–1849). Chopin could express his sweet sorrows in lilting nocturnes, his sunny gaiety in bright waltzes and

FIGURE 41.4 Josef Danhauser, *Liszt at the Piano*, 1840 This romantic painting brings together key figures of romanticism. At the center, Franz Liszt plays the piano for his friends. Standing, from left to right, are Victor Hugo, Niccolò Paganini, and Gioacchino Rossini. Sitting are Alexandre Dumas, George Sand (in men's clothes), and Marie d'Agoult. Above them is a portrait of Lord Byron and a bust of Ludwig van Beethoven. (Bildarchiv Preussischer Kulturbesitz, Berlin)

mazurkas, his national patriotism in stirring polonaises, or his deeper, dramatic moods in more formal ballades and concertos—all with equal skill and all in the romantic tradition. Meanwhile, other notable Frenchmen were writing romantic symphonies and operas. Charles-François Gounod's *Faust* is an operatic version of Goethe's great theme. The haunting melodies of Georges Bizet's (1838–1875) *Carmen* are widely known and sung. The greatest Italian romantic composer was Giuseppe Verdi (1813–1901). His operas *Aïda*, *La Traviata*, *Il Trovatore*, and *Rigoletto* are still sung every season in opera houses all over the world. Verdi was Italy's national cultural hero during the long, uphill fight for freedom and unity.

Richard Wagner (1813–1883) brought the romantic era in music to a dramatic climax. Wagner's tempestuous life, like his music, illustrates and marks the transition from the romantic, moderately liberal and nationalistic early nineteenth century to the more violent and restless spirit of the late nineteenth and early twentieth centuries. In his youth Wagner was a radical and

was exiled from Saxony in 1849 for his revolutionary activities. Later he became an extreme German nationalist—even a German "master racist" of the type that has brought so much violence to the twentieth-century world. His operas, though containing some of the world's greatest music, are also grandiloquent and often stridently nationalistic. *Tannhäuser*, *The Meistersingers*, *Siegfried*, *Götterdämmerung*, *Lohengrin*, and *Das Rheingold* are an important part of the opera repertory today.

Romanticism in the arts, as in literature and philosophy, reflected a new recognition that human beings are complex, emotional, and only sometimes rational creatures. In a civilization that was becoming more scientific, materialistic, industrial, and urban, romanticism was a counterweight for the human experience. Although new cultural trends such as realism would appear during the middle of the nineteenth century (see Color Plate 22), romanticism would remain a strong current in Western civilization well into the twentieth century.

SUGGESTED READING

General

K. Clark, *The Romantic Rebellion* (1973). Clearly written and useful.

M. LeBris, *Romantics and Romanticism* (1981). A well-illustrated survey of romanticism in its political context.

S. Prawer, ed., *The Romantic Period in Germany* (1970). A good collection of essays.

H. B. Schenk, *The Mind of the European Romantics* (1966). A solid survey.

J. L. Talmon, *Romanticism and Revolt: Europe, 1815–1848* (1967). A survey of romanticism in its broad historical context.

The Philosophy of Idealism

E. Cassirer, *Kant's Life and Thought* (1981). Excellent, though difficult.

R. Stromberg, *European Intellectual History since 1789* (1975). Surveys the topic well.

C. Taylor, *Hegel* (1975). Excellent introduction.

Romantic Literature

M. H. Abrams, *Natural Supernaturalism: Tradition and Revolution in Romantic Literature* (1971). A good survey of romantic literature.

J. S. Allen, *Popular French Romanticism* (1981). Relates literary romanticism and popular culture.

J. Wordsworth, *William Wordsworth and the Age of English Romanticism* (1987). Covers English romanticism well.

Romanticism in the Arts

A. Hauser, *Social History of Art* (1958). Relates artistic trends to social developments.

H. W. Janson, *History of Art* (1977). The standard survey with a section on romanticism.

CHAPTER 42

Conservatism, Restoration, and Reaction, 1815–1830

FIGURE 42.1 George Cruikshank, ***The Peterloo Massacre,*** **1819** This painting by Cruikshank depicts the troops of the conservative British government breaking up a rally for liberal political reform, including demands for universal suffrage and religious freedoms. During the restoration, many European governments attempted to repress liberal movements. (The Mansell Collection)

The overthrow of Napoleon in 1815 brought to an end, in Europe at least, the heroic and tumultuous epoch that had begun in 1789 with the meeting of the Estates General. The intervening twenty-six years had been filled with great expectation, experimentation, turmoil, and war. Now there were disillusionment and weariness. The European royalty and aristocracy, at long last triumphant over revolutionary France, were determined to put an end not only to the Mirabeaus, Robespierres, and Napoleons but also to the ideas of the Enlightenment.

The returning holders of power—the monarchs, the aristocrats, the established Christian churches, and the elite of the governmental and military bureaucracies—generally subscribed to a conservatism that was dominant between 1815 and 1830 and that would remain a powerful force throughout the nineteenth century. Conservatives tended to believe that a hierarchical Christian society authoritatively guided by traditional monarchs, aristocrats, and clergy was time tested and best. Edmund Burke (1729–1797), Great Britain's most influential conservative thinker, and conservatives in general rejected the abstract rationalism of the Enlightenment and the reforms of the French Revolution. Any rapid change was suspect, and the attempt by the middle class to grasp political power had been a presumptuous act by individuals who simply did not know how to rule. For conservatives the experience of the French Revolution was a lesson in what to avoid.

In order to achieve their conservative goals, to redraw territorial boundaries, and to establish lasting stability in Europe, the leaders of the victorious powers gathered at the Austrian capital of Vienna in the autumn of 1814. To this conference also flocked representatives of every state in Europe, hundreds of dispossessed princes, agents of every conceivable interest, and adventurers.

1. THE CONGRESS OF VIENNA, 1814–1815

The Congress of Vienna was dominated by the four major victors over Napoleon (see Figure 42.2). Great Britain was represented by her able foreign minister, Lord Castlereagh. Prussia's mediocre king, Frederick William III, headed his own delegation, as did Russia's tsar, the idealistic young Alexander I. Austria's emperor, Francis I, played host to the assembled great. However, the real leader of the Austrian delegation—and, indeed, the dominant figure of the whole congress—was the Austrian chancellor, Prince Klemens von Metternich. As guiding principles on which to base their decisions, the conferees decided on "legitimacy" and "stability." By *legitimacy* they meant that in the redistribution of various territories, attention would be paid not to the desires or interests of the people concerned but to the claims of the victorious—the former and future sovereigns. By *stability* they meant establishing and maintaining a balance of power within Europe, with particular focus on restraining France. Many of the decisions formalized at Vienna had already been made by the four major powers shortly before and after Napoleon's overthrow in April 1814 (see Map 42.1).

Thanks in no small measure to the presence of the clever and able Talleyrand, France, the cause of all the turmoil, got off lightly. Prussia would have severely punished and weakened France, but her three major colleagues were fearful of upsetting the balance of power. Already saddled with the restored Bourbons, France was merely reduced to almost the same boundaries it had had before the wars of the revolutionary era. The Congress of Vienna had originally imposed no indemnity on France. But because of Napoleon's return from Elba in the midst of the congress and his hundred-day fling that ended at Waterloo, the four great powers compelled France to cede the Saar Basin to Prussia, to pay an indemnity of 700 million francs, and to return the art treasures stolen by Napoleon from the various galleries of Europe. Allied forces were to occupy France until the indemnity was paid. To contain France within its frontiers and to discourage future French aggression, Prussia was given a sizable block of territory along the Rhine, the Austrian Netherlands (Belgium) was annexed to the Dutch Netherlands, and Piedmont was enlarged by the annexation of the city-state of Genoa.

The main powers, taking advantage of political changes that had occurred over the previous twenty-six years and trading among themselves, received new territories. Great Britain gained several strategic islands and colonies, increasing

Figure 42.2 Jean-Baptiste Isabey, *Congress of Vienna* The principal figures of the Congress of Vienna are portrayed by Isabey. From left to right: Metternich is standing before a chair, Castlereagh is sitting with crossed legs, and Talleyrand is sitting with his right arm on the table. (Culver Pictures)

her sea power and overseas dominance. Prussia added some areas in central Europe that made it more homogeneously German and Western. However, the Rhineland territory was not contiguous to the Prussian homeland—a situation that invited further aggression. Russia's acquisition of Polish territory made the great majority of the Polish-speaking people subjects of Russia and brought Russia farther into the heart of central Europe. Austria, in exchange for the Belgian Netherlands, took the two rich Italian provinces of Lombardy and Venetia. Its preeminence in Italy, together with its presidency over the German Confederation, made Austria the dominant power in central Europe. The Holy Roman Empire, which Napoleon had destroyed, was not restored, but in its place was erected the weak German Confederation under the permanent presidency of Austria. Napoleon's consolidation of the more than three hundred German states into thirty-nine was allowed to stand, bringing

the German people that much more political unity.

The Congress of Vienna has been both admired and criticized by observers ever since 1815. Critics point out that the peoples and territories of Europe were moved about by the great powers at Vienna like pawns on a chessboard, in complete disregard for the wishes of the people or for the spirit of nationalism that was now an increasingly virile force. Instead of trying to deal constructively with the budding forces of liberalism and nationalism, the great powers tried to ignore or repress them. Admirers point out that the Vienna settlement was not vindictive toward France and did establish a reasonable balance of power, both of which contributed to a century of freedom from Europe-wide war. While one may not agree with the conservative goals of the conferees, a settlement was achieved at Vienna and at least temporarily maintained in succeeding years.

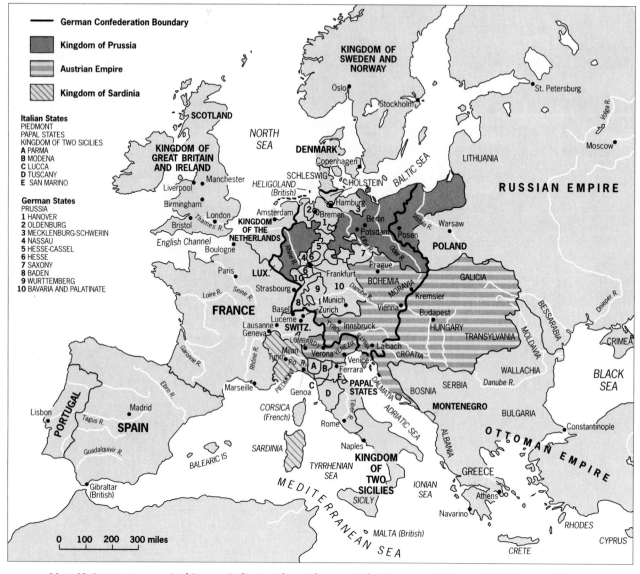

Map 42.1 EUROPE, 1815 As this map indicates, the settlement at the Congress of Vienna left France with its lands little changed from 1789, but now France was bordered by strengthened states: the Kingdom of the Netherlands, Prussia, and the Kingdom of Sardinia. The victorious powers gained territories, but a balance of power was maintained.

2. THE CONCERT OF EUROPE

Metternich and his colleagues, pleased with their work, set up machinery for perpetuating it. Conveniently at hand was the Holy Alliance, conceived by Alexander to establish and safeguard the principles of the Christian religion. Russia (Orthodox), Austria (Roman Catholic), and Prussia (Protestant), the three bastions of conservatism, were to form the nucleus of the alliance. All the Christian states of Europe were invited to join, and only Great Britain and the Papal States did not. Metternich considered the Holy Alliance a "sonorous nothing" but saw in it an opportunity for influencing the tsar. Intended by Alexander I as a bulwark of Christianity, the Holy Alliance became a symbol of reaction and repression.

Much more earthly an agency for perpetuating the Vienna settlements was the Quadruple Alliance. This was a military alliance of Austria, Russia, Prussia, and Great Britain created in November 1815 for the purpose of guaranteeing for twenty years the territorial boundaries established by the Vienna settlement. Metternich was determined to make of the alliance an international military police force that would suppress any liberal or national movements. It was arranged that the four member powers should hold periodic congresses to carry out the purposes of the alliance.

The first congress was held at Aix-la-Chapelle in northwest Germany in 1818. The purpose was to arrange the withdrawal of occupying forces from French soil. Since France had demonstrated good behavior under the restored Bourbon king, Louis XVIII, it was not only freed of occupying forces but was admitted to the Quadruple Alliance. Congresses at Troppau in 1820 and at Laibach in 1821, both on Austrian soil, concerned themselves with an insurrection that had broken out in Naples against the tyrannical Bourbon king, Ferdinand I. An Austrian army was authorized to put down the insurrection and reestablish the hated Ferdinand I on his throne. The Neapolitan liberal volunteers, no match for the Austrian regulars, were soon defeated and their leaders executed, imprisoned, or exiled. What turned out to be the last of the congresses met in 1822 at Verona to deal with a liberal revolt in Spain against the reactionary Ferdinand VII. With the sanction of the Congress of Verona a French army crossed the Pyrenees and easily put down the rebellion.

The first of the alliance powers to repudiate the Metternich system was Great Britain. At the Troppau congress, the British clearly indicated their opposition to interfering in the internal affairs of other states. When the Verona congress decided, over British protest, on intervention in Spain, Britain's representative withdrew.

The Metternich system soon received further blows, some from unexpected quarters. At the Congress of Verona, the like-minded Austrians, Russians, and Prussians had been alarmed not only by the rebellion in the Spanish homeland but also by the revolt of Spain's New World colonies. When the corrupt government of Ferdinand VII proved incapable of putting down the revolt, Alexander I, with Metternich's blessing, proposed to send a Russian fleet to help coerce the colonies. Great Britain, enjoying a lucrative trade with the rebellious colonies, did not wish to see them restored to Spanish dominion and commercial monopoly. The British minister, George Canning, who had succeeded Castlereagh in 1822, proposed to the government of the United States that Great Britain and the United States issue a joint statement against interference by the "Holy Alliance" in the affairs of the Western Hemisphere. However, Secretary of State John Quincy Adams foresaw that the time might come when the United States would wish to invoke such a policy alone, perhaps even against Great Britain. In 1823, President Monroe announced what has come to be called the Monroe Doctrine: The United States would regard any interference on the part of European powers in the affairs of the Western Hemisphere as an "unfriendly act." The United States was at the time, of course, a new and relatively weak nation, but Canning's immediate support of the American policy killed any further thought of "Holy Alliance" intervention in the New World, for Great Britain had unchallenged dominance of the seas. The Monroe Doctrine marked the beginning of active participation by the United States in affairs beyond its own immediate shores.

The next blow to Metternich's concert of Europe came when the Greeks turned against their Moslem Turkish overlords in the revolt of 1821–1829. The valiant efforts of the Greeks were not sufficient, however, to resist the power of the Ottoman Empire. By 1827 they were on the point of being hopelessly crushed. However, the sympathies of the great powers were being aroused for the courageous Greeks. Russia, Great Britain, and France in particular displayed a growing concern over the events in Greece. Russia's Orthodox Christian religion was the same as that of the Greeks. Furthermore, the Russians had long desired Constantinople, which controlled Russia's natural strategic and commercial outlet to the Mediterranean. Great Britain was concerned over the possibility of Russia's dominance in the Near East. In addition, the ruling classes in Great Britain and France were steeped in the classical culture of ancient Greece. Lord Byron, the most popular literary figure in Europe, lost his life fighting as a volunteer for Greece. In 1827 these three powers, over Metternich's protest, intervened in the Greek revolt and defeated the Turks on land and sea. The Treaty of Adrianople in 1829 granted independence to most of the Greeks on the home peninsula and local autonomy to the Serbs and Rumanians. The successful revolt of the Greeks was a victory for the resurging revolutionary principles of liberalism and nationalism. The intervention of Russia, Great Britain, and France further weakened the already battered Concert of Europe.

3. THE BOURBON RESTORATION IN FRANCE

When the victorious armies of the coalition powers entered France and deposed Napoleon in the spring of 1814, they brought "in their baggage" the members of the Bourbon royal family who had fled the Revolution. In their wake trooped the émigré nobility. A younger brother of the guillotined Louis XVI was placed on the throne as Louis XVIII. (The son of Louis XVI, who had died in prison in 1795, without having ruled, was considered to be Louis XVII.) The "restored" Bourbon king was now fifty-nine and too fat and gouty to walk unassisted. He had traveled much and unwillingly during the long, lean years of his exile. When Napoleon returned from Elba in 1815, Louis XVIII had to flee once more. After Waterloo he returned to his throne, which he considered "the most comfortable of armchairs," determined to do nothing that might force him to leave it again.

Upon assuming the throne, Louis XVIII issued a charter, or constitution, that retained Napoleon's administrative and legal system and civil and religious liberty. Lawmaking was placed into the hands of a two-chamber legislature. The upper house was made an aristocratic stronghold, and the lower house was elected by a highly restricted electorate. Only those who paid direct annual taxes of three hundred francs could vote; this limited the suffrage to about one hundred thousand out of a total population of nearly 30 million. The lower house could be dis-

solved by the king. Since the king also appointed and controlled his own ministers and the host of civilian and military officials, carried on foreign relations, controlled the military forces, and enforced the laws, his power was only somewhat limited by the charter.

Louis XVIII set out to use his powers with moderation so that tranquillity might be restored. There was no wholesale punishment of revolutionary leaders. The peasant and bourgeois purchasers of church and noble lands were not dispossessed. However, most of the returned émigrés—largely from the highest ranks of the clergy and the nobility—were of a different spirit. They came back from their unhappy exile angry and vengeful, demanding their old privileges and indemnification for their lands. Their leader was the king's younger brother, the Comte d'Artois—a typical Bourbon who had "never learned anything and never forgotten anything." The reactionaries controlled both houses of the national legislature, since even in the lower elected house, suffrage restrictions heavily favored the aristocracy and the *nouveaux riches* bourgeoisie. Louis XVIII found it increasingly difficult to hold these fire-eating reactionaries in check. Shortly before he died in 1824, he warned his incorrigible brother of the danger to the Bourbon dynasty if he did not adopt a more moderate attitude.

Unfortunately, Charles X, as the Comte d'Artois now styled himself, was a stranger to moderation. He quickly aroused animosity against his regime to an explosive pitch. The Napoleonic generals who had brought so much glory to France were immediately retired from duty. An indemnity was voted the émigrés for their confiscated lands, the money to be raised by reducing the interest on government bonds from 5 percent to 3 percent. This angered the upper bourgeoisie, who were the chief bondholders. The peasants were alarmed by a proposed establishment of primogeniture, which seemed to endanger the principle of equality and the security of land titles. The Jesuits were brought back to France, and favors were bestowed on the Catholic church. Opposition mounted rapidly. By 1827 Charles X had lost his majority in both houses of the national legislature. Totally blind to the political realities of the day, he twice dissolved the lower chamber and attempted to force the election of a friendly majority by censoring the press and using official pressure on the electorate. The hostile majorities only increased in number. Finally, in July 1830, the king dissolved the newly elected chamber, called for new elections, restricted the suffrage so drastically that only about twenty-five thousand very rich citizens could vote, and completely abolished the freedom of the press. These measures set off an uprising in Paris. The Parisian proletariat erected barricades in the streets that the disaffected rank and file of the army were "unable" to break. After three days of desultory fighting, the insurgents had the upper hand, and the last Bourbon king of France was on his way to exile in England.

4. RESTORATION AND REPRESSION IN THE GERMANIES

In central and eastern Europe, particularly in the Germanies, Italy, and Russia, the conservatives and the Metternich system were more secure. The Germanies in 1815 consisted of thirty-seven little states and two large ones—Prussia and Austria. In all of them the influence of Metternich was strong. The German Confederation was an improvement over the old Holy Roman Empire, which Napoleon had destroyed, only in the sense that Napoleon's consolidation of the more than three hundred states down to thirty-nine was allowed to stand. The Diet was only a gathering and debating place for the representatives of the rulers of the thirty-nine states. The confederation had no treasury and no army at its command. There was not even a flag to symbolize its German national character. Reactionary Austria enjoyed a permanent presidency over it.

The German nationalism and liberalism that existed in 1815 centered primarily in the little states, some of whose rulers defied Metternich by granting liberal constitutions. The national and liberal activities here were largely the work of university students and professors, who shortly after 1815 began to form *Burschenschaften*, or brotherhoods, for the purpose of promoting German nationalism, liberalism, and the Christian religion. In 1817, in commemoration of the three hundredth anniversary of Luther's publication of his Ninety-five Theses, the Burschen-

schaften staged a giant festival at Wartburg, where Luther had hidden and had begun his translation of the Bible. Although the festivities were primarily religious in character, enough enthusiasm for German nationalism and liberalism was displayed to fill Metternich with anxiety. The murder two years later of a reactionary propagandist by a fanatical student gave Metternich his opportunity to strike. Calling together the princes of the leading German states at Carlsbad, he joined them in drawing up a set of harsh decrees designed to crush the embryonic national and liberal movements. The Burschenschaften were outlawed. Strict censorship was established. Classrooms and libraries were supervised. Liberal students and professors were terrorized by spies and police. The Carlsbad Decrees succeeded in suppressing for a number of years this first outcropping of the revolutionary spirit in Germany since the overthrow of Napoleon.

In Prussia the militaristic, paternalistic, despotic Hohenzollerns reigned. Behind them stood the equally reactionary landed aristocracy, the *Junkers*. The Junkers served as officers in the Prussian army and filled the key posts in the civil service and administration. These military lords hated not only liberalism in any form but also German nationalism. They did not wish to see virile, martial Prussia contaminated by association with the lesser German states, which were now infected with the French disease of liberalism. It was only in the economic field that German unity received any encouragement from Prussia. Because its territory was separated into two noncontiguous segments, Prussia in 1819 began making commercial treaties with its smaller German neighbors, providing for the free flow of trade among them. By 1834 nearly all the states of the German Confederation except Austria had joined the Prussian-sponsored *Zollverein* (customs union). Though it was not so intended, the Zollverein proved to be a forerunner of German political unity under Prussian leadership.

As was to be expected, conservatism reached its height in Austria. The spirit of the French Revolution and Napoleon, with the one exception of nationalism, had hardly touched the Hapsburg state and its feudal society. In addition to the natural conservatism of the Hapsburgs and their chief minister, Austria had a language problem that caused its rulers to fear liberalism and nationalism like the plague. Austria proper is German-speaking, but during the sixteenth, seventeenth, and eighteenth centuries the Hapsburgs had annexed territories inhabited by Hungarian (Magyar), Czech, Slovak, Ruthenian, Polish, Rumanian, Serb, Croat, and Slovene language groups. In 1815 two Italian-speaking provinces were added. Before 1789 these various language groups had remained relatively quiet under their feudal lords, the Hapsburg dynasty, and the Roman Catholic church, but in the wake of the French Revolution, they began to stir with national consciousness.

Metternich saw clearly that if this new force were not suppressed, the Hapsburg state would fall apart. Furthermore, nationalism unchecked would cause Austria to lose its dominance over Germany and Italy. The various German and Italian states would be drawn together into powerful national states from which Austria would be excluded, for most of the people in the Hapsburg state were neither German- nor Italian-speaking. When these facts are considered, it is not surprising that Austria in 1815 was the most reactionary state in Europe save Russia. In the Hapsburg provinces Metternich's police and spies were everywhere. Permission to enter or to leave the country was made very difficult, lest dangerous ideas be brought in from the West. Classrooms, libraries, bookstores, and organizations of all kinds were considered suspicious and closely supervised. Even music (in the country of Mozart and Beethoven) was censored for fear that musical notes would be used as a cryptic code for conveying revolutionary ideas. On the surface, these policies appeared for some time to succeed. Nevertheless, Metternich was aware that the Hapsburg state stood on shaky ground.

5. RESTORATION AND REPRESSION IN ITALY

Austria dominated Italy even more completely than Germany. Lombardy and Venetia were annexed outright. Modena, Parma, and Tuscany were ruled by Austrian princes. The Papal States and Naples were under Austria's protection and guidance in both domestic and foreign affairs. In all these states the deposed aristocracy and clericals trooped back, full of hatred for French institutions and for the Italian liberals who had

cooperated with Napoleon (see Figure 42.3). Nearly all the Italian intelligentsia were soon in prison or in exile. In the Papal States the Inquisition and the Index were restored, and such Napoleonic innovations as street lighting were done away with. Of all the Italian states, only Piedmont in the extreme northwest was free of Austrian control, but even here the restored heads of the House of Savoy were so reactionary as to cause Metternich only joy.

6. CONSERVATISM IN GREAT BRITAIN

Although Great Britain had been for years a home of representative government, its government in 1815 was far from democratic. The suffrage was so severely restricted by property qualifications that only about 5 percent of the adult males could vote. Furthermore, the industrial cities of the north, which had emerged since the last distribution of seats in Parliament, were not represented at all. Both houses of Parliament were therefore monopolized by the landed aristocracy. It must be remembered, however, that the cleavage between the middle class and the aristocracy was not so sharp in Great Britain as on the Continent. The law of primogeniture in Great Britain granted the eldest son the entire landed estate and permitted him alone to assume the title. Younger sons sought careers in the church, in the military, or in business. This process brought about much intermingling between the upper and the middle classes. The long-sustained prosperity of British commerce had produced a merchant class wealthy enough to purchase respectability, lands, and sometimes titles. The aristocracy frequently invested in commercial enterprises and later in industry. These facts help to explain why the great political and social struggles in nineteenth-century Britain, though sometimes bitter, lacked the violence of those on the Continent.

A period of economic depression and unrest in Great Britain followed the ending of the Napoleonic wars in 1815. For twenty-two years, with only one brief interruption, Britain had been engaged in a desperate struggle with France, a struggle that was economic as well as military. Meanwhile, British industrial expansion had gone on apace. The war's end found British

FIGURE 42.3 Repression in Italy This illustration shows Italians being shot as suspected revolutionaries; it epitomizes the spirit of reaction and repression as the great powers of Europe tried to restore the old order and stifle the new currents of liberalism and nationalism. (Historical Pictures Service, Chicago)

warehouses piled high with unsold goods. Thousands of returning veterans found no jobs. Strikes and riots, which had begun during Napoleon's blockade, increased. The conservative Tory party, which had seen the country through the war, was strongly entrenched in power. Both the Tories and the slightly more liberal Whigs were still badly frightened by the specter of French revolutionary Jacobinism. The government therefore took strong measures against the restless workers. Writs of habeas corpus were suspended. The climax came in 1819 when troops fired on a crowd that had assembled outside Manchester to listen to reform speeches. A number were killed and hundreds injured in this "Peterloo Massacre" (see Figure 42.1).

Within a few years, however, as the postwar crisis of depression and unrest eased, the Tory government yielded slightly to the pressure for reform. We have already seen how Foreign Secretary Canning by 1822 had deserted Metternich's reactionary Concert of Europe and aided independence movements in Latin America and Greece. During the 1820s the navigation laws were somewhat relaxed and the tariff slightly lowered. The Combination Laws were partially repealed, permitting laborers to organize unions, though not to strike. The civil disabilities against nonconforming Protestants and Roman Catholics were removed, permitting them to participate in political life on an equal basis with Anglicans. These measures, however, welcome as they were, did not get at the fundamental issue: a broadening of popular participation in the government. The pressure for suffrage reform would continue to mount, particularly from the industrial bourgeoisie, which was rapidly gaining in wealth.

7. REACTION AND REPRESSION IN RUSSIA

Even Russia had not escaped the influence of the French Revolution and Napoleon. Russia had joined in the second, third, fourth, and fifth coalitions against France, had been invaded and ravaged as far as Moscow in 1812, and had played a major role in the wars of liberation against Napoleon in 1813–1814. Meanwhile, the young tsar, Alexander I, and many of his aristocratic young army officers had picked up romantic and liberal ideas from the West. But Russia was not yet ripe for Western liberalism. It was a vast agricultural nation with a feudal social structure and a very small urban bourgeoisie that could serve as a liberal base. The Orthodox Christian church, dominated by an upper clergy drawn from the aristocracy, was a handy governmental agency for controlling the masses. The unstable Alexander I soon fell under the influence of Metternich and of his own reactionary boyar magnates and repented of his liberalism.

There was no trace of romanticism whatever in Nicholas I, Alexander's younger brother, who succeeded him in 1825. Nicholas was a handsome, austere autocrat whose military career wedded him to the concepts of discipline and authority. A quixotic revolt by a group of young liberal officers on the occasion of his ascension to the throne and a full-scale revolt by his Polish subjects in 1831 further embittered him against liberalism in any form. Both revolts were crushed with an iron hand. For thirty years (1825–1855) Nicholas I was to stand as the perfect symbol of absolute reaction and the armed guardian of the Metternich system. When at the end of the nineteenth century Russia did begin to yield to liberal and revolutionary forces, it was with disorder and violence.

8. CONSERVATISM AND THE CHALLENGE OF LIBERALISM

Between 1815 and 1830 the forces of conservatism were dominant. They acted both in reaction to the events of the French Revolution and the era of Napoleon and in accordance with their own ideology—a set of beliefs and policies in support of a traditional Christian, ranked, aristocratic society wedded to old institutions and suspicious of change. In the international field this conservatism was epitomized by Metternich's policies, the Holy Alliance, and the concert of Europe. In domestic politics, this conservatism was characterized by the restoration of power to the traditional monarchs and aristocrats, the renewed influence of Christianity, and the suppression of liberal and nationalistic movements. Yet conservatives were faced with formidable opponents even during the early years after the fall of Napoleon. The struggle between conservatism and liberalism, which would last into the twentieth century, had just begun.

SUGGESTED READING

General

F. Artz, *Reaction and Revolution, 1814–1832* (1968). The standard survey of the period.

R. Gildea, *Barricades and Borders: Europe 1800–1914* (1987). A good recent survey covering this period.

J. Weiss, *Conservatism in Europe, 1770–1945* (1977). A good analysis of conservatism in its broad context.

The Congress of Vienna

F. Bridge, *The Great Powers and the European States System, 1815–1914* (1980). Covers international developments of the whole period.

H. Nicolson, *The Congress of Vienna: A Study in Allied Unity 1812–22* (1970). An excellent volume on the subject.

The Bourbon Restoration in France

A. Jardin and A. J. Tudesq, *Restoration and Reaction* (1984). Covers France well.

P. Mansel, *Louis XVIII* (1981). A good biography.

Reaction in Central Europe

T. Hamerow, *Restoration, Revolution, and Reaction: Economics and Politics in Germany, 1815–1871* (1958). A respected, difficult analysis encompassing the period.

A. Sked, *The Decline and Fall of the Habsburg Empire, 1815–1918* (1989). A new interpretation stressing Habsburg strengths.

Conservatism in Great Britain

N. Gash, *Aristocracy and People. Britain, 1815–1867* (1979). A balanced coverage.

Reaction and Repression in Russia

A. Palmer, *Alexander I: Tsar of War and Peace* (1974). A thorough biography.

A. Ulam, *Russia's Failed Revolutionaries* (1981). Contains a good analysis of the Decembrists.

CHAPTER 43

Liberalism and Revolution, 1830–1850

FIGURE 43.1 The Reform Bill of 1832 This engraving from the April 15, 1832, issue of *Bell's Weekly Messenger* depicts the successful struggle to enact the liberal Reform Bill of 1832 in Great Britain. At the top, under the banner of reform, Whig leaders unite with the king to pass the bill. At the bottom, the British lion uses reform to defeat the fleeing Tories and the dragon representing the rotten borough system. (The Mansell Collection)

During the Restoration years following the defeat of Napoleon, liberalism was suppressed by the conservatives who came back into power. Between 1830 and 1850 liberals gained a series of victories, often by way of revolutions or threatened revolutions, marking this period as a heyday for liberalism (see Map 43.1). By the early 1830s Greece, Belgium, and most of Spain's New World colonies had gained their freedom. The restored French Bourbons had been overthrown in a liberal revolt. In Great Britain the Reform Bill of 1832 marked a new liberal era. A new constitution in 1834 brought liberal institutions to Spain. Liberal revolts and movements had at least raised their heads in Poland, Italy, and parts of Germany. By 1850 liberal institutions had spread and revolutions, almost all of which included strong liberal elements, had occurred in nearly every country of continental Europe.

1. THE GENERAL NATURE OF NINETEENTH-CENTURY LIBERALISM

Liberalism is a difficult term to define. It has various shades and from time to time changes its complexion. During the nineteenth century, liberalism had developed into an ideology—a loose set of beliefs about the world and how it should be.

The roots of liberalism stretch back through the French Revolution and the Enlightenment to the seventeenth-century political thoughts of John Locke and others. At the base of liberalism was a belief in individualism. Liberals optimistically believed that individuals, unaided and free from outside forces or institutions, should pursue their own interests. Individuals deserved equality before the law and the right to embark on careers open to talent. Government should be constitutional and based on popular sovereignty. The people should be represented by an elected legislature to which government ministers would be responsible. Government should be limited in its powers, with such individual freedoms as freedom of the press, of speech, and of assembly guaranteed. The role of the government should be that of a passive police officer, enforcing laws and contracts. Government should interfere in economic life as little as pos-

sible, leaving that realm to private enterprise. Liberals were also anticlerical; that is, they opposed interference in government by organized religion. During the first half of the nineteenth century, liberals were usually nationalists, since nationalism at that time was primarily concerned with freeing peoples from alien rule and uniting them under one flag, and nationalism seemed consistent with popular sovereignty, constitutional government, and people's rights. Liberals, particularly during the first half of the nineteenth century, were not democrats; liberals wanted to limit the right to vote to those holding wealth and the educated. Only later in the nineteenth century did liberals begin to favor universal male suffrage.

Liberals typically came from the middle class—the commercial and industrial bourgeoisie, the professionals, and the intellectuals. Their chief opponents were the vested interests of traditional society—the aristocracy, the clergy, and the military—seeking to retain their favored positions. The peasantry was still generally conservative, strongly influenced by the clergy and sometimes by the aristocracy, and not very active in politics. Liberals were sometimes contemptuous of the propertyless masses below, forming alliances with them against conservatives only so far as necessary. Middle-class liberals' contempt for those below them was often a mask for fear; their contempt of the aristocrats above them was tinged with envy.

Liberals stood in contrast to conservatives. Liberals were optimistic about the individual; conservatives were pessimistic. Liberals had great faith in reason; conservatives argued that reason was too abstract. Liberals favored many of the ideas and reforms of the Enlightenment and French Revolution; conservatives attacked them. Liberals valued the individual over society; conservatives felt the individual was secondary. For liberals the state was an agent of the people; for conservatives the state was a growing organism not to be tampered with.

After 1850 the nature of liberalism would change. The outcomes of the revolutions occurring between 1848 and 1850 were a blow to liberals. As commerce and industry spread, the bourgeoisie acquired wealth and power, and soon the vested interests of this class made it more hostile to rapid political and social changes.

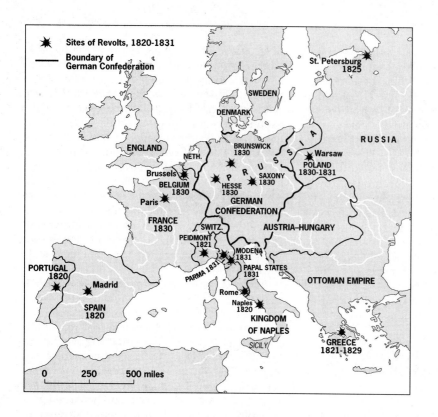

Sites of Revolts, 1820-1831

— **Boundary of German Confederation**

St. Petersburg 1825

SWEDEN

DENMARK

RUSSIA

ENGLAND

NETH.

BRUNSWICK 1830

Warsaw

Brussels

P R U S S I A

POLAND 1830-1831

BELGIUM 1830

HESSE 1830

SAXONY 1830

Paris

GERMAN CONFEDERATION

FRANCE 1830

SWITZ.

AUSTRIA–HUNGARY

PEIDMONT 1821

MODENA 1831

PARMA 1831

PAPAL STATES 1831

OTTOMAN EMPIRE

PORTUGAL 1820

Madrid

Rome

SPAIN 1820

Naples 1820

KINGDOM OF NAPLES

SICILY

GREECE 1821-1829

0   250   500 miles

Sites of Revolts, 1848-1849

— **Boundary of German Confederation**

SWEDEN

DENMARK

RUSSIA

ENGLAND

NETH.

Berlin

BELGIUM

Frankfurt

P R U S S I A

SAXONY

Paris

GERMAN CONFEDERATION

Prague

FRANCE

Vienna

Budapest

SWITZ.

Milan

AUSTRIA–HUNGARY

Novara

Venice

Turin

Custozza

PORTUGAL

Florence

PAPAL STATES

SPAIN

Rome

OTTOMAN EMPIRE

Naples

KINGDOM OF NAPLES

Palermo

SICILY

0   250   500 miles

Map 43.1 EUROPEAN REVOLTS, 1820–1831 AND 1848–1849 The first map indicates the location and dates of revolts, both major and minor, taking place between 1820 and 1831. The second map indicates the location of revolutions between 1848 and 1849. While the specifics of each outburst differed, most involved demands for liberal reform. Together, these maps reveal the geographical breadth of revolutionary activity during this period.

Its place in movements for political and social change was taken by the industrial working class, which was slowly becoming politically active. Groups deriving from the working classes, lower middle classes, and intelligentsia began to advocate greatly increased government intervention in economic affairs on behalf of the masses as well as the participation of the masses in political life. More progressive advocates of liberalism joined these groups in arguing for greater democratization of political life and government intervention in economic and social affairs. This, however, takes us beyond the primary concerns of this chapter. Liberalism flowered between 1830 and 1850, and this story needs to be told.

2. POLITICAL AND SOCIAL REFORM IN GREAT BRITAIN

During the 1820s Great Britain had already taken some moderate steps on the road to liberal reform (see pp. 546–547), but these steps did not go to the heart of the matter—broadening the franchise. Pressures mounted on the conservative Tories to effect electoral reform, but they were unwilling or unable to do it. Finally in 1830 the aristocratic but more liberal Whigs, long out of power, drove the Tory government from office.

The new prime minister, Earl Grey, immediately introduced and forced through Parliament the Reform Bill of 1832 (see Figure 43.1). This bill redistributed the seats of the House of Commons, taking many away from the "rotten boroughs" (once-important towns that had dwindled in population or even disappeared) and giving them to the industrial cities of the north. The suffrage was extended to all those who owned or rented property with an annual value of ten pounds. It is estimated that the number of eligible voters was thereby increased from approximately four hundred fifty thousand to eight hundred thousand out of a total population of some 16 million. Although on the surface the Reform Bill of 1832 appears innocuous, it represents a great turning point in British history. The long era of dominance of the conservative landed aristocracy was ending, and that of more liberal property owners, including the commercial and industrial bourgeoisie, had begun. The supremacy of the House of Commons over the House of

Lords, which had opposed the Reform Bill, was established. A new period of political and social reform had opened.

Both political parties recognized the new era. The Whig party, supported by the industrial bourgeoisie but containing a right wing of liberal aristocrats and left wing of intellectual radicals, changed its name to the Liberal party. For the next half century the Liberals were often in power, under the leadership of such personalities as Lord Grey, Lord John Russell, Viscount Palmerston, and eventually William E. Gladstone. The Tory party was still predominantly the party of the landed aristocracy, but it contained some bourgeois elements, and its more liberal wing, led first by Sir Robert Peel and later by Benjamin Disraeli, was now in ascendancy. The somewhat discredited "Tory" designation was changed to "Conservative."

Both parties, conscious of the rising importance of public opinion, supported a series of reforms. In 1833 slavery was abolished in the British Empire with compensation for slave owners. The Municipal Corporations Act applied the principles of the Reform Bill of 1832 to local government. The old penal code was reformed, reducing the number of capital offenses and generally softening the punishment of criminals. The penny post increased the circulation of mail and literature. Parliament granted small but gradually increasing subsidies to the schools, most of which were run by the Anglican church. Between 1833 and 1847 Parliament passed a series of laws that prohibited the employment in textile mills of children under nine and limited the hours of older children and women to ten hours a day. The employment of women and children in underground mines was prohibited. In 1846 the Corn Laws (the import tariff on grain), long opposed by liberals and the object of a major reform movement, were repealed, reducing the price of bread.

These reforms were the work not of the masses but of wealthy middle-class and aristocratic liberals along with a few intellectual radicals. The only reform movement initiated by the laboring classes in this period was the Chartist movement (see Figure 43.2). The hard-pressed urban workers, bitterly aware that they had been bypassed by the Reform Bill of 1832 and that they were not sharing in the unprecedented national prosperity, were dissatisfied with the reforms of

FIGURE 43.2 Chartist Print This print shows Chartists in a powerful but peaceful procession in London. (The Mansell Collection)

the bourgeois liberals. In 1838 working-class leaders drew up a People's Charter, which demanded (1) universal male suffrage, (2) the secret ballot, (3) removal of property qualifications for members of Parliament, (4) pay for members of Parliament, (5) annual elections, and (6) equal electoral districts. The charter was twice presented to Parliament and twice summarily rejected. In 1848, the Chartists planned a huge petition and demonstration in London. The frightened government prepared to use force. However, only a few mild disorders followed the third rejection, and the movement came to an end. Nevertheless, the Chartist movement had its influence. The most immediate result of the movement was to make both political parties aware of the growing influence of the working classes and the advisability of winning their favor. In the following decades, all the demands in the charter were enacted into law.

3. LIBERAL REVOLUTIONS IN BELGIUM AND FRANCE

The year 1830 was a bad one for conservatives in Belgium and France. The union forced upon Belgium and the Netherlands at Vienna had never been a happy one, and Belgian discontent with Dutch rule had been mounting for fifteen years. In addition to differences in language, the Belgians were Roman Catholic, whereas the Dutch were predominantly Calvinist. The Belgian economy was based on industry, the Dutch on commerce. Belgium, more populous than the Netherlands, was not given its fair share of representation in the government. When the halfhearted efforts of the Dutch failed to suppress the revolt, Austria and Russia threatened to intervene in the interests of legitimacy and tranquillity. They were deterred by British and French support of Belgian independence, which

FIGURE 43.3 Honoré Daumier, *The Chamber of Deputies* This print by the French artist Daumier presents a satirical view of the French Chamber of Deputies during Louis-Philippe's July Monarchy. This governmental body, though clearly more liberal than its predecessor under Charles X, was dominated by the relatively wealthy, satisfied upper classes. (The Art Institute of Chicago)

was thus achieved. Belgium soon adopted a liberal constitution and would remain a liberal nation throughout the nineteenth century.

The July Revolution in France was an even more serious blow to conservatism. Liberals and the people of Paris had toppled the reactionary regime of Charles X, the last of the Bourbons. There was strong sentiment to form a republic, but a coalition of liberal legislators and leaders of the wealthy bourgeoisie wanted only a constitutional monarchy. They set themselves up as a provisional government and named a new king: Louis-Philippe (1830–1848), head of the house of Orléans and a cousin of the departed Bourbon.

Louis-Philippe, recognizing that a new era had come to France, catered to the rich. He assumed the role of Citizen King, casting aside the

trappings of royalty and donning those of the Parisian upper middle class. His eighteen-year reign came to be called the bourgeois monarchy (see Figure 43.3). His twofold policy, from which he never veered, was order and prosperity at home and peace abroad. One of his first acts was to lower the taxpaying requirements for voting from three hundred francs to two hundred francs per year. This act raised the electorate from approximately one hundred thousand to two hundred fifty thousand in a nation of some 32 million people and placed political control into the hands of the wealthy. Louis-Philippe's chief minister during the 1840s was the historian François Guizot, a thoroughgoing liberal who believed in government by the property-owning classes, particularly the bourgeoisie, and therefore opposed any further extension of the suffrage, even to members of the intelligentsia like himself.

Beneath the surface, problems simmered. The national prosperity was not shared by the working class, who suffered the usual hardships, insecurity, and maladjustments that accompanied the advent of industrialization. Slums mushroomed in Paris and the industrial cities of the northeast. Workers clamored for the right to vote and the right to organize unions but got neither. Poor harvests, financial crises, and growing unemployment in 1846 and 1847 heightened the frustration.

4. THE REVOLUTION OF 1848 IN FRANCE

The mounting discontent came to a climax in February 1848 when the government prohibited the holding of a reform banquet. Street brawling broke out in Paris. Louis-Philippe attempted to quiet people by dismissing Guizot, but the appeasement failed. A shot fired during a brawl between a mob and the troops guarding the residence of Guizot unnerved the troops, who fired a murderous volley into the mob and set off a full-scale insurrection. Barricades flew up all over Paris, and when the disaffected national guardsmen began going over to the rebels, Louis-Philippe followed Guizot into exile in Great Britain.

The working classes of Paris had triumphed, but only for a fleeting moment. A group of bourgeois liberals led by Alphonse de Lamartine hastily set up a provisional government that was republican in sentiment but in which the only prominent radical member was the socialist Louis Blanc. The provisional government immediately called for the election by universal male suffrage of an assembly to draw up a new constitution. Under the pressure of the Paris populace, the provisional government admitted the workingmen to the national guard, thereby arming them, and set up national workshops for emergency relief. The workshops, however, were a parody of those outlined by Louis Blanc, who cried that they were deliberately planned so as to ensure their failure. Workers of all kinds were assigned to hastily arranged projects, and when more workers enrolled than could be used, the

surplus workers were paid almost as much to remain idle. Tens of thousands rushed to Paris to join the workshops. The resulting demoralization of labor and the cost to the taxpayers thoroughly frightened all property owners, the peasants as well as the bourgeoisie. The elections held in April 1848 resulted in an overwhelming victory for the conservative republicans and limited monarchists, in part thanks to the conservatism of the landowning peasants, who constituted the great majority of the French population. The socialists were crushed. Even in Paris, their only real stronghold, they won a mere handful of seats.

One of the first acts of the newly elected Constitutional Assembly was to abolish the national workshops. The workers were told either to join the army or to go look for work in the provinces. The desperate Paris working class resorted to arms and the barricades: "Better to die from bullets than from starvation!" For four days all-out war raged in the streets of Paris between the working class, armed with national guard rifles, and the regular army of the conservative constitutional assembly, using artillery in addition to small arms. When the last barricade had been destroyed, some fifteen hundred, mostly workingmen, had been killed. Several hundred were sent overseas to French colonial prisons. Louis Blanc fled to Great Britain. The bloody "June Days" widened the cleavage between radical urban Paris and conservative rural France—a cleavage that has long complicated France's public life.

The inexperienced constitutional assembly hurriedly drew up a constitution establishing the Second French Republic. (The First French Republic had been declared by the revolutionists in 1792 and had been overthrown by Napoleon in 1804.) Legislative power was given to a single-chamber legislature elected by universal male suffrage. All executive and administrative powers were placed in the hands of a president, also elected by universal male suffrage. The first presidential election, in December 1848, resulted in a sweeping victory for Louis-Napoleon Bonaparte, nephew of Napoleon Bonaparte, as president. It took this ambitious and clever politician only three years to destroy the weak constitution and to take power in a coup d'état.

The Revolution of 1848 in France involved the first violent reaction of the urban working class

FIGURE 43.4 Revolution in Germany In central Europe in 1848, liberal sentiment emerged in the form of public demonstrations by the intelligentsia—particularly the university students. Here, in June 1848, German students convene at Wartburg, the castle that had once served as a refuge for Martin Luther. (Copyright Staatsbibliothek, Berlin)

against bourgeois liberalism. The working class was too small as yet to make any headway outside Paris. The revolution shattered against the solid mass of landowning peasantry allied with the propertied bourgeoisie. Its bloody suppression left a heritage of bitterness that would cloud the future of France.

5. THE REVOLUTION OF 1848 IN CENTRAL EUROPE

The February explosion in Paris set central Europe aflame with revolt (see Figure 43.4). However, the Revolution of 1848 in central Europe was a rising of the intelligentsia and the middle classes with a little support from the working class. Furthermore, in 1848 the cause of liberalism in central Europe was entwined with that of nationalism. The two forces frequently conflicted with each other, nationalism proving to be the more virile of the two.

The most crucial center of revolution was Vienna. This beautiful metropolis was the seat of the Hapsburg government, which not only ruled over the various language groups of the Austrian Empire but also dominated both the German Confederation and Italy. When early in March 1848 news of the events in Paris arrived in Vienna, the long-repressed student liberals began rioting in the streets and clamoring for an end to the Metternich system. As the uprising gained in momentum, Metternich was forced to flee for his life. The Hapsburg emperor, Ferdinand I, hastily abolished the repressive laws, ended serfdom, and promised constitutional representative government. However, he too was soon forced to flee his own capital. Meanwhile, the Magyars in Hungary, under the leadership of the eloquent Louis Kossuth, set up a liberal autonomous Hungary. The Czechs did the same in Bohemia and called for a Pan-Slavic congress to meet at Prague. In Austria's Italian provinces of Lombardy and Venetia the rebellious populace drove the Austrian garrisons into defensive fortresses and declared their independence. By June 1848 it appeared that the Hapsburg Empire would become liberalized, fall apart along national (language group) lines, or both.

In Berlin, the capital of Prussia, the news from Paris and Vienna set liberals demonstrating in the streets. The vacillating Hohenzollern king, Frederick William IV, promised a liberal constitution and support for German national unity. As in Paris, an unauthorized volley into the mob set off bloody street fighting, which the king ended by making further concessions to the liberals. Hohenzollern Prussia, like Hapsburg Austria, appeared for the moment to be on the road to liberal government.

Meanwhile, in the rest of the German states a group of self-appointed liberals called for a popularly elected assembly to meet at Frankfurt to construct a liberal German nation. The two questions confronting the Frankfurt Assembly were whether the German-speaking portions of the multilingual Hapsburg Empire should be included in the projected German nation and who should head the new nation. Tied in with the Austrian question was that of religion. With Austria (and Bohemia, which was alleged to be predominantly German), the Roman Catholics would predominate, and without Austria and Bohemia, the Protestants. For eleven precious months these knotty problems were debated. Eventually Austria virtually excluded itself by refusing to consider coming into the new German nation without its non-German provinces. By a narrow margin it was decided to offer the emperorship to the king of Prussia. But now it was too late, for the situation in Vienna and Berlin had changed drastically.

In Austria the inexperience and weakness of the liberals and the rivalries and conflicts among the various language groups played into the hands of the Hapsburgs. Skillfully playing off one group against another, the Austrian rulers beat down the liberal and national revolts one after the other. In Hungary they had the help of the reactionary Nicholas I of Russia, whose army crushed the rebels.

In Prussia, too, the liberals were weak and inexperienced. The unstable Frederick William IV, after his first uncertainty, gradually fell under the influence of his militaristic and reactionary Junker advisers. Further stiffened by the news from Vienna that the Hapsburgs had regained their autocratic position, he spurned the German crown offered him by the Frankfurt Assembly and replaced the constitution drawn up by Prussian liberals with one that was a travesty of liberalism.

The Hohenzollerns' rejection of the crown of a united liberal Germany blasted the hopes of the Frankfurt Assembly. When a few of the most determined attempted to continue their efforts, they were dispersed by Prussian troops.

6. REVOLUTION IN ITALY

On the Italian peninsula 1848 was a year of revolution. These revolts reflected an already long history of liberal and nationalistic movements in Italy. Soon after 1815 Italian nationalists began to form secret societies called *Carbonari* (charcoal burners), which met at night around charcoal fires to plot freedom from Austrian and local tyranny and to plan for national unification. In 1821 revolts erupted in Naples, Sicily, and Piedmont, but all were short-lived. In the early 1830s a romantic young intellectual, Giuseppe Mazzini (1805–1872), organized the Young Italy society, which was dedicated to the task of achieving a free, united Italian nation. Although the first uprisings inspired by the Carbonari and Young Italy were crushed by Austrian arms, the Italian national movement, once aroused, could not so easily be suppressed.

In 1848 revolutions occurred in Sicily, Naples, Piedmont, and Tuscany. By 1849 republics had been established in Rome and Venice, and other Italian states had adopted liberal constitutions. Yet the time for the permanent overthrow of

Austrian rule and the unification of Italy had not yet arrived. Austrian arms (and, in Rome, French arms) prevailed. It would be another ten years before liberalism and nationalism, under the leadership of Piedmont, would gain a more lasting victory in Italy.

7. AN ASSESSMENT

The struggles between liberals and conservatives, which had resulted in several liberal victories since 1830, came to a climax with the revolutions of 1848. Economic turmoil, demands for liberal reform, nationalistic sentiments, and ineptitude by frightened governments combined to spell a series of stunning victories for revolutionaries in almost every major country in Europe. The major exceptions were England, which had compromised in response to demands for liberal reform, and Russia, which remained the bastion of reaction. Once in power, the revolutionaries initiated major reforms, most of which fit well with the recognized canons of liberalism.

Nevertheless, the revolutionaries' victories were short-lived. By 1850 the conservative forces of order had regained control. Louis-Napoleon, soon to be Napoleon III, sat as president in France. The Prussian king regained control over his lands and ended hopes for a liberal unified German nation. In Austria and Hungary the Hapsburgs were again in power, just as they were in their Italian lands. Liberalism and nationalism were not yet strong enough to form new, lasting governments in these areas.

Several factors account for the defeat of liberal and nationalist forces, though the situation differed in each case. First, the alliance among middle-class liberals, radicals, socialists, artisans, and workers was one of convenience. Once revolutionary forces were in power, the interests of the various groups were too divergent for the alliance to hold. This division was most clearly evident in France, where the frightened middle class and conservative peasantry broke with the Parisian working classes, as revealed by the outcome of the elections and the bloody June Days. Second, liberalism and nationalism were forces that worked together when out of power; once in power they often were at cross-purposes. This lack of harmony between liberalism and nationalism was particularly pronounced in central Europe, where the aspirations of German, Polish, Magyar, Croatian, Serbian, and other nationalities conflicted with efforts to form new governments with liberal institutions. Third, the strength of conservatism and the forces of order should not be underestimated. With industrialization only beginning in central Europe, the main source of liberal strength, the industrial middle class, and an important source of revolutionary urban discontent, the working class, were weak. Revolutionary liberal leaders were inexperienced, particularly in central Europe and Italy. Once the shock of initial defeat was over, experienced conservatives marshaled their resources, and forces of order overcame the now divided revolutionary forces.

The reestablished governments had learned lessons from 1848 and maintained themselves with new vigor. In a few cases liberal reforms initiated between 1848 and 1850 were retained, and in other cases those reforms in modified form would be passed in succeeding years. But the great period of revolutionary liberalism ended in 1850.

SUGGESTED READING

General

C. Church, *Europe in 1830: Revolution and Political Change* (1983). A good starting point.

W. L. Langer, *Political Upheaval, 1832–1852* (1969). An excellent survey of the period.

Liberalism

A. Arblaster, *The Rise and Decline of Western Liberalism* (1986). A good recent account.

J. Gray, *Liberalism* (1986). An effective introduction.

Reform in Great Britain

D. Beales, *From Castlereagh to Gladstone, 1815–1885* (1969). A useful study of political history.

M. Brock, *The Great Reform Act* (1974). Solid, scholarly, respected.

D. Thompson, *The Chartists: Popular Politics in the Industrial Revolution* (1984). A thorough recent study.

The Bourgeois Monarchy in France

A. Jardin and A. Tudesq, *Restoration and Reaction, 1815–1848* (1984). A thorough coverage of France.

D. Pinkney, *The French Revolution of 1830* (1972). An excellent study of the topic.

Central Europe and Italy

I. Deak, *The Lawful Revolution: Louis Kossuth and the Hungarians, 1848–9* (1979). An excellent study of the individual and the revolution.

T. Hamerow, *Restoration, Revolution, Reaction 1815–1871* (1966). A highly respected analysis of Germany.

S. Wolf, *A History of Italy, 1700–1986* (1986). A good general account.

The Revolutions of 1848

M. Agulhon, *The Republican Experiment, 1848–1852* (1983). An excellent analysis of all aspects of the revolutions.

G. Duveau, *1848: The Making of a Revolution* (1967). An excellent study of the 1848 revolutions in France.

L. B. Namier, *1848: The Revolution of the Intellectuals* (1964). An eminent historian shows how nationalism wrecked the liberal movement.

P. Stearns, *1848: The Revolutionary Tide in Europe* (1974). A good summary.

CHAPTER 44

Nationalism and the Nation-State, 1850–1871

FIGURE 44.1 Garibaldi Landing in Sicily The period between 1850 and 1870 was marked by a strong growth of nationalism and the successful unification of Italy and Germany. Here the lifelong nationalist Garibaldi is heroically portrayed landing in Sicily in 1860 as part of the struggle for Italian unification. (Historical Pictures Service, Chicago)

By 1850 many of the revolutionaries' liberal and nationalistic aspirations were dashed as conservative, authoritarian rulers came to power. However, nationalism as a dynamic force remained powerful and would continue to increase in strength during the nineteenth and twentieth centuries. Between 1850 and 1871 almost all political leaders, whether liberal or conservative, recognized the strength of nationalism. Nationalism's political impact was manifested most dramatically in Louis-Napoleon's rise to power in France and in the successful struggles for national unification in Italy and Germany. More broadly, nationalism played a crucial role in the growing authority of the nation-state. Increasingly, central governments had to justify and bolster their authority by reference to a nation of citizens rather than dynastic links to the past. The period from 1850 to 1871, then, marks a time when nationalism grew from earlier roots to become a dominant force in Western political life and when the nation-state took on new authority and new functions.

1. THE NATURE OF NATIONALISM

Nationalism may be defined as feelings of common cultural identity and loyalty to one's country. What are the essential factors that contribute to these feelings? What makes a person a German or a Pole, even when there is no German or Polish national state?

The most important factor is language. Language brings people together in understanding and separates them from those they cannot understand. Probably second in importance is a historical tradition of unity. The Belgians with their two languages and the Swiss with their three languages and two religions illustrate the importance of this factor. Religion can be a powerful factor, too, though not so important as language. The German Empire with its common language came and held together in spite of a serious religious cleavage, and the Austrian Empire fell apart along language lines in spite of a common religion and a long tradition of unity under the Hapsburgs. Territorial compactness and natural boundaries frequently contribute to nationalism.

Until the French Revolution, national loyalty was chiefly centered on the ruling monarch or dynasty and was limited for the most part to the educated upper classes who participated in the government of the nation. The French Revolution gave birth to a new and more virile kind of nationalism. The establishment of equal rights and popular representative government, together with the abolition of old provincial boundary lines, brought the masses of people into direct partnership with the national government. Universal conscription into the revolutionary armies gave the people a sense of fraternity in a righteous cause—a crusade. Nationalism acquired the attributes of a religion. Such mass dynamism helped make the revolutionary and Napoleonic armies irresistible.

Nationalism soon spread to the other peoples of Europe. In the decades following the Napoleonic era industrialization and policies toward industrialization were becoming connected with nationalism. The revolutions of 1848 clearly demonstrated the revolutionary potential of nationalism. By midcentury nationalism had grown from its deeper roots to become entwined with the central political, economic, and social forces of modern times.

2. THE SECOND EMPIRE OF NAPOLEON III

In France, Louis-Napoleon Bonaparte blended support from below, reform, and authoritarian nationalism in his Second Empire, which was established in 1852 and lasted until 1870. Louis-Napoleon was originally elected president of France's Second Republic in 1848. He benefited from his illustrious name, his appeal to property owners longing for order, and his well-publicized promises to link democracy from below with reforming leadership from above. When the National Assembly refused to change the constitution so that he could run for a second term, he organized a coup d'état and seized power on December 2, 1851. Resistance was limited, though thousands were arrested and deported. He quickly granted universal male suffrage, and during the following year he held two plebiscites in which over 90 percent of the voters supported him and made him hereditary emperor—Napoleon III.

Under the new constitution, most power re-

FIGURE 44.2 Rebuilding Paris under Napoleon III Under Napoleon III, numerous slums and old, winding streets were torn down to make room for new, wide boulevards. The boulevards made it easier for authorities to maintain order and more difficult for revolutionaries to raise barricades. (The Mansell Collection)

sided in the emperor. Although there was an elected legislative body, it could not initiate legislation or exert control over Napoleon III's ministers. The emperor controlled elections by manipulating the electoral machinery, exerting official pressure, and supporting official candidates. He kept the press under scrutiny. Thus politically the Second Empire was clearly authoritarian, at least during the 1850s.

It was also during the 1850s that Napoleon III enjoyed his greatest successes. Economically France prospered, in part thanks to Napoleon III's policies. He encouraged industrialization and economic growth by promoting railroad construction, public works, and financial institutions. Two giant investment banking corporations, the Crédit Mobilier and the Crédit Foncier, mobilized huge amounts of capital for industry,

railroads, and real estate. The Bank of France expanded until each of the country's eighty-six departments had at least one branch. Georges Haussmann, the prefect of Paris, had large parts of Paris torn down and rebuilt (see Figure 44.2). With a new sewer system, new parks, and new wide boulevards, Paris took on an envied image that would last well into the twentieth century.

Napoleon III also encouraged educational and social reforms, thereby increasing his popularity among a variety of groups. Hospitals, nurseries, and homes for the aged were built. Government subsidies kept the price of bread low. A system of voluntary social insurance for workers was instituted. Cooperatives were encouraged, and labor unions with limited rights to strike were partially legalized for the first time.

The peak of France's revived national prestige was reached during the Crimean War (1854–1856). Like his uncle, the second Napoleon was not satisfied with spectacular domestic achievements. His opportunity for glory in foreign affairs came when Tsar Nicholas I of Russia attempted to dismember the Ottoman Empire, "the sick man of Europe," and to achieve Russia's historic goal: Constantinople and access to the world through the Turkish Straits. France did not relish the prospect of an ambitious new rival in the Mediterranean. (Great Britain, with its vast holdings and interests in the Near and Far East, was even more sensitive to this threat than was France.) A second source of Franco-Russian conflict arose when the tsar, as the great champion of Orthodox Christianity, attempted to gain a protectorate over all Christians in the Ottoman Empire and over the Christian holy places in the Turkish province of Palestine. Since the Crusades France had been the leading champion of Catholic interests in the Near East, including the Christian shrines in the Holy Land. And Napoleon III's strongest ally in France was the Catholic church.

In 1853 the Russian army and navy suddenly attacked the Turks. Early the next year Great Britain and France sent their naval and military forces into the Black Sea and laid siege to Russia's naval base, Sebastopol, on the Crimean Peninsula. Sardinia came into the war to gain the friendship of France and Great Britain. Austria maintained a hostile and Prussia a friendly neutrality toward Russia. The war was fought with gross inefficiency on both sides. The only real hero was the British nurse Florence Nightingale, whose efforts helped to inspire the creation of the International Red Cross a few years later (1864).

Nicholas I died in 1855, humiliated by the knowledge that his creaking military machine was going to fail. The Peace of Paris in 1856 prohibited Russia's naval forces on the Black Sea and maintained the integrity of the Ottoman Empire. The autonomy of Serbia and the Rumanian provinces of Moldavia and Wallachia under the suzerainty of Turkey was guaranteed by the great powers. The Catholics were left in control of their shrines in the Holy Land. Great Britain at long last agreed to neutral rights on the high seas.

The chief loser of the Crimean War was Russia, whose massive military no longer looked so formidable. But more broadly a loss was suffered by the already crumbling Concert of Europe, which could no longer wield significant influence on behalf of a conservative international status quo. An immediate beneficiary of the Crimean War was Napoleon III. He played host to the peace conference and, of course, made it into a colorful spectacle. French nationalism and international prestige rose to new heights.

By 1859 Napoleon III had obtained not only the loyalty of the great majority of his own people but also some hegemony in the affairs of the European continent. France was prosperous and powerful. Then things began to go wrong. The dynamic force of nationalism, which he understood and used so well in France, he greatly underestimated abroad. In his efforts to control the Italian and German national movements he failed dismally—in the latter case fatally.

The first serious blunder came in 1859, when he made war on Austria in behalf of Italian freedom. The defeat of Austria set off a frenzy of Italian nationalism that threatened to dispossess all the rulers of the local states of Italy, including the pope. This situation alarmed and angered the French Roman Catholics, who blamed Napoleon. But when the French emperor deserted the Italian nationalists in the midst of the campaign, with the agreed-upon job only half done, he further alienated the French liberals, who were already unsympathetic to him.

Napoleon's efforts to create an overseas empire brought France little immediate profit and much trouble. The most ambitious and disastrous was his attempted conquest and control of Mexico. In 1862 he joined with Great Britain and Spain and seized several Mexican ports, ostensibly to collect debts owed by the revolutionary Juárez government. As soon as the British and Spaniards saw that Napoleon had more ambitious plans in mind, they withdrew. The French armies then marched on to Mexico City, drove the Juárez government into the hinterland, and set up a Hapsburg prince, Maximilian, as puppet emperor for France. The government of the United States protested vigorously in the name of the Monroe Doctrine, but embroiled in its own Civil War, it could do no more. As soon as the Civil War ended early in 1865, the American government dispatched victorious Union troops to the Mexican border. Napoleon III, now hard-pressed at home, agreed to withdraw his troops. No sooner had the last French soldiers left Mexico City in 1867 than the Juárez forces captured and shot the well-meaning puppet emperor Maximilian. The Mexican fiasco added to the growing unpopularity of Napoleon III with the French people.

On the Continent, Napoleon III was attempting to slow the rapid growth of Prussia and to offset it by annexing territories on the left bank of the Rhine. His failures in this area of foreign policy would eventually prove fatal to his regime.

Meanwhile, the booming prosperity subsided after 1860. The Cobden Treaty, which lowered tariffs between Great Britain and France, flooded France with cheap British manufactured goods with which the less advanced French industries could not compete. The French textile industry also suffered heavily as a result of the American Civil War, which cut off its cotton supply. Both the industrial bourgeoisie and the proletariat were hard hit. Overexpansion and speculation began to take their toll.

The emperor attempted to allay the mounting discontent of liberals and workers. Beginning in 1859 he made one concession after another until by 1870 the Second Empire was, at least on paper, a limited constitutional monarchy with a liberal parliamentary government. But 1870 was too late. The showdown with Bismarck's rapidly forming German nation was at hand. The sick and discouraged Napoleon III blundered into a war with Germany for which his armies were woefully unprepared (see p. 571). He was defeated and captured, and his government was overthrown.

3. CAVOUR AND THE MAKING OF ITALIAN UNITY

For centuries Italy had been politically divided into various city-states, kingdoms, and provinces. After 1815 nationalistic sentiments and movements stirred throughout Italy. By 1848 three different plans for uniting Italy into a sovereign state had been developed; each had its own following. One plan was to make Italy a liberal democratic republic. This was the plan of Giuseppe Mazzini, an inspiring speaker and

writer but not a very practical organizer or man of action. His movement was called Young Italy. The second plan was to form an Italian confederacy under the leadership of the pope. The third plan was to make Italy a limited monarchy under the leadership of the House of Savoy, the ruling dynasty in Piedmont-Sardinia. During the Revolution of 1848, the first two plans were discredited. Mazzini's chaotic Roman Republic, which he set up after the rebellious populace had driven out the pope, outraged the Roman Catholic world and was overthrown by a French army of Louis-Napoleon. After this experience the pope bitterly opposed the unification of Italy, fearing that it would mean the loss of his political control over the Papal States.

At the same time, the heroic role played by Piedmont-Sardinia in battling the Austrians against hopeless odds won for the House of Savoy the devotion and confidence of Italian nationalists. However, the powerful Austrians were still in Lombardy and Venezia, the unsympathetic pope still ruled the Papal States, and the rest of the Italian states were weak and divided. Despite the new prestige of Sardinia, however, the task of uniting Italy required the work of a great political leader. He soon appeared: Camillo Benso, Count of Cavour (1810–1861).

Cavour was born into a well-to-do noble family of Piedmont. By the 1840s he was a successful businessman and had become enamored with moderate liberal ideas. Shortly before the Revolution of 1848, he founded a newspaper called *Il Risorgimento (The Resurgence)*, which never ceased to preach Italian unity. In 1850 Cavour was made minister of commerce and agriculture and two years later prime minister of Sardinia.

Cavour's goals were limited: to modernize Piedmont economically, to make Piedmont the center of the national unification movement, and to form a new Italian state as a constitutional monarchy rather than a democratic republic. To these ends, he worked to lower tariffs, build railroads, and balance Piedmont's budget. He supported the nationalistic Italian National Society, which worked toward national unification under Piedmont. Finally, he used diplomacy and Piedmont's relatively small army to gain international support and overcome the primary obstacle to unification—Austria.

Cavour sent Piedmont's army into the Crimean War in the hopes of winning French sympathy. The plan worked, and at the Paris Peace Conference in 1856 he was given an opportunity to state Italy's case against Austria impressively to the world. In 1858 Cavour and Napoleon met at Plombières, a French spa, and there Cavour persuaded Napoleon to fight Austria. Sardinia would provoke Austria into a declaration of war; France would help Sardinia drive the Austrians out of Lombardy and Venezia, which would then be annexed to the Kingdom of Sardinia. In payment Sardinia would cede the two little French-speaking provinces of Savoy and Nice to France.

When everything was in readiness in April 1859, Cavour easily provoked unsuspecting Austria into a declaration of war. To Austria's surprise, French armies poured across the Alps to fight alongside the Sardinians. In the two bloody battles of Magenta and Solferino, the Austrians were defeated and driven out of Lombardy. But to the dismay of Cavour, Napoleon suddenly made a separate peace with Austria (the Agreement of Villafranca) on condition that Sardinia receive Lombardy but not Venezia. Napoleon appears to have been motivated by the surprising bloodiness of the battles, the threatening attitude of Prussia, and the anger of the French Roman Catholics, who feared that the wild outburst of nationalism all over Italy following the victories over Austria threatened the independence of the Papal States. News of Magenta and Solferino set all Italy aflame with nationalistic fervor. Early in 1860, under Cavour's supporters, Tuscany, Modena, Parma, and Romagna (the northernmost of the Papal States) joined Piedmont, bringing together all of northern Italy except Venezia.

At this juncture, the rawboned Giuseppe Garibaldi, the most colorful of all the makers of the Italian nation, performed a daring exploit (see Figure 44.1). With a thousand civilian warriors dressed in red shirts and slouch hats, he sailed for southern Italy aboard two little Piedmontese ships. His goal was the conquest of the Kingdom of Naples, the largest and most populous of the Italian states, with a regular army of 124,000 men and a sizable navy. Cavour officially condemned the seemingly foolhardy expedition of the thousand but secretly aided it. Garibaldi's exploits read like a fairy story. He conquered the large island of Sicily, crossed the Strait of Messina, and entered triumphantly into Naples. The opposing troops had little heart for their cause and deserted to Garibaldi by the thousands after his first victories. Moving northward in the direction of Rome, Garibaldi defeated the last Neapolitan forces.

Not wanting to lose control of the situation and fearful that the daring but undiplomatic Garibaldi would march on Rome and bring down French armies, Cavour sent troops southward and seized all the pope's remaining territory except Rome and the territory immediately surrounding it. When Victor Emmanuel at the head of his army approached the forces of Garibaldi, the gallant warrior and patriot submitted to his king and retired to the rocky island of Caprera (see Figure 44.3). The Kingdom of Italy was formally declared in March 1861, with Victor Emmanuel II as king and the liberal Sardinian Constitution of 1848 as the national charter. The red, white, and green Sardinian flag now flew over all of Italy from the Alps to Sicily except Venezia and Rome (see Map 44.1). Those two provinces were not joined to the Italian state until 1866 and 1870, respectively, when, as we shall soon see, first Austria and then France were defeated by Prussia.

Cavour did not live to enjoy the fruits of his labors. Less than three months after the birth of his beloved Italian nation, he was dead. Paunchy, with ill-fitting glasses and a myopic stare, he was anything but impressive in appearance. Neither was he an orator. "I cannot make a speech," he once truthfully said, "but I can make Italy."

4. GERMAN UNIFICATION

During the 1850s both liberalism and nationalism began to make rapid headway in the German states. The area was industrialized rapidly. In Prussia the rise of a middle class, imbued with liberalism and German nationalism, challenged for the first time the dominance of the Junker aristocracy, who abhorred liberalism and whose national loyalty was limited to Prussia. The conversion of the Hohenzollerns and the Prussian Junkers to German nationalism was facilitated by the "Humiliation of Olmütz" in 1850. Shortly after the vacillating Frederick William IV had spurned the German national crown offered him by the Frankfurt Assembly in the spring of 1849,

FIGURE 44.3 Victor Emmanuel and Garibaldi This English engraving portrays King Victor Emmanuel and the heroic Garibaldi shaking hands in 1860, culminating the unification of Italy. (Culver Pictures)

he attempted to reorganize the German Confederation under Prussian leadership. The Hapsburg government of Austria, now completely recovered from its embarrassments of 1848–1849, mobilized its superior army and ordered him to cease. At the town of Olmütz in Austrian territory, the king of Prussia abjectly yielded. After this, the Hohenzollerns and more and more of the proud Junkers sought an opportunity to avenge the national insult to Prussia and replace Austria as leader of the Germanies (see Map 44.2).

In 1858 the unstable mind of Frederick William IV gave way, and his younger brother, who three years later became King William I, assumed leadership of the Prussian government as regent. Unlike his romantic, idealistic brother, William I was a militarist. His first move was to rejuvenate and greatly strengthen the Prussian military machine. The liberals, now strong in the Prussian Landtag, began to take alarm. Might not

this all-powerful military machine be used to suppress liberalism? The liberals hoped that by holding up the military budget they might bargain for a stronger role for the legislature in the Prussian government. In 1862, after several years of haggling, the liberals finally defeated the military budget. Liberalism and nationalism had collided head-on. William I, unskilled in and unsympathetic with parliamentary government, threatened to resign. As a last resort, he called to the chancellorship Otto Eduard Leopold von Bismarck (see Figure 44.4).

Bismarck would remain chancellor for the next twenty-eight years. He stamped his iron will and his domineering personality not only on Prussia and Germany but also to a considerable degree on the rest of Europe. Upon assuming the chancellorship of Prussia in 1862, Bismarck, with the backing of the king and army, defied the liberal opposition in the Landtag, violated the constitution, and illegally collected the funds

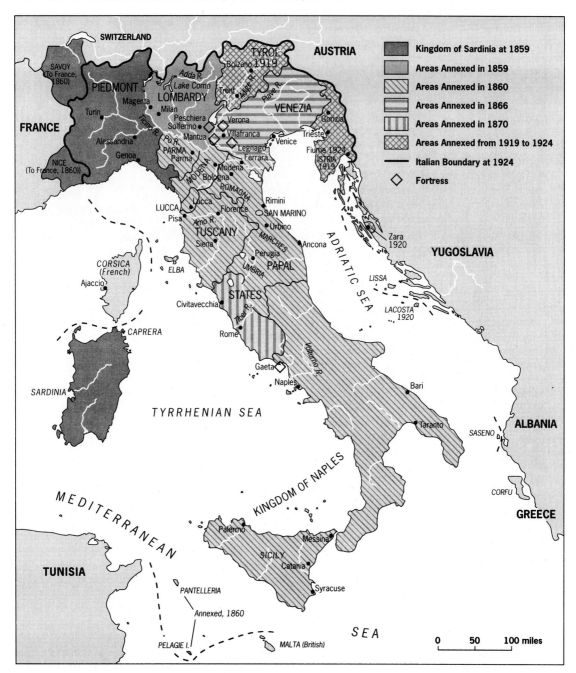

Map 44.1 **THE UNIFICATION OF ITALY** This map shows the various stages of Italian unification after 1859. Most of Italy was unified under the leadership of Piedmont by 1860. The new Italian nation took advantage of international affairs to gain other territories after 1860.

Map 44.2 THE UNIFICATION OF GERMANY During the 1860s Prussia won its struggle with Austria for leadership in Germany. Through wars and diplomatic maneuvering, Bismarck welded numerous German states into a single nation by 1871.

necessary for the military program. "Not by speeches and majority resolutions," said Bismarck, "are the great questions of the time decided"—that was the mistake of 1848 and 1849—"but by blood and iron." He came to be known as the "Iron Chancellor." Prussian liberalism was crushed. Bismarck believed that military victories won on foreign soil would turn the Prussian

liberals into fervent German nationalists. This prediction soon came true.

Bismarck lost little time in putting his new military machine to work. An opportunity soon presented itself in the form of a dispute with Denmark over the long-standing and complex Schleswig-Holstein question. Schleswig and Holstein were two little provinces lying between

FIGURE 44.4 Bismarck Otto Von Bismarck had little faith in democratic processes for achieving purposes of state. Rather, he trusted "blood and iron." The German Empire bore in large measure the stamp of his personality and ideals. (The Granger Collection)

Prussia and Denmark. Their population was partly German speaking and partly Danish speaking. Since 1815 they had been ruled by the king of Denmark, though they had not been incorporated into Denmark. In 1863 the Danish king suddenly annexed Schleswig outright. Bismarck, seeing an opportunity to test the Prussian army, to annex some territory, and also to embroil Austria, declared war on Denmark in 1864. Since Holstein was a member of the German Confederation, Austria also entered the war against Denmark lest the leadership of the confederation pass to Prussia. Denmark sued for peace, and Bismarck made the peace settlement as complicated as possible. Schleswig and Holstein were to be ruled jointly by Prussia and Austria.

Bismarck soon used this unworkable arrangement to stir up trouble with Austria. His first task

was to obtain the support or neutrality of the other three continental powers, Italy, Russia, and France. Prussia had been the first great power to recognize the new Kingdom of Italy. Now, promising Venezia as a prize, Bismarck drew the new nation into an alliance against Austria. It was always a cardinal principle of Bismarck to maintain friendly relations with Russia (at Prussia's back door). When Russia's Polish subjects revolted once more in 1863, Prussia alone of the great powers supported Russia. Bismarck neutralized Napoleon III by personal persuasion and deception. By the spring of 1866, with everything in readiness, Bismarck created by threats and maneuvers a state of alarm in Austria, finally manipulating Austria into a declaration of war.

In the Austro-Prussian War most of the little German states supported Austria. Their military forces, however, were quickly crushed beneath the Prussian steamroller. Prussia's armies overwhelmed Austria, a nation of twice the size and population of Prussia and long the dominant power in central Europe. Bismarck saw that Austria was now harmless to Prussia and would make a valuable ally or at least friend in Prussia's future wars. Restraining his king and his generals, he made the terms of the Treaty of Prague extremely lenient. Austria was to pay no indemnity and to accept the rearrangement of Germany by Prussia. Austria was also forced to cede Venetia to Italy as Italy's reward for fighting on the side of Prussia.

Following the victory over Austria, Bismarck reorganized Germany. Hanover, Nassau, Frankfurt, and Hesse-Cassel were annexed to Prussia outright, bridging the gap between Prussia's Rhine province and the main body. The remaining twenty-one states north of the Main River were bound to Prussia in a North German Confederation. The confederation was completely dominated by Prussia, which alone constituted four-fifths of its area and population. Prussia's king and prime minister were made president and chancellor of the confederation, for which Bismarck drafted the constitution.

Its government was fundamentally autocratic, despite some democratic and liberal forms. The chief administrative officer was the chancellor (Bismarck), who was responsible only to the king of Prussia as president, by whom he was appointed. The legislative body was composed of the Bundesrat, whose members were really ambassadors of the twenty-two state governments, and the Reichstag, whose members were elected by universal male suffrage. All new laws required the approval of both bodies. The Reichstag had no control over the chancellor and his cabinet, as in Great Britain, and little control over the budget and the army and navy. If the Reichstag failed to vote a new budget, the old one automatically continued in force. This document later became the constitution of the German Empire.

Meanwhile, the former liberals in the Prussian Landtag, caught up in the nationalistic fervor following the victory over Austria, repented of their sin of having opposed Bismarck and voted him exoneration for having violated the constitution. The four predominantly Roman Catholic states south of the Main River (Bavaria, Württemberg, Baden, and part of Hesse-Darmstadt) were left out of the North German Confederation at the insistence of Napoleon III and because Bismarck preferred to have them come in later by their own choice. Bismarck recognized that the reluctant German states could be brought into the fold if German nationalism could be rallied against a foreign threat. France, itself stirred by nationalistic ambitions, provided that threat.

Bismarck's opportunity to confront France came in 1870, when the Spanish crown was offered to a Hohenzollern prince. Bismarck persuaded the reluctant prince to accept the Spanish offer, and the French immediately took alarm at the prospect of being surrounding by Hohenzollerns. Heavy French pressure was exerted on Prussia, to which both the prince and King William I yielded. However, the French ministers were still not satisfied and demanded more. After a meeting at Ems between the French ambassador and the Prussian king, the chancellor saw an opportunity to provoke the French into war. Cleverly editing the Ems dispatch so as to make it appear that the French ambassador and the Prussian king had insulted each other, he published it to the world. The French government, walking into Bismarck's trap, declared war.

The prevailing world military opinion was that this time Prussia had overreached herself and that Bismarck's work would be undone. But as in the case of the Austro-Prussian War, the military might of Prussia was grossly underestimated. The four predominantly Catholic south German states, far from joining Catholic France as Napoleon III had hoped, threw in their lot with Protestant, German-speaking Prussia as Bismarck had anticipated.

The issue of the war was decided in a matter of weeks. Count Helmuth von Moltke's superior hosts moved into France. The French were overwhelmed. One French army was surrounded at the fortress city of Metz, where it surrendered three months later. Another French army under Marshal MacMahon and Emperor Napoleon III was surrounded at Sedan and surrendered on September 2. Napoleon III himself was one of the captives. When this news reached Paris two days later, the liberals overthrew the government of the Second Empire and declared the Third French Republic. Within a matter of weeks Paris was surrounded by the Germans. For four months the great city held out; starvation forced it to surrender on January 28, 1871 (see Figure 44.5).

Bismarck forced stricken and helpless France to sign a treaty designed to cripple the nation beyond recovery. The Treaty of Frankfurt required France to pay an indemnity of 5 billion francs in gold. German troops would remain on French soil until this amount was paid in full (which Bismarck mistakenly hoped and expected would take a long time). The province of Alsace and the greater part of Lorraine were ceded to Germany. Since these provinces contained much of France's vital iron reserves, the seizure of Alsace and Lorraine long poisoned Franco-German relations.

On January 18, 1871, while the big German guns were still battering Paris, the heads of the twenty-five German states at war with France met on Bismarck's call at Versailles (behind the German lines) and in the Hall of Mirrors proclaimed William I emperor of the German Empire. The constitution that Bismarck had drafted for the North German Confederation became the constitution of the German Empire. Bismarck, of course, became its chancellor, and he lived to rule over his creation for the next nineteen years. The German Empire had now replaced France as the dominant power on the European continent and became a new rival of Great Britain for world hegemony.

FIGURE 44.5 Victorious German Troops in Paris Victorious German troops march down the Champs-Elysées (with the Arc de Triomphe in the background) at the end of the Franco-Prussian War. (Historical Pictures Service, Chicago)

In Germany, as in Italy, nationalism had succeeded. In the decades after 1871 the two new nation-states would join the competition in international affairs. And nationalism was strengthening the political institutions of other nation-states, furthering a trend that had already become apparent in France during the 1850s and 1860s. Nationalism would also contribute to the new imperialism of the late nineteenth century, which in turn would further increase the power of the nation-state and eventually help spread nationalism to the non-Western world.

SUGGESTED READING

General

W. E. Mosse, *Liberal Europe, 1848–1875* (1974). A useful comparative history.

N. Rich, *The Age of Nationalism and Reform* (1976). A solid survey.

The Nature of Nationalism

B. Shafer, *Faces of Nationalism* (1972). A good summary.

A. Smith, *Theories of Nationalism* (1983). A comparative approach.

The Second Empire of Napoleon III

A. Plessis, *The Rise and Fall of the Second Empire* (1985). A recent account.

N. Rich, *Why the Crimean War? A Cautionary Tale* (1985). A concise political and diplomatic interpretation.

T. Zeldin, *France, 1848–1945*, 4 vols. (1973–1980). Sophisticated, insightful, and thorough.

Cavour and the Making of Italian Unity

D. Beales, *The Risorgimento and the Unification of Italy* (1982). A brief survey with accompanying documents.

R. Grew, *A Sterner Plan for Italian Unity* (1963). An excellent analysis of the movement for Italian unification.

D. M. Smith, *Cavour* (1985). A highly respected work.

D. M. Smith, *Italy: A Modern History* (1969). A scholarly survey covering the period.

German Unification

E. Crankshaw, *Bismarck* (1981). A good biography that also covers unification.

T. S. Hamerow, *The Social Foundations of German Unification, 1858–1871* (1972). Relates the economic, social, and political factors behind German unification.

H. Holborn, *A History of Modern Germany*, 3 vols. (1959–1969). A detailed, scholarly survey.

M. Howard, *The Franco-Prussian War* (1969). An excellent analysis.

CHAPTER 45
Industrial Society, Social Classes, and Women

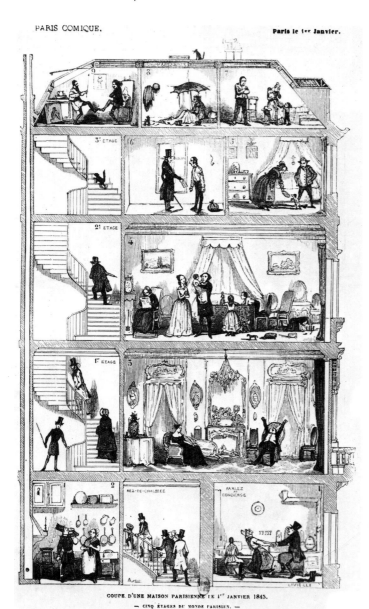

FIGURE 45.1 **The Urban Classes** This French cartoon of 1845 shows a typical Parisian apartment house in which the various social classes live in close proximity but different conditions. The bourgeoisie live on the first (American second) and second floors in wealth and prudent comfort. The lower classes, and aspiring artists, live on the bottom and upper floors in increasing poverty—thanks to their imprudence. (Bibliothèque Nationale, Paris)

Between 1850 and 1914 new areas in the West were industrializing, new industries were being developed, new methods of production were being used, and new business structures were emerging. The quantity and quality of industrial production underwent such a great change that historians have come to call these industrial developments the "second Industrial Revolution." During the same period social developments initiated during the earlier period of industrialization were maturing and evolving. Some, such as the rise of working-class organizations and ideologies, were directly connected to the industrial process. Others were more broadly based—the growth and movement of populations, the evolution of classes, and the developing experiences of women in an increasingly urbanized society. In short, mature, modern industrial economies and societies were becoming firmly established throughout the West.

1. THE SECOND INDUSTRIAL REVOLUTION

The first Industrial Revolution was initiated in Great Britain during the last decades of the eighteenth century. It spread to certain limited areas of western Europe and the United States during the first half of the nineteenth century. This early industrialization was based primarily on steam, iron, and textiles. During the 1850s and 1860s industrial production continued to expand, but mostly in the same areas and along the same lines as in earlier decades. In 1871 Great Britain was still the industrial leader, producing more industrial goods than the rest of the world combined. Besides Great Britain, only Belgium and parts of France, Germany, northern Italy, and the United States were industrially well developed.

The second Industrial Revolution was initiated in the last third of the nineteenth century. It was more widespread than the first Industrial Revolution and was based more on electricity, oil, steel, and chemicals. Great Britain, failing to invest sufficiently in new processes, falling behind in marketing techniques, and relying too heavily on old plants, lost its industrial leadership. Between 1871 and 1914 the United States and Germany surpassed Great Britain. By 1914

the Industrial Revolution had penetrated central and eastern Europe, Japan, Canada, Australia, and New Zealand; even India had a small textile industry. However, it was still in western Europe and the United States that most of the world's industry was to be found, and the greater part of Asia, Africa, and Latin America was still not industrialized. Moreover, it was in western Europe that both the prosperity and the uncertainties of economic life—exemplified by the industrial boom of 1850–1873 and the depression between 1873 and 1896—were experienced most.

New Products and Processes

Steel has been the mainstay of industry and transportation since the latter part of the nineteenth century. Until the mid–nineteenth century, steel was hard to make and very expensive. The discovery of the Bessemer process (1856) and the Thomas-Gilchrist process (1878) of removing impurities from molten iron greatly speeded up and cheapened the production of steel. In 1871 the total annual steel production of the entire world was approximately 1 million tons, of which about half was produced by Great Britain, a fourth by Germany, and an eighth by the United States. By 1914 the world's annual production had increased more than fiftyfold; the United States was producing approximately half the total, Germany a fourth, and Great Britain an eighth. Out of this steel were made tools and machines that constantly increased in numbers and efficiency. By 1914 in the industrialized countries, these increasingly automatic machines fabricated most metal, textile, leather, and wood products (see Figure 45.2).

The power to drive the steel machines was increasing in like proportion. In 1914 probably nine-tenths of the world's industrial power was still provided by the steam engine. Other and more efficient power generators, however, were rapidly coming to the fore. Between 1831 and 1882 the dynamo for generating electricity was developed by a number of inventors, the most important of whom were Michael Faraday (British), the Siemens brothers (German), and Thomas A. Edison (American). Sir Charles Parsons (British) patented the steam turbine in 1884. The turbine proved to be so efficient that it was soon used to drive the largest ships and even-

FIGURE 45.2 Krupp Works Germany industrialized rapidly during the last quarter of the nineteenth century. This photo shows the armaments factory at the Krupp works in Essen, Germany. (Culver Pictures)

tually to generate most of the world's electric power. In 1888 the electric motor was invented by Nikola Tesla, a naturalized American born in Croatia. The first practical internal combustion engine was invented by Gottlieb Daimler (German) in 1886. One year later he put it to work in the first automobile. In 1892 the diesel engine, which efficiently burned cheap crude oil, was invented by Rudolf Diesel (German). The invention of these two engines gave impetus to the oil industry.

In the last decades of the nineteenth century pure science was playing an increasingly vital role in industry, and both science and industry were being applied to agriculture. Physics contributed most heavily to the rapidly growing electrical industry. Chemistry made possible such important industries as synthetic dyes, wood pulp, paper, plastics, synthetic fibers, photography, and motion pictures. The electrical and chemical industries were most highly developed in Germany. The mechanization of agriculture made its first big advances in the great grain-growing areas of the United States, Canada, and Australia, although western Europe was also steadily increasing its agricultural yields through the use of farm machinery and scientific farming techniques.

Transport and Communications

Between 1850 and 1914 a large part of humanity became mobile. Whereas before 1850 relatively few people had ever seen more of the world than could be seen on journeys by foot or on horseback, by 1914 millions of people were traveling considerable distances, often by rapid conveyance. Even in places such as China, Turkey, and Brazil, trains chugged along, hauling people for distances and at speeds unknown before.

This was the greatest era of railroad building in history. There had been a rather lively building of railroads before 1850 in western Europe and the United States. However, between 1850 and 1914 the world's railway system was fundamentally completed. There has been relatively little railroad building since.

At the same time, the steamship was making comparable progress, although it had stiff competition from the sailing ship until near the end of the nineteenth century. Steel hulls of great size, turbine engines, and screw propellers were too much for the beautiful sails. The opening of the Suez Canal in 1869 and the Panama Canal in 1914, together with the increase in the size and speed of ships, brought the world and its peoples, commodities, and markets much closer together.

During the last three decades of the nineteenth century, the humble bicycle became a common and important means of locomotion, especially in Europe. But the bicycle was not fast enough for the industrial age. When Gottlieb Daimler attached his little combustion engine to a wagon in 1887, the automobile was born. It quickly captured the imagination of daring pioneers. Daimler sold his patent to a French company, and until the end of the century the French led the field in automobile development and production. Leadership passed to America with the founding of the Ford Motor Company in 1903. Henry Ford, who started out as a bicycle mechanic, applied the assembly-line method of mass production to the new automobile industry. The rapid spread of the automobile created vast new industrial empires in oil, rubber, and concrete.

After the turn of the century the airplane was invented. The first successful heavier-than-air flying machine was flown by Wilbur and Orville Wright in 1903 over the sand dunes at Kitty Hawk, North Carolina. Aviation was still in its infancy in 1914, but already its tremendous future was obvious.

Communications were developing faster yet. In 1844 Samuel F. B. Morse sent a message by wire forty miles from Baltimore to Washington. The telegraph, which transmitted messages almost instantaneously from one end of any length of wire to the other, caught on rapidly. In 1866 a telegraph cable was laid across the Atlantic, enabling news to travel from New York to London as quickly as from New York to Brooklyn. Ten years later Alexander Graham Bell, an American born in Scotland, invented the telephone, and in 1895 Guglielmo Marconi, an Italian, sent the first message by wireless telegraphy. Together with the revolution in transportation, these developments in communications accelerated the Industrial Revolution by greatly facilitating the large-scale mobilization of capital, raw materials, labor, and markets.

The Growth of Corporations and Monopolies

At the same time that industry was growing, individual companies were growing larger and combining to form monopolistic mergers or trusts. Such undertakings as railroads, shipping lines, and iron-and-steel mills were too large for all but a very few individuals to finance. As a rule, therefore, enterprises of this scope were carried on by joint stock companies. Entrepreneur capitalists would raise the necessary capital outlay by organizing a corporation and selling stock in it to other capitalists. All the industrialized countries encouraged the investment of capital in corporations by passing laws that limited the liability of stockholders to the amount of money invested (hence the "Ltd." usually seen after the name of a British corporation or combine). By 1914 most of the world's industry was controlled by large corporations and trusts. Although their stockholders were numbered by the thousands, they were really controlled by a relatively few banks and wealthy individuals. And between the owners of these corporations and the millions of workers lay a great gulf. The actual operation of the larger industries was carried on by hired managers, who hired, fired, and supervised the workers.

The giant corporations were ruthless in dealing with one another. In this era of unrestrained competition, the big and strong frequently destroyed the small and weak. The premium was on size and strength. The results were combines, mergers, and monopolistic trusts. The spectacular success of Rockefeller's Standard Oil Trust in the 1880s soon made it the model for many others, particularly in the United States, Germany, Japan, and to a lesser extent Great Britain. The German monopolistic combinations such as the giant I. G. Farben Industries (chemicals and dyes) were called *cartels*. They received government encouragement and support, particularly in their operations abroad. In Japan three-quarters of the nation's industry was controlled by five giant family corporations.

2. THE RISE OF WORKING-CLASS ORGANIZATIONS AND IDEOLOGIES

Labor Unions and Cooperatives

Wherever industrialization occurred, distressed laborers almost immediately attempted to protect themselves by banding together. However, until the 1870s inexperience, poverty, hostile governments, and unfavorable public opinion effectively hindered their efforts. Anti–labor union laws were not fully repealed in Great Britain until 1875 and in France until 1884. In Germany Bismarck persecuted labor unions until his dismissal in 1890. Until the 1880s the union movement in Europe was limited chiefly to skilled workers, organized by crafts, who were moderate in their aims and methods.

In the 1880s unionization spread rapidly to unskilled workers, cut across craft lines, and adopted socialistic programs (often Marxist) and more radical methods. In Great Britain the labor unions formed the national Trades Union Congress in 1868, and later they became identified with the Labour party, which was founded between 1881 and 1906. In Germany the individual unions in 1890 formed a national organization that was frankly Marxist. In France in 1895 the various unions banded together in the giant CGT

(Confédération Générale du Travail—General Confederation of Labor) with a radical program. By 1914 the working class in the industrialized countries was sufficiently large and organized (though only a minority was as yet unionized) to make itself a power to be reckoned with, both in the factories and mines and at the polls.

Meanwhile, a much bigger portion of the working class was participating in the milder cooperatives of various types. In 1910 in Great Britain membership in cooperative retail stores, fraternal insurance (friendly) societies, and credit associations is estimated to have been some 14 million, the great bulk of whom were wage earners. These organizations also provided much-needed social fellowship for workers. In the 1880s Denmark became the home of the agricultural cooperative movement. By 1914 nearly all of Denmark's agricultural commodities were cooperatively produced and marketed, and the movement had spread to most of northern Europe, to Italy, and to the United States.

Socialism

During the second half of the nineteenth century socialism became a major ideological force within the working class and came to influence the society and politics of the West in important ways. The most prominent source of socialism was Karl Marx, who, along with Friedrich Engels, had already produced *The Communist Manifesto* in 1848 (see Chapter 40). Marx argued that modern industrial society in the capitalist West was increasingly being split into two opposing classes: the capitalists (factory owners) and the workers. According to Marx, capitalism was doomed to be overthrown by a revolution of the working class and replaced by a socialist system.

Marx continued to write during the 1850s, 1860s, and 1870s, publishing his most important book, *Das Kapital*, in 1867. He played a key role in translating his ideas into actions by helping union organizers to form the International Working Men's Association (the First International) in 1864. The association was an amalgam of non-Marxian socialists (such as followers of Louis-Auguste Blanqui and Pierre-Joseph Proudhon), anarchists (such as Mikhail Bakunin), and Marxists, and it was divided at the start. Soon, however, Marx and his followers gained control. Although this organization proved to be fragile, falling apart in the 1870s after the Paris Commune, it helped spread Marx's socialism, particularly in Germany. The Second International was formed in 1889 and lasted until 1914. An international federation of socialist parties, it worked to spread socialism, maintain doctrinal purity, and develop socialist strategies.

After Marx's death in 1883, his followers split into various groups and often disagreed over the "correct" meaning of Marxism. The most important modification of Marxism was a moderate revisionism led by the German socialist Eduard Bernstein (1850–1932). Bernstein argued that Marx had made some errors and that a revolution would not be necessary. He advocated cooperation with the capitalistic classes to obtain all the immediate benefits possible for labor and a gradual approach to socialism. Others, such as the Polish-born socialist Rosa Luxemburg (1870–1919), attacked Bernstein's position as being too much of a compromise with bourgeois liberalism and nationalism. Active in Germany, Poland, and Russia, Rosa Luxemburg would later become a founding leader of the radical Spartacus League and the German Communist party.

In Germany, where socialism had its greatest success before 1914, the Social Democratic party formally rejected Bernstein's moderate revisionism but in practice often tended to follow it after the 1890s. By 1914 the party was able to poll some 4.5 million votes and had become the largest party in Germany. The French Socialists were more radical than the Germans. In 1905 the orthodox and revisionist wings of the French Socialists joined to form the United Socialist party under the leadership of the scholar-orator Jean Jaurès. By 1914 they numbered 1.5 million voters and had 110 seats in the Chamber of Deputies. Contrary to the expectations of Marx, socialism in Great Britain was weak and mild. Among the earliest British Socialists were George Bernard Shaw, H. G. Wells, and Sidney and Beatrice Webb. These intellectual radicals formed the Fabian Society, which was committed to moderation and gradualism. The Labour party, founded between 1881 and 1906, was also mild and grew slowly before 1914. Neither the Fabian Society nor the Labour party could be called Marxist, although both were influenced by Marx. In the United States, the socialist movement was relatively weak and (in retrospect) mild. The first prominent American Socialist, Eugene V. Debs, did manage to poll nearly a million votes for president in 1912 and again in 1920.

Anarchism

Anarchism was an extremely radical movement that has often been confused with Marxism. While both were anticapitalist and gained most of their support from the working classes, anarchists stressed much more the elimination of the state and any authority that impinges on human freedom. Anarchists optimistically believed that human beings, once freed from the corrupting institutions that oppressed them, would naturally cooperate with one another. Anarchism's two most influential leaders were the Russian activist Mikhail Bakunin (1814–1876) and the exiled Russian theoretician Prince Pyoter Kropotkin (1842–1921). Anarchism became particularly influential in France, Spain, and Italy and among artists and intellectuals as well as members of the working classes. A relatively small wing of the anarchist movement turned to violent means to gain their ends. Among its victims were Tsar Alexander II of Russia in 1881, President Sadi Carnot of France in 1894, King Umberto I of Italy in 1900, and President William McKinley of the United States in 1901. This image of violence has tainted the general perception of anarchism ever since.

3. THE GROWTH AND MOVEMENT OF POPULATION

Since the eighteenth century, European population had been growing at a rapid pace. This growth continued as industrialization spread throughout Europe in the nineteenth century. Between 1850 and 1914 Europe's population expanded from 266 million to 450 million. However, there were important changes underlying this growth of population during the second half of the nineteenth century, particularly after 1870.

In many areas, particularly western Europe, increasing birthrates were no longer a prime generator of population growth; in fact, the birthrates were declining. A trend starting in the middle class and spreading to the working classes of marrying later and intentionally having fewer children was limiting the size of families. Because parents could rely more on infants surviving into adulthood, there was less need to have so many children. Moreover, parents who wanted to ensure their own and their children's rising economic well-being and social position elected to have smaller families, which were less expensive and required less division of assets. Despite the declining birthrate, population grew, fueled by an even greater decline in the death rate. This decrease was caused by a combination of improved public sanitation, economic growth, and medical advances.

This European population was not only growing but also moving in vast numbers in two main ways: from Europe to overseas areas, particularly the United States, and from the countryside to the city.

The overseas emigration of Europeans between 1850 and 1914 was phenomenal. Ever since the first settlements in the New World, there had been a sizable trickle of Europeans to the Americas. This trickle became a flowing stream in the mid–nineteenth century. Great numbers of British, Irish, and then German immigrants landed in the United States during the 1840s, 1850s, and 1860s. After 1870 the stream of Europeans emigrating overseas swelled into a rushing torrent as peoples from southern and eastern Europe joined the flow. In the brief span of forty-three years between 1871 and 1914, more than 30 million Europeans left their homelands and emigrated to the New World or to the British dominion territories. The great bulk of them came to the United States.

Several factors help explain this massive movement of Europeans overseas. Perhaps the greatest impetus was the growth of population. The growing numbers led to increasing competition for land in rural areas and for living space and jobs in urban areas. As different areas of Europe underwent the economic and social transformations connected with industrialization, people were uprooted from their traditional ways of life. When these upheavals were accompanied by political turmoil, many found additional reasons to emigrate. As these developments pushed Europeans from their homelands, opportunities in the New World, both real and imagined, pulled them across the Atlantic (see Figure 45.3). Land and economic opportunity

seemed abundant in such places as the United States, Canada, Argentina, and Brazil. Improvements in transportation—railroads and steamships—made travel to these faraway places easier. This combination of push from Europe and pull from the New World induced millions of relatively poor, young, and often unmarried Europeans to emigrate overseas. Although it is difficult to know how most of them experienced this change, clearly not all of them were satisfied. Approximately one-third of those emigrating overseas from Europe eventually returned.

Europeans were moving from the countryside to the city at an even faster pace than they were moving overseas. In 1850, despite a long process of urbanization, in no country did those in cities outnumber rural inhabitants. This picture changed rapidly during the second half of the nineteenth century. By the turn of the century more than half the population of western Europe lived in urban areas. Agriculture had become an occupation for the minority in Great Britain, Belgium, the Netherlands, Germany, and France.

The movement to the city was brought about by the opportunities in industry and commerce, the growing attractiveness of urban life, and the application of mechanization and science to agriculture, which now required far fewer workers to produce greater yields. The social problems of the cities were being recognized and attacked. A public health movement to improve water supplies and public sanitation by introducing piped water and sewer systems was initiated in England during the 1840s. Urban areas in other countries followed England's lead in the succeeding decades. Urban life was altered by the introduction of mechanized, regular, and reliable means of public transportation, particularly electric streetcars in the 1890s. This development widened opportunities for better housing, since people no longer had to live so close to work. The central areas, which had housed people of all social classes together, were becoming dominated by public buildings, retail outlets, businesses, and theaters (see Figure 45.1). Around the central areas new residential districts and suburbs formed, often separated into working-class and middle-class sections. Some limited private and public programs were initiated to facilitate the construction of cheap housing.

Cities were thus becoming more attractive. Urban planning spread throughout Europe in

FIGURE 45.3 *Welcome to the Land of Freedom* In this romanticized painting a variety of emotions is displayed on the faces of immigrants as they pass the Statue of Liberty in New York Harbor on their way to a new life. Between 1871 and 1914, more than 30 million Europeans emigrated overseas, most of them to the United States. (The Granger Collection)

the second half of the nineteenth century. The general pattern was initiated in Paris during the 1850s and 1860s, when the government tore down old, overcrowded, and almost inaccessible areas of the city, built large boulevards and parks, and provided for more open spaces. Other cities, such as Vienna and Cologne, followed the example of Paris. Together the spread of sanitation facilities, public transportation, urban planning, and new housing in Europe's cities was making life in the urban areas relatively safe and appealing compared to life in the countryside.

4. SOCIAL CLASSES

The class divisions of industrial society continued to develop along the lines already estab-

lished during the first half of the nineteenth century. The aristocracy continued to shrink in size and significance, yet it still retained some vestiges of wealth, prestige, and position. In part, it was supported by the increasingly conservative elite of the upper middle class. These families, who had gained great wealth from industry, commerce, and banking, mingled with the old aristocracy and copied much of its exclusive and expensive lifestyle. Numerous servants, at least one country house surrounded by an estate, membership in exclusive clubs, extensive travel, major contributions to good causes, and support of culture were almost requirements for full membership in this elite, which constituted less than 5 percent of the population.

The bulk of the middle class, ranging from small factory owners, shopowners, schoolteachers, and professionals to clerks and minor officials, continued to benefit from industrial expansion and urbanization. During the second half of the nineteenth century, however, there were some important changes in the outlook and composition of this class. Before 1848, the middle class was often revolutionary and certainly at the forefront of progressive political change. After 1848, the middle class ceased to be revolutionary and more often fought to retain the status quo rather than promote progressive reform. For the most part, the middle class was gaining what it wanted and was achieving dominance in Western society. In composition, the middle class was not only growing (to some 20 percent of the population) but also adding new groups to its numbers. The two most important of these new groups were professionals and white-collar employees. The professionals included people such as engineers, chemists, accountants, and architects as well as public and private managers. These people utilized their education and expertise to carry out the specialized tasks created by industrialization. In wealth, attitudes, and style of life they resembled the traditional middle-class entrepreneurs, merchants, and bankers they served. The white-collar employees were placed toward the bottom of the middle classes. They included the growing numbers of clerks, secretaries, bureaucrats, and salesmen who usually worked for large firms and earned little more than members of the skilled working class. But they self-consciously considered themselves apart from the working classes below them, subscribed to middle-class attitudes, and tried their best to follow a middle-class style of life—at least in appearances.

Generally, members of the middle class copied as much of the envied lifestyle of the wealthier upper middle class as they could. With care, most could afford one domestic, good food, a well-furnished apartment or house, schooling and perhaps music lessons for the children, attendance at cultural events, fashionable clothes, and travel. The middle-class home became a symbol of accomplishment and status, displaying wealth in a bounty of utensils, pictures, furnishings, and knickknacks. Magazines and stores appeared that both appealed to and channeled middle-class tastes. New department stores, such as the Bon Marché in Paris, offered to fulfill the desire for goods easily.

In values and beliefs, middle-class people thought that they represented what was correct and best in Western society. They believed that prudence, control, rationality, and hard work were the keys to success. They respected traditional Christian morality, sexual purity, and marital fidelity, while they denounced drinking, crime, excesses, and even poverty as vices. They felt they should be able to live up to these standards, at least in appearances if not always in practice. Money remained an important consideration for marriage, but a union was supposed to be centered on sentiment. While this was the period of Victorian sexual propriety for the middle class, it now appears that there was increasing acceptance and expectation of sexual enjoyment within the marriage. Children were at the center of the family and fewer in number; they remained at home through the adolescent years and were more extensively educated.

The working classes—the wage laborers with little if any capital—were headed by an elite of workers whose skills as artisans, machinists, foremen, or specialists were in great demand. Often they struggled to distinguish themselves from the bulk of the working classes below them by adopting a stern, moralistic attitude, copying the appearance of the middle class, and striving to ensure that their children would maintain or surpass their own position in the social hierarchy. The bulk of the working classes were factory laborers, construction workers, transport workers, unskilled or semiskilled day workers, and domestics.

Clearly, the working classes were benefiting from industrialization during the second half of the nineteenth century. Real wages were on the rise, perhaps doubling in Great Britain between 1850 and 1914. The working classes engaged in the proliferating leisure-time activities, which included public drinking and socializing in cafés and pubs, watching organized sports such as soccer, boxing, and racing, and attending music halls, vaudeville theaters, and amusement parks. Nevertheless, the working classes were still located toward the bottom of the social and economic scale, continually experiencing or being threatened by poverty, unemployment, poor housing, and insecurity. They may have been participating in an expanding industrial society, but that expansion did not benefit all equally. The gap between rich and poor remained wide;

FIGURE 45.4 Jules Adler, *An Atelier for the Cutting of False Diamonds at Pré-Saint-Gervais* Working-class women often took jobs in certain kinds of small factories and workshops for relatively poor pay. This painting shows the interior of a late-nineteenth-century Parisian workshop where women are making costume jewelry. (Musée Baron-Gérard, Bayeux)

the upper 20 percent of the population usually received more national income than the combined total of the remaining 80 percent.

This society of the late nineteenth and early twentieth centuries had acquired some permanence that reflected its mature industrial base. It was a society that was more affluent than ever but was still divided into classes of greatly differing status and wealth. Tensions ran through this society, as did great movements of people and ideas. Nevertheless, when the generations after World War I looked back to this society, it seemed enviable despite its faults.

5. WOMEN'S ROLES AND EXPERIENCES

It is difficult to summarize the situation of women between 1850 and 1914. Women's roles and experiences differed sharply according to class lines, and even within classes many of the relevant developments were contradictory. What generally unified women's experiences during this period, as before, was their legal inequality with men, their lack of political rights, their eco-nomic dependence and inferiority, and their social restrictions. In an age in which liberal values—stressing individualism, political rights, and equality before the law—were becoming firmly established, women were still relegated to a secondary position or actually excluded from most aspects of public life.

For middle-class women, the contradictions were greatest. The sexual division of labor, which separated the woman's sphere from the man's sphere, was rigidified by the growing cult of domesticity. Accordingly, women were glorified as caring mothers, supportive wives, and religious beings. Their place was in the home, where they were in charge of the domestic scene. The wife was supposed to defer and cater to her husband and take personal responsibility for nursing and rearing the children. The children's education and the religious well-being of the family were her realm. As domestic manager, she was supposed to have expertise as a consumer, and in turn she was the object of consumer advertising. She was also assumed to be interested in charity and willing to donate time for worthy causes. The middle-class wife was not expected to engage in paid occupations outside the home.

The more successfully middle class the family was, the less likely it was that the wife engaged in paid work. Nevertheless, toward the end of the nineteenth century some professions such as schoolteaching, social work, and nursing were expanding and opening to even married middle-class women. Still, most of these occupations were associated with women's domestic roles, were relatively low paying, and were considered most appropriate for unmarried women.

Within the working class, middle-class views about the separate spheres of women and men and the particular domestic nature of women hovered and had some important effects, but the actual experience of women differed. In general working-class women were much more likely to work for wages than middle-class women (see Figure 45.4). A common pattern was for young women to take jobs as domestics before they were married—often moving to cities for this purpose. In addition to the more traditional jobs for women in textiles, food processing, and retail outlets, some of the newer occupations in nursing and secretarial work were opening to women. When jobs were unavailable, prostitution (generally legal and regulated) remained at least a temporary alternative for some. After marriage, women were effectively excluded from several of the options they had when single. One of the main ways for working-class women to earn money was in "sweated industries," where they worked in small factories or at home, usually in textiles or decorating, and were paid by the piece. In all these occupations women continued to be discriminated against; they received lower pay than men for the same work and were excluded from many jobs open to working-class men. Often middle-class notions of domesticity were used to justify the lower pay and status of women's work, employers arguing that women's primary role was not in paid labor. Women were the first to be affected by new legislation controlling the hours and conditions under which workers could be employed, although these laws were often poorly enforced.

The image of domesticity was often in contrast to the realities of life for women. Venereal diseases rose to the point where they were a major cause of death. Illegitimacy was widespread, particularly in urban areas. Many more women were working for wages and in "inappropriate"

FIGURE 45.5 Emmeline Pankhurst Women led numerous demonstrations in their struggle to gain the vote, particularly in Great Britain. Here a policeman is arresting a leading suffragette, Emmeline Pankhurst. (Culver Pictures)

jobs than accepted notions of morality dictated. While working-class women may have suffered most from these realities, they affected women of all classes.

During this period some organized efforts to challenge the role and status assigned to women arose. The strongest feminist movements, particularly movements to extend voting rights to women, arose in Great Britain and the United States. In Great Britain organizations such as the National Union of Women's Suffrage Societies, led by Millicent Fawcett (1847–1929), and the more radical Women's Social and Political Union, led by Emmeline Pankhurst (1858–1928), petitioned, lobbied, and marched for the franchise (see Figure 45.5). Increasingly, women's organizations publicized their positions and used rallies to further their causes. Mass demonstrations occurred more often in the years before World War I. In 1908 a rally for female suffrage drew some 250,000 women to Hyde Park in London. Some women used more violent means to bring attention to their cause. But the government resisted, and success was achieved only at the end of World War I.

In other countries, women's organizations argued for the right to vote and for changes in women's social and economic position, but these organizations were often splintered and rarely achieved their goals. Many continental feminist leaders such as Louise Michel in France, Clara Zetkin in Germany, and Anna Kuliscioff in Italy associated themselves with socialist or radical movements. Only in Norway did women gain the right to vote in national elections before World War I. However, the issues of feminism were now being raised publicly as never before and would become more powerful during the twentieth century.

SUGGESTED READING

General

E. J. Hobsbawm, *The Age of Capital* (1975). Examines middle-class life during the second half of the nineteenth century.

N. Stone, *Europe Transformed, 1878–1919* (1984). A broad survey.

E. R. Tannenbaum, *1900: The Generation Before the Great War* (1976). Good essays on social history.

The Second Industrial Revolution

F. Crouzet, *The Victorian Economy* (1982). Good sections on this period.

D. S. Landes, *The Unbound Prometheus: Technological Change and Industrial Development in Western Europe from 1750 to the Present* (1969). An excellent survey emphasizing technological change.

A. S. Milward and S. B. Saul, *The Development of the Economies of Continental Europe, 1850–1914* (1977). A good treatment of the second Industrial Revolution.

The Rise of Working-Class Organizations and Ideologies

L. R. Berlanstein, *The Working People of Paris, 1871–1914* (1985). A comprehensive study.

J. Joll, *The Anarchists* (1964). A good examination of anarchism and anarchists.

G. Lichtheim, *Marxism* (1971). A highly respected treatment.

A. Lindemann, *A History of European Socialism* (1983). Connects thought and practice.

W. Sewell, Jr., *Work and Revolution in France* (1980). A good treatment of French socialism.

The Growth and Movement of Population

A. Briggs, *Victorian Cities* (1970). A good examination of Britain's industrial cities.

T. McKeown, *The Modern Rise of Population* (1976). A good introduction.

J. Merriman, ed., *French Cities in the Nineteenth Century: Class, Power, and Urbanization* (1982). A good selection of recent essays.

Social Classes

J. Donzelot, *The Policing of Families* (1979). An important interpretation stressing governmental interference with family life.

P. Gay, *The Bourgeois Experience: Victoria to Freud,* 2 vols. (1984–1986). An excellent study of sexuality and the middle class.

P. Joyce, *Visions of the People: Industrial England and the Question of Class, c. 1848–1914* (1991). An excellent recent interpretation.

Women

M. Boxer and J. Quataert, eds., *Connecting Spheres: Women in the Western World, 1500 to Present* (1987). Fine chapters covering the period.

P. Branca, *Women in Europe since 1750* (1978). A useful study.

R. Bridenthal and C. Koonz, *Becoming Visible: Women in European History* (1987). Contains good chapters covering the period.

M. Vicinus, *Suffer and Be Still: Women in the Victorian Age* (1972). Good essays on Victorian women.

CHAPTER 46

Science and the Challenge to Christianity

FIGURE 46.1 Thomas Eakins, *The Gross Clinic*, 1875 This realistic painting by Eakins of an operation in progress conveys the sense of power of modern science and the optimism with which science was viewed in the nineteenth century. The lack of religious references in this medical scene indicates some of the potential challenge of secular science to Christianity. (Jefferson Medical College, Thomas Jefferson University, Philadelphia)

B y the middle of the nineteenth century, science had gained much prestige. It was increasingly connected with the inventions and technology of industrialization, which provided wealth and power. It seemed to go hand in hand with the rationalism and prevailing bourgeois liberalism of the period. Over the course of the nineteenth century, people assumed that scientists had, or soon would have, a firm understanding of the physical world. They were optimistic that scientific methods would provide a similar understanding of human society. Although this sense of certainty and optimism would be somewhat undermined in the decades surrounding the turn of the century, the period between 1850 and 1914 must be considered one of great progress in the sciences.

At the same time Christianity faced serious and fundamental challenges. It was attacked from several quarters, but at the base of the many challenges were the successes and increasing prestige of science. Christian leaders often had difficulty adjusting their theology and institutions to the scientific, liberal, and secular assumptions of the period.

1. THE PHYSICAL, BIOLOGICAL, AND MEDICAL SCIENCES

The greatest advances in the field of the physical sciences in the nineteenth and early twentieth centuries centered on discovering the nature of matter, energy, and electricity. John Dalton (1766–1844), a gifted British scientist and teacher, started a fruitful line of inquiry by reviving the theory that all matter is composed of atoms. Dalton eventually concluded that what distinguishes the various chemical elements is the weight of the atoms of which each element is composed. Building on Dalton's theories, the Russian chemist Dmitri Mendeléev (1834–1907) in 1870 worked out a periodic chart showing the atomic weight of all the known elements and indicating by gaps in the chart that others remained to be discovered. Both Dalton and Mendeléev thought that the atom was an indivisible solid. But in the 1890s the British physicist Joseph Thomson (1856–1940) and the Dutch physicist Hendrik Lorentz (1853–1928) independently discovered that atoms are composed of small particles, which Lorentz named electrons. Shortly thereafter another British physicist, Sir Ernest Rutherford (1871–1937), further developed Thomson's theories. Rutherford conceived of each atom as a miniature solar system, the nucleus being the sun and the electrons the planets. Furthermore—and this was most startling—Thomson and Rutherford suggested that the protons and electrons might not be matter at all but merely positive and negative charges of electricity.

Meanwhile in the 1890s the German physicist Wilhelm von Roentgen (1845–1923) discovered X rays, and the French physicist Pierre Curie (1859–1906) and his Polish wife Marie Curie (1867–1935) discovered radium and added to what was known about radioactivity.

During this same period, Albert Einstein (1879–1955), a German physicist who later fled to America, was assailing time-honored concepts not only about the stability of matter but also about time, space, and motion (see Figure 46.2). Einstein derived a formula equating mass and energy: $E = mc^2$ (E = energy in ergs; m = mass in grams; c = speed of light in centimeters per second). According to this formula, the atomic energy in a lump of coal is some three billion times as great as the energy obtained by burning the coal—a truth that was proved several decades later with the development of the atomic bomb. In 1905 Einstein proposed his theory of relativity, which made time, space, and motion relative to one another and to the observer, not the absolutes they had always been conceived to be.

These stunning discoveries in physics and chemistry were triumphs, reflecting a new sophistication in scientific theory and experimentation. But by the turn of the century a sense of uncertainty was creeping into elite scientific circles—a sense that the more we learn, the less solid and reliable the material world seems. This sense of uncertainty, particularly in physics, would spread in the early decades of the twentieth century.

The intellectual world was even more interested in and influenced by developments in the biological sciences. Evolution, like the atomic theory, had been suggested by the ancient Greeks and from time to time afterward. With the revival of scientific interests and attitudes in

FIGURE 46.2 **Einstein** Albert Einstein (1879–1955) became one of the most recognized figures of the twentieth century. His theory of relativity, first proposed in 1905, undermined the concept of a stable material universe that Newton had so beautifully formalized early in the eighteenth century. (Karsh, Ottawa/Woodfin Camp & Associates)

the seventeenth and eighteenth centuries, the thoughts of a number of scientists turned to the problem of the origin of the present world and its phenomena. By the mid–nineteenth century, the concept of a slow and gradual development of the earth's crust and its inhabitants was not at all uncommon among intellectuals. The time was ripe for a first-rate scientist to supply the evidence. That man was Charles Darwin (1809–1882).

Darwin was of a distinguished British family. His study of medicine at Edinburgh and theology at Cambridge failed to challenge him. The world of plants and, to a somewhat lesser extent, animals was his first love—or rather, his consuming passion. In spite of frail health, he turned his powers of observation and reflection to the amassing of biological knowledge. Gradually he developed his concept of evolution. Of great influence on his thinking was Malthus' *Essay on Population* (1798), which described the struggle

of human beings for food and survival, and Sir Charles Lyell's *Principles of Geology* (1830–1833), which was the first truly scientific treatise on geology. Lyell demonstrated by the study of fossils the likelihood of a gradual evolution of the earth's crust and of plant and animal forms over eons of time. Darwin published *On the Origin of Species by Natural Selection* in 1859. In this historic work he described, with an impressive array of factual data, convincing reasoning, and lucid prose, the long, slow evolution of present plant and animal species from simpler forms through a process of natural selection. In the struggle for survival in nature's jungle, the fittest survived. Those specimens that possessed the more useful characteristics—for instance, the horse with the longer legs—survived to produce more offspring and to transmit their superior qualities, both inherited and acquired, to future generations. Twelve years later (1871) in his *Descent of Man*, he undertook to show how humans had evolved from more primitive species by the same process. Although Darwin's work left many fundamental questions unanswered, his main thesis quickly gained general acceptance in the scientific world.

Few books in history have had so much influence as *On the Origin of Species*. The industrial bourgeoisie seized upon Darwin's theory as an explanation of and justification for its own success. Rulers and dominant groups everywhere derived comfort from it. Philosophers, notably Herbert Spencer, undertook to broaden the principle of evolution to make it the key to all truth. Meanwhile, Darwin's brilliant work not only popularized but also significantly contributed to the advancement of the biological sciences.

Medical science lagged far behind the physical and biological sciences at the opening of the nineteenth century. The seventeenth- and eighteenth-century scientists had made great progress in discovering the secrets of the stars, of the elements, and of plants and animals, but where the ailments of the human body were concerned, most were still holding to the theories of Galen, a Greek physician of the second century A.D. George Washington was bled to death in 1799 by a physician who was following the standard practice of the time.

Much groundwork had been laid, however, for medical progress. In the sixteenth century Andreas Vesalius made great advances in the study of human anatomy. In the seventeenth century William Harvey discovered the circulatory system and Antoni van Leeuwenhoek and Marcello Malpighi were using the newly invented microscope to explore the structure of human tissue and to discover the existence of microbes. By the late eighteenth century the British physician Edward Jenner was successfully inoculating against smallpox, though he did not understand the secret of its success. During the 1840s anesthesia was discovered and used successfully. But the whole field of germ diseases and infections was still a mystery.

The secrets of bacteria, their nature and their control, were first explored by the French chemist Louis Pasteur (1822–1895). During the 1860s Pasteur, after intensive and imaginative research, discovered that fermentation is caused by airborne bacteria that can be destroyed by boiling (or "pasteurization"). Later he discovered that many diseases of humans and animals are also caused by bacteria and that some of them can be prevented by vaccination. His spectacular services to French agriculture and to humankind made him the most honored man in France. Robert Koch (1843–1910), a country doctor in eastern Germany, hearing of Pasteur's first discoveries, picked up the trail and discovered the germs causing anthrax (a deadly disease of cattle), tuberculosis, sleeping sickness, and many other diseases. He became a professor at the University of Berlin and was awarded the Nobel Prize.

Also building on Pasteur's foundations was the renowned British surgeon Joseph Lister (1827–1912), who applied the new knowledge of bacteria to the use of antiseptics and disinfectants in surgery. His amazing success in controlling infection opened a new era in surgery, and Lister was raised to the peerage by the British government. The honors bestowed on Pasteur, Koch, and Lister, in contrast with the persecutions suffered by many of the sixteenth- and seventeenth-century scientists, are striking evidence of the triumph of science and the scientific spirit in the nineteenth century.

New discoveries in the physical, biological, and medical sciences did not, however, mean that women gained stature in the eyes of scientists. Darwin believed his findings showed men to be superior to women. Men in the sciences generally found support for their views that women were inferior to men and were appropriately dependent upon men. As with attitudes toward race, science was often used to justify assumptions about women and their proper domestic roles in a male-dominated family. Most universities, in fact, remained closed to women, though some separate women's colleges were starting to open in the last decades of the nineteenth century.

2. THE RISE OF SOCIAL SCIENCE

The spectacular successes of the natural sciences in the nineteenth century encouraged scholars to apply the techniques and principles of natural science to the study of the human mind and society. The result was the birth of modern psychology and sociology, both of which soon became popular.

Until the middle of the nineteenth century the mechanistic and associational approach to psychology stemming from the theories of John Locke (1632–1704) still prevailed. In the second half of the nineteenth century a number of psychologists began to systematically apply an empirical approach to the study of human behavior. One of the first to bring psychology into the laboratory was Wilhelm Wundt (1832–1920). In his famous laboratory at Leipzig he and his enthusiastic students tested human reactions and tried all sorts of carefully controlled and measured experiments on cats and dogs, assuming that the findings would also be applicable to human beings.

The Russian scientist Ivan Pavlov (1849–1936), pursuing Wundt's line of attack, excited the intellectual world with the discovery of the conditioned reflex. Pavlov showed meat to a hungry dog, and the dog's mouth watered. Then Pavlov rang a bell while showing the meat. Eventually the dog's mouth watered when only the bell was rung. The implication was that many of our human responses are purely mechanical reflexes produced by stimuli of which we are often unaware.

Sigmund Freud (1856–1939) created the greatest stir of all in the rapidly growing field of psychology. Freud was a Viennese neurologist who became the father of psychoanalysis. Freud concluded that much of human behavior is irrational, unconscious, and instinctual. He argued that conflict is a basic condition of life, particularly conflict between our innate biological drives (such as sex or aggression) and our social selves. These conflicts are worked out on a mostly unconscious level and in stages during childhood. These conflicts invariably cause frustration. Freud believed that much neurosis and psychosis stemmed from the suppressed and frustrated drives of early life—frustrations that then festered in the subconscious. He concluded that the correct therapy for such neuroses was to make the sufferer conscious of the facts and circumstances of the original frustration. He stressed the interpretation of dreams as a key tool for revealing the unconscious. Freud and his followers developed psychoanalysis into an influential theory of human behavior, an insightful method of psychological investigation, and a useful therapy for certain problems.

During the second half of the nineteenth century sociology acquired status as a social science. This new discipline was founded and named by Auguste Comte (1798–1857), an eccentric Frenchman of great energy and imagination. The history of humankind, said Comte, can be divided into three epochs. The first was religious, when mystical or supernatural explanations were assigned to all phenomena. The second was metaphysical, when general laws and abstract principles were taken as explanatory principles. The third, which humankind was on the point of entering, was the specific or positive, when the truth would be discovered by the scientific gathering of factual data. Comte had utter scorn for the first and little respect for the second epochs. He believed that humans and society are as susceptible to scientific investigation as minerals, plants, and the lower animals. His religion was the worship of humanity, and he had great faith in its future. These ideas were called *positivism.* Comte's followers, eager and numerous, placed great faith in statistics. They amassed vast arrays of statistical data on every conceivable social problem.

Second only to Comte in importance in the founding and promotion of sociology was the Englishman Herbert Spencer (1820–1903). Spencer shared Comte's scorn for mystical religion and denied that morals should be based on religion. He also shared Comte's faith in the progress of humanity. In his ten-volume *System of Synthetic Philosophy,* Spencer undertook to synthesize all human and social phenomena into one grand evolutionary system.

People's interest in themselves and in human society, together with the scientific spirit of the times, guaranteed great popularity for the social sciences. Anthropologists and archaeologists dug feverishly into the physical and cultural past of the human race. Political scientists and economists tended to forsake theory for the statistical and "practical." Strenuous efforts were made to make history a social science. Leopold von Ranke (1795–1886) strove to make history coldly scientific and morally neutral. History, he insisted, should be based on an exhaustive accumulation and analysis of documentary evidence. Ranke's historical attitude and methodology were imported from Germany into the United States, becoming the standard in both countries.

Between 1850 and 1914 natural scientists appeared to be solving the last mysteries of the material universe. Medical scientists appeared to be banishing pain and disease from the earth. Social scientists were amassing voluminous knowledge about the human mind and social relationships. Science had become one of the mainstays of the widely popular belief in progress.

3. CHALLENGES TO CHRISTIANITY

The rapid growth of science was just one of several challenges faced by organized religion in the West. Christianity also seemed to be threatened by most of the other major forces of modernization.

Industrialization was in many ways inimical to Christian faith and practices. Industrialization contributed to the mass migration of people from farm to city and from country to country, tearing them loose from old social patterns and institutions, of which the Church had long been one of the most important. Members of the flocks became separated from their pastors. Once in the active and exciting industrial cities, many of the newcomers seemed no longer to need the Church for their social life and entertainment.

The liberal and radical political movements of the late nineteenth century were for the most part anticlerical. The established churches in Europe, particularly the Catholic church, had long been allied with the conservative aristocracy and royalty. Liberals, when they came to power, often attacked the powers, the privileges, and the property of the established Church. France is a good example. After the revolutionary era ended with the overthrow of Napoleon, the Catholic church made a comeback. It allied itself with the Bourbon regime and with Napoleon III's Second Empire, and it opposed liberal movements, including the setting up of the Third French Republic. The liberal leaders of the Third Republic soon adopted anticlerical policies. During the 1880s the Ferry Laws loosened the hold of the Church on education by setting up a rival and favored system of public secular schools, in which the teaching of religion was banned. In 1901 the Associations Law virtually destroyed the Church's schools by outlawing the Catholic teaching orders or associations. In 1905 church and state were completely separated. In all the industrialized countries in this period, public secular education made great strides, usually under the sponsorship of liberal parties.

Another factor inimical to organized religion during the second half of the nineteenth century was the growth of nationalism, which afflicted all the great industrialized powers. International Catholicism and international Judaism were seen as competitors for nationalistic allegiance. Between 1872 and 1878 Bismarck waged *Kulturkampf* (battle for civilization) against the Catholic church in Germany (see p. 610). Bismarck regarded as intolerable the allegiance of millions of German citizens to a non-German pope and the formation of a Catholic political party in Germany. The anti-Semitism that arose in many countries at this time may be attributed in part to the resentment against the international character of Judaism and also to racism, which was often connected to strong nationalism. The Dreyfus case in France is an example (see p. 608). Bloody pogroms in Russia drove tens of thousands of Russian and Polish Jews to America. Many Jews themselves, after centuries of dispersion, became nationalistic and started a movement (Zionism) to set up a Jewish national state in Palestine.

In most of these challenges to Christianity, science—whether through use or abuse—was used to bolster or lend some credibility to the attack. During the twentieth century Christianity would learn to coexist with science, but in the nineteenth century the two were at odds with each other.

With the exception of the evolutionary hypothesis, the challenge to Christianity by natural science was more indirect than direct. The discovery of more and more of the secrets of the material world allowed people to attribute to natural causes many phenomena that previously had been attributed to divine intervention. Disease germs, for instance, now appeared to be doing things that had long been ascribed to God (see Figure 46.1).

The greatest conflicts between natural science and the Christian religion to emerge in the nineteenth century grew out of Darwin's evolutionary hypothesis. The publication of *On the Origin of Species* created an immediate religious storm. The proposal of a long, gradual, and seemingly mechanistic evolution of all present species from simpler forms appeared to contradict the account of divine creation given in the first chapter of Genesis. The whole process of evolution as suggested by Darwin appeared to leave God entirely out of the affairs of the universe. Any doubt concerning Darwin's place for human beings in his evolutionary hypothesis was removed when he published *The Descent of Man*. Human beings, he theorized, like all other living things, evolved from more primitive species. According to Darwin's hypothesis, in the view of many readers, a human being seemed to be just another animal, albeit the highest.

Clerics raged against Darwin and his hypothesis. Efforts were made, sometimes successfully, to suppress the reading of Darwin's books and the teaching of the evolutionary hypothesis in the schools. Darwin was not lacking in champions able and willing to assail the forces of religion. Thomas Huxley (1825–1895), a biologist, surgeon in the British navy, and president of the Royal Society, popularized Darwin's work in dozens of vigorous and lucid books and pamphlets and heaped withering scorn upon the clergy. He called himself "Darwin's bull-dog." Herbert Spencer was carried away with Darwin's thesis and built a whole system of philosophy around the idea of evolution. Spencer considered evolution the key to all truth and all progress. Ernst

Haeckel (1834–1919), a prolific German scientist and popularizer, made great claims for evolution and for science. He proclaimed that scientists would very soon be solving all the remaining mysteries of life and even creating life. The conflict between the evolutionists and the Christian clergy that raged in western Europe in the last four decades of the nineteenth century did not reach its climax in the United States until the 1920s.

The assault of social science upon Christianity was much more direct and severe than that of natural science. Anthropologists dug into the human race's distant past to unearth the primitive origins of its culture, of which religion is always an important part. Nearly all of them concluded that religion is based on primitive superstition. In 1890 Sir James Frazer (1854–1941) published *The Golden Bough,* a vast and fascinating history of early myths, superstitions, and cults from which he believed that modern religions, including Christianity, were derived.

Psychologists often viewed religion as a fantasy or illusion created by human beings. God, they felt, serves as a powerful parental figure to turn to when difficult problems drive human beings into a more childlike psychological state—someone who can be relied on to deal with a threatening world. Religion also provides psychological ecstasy as well as ways of enforcing constraint and control.

But it was the sociologists who were the most persistently and pointedly hostile to religion. Supernatural religion had no place whatever in Comte's positivism, humanity itself being the object of worship. Through volume after volume of Herbert Spencer's sociological writings ran a vein of hostility to mystic religion in general and to Christianity in particular. Mechanical evolution became, for Spencer, the key to all social progress; even morals evolved. Religious faith, said Spencer, retarded social progress and obscured human vision of the evolutionary social process.

Finally, the scientific spirit brought forth a number of biblical scholars who subjected the Bible to searching scrutiny and analysis—some for the purpose of establishing its exact meaning, others for the purpose of detecting error or fraud. This type of scholarship is called "higher criticism."

The first prominent nineteenth-century "higher critic" of the Bible was David Strauss (1808–1874), a Lutheran theologian at the University of Tübingen in Germany. After long years of laborious work, Strauss brought out a *Life of Jesus* in two volumes that stripped Christ of his divinity and undertook to explain in natural terms the miracles and prophecies recorded in the New Testament. Strauss asserted that the New Testament was a very unreliable document, that the authorship of the four Gospels could not be proved, and that the four accounts of the life of Jesus were contradictory.

Much more popular and influential was the charming one-volume *La Vie de Jésus* by Ernest Renan (1823–1892), a French scholar and a Catholic. Renan pictured Christ in solely human and natural terms. Renan attributed Christ's belief in his own divinity to hallucinations. But it was these psychological aberrations, Renan said, that gave him his power and drive and much of his appeal. The work of Strauss, Renan, and the numerous other "higher critics" appeared to many to bring religion within the compass of onrushing science.

4. THE CHRISTIAN RESPONSE

The first reaction of Christianity to the new challenges was angry rejection of the new ideas and forces. In 1864 Pope Pius IX (1846–1878) issued a *Syllabus of Errors,* errors that Roman Catholics were to avoid. These errors, eighty in all, included separation of church and state, civil marriage, secular education, freedom of speech and press, religious toleration, liberty of conscience, liberalism, and materialism. In 1870 Pius IX called a Vatican council (the first general council since that at Trent in the sixteenth century), which pronounced the doctrine of papal infallibility. According to this doctrine, the pope, when speaking *ex cathedra* (that is, officially *from the chair* of St. Peter) on a matter of faith or morals, is not subject to error. This was the most authoritarian position that the Church and the pope had ever taken, and it came at a time when the intellectual, political, and religious trends seemed to be in the opposite direction. In the late nineteenth and early twentieth centuries, the Catholic hierarchy excommunicated numerous members and several priests who had compromised the official doctrines of the Church.

Many Protestants also rejected the new ideas and forces, particularly fundamentalist sects that interpreted the Bible literally. More established churches, such as the Anglicans in Great Britain and Lutherans in Germany, resisted but had to contend with undisciplined dissent within their ranks and secular authorities that supported the new developments.

The second reaction of Christianity to the nineteenth-century challenges and assaults was to surrender to them. Many Christians, Catholics and Protestants alike, lost their faith and left their church. But many more who lost the traditional faith remained in their church and attempted to change its doctrines. They granted the claims of science and the "higher criticism," and they sympathized with the materialism, liberalism, and nationalism of the day. They continued to go to church, to sing the hymns, to say the prayers, and to recite the creeds, but they did not believe what they sang, said, and recited. They would reject the supernatural and deny the divinity of Christ. They would make the Bible a book of good literature and high ethical ideals; Christ, a great social reformer; and the Church, an instrument for the promotion of good will, wholesome fellowship, racial tolerance, temperance, charity, patriotism, and so on. These Christians came to be called *modernists*. The Catholic church declared officially against modernism in 1907, and by 1914 it appeared to have either suppressed the modernists in its ranks or driven them under cover. In the various Protestant churches in Europe modernism competed with fundamentalism, both extreme and moderate, and by 1914 modernism had tended to gain the upper hand. In the United States modernism in the Protestant churches did not reach its peak until the 1920s and 1930s.

The third reaction of Christianity was moderate compromise: an acceptance of proved scientific facts and reasonable deductions therefrom together with attempts to harmonize the findings of science with the fundamentals of the Christian faith. This attitude involved interpreting certain passages in the Bible figuratively, particularly the first chapter of Genesis, and admitting to a few errors in various versions of the Bible. This harmonizing Christian reaction led to an in-

FIGURE 46.3 Pope Leo XIII Leo XIII (1878–1903) was the first pope to face up to issues raised by science and modernization. While clinging to the traditional doctrines of the Church, he accepted new scientific discoveries and supported some liberal reform movements. (UPI/Bettmann Newsphotos)

creased awareness of the responsibility of the Christian churches to participate actively in the social and political problems of the day.

The Catholics were the first to reach this middle position. Leo XIII (see Figure 46.3), pope from 1878 to 1903, promoted the theology of Thomas Aquinas, which stressed the compatibility of faith and reason. He welcomed new scientific beliefs on condition that they be proved. He and his successors gradually took the position that natural science was not the province of the Church; that evolution could be taught in the Church's schools as a hypothesis; that the first chapter of Genesis should be taken figuratively; and that within these premises belief in evolution was a private and individual matter.

Leo XIII also faced up to some of the economic and social challenges of industrialization. In 1891, in the most famous of all his encyclicals, *Rerum Novarum* ("of new things"), he denounced materialism and Marxian socialism and proclaimed the sanctity of private property. He did, however, declare limits to the use of private property. Labor must not be treated as a commodity; workers must be paid a fair living wage and protected against too long hours, injury, and disease. Leo XIII advocated a wider distribution of property, labor unions for collective bargaining, and farming cooperatives. Roman Catholic labor unions were soon organized to challenge the socialist-dominated unions.

Christianity, so beset on its home grounds by challenges, assaults, and internal divisions during the late nineteenth century, was never more zealous in sending out missionaries to propagate the faith abroad. Roman Catholic, Protestant, and Eastern Orthodox missionaries vied with one another in Asia and Africa. By 1914 more than 40 million people outside western Christendom professed the Christian faith. But since the Christian missionaries in Asia and Africa were often associated with Western imperialism and exploitation, they frequently aroused resentment. In 1914 Christianity in the West was still on the defensive.

SUGGESTED READING

General

O. Chadwick, *The Secularization of the European Mind in the Nineteenth Century* (1975). A useful, well-written study.

P. A. Dale, *In Pursuit of a Scientific Culture: Science, Art, and Society in the Victorian Age* (1990). A thoughtful recent study.

The Physical, Biological, and Medical Sciences

E. Mayr, *The Growth of Biological Thought* (1982). A good recent survey.

M. Ruse, *The Darwinian Revolution* (1979). An excellent introduction.

The Rise of Social Science

R. Aron, *Main Currents in Sociological Thought*, 2 vols. (1965, 1967). An excellent survey of the founders of modern sociology.

P. Gay, *Freud: A Life for Our Time* (1988). A well-regarded study.

Challenges to Christianity

J. L. Altholz, *The Churches in the Nineteenth Century* (1967). A solid survey.

H. McLeod, *Religion and the People of Western Europe, 1789–1970* (1981). Useful chapters on the period.

J. McManners, *Church and State in France, 1870–1914* (1972). Solid and scholarly.

J. Moore, *The Post-Darwinian Controversies: A Study of the Protestant Struggle to Come to Terms with Darwin in Great Britain and America, 1870–1900* (1979). A respected analysis.

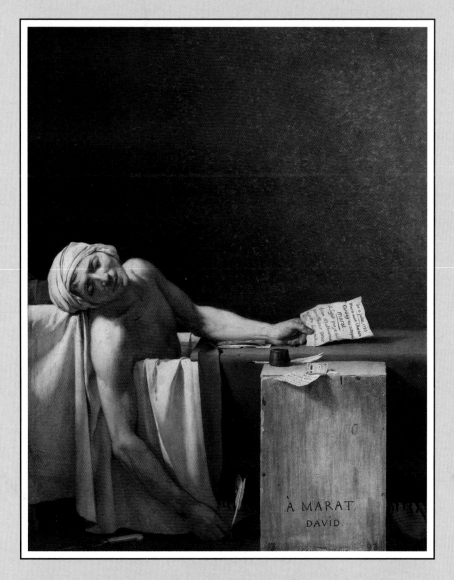

PLATE 18. Jacques-Louis David, *The Death of Marat,* 1793 The French artist David was an active figure in the French Revolution. Here he shows the death of Marat, one of the chief leaders of the radical second phase of the Revolution. Marat was working in his bathtub when Charlotte Corday assassinated him. The subject matter and the political message are in sharp contrast to earlier eighteenth-century art, which reflected aristocratic tastes. (Musées Royaux des Beaux-Arts de Belgique, Brussels)

PLATE 19. John Constable, *The White Horse,* 1819
Like many romantic painters, John Constable (1776–1837) was fascinated by nature. Here he depicts a rural scene that is naturalistic (a real scene the viewer might come across) and idyllic. The painting, with its vast living sky and detailed foliage, pulls the viewer into nature. The reality of this image of rural life in nature was already starting to disappear as commercial agriculture, industrialization, and urbanization spread throughout England. (Copyright The Frick Collection)

PLATE 20. Joseph Mallard William Turner, *The Fighting Temeraire,* 1839
Turner is considered the greatest of the English romantic painters. In paintings dominated by light and color, he depicted heroic, tragic struggles mirrored by the overwhelming forces of nature. Here an antiquated battleship sails off into the eternity of the setting sun. The grand ship of the past is replaced by a modern steamship, the smoke from its stack merging into the clouds that frame the sun. (National Gallery, London: Art Resource)

PLATE 21. Eugène Delacroix, *Entrance of the Crusaders into Constantinople,* 1840 Romantic painters such as Delacroix (1793–1863) often glorified the medieval past and the exotic. In this dramatic scene, Byzantine patricians humble themselves before the intruding Crusaders. The scene swirls with passion and color—a romantic vision of the past in sharp contrast to the reality of mid-nineteenth century France. (The Louvre, Paris)

PLATE 22. Gustave Courbet, *The Stone Breakers,* 1849 Realism rejected almost all elements of the Romantic movement. Realistic artists such as Courbet (1819–1877) depicted the mundane, everyday life of workers. Here he portrays stone breakers as a passerby might see them. While there is dignity in their work, Courbet does not glorify them or nature. (Staatlichen Kunstsammlungen, Dresden)

PLATE 23. Auguste Renoir, *Le Moulin de la Galette à Montmartre*, 1876 Impressionist painters emphasized the appearance of things as one might see them at a glance. Using new techniques that emphasized applying dabs of colors to the canvas so the eye could mix them, these paintings had great immediacy. Here Renoir (1841–1919), a leading French impressionist most known for his fleshy, optimistic paintings, portrays a festive scene at a Parisian outdoor dance hall. Youthful middle- and working-class figures brim with health and pleasure in this artificial urban environment. (Musée d'Orsay, Paris; Scala/Art Resource)

PLATE 24. Georges Seurat, *A Sunday on La Grande Jatte*, 1884–1886 Some neo-impressionists such as the French artist, Georges Seurat (1859–1891), reflected the growing influence of science during the second half of the nineteenth century. Using a compulsive style of painting based on the latest scientific understanding of light and color, Seurat carefully composed this canvas portraying the urban bourgeoise at leisure. The scene emphasizes the inhibited stiffness of this class, its emotional separation from other classes, and the isolation of individuals and small groups within the bourgeoisie. (Oil on canvas, 207.6 × 308 cm, Helen Birch Bartlett Memorial Collection, 1926.224. © 1993 The Art Institute of Chicago.)

PLATE 25. Paul Cézanne, *Mont Sainte-Victoire*, 1902–1904 Cézanne (1839–1906) had roots in impressionism but ultimately rejected it. He tried to display the essence rather than the surface of reality by emphasizing the geometric principles of form and an analytic understanding of color. This landscape is one of a series of paintings of Mont Sainte-Victoire in southern France. Both Cézanne and van Gogh created foundations for twentieth-century painting. (Philadelphia Museum of Art, George W. Elkins Collection)

PLATE 26. Vincent van Gogh, *The Starry Night*, 1889 Like Cézanne, van Gogh (1853–1890) had roots in impressionism but went beyond it. He was able to express his own intense emotions in bold, dynamic paintings. Here he seems to have poured himself into this scene he painted toward the end of his life while at a sanatorium in St.-Rémy. The scene swirls with color applied in distinct, broad strokes. It is not a scene of reality one might see, but rather an expression of feelings that mingles with external reality. (Oil on canvas, 29 x 36¼″. Collection, The Museum of Modern Art, New York; acquired through the Lillie P. Bliss Bequest)

PLATE 27. James Ensor, *Intrigue*, 1890
During the late nineteenth century a sense of dissatisfaction and a criticism of middle-class life grew. This is reflected in expressive paintings such as those by the Belgian painter James Ensor (1860–1949). Here people are shown as indistinct from the obnoxious masks they seem to wear. (Royal Museum of Fine Arts, Antwerp)

PLATE 28. Edvard Munch, *The Scream*, 1893 Like Ensor, Edvard Munch (1863–1944) expressed an undermining of middle-class life, but on a deeper, more individual level. In *The Scream,* a nightmare-like fear is revealed, reflecting an anxiety and a turning inward toward the unconscious that was growing in late-nineteeth-century intellectual and cultural circles. Similarities to van Gogh's paintings can be seen in how paint is used boldly to express emotion. (National Museum, Oslo)

PLATE 29. Max Ernst, *Europe after the Rain,* 1940–1942 Max Ernst (1891–1976) became a leader of the surrealists during the 1920s. He painted *Europe after the Rain* while hiding in Paris during World War II. The painting seems to represent the illogical horror and destruction of that era, and it stands as a perhaps prophetic warning to us all. (Wadsworth Atheneum, Hartford, Ella Gallup Sumner and Mary Catlin Sumner Collection)

PLATE 30. Salvador Dalí, *The Temptation of St. Anthony,* 1947 Surrealism, a relatively popular style of twentieth-century painting, emphasizes the power of dreams and the unconscious. The aim is to depict an unfiltered psychic reality that visually may seem shocking and impossible. One of the most well known surealists was Salvador Dalí (1904–1989). Here the subject is apparently traditional (St. Anthony trying to fend off temptations), but the painting has the feeling and appearance of an improbable nightmare. (Musées Royaux des Beaux-Arts de Belgique, Brussels)

PLATE 31. Piet Mondrian, *Composition*, 1929
The twentieth-century trend away from art that represents external reality toward abstract art was carried to an extreme by the Dutch painter Piet Mondrian (1872–1944). Here he uses only black, white, and the three primary colors to express his logical, harmonious vision. (National Museum, Belgrade: Scala/Art Resource)

PLATE 32. Fernand Léger, *The Great Constructors*, 1950 This painting by the French artist Léger (1881–1955), reflects several trends in twentieth century art. Clearly this is an urban scene, showing construction workers and the steel frame of a skyscraper; yet the lines, proportions, and colors scarcely conform to reality. Elements of expressionism—the attempt to convey a feeling about people in this mechanical age—and abstract art—the concern with nonrepresentational lines and colors—abound in this work. (Musée de Biot, France: Josse/Art Resource)

CHAPTER 47
Thought and Culture in an Age of Nationalism and Industrialization

FIGURE 47.1 Pablo Picasso, *Les Demoiselles d'Avignon*, 1906–1907 Between 1850 and 1914 artistic styles evolved rapidly, moving from realism to the beginnings of modernism. Picasso (1881–1973) was one of the most influential artists during the latter part of this period and throughout the twentieth century. This painting reflects the sense of revolt, the rapidly changing values, and the tendency to turn inward that characterized many cultural products of the late nineteenth and early twentieth centuries. (Oil on canvas, 8' × 7'8". Collection, The Museum of Modern Art, New York. Acquired through the Lillie P. Bliss Bequest)

The nationalism of the increasingly powerful Western nation-states, the challenges to established religious and moral values, and the tensions of industrial society are reflected in the thought and art of the period between 1850 and 1914. There was no sudden or drastic break with the spirit of idealism and romanticism that prevailed in the thought and art of the first half of the nineteenth century. Both idealism and romanticism continued throughout the nineteenth century and beyond. Nevertheless, after midcentury, realism tended to replace the romanticism of the early nineteenth century. As the bourgeoisie played a more dominant role in the culture of the period, artists, writers, and intellectuals became more of an avant-garde—increasingly critical of bourgeois values and tastes. By the end of the nineteenth century and the beginning of the twentieth, these artists, writers, and intellectuals were injecting a theme of pessimism and painful introspection into Western culture.

The nationalism that was such an important component of political and social developments during the period was reflected in a growing body of thought. Nationalism was also one of the elements behind the spread of state-sponsored educational reforms, which led toward expanded literacy and the growth of popular journalism.

In literature a stream of realism and naturalism, characterized by an almost scientific examination of life, seemed to focus on individual and social failings. Art tended to slip away from the grasp of the ordinary viewer as photography displaced traditional representational art and impressionists applied a new understanding of the physical world and optics to their paintings. Post-impressionists veered into even more disturbing styles as art, like the new scientific disciplines, became more specialized.

1. POPULAR EDUCATION, JOURNALISM, AND CULTURE

During this era of nationalism and spreading industrialization, and particularly after 1871, there were great advances in popular education. In 1871 northern Germany and Scandinavia were the only places in the world where practically everyone could read and write. In the United States most of the states had free public elementary schools, but a fifth of the total population was still illiterate. In Great Britain a third of the people were still illiterate, in France and Belgium a half, in Spain and Italy three-fourths, in Russia and the Balkans nine-tenths. Between 1868 and 1881 national systems of free and compulsory public education were established in nearly all the nations of western and central Europe and the United States. There was a variety of reasons for this growing commitment to public education. Public schooling was seen as a way to create more patriotic, nationalistic citizens. At the same time schools could help provide workers with the skills and discipline that modernizing economies and military establishments demanded. For the most part, the compulsory public school systems were limited to elementary education. While the core of the curriculum was generally the same for boys and girls—reading, writing, history, mathematics, and a few other subjects—boys were usually taught more science and skills such as carpentry while girls were taught domestic skills. By 1914 illiteracy had practically ceased to exist in Scandinavia, Germany, Great Britain, and the Netherlands. The illiteracy rate was less than 10 percent in the United States, Canada, France, and Belgium. In Italy it had been reduced to 50 percent and in Spain, Russia, and the Balkans to a little more than 50 percent. Literacy, of course, is only the first step toward education.

The rise in literacy was reflected in a growth of popular journalism. In 1850 newspapers were relatively few, small, expensive, and written for a limited educated clientele. The London *Times*, probably the world's most influential newspaper, had a daily circulation of less than fifty thousand. During the second half of the nineteenth century, nationalism and industrialization were accompanied by a new kind of newspaper, one that was cheap, sensational, and popular in its appeal. One of the pioneer popular journalists was Joseph Pulitzer (1847–1911), a Hungarian immigrant to the United States. Pulitzer founded the St. Louis *Post Dispatch*. He bought and built up the New York *World* until it became the country's biggest newspaper. With screaming headlines, flag-waving patriotism, an easy, catchy style, sensational news, popular causes and features, and above all comics, he made a fortune and became influential in politics. In the 1890s William Randolph Hearst built a great newspaper empire patterned after Pulitzer's. In Great Britain Alfred Harmsworth founded the halfpenny popular *Daily Mail*, made a fortune, and then bought the London *Times*. Before the end of the century five newspapers—two in London, two in Paris, and one in Berlin—had a daily circulation of more than a million each. *Le Petit Journal* in Paris had a circulation of more than two and a quarter million. This type of newspaper not only catered to the masses but also became a powerful molder of public opinion. Hearst boasted, with a modicum of truth, that he had manufactured the Spanish-American War. Since the popular newspapers made their money chiefly from advertising rather than from sales, they came increasingly to reflect the viewpoints of their chief advertisers, the great corporations. The big newspapers were themselves, of course, big business. Although they catered to the masses, they generally did not represent the interests of the masses.

Newspapers were part of the literature of popular culture. Pulp fiction was also spreading rapidly, as were other cultural outlets of the masses. The phonograph increased the demand for popular music, as did the growing number of urban music and dance halls. After the 1890s commercial films were produced. By 1914 millions of people were watching movies every week. New public libraries and museums were institutions that could serve all classes and blur the lines between popular and elite culture. Nevertheless, divisions between the classes were strong, and this was reflected in the differences between popular and elite culture.

2. CURRENTS OF THOUGHT: NATIONALISM, RACISM, AND DISENCHANTMENT

During the nineteenth century a strong current of thought reflected and supported the growing nationalism of that era. German thinkers in particular contributed to the intellectual foundations of nationalism. In the first half of the century, Georg Wilhelm Hegel (1770–1831) was most influential. Among other things, he argued that individual freedom depends on ordered discipline under a strong state and that the zeitgeist (spirit of the time) of the nineteenth century was the spirit of German civilization.

Even more directly supportive of nationalism were the ideas of people such as Heinrich von Treitschke, probably the most influential German historian of the decades surrounding the turn of the century, who proclaimed that Germany's victory over France demonstrated the superiority of military autocracy over liberalism. Only strong states ought to exist, he felt; dissident minorities, individualism, and parliamentary inefficiency must not be tolerated.

German thinkers were not the only ones to reflect the nationalism of the period in their ideas. The French historian Hippolyte Taine blamed France's defeat in 1870–1871 on the corrupting influence of liberalism born in the French Revolution and bred during the nineteenth century. He wanted to take France back to the days of the Old Regime. In Great Britain, Thomas Carlyle exalted heroes and hero worship, specifically the Prussian variety, in thunderous prose. Rudyard Kipling put his poetic gifts to use to sing of the glorious British Empire and the "white man's burden" of ruling and civilizing "backward" peoples.

The most extreme set of ideas underlying nationalism during the second half of the nineteenth century was racism (see p. 615). People of every nation began to think and talk of themselves as a distinct and superior breed. Language was more than ever confused with race. Thus one spoke of the various "races" in the Austro-Hungarian Empire. By far the most popular and serious of all the racial cults was the Aryan myth. The term *Aryan,* which was originally a linguistic term referring to the ancient Persians (Iranians) and later to all peoples speaking Indo-European languages, was now applied to the Germanic- or Teutonic-speaking peoples or to the Nordic (tall blond) type of northern European. After Germany's spectacular military triumphs and economic developments under Bismarck, the term *Aryan* came to be applied more specifically to Germans and to the energetic, aggressive, military qualities they were supposed to possess. Oddly, the two chief formulators of the Aryan myth were a Frenchman, Comte de Gobineau, and the renegade Englishman Houston Stewart Chamberlain, who left his homeland and became a German citizen. Their ideas, however, were taken much more seriously in Germany than in France or Great Britain. They argued that race was the key determinant of history. Chamberlain's racist ideas veered off into anti-Semitism, as did the ideas of other racist writers such as Richard Wagner. Wagner wrote violent propaganda tracts and composed grandiose operas that stridently extolled the virtues of the early Nordic (German) supermen—Siegfried and the Nibelungs.

Although many philosophers of Social Darwinism and liberalism remained optimistic about the evolution of human beings and human society ever onward and upward, a new, strong strain of disenchantment surfaced in late-nineteenth-century philosophy. A forerunner of these pessimistic philosophers who were to have so much influence on the twentieth century was Arthur Schopenhauer (1788–1860). In *The World as Will and Idea,* published in 1819, forty years before *On the Origin of Species,* this German thinker set forth the idea that one force governs and motivates the whole world of animate life, and that force is will—the will to survive. The world, therefore, is a cruel and heartless place full of struggling and competing creatures, a place where the strong and fierce devour the weak and gentle. The only possible happiness to be found in it is by ascetic denial and withdrawal. They suffer least who participate least in the hard, competitive world.

This line of thinking (at least a variation of it) was carried to its ultimate by an admirer of Schopenhauer, Friedrich Nietzsche (1844–1900). Nietzsche was a disillusioned German theological student turned philosopher. He was a pain- and nerve-racked genius. Two of his most influential works are *Thus Spake Zarathustra* and *Beyond Good and Evil.* Like Schopenhauer, he believed that the greatest force in the animate world is will. However, this will is not only to survive but also, in the strong at least, to achieve power. "The will to power" was Nietzsche's key phrase. If a superior society is to emerge, it will have to come about through the efforts of strong and gifted individuals who will rise to power because of their superior strength, will, and intelligence. Anything that contributes to power is good, be it strength of will, boldness, cunning, or intelligence. Whatever leads to weakness is

bad, be it gentleness, modesty, generosity, or compassion. The two greatest enemies of the good society are democracy and Christianity. Democracy is the rule by mediocre masses, cattle. But it was against Christianity that Nietzsche hurled his sharpest invective; he believed Christianity to be the greatest curse of Western civilization: a religion that extols the vices of slavery, such as meekness, compassion, sacrifice, and charity to compensate for actual weakness. He went on to attack many other accepted foundations of nineteenth-century civilization, including liberalism, rationalism, and science. Although not a nationalist or racist himself, his ideas would later be used by others to support militant nationalism and even racism.

Less caustic and far more popular was the French philosopher Henri Bergson (1859–1941). Like Nietzsche, he attacked bourgeois liberalism and extolled the instincts and the subjective will. His sense of the world as an evolving, vital, spontaneous place fit well with other trends in thought and the arts during the early decades of the twentieth century.

Also popular was the philosophy of pragmatism. The chief expounder of this school of thought, which has been so potent and widespread in the twentieth century, was William James (1842–1910), a professor of psychology and philosophy at Harvard University. Pragmatism reflected the uncertainties aroused by atomic physicists around the turn of the century. James rejected all absolutes of logic and religion. Truth, he stated, is relative, depending on the individual and the circumstances. A thing is true if it works and is useful. We cannot know ultimate religious or moral truths, for instance, but if a particular religious faith gives an individual confidence and peace of mind, then it is practical and therefore true for that person. Thus spiritual, moral, and human values became as relative in the minds of William James and the pragmatists as the physical world in the mind of Albert Einstein.

3. REALISTIC LITERATURE

Much of the literature of the second half of the nineteenth century, like the philosophy, reflected the materialism, the cynicism, and the pessimism of the age. However, there was a strong carryover of romanticism beyond 1850 and into the twentieth century. The romantic Victorian poets Victor Hugo, Robert Browning, and Alfred Tennyson lived on until 1885, 1889, and 1892, respectively. Although Browning was a rugged, analytical realist when probing the depths of human psychology and emotions, he tended at times to be an idealist and optimist, believing that "God's in his heaven, all's right with the world." And although in 1850 the young Tennyson in his *In Memoriam* revealed a religious skepticism bold for the time, in 1889 he hoped to see his "Pilot face to face" when he had "crossed the bar." Nevertheless, the prevailing and most significant trend in literature was realism. It was expressed most generally in the novel and drama rather than poetry. Realism tended to depict the seamy, sordid side of human nature and society. It villainized the *nouveau riche* industrial bourgeoisie and its religious and moral hypocrisy without idealizing the uprooted and distressed working class.

France took the lead in realistic literature. Honoré de Balzac (1799–1850) foreshadowed realism. In his scores of novels and tales he subjected the dominant middle class to increasingly exact and severe scrutiny. The first French novelist to catch the full flavor of realism was Gustave Flaubert (1821–1880). His *Madame Bovary* related the illicit sex life of the wife of a small-town French physician in such full and unblushing detail that it scandalized a public not yet accustomed to such unrestrained "realism." *Madame Bovary* became a model for other novelists.

Émile Zola (1840–1902), though like Flaubert interested in individual personality, was more concerned with social problems, particularly those created by industrialization. Zola was a bold and radical republican who played a major role in finally securing justice for Alfred Dreyfus (see p. 608). In twenty penetrating but sometimes tedious novels he depicted and analyzed the problems of a changing society. His sympathy was with the industrial working class, but he suffered from no illusions as to the natural goodness of people, including the distressed lower classes.

Charles Dickens (1812–1870) in Great Britain combined romanticism and realism. In his sentimentality, his moralizing, his optimism, and his spontaneous gush of words, he was a romantic. In his zeal for social reform, his pillorying of bourgeois arrogance and corrupt bourgeois institutions, and his graphic and often sordid detailing of the life of the urban working class, he was the first of the British realists. In *David Copperfield, Oliver Twist,* and *The Pickwick Papers,* three of the best known of his numerous and lengthy novels, a galaxy of characters of the middle and lower walks of life in industrial Britain parade realistically before us.

Mary Ann Evans (1819–1880), writing under the pen name George Eliot, wrote popular novels depicting the realities of British social life. In *Middlemarch: A Study of Provincial Life,* she sensitively related psychological conflicts to the determining social realities that surround her characters.

Thomas Hardy (1840–1928), unlike Dickens, had a pessimistic view of the universe. His vivid characters—ordinary English countryside folk—struggle Darwin-like against fate, environment, and their own frail natures without any help from God or Hardy. *The Return of the Native, The Mayor of Casterbridge,* and *Tess of the D'Urbervilles* are some of the best examples of the realistic novel in any language.

Probably the most typical of all the British realists was George Bernard Shaw (1856–1950). Of Irish birth, Shaw early crossed over to London, where he long remained the gadfly of bourgeois society. In scores of urbane and sophisticated novels, essays, and plays, he charmingly but caustically taunted Christianity, capitalism, and democracy. Shaw was a cynic, a socialist, and a stark materialist. He was the epitome of late-nineteenth-century and early-twentieth-century realism.

In the United States, the era of the realistic novel began with the works of Theodore Dreiser (1871–1945). Dreiser's novels depicted in hard, rough detail the life and the philosophy of the disenchanted, uprooted proletariat living in a materialistic, industrial world of changing values. His first novel, *Sister Carrie,* which appeared in 1900, was an American industrial version of *Madame Bovary* told with raw unrestraint. To escape poverty, Carrie became the mistress of a succession of men. The progressive degeneration of the characters constitutes the theme of the novel. Editors were so shocked at the frank and open presentation of lurid details that Dreiser had great difficulty getting the book published. The success of *Sister Carrie* was immediate, and other novels in a like vein followed.

One of the most influential of the realists was the Norwegian playwright Henrik Ibsen (1828–1906). A frustrated artist embittered by youthful poverty, Ibsen ridiculed bourgeois society in his popular dramas. In what is probably his best-known play, *A Doll's House,* one of his heroines rebels against the "doll's house" that her stodgy, hypocritical, middle-class husband has created for her. In *An Enemy of the People,* Ibsen reveals the fickleness of the masses and their unfitness for democratic government. *Ghosts* deals with the social and personal problems of syphilis.

In Russia, Ivan Sergeyevich Turgenev (1818–1883) and Fyodor Dostoyevski (1821–1881) combined realism with romanticism in much the same manner as did Dickens in Great Britain. In his masterpiece, *Fathers and Sons,* Turgenev grapples powerfully with the problems of the older, conservative Russian generation versus the modern, sophisticated, and radical younger generation. Dostoyevski's two greatest novels are *Crime and Punishment* and *The Brothers Karamazov.* In them he delves psychologically and mystically into the problems of evil and purification through suffering. He was deeply religious, but not in any formal or orthodox sense. Leo Tolstoy (1828–1910) was more completely dedicated to realism and devoted his life and writing almost exclusively to social reform. His masterpiece is *War and Peace.* In this gigantic novel, scores of personalities along with more impersonal social forces so interlace with and influence one another that not even the strongest individual—not even Napoleon—can work his will alone. In his later years Tolstoy sought to combine Christianity with socialism, giving up his great inherited wealth to set a good example. Anton Chekhov (1860–1904) wrote polished but realistic and pessimistic plays about Russian life. Maxim Gorky (1868–1936), up from the proletarian ranks, analyzed the social problems of the Russian masses in his dramas and novels.

The various veins of realistic literature, with all their variety, had many things in common. The literature almost invariably reflected the social dislocation brought about by the Industrial Revolution, particularly in its more advanced second phase. It reflected the materialism of an age of science and technology. It displayed over and over again the influence of Darwin and, later, of Freud. It was increasingly concerned with the disillusionment and cynicism brought about by changing religious and moral values.

4. IMPRESSIONIST AND MODERN PAINTING AND SCULPTURE

France, the birthplace of realistic literature, was also the chief seat of the impressionistic and modern painting and sculpture that predominated during the second half of the nineteenth century. Impressionism was a mild, sophisticated revolt against the artistic standards that had prevailed since the late fifteenth century. It reflected the intellectual challenge to traditional values and institutions that arose after midcentury. It took its chief inspiration from the seventeenth-century Spanish painters Velásquez and El Greco, from Japanese art, which was rediscovered after 1853, and from new scientific knowledge concerning the nature of color and light. Impressionistic painting was informal, unposed, and random-angled. It sought to convey by studied casualness the impression of a view one gets at a glance. The chief founder of the impressionistic style of painting was the Frenchman Édouard Manet (1832–1883). Among his more illustrious disciples were Claude Monet (1840–1926), Auguste Renoir (1841–1919), and Camille Pissarro (1830–1903) (see Color Plate 23 and Figure 47.2). These artists painted sunlit parks and landscapes, shimmering lakes and rivers, and subtle, sophisticated portraits. They omitted much detail, painting in only suggestive shapes, forms, and colors as first impressions and leaving the rest to the imagination. Their work was sensuous, decorative, and mildly iconoclastic.

The breach the impressionists made with long-established traditions was greatly widened near the end of the nineteenth century and early in the twentieth by more radical modern painters. The new trend was led by Paul Cézanne (1839–1906), a lifelong friend of Émile Zola (see Color Plate 25). Cézanne distorted freely in order to achieve a more powerful effect and applied thick paint to attain the appearance of solidity and roundness. Going far beyond Cézanne, the gifted but eccentric Frenchman Paul Gauguin

FIGURE 47.2 Claude Monet, *La Grenouillère*, 1869 Monet was a leading French impressionist. His bold use of color, his emphasis on the play of light, and his focus on the appearance of things were typical of impressionist painters. (The Metropolitan Museum of Art, Bequest of Mrs. H. O. Havemeyer, 1929. The Havemeyer Collection)

(1848–1903) and the Dutchman Vincent van Gogh (1853–1890) broke openly with the artistic standards of the past. Gauguin was interested in painting not the literal document of his subject but only what the subject meant to him. He painted the patterns formed in his mind by objects rather than the objects themselves, using violent reds, yellows, and greens. He finally became primitive, deserting Western civilization for the South Sea Islands. Gauguin's friend, van Gogh, would squeeze paint directly from the tube onto the canvas to achieve striking effects (see Color Plate 26). Like Gauguin, van Gogh was an expressionist, freely distorting the images of nature to make them express his own feelings. Cézanne, Gauguin, and van Gogh were the forerunners of many iconoclastic schools, such as cubism and futurism, that marked twentieth-century painting.

Two of the most influential of the revolutionary modern painters were the Frenchman Henri Matisse (1869–1954) and the Spanish-born (French by adoption) Pablo Picasso (1881–1973), both of whom received their chief inspiration from Cézanne. In some of their work they carried distortion to great extremes. Matisse became enamored with primitive culture. Picasso's figures

during one phase of his long career became geometric (hence cubism) and disjointed (see Figure 47.1). He occasionally gave up color entirely for black and white.

It is characteristic of an age of intellectual revolt and changing values that artists turn inward (see Color Plates 27 and 28). During the late nineteenth and early twentieth centuries, painting became highly individualistic. Artists tended to paint such objects as fruit, still life, and mandolins. Furthermore, they turned to figures on the periphery of a disintegrating society, such as prostitutes, solitary drinkers, blind beggars, and circus performers. The figures were separate from one another. This disjointedness and the symbols of science, machinery, and speed, which were so prominent in this painting, represented an age of intellectual revolt against traditional values, of materialistic science and technology, and of social tension. Unfortunately, much of this painting was so technical and highly specialized that it could be appreciated only by a relative few at a time when many were seeking enlightenment.

The rapid growth of cities and wealth during the second Industrial Revolution was responsible for the production of a large quantity of sculp-

FIGURE 47.3 Auguste Rodin, *Heroic Head* (Pierre de Weissart), 1889, bronze Rodin's powerful figures represent both a new departure in sculpture and a bridge from the nineteenth century to the twentieth. He brought the impressionist spirit to his work, and he was a forerunner of much of the abstract and symbolist sculpture of the twentieth century. (Norweb Collection, The Cleveland Museum of Art)

ture to decorate the new public buildings, squares, and parks. Most of it was patterned after the styles of the past, either classical or baroque, more often the latter. Probably the two sculptors of the period who most truly reflected the spirit of their own time and of future trends were Constantin Meunier (1831–1905) in Belgium and Auguste Rodin (1840–1917) in France. Meunier was the first great sculptor to recognize the importance of the industrial proletariat. Among his rugged and realistic statues are "The Hammersmith," "The Puddler," "The Mine Girl," and

"The Old Mine Horse." Rodin introduced impressionism into sculpture (see Figure 47.3). His most famous statue, "The Thinker," illustrates not only impressionistic art but also the influence of the classical, Renaissance, baroque, and romantic styles. Rodin was the forerunner of much of the modern, abstract, and symbolist sculpture of the twentieth century.

5. FUNCTIONAL ARCHITECTURE

The architecture of the period 1850–1914, like the sculpture, combined the old with the new. The prevailing style in the numerous and increasingly large public buildings continued to be classical or baroque. Gothic architecture, which had enjoyed a revival in the early part of the nineteenth century, was now limited primarily to university buildings and to churches. Even Byzantine, Moorish, and Oriental models appeared here and there throughout the West as the world was brought closer together by rapid communications.

The first great architect to develop a style appropriate to an age of steel, science, and speed was the American Louis Henry Sullivan (1856–1924). Sullivan argued that "form follows function"; that is to say, the style of buildings should be determined by their intended use and by the materials used in their construction (see Figure 47.4). The architectural devices of the past had lost their utility, were purely decorative. And in fast-moving, crowded, and growing New York and Chicago, what sense did horizontal Greek or Moorish lines make? Sullivan designed the first steel-supported skyscraper.

But Sullivan and his followers were not satisfied with the principle "form follows function." They decided that function is the prime purpose of architecture. The application of this principle came to be known as "functional architecture." Structural steel, reinforced concrete, and glass brick made it possible for the functional architects to achieve unbroken horizontal lines impossible for the Greeks and towering heights combined with gracefulness and light that the medieval Gothic builders could not have contemplated. Furthermore, the spirit of intellectual revolt against the standards and values of the past gave architects a freedom to experiment never before enjoyed. Finally, unprecedented wealth and technological advances provided them with the means to execute their ideas. Some of the massive utilitarian structures of this and later periods are creditable monuments to an age of materialism.

6. MUSIC OLD AND NEW

Of all the arts, music showed the least responsiveness to the economic and social trends between 1850 and 1914. Some of the greatest romantic composers lived well on into the second half of the nineteenth century. Wagner lived until 1883, Verdi until 1901. Their ranks were joined in the late nineteenth century by such great romanticists as Camille Saint-Saëns (1835–1921) in France and Peter Tchaikovsky (1840–1893) in Russia. Nor was there any lessening in the spirit of nationalism in music, which was such an important ingredient of romanticism. Wagner's nationalism became more militant after 1870. Tchaikovsky combined Russian nationalism with his romanticism. More strictly nationalist in their themes and folk tunes were the Russian Nikolai Rimsky-Korsakov (1844–1908), the Czech Antonín Dvořák (1841–1904), the Norwegian Edvard Grieg (1843–1907), and the Finn Jean Sibelius (1865–1957).

Not only romanticism but also classicism was carried over into the late nineteenth century by the great German composer Johannes Brahms (1833–1897). Spending the last thirty-five years of his life in the Hapsburg capital of Vienna, Brahms became an ardent Hungarian nationalist without giving up his loyalty to his native Germany. Probably more than any other musician, Brahms resembles Beethoven in style. Like Beethoven, he combined the classical spirit with the romantic.

One of the most important innovators in music of the period was the French composer Claude Debussy (1862–1918). Debussy was the father of impressionistic music. Experimenting with subtle and sophisticated dissonances, he was to music what Manet and Renoir were to painting. Meanwhile, in Germany Richard Strauss (1864–1949) was startling and scandaliz-

FIGURE 47.4 Louis Sullivan's Carson-Pirie-Scott Department Store The Carson-Pirie-Scott Department Store in Chicago was designed by the American architect Louis Henry Sullivan (1856–1924), who was the first to determine that function is the sole purpose of the style of a building. Sullivan designed the world's first steel-supported skyscraper. (Hedrich Blessing)

ing his pre–World War I audiences with his complex and sometimes harshly dissonant "realistic" tone poems. He is often said to have ushered in the "modern" period in music. In Russia, Igor Stravinsky (1882–1971) was beginning his long career of composing music that was still more iconoclastic and abstract. He is called the father of the expressionist school. Stravinsky, with his more violent and impetuous dissonances, bears somewhat the same relationship to Debussy as Picasso does to Monet in painting.

SUGGESTED READING

General

F. L. Baumer, *Modern European Thought* (1977). A good general introduction.

H. S. Hughes, *Consciousness and Society* (1979). A superb study of intellectual history during the period.

S. Kern, *The Culture of Time and Space, 1880–1918* (1983). An important, interpretive work.

P. Monaco, *Modern European Culture and Consciousness, 1870–1980* (1983). The early chapters cover the period well.

C. E. Schorske, *Fin-de-Siècle Vienna: Politics and Culture* (1980). An excellent study of one of Europe's cultural centers.

R. Shattuck, *The Banquet Years* (1968). A well-written account of the social and cultural life of late-nineteenth-century Paris.

Popular Education, Journalism, and Culture

C. M. Cipolla, *Literacy and Development in the West* (1969). Covers the rise in literacy during the period.

C. Cross, *A Social History of Leisure since 1600* (1990). A recent history that covers the period.

A. J. Lee, *The Origins of the Popular Press in Britain, 1855–1914* (1978). Covers aspects of popular culture and journalism.

M. Maynes, *Schooling in Western Europe: A Social History* (1985). Covers popular education well.

Currents of Thought

W. Kaufmann, *Nietzsche: Philosopher, Psychologist, Anti-Christ* (1974). A highly respected analysis of Nietzsche and his thought.

K. Löwith, *From Hegel to Nietzsche: The Revolution in Nineteenth-Century Thought* (1964). A good analysis.

L. Poliakov, *The Aryan Myth: A History of Racist and Nationalist Ideas in Europe* (1971). An excellent introduction.

Realistic Literature

R. Pascal, *From Naturalism to Expressionism: German Literature and Society, 1880–1918* (1973). A good survey.

Art, Architecture, and Music

P. Collaer, *A History of Modern Music* (1961). A well-written survey.

R. Herbert, *Impressionism: Art, Leisure, and Parisian Society* (1988). An insightful cultural history.

H. R. Hitchcock, *Architecture: 19th and 20th Centuries* (1958). A good survey.

R. Hughes, *The Shock of the New: Art and the Century of Change* (1981). Extremely well written.

J. Rewald, *Post Impressionism: From van Gogh to Gauguin* (1979). A respected study.

CHAPTER 48
Politics, Democracy, and Nationalism, 1871–1914

KEEPING IT DOWN!

FIGURE 48.1 Bismarck and the Socialists This satirical illustration from the September 28, 1878, edition of the British magazine *Punch* shows German Chancellor Bismarck in military dress vainly struggling to keep down the socialist "Jack in the Box." Although Bismarck banned the Social Democratic party in 1878, it would not die. In the years just prior to World War I it became Germany's largest single party. Other socialist parties grew throughout Europe during the same period. (*Punch,* September 28, 1878)

From the end of the Franco-Prussian War in 1871 until the outbreak of World War I in 1914, the West was free from major wars. Despite some changes and shaky beginnings, European nations survived the period with their governments intact. When the considerable economic expansion, cultural production, and imperial success are added to this political picture, the years between 1871 and 1914 may be viewed as a time of great progress for Europe.

Nevertheless, some disturbing trends were evident. The freedom from war was accompanied by a growing militarism in several nations and a new precarious complexity in international affairs. Moreover, governmental survival did not mean political peace; political unrest and even some revolutionary activity threatened many European nations. Imperial success was purchased at a price of heightened international rivalries. These disturbing trends would bear bitter fruit with the outbreak of World War I in 1914.

The strongest political forces of the period were the spread of democratic institutions and nationalism. Both forces had been under way since the first half of the nineteenth century. However, the spread of democratic institutions occurred quite unevenly. And nationalism, while it differed according to the conditions in each country, took on more conservative, aggressive, militaristic, and even racist overtones. The political developments between 1871 and 1914 can be well expressed by stressing the themes of democracy and nationalism and dividing our examination of European nations roughly between western and eastern Europe.

1. WESTERN EUROPE: THE SPREAD AND REFORM OF DEMOCRATIC INSTITUTIONS

Most of the western European countries had formed a national identity and initiated democratic reforms before the eastern European countries did. Between 1871 and 1914 democratic institutions continued to spread in western Europe and, in general, encountered fewer problems than in eastern Europe.

Great Britain

During the second half of the nineteenth century Great Britain was in a strong position. The country had avoided the revolutionary turmoil that struck the European continent between 1848 and 1850, largely due to the government's ability to reform and adapt just enough to contain the pressures for radical change. Liberalism seemed to be working well. The British economy was the most modern in the world, and the British people were relatively wealthy (although the condition of the working class was still unenviable). Yet Great Britain was not immune to the forces of nationalism that were growing everywhere in the West. In the decades following 1850 British nationalism grew, and liberal and conservative British politicians increasingly used it to gain support, increase the responsibilities of the national government, and justify foreign policy.

For most of the 1850s and 1860s liberals controlled the government. Lord Palmerston, a liberal Whig, was prime minister and leader of the Whigs for much of the period between 1855 and 1865. While modest domestic reforms to modernize government and increase the allegiance of the people to the government were instituted under his ministry, he relied on nationalistic sentiment for support. He willingly paraded British naval might whenever possible and sympathetically supported movements for national liberation abroad. But he did not bend to those who demanded greater inclusion in the political system by increasing suffrage.

By 1865 William E. Gladstone had risen to leadership within the Whig party and was transforming it into the more modern Liberal party. In 1866 he and the Liberal prime minister, Lord Russell, introduced a suffrage reform bill. Although the bill was defeated and the Liberal ministry was forced to resign, the narrowness of the defeat plus the popular demand for suffrage reform convinced the rising young leader of the Conservatives, Benjamin Disraeli (1804–1881), that reform was inevitable. The shrewd Disraeli decided to seize credit for the inevitable by introducing his own reform bill. The result was the Reform Bill of 1867, which, as amended by the Liberals, doubled the electorate and gave the vote to males in the lower middle class and upper working class for the first time. William E. Gladstone's Reform Bill of 1884 enfranchised most of the rural males. After 1884 virtually every male householder or renter in Great Britain could vote. Restricted woman's suffrage would come in 1918 and full suffrage in 1928.

Several liberal reforms were enacted during the 1850s, 1860s, and 1870s, making government responsible for primary schools, requiring competitive examinations for civil service, and removing some religious restrictions on non-Anglicans. Yet, until the end of the nineteenth century, both the Conservative and Liberal parties were still controlled by the aristocracy and the wealthy bourgeoisie. Although both parties were fairly benevolent toward the working classes, the large and discontented industrial proletariat wanted its fair share in the government. Between 1881 and 1906 its leaders turned to a program of moderate socialism, and with the aid of a number of intellectual radicals, notably George Bernard Shaw, H. G. Wells, and Sidney and Beatrice Webb, the Labour party was formed.

In 1906 the rejuvenated Liberal party came to power under the actual, if not official, leadership of the fiery young Welshman David Lloyd George, who also had the backing of the Labour party. Between 1906 and 1911 Lloyd George put through Parliament a revolutionary program of accident, sickness, old-age, and unemployment insurance. To meet this and other increased costs to the government, he forced through the reluctant House of Lords his famous budget of 1909, which shifted the "heaviest burden [of taxation] to the broadest backs." A steeply graduated income tax and high taxes on unearned income, inheritances, the idle parks of the landed aristocracy, and mining royalties struck heavily at the rich. The Parliamentary Reform Act of 1911 stripped the House of Lords of most of its former power and made the popularly elected House of Commons supreme. In 1914 the long-festering Irish question was resolved by granting self-government to Ireland, although the outbreak of World War I in that year delayed its implementation. And conflict between Protestants and Catholics in northern Ireland promised to persist. However, by 1914 Great Britain was on the road to greater social, economic, and political democracy.

Between 1871 and 1914 Britain increased its imperial holdings (see Chapter 50) and joined other nations in a dangerous international rivalry that combined nationalism and militarism. In the face of Germany's swift rise to power and prestige, the British took renewed pride in their dominant navy and in their empire, which contained one-fourth of all the earth's territory and people. Many well-to-do Britishers thought themselves to be so superior to the other peoples in Europe that they became the most unpopular of all travelers on the Continent. To some observers, it appeared that Great Britain was as big a bully on the seas and overseas as Germany was on the continent of Europe.

France

With the end of the Second Empire of Napoleon III during the Franco-German War of 1870–1871, the Third French Republic was proclaimed. However, the first elections, held in February 1871 after the surrender of Paris, resulted in a sweeping victory for the monarchists. This somewhat surprising result may be explained by the fact that the republican leaders wanted to continue the hopeless war with Germany. The city of Paris, made up largely of the liberal bourgeoisie and the radical proletariat, was unwilling to submit to the domination of conservative rural France. It declared its independence from the rest of France and set up its own city government, or commune. The Paris Commune gained a reputation as an experiment in Marxist socialism. In reality the Commune was dominated by a mix of different socialist and republican groups and was more radically democratic than anything else. Two months (April–May 1871) of fighting, culminating in a week of all-out warfare in the streets of Paris, were required for the rest of the French nation (with the regular army) to subdue the Commune (see Figure 48.2). Some twenty thousand Parisians were executed after they had surrendered, and seventy-five hundred were deported. The fall of the Paris Commune ended a threat to the integrity of France, heartened conservatives, and created martyrs for socialism.

The royalists, though in the majority, were split into a Bourbon faction and an Orléanist faction, neither of which was willing to yield to the other. Meanwhile, as this stalemate dragged on for several years, the liberals grew in strength. Finally, in 1875, the frustrated and frightened monarchists consented (by a single vote) to the adoption of a republican constitution. The constitution provided for a Chamber of Deputies elected by universal male suffrage, a Senate elected by a complicated indirect method, and a rather powerless president to be elected by the

FIGURE 48.2 Executions During the Paris Commune Bloodshed and bitter reprisals were common on both sides during the Paris Commune. Here, in 1871, Communards (including women) execute hostages in response to a previous execution of Communard leaders. (BBC Hulton/The Bettman Archive)

two legislative bodies. Most of the executive functions of the republic were to be carried on by a cabinet of ministers dependent on the Chamber of Deputies. It was not until four years later, however, that the liberal republicans under the leadership of the eloquent Léon Gambetta gained actual control of the republic.

But the Third French Republic, so furtively born, was still not safe. Powerful groups were hostile to it. The chief of these were the various factions of monarchists (Bourbons, Orléanists, and Bonapartists), the professional military, the Roman Catholic hierarchy, and large numbers of peasant proprietors. In the late 1880s these factions rallied around a handsome man on horseback, General Boulanger, who became so popular that he might have overthrown the republic had he been bolder and more skillful or had the republican leaders been less courageous. As it turned out, when he was summoned to answer charges of treason against the republic, he fled the country and eventually committed suicide.

In the 1890s the antirepublican forces rallied again around a group of army officers who had falsely accused a Jewish army captain, Alfred Dreyfus, and sent him to prison on Devil's Is-

land. This time the enemies of the republic were aided by a rising militant nationalism and anti-Semitism. It required twelve years for the republicans, inspired by the novelist Émile Zola, to get Dreyfus acquitted and the army officers who had imprisoned him punished. The Dreyfus case strengthened the republic and discredited its enemies.

Democratic government did not work as smoothly in France as in Great Britain. The tradition of extreme individualism, the animosity between clericalist and anticlericalist, the sharp cleavage between radical urban Paris and conservative rural France, lingering provincial loyalty, and a historic suspicion of strong government and high taxes—all contributed to the formation of a multiplicity of political parties. Thus the cabinet was forced to rely on the support of a precarious combination of parties (a *bloc*) in order to carry on the executive functions of government. In France the Chamber of Deputies could overthrow a cabinet without having to risk an immediate national election, as was the case in Great Britain. As a result, there was a rapid turnover of French ministries. During the forty-three years from 1871 to 1914, no fewer than fifty-one ministries attempted to govern France. Nevertheless, the French government was not as unstable as it might appear. The same groups of ministers often rotated in and out of office, sometimes simply exchanging one ministry for another. Moreover, the actual details of administration were carried on with relatively little interruption by a stable civil service, firmly built on the tradition of Richelieu and Napoleon I.

As the twentieth century opened, democratic government in France appeared to be firmly established and increasingly responsive to the will of the masses. Trade unions had been legalized, a modern system of public education that bolstered support for the republic was well established, and in 1905 all formal ties between the state and the Catholic church were broken. Factory laws were giving the workers increased protection. Between 1905 and 1910 a limited program of unemployment, old-age, accident, and sickness insurance was inaugurated. This program of social legislation, however, was only a modest beginning. The French masses, becoming more politically conscious and active, expressed their discontent in strikes and more votes for the Socialists.

France, like Great Britain, was subject to the growing nationalism of the period, which was related to international rivalries, imperial expansion, and military buildup. The already strong French pride had only been intensified by France's defeat at the hands of Germany in 1870–1871. The statue dedicated to the city of Strasbourg in the Place de la Concorde in Paris was draped in perpetual mourning as a constant reminder of the day of revenge. France greatly speeded up its overseas empire building and increased the size of its armed forces until they were larger in proportion to the population than those of the German Empire. France sought and found military allies. When a general strike in 1910 threatened the nation's military security and war preparations, Aristide Briand, himself a radical and former Socialist, did not hesitate to use the armed forces to break it up.

Italy

Italy entered the 1870s in a much weaker position than France or Great Britain. Italy had only just become a nation-state, and even that status was weakened by strong regional differences, particularly between the more economically developed north and the poorer south. Italy's new government was liberal, but the right to vote was limited to the middle and upper classes, who constituted a small minority of the nation's population.

Between the 1870s and World War I Italian governments weathered various political crises that sometimes reached revolutionary proportions. The nation was painfully modernizing and entering into the international arena. Italian governments became involved in the shifting international alliances of the period and the nationalistic race for colonial possessions. Toward the end of the period there were signs that Italy would follow the democratic pattern set by other Western nations. Economic and social reforms to benefit the working classes were enacted under the government of Giovanni Giolitti, and in 1911 universal male suffrage was enacted.

The Smaller Countries of Northern Europe

The people of the smaller countries of northern Europe also witnessed the triumph of democratic government during this period. Belgium adopted universal male suffrage in 1893. Here the weighted vote was established, men of wealth and education getting two or three additional votes. The Dutch Netherlands extended the suffrage in 1887 and again in 1896; in 1917 all adult men and women were given the right to vote. Norway adopted universal male suffrage in 1898, Sweden in 1909, and Denmark in 1914. In 1913 Norway became the first European country to grant the vote to women. In these five nations the traditional respect for government and the relatively high degree of literacy made democracy a vigorous reality.

2. EASTERN EUROPE: CONSERVATISM, MILITARISM, AND NATIONALISM

The democratic trends characteristic of western Europe were also occurring in eastern Europe, but they were longer in arriving, less firmly established, and not as complete as in western Europe. Moreover, nationalism, which was a general phenomenon, took on more strident, aggressive tones in eastern Europe, where national identity was less comfortably fixed. Most of eastern Europe remained in the control of conservative groups. The governments were autocratic in nature and more dependent on the military for support.

The German Empire under Bismarck and Kaiser Wilhelm II

The center of these trends in eastern Europe was the German Empire. Its creation by the blood-and-iron method, its autocratic constitution (despite the establishment of universal male suffrage), and its strong-handed leadership, first by the Iron Chancellor and then by Kaiser Wilhelm II, guaranteed that the German Empire would be an enlarged Prussia. The German Empire possessed a powerful army, a large, energetic, and disciplined population, a rapidly growing industrial machine, a fervent and restless national spirit. Bismarck ruled over his creation as chancellor for almost twenty years.

His first concern after the defeat of France and the declaration of the empire in 1870–1871 was to complete the consolidation and nationalization of the German states and people. The law codes, currencies, and military forces of the twenty-five lesser states were brought into conformity with those of Prussia. Banking and railroads were placed under control of the national government. The empire's spawning industry was protected against British competition by a high tariff. The French in Alsace-Lorraine, the Danes in Schleswig, and the more than 3 million Poles in the eastern districts were pressured to give up their language and traditions.

Two other groups in Germany excited Bismarck's suspicion and wrath: the Roman Catholics and the Socialists. Any German who had a foreign loyalty was intolerable to Bismarck. From 1872 to 1878, Bismarck waged a political power struggle with the Roman Catholics that came to be called the *Kulturkampf* (battle for civilization). The Jesuits were expelled, civil marriage was made compulsory, and all education, including that of Roman Catholic priests, was brought under state control and largely secularized. When the Roman Catholic clergy and most of the laity, which constituted approximately one-third of the total German population, resisted and rallied

to the pope, hundreds of priests and six bishops were arrested. But it was all to no avail. The Roman Catholic Center party in the Reichstag became stronger, and by 1878 Bismarck wanted its support for what he considered to be a struggle of greater importance—that against the Socialists. In 1878, upon the accession of a more conciliatory pope, Leo XIII, Bismarck "went to Canossa" and had the most severe of the anti-Catholic laws repealed.

In the same year he began a twelve-year crusade against the internationally minded Socialists (see Figure 48.1). He outlawed their publications, their organizations, and their meetings, and set the German police force upon them. But he only drove them underground. Throughout the decade of the 1880s, Bismarck sought to undercut the Socialists' appeal to the working class by setting up a comprehensive system of social insurance. Accident, sickness, and old-age insurance was provided for the industrial proletariat, the funds being raised by compulsory contributions from the workers, the employers, and the state. Although Bismarck's motives were not benevolent or humanitarian, his measures gave impetus to a trend toward state responsibility for social security. Nevertheless, the Socialists were not appeased, and Bismarck continued to fight them as long as he remained chancellor.

Bismarck's foreign policy after 1871 was one of security and retrenchment. He knew that France would be unforgiving and revengeful, forever seeking an opportunity to regain Alsace and Lorraine. Of France alone he had little fear, but France in league with other powers, particularly Russia and Great Britain, would be formidable. Therefore, his consistent policy was to maintain a close military alliance with Austria-Hungary and cordial relations with Russia and Great Britain. In 1873 Bismarck formed the Three Emperors' League among Germany, Austria-Hungary, and Russia. When the interests of Austria-Hungary and Russia proved to be incompatible, this league was replaced in 1879–1882 by the Triple Alliance among Germany, Austria-Hungary, and Italy. A separate "reinsurance treaty" of friendship and neutrality was made with Russia. Of course, Bismarck did not depend wholly on diplomacy. Throughout this period, the German military machine was made even more powerful.

In 1888 Wilhelm II (1888–1918) became kaiser. Wilhelm II was twenty-nine years of age when he ascended the throne. He had been brought up in the army, which was his first love. Egotistical and bombastic by nature, he was a dabbler in theology, history, and the arts and freely gave advice and instructions to the leading figures in those fields. He was also an eloquent, willing speaker and had his generous and humanitarian moments.

The young kaiser's personality and policies soon clashed with those of Bismarck. In 1890, just two years after he became emperor, Wilhelm II accepted Bismarck's reluctant resignation as chancellor. The immediate cause of the break was a disagreement over the control of the ministry and the repeal of the anti-Socialist laws, which Bismarck wished to be continued. The real reason, however, was that there was simply not room enough in Germany for two such prima donnas.

Bismarck's foreign policy was quickly reversed. The reinsurance treaty with Russia was immediately allowed to lapse, as the kaiser assumed a keen interest in extending German hegemony over the Balkans and the Ottoman Empire, areas the Russians considered to be vital to their own interests and ambitions. In 1894 Russia formed an alliance with France, the very thing that Bismarck had worked so hard to prevent. Wilhelm II also soon alienated Great Britain. His extension of German influence in the Near East, particularly his Berlin-to-Baghdad railroad project (see pp. 631–632), threatened an area in which Great Britain had many vital interests and through which ran its "lifeline" to India and the Far East. In China, too, German interests began to rival those of the British.

It was the kaiser's naval policy, however, that alarmed the British the most. Wilhelm was an ardent and lifelong navalist. "The waves beat powerfully at our national gates," he cried, "and call us as a great nation to maintain our place in the world. . . ." Germany's "place in the sun" was a favorite phrase of the Hohenzollern emperor. The Reichstag voted an enormous naval building program that was steadily increased until in 1908 it called for twenty-eight new battleships of the biggest and latest design. The purpose of this program was to give Germany a battle fleet so great that "a war against the might-

iest naval power would endanger the supremacy of that power."

Great Britain, whose food supply as well as her empire depended on naval supremacy, took utmost alarm. Failing in efforts to reach an understanding with the kaiser's government, Britain launched a huge and costly naval building program of its own. In 1904 Britain joined France, and in 1907 Russia, in the Triple Entente, which was in reality a defensive military alliance. The interests and policies of Great Britain, France, and Russia had long been so discordant that nothing less than maximum alarm could have brought them together. Thus in seventeen years Wilhelm had undone Bismarck's work and brought about the "encirclement" of the fatherland by three of the world's greatest powers.

Germany's economic exploits under Bismarck and Wilhelm II were no less phenomenal than those in the military realm. In 1871 Great Britain was the world's leading nation in manufacturing and commerce; the Industrial Revolution was still in its early stages in Germany. By 1914 Germany was a close second to Great Britain in industry and commerce; in many areas, such as the production of steel and machinery, Germany had far outstripped Britain. In the up-and-coming chemical and electrical industries and in scientific agriculture and forestry, Germany was far in advance of all other nations. Germany was also first in the application of science to industry and in industrial and scientific research. By 1914 the German merchant marine had captured the lion's share of the lucrative transatlantic passenger traffic.

At a time when other industrial nations, particularly the United States, were beginning to restrict the giant monopolistic trusts, the German imperial government was encouraging and subsidizing its cartels in order that they might compete with foreign companies more effectively. More and more of the world's market was captured by German business. "Made in Germany" became a familiar mark from the Andean plateau to the Congo jungles. Germany's population, keeping pace with its economy, increased from 41 million in 1871 to 65 million in 1914. Meanwhile, heavy emigration (which had reached a peak in the 1880s of some two hundred fifty thousand a year, most of it to the United States) dwindled to a mere trickle. In 1914 the number of German emigrants was less than the number of workers coming into Germany from neighboring countries. Only the United States was keeping pace with Germany in overall economic advancement.

The industrialization of Germany, although accompanied by the growth of a large and prosperous bourgeoisie, did not produce a tide of liberalism as it had in the other Western industrialized nations. The middle classes allied themselves with the conservative government. Only the Social Democratic party (working class) and the small and weak Progressive party (intellectuals, professionals, and small-business people) advocated liberal or radical reforms. But even the Social Democratic party, by 1914 the largest party in the empire, was inundated by the flood of nationalism that welled up during the international crises that preceded World War I.

Russia

Until the 1850s Russia had remained relatively untouched by the Industrial Revolution and liberalism. Russia's government was autocratic under the tsar, its society was still feudalistic with serfs bound to the land and their lords, and its large army enjoyed an aura of near-invincibility. Russia had earned the reputation of being the most conservative and unreforming of the European powers. After the Crimean War of 1853–1856, it was clear that things would have to change soon.

Russia's army was humiliated in the war. Its leaders quickly realized that Russia was being left behind by the other powers, that the country lacked the economic and social foundations for a modern war—the railroads, the armaments industry, the social support. The new tsar, Alexander II (1855–1881), announced a series of reforms. The most important was the freeing of the serfs in 1861. While the measure put an end to that form of human bondage and did transfer land to the freed peasantry, it did not make the peasants fully independent and self-sufficient. In general they received only the poorest land, they remained burdened by payments owed to the state, and they were tied by collective ownership to their village commune (the *mir*). Other reforms

made the local judicial system more independent, created local political institutions with elected officials, encouraged primary and secondary education, relaxed censorship, and modernized the military. At the same time, the government initiated a program of railway construction, which stimulated related industries. In Russia's cities a still-small middle and working class began to grow.

A strong wave of dissatisfaction arose during the later years of Alexander II's rule. The former serfs had been cruelly disappointed by the fruits of emancipation. Another revolt of Russia's Polish subjects in 1863 made Alexander II more reactionary. His failure to follow through with more sweeping reforms after the emancipation of the serfs disappointed liberals, populists, and others, who were mostly intellectual young aristocrats. In despair over the possibility of reforming the huge Russian Empire by orderly methods, these young intellectuals became radical. They set out to undermine Russia's society, government, and church in order to build a new and modern Russia from the ruins. When their efforts were spurned by the masses whom they were seeking to uplift, a more violent wing of the revolutionaries turned to terror and assassination to achieve their ends. Numerous bureaucrats and police officials were slain by terrorists, and Tsar Alexander II himself was killed by a bomb.

The new tsar, Alexander III (1881–1894), was a harsh, reactionary autocrat. Blaming his father's death on softness, he set out to exterminate all liberalism in Russia. The ruthless Vyacheslav Plehve was made head of the secret police, and its agents were soon everywhere. Thousands of suspects were arrested. Some were shot or exiled to Siberia. Alexander initiated a sweeping reactionary program of Russianization. The censored press, the closely supervised schools, the secret police, and above all the clergy of the Orthodox church became potent agencies for Russianization. Non-Orthodox religions were persecuted. Language minority groups—the Poles, the Baltic peoples, the Finns, even the Ukrainians—were forced to use the Russian language. The Jews suffered the harshest persecution. They were subject to such abuse, including bloody pogroms, that more than a quarter million of them fled, mostly to the United States.

Alexander III was succeeded by Nicholas II (1894–1917), who was also reactionary but was less effective. Although Nicholas attempted to continue the policies of his father, he was unable to make them work. During the 1890s, Russia experienced a new surge of industrialization stimulated by the aggressive policies of Sergei Witte, the finance minister, and an infusion of foreign capital into Russia. A larger industrial bourgeoisie and proletariat emerged and with them movements for liberal and radical reform. Of the various liberal and radical parties that emerged, the one of greatest significance for the future was the Social Democratic party. This was a Marxist party whose leadership was made up almost entirely of intellectual radicals. Their chief concern was for the industrial proletariat. In 1903 the Social Democrats split into a moderate, gradualist wing called the Mensheviks (minority) and a violent revolutionary wing called the Bolsheviks (majority). The Bolsheviks were led by the brilliant, dynamic Vladimir Lenin, who was living in exile in Switzerland.

Taking advantage of the embarrassment of the tsar's government because of Russia's defeat by Japan in 1904–1905 (see p. 000), the various liberal and radical groups clamored for reform. In July 1904 the hated Plehve was assassinated. In January 1905 hundreds of peaceful demonstrators were shot down in front of the royal palace in St. Petersburg by the tsar's guard. This bloody event, known as "Red Sunday," fanned the flames of discontent (see Figure 48.3). In October 1905 a general strike completely paralyzed the country for ten days. Nicholas II, yielding at last, issued a manifesto that promised civil liberties and a popularly elected Duma. However, before the Duma could be elected, the return of the Russian troops from the Far East and a huge loan from Russia's ally, France, strengthened the hand of the tsar. During the next two years he and his advisers succeeded in reducing the Duma to a non–democratically elected body that had little real control over the government. Nevertheless, a break had been made in Russia's autocratic system. Russia's rural society had broken from its feudal bonds, its economy was industrializing, and its political system included parliamentary institutions that promised to gain authority in the future.

FIGURE 48.3 Red Sunday In January 1905 the tsar's guards shot down hundreds of peaceful demonstrators in front of the royal palace in St. Petersburg. This event, known as "Red Sunday," left a bitter memory with Russia's liberals and radicals. (The Granger Collection)

National Movements in Southeast Europe

While nationalism between 1871 and 1914 was crushing minority language groups in the German and the Russian empires, it was pulling the Austrian and Ottoman empires apart along language lines. After Austria's defeat by Prussia in 1866, the dominant German minority in Austria felt obliged to take the aggressive and restless Magyars of Hungary into partnership. The *Ausgleich* (compromise) of 1867 set up the Dual Monarchy of Austria-Hungary. Each country had its own separate parliament. But the two were united under a common ruler, the head of the House of Hapsburg; common ministries of war, finance, and foreign affairs; and joint delegations from the two parliaments, whose duty was to coordinate policies wherever possible. This arrangement was essentially an alliance between the Germans of Austria and the Magyars of Hun-

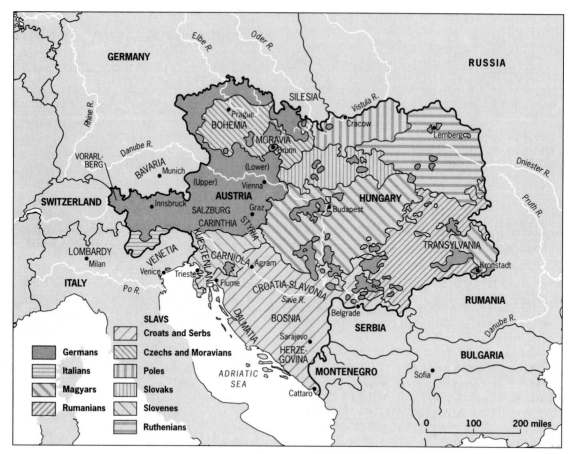

Map 48.1 LANGUAGE GROUPS, AUSTRIA-HUNGARY This map indicates the difficulties facing the Austro-Hungarian Empire in an age of growing nationalism. Satisfaction of demands for independence by the various ethnic or language groups would spell dismemberment of the empire.

gary against the Slavic, Rumanian, and Italian language groups, which constituted a majority of the total population of the Dual Monarchy. In effect, the Germans said to the Magyars: "You take care of your subject language groups [mostly Slavs], and we will take care of ours" (see Map 48.1).

Austria followed a relatively moderate policy in dealing with its subject language groups. Cultural autonomy was granted, and the suffrage was gradually extended until in 1907 all adult

males were given the vote. However, the subject peoples were more interested in nationalism than in democracy. The various language groups developed images of a glorious cultural and political past. The prosperous Czechs of Bohemia were especially adamant. The problem was confounded by the fact that many of the language groups had kinspeople outside the Dual Monarchy whom they wished to join and who deliberately stirred up their disloyalty. Such groups were the Italians, the Poles, the Ruthenians

(Ukrainians), the Serbs, and the Rumanians. Parliamentary sessions in Austria frequently degenerated into shouting, inkstand-throwing melees among the various language groups. Moreover anti-Semitism in Austria was growing, a development not unrelated to these problems among different ethnic groups.

Hungary made no pretense of conciliation. The Magyar aristocracy ruled over the Slovak, Rumanian, Serb, and Croat minorities with an iron hand. The aristocracy also refused to permit its own Magyar masses to participate in the government. The nationalist discontent in Hungary was even greater than it was in Austria; the Yugo (southern) Slavs (Croats and Serbs) were particularly troublesome. This explosive nationalism threatened to blow the Austro-Hungarian monarchy apart and, because of the network of entangling alliances, to draw the other major powers into a world conflict.

Between 1871 and 1914 the Balkan portion of the Ottoman Empire was a hornets' nest of nationalism (see Map 48.1). The hatred of the Christian Balkan language groups for their Islamic Turkish masters was equaled only by their distrust for each other. The once-potent Ottoman Empire crumbled throughout the course of the nineteenth century, and one Balkan language group after another, now aflame with national pride and ambition, emerged as an independent nation. Meanwhile, all the great powers of Europe became involved in the strategic and troubled area of the Near East. Russia, Austria-Hungary, Great Britain, France, Germany, and Italy had important imperial, economic, and military interests in the Balkans. In addition, Russia and Austria-Hungary had serious nationalistic interests there. Russia considered itself the big brother and protector of the Slavic-speaking Serbs and Bulgarians. Austria-Hungary's large Rumanian and Yugoslav populations desired union with their free kinspeople in Rumania and Serbia. Between 1829 and 1913 first the Greeks, then the Serbs, Rumanians, and Bulgarians, and finally the Albanians gained their independence from the Ottoman Empire. In each case a major crisis occurred among the great powers. These Balkan crises became progressively more severe, until finally one crisis got out of control and exploded into World War I.

Nationalism and Anti-Semitism

Jews had long suffered from anti-Semitism, but between 1789 and 1871 there were signs of change. The ideals of the Enlightenment, the French Revolution, and liberalism worked against anti-Semitism. In several countries Jews gained new rights and legal equality, though rarely full acceptance.

During the second half of the nineteenth century, particularly after the 1880s, anti-Semitism was on the rise. The situation was worst in central and eastern Europe, where most Jews lived and where conservative, militant, aggressive nationalism was thriving. Right-wing anti-Semitic organizations, such as the Pan-German Association and the Christian Social Workers' party, formed and grew in Germany. In Austria the leaders of the Christian Socialist party and the German National party became openly anti-Semitic. In Rumania Jews were not allowed to vote. Some of the most violent anti-Semitic acts in the decades before 1914 occurred in Russia, where legal restrictions, persecutions, and pogroms caused much displacement, suffering, and loss of life among Jews.

One result of this mixture of liberation for Jews in some cases and increasing anti-Semitism in others was the growth of Zionism, a Jewish nationalist movement to create an independent state for Jews in Palestine. Theodor Herzl (1860–1904) became the leading figure in the Zionist movement. He gained financial support from the French banker Baron de Rothschild and others. By the turn of the century an international Zionist organization was formed and efforts were being made to establish a Jewish homeland in Palestine. It would be several decades before these efforts would bear fruit.

Of greater immediate consequence was migration. Between 1871 and 1914 some two million eastern European Jews moved westward, many crossing the Atlantic to the United States. Certainly there were also other reasons for this migration (see p. 580), but the anti-Semitism that accompanied right-wing nationalism in eastern Europe helped push Jews from their homes in search of better lives elsewhere.

SUGGESTED READING

General

A. J. Mayer, *The Persistence of the Old Regime in Europe to the Great War* (1981). A controversial interpretation.

N. Stone, *Europe Transformed, 1878–1919* (1984). A fine recent survey.

A. J. P. Taylor, *The Struggle for Mastery in Europe, 1848–1918* (1971). A good, interpretive study of international politics.

Great Britain

M. Bentley, *Politics Without Democracy, 1815–1914* (1984). Good political coverage.

D. Read, *England, 1868–1914. The Age of Urban Democracy* (1979). Relates politics and socioeconomic developments.

France

D. Johnson, *France and the Dreyfus Affair* (1967). Excellent study.

J. M. Mayeur and M. Rebérioux, *The Third Republic from Its Origins to the Great War, 1871–1914* (1984). A thorough synthesis.

R. Tombs, *The War Against Paris, 1871* (1981). A good analysis of the Paris Commune.

Italy

D. M. Smith, *Italy: A Modern History* (1969). A good survey.

J. A. Thayer, *Italy and the Great War: Politics and Culture, 1870–1915* (1964). A solid analysis of Italian political history.

Germany

G. Craig, *Germany, 1866–1945* (1980). Particularly good on German political history during this period.

H. U. Wehler, *The German Empire, 1871–1918* (1985). A recent interpretive study.

Russia

W. Blackwell, *The Industrialization of Russia* (1982). Good on this important topic.

H. Rogger, *Russia in the Age of Modernization and Revolution, 1881–1917* (1983). An excellent synthesis.

A. B. Ulam, *Russia's Failed Revolutionaries* (1981). A good study of Russia's revolutionary groups prior to 1917.

Southeast Europe

B. Jelavich, *History of the Balkans* (1983). A useful survey.

A. Sked, *The Decline and Fall of the Habsburg Empire, 1815–1918* (1989). Some good coverage of this area.

Nationalism and Anti-Semitism

G. L. Mosse, *Toward the Final Solution: A History of European Racism* (1978). A useful introduction.

P. Pulzer, *The Rise of Political Anti-Semitism in Germany and Austria* (1988). A respected analysis.

D. Vital, *The Origins of Zionism* (1975). The standard introduction.

CHAPTER 49

Democracy, Expansion, Civil War, and Reform in the United States, 1800–1920

FIGURE 49.1 John Gast, *Manifest Destiny* This painting reveals the idealized myth of westward expansion. Moving from the Atlantic coast cities of the East across the plains and mountains toward the Pacific, the goddess of Destiny carries a schoolbook in one hand and a telegraph wire in the other. Below her come white male hunters and settlers, pushing Indians and buffalo further west in retreat. In her wake follows the railroad. (Library of Congress)

By the end of the eighteenth century the United States was experiencing many of the same trends and developments as other nations of Western civilization. As we saw in Chapter 37, the United States was influenced by Enlightenment ideas, experienced a revolution, and established liberal political institutions—a pattern familiar to France and some other European nations. With the exception of the African slaves, almost all citizens of the new nation were of European stock. Most people worked the land, but there were some growing cities and early industrial establishments—again a pattern not too different from that of many areas in Europe.

There were some important differences between the United States and other Western nations in 1800. It had only recently emerged from colonial status and remained separated from Europe by the Atlantic Ocean. Politically and socially, the United States did not carry a strong legacy of monarchical rule or aristocratic distinctions. There was a surplus of land, thanks to the willingness of American citizens to take from the Indians, and a supply of cheap, noncompetitive labor, thanks to slavery.

During the nineteenth century the United States again shared in trends sweeping through the West while remaining strikingly distinct in some important ways. In this chapter we will emphasize the pattern of shared trends and distinctions as we trace major elements of U.S. history in rough chronological order. By the end of the second decade of the twentieth century, the United States will have reached a point where its development can be better viewed as integrated with that of other Western nations.

1. DEMOCRACY AND GEOGRAPHIC EXPANSION, 1800–1861

Democracy in the young American republic received a boost with the election of Thomas Jefferson as president in 1800. Jefferson represented the ideals of a nation of small farmers and the realities of a political democracy with a party system. The coming to power of this liberal theorist—the author of the Declaration of Independence—was a shock to the more elitist Federalists, who had flourished under presidents Washington and Adams. The conservative Founding Fathers had felt that the capable elite should rule and that political parties, or "factions," would undermine the new political system. Although the rich and well-born raised a cry of anguish at the triumph of Jefferson, he was a moderate individual who in fact did little that was radical as president. Although he was supported in the election by the yeoman farmers, he was an elegant Virginian and scholarly philosopher rather than a man of the masses.

The War of 1812 with Great Britain resulted in an upsurge of American nationalism, which helped mold America's evolving political institutions. A new crop of nationally minded statesmen appeared, the ablest of whom were Henry Clay, John C. Calhoun, and Daniel Webster. The war itself ended indecisively, yet the United States emerged with a stronger national economy and a greater sense of being a nation with its own character and institutions rather than a former British colony.

The War of 1812 also produced a hero, Andrew Jackson. His rise to the presidency signaled a new stage in the development of America's democratic institutions. Not only did it represent the rise of a common man to the presidency—he defeated formidable, established, sophisticated political giants—it also marked the rise of the western frontier states to national political importance and the early development of modern, mass-based political parties. During the Jacksonian era, which extended for some two decades after his election in 1828, democracy advanced as new states without property qualifications for voting were rapidly admitted to the Union and as the older states eliminated property qualifications from their voting requirements. Artisans and small farmers used the egalitarian rhetoric of the Jacksonian era to assert their own interests and power. Yet much of the so-called Jacksonian "revolution" was more superficial than substantial. American Indians fared worse during the Jacksonian era than before, and, like Jefferson, Jackson as president did little that was radical.

Meanwhile, the United States was expanding (see Map 49.1). Between 1800 and 1861 the United States was the most rapidly growing nation in the world, both in area and in population. The purchase of the Louisiana Territory by

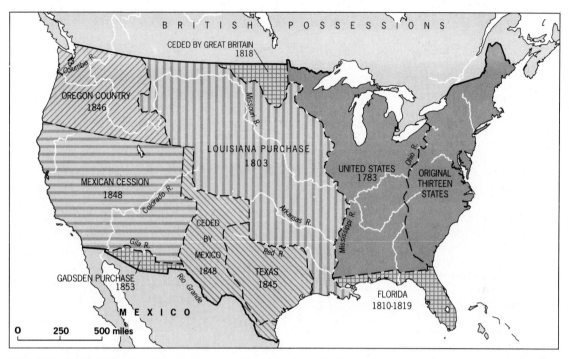

Map 49.1 **TERRITORIAL EXPANSION OF THE UNITED STATES, 1783–1853** Through a variety of means, including wars, purchases, treaties, and expropriation, the United States more than trebled its territory between 1800 and 1861. This territorial expansion kept land in surplus despite an unprecedented rate of population growth.

Thomas Jefferson from Napoleon in 1803 for some $16 million doubled the original area of the United States. In 1819 Florida was purchased from Spain for $5 million. Texas, which was even bigger than now, was annexed in 1845. The next year the Oregon Country was annexed after the settlement of a long-standing dispute with Great Britain. The annexation of Texas resulted in a war with Mexico (1846–1848). After a quick and easy victory, the United States took a huge block of Mexican territory, comprising the present states of California, Arizona, New Mexico, Nevada, Utah, and parts of Colorado and Wyoming. This territory was enlarged to the south in 1853 by the Gadsden Purchase from Mexico ($10 million). These additions within a period of fifty years more than trebled the original territory of the young American nation. Yet the cost was higher than the money paid for some of the territory. Indians had to be slaughtered and dispossessed.

Wars of conquest had to be fought (Mexico), and other wars had to be risked (Great Britain). Westward expansion was not simply a sanitary, heroic struggle to a predestined end (see Figure 49.1).

The growth in population was keeping pace with the increase in area. Between 1800 and 1861 the population of the United States increased from approximately 5 million to 32 million. Adding to the high rate of natural increase was an ever-increasing tide of immigration from Europe. After 1840 the largest immigrant groups were the Irish, most of whom settled in the cities of the Northeast, and the Germans, most of whom pushed on to the fertile lands of the Middle West.

Between 1800 and 1861, then, American political institutions had evolved along democratic and nationalistic lines. Voting rights had been extended to essentially all adult white males. Po-

FIGURE 49.2 A Northern Factory This lithograph of the Stillman, Allen & Co. Novelty Iron Works of New York City shows the more industrial, urban nature of the North in the middle decades just prior to the Civil War. (Museum of the City of New York)

litical power had been wrested from the elite circles of the old colonial well-to-do. A modern political party system had been developed. Americans pridefully thought of themselves and their institutions as distinct within Western civilization. The United States had expanded westward to the Pacific Ocean. The western frontier itself was one of the greatest of nationalizing influences. To it came people from all the seaboard states and from abroad who looked to the national government for protection, for roads and canals, and for land titles. It was in this period that American culture began to free itself from strictly European influence. The American Indian was idealized by Henry Wadsworth Longfellow and James Fenimore Cooper. Washington Irving's pen made the legends of American colonial days enchanting. Gilbert Stuart and Charles Willson Peale painted idealized portraits of American heroes. American schools and universities were teaching a particularly American version of civilization and world affairs.

2. SLAVERY, CIVIL WAR, AND RECONSTRUCTION, 1861–1877

The central event for American history during the nineteenth century was the Civil War, which broke out in 1861 and lasted until 1865. The nature of the Civil War has been debated endlessly, but certain features stand out. The North was increasingly a growing, urban, industrial society based on free labor (see Figure 49.2). The South remained agricultural, dependent on large plantation crops such as cotton, and based on slave labor (see Figure 49.3). The North was enjoying an increasing influence over national policies and generally favored federal over state power. The South saw its influence over national policies slipping and increasingly favored states' rights over federal power. The North seemed to represent a modernizing, democratic, nationalistic society; the South a traditional, unegalitarian, regional society. In great part, the Civil War was a clash between these increasingly different socie-

FIGURE 49.3 A Southern Plantation This picture, Charles Giroux's "Cotton Plantation," shows the contrasting rural society with a large population of slaves typical of the South. (Courtesy, Museum of Fine Arts, Boston, M. and M. Karolik Collection)

ties with different interests. But the issue that provided much of the emotional energy to this clash and that prior to 1861 tied together the issues dividing North and South was slavery.

The first boatload of slaves was brought to Virginia in 1619, one year before the Pilgrims landed at Plymouth Rock. Because of the tremendous amount of labor required to clear the American wilderness, the African slave trade flourished throughout the colonial period. By the time of the American Revolution, slaves constituted approximately one-fifth of the total population of the thirteen colonies. Slavery was recognized and protected by the national constitution. Because of the climate and the diversified economy, however, slavery proved to be unprofitable in the Northern states, and between 1777 and 1804 all the states north of Maryland passed emancipation laws. South of the Mason and Dixon line (the boundary between Maryland and Pennsylvania), where agriculture reigned supreme, slavery continued to be profitable and prevalent. But

by 1789 many Americans, in the South as well as in the North, disliked the institution. After the Revolution scores of antislavery societies were founded. It appeared possible that slavery in America was on its way to an early and peaceful end.

Some unforeseen developments, however, changed the attitude of the South toward emancipation, and a sharp line was drawn between the North and South over the slavery issue. The first of these developments was Whitney's invention of the cotton gin in 1793. This machine made the raising of cotton so profitable that soon large cotton plantations worked by slaves grew up throughout the South. The American South became the chief supplier of Britain's textile mills. By the mid–nineteenth century, slaves outnumbered whites in South Carolina and Mississippi, and in the rest of the Deep South slaves were about equal in number to whites. The Southern economy had become so wedded to cotton and to slavery that the Southern antislavery movement had faltered and the defense of slavery had gained momentum. Even more important than economic considerations in the development of proslavery sentiment in the South was the social problem. Slaves were seen not only as the basis of wealth but also as the basis of power and status by southern slaveholders. Slaveholders accepted as given the inferiority of African Americans. Southern whites did not believe that they could absorb into their society or even live alongside so many free African Americans under any circumstances. Meanwhile, in the free-labor North, antislavery sentiments were growing. Movements for the abolition of slavery became more prominent and forceful.

The critical issue became the extension of slavery to the western territories. The population of the northern states, with their growing industry, was rapidly outstripping that of the South. As the northwestern territories clamored for statehood without slavery, the Southerners took alarm. Already they were hopelessly outnumbered in the House of Representatives, whose membership is based on population. Their only security in the national government lay in the Senate, where each state has two members. The Southerners did everything in their power to slow down the settlement of the West and insisted that the admission of every free state must be accompanied by the admission of a slave state in order that equality in the Senate be maintained. But time and tide were on the side of the North. Geography, population, the growth of industrialization, and the march of liberalism in the Western world were irresistible.

In 1854 the Republican party was founded as a strictly Northern party committed to the restriction and, seemingly, ultimate extinction of slavery. In 1860, with Abraham Lincoln as its candidate, it won a sweeping victory over the Democrats, now split between North and South over the question of slavery. Rather than accept an inferior position in the nation and face the prospect of eventually having their power and status destroyed by some 4 million slaves forcibly freed in their midst, eleven southern states (about half the territory of the Union and a third of its population) seceded and set up an independent government.

The North had an overwhelming preponderance in population, wealth, industry, transpor-

tation, and naval power. But the South enjoyed brilliant military leadership and the further advantage of fighting on its own soil for what it believed to be the survival of white civilization. The war lasted four bloody years. For three of the four years it looked as if the Union could not be restored. But after numerous discordant elements in the North were brought together, Great Britain and France tactfully neutralized, and, the winning commanders and strategy found, the southern armies were finally crushed.

Slavery was abolished and the authority of the national government restored, never to be seriously threatened again. However, the war left a legacy of sectional bitterness. The conciliatory Lincoln was assassinated just five days after the war ended. The radical Republican congressional leaders, who now gained control of the government, treated the defeated and devastated South as a conquered province. They sought to achieve basic reforms and to ensure political and civil rights for the freed slaves. The effort ended by 1877, when the last federal troops were finally withdrawn from the South. Over the course of the next twenty years many of the gains made by African Americans were lost. By this time a different dynamic was taking hold of American life and changing it in unprecedented ways: industrialization.

3. INDUSTRIALIZATION AND URBANIZATION, 1865–1901

Although the earliest factories were already present in the United States by the end of the eighteenth century, the growth of industrialization during the nineteenth century was at first quite slow. The French and British blockades during the Napoleonic wars and the War of 1812 with Britain cut the United States off from British manufacturers and caused much American commercial capital to be diverted to manufacturing. By the middle decades of the nineteenth century, industrialization was spreading, particularly in the Northeast. However, it was not until the years immediately following the Civil War that the United States joined other Western nations as a leading industrial power.

In most ways industrialization in the United States proceeded much as it did in other Western countries. New machines and sources of power were applied to the manufacturing process. Large factories sprang up in the East and Midwest, turning raw materials into finished products in great quantities. Working-class and urban populations connected with industrialization grew, fed both by migration from rural areas and by massive immigration from Europe. The United States proved to be subject to the same problems that plagued other industrializing nations: poor working conditions, low pay, child labor, urban slums, inadequate sanitation, and few social services.

However, there were a few elements that seemed to characterize the United States' growing industrialization between 1865 and 1901. Above all, the degree to which business became concentrated in the hands of a few individuals and corporations was striking. Industrial capitalists such as Andrew Carnegie (steel), John D. Rockefeller (oil), Cornelius Vanderbilt (railroads), and J. P. Morgan (finance) amassed unbelievable fortunes and power (see Figure 49.4). The corporations they founded, such as U.S. Steel and Standard Oil, soon gained monopolistic control over vast resources.

More than in most other nations, governmental policies during this period favored business in general and these huge industrial firms in particular. Not surprisingly, then, in the United States the unionization of labor was relatively slow to emerge. In part this was due to the continued abundance of cheap land and the influx of cheap, mobile labor from Europe. But unionization was also deterred by the determined resistance of industrial capitalists backed by private and public police power and by governmental policies and officials unsympathetic to unionization. Despite some earlier beginnings in various trades (such as the Knights of Labor), it was not until 1886 that Samuel Gompers, an immigrant from Great Britain, organized the American Federation of Labor—the first successful national labor organization in America.

By the end of the nineteenth century the United States not only was a major industrial power but also had outstripped the world in industrial production. The government and the economy of the country were still dominated by big-business interests that controlled the dominant "Old Guard" wing of the Republican party.

FIGURE 49.4 Cornelius Vanderbilt This cartoon attacks Cornelius Vanderbilt, who in the 1860s gained control over several railroads and amassed a great fortune. He is portrayed exercising monopolistic corporate power over the nation's railroads. (Culver Pictures)

Although the United States enjoyed enormous overall economic development, wealth was very unequally distributed, causing widespread discontent. Western and southern farmers had been clamoring for public regulation of the railroads, on which they were dependent. Small business, labor, and consumers demanded protection against the monopolistic practices and prices of the great trusts and corporations, which were protected by a prohibitively high tariff. The U.S. government remained behind almost that of all other industrial nations in its willingness to deal with social abuses stemming from industrialization. Millions deplored the city slums, the corrupt spoils system in the civil service, and the squandering of natural resources by private interests. The forces of reform were growing and would break out in the two decades following the turn of the century.

4. REFORM AND PROGRESSIVISM, 1901–1920

The great reforms of the progressive era are usually dated from 1901, when Theodore Roosevelt assumed the presidency. Roosevelt firmly believed in the capitalist system, but he was convinced that the time had come when the superiority of the government over private business must be asserted. After assuming the presidency in 1901 upon the assassination of William McKinley, "T.R.," as he was popularly known, immediately launched a vigorous program of reform. The Interstate Commerce Act of 1887 and the Sherman Antitrust Act of 1890, which had lain dormant, were activated. Organized labor was given a little support in its unequal fight with organized capital. Pure food and drug acts were designed to restrict the corporations and safeguard the public health. More than 200 million acres of forest and mineral lands and water power sites were withheld from private exploitation. He strengthened the merit system in the federal civil service. Many of his reform efforts were blocked by Congress and the federal courts, which were still controlled by the Republican Old Guard.

In 1912 the Democrats, under the leadership of Woodrow Wilson (1856–1924), gained their first clear-cut victory since the Civil War. Wilson proved to be more liberal than Roosevelt. With the Democrats in control of both houses of Congress, Wilson's administration sharply lowered the tariff, passed the Clayton Antitrust Act (more specific than the Sherman Act), gave further encouragement to organized labor, and set up the Federal Reserve Banking System, which removed control of the nation's financial policies from the hands of private interests on Wall Street and placed them in the hands of the federal government.

The passage of the long-struggled-for women's suffrage act in 1920 was the last reform of the progressive era. The return to power of the conservative Republicans under Warren Harding in 1920 brought the progressive period to a close. However, in those two decades American institutions and policies had adjusted to at least some of the social and economic realities of a modern democratic industrial society. At the same time the United States had joined other imperial powers with its acquisition of territories in Latin America, the Pacific, and Asia. Finally, the United States had become embroiled in World War I. From this point on, the United States would be too integrally connected to worldwide economic and political affairs to act in isolation.

SUGGESTED READING

General

R. Current et al., *American History: A Survey* (1987). A balanced, solid text.

Democracy and Geographic Expansion, 1800–1861

R. Billington, *Westward Expansion: A History of the American Frontier* (1974). An excellent survey.

J. Ellis, *After the Revolution: Profiles of Early American Culture* (1979). A useful survey of culture.

J. R. Howe, *From the Revolution Through the Age of Jackson: Innocence and Empire in the Young Republic* (1973). A good study of political development.

E. Spicer, *A Short History of the Indians of the United States* (1969). A useful introduction to the topic.

Slavery, Civil War, and Reconstruction, 1861–1877

M. Berry and J. Blassingame, *Long Memory: The Black Experience in America* (1982). A good survey.

E. Foner, *Reconstruction: America's Unfinished Revolution, 1863–1877* (1988). By a leading historian of the period.

E. D. Genovese, *Roll, Jordan, Roll: The World Slaves Made* (1974). A scholarly study of slave society.

J. M. McPherson, *Battle Cry of Freedom: The Civil War Era* (1988). Extremely well written.

Industrialization and Urbanization, 1865–1901

D. J. Boorstin, *The Americans: The National Experience* (1965). Useful sections on the impact of modernization.

D. Cashman, *America in the Gilded Age: From the Death of Lincoln to the Rise of Theodore Roosevelt* (1984). A well-written survey.

T. C. Cochran and W. Miller, *The Age of Enterprise* (1968). A broad, scholarly study covering the period.

Reform and Progressivism, 1901–1920

J. M. Cooper, Jr., *The Warrior and the Priest: Woodrow Wilson and Theodore Roosevelt* (1983). A comparative biography.

R. Hofstadter, *The Age of Reform: From Bryan to FDR* (1955). A classic.

A. Link and R. McCormick, *Progressivism* (1983). A succinct modern review.

S. M. Rothman, *Woman's Proper Place* (1978). Focuses on women's changing roles.

R. H. Wiebe, *The Search for Order, 1877–1920* (1968). Contains good material on reform and progressivism.

CHAPTER 50
Imperialism

FIGURE 50.1 Imperial Glory This picture of colonial troops parading in London in celebration of Queen Victoria's Diamond Jubilee in 1897 reveals some of the forces behind late-nineteenth-century imperialism: nationalistic pride, military power, social cohesion, and romantic sentiment. (Culver Pictures)

Between the fifteenth and eighteenth centuries European nations gained control over most of the Western Hemisphere, the west coast of Africa, and Southern Asia. Then, from the 1760s to the 1870s, there was a relative lull in expansion. Imperial powers such as Spain, Portugal, and France lost many of their overseas holdings during this period; even some of Britain's holdings in North America had been lost during the American Revolution. In the period between 1880 and 1914, however, there was a new burst of imperial expansion, the "new imperialism." Western powers engaged in a sudden quest for control over new territories in Asia, Africa, and the Pacific. Rapidly the West greatly increased its dominance over much of the rest of the world, taking Western culture and institutions to indigeous societies whether they wanted them or not.

1. CAUSES OF THE NEW IMPERIALISM

One of the chief impulses behind the new imperialism was economic. The rapid expansion of industry in Europe and the United States created a demand for greater markets, new sources of raw materials, and investment outlets for surplus capital. Many people in Western nations pushed for imperial expansion, optimistically assuming that the new markets, new sources of raw materials, and new investment outlets could be found. These advocates of imperialism were primarily those most directly in a position to profit from it—certain financiers, merchants, shippers, settlers, and colonial officials as well as industrialists with specific economic interests in non-Western lands.

Probably a greater impulse to the new imperialism was nationalism (see Figure 50.1). The outbreak of the new imperialism occurred shortly after the unification of Italy and Germany and during a period in which nationalism was on the rise throughout Europe. This nationalism turned into a new competitive struggle for international prestige among Western nations that spilled over into non-Western areas after 1880. Whether it was economically profitable or not, the national ego was flattered to see its colors spread over the map. Imperial conquest became

a measure of status, proof that a nation had become first rate. To be left behind in the imperial race was to be marked as a second-class nation. National egotism also gave the citizens of the great Western powers a sense of mission: They were bringing the blessings of their civilization to backward peoples. Rudyard Kipling expressed the belief of many Westerners when he sang in rhyme of the "white man's burden" to hold in tutelage and to civilize the "lesser breeds" of the earth.

Another motivating factor in the new imperialism was the evangelizing zeal of the Christian religion. Christianity had long taken to heart the command "Go ye into all the world and preach the gospel to every creature." At the very time that Christianity was wavering under attack in its homeland in the West, it was carrying on foreign missionary activity of unprecedented scope and intensity. More often than not, where the missionaries went, there went Western explorers, traders, troops, and officials.

In addition, political and diplomatic developments became intertwined after the 1880s to make colonial claims increasingly valuable assets. Here Bismarck set a pattern of making claims to colonial territories and using those claims as bargaining chips against other powers. His tactics forced other nations to make their own claims. Soon these claims were being used by Western nations to forge alliances or bargain with competitors in the growing international disputes of the period. The result was the virtual partition of Africa.

Finally, the processes involved in imperial expansion and the circumstances of the West help explain the new imperialism. Science and technology gave industrialized nations such a military advantage that they could easily conquer and control the nonindustrialized lands. Almost any penetration into such areas as Africa, southern Asia, or the Pacific quickly led to greater involvement and eventual control. Once missionaries or traders established their presence in a new area, their home governments were called on to provide support, enforce contracts, and protect private interests. To provide that support and protection, they had to create new facilities in the new lands, thus increasing the Western presence. The governments soon requested the cooperation of the native political leaders, and

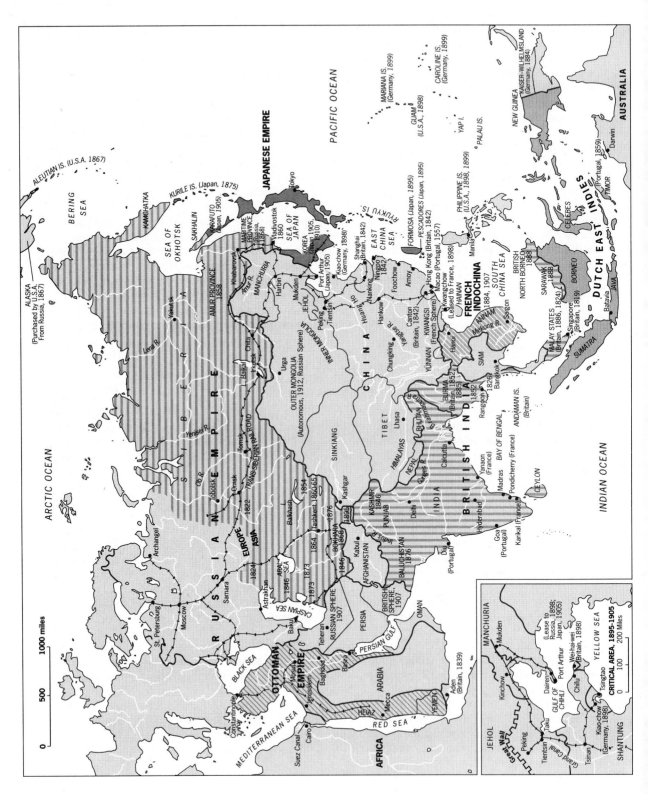

ARCTIC OCEAN

ALEUTIAN IS. (U.S.A. 1867)

ALASKA
(Purchased by U.S.A.
From Russia, 1867)

BERING
SEA

KAMCHATKA

SEA OF
OKHOTSK

KARAFUTO
(Japan, 1905)

SAKHALIN

KURILE IS. (Japan, 1875)

MARITIME
PROVINCE
(Russia,
1858)

Vladivostok
1860

SEA OF
JAPAN

Tokyo

JAPANESE EMPIRE

PACIFIC OCEAN

MARIANA IS.
(Germany, 1899)

CAROLINE IS.
(Germany, 1899)

GUAM
(U.S.A., 1898)

YAP I.

PALAU IS.

NEW GUINEA

KAISER-WILHELMSLAND
(Germany, 1884)

AUSTRALIA

Darwin

Timor
(Portugal, 1859)

S I B E R I A

Yakutsk

Lena R.

Khabarovsk

Chita

Irkutsk

Lake Baikal

MANCHURIA

Amur R.

Harbin

AMUR PROVINCE
1858

JEHOL

Mukden

Port Arthur
(Japan, 1905)

Peking

Tientsin

KOREA
(Japan,
1910)

RYUKYU IS.

FORMOSA (Japan, 1895)

PESCADORES (Japan, 1895)

HAINAN

PHILIPPINE IS.
(U.S.A., 1898, 1899)

Manila

SOUTH
CHINA SEA

CELEBES

DUTCH EAST INDIES

Batavia

JAVA

BORNEO

BRITISH
NORTH BORNEO
1888

SARAWAK
1888

SUMATRA
(Britain, 1819)

MALAY STATES
(Britain, 1886, 1824)

Singapore
(Britain, 1824)

RUSSIAN EMPIRE

EUROPE
ASIA

St. Petersburg

Moscow

Archangel

Samara

Ob R.

Tobolsk

Omsk

Tomsk

TRANS-SIBERIAN RAIL ROAD

1822

1854

1860

1865

Urga

OUTER MONGOLIA
(Autonomous, 1912, Russian Sphere)

INNER MONGOLIA

SINKIANG

Kashgar

Yenisei R.

Balkhash

Tashkent 1865

1876

1895

BOKHARA 1876

1868

1846

1873

1873

1864

1824

ARAL
SEA
1846

CASPIAN SEA

Baku

Astrakhan

Teheran

PERSIA

RUSSIAN SPHERE
1907

BRITISH
SPHERE,
1907

AFGHANISTAN

Kabul

BALUCHISTAN
1876

Indus R.

KASHMIR
1846

PUNJAB

Delhi

NEPAL

TIBET

Lhasa

HIMALAYAS

BHUTAN

Brahmaputra R.

Ganges R.

BURMA
Britain, 1852,
1885

Rangoon

SIAM
1826

Bangkok

ANDAMAN IS.
(Britain)

BAY OF BENGAL

Calcutta

B R I T I S H   I N D I A

I N D I A

Hyderabad

Madras

Pondicherry
(France)

Yanaon
(France)

Karikal (France)

Goa
(Portugal)

Diu
(Portugal)

CEYLON

INDIAN OCEAN

C H I N A

Huang Ho (Yellow R.)

Shanghai
(Britain, 1842)

Ningpo
1842

Nanking

Hankow

Foochow

Amoy

Canton
(Britain, 1842)

Chungking

YUNNAN

KWANGSI
(French Sphere)

Kiao-chow
(Germany, 1898)

Hong Kong (Britain, 1842)

Macao (Portugal, 1557)

Kwangchow
(Leased to France, 1898)

FRENCH
INDOCHINA

ANNAM
1884, 1907

Hanoi

Mekong R.

Saigon

EAST
CHINA
SEA

Yangtze R.

OTTOMAN EMPIRE

Constantinople

BLACK SEA

Jerusalem

Cairo

Suez Canal

MEDITERRANEAN SEA

Baghdad

Mosul

Basra

PERSIAN
GULF

ARABIA

Mecca

HEJAZ

RED SEA

Medina

YEMEN

Aden
(Britain, 1839)

OMAN

AFRICA

0   500   1000 miles

INSET MAP:

JEHOL

MANCHURIA

Mukden

SHANTUNG

Peking

Tientsin

Taku

Tsinan

Tsingtao

Kinchow

Chifu

Wei-hai-wei
(Britain, 1898)

Dairen

Port Arthur

(Lease to
Russia, 1898;
Japan, 1905)

Kiao-chow
(Germany, 1898)

GULF OF
CHIHLI

YELLOW SEA

Grand Canal

Great Wall

CRITICAL AREA, 1895–1905

0   100   200 Miles

628

when it was not forthcoming, they used force. Indirect control could quickly turn into direct control as problems arose and then into expanding control as neighboring areas became of interest. Thus, the initial contacts by Western explorers, missionaries, or traders blossomed into full imperial control by Western nations.

2. THE EXPLOITATION AND AWAKENING OF CHINA

One of the most important scenes of European imperialism during the nineteenth century was China. This huge, populous country was the seat of the oldest continuous civilization in the world. For over three thousand years China had been a vast melting pot, absorbing invading peoples and cultures and welding them into a tough but resilient civilization. The military conquerors had always been swallowed up or conquered by Chinese culture.

Over time, the Chinese chose to isolate themselves from the outside world. A great wall (never completed), originally constructed to defend China's northern border, later symbolized its effort to retain the old and keep out the new. Although they admitted some European traders and Christian missionaries in the sixteenth and seventeenth centuries, they closed their doors rather tightly thereafter. By the mid–nineteenth century their society, weakened by internal problems under the declining Manchu dynasty, constituted a power vacuum that tempted exploitation by the West.

The first Europeans to force themselves upon the Chinese were the British. Going to war in 1839, when Chinese officials interfered with their sale of opium in China, the British, with their modern weapons, easily defeated the Chinese. By the terms of the Treaty of Nanking (1842), the Chinese ceded Hong Kong to the British, opened many of their ports to foreign trade free of restricting tariffs, and granted the foreigners extraterritorial rights. This was the first of a series of

unequal treaties and the signal for all the great Western powers to rush into China and seize what they could. In the ensuing scramble it was the rivalry among the great powers themselves as much as Chinese resistance that saved China from complete loss of independence.

The British got the lion's share. In addition to Hong Kong and concessions in the Canton area of the southeast, they gained a virtual trading monopoly in the Yangtze Valley, which was the richest and most populous part of China. In the north they gained footholds in the capital city of Peking and its port city of Tientsin, in the Shantung peninsula, and in Manchuria. They gained dominion over Tibet. In the 1880s they seized control of Burma, which owed a tenuous allegiance to China. The French took large areas in southeast China and Hainan Island as their sphere. In the 1880s they completed the detachment of Indochina from Chinese sovereignty. The Russians took Manchuria as their sphere, annexed a large strip of China's northeast coast, including the port of Vladivostok, and became active in Korea. The Germans carved out for themselves much of the strategically located Shantung peninsula and built a powerful naval base at Kiaochow. In 1894 the rejuvenated and modernized Japanese went to war with China. They easily defeated China and not only took away Formosa and Korea but also forced China to pay a huge indemnity. Even the United States got into the act. The United States had launched an imperialist program in the Far East in 1898 by seizing the Philippine Islands and Guam from Spain. Now, fearful for its growing trade with China, the United States attempted to gain a sphere of influence in Fukien Province and demanded an Open Door policy in China with equal trading opportunities for all.

Meanwhile, Chinese nationalism was being aroused by the Western and Japanese aggressions against the "Celestial Empire." In 1899–1900 a serious uprising against the foreign exploiters, known as the Boxer Rebellion, took place. Thousands of Chinese Christians and a

---

Map 50.1 IMPERIALISM IN ASIA, 1840–1914 As the map on opposite page indicates, almost all the Western powers participated in the imperial expansion into Asia. Once Japan westernized, it too joined the imperial race.

number of foreigners were slain. This liberation movement was put down by British, French, German, Russian, Italian, Japanese, and American troops. The nationalist leaders were severely punished, and China was forced to pay the foreign governments a large indemnity.

A more far-reaching revolutionary movement, aimed not only at freeing China from foreign exploitation but also at modernizing and democratizing its society and government, was being organized by Dr. Sun Yat-sen (1866–1925). Sun, the son of a poor Chinese farmer, studied in a British mission school in Hawaii, became a Christian, and later graduated from the British medical school at Hong Kong. Eloquent and dynamic, he organized his followers into the Kuomintang party, which was committed to a three-point program: (1) national independence, (2) democratic government, (3) social justice. In 1911 the reformers launched a revolution against the Manchu dynasty, declared a republic, and elected Sun as provisional president. The revolution swept most of China. The Manchu officials in Peking, their power having evaporated, declared China a republic and abdicated in favor of General Yuan Shi-kai, organizer of the New Army of North China. Early in 1912 the idealistic Sun, in behalf of national unity and fearful of rising anarchy and warlords within and the possibility of Japanese and Russian intervention from without, yielded to General Yuan. Yuan, however, soon proved to be more interested in power than in liberal reform. When the Kuomintang party won the elections of 1913, he suppressed the party and had its most promising young leader assassinated. Sun disassociated himself from Yuan's dictatorship and resumed his liberal activities in South China. When World War I opened a new era in 1914, China was torn with revolution and division.

3. THE EMERGENCE OF JAPAN

Japan's reaction to Western intrusion was quite different from that of China. The Japanese people inhabit four large islands and some three thousand small ones stretching along the eastern coast of Asia for a distance of about two thousand miles. Like China, Japan had admitted the sixteenth- and seventeenth-century European traders and Christian missionaries but had evicted them and closed its doors after observing what was happening everywhere in Asia where Europeans were admitted. At mid–nineteenth century the Japanese were living in isolation.

In 1853, eleven years after the Treaty of Nanking opened up China, an American fleet commanded by Commodore Matthew C. Perry steamed into Tokyo Bay and pressured the Japanese to open their ports to American trade. The Japanese were much impressed by the technological superiority of the Americans. In 1868, just fifteen years later, a group of young Japanese overthrew the existing government and began reorganizing the Japanese government and society along modern Western lines (the Meiji Restoration). Taking what they considered to be the best from the various Western nations, they patterned their business methods after those of the United States, their legal system after the French, and their navy after the British. But it was Bismarck's Germany that impressed the Japanese the most. They built a military machine and an authoritarian governmental and educational system on the model of the German Empire.

In an incredibly short time Japan became a modern, industrialized, military, and, on the surface at least, westernized power (see Figure 50.2). In 1894 Japan attacked China, defeated it with ease, and forced it to pay a large indemnity and to give up Korea (which Japan annexed in 1910) and the island of Formosa. In 1902 Great Britain became the first Western power to treat an Asian nation as an equal by entering into a military alliance with Japan. Thus strengthened and reassured, Japan attacked Russia in 1904 and, to everyone's surprise, defeated Russia both on land and at sea. As a reward, Japan took the southern half of Sakhalin Island and Russia's railroad and port concessions in southern Manchuria, thereby becoming the dominant power in that large and valuable section of China. By 1914 Japan was a first-rate westernized power—industrialized, militaristic, and imperialistic.

4. COMPETITION FOR THE STRATEGIC NEAR AND MIDDLE EAST

The term *Near East* usually refers to the area at the eastern end of the Mediterranean: Egypt, the old Ottoman Empire, and the Balkan peninsula.

FIGURE 50.2 Japanese Silk Factory, 1905 By the early twentieth century Japan had successfully adopted Western industrial methods. In this 1905 photograph of a silk-weaving factory, supervising men are in formal Western attire and women work on the machines. (California Museum of Photography, University of California, Riverside)

In the nineteenth century the term *Middle East* usually meant the area of the Persian Gulf, the territory northwest of India, and sometimes Tibet. (By the middle of the twentieth century the term *Middle East* was generally used to designate the whole area from and including Egypt and Turkey to the western borders of India.) Before the development of its oil resources after World War I, this area (with the exception of the Balkan peninsula) was relatively poor. It was inhabited chiefly by Moslems, who were hostile to Europeans. The main importance of the area, therefore, was strategic. It is the land bridge between the world's two largest land masses—the continents of Eurasia and Africa. The opening in 1869 of the Suez Canal, which shortened the sailing distance between western Europe and the Far East by five thousand miles, doubled the strategic value of the Near and Middle East. Indeed,

Suez quickly became one of the most vital single commercial and military focal points in the world.

The Suez Canal was built by a French company between 1859 and 1869. However, in 1875 Great Britain, taking advantage of the Egyptian government's financial distress, purchased the khedive's controlling portion of the canal stock. Seven years later, to quell an anti-European insurrection, the British occupied Egypt with their military forces. The French acquiesced in the establishment of Britain's control over Egypt and the Suez Canal in return for British support of French dominance in Morocco.

Serious competition for the British in the Near East soon came from an unexpected source. Wilhelm II, upon becoming kaiser of the German Empire in 1888, immediately began to show a keen interest in the Ottoman Empire. In 1889

Wilhelm II visited Constantinople and declared himself to be the friend and benefactor not only of the Turks but also of all Moslems. Friendship was followed by economic concessions and German investments in the Ottoman Empire. A second visit by the kaiser in 1898 led to a concession to Germany to build a railroad from the Bosporus to the Persian Gulf. This, with its European connection, was the famous Berlin-to-Baghdad railroad. The British took alarm. The Baghdad Railroad, with a fortified terminus on the Persian Gulf, would undercut Britain's longer water route to the East and threaten India, Britain's richest colonial prize. A projected branch running down through Syria and Palestine to Hedjaz would menace the Suez Canal itself.

Russia was equally concerned. Since the days of Ivan III in the fifteenth century, one of Russia's major ambitions has been to gain a warm water outlet to the world through the Turkish Strait at Constantinople. Russia had long looked to Constantinople as the seat and legitimate capital of its Orthodox religion and Byzantine culture. The decay of the Ottoman Empire in the nineteenth century encouraged Russia to try for Constantinople, and only the intervention of Great Britain and France in the Crimean War (1854–1856) prevented Russia from attaining its goal. In 1877–1878 Russia defeated Turkey and threatened to dominate the whole Balkan peninsula. This time Great Britain and Austria-Hungary forced Russia to submit to a general settlement by the European powers. At the Congress of Berlin, 1878, Russian ambitions in the Near East were once more thwarted. Bismarck's support of Austria-Hungary and Great Britain at the Congress of Berlin marked the beginning of German-Russian estrangement. Russia's defeat by Japan in 1904–1905 caused Russia to intensify its pressure toward the Middle and Near East. Russia's southward expansion so menaced India that Great Britain extended the northwest Indian frontier to the Khyber Pass and crossed over the Himalayas to checkmate Russian influence in Tibet, Afghanistan, and Persia.

The new German threat in the Near and Middle East, however, caused the British and the Russians to settle their long-standing differences. In 1907 they neutralized Tibet and Afghanistan and divided Persia into three spheres of influence—a Russian sphere in the north, a British sphere in the south, and an "independent" sphere in the center. Great Britain, Russia, and France, now diplomatic allies, prevented the sale of Baghdad Railroad bonds in their respective countries in an effort to embarrass the financing of the costly undertaking. Germany went right ahead, however, with the extension of its influence in the Balkans and the Ottoman Empire. In 1913 Germany dispatched a military mission to Constantinople to reorganize and instruct the Turkish army. The Ottoman Empire's friendship and eventual alliance with Germany was undoubtedly motivated by a greater fear of Russia. By 1914 the area of the Near and Middle East was a giant powder keg with fuses leading to St. Petersburg, Berlin, and London.

5. THE SCRAMBLE FOR AFRICA

At the opening of the nineteenth century, Africa was the seat of several civilizations. In the north the long-established Islamic societies continued to evolve, though at a slow pace. In sub-Saharan Africa, particularly in the western and central Sudan where the Sahara Desert gave way to grasslands and trade flourished, many societies and states had developed over the centuries. Africa was affected by trade and contact with Europeans, but except for coastal and certain other limited areas, such as South Africa, most of Africa was generally free from western European control. The Portuguese, Spanish, British, and French had trading posts on the west coast, while the Dutch and Portuguese had posts and settlements around the southern cape.

By the middle decades of the nineteenth century the French had conquered Algeria and made it a part of France and had pushed up the Senegal River in the west. The British had taken the Cape Colony from the Dutch during the Napoleonic wars, and the Dutch settlers had moved northward into the interior.

After 1880, however, the tempo of European activity changed drastically. Such a mad scramble for Africa took place among the powers of western Europe that by 1914 the only independent areas left were Ethiopia in the east and Liberia in the west. Ethiopia, with French aid, had

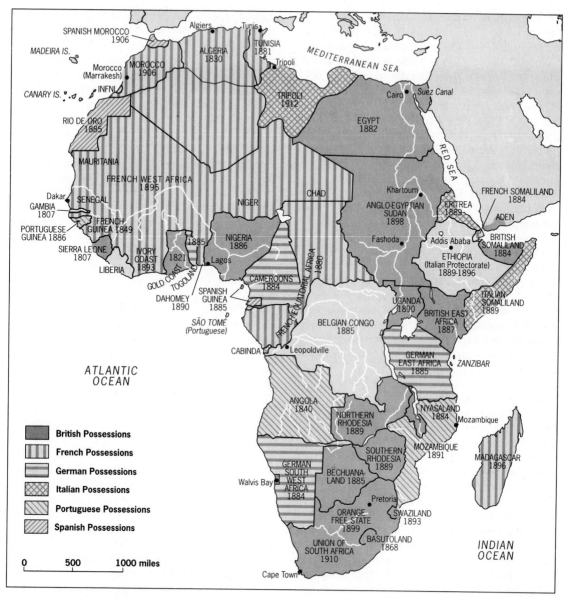

Map 50.2 IMPERIALISM IN AFRICA, 1914 This map indicates how the vast majority of Africa was carved up by European nations in the two decades of the 1880s and 1890s.

repulsed an invading Italian army, and Liberia had been sponsored by the United States as a hoped-for receptacle for liberated slaves. The rest of the huge continent had been seized by France, Great Britain, Germany, Portugal, Belgium, Italy, and Spain (listed in the approximate order of size of territory held) (see Map 50.2). The treatment of Africans was often similar to that accorded the native Americans in the sixteenth and seventeenth centuries.

The seizure of so much territory did not occur, of course, without serious international incidents and crises. One such incident occurred at Fashoda in the Sudan in 1898. A French expedition under Major Jean-Baptiste Marchand, bent on establishing an all-French axis across Africa from west to east, arrived at Fashoda and hoisted the French flag. The British, however, claimed the Sudan as an appendage of Egypt. Furthermore, they were interested in a Cape-to-Cairo railroad running through all British territory, even though they were already blocked by German East Africa. Lord Kitchener therefore hurried down from the north with a superior British force and compelled the French to withdraw.

In South Africa the British fought a major war with the Dutch settlers (1899–1902). When British settlers began to move into the Cape Colony early in the nineteenth century, the Calvinist Dutch Boers (farmers) who had settled there in the seventeenth century trekked northward far into the interior. Eventually the British recognized the independence of the two Boer states, Transvaal and Orange Free State. When, however, the richest gold mines in the world were discovered in the Transvaal in the 1880s, British immigrants (Uitlanders) flooded in. The unwelcome Uitlanders were badly treated by the Dutch Boers. The British empire builder Cecil Rhodes, with the support of powerful interests back home, was determined to brush aside the two little Boer republics. When the able Boer president, Paul Kruger, saw the British intent, he opened hostilities. What the world expected to be an easy victory for the British took three years of all-out military effort involving severe casualties and enormous costs. Britain's treatment of the defeated Boers, however, was lenient. They were taken into partnership in the Union of South Africa, and their war hero, General Louis Botha, was elected the Union's first prime minister. During the course of the struggle, a telegram of congratulation from the German kaiser to President Kruger and the British seizure of a German ship attempting to violate the British blockade caused great tension between Great Britain and Germany. As the kaiser admitted, only the superiority of the British navy prevented him from going to war.

The British navy also proved decisive in two crises over Morocco. In 1905 France, with the approval of Great Britain, Italy, and Spain, began the conquest of Morocco. France claimed that it was necessary because of continual raids by Moroccan tribes on French Algeria. The German kaiser, seeing an opportunity to assert his own power and possibly to break up the Triple Entente, which France, Great Britain, and Russia were then forming, appeared at the Moroccan port of Tangier on a German warship and indicated his support of Moroccan independence. Great tension followed. At an international conference at Algeciras in Spain, France, supported by her own ally, Great Britain, and by Germany's ally, Italy, won limited control over Morocco. Disorder continued, however, and in 1911 France sent a conquering army into Morocco, at which point Germany dispatched a cruiser to the Moroccan port of Agadir. Again tension mounted. In the face of Germany's threat to France, Britain's chancellor of the exchequer, Lloyd George, talked loudly of war. Again Germany backed down. Between Germany and Morocco stood the British navy. These two efforts of the kaiser to drive a wedge between the Entente powers had the effect of driving them closer together. Moreover, his own ally, Italy, had proved uncertain. These two crises growing out of imperialism hastened the coming of World War I.

6. THE BRITISH EMPIRE

Of all the European overseas empires, the British was by far the most successful. Indeed, it was the dazzling size and wealth of the British Empire that helped to excite the other European powers to greater imperialistic activity. By 1914 the British Empire included one-fourth of all the land and people of the earth.

Great Britain's commerce with its empire was enormous. In 1914 Britain's foreign investments, most of which were in the empire, totaled $20 billion—one-fourth of the total wealth of the homeland. (By comparison, France had $9 billion invested abroad; Germany, $6 billion. The United States was a debtor nation.) The empire, furthermore, provided lucrative and often glamorous careers for thousands of British governors, army and navy officers, diplomats, and civil servants of every description.

In the latter part of the nineteenth century,

FIGURE 50.3 The British in India This photo of Indian servants catering to a British gentleman indicates the gulf between the British ruling class and the Indians they governed. It also reveals the appeal to Britishers of the foreign service. (BBC Hulton/The Bettmann Archive)

Great Britain adopted the policy of granting self-government to the English-speaking portions of its empire. Canada, which had gained self-government in 1849, was granted dominion status in 1867. With dominion status, the only remaining effective bond was allegiance to the British crown. The British governor-general was only a figurehead like the king at home. Australia was made a self-governing dominion in 1901, New Zealand in 1907, and the Union of South Africa in 1910. The policy was successful. All the dominions rallied to the mother country in both world wars.

Great Britain's richest imperial prize was India (see Figure 50.3). India's more than 300 million inhabitants accounted for at least three-fourths of the total population of the whole empire. India was nearly twenty times as large as Great Britain and more than seven times as populous. It was the mother country's best customer and supplied many minerals and raw materials.

Until 1858 India was governed by the British East India Company, a private stock company. However, the great Sepoy Mutiny of 1857, the first large-scale uprising of the Indians against British rule, caused the British government to take over the government of India from the company. Between 1858 and 1914 Great Britain spent millions of dollars in India on railroads, industries, education, and public health. The enormous growth of India's population, which more than doubled during the period, is testimony to some improvement in the conditions of life under British rule. But the British took out of India more than they brought in, and they showed no inclination to grant self-government. Indian dissatisfaction with British rule mounted steadily. In the late nineteenth century, nationalism, which had provided so much aggressive energy for Europe, was coming to Asia—to India as well as to Japan and China. In 1885 the All India Congress party was formed for the purpose of achieving Indian

FIGURE 50.4 Imperialism Satirized This cartoon, which appeared in 1899, satirizes the attitudes of smug righteousness and superiority with which the Americans, the British, and the European nations extended their dominance over the rest of the world. The United States was dominant in the Western Hemisphere, the European imperialist powers in the Eastern Hemisphere. (New York Public Library Picture Collection)

independence. By 1914 it was becoming obvious that India would not remain a placid, profitable colony much longer.

7. THE LEGACY OF IMPERIALISM

The Western world's technology, its dynamic capitalism, and above all its aggressive nationalism had enabled it between 1880 and 1914 to subject most of the rest of the world to its domination (see Figure 50.4). Western peoples and their economies became entwined in large parts of Africa and Asia as never before (see Maps 50.1 and 50.2). Rather than striving for a better understanding of these non-Western societies, Westerners were usually encouraged to view others in condescending, arrogant, or racist terms.

In the process of dominating the non-Western world, Western nations not only exploited the natural and human resources of conquered lands but also profoundly undermined the cultures, societies, and political organizations of native peoples. Economies that had been balanced and well-functioning in the environment were distorted and ruined as they were transformed to serve the demands of Western commerce. New activities, such as mining and railroad building, often employed native laborers in inhumane ways and at great cost to lives. Political structures that had long functioned effectively were distorted or destroyed in just a few years. New social and political divisions were created as Western administrators favored certain groups to pass on their orders to others.

Few in the West were able or willing to recognize how destructive the policies of imperialism could be. By 1914 most people in the Western world had come to view imperialism as a normal and permanent state. In the course of the twentieth century, however, some of the very forces that had accounted for the new imperialism would lead to its demise. The non-Western world was irreversibly changed by Western imperialism, but it would not remain under the thumb of Western nations for long.

SUGGESTED READING

General and Causes

M. Doyle, *Empires* (1986). Imperialism in a comparative context.

D. K. Fieldhouse, *The Colonial Experience: A Comparative Study from the Eighteenth Century* (1982). A good introduction.

D. Headrick, *Tools of Empire* (1981). Examines what made imperial expansion relatively easy.

T. Smith, *The Patterns of Imperialism* (1981). A good survey.

The Exploitation and Awakening of China

J. K. Fairbank, *The United States and China* (1979). A scholarly, lucid history of China by a leading expert.

I. Hsu, *The Rise of Modern China* (1975). A useful survey.

The Emergence of Japan

W. Beasley, *The Meiji Restoration* (1972). A good analysis of this crucial development.

R. Storry, *A History of Modern Japan* (1982). Good on the period.

Competition for the Near and Middle East

S. N. Fisher, *The Middle East: A History*, 2nd ed. (1969). A reliable text.

The Scramble for Africa

A. Christopher, *Colonial Africa* (1984). A useful introduction.

J. Gallegher, R. Robinson, and A. Danny, *Africa and the Victorians: The Climax of Imperialism* (1961). A good, controversial analysis.

The British Empire

W. Baumgart, *Imperialism: The Idea and Reality of British and French Colonial Expansion* (1982). An up-to-date study.

P. Moon, *The British Conquest and Domination of India* (1989). Good chapters on the period.

B. Porter, *The Lion's Share, A Short History of British Imperialism, 1850–1970* (1975). A solid survey.

The Legacy of Imperialism

D. Headrick, *The Tentacles of Progress: Technology Transfer in the Age of Imperialism, 1850–1940* (1988). Focuses on the economic disruption caused by Western technology.

D. Mannoni, *Prospero and Caliban: The Psychology of Colonization* (1964). An excellent analysis from a psychological perspective.

RETROSPECT

The first half of the era between 1776 and 1914 was a period of great political, economic, and social upheaval. Politically and socially, it was a time of high expectation and excitement. In a matter of weeks—and sometimes days—the kind of fundamental changes that usually require decades took place. Time-honored institutions, privileges, and customs toppled. Wealth, power, and rights were redistributed. Economically, changes came somewhat slower but were even more fundamental. Goods and services were produced in different ways and in different places. Where people lived, how they made a living, and how they related to one another were changing in irreversible, revolutionary ways.

The Western Hemisphere was the stage for

the first of these revolutions. The American Revolution was primarily a matter of the thirteen English colonies winning their independence from the mother country. As a result of the Revolution, loyalist lands were redistributed and the royal governors and their aristocratic councils gave way to the more democratic legislatures. The Declaration of Independence and the new Constitution were filled with the ideas of the Enlightenment.

The changes brought about by the French Revolution were more dramatic and significant for Western civilization. French society on the eve of the Revolution was still essentially feudal, with its privileged clergy and nobility. Government was in the hands of a monarch. Within a few months of the outbreak of the Revolution in 1789, a series of sweeping reforms had occurred—the end of feudalism, the Declaration of the Rights of Man, and the drawing up of a liberal but moderate constituion.

But the nobility and clergy were not willing to see their privileges so easily lost. Nor were the radical Jacobins convinced that the Revolution had gone far enough. They wished to see the principles of "Liberty, Equality, Fraternity" extended beyond France's borders. When Austria and Prussia intervened in behalf of the French royalty and nobility, the radicals deposed and beheaded Louis XVI. All the great powers of Europe except Russia formed a coalition for the purpose of ending this threat to the established order. The revolutionary radicals, now in control, inaugurated a Reign of Terror for the purpose of uniting and mobilizing the nation. It was remarkably successful; the internal enemies of the Revolution were terrorized into silence or support, and the foreign enemies were defeated and driven back beyond the frontiers. But no one seemed able to consummate the Revolution and restore peace. The radical Jacobins were overthrown by the bourgeois moderates, and the Terror ended; but the moderates, too, proved unable to bring peace at home and abroad.

In 1799 a coup d'état brought Napoleon Bonaparte to power. Over the next few years he instituted stabilizing reforms that affirmed some of the changes wrought by the French Revolution and destroyed others. His fifteen-year rule was marked by almost continual warfare.

Meanwhile, another kind of revolution was taking place in western Europe—the Industrial Revolution. By the end of the eighteenth century new factories, using new sources of power, new machines, and new methods of production, were sprouting up in Great Britain in great numbers. Great Britain's economy was experiencing unprecedented, sustained growth. The Industrial Revolution had begun. Over the course of the nineteenth century it spread to continental Europe and other parts of the world. Great social changes followed in the wake of industrialization. Cities grew, the class structure changed, new social institutions developed, and even the function of the family and the role of women evolved. The first beneficiaries of the Industrial Revolution were the industial bourgeoisie—the factory owners. Whether the industrial proletariat benefited during the early period of industrialization is questionable. While their wages may have risen, they lost skills and security and became the virtual slaves of factory owners. These radical changes in production and distribution and the ensuing stresses prompted new economic and social thought—economic liberalism, Utopian Socialism, and Marxism.

Both an affirmation of and a reaction to the revolutionary spirit that engulfed the Western world between 1776 and 1850 were reflected in the romanticism that characterized the philosophy, literature, and arts of the period. For liberals, romanticism affirmed the optimism, individualism, and heroism epitomized by the French Revolution, Napoleon, and the revolutions of the first half of the nineteenth century. For conservatives, romanticism rejected the rationalism of the Enlightenment and affirmed the glories of the prerevolutionary and preindustrial world, where the mysteries of nature and religion dominated. Although romanticism would remain an influential and popular cultural style after midcentury, the ensuing period would be more accurately reflected by realism.

At the Congress of Vienna in 1814–1815, the major powers structured a peace settlement at the end of the Napoleonic wars in accordance with the principles of conservatism. In many ways the ensuing decades between 1815 and 1850 were a struggle between these forces of conservatism and the newer forces of liberalism. Despite various revolutionary rumblings, the forces of conservatism generally remained in control until 1830. After 1830 reform and revolution in the name of liberalism started to wrestle control from the conservatives, culminating in the great liberal and nationalistic revolutions of 1848. Yet this great defeat for the conservative forces of order was short-lived. By 1850 most were back in power again and the great period of liberal revolution was over.

Between 1850 and 1914 developments in Western civilization were dominated by the spread of nationalism and industrialization. Both had their roots in the preceding decades, but until the middle of the nineteenth century they were relatively limited in scope and intensity. During the second half of the century nationalism spread to new areas, achieved new successes, and took on a more pragmatic, aggressive quality. At the same time, industrialization matured in Western societies and spread into the non-Western world.

Between 1850 and 1871 nationalism was used to strengthen the political institutions of the nation-state. The Second Empire of Napoleon III provides an outstanding example of nationalistic state building during this period. Domestically, Napoleon III involved the government in a series of new economic and social programs; in foreign affairs he intervened in areas stretching from Russia to Mexico. However, the fruits of nationalism were even more significant in Italy and Germany. First Italy, under the guidance of Piedmont and its prime minister, Cavour, unified most of the diverse states of the Italian peninsula into a single nation in 1860. Then Prussia, under the leadership of Bismarck, used war and diplomacy to unify Germany into a powerful new nation in 1871.

Meanwhile, the second Industrial Revolution was taking place in the West. Steel, chemicals, and electricity were replacing iron, textiles, and steam as the basis of new industrial development. Countries such as Germany and the United States successfully challenged the long leadership of Great Britain in industrial production. The industrial societies became much more urbanized and were dominated by the middle class, but the working classes were now rising to the fore with their own organizations and ideologies. Most significant was the rise of Marxist socialism, a powerful ideology that won many adherents and that was thrust into public life by socialist unions and socialist political parties.

Thought and culture between 1850 and 1914 reflected the influence of nationalism and industrialism. Both stressed secular beliefs and a certain pragmatic scientific approach. Both contributed to the growing problems facing Christianity during the period. The spread and prestige of the natural and social sciences were particularly strong and were reflected in some of the literary and artistic trends of the period. Toward the end of the nineteenth century and the beginning of the twentieth century, however, a new strain of disillusionment, uncertainty, and even pessimism was appearing in philosophy, literature, art, and even science. This disturbing cultural trend foreshadowed the devastating turmoil of the decades following the outbreak of World War I in 1914.

Between 1871 and 1914 Europe was characterized politically by the spread of democratic institutions and the growth of a more militant nationalism. While the spread of democracy occurred in some form throughout Europe, it was more complete and more closely associated with liberalism in western Europe. In eastern Europe the spread of democracy was much less complete and, in some cases, more a matter of form than substance. There, governments such as those under Kaiser Wilhelm II in Germany, the tsars in Russia, and the emperor in Austria-Hungary tended to be conservative and authoritarian.

Meanwhile, in the United States many of the main developments occurring during the nineteenth century roughly paralleled European developments. Democratic institutions, along with a growing sense of nationalism, were spreading as the country expanded. At the same time that the Industrial Revolution was spreading from Great Britain to other areas of Europe, the United States was industrializing its economy—particularly after the Civil War ended in 1865. And like other Western governments, the American government attempted to adjust to the pressures of a mature industrial society by instituting political reforms toward the end of the nineteenth and the beginning of the twentieth centuries.

After 1880 nationalism and industrialization combined to thrust the leading nation-states of the West into a new imperial race. Within two decades the Western powers carved vast areas of Africa, Asia, and the Pacific into colonies and territories of imperial interest. As a result of this imperial expansion, non-Western societies were undermined and irreversibly changed, and the Western powers became locked into added rivalries that would bear the fruits of war in 1914.

PART SEVEN

WAR AND GLOBAL INTERDEPENDENCE, 1914–PRESENT

The outbreak of total war in 1914 initiated a new era of destruction, upheaval, and revolutionary change in the West. At great cost, liberal democratic powers won the war, but the developments that followed were not encouraging. Revolutions in Russia had not only brought down the tsarist government but also brought the Bolsheviks to power. The Bolsheviks transformed Russia into the Communist Soviet Union, which by the 1930s was a totalitarian nation pursuing policies in fundamental opposition to those of the capitalistic West. Fascism, which directly and violently identified liberalism and democracy as enemies, arose in Europe, first in Italy and later in Nazi Germany. Meanwhile, hopes for the spread of liberal democracy in southern and eastern Europe, and Japan were dashed as these areas turned to authoritarian forms of government. The Great Depression of the 1930s increased strains in this already tense environment. World War II, which broke out in 1939, seemed to many to be a destructive continuation of the violence unleashed by World War I.

For most of the period after 1945 the basic trends were toward recovery, growth, and relative stability. Two competing superpowers, the United States and the Soviet Union, were the dominating nations in the West and, to a considerable extent, the world. Colonies controlled by the old imperial powers gained their freedom. Rather than by direct control, the West became tied to the non-Western world by expanding communications, economic interdependence, international organizations, systems of alliances, ideological competition, and cultural exchange.

In recent years stunning new developments seem to have altered the course of history. In the Soviet Union and Eastern Europe, communism has collapsed. In western Europe, new steps toward greater union have been taken. Along the rim of the Pacific Ocean, economic development has shifted the economic balance of power in the world toward Asia.

CHAPTER 51
World War I, 1914–1918

FIGURE 51.1 Trench Warfare This photo of French troops on the western front in World War I illustrates the type of war it was: fought in deep, barbed-wire-covered trenches by foot soldiers wearing masks against poison gas. Despite the assumptions to the contrary by offense-minded generals, the advantage was with the defense. (Roger-Viollet)

The first blow that rocked the twentieth-century world was World War I. To most people, busy with their daily tasks, it seemed to be a sudden and unforeseen disaster. To statesmen and informed students of world affairs, it was the snapping of long-developing tensions.

1. ORIGINS OF THE WAR

National, imperial, and economic rivalry underlay the developments that led to the outbreak of World War I (see p. 644). The increasingly militant nationalism that had been growing since the mid–nineteenth century encouraged nations to view one another as dangerous rivals in the struggle for national power and prestige. The outburst of imperialism in the decades before 1914 pitted these nationalistic rivals against one another in the race to acquire colonies and expand their international influence. The growth of industrial and financial capitalism created a context of competitive economic struggle.

These rivalries were reflected in international affairs, particularly in the system of alliances among the European states. During the last decades of the nineteenth century, the various powers bound themselves into alliances based on shared interests with an eye toward maintaining a balance of power in the potentially dangerous international arena (see pp. 610–611). Although the alliances were not always steady, they may have helped maintain a sense that major wars could be avoided. By 1904, ten years before the outbreak of World War I, Europe was divided into two powerful alliance systems: the Triple Alliance, composed of Germany, Austria-Hungary, and Italy, and the Triple Entente, composed of France, Russia, and Great Britain.

Suspicion and fear between the two power combinations mounted steadily. A ruinous armaments race ensued; the powers of the Triple Entente strove desperately to overcome Germany's long lead in land forces, while Germany sought to erase Great Britain's naval advantage. Rivalries and conflicts among the various members of the two alliances cropped up all over the world, threatening to embroil all the other members. In 1905–1906 and again in 1911 two such clashes occurred in Morocco between France and Germany (see p. 634).

It was in the Balkans that these rivalries and conflicts entwined into a series of crises after 1908 that would result in a fatal explosion. Austria-Hungary had vital interests in the Balkans that grew out of the history and polyglot nature of its empire. It was composed of numerous language groups, some of which, particularly the Serbs, Croats, Slovenes, and Rumanians, had linguistic kin in the Balkans. As the Ottoman Empire in the Balkan peninsula disintegrated in the nineteenth and early twentieth centuries, the various Balkan language groups emerged as independent nations. These free peoples constituted a strong attraction for the members of their language groups in Austria-Hungary, who wished to break loose and join them. This was particularly true of Serbia, which attracted the Hapsburg's Yugoslav subjects (the Serbs, Croats, and Slovenes). But if the Yugoslavs should join Serbia, Austria-Hungary's other language minorities—Italians, Czechs, Slovaks, Poles, Rumanians, and Ruthenians—would also demand their freedom from Austrian and Hungarian rule and the Dual Monarchy would fall apart. Austria-Hungary therefore felt it must control the Balkan peninsula in self-defense. It was also the only direction in which it could expand, particularly after its exclusion from Germany in 1866.

Overlying the interests of Austria-Hungary in the Balkans were those of Russia and Germany. Russia had long pursued ambitions for influence and expansion in the Balkans. Germany, which also had its own interests in the area (see p. 611), felt it must support Austria-Hungary, its most effective and reliable ally. Italy, Great Britain, and France also had interests in the Balkans and in the Near and Middle East, although their primary concern was their commitments to their respective allies.

The first Balkan crisis occurred in 1908, when Austria-Hungary suddenly annexed two provinces, Bosnia and Herzegovina, which were inhabited by Serbs and Croats. Serbia had planned to annex these territories, peopled by its own linguistic kin. Serbia appealed to Russia, and Russia threatened Austria-Hungary, whereupon Germany rattled its mighty sword and forced Russia to back down.

A second Balkan crisis occurred in 1912–1913. The various Balkan states defeated Turkey and then fought among themselves over the spoils.

WHERE HISTORIANS DISAGREE

Causes of World War I

World War I shattered the world of 1914 and nearly destroyed a whole civilization. It is natural, then, that many historians and others should spend a great deal of time and thought trying to assess the causes of and assign responsibility for such a disaster.

Initially, people had great difficulty distinguishing causes from responsibility. Most nations were allies or supporters of the victors, and they held Germany responsible for the war. To them, that was little different than concluding that Germany had caused the war. This view was formalized in Article 231 of the Treaty of Versailles.

During the 1920s a reaction against this harsh judgment set in. Several historians offered "revised" analyses of responsibility for World War I. Harry Elmer Barnes concluded that primary blame rested not with Germany but rather with Russia, France, and Serbia. Sidney Bradshaw Fay argued that World War I was a war that no one had really wanted, and that if blame must be assigned, it should go to Russia, France, and England as much as anyone.

Responses to these "revisionist" judgments soon appeared. Since then the scholarly and ideological struggle has continued, some historians pointing to Germany, others to the Allies, still others to Austria-Hungary.

In recent decades scholars have tended to avoid assigning responsibility or blame for the war and instead to focus on what were the crucial causes of the war. Many historians point to the system of alliances that developed in the decades prior to 1914. These alliances divided nations into hostile, distrustful camps. In this system of alliances the acts of one nation became tied to the acts of others. Increasingly, each nation lost its ability to be flexible. Thus, when a relatively local problem between Serbia and Austria-Hungary got out of control, other nations were sucked into a conflict they did not want by the terms of the alliances they had formed and feared to violate.

Other historians focus on nationalism as the real underlying cause of the war. They argue that it was nationalism that caused nations to view everything in terms of rivalry. It was nationalism that spurred the imperial struggle, the buildup of arms, the willingness to fight, the refusal to compromise, and the underestimation of war costs.

More recently, some historians have emphasized the social tensions of European nations as the more profound underlying cause for the war. They point to growing social unrest in almost all European nations and the revolutionary threat in some. These social tensions made governments and people unusually willing to go to war as a means of letting off social pressure and bringing internal unity in the face of an external threat. The near-collapse of all opposition to war once war was declared (even among committed socialists) seems to support this view.

Finally, there are those, particularly Marxist scholars, who argue that World War I stemmed from economic rivalries. They emphasize that as industrial and financial capitalism developed, so did the international interests of influential economic groups. Economic rivalry led to imperial rivalry and eventually to military rivalry. It was these economic factors that set the stage for the particular events leading to the outbreak of World War I.

Ultimately, there are always individuals who make the decisions leading to war. The deeper question is what forces create a situation in which such decisions occur and result in a major war such as World War I.

Victorious Serbia threatened to expand. Austria-Hungary not only thwarted Serbia's expansion to the Adriatic Sea but also threatened to annihilate Serbia. Again Serbia appealed to Russia, and again Germany forced Russia to back down. Each of these crises brought the world close to war, increased international tension, and speeded up preparations for a final showdown.

When a third crisis occurred in the Balkans in the summer of 1914, all the great powers of Europe were bound by their alliances to become involved. This time, all it seemed to take was an incident.

On June 28, 1914, Austrian Archduke Franz Ferdinand was shot by Gavrilo Princip, a Bosnian Serb, in Sarajevo, the capital of the Austro-Hungarian province of Bosnia. The assassination was a deliberate plot involving numerous Serbian army officers. Franz Ferdinand, heir to the Austro-Hungarian throne, was singled out because the Serbs feared that his liberal policy toward the Yugoslavs in Austria-Hungary would allay their discontent, thereby lessening their desire to break away and join Serbia. After the assassination, the government of Austria-Hungary decided to crush Serbia and establish its own dominance in the Balkans once and for all. This tactic would require the backing of Germany, for clearly Russia would not stand aside and allow its Serbian kin and allies to be so treated or its own national interests to be thus violated. At a fateful conference in Berlin eight days after the shooting, the German government gave Austria-Hungary a ''blank check.'' The Germans urged Austria-Hungary to act quickly while world opinion was still outraged by the assassination and promised support in any emergency.

Armed with Germany's blank check, Austria-Hungary presented Serbia with an impossible ultimatum. When Serbia failed to yield to all of its terms, Austria-Hungary declared war and invaded Serbia. Russia mobilized its forces in anticipation of becoming involved in the war. Given the nature of current military strategies, the demands of military timetables, and in particular the circumstances of Russia's clumsy military establishment, Russia's military mobilization was understood to require Germany's military mobilization. In turn, such general mobilization on both sides made it extremely diffi-

cult to prevent the outbreak of war. Germany sent harsh ultimatums to both Russia and France. When Russia failed to reply and France gave an unsatisfactory reply, Germany declared war on Russia on August 1 and on France two days later. The next day, August 4, when German troops violated Belgian neutrality on their way to attack France, Great Britain declared war on Germany. Thus, by August 4, 1914, all the great powers of Europe except Italy were at war (see Map 51.1). Italy claimed that it was not obligated to aid its allies, Germany and Austria-Hungary, since they were the aggressors. The following year, after receiving promises from France and Great Britain that it would reap the spoils of victory, Italy entered the war on the side of the Entente powers. To the side of Germany and Austria-Hungary came Turkey and Bulgaria; these were referred to as the Central Powers. To the side of the Entente powers, which came to be called the Allies, eventually came much of the rest of the world—some thirty-two nations in all. This was truly a world war.

2. THE WESTERN FRONT

Almost everywhere the unwanted war was nevertheless greeted with expressions of nationalistic joy. Most expected the war to be short and easy, perhaps like the Franco-Prussian War of 1871. All expected to win.

The German high command had long anticipated the situation that confronted it in August 1914 and had developed a plan of operation known as the Schlieffen plan. This plan called for a holding action against the slow-moving Russians while the main German forces thrust through neutral Belgium to quickly knock out France, which possessed the only army in the world that gave the Germans any real concern. Then the Germans would concentrate on and destroy Russia with relative ease. Great Britain, her allies gone, would sue for peace.

The Schlieffen plan nearly succeeded. Four weeks after the beginning of hostilities, the German forces were outside Paris ahead of schedule. Nevertheless, the Germans were increasingly vulnerable. Stubborn Belgian resistance had held up the Germans long enough for the French to

Map 51.1 WORLD WAR I This map indicates the surrounded position of the Central Powers and the areas of greatest fighting (and greatest destruction) during World War I.

redeploy their forces to the north and for the British to throw their small army across the Channel. Germans were suffering unanticipated casualties along the western front. Transportation and logistics were difficult. At a critical moment, some one hundred thousand of their best troops under generals von Hindenburg and Lu-

dendorff were detached and sent east for use against the Russians, who had invaded Germany with unexpected speed. Nearing Paris, there was a gap in the German First Army's eastern flank and its western flank lay exposed. At this juncture, the desperate French and British armies turned on the Germans and in the bloody seven-day Battle of the Marne not only halted the Germans but drove them back several miles. Both sides extended their lines from the Swiss border to the North Sea and entrenched.

This was the beginning of a war of attrition. Generals and military strategists had anticipated a short war dominated by rapid movements of men and arms and dramatic offensive thrusts. The reality was a long war dominated by fixed positions and defensive forces. Generals failed to realize that the machine gun, modern artillery, mass mobilization, and trenches were changing the nature of warfare (see Figure 51.1). Acting on old assumptions and flying in the face of these new military realities, generals on both sides ordered offensive thrusts again and again over the next three years. Each time the results moved lines only yards or a few miles, and each time the human costs were staggering. In the nine-month Battle of Verdun, the French held the Germans back; some 700,000 lives were lost. The four-month Battle of the Somme between the British and Germans was even bloodier. Like Verdun, it ended in a stalemate. In the indecisive Passchendaele offensive, the British alone lost some 400,000 soldiers.

Battles were also fought in the air and on the seas. The British navy set up a blockade of Germany. However, the Germans soon overcame Britain's Achilles' heel with a new weapon: the submarine. Eventually the Allies developed mines, depth charges, and tactics to counter German submarines. In the Battle of Jutland, the only major naval battle of the war, the British fleet thwarted the effort of the German fleet to break the blockade but suffered serious losses. But it was on the ground that most of the massive struggle was taking place. After three years of fighting, neither side could break through on the western front.

3. THE EASTERN FRONT

On the eastern front the war was not the immobile defensive struggle that characterized that on the western front. Initially Russia, with its huge but inadequately supplied army, pushed into German and Austro-Hungarian lands. But by the end of August the German armies, reinforced by troops from the western front, trapped the Russians at Tannenberg and administered a crushing defeat that sent them reeling back into Russia.

Further south, however, the Russians were victorious at Lemberg against the Austro-Hungarian army. This victory was only temporary. In 1915 the Germans delivered a series of hammer blows on the Russians, driving deep into Russia and inflicting immense casualties. Disertions, lack of effective leadership, and insufficient supplies plagued Russian efforts. That same year the Serbs were defeated by German, Austrian, and Bulgarian forces and eliminated from the war. An Anglo-French effort to come to the aid of the hard-pressed Russians by breaking through Turkish defenses at the Dardanelles was beaten back with heavy losses.

In 1916 Russia made one more great effort against the Austro-Hungarian forces in the south. Under General Aleksei Brusilov, Russian armies almost forced the Austro-Hungarians to withdraw from the war. A year later, overwhelmed by German forces and a revolution of its own, Russia withdrew from the war. Under the harsh Treaty of Brest-Litovsk Germany gained much territory from Russia, as well as the ability to transfer more of its forces to fight against the weary French and British troops on the western front.

Meanwhile, in northeastern Italy, Austrian and German troops won some battles that were costly on both sides, but their advances were limited and not decisive for the war as a whole. Further south and east, Allied and Arab forces were gaining the upper hand against the Ottoman Turks. In addition to their own importance, these battles drew men and materials from the western front, all of which added to the burdens being carried on the home fronts.

4. THE HOME FRONT

As the months dragged on and the toll of lives and material spent on the war rose, it became apparent that whole societies would have to be mobilized to support the war effort. World War I would be a total war that blurred distinctions between combatants and civilians, between the battle lines and the home front.

FIGURE 51.2 Women War Workers During World War I the British created large armaments plants under the Ministry of Munitions. Under the wartime pressure women replaced men in numerous occupations usually reserved for men. (Imperial War Museum, Great Britain)

The most pressing need was to organize the economy to produce the materials consumed by modern warfare—most obviously the high quantities of bullets, shells, guns, and armaments of all types (see Figure 51.2). But a vast array of other materials were also necessary—everything from food and uniforms to trucks and railway cars. Over the long haul, the war demanded both an advanced industrial capability and efficient organization of that capability to produce what was needed and get it where it could be used. To varying degrees, the governments of the major powers, particularly Germany, Great Britain, and France, took control of their economies. Production, consumption, wages, and prices were determined by governmental agencies rather than the free marketplace.

The mobilization of resources included human resources. Not only were men drafted into the armed services, but women and men on the home front were often required to work in accord with priorities determined by the government. Labor unions were brought into partnership with the government. Class distinctions blurred as more and more members of society were included in the war effort.

Women's roles changed as they assumed jobs previously reserved for men. They took over jobs ranging from work in munitions industries to clerical positions in the armed services. In Great Britain alone the number of women working outside the home increased twentyfold to some 5 million by 1918. Similar patterns held in other countries. Although these new patterns of work for women would not last beyond the war's end, they were a crucial part of the massive mobilization necessary to support total war.

Politically, governments became intolerant of dissent. Constitutional and democratic processes were often ignored in the name of authority and efficiency. Propaganda was used to create support for the government and hatred for the enemy.

Those nations less able to organize and maintain this vast effort—such as the Austro-Hungarian and Russian empires—faltered first. They lacked the strong industrial base and organizational strength of Germany, France, and

Great Britain. But over time, even the strongest nations weakened under the strain. By 1917 the threat of mutiny by the troops was accompanied by political and social protests against the war. It had become clear that the war would be won or lost on the home front as much as on the battle lines.

5. THE ENTRY OF THE UNITED STATES AND THE VICTORY OF THE ALLIES

When the war began in 1914, President Woodrow Wilson admonished the American people to remain neutral in thought as well as in deed. However, from the beginning, the great majority of public opinion in the United States was that Germany and its allies were the aggressors. During the course of the war, the United States increasingly became economically tied to the Allied cause. The sinking of American ships by German submarines, however, provided the immediate impetus for the entry of the United States into the war. When the Germans first began large-scale sinkings of merchant and passenger ships in 1915, President Wilson protested so vigorously that the Germans finally agreed to desist. Great Britain and France, it is true, had seized some American ships attempting to evade the blockade of Germany, but no lives had been lost and damages had been paid. Early in 1917 the German high command decided to launch an unlimited submarine campaign against enemy and neutral shipping alike. At about the same time, British intelligence turned over to the United States the Zimmermann note, in which Germany offered U.S. territory to Mexico as a reward for attacking the United States.

German leaders fully expected that these policies would bring the United States into the war, but they also believed that Great Britain and France would be crushed before any appreciable American weight could be brought to bear in Europe. The American government immediately broke off diplomatic relations with Germany. After several American ships had been sunk, Congress, on April 6, 1917, at the request of President Wilson, declared war on the German imperial government.

Although a full year elapsed before American troops were able to play an important role at the front, the boost in Allied morale was immediate, and the Americans lost no time supplying financial, material, and naval aid. The total contribution of the United States to the Allied victory was relatively small compared with that of France and Great Britain, but America's role, coming as it did when both sides were approaching exhaustion, was probably decisive. At the beginning of 1918 the race was between Germany and the United States. Germany transferred troops from the Russian front to overwhelm Great Britain and France before large numbers of American troops could arrive, while the United States strove to raise, train, and transport sufficient forces to France to stem the German tide.

In March 1918 Field Marshall Erich Ludendorff, now in command of the German armies, launched the first of a series of massive blows on the western front designed to end the war. The British and French were driven back with heavy losses. In desperation, they at long last agreed to a unified command under France's General Ferdinand Foch. The Americans, under General John J. Pershing, also accepted his command. By the middle of June, Ludendorff had launched four great drives, and the Allied lines had been battered so thin that when the climactic fifth drive began along the Marne River in mid-July 1918, Ludendorff wired the kaiser: "If the attack succeeds, the war will be over and we will have won it." When Foch heard the opening German barrage, he wired his government: "If the present German attack succeeds, the war is over and we have lost it." The Germans were stopped by a narrow margin. Foch, now receiving a swelling stream of fresh American troops and armaments, immediately ordered a counterattack. In the Allied counterattack, the tank, developed by the British, proved to be the breakthrough weapon. German strength and morale waned rapidly; the war was lost.

The first of the Central Powers to go out of the war was Bulgaria, which at the end of September 1918 surrendered to French, British, and Serbian forces operating from the Greek port of Salonika. A month later Turkey surrendered to British imperial forces in the Near East. Austria-Hungary, its various language groups in revolt,

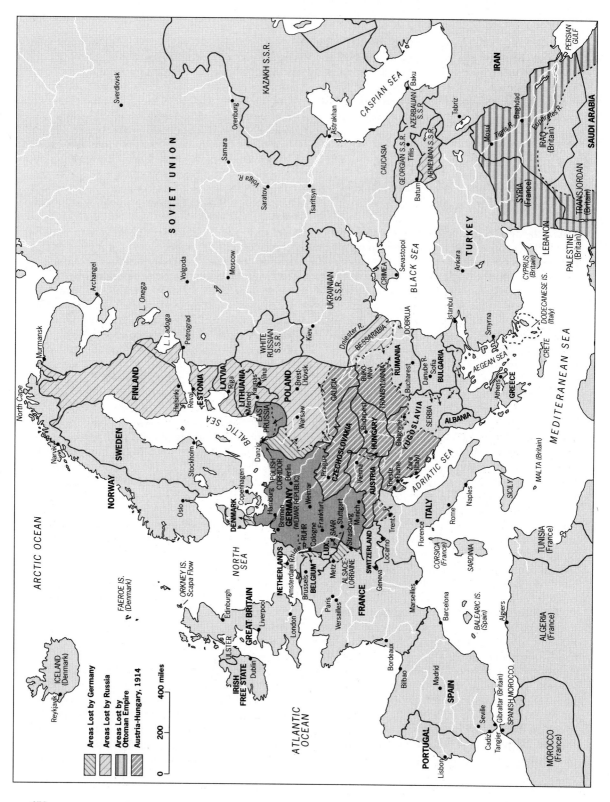

ARCTIC OCEAN

North Cape

Murmansk

SWEDEN

NORWAY

Narvik

Oslo

Stockholm

Reykjavik

ICELAND
(Denmark)

FAEROE IS.
(Denmark)

ORKNEY IS.
Scapa Flow

Edinburgh

GREAT BRITAIN

Liverpool

ULSTER

Dublin

IRISH
FREE STATE

NORTH
SEA

London

Amsterdam

NETHERLANDS

BELGIUM

Brussels

Paris

Versailles

FRANCE

Bordeaux

Bilbao

SPAIN

Madrid

Seville

Cadiz

PORTUGAL

Lisbon

Tangier

MOROCCO
(France)

SPANISH MOROCCO

Gibraltar (Britain)

ALGERIA
(France)

BALEARIC IS.
(Spain)

Barcelona

Algiers

Archangel

L. Onega

L. Ladoga

Petrograd

FINLAND

Helsinki

Reval

ESTONIA

LATVIA

Riga

Libau

LITHUANIA

Memel

Vilna

EAST
PRUSSIA

Danzig

POLISH
CORRIDOR

POLAND

Warsaw

Brest
Litovsk

Kiev

Sverdlovsk

SOVIET UNION

Orenburg

Samara

KAZAKH S.S.R.

Volga R.

Saratov

Tsaritsyn

Volgoda

Moscow

WHITE
RUSSIAN
S.S.R.

UKRAINIAN
S.S.R.

Dniester R.

BESSARABIA

BUKO-
VINA

GALICIA

DOBRUJA

CASPIAN SEA

Astrakhan

CAUCASIA

GEORGIAN S.S.R.

Tiflis

Batum

Baku

AZERBAIJAN
S.S.R.

ARMENIAN S.S.R.

CRIMEA

Sevastopol

BLACK SEA

Istanbul

Ankara

TURKEY

Smyrna

AEGEAN SEA

Athens

GREECE

CRETE

DODECANESE IS.
(Italy)

IRAN

PERSIAN
GULF

Baghdad

Mosul

Tigris R.

Euphrates R.

IRAQ
(Britain)

Tabriz

SAUDI ARABIA

SYRIA
(France)

TRANSJORDAN
(Britain)

LEBANON

PALESTINE
(Britain)

CYPRUS
(Britain)

MEDITERRANEAN SEA

MALTA (Britain)

TUNISIA
(France)

SICILY

Naples

Rome

ITALY

Florence

SARDINIA

CORSICA
(France)

Marseilles

Geneva

SWITZERLAND

Locarno

Trent

Trieste

Fiume

Zara (Italy)

ADRIATIC SEA

YUGOSLAVIA

SERBIA

Belgrade

ALBANIA

Bucharest

RUMANIA

TRANSYLVANIA

HUNGARY

Budapest

AUSTRIA

Vienna

CZECHOSLOVAKIA

Prague

Munich

Stuttgart

Strasbourg

Metz

ALSACE
LORRAINE

SAAR

LUX.

Cologne

RUHR

GERMANY
(WEIMAR REPUBLIC)

Weimar

Berlin

Frankfurt

Bremen

Hamburg

Amsterdam Rhine R.

Copenhagen

DENMARK

BALTIC SEA

BULGARIA

Sofia

Danube R.

BLACK SEA

ATLANTIC OCEAN

0   200   400 miles

Areas Lost by Germany

Areas Lost by Russia

Areas Lost by
Ottoman Empire

Austria-Hungary, 1914

650

surrendered on November 3 to Italian, British, and French forces driving in from Italy. The following day a full-fledged mutiny that had been brewing for several days broke out in the German navy and quickly spread throughout Germany. Popular uprisings brought down the kaiser's government. On November 11 the German commanders, their armies hopelessly beaten and in full retreat from France and Belgium, accepted Foch's armistice terms, which amounted to outright surrender. However, the German commanders manipulated events so that most of Germany's population was unaware of the extent of Germany's military collapse (no foreign soldiers were yet on German soil), and a new civilian government of republicans and socialists had to accept responsibility for the surrender. This tactic set the stage for future charges that Germany had not really been beaten but had been "stabbed in the back" by the political forces that would rule Germany during the 1920s.

6. THE PEACE SETTLEMENT

The Allied statesmen who gathered in Paris in January 1919 to try to make a lasting peace were confronted with a formidable task. Hate and disillusionment poisoned the atmosphere. Although all thirty-two of the victorious Allies were represented at the Paris Peace Conference, the great decisions were really made by the leaders of France, Great Britain, and the United States (see Figure 51.3). The French delegation was headed by Premier Georges Clemenceau, the aged "Tiger of France." As host of the conference and head of the nation that had done the most to defeat Germany and that had suffered greatly, he expected to dominate the decisions. Leading the British delegation was the eloquent and fiery "Little Welsh Attorney," Prime Minister David Lloyd George. As spokesman for the British Empire, which comprised one-fourth of all the land and people in the world, he also expected to dominate the conference. At the head of the American delegation was the idealistic President Woodrow Wilson.

A fundamental and bitter clash immediately developed between Clemenceau, who wanted a hard peace that would mutilate Germany and make it harmless in the future, and Wilson, who wanted a "just" peace free of vindictiveness of any kind. In the end Wilson received support from Lloyd George. Great Britain needed the trade of a recovered Germany and did not wish to see France become too dominant on the Continent. The Treaty of Versailles with Germany reflected Wilson's ideas in fundamental principles, though not in every detail.

Six months of hard work and bitter wrangling were required to draw up the treaty (see Map 51.2). Its most important terms were, in brief, as follows: Germany and its allies were forced to accept full responsibility for the war. Germany was compelled to give up all its overseas colonies and concessions. Alsace and Lorraine were returned to France. The Polish-speaking areas of eastern Germany were ceded to the resurrected Polish state. With one exception, wherever doubt existed as to the wishes of the people in the affected areas, plebiscites were held to determine their desires. The exception was the "Polish corridor," which was cut along the Vistula River to give Poland an outlet to the sea. Germany's armed forces were severely cut down and saddled with permanent limitations. Its general staff was to be dismantled and its top war leaders tried for violations of the rules and customs of war and, if found guilty, punished. (The kaiser fled to the Netherlands just before Germany collapsed, and the Netherlands refused to give him up.) Finally, Germany was held liable for an indemnity that in 1921 was set by an Allied reparations commission at approximately $33 billion. Wilson and Lloyd George believed these terms to be just. Clemenceau considered them to be suicidally lenient.

The treaties with Germany's allies were ac-

Map 51.2 EUROPE, 1923 As a result of World War I the Austro-Hungarian and Ottoman empires were dismembered and both Germany and Russia suffered important losses of territory. However, the newly established states of eastern Europe were vulnerable and cut off from their strongest potential support: France and Great Britain.

FIGURE 51.3 The Big Four
The "Big Four" as they posed for newsreels at Versailles in 1919. Left to right, David Lloyd George, Vittorio Orlando, Georges Clemenceau, Woodrow Wilson. The biggest controversy that developed at the peace conference was between Clemenceau, who demanded a harsh treaty with Germany, and Wilson, who insisted upon a "just" treaty. (UPI/Bettmann Newsphotos)

tually more severe than the Treaty of Versailles because the principle followed in territorial rearrangements was freedom or union of all national language groups, and Germany was more homogeneous linguistically than were its allies. The polyglot Austro-Hungarian Empire was split up along language lines. The Czechs and Slovaks were formed into the new state of Czechoslovakia, which unfortunately also included sizable German and other minorities. The Poles were joined to Poland, the Rumanians to Rumania, the Italians to Italy, and the Serbs, Croats, and Slovenes to Serbia, which now became Yugoslavia. Thus the Dual Monarchy was cut down from a nation of 50 million, second in area only to Russia among the nations of Europe, to an Austria of 6.5 million German-speaking Austrians and a Hungary of 8 million Magyars. Turkey was shorn of its far-flung non-Turkish territories. The new national boundaries, in spite of the painstaking care with which they were drawn, left many pockets of discontent to breed future conflicts.

Wilson placed his chief hopes for peace in an association of nations that would peaceably settle the tensions and conflicts that were certain to arise in the future. He insisted that its framework be incorporated in the treaty with Germany. The first twenty-six articles of the Treaty of Versailles therefore constitute the covenant of the League of Nations.

The League of Nations had no military forces at its command. Its only teeth, so to speak, were Article X and Article XVI. Article X stated that every member undertook to guarantee the territorial integrity of every other member. In other words, if one member was attacked, all the other members were morally obligated to come to its aid. However, there was no way to compel them to do so. Article XVI stated that if a nation went to war in violation of a decision of the League, all the members of the League were to boycott the aggressor. This weapon (economic sanctions) could have been a potent deterrent if faithfully applied.

In the last analysis, however, the success of the League of Nations depended primarily upon the support of the Big Three victorious democracies—the United States, Great Britain, and France. The refusal of the United States to join the League (see pp. 681–682) was a body blow. Great Britain and France immediately lost faith in it and began to pursue their traditional nationalistic aims. Moreover, a defensive alliance among France, Great Britain, and the United States, desperately wanted by France and agreed to at the conference, was not ratified by the governments of Great Britain or the United States. France felt betrayed and left alone to face a resentful Germany.

7. THE EFFECTS OF WORLD WAR I AND THE PEACE SETTLEMENT

World War I profoundly affected the West. Much of Europe was shattered by this war of unprecedented scope and destructiveness. Over 10 million people had been killed, some 3 million of them civilians. Even more had died of diseases or hardships traceable to the war. More than 20 million had been wounded. The cream of a generation of Europe's future leaders had been lost, a reality that helps account for the poor quality of leadership during the 1920s and 1930s. The financial and material losses were incalculable. A tenth of the richest part of France had been laid waste. The most developed part of Russia was devastated. The European nations were saddled with heavy debts. The German, Austro-Hungarian, Ottoman, and Russian empires had collapsed. The British and French empires were seriously weakened. The economic system of capitalism, based on a relative lack of governmental control over economic and social affairs, was undermined during the war as central governments mobilized and managed their nations' economies as never before. Propaganda was unleashed on a massive scale and would thereafter become an important fixture of twentieth-century life.

The peace settlement negotiated in Paris left no one satisfied and many deeply resentful. Russia, which had suffered great losses, was not even invited to the conference. Germany, which would have to play an important role in postwar Europe, was not allowed to participate in the talks—rather, its representatives were presented with a treaty and offered little choice but to sign a humiliating and weakening settlement. The U.S. government refused to sign the treaty. France's thirst for revenge was not satisfied, and France soon felt itself isolated. The settlement left the newly established nations in eastern Europe in a weak position. Certainly, the task facing the negotiators was difficult and perhaps overwhelming. The passions and destruction unleashed by the war may have been so great that no settlement would have been satisfactory. However, the Treaty of Versailles left a legacy of disappointment and resentment to be built upon during the two decades separating World Wars I and II.

SUGGESTED READING

Origins of World War I

F. Fischer, *Germany's Aims in the First World War* (1967). A controversial account stressing Germany's responsibility for the war.

J. Joll, *The Origins of the First World War* (1984). An excellent analysis.

L. Lafore, *The Long Fuse* (1971). A good analysis of the causes of the war.

The War

G. Hardach, *The First World War: 1914–1918* (1977). A useful, broad survey.

K. Robbins, *The First World War* (1984). Covers all aspects of the war.

A. Solzhenitsyn, *August 1914*. An inspired, detailed account of the Tannenberg campaign, which virtually knocked Russia out of the war.

B. Tuchman, *The Guns of August* (1963). A well-written account of the immediate background to and opening campaigns of World War I.

The Home Front

F. L. Carsten, *War Against War* (1982). A good study of radical movements in Great Britain and Germany.

J. Williams, *The Home Fronts: Britain, France, and Germany, 1914–1918* (1972). A comparative study of the domestic impact of the war.

J. Winter and R. Wall, eds., *The Upheaval of War: Family, Work and Welfare in Europe, 1914–1918* (1988). Covers economic and social developments.

The Peace Settlement

H. Nicolson, *Peacemaking 1919* (1965). A good examination of the Versailles process and settlement.

D. Stevenson, *The First World War and International Politics* (1988). Good on the difficulties of the peace.

The Effects of World War I

R. Albrecht-Carrie, ed., *The Meaning of the First World War* (1965). Stresses international affairs.

P. Fussell, *The Great War and Modern Memory* (1975). Stresses the psychological significance of the war.

J. Roth, ed., *World War I* (1967). An excellent collection of essays analyzing the significance of the war.

B. Schmitt and H. Vedeler, *The World in a Crucible, 1914–1919* (1984). Includes an analysis of the consequences.

Historical Fiction

E. Hemingway, *A Farewell to Arms.* A famous novel based on the author's experiences on the Italian front.

E. M. Remarque, *All Quiet on the Western Front.* Has brought home to millions the horrors of trench warfare in World War I.

CHAPTER 52
Revolution and Communism in Russia

FIGURE 52.1 Serov, *Lenin Proclaiming Soviet Power* This painting shows Lenin, with Stalin and other Bolshevik leaders, proclaiming to the revolutionary forces the Bolsheviks' assumption of power in 1917. The style of the painting, social realism, is typical of Soviet art during the 1920s and 1930s. (Sovfoto)

World War I not only was militarily devastating for Russia but also was something the centuries-old tsarist government could not survive. In March 1917 the government of Nicholas II was swept from power by a revolution. This was the beginning of an extended period of revolutionary events in Russia that eventually resulted in the rise to power of the Bolsheviks, who in turn attempted to establish their vision of a Communist society in Russia. By the 1930s Russia was ruled by a totalitarian government that was effecting a massive economic, social, and cultural transformation of the nation and that was seen as a threat by most nations of the West.

1. THE RUSSIAN REVOLUTION OF 1917

Without the strain of World War I, revolution might not have occurred as and when it did, but that a revolution occurred should not be surprising. The violent Russian upheaval of 1917 was the result of maladjustments and discontent that had long been developing. Russia, except for a handful of intelligentsia, had been virtually bypassed by the great liberalizing movements, such as the Enlightenment and the French Revolution, that had influenced western Europe. The Industrial Revolution, which brought in its wake liberalism and radicalism, reached Russia only in the 1890s. While western Europe and parts of central Europe and the United States were becoming politically, economically, and socially modernized, Russia remained a land of peasantry, feudal aristocracy, and tsarist autocracy. In the latter half of the nineteenth century many of the frustrated Russian intelligentsia turned to revolutionary doctrines and even terrorism in an effort to effect rapid change. Others, including elements from the small but growing middle class, hoped for more moderate liberal reforms. But the tsarist government, particularly under Nicholas II (1894–1917), was generally reactionary and unbending.

The growing pressures for change exploded in the revolution of 1905. With little support and faced with dissension and revolt on all sides, Nicholas II was forced to grant some liberal reforms and promised to give the elected Duma some real powers. But as soon as the crisis passed, Nicholas II returned to his old policies and rejected the substance of the liberal reforms.

The outbreak of the war in 1914 brought some temporary national unity as most factions rallied to the support of the nation. Soon, however, the strains of war proved too much for the inept Russian government. Russia suffered staggering losses at the hands of the German armies. Behind the lines the suffering of the civilian population, much of which could be attributed to the corrupt bureaucracy of the tsar, was acute. Members of the Duma and others increasingly demanded liberal reform, but the tsar and his ministers refused to share power. The disintegration of Russia's military forces was reflected in the disintegration of Russia's government. The tsar increasingly fell under the influence of his unbending wife, Alexandra. She in turn fell under the influence of Grigori Efimovich Rasputin (1871?–1916), an uneducated Siberian monk who claimed to have the power to heal the tsar's hemophilic son. Even the tsar's aristocratic supporters, a group of whom murdered Rasputin late in 1916, were demanding fundamental change.

In early March 1917, the dam broke. Demands for bread in Petrograd quickly turned into riots and strikes. The tsar's troops were unable to restore order, often refusing to fire on the rioters—many of them led by women—or actually joining them. On March 12 the Duma organized a Provisional Government and three days later Nicholas II resigned. The new Provisional Government was dominated by liberals and moderate socialists. The leading figures of this government were Pavel Milyukov and Prince Georgi Lvov, both relatively moderate liberals. The Provisional Government enacted into law civil liberties, religious freedom, equality before the law, union rights, and other typical liberal reforms. Its more moderate faction promised to turn Russia into a Western-style political democracy and enact fundamental social reforms; others demanded more radical change. However, in addition to its inexperience, its differing factions, and the pressures for change, the Provisional Government labored under two burdens. First, it had to share power with the newly organized soviets—political organizations of workers, soldiers, and radical intellectuals—particularly the powerful Petrograd soviet. Second, it chose to continue the war that was draining Russia. Some of the crucial connections between these two burdens are indicated by the Petrograd Soviet's issuance of Order Number 1, which declared that military officers would be democratically elected by soldiers and military decisions would be democratically made. Order Number 1 contributed to the continuing disintegration of the Russian forces.

In May the liberal leaders of the Provisional Government resigned and the socialist Alexander Kerensky (1881–1970) became the leading figure in the government. By this time, however, the Bolshevik wing of the Marxist Social Democratic party was starting to play an important role in Russian affairs.

2. THE RISE OF THE BOLSHEVIKS

Marxism became influential among some intellectuals toward the end of the nineteenth century. In 1898 Russian Marxists formed the Social Democratic party, whose principal leaders were Gregory Plekhanov (1857–1918) and his disciple Vladimir Ilich Ulyanov (Lenin) (1870–1924). Repression by the tsar's government forced the Social Democrats into exile. At a London conference in 1903 the radical Bolshevik wing under Lenin split from the more moderate Mensheviks.

Until 1917, Lenin's Bolsheviks remained only a minor party. Its leaders were hunted down by the state police and shot, imprisoned, or exiled. For some seventeen years Lenin remained in exile in Switzerland, keeping his party alive and plotting the eventual overthrow of the tsar's government. During that time he developed theoretical and tactical principles for the successes the Bolsheviks would enjoy in 1917. Three of these principles were crucial. The first was that the party should not be open and democratic but rather should be an elite, highly trained, and constantly purged group of dedicated Marxist revolutionaries. The second was that the socialist revolution need not be a revolution of only the industrial working class; in Russia it could also be a dual revolution of workers and peasants—all part of an even broader socialist revolution that would sweep other countries of Europe. The third was a continuing opposition to World War I.

Lenin and the Bolsheviks' chance came in the months after the fall of the tsar's government in March 1917. In April 1917 the German government transported Lenin from his place of exile in Switzerland to the Russian border in an effort to increase the chaos and remove Russia from the war. Lenin refused to cooperate with the Provisional Government and instead unleashed a barrage of appealing slogans such as "peace to the army, land to the peasants, ownership of the factories to the workers." Meanwhile, the Socialist Kerensky came to power, but he was unable to extract Russia from the war. Bolshevik influence was growing, particularly among the Petrograd workers and soldiers. In July the Bolsheviks decided the time was ripe to seize power, but the effort failed. The Bolsheviks were not yet a dominant force, and the Kerensky government arrested many Bolsheviks and forced others, including Lenin, to flee to exile in Finland. The Kerensky government was further weakened by the failure of a new Russian offensive in the war and a threatened coup d'état by General Lavr Kornilov. This threat led Kerensky to release the Bolsheviks and rely on the soviets to defend the capital in September. By October the Bolsheviks, under the leadership of Lenin and the brilliant Leon Trotsky (1877–1940), gained control over the Petrograd and Moscow soviets. Lenin again judged the time was ripe for revolution, and this time he was right. On November 6 Trotsky conducted a well-organized revolution, seizing the crucial centers of power and arranging for the transfer of power to the soviets and Lenin. On November 7 the Bolshevik majority elected Lenin the head of the new government (see Figure 52.1).

3. THE BOLSHEVIKS IN POWER, 1917–1927

The Bolsheviks immediately moved to fulfill their promises and consolidate their power. In place of the old tsarist hierarchy, a pyramid of people's councils, or soviets, was set up. These councils were elected by universal suffrage but were actually dominated by a relatively few Communist party members. When national elections failed to return a Bolshevik majority to a Constituent Assembly, Lenin had the Red Army disperse it. Capitalism was abolished. A barter system of exchange replaced money, the value of the ruble having been destroyed by inflation and devaluation. All industry and commerce were placed under the management of committees of workers responsible to party commissars. The land was nationalized and its management turned over to local peasant committees. They in turn distributed it to individual peasants to be worked by their own labor. All crop surpluses were turned over to the state. Church lands were expropriated by the state.

In order to free the new regime for the enormous task of refashioning Russian society, Lenin immediately opened peace negotiations with the Germans. The Germans, realizing Russia's helplessness (Russian troops were deserting in droves), demanded the harshest of terms. Lenin attempted to stall them off, but when the Germans threatened to march on Petrograd and Moscow, he was forced to sign the Treaty of Brest-Litovsk in March 1918. Russia lost Finland, Estonia, Latvia, Lithuania, the Ukraine, Bessarabia, its Polish provinces, and some of its Trans-Caucasian territory. These lands contained one-third of Russia's European population, three-fourths of its iron, and nine-tenths of its coal. In addition, Russia was compelled to pay a heavy indemnity.

But these hard terms were not the end, nor the worst, of Lenin's woes. Two years of bitter civil war followed the peace with Germany. The aristocracy, including most of the higher army officers, launched a counterrevolution against the Bolshevik regime. These "White" forces were aided by various other disaffected groups and by French, British, Polish, Japanese, Czech, and U.S. troops. It was with the greatest of difficulty that the "Red" armies, hastily organized by Trotsky, finally defeated the "Whites." In doing so, the Bolsheviks regained the Ukraine. However, a large additional strip of territory was lost to Poland, thanks largely to French armed intervention on the side of the Poles. Moreover, military and civilian deaths stemming from the civil war and the accompanying disease and starvation probably approached some 4 to 6 million people.

Russia's war-torn economy was a shambles. The civil war compounded the destruction already suffered in World War I. Indeed, part of the reason for the Bolshevik victory in the civil war was their policy of "war communism," which succeeded in mobilizing Russia's economy and society for the war effort but also further disrupted normal economic activities. Lack of experience and some unpopular policies added to the economic difficulties. Often workers did not know how to run factories and trains. The distribution of goods was in inexperienced hands. When peasants saw that their surpluses would be seized by the government, they often resisted or refused to raise more than they needed for themselves. By 1921 some 30 million Russians were threatened with starvation, and in spite of considerable foreign relief, particularly from the United States, many did starve.

Lenin, a realist, saw the necessity for retreat. In 1921 he launched the NEP (New Economic Policy), which was a temporary compromise with capitalism. The popular Nikolai Bukharin (1888–1938) was chosen to carry out the new policy. In order to provide incentive, industries employing fewer than twenty workers were permitted to operate under private ownership. These little industrial capitalists were called *nepmen*. Enterprising peasants, called *kulaks,* were permitted to own and rent land and hire laborers. Money and credit were restored. This small-scale capitalistic activity was closely supervised and regulated by the state. However, the NEP provided enough incentive to pull the Russian economy out of chaos. In 1923, just as the new policy was beginning to function, Lenin suffered a paralytic stroke. He died the following year.

Lenin's death precipitated a power struggle among his chief associates (see Figure 52.2). Most assumed that his successor would be Leon Trotsky, who had been the chief organizer of the Red Army and had planned its victory over the Whites. A brilliant, eloquent Communist theorist, he was an apostle of world revolution. Trotsky, however, underestimated Joseph Stalin, executive secretary of the Communist party. This unobtrusive, taciturn man was an unscrupulous behind-the-scenes operator. Stalin was the son of poverty-stricken ex-serfs. Expelled from an Orthodox seminary because of his Marxist views and activities, he became a professional revolutionist and terrorist. (*Stalin* is a pseudonym meaning "man of steel.") He was repeatedly arrested and imprisoned and repeatedly escaped. World War I found him in exile in Siberia. Taking

FIGURE 52.2 Trotsky and Stalin This rare photograph, taken in 1923 at a party meeting, shows the feud between Stalin (seated, at right) and Trotsky (standing, at left) that ended with Trotsky's murder in Mexico in 1940. As the brilliant, eloquent Trotsky speaks, the taciturn Stalin, son of ex-serfs, eyes him coldly. (UPI/Bettmann Newsphotos)

advantage of the amnesty granted to all political prisoners by the Kerensky regime in 1917, Stalin hastened to Petrograd, where he became a devoted associate of Lenin. He played a prominent role in the civil war against the Whites and became executive secretary of the Communist party. In this key position he made himself master of the all-important party machinery.

In this struggle for leadership, Trotsky took the position that all efforts must be made to bring the socialist revolution to other parts of Europe, and that without support from other, more advanced socialist nations, socialism in Russia would fail. Trotsky also favored ending the NEP and immediately launching a policy of massive industrialization. Stalin took a more moderate stand, arguing that socialism in one country (Russia) was possible and therefore all efforts should be pointed toward securing what had already been gained in Russia. Trotsky was the more compelling speaker and accomplished theorist, but he also conveyed an element of arro-

FIGURE 52.3 *The Five-Year Plan in Four Years* In this 1930s Soviet propaganda poster, *The Five-Year Plan in Four Years,* Stalin is portrayed leading industrial development against the reactionary forces of capitalism and religion. (The Fotomas Index, London)

gance. Stalin was more adept at political in-fighting. By conspiring with prominent groups of Bolsheviks and playing one faction against another, Stalin isolated Trotsky and had him expelled from the party and exiled from Russia. By the end of 1927 Stalin had maneuvered himself into a position of dominance over the Communist party and dictatorship over the Soviet Union.

4. THE FIVE-YEAR PLANS AND THE PURGES

In 1928 Stalin launched the first of a series of five-year plans (see Figure 52.3). They were units of planned economy with certain specific goals or objectives to be achieved every five years. They marked the end of the NEP, which had served its purpose of pulling the Communist economy through its first major crises. The objectives of the First Five-Year Plan were (1) the elimination of the last remnants of capitalism, (2) the industrialization of the Soviet Union, (3) the collectivization and mechanization of agriculture, and (4) national defense. However, underlying these objectives were even more fundamental goals: transforming the economy and

society of the Soviet Union into a Communist economy and society and training and socializing Soviet citizens to be adaptive participants in this Communist system. Rarely has such an ambitious program been undertaken.

Achievement of the first goal meant the liquidation of the *nepmen* and the *kulaks.* When tens of thousands of the independent peasant-proprietor *kulaks* resisted, Stalin simply eliminated them. The consolidation of their farms into mechanized collectives and the organization of giant state farms went on apace. The state farms were huge areas of up to three hundred thousand acres in size run by party managers and hired laborers. Every effort was made to mechanize them. Vast tracts of land in southeast Russia and Siberia were brought under cultivation for the first time. The collective farms were of various types. In the most common type independent farmers surrendered their lands and horses but retained their houses, gardens, cattle, pigs, and chickens for their own private use. The collective farm was run by elected managers who were instructed and supervised by party officials. Elimination of the tiny individual tracts, each one of which had been surrounded by ditches or hedgerows, made mechanization possible. A certain amount of the harvest was set aside for taxes, insurance, improvements, and feed. A large part had to be sold to the state at a fixed price. The rest was distributed to the peasant members in proportion to the amount of their original contribution to the collective in land and horses and to the amount and quality of their work. The mechanization of Russia's agriculture required the construction of huge quantities of tractors and farm machinery.

Since the Industrial Revolution was still in its infancy in Russia in 1928, industrialization meant building almost from the ground up and concentrating on producer rather than consumer goods. Western engineers and technicians were lured to Russia with high salaries. Capital was obtained by exporting scarce supplies of wheat, often at ruinously low prices. At the cost of much privation, enormous strides were made. Steel mills, power plants, foundries, mines, refineries, and railroads were built all over the Soviet Union. At Dnepropetrovsk on the Dnieper River, the world's largest dam and hydroelectric power plant were constructed. At the end of 1932 it was announced that all the goals of the First Five-Year Plan had been reached several months ahead of time.

During the 1930s the Second and Third Five-Year Plans were launched. In general, the stress remained on collectivization and mechanization of agriculture and on heavy industrialization. However, there was a new emphasis on the production of consumer goods that enabled the masses to enjoy a slowly rising standard of living.

The results of the five-year plans are difficult to evaluate accurately. What might have happened if the policy choices had been different is unknown. The results in agriculture were most questionable. Clearly millions of people suffered as Stalin tried to make the peasantry pay for industrialization one way or another. Rural families, communities, and established ways of life were torn apart. There was tremendous resistance to collectivization as well as mismanagement and drought. At times famine became a reality, as did a state of near civil war in the countryside. At one point Stalin admitted that problems with collectivization had claimed some 10 million human victims and brought about the destruction of half of the nation's draft and farm

animals. Yet by 1939 over 90 percent of Soviet agriculture was collectivized and much of it was mechanized.

The results of the five-year plans in industry and defense were more gratifying and, in many ways, phenomenal. In 1928, at the beginning of the First Five-Year Plan, the Soviet Union was far behind other nations in industrial production. During the First Five-Year Plan industrial production doubled, a record equaled again in the Second Five-Year Plan. During this period the Soviet Union managed to achieve an unprecedented rate of growth in industrial output, but at great human cost. By 1941, when the Germans invaded the Soviet Union, it had become the fourth greatest industrial power in the world. In a number of categories it had surpassed both Great Britain and Germany and was second only to the United States. The Soviet Union could never have withstood the German assault had this not been true.

The 1930s were also the time of the Great Purges. In 1934 Sergei Kirov (1888–1934), a high Soviet official, was assassinated. It is unclear whether Stalin's enemies were responsible or whether Stalin himself ordered the assassination only to use it as an excuse to eliminate potential rivals. However, a long period of party purges, arrests, trials, imprisonments, and executions soon followed. Eventually almost all the original Bolshevik leaders were removed from power and from the party, as were most of the Red Army's top officer corps. By the end of the Great Purges in 1939, hundreds of thousands—perhaps millions—of people had been affected. The government, the Communist party, and the military were now staffed by new, generally younger figures all beholden to Stalin.

Stalin's motives for the Great Purges are a matter of debate. Some argue that the purges were a manifestation of his paranoia; others argue that they were a logical step in the process of moving the Soviet Union from a revolution in 1917 to a totalitarian Communist state in the 1930s. In any case, they did consolidate Stalin's power and eliminate all potential pockets of resistance to him. But the price was high. The purges were part of a pattern of repression that Stalin used during his five-year plans and would continue to use until his death in 1953. Some scholars estimate that in all, the starvation, the executions, and the force-labor camps may have caused the deaths of up to 40 million Soviet citizens.

5. TOTALITARIAN CONTROL

Between 1917 and 1939 the government effected totalitarian rule in the Soviet Union. The government was dominated by the Communist party, and the party head served as virtual dictator. Not only did the party enjoy a monopoly over political affairs and the armed forces, it also controlled the economic, social, religious, and cultural life of the nation to an unprecedented degree.

The Soviet Political System

On coming to power, the Bolsheviks divided the Russian Empire into eleven socialist republics—Russia proper and ten other language or dialect areas. In 1939–1940 five more were added from territories seized by Russia at the outbreak of World War II. The Soviet Union was in theory a union of autonomous republics. (U.S.S.R. stands for "Union of Soviet Socialist Republics.") Actually, however, Russia itself constituted at least four-fifths of the total area and population and dominated the Union.

The Soviet system of government as originally set up consisted of a pyramid of elected councils—village, district, county, and provincial—culminating in the Union Congress of Soviets, which met once every two years and chose executive and administrative boards. Voting was by show of hands in mass meetings. The urban vote was given more than double the weight of the rural vote, since bolshevism's chief concern was the industrial proletariat. In 1936 Stalin promulgated a new constitution, which appeared to be more democratic. Voting was to be by secret ballot, the differential between the urban and the rural vote was abolished, and the members of the various soviets in the pyramid were to be elected directly by the local districts. The member republics in the Union were allegedly granted complete autonomy.

Only the Communist party was permitted to engage in organized political activity. It named the official candidates, made all political policies

and platforms, and conducted all election promotion and propaganda. Opposition to the party's official candidates and program was considered to be disloyal and was ferreted out and crushed by the state police, both secret and regular. The all-powerful Communist party was organized on an authoritarian basis. The Politburo, sixteen men meeting in secret and responsible only to the secretariat of the party, made all decisions, which were transmitted without question down through the chain of command to the local cells. The real center of power in the Soviet system was the secretariat of the Communist party, and the first (or general) secretary of the party was the most powerful figure in the Soviet Union. Obedience to superiors was demanded of all party members. Party members were carefully selected and trained. As set up by Lenin, the total number was kept relatively small.

Soviet Culture and Society

In 1917 more than 60 percent of the Russian people were illiterate. It was Lenin's belief that a Communist state required an educated populace in order to succeed. Nearly all the top Bolsheviks themselves were educated—in fact, they would be considered members of the intelligentsia in almost any time or place. Little could be done in the educational field in the first turbulent years of the Communist regime, but education received major attention in Stalin's five-year plans. In 1928 the Communists launched a vast program of free compulsory secular education. The program covered all levels—elementary, secondary, and higher—for both young and adults. It included a comprehensive system of technical and on-the-job training. Science and engineering were particularly stressed. Of course, Soviet education was interlarded with Communist propaganda, but its standards were high, and it turned out the trained people who were needed.

Advanced scholarship and the arts were not neglected. An extensive program of scholarships, prizes, and institutes was inaugurated for the purpose of encouraging and subsidizing superior talent. Soviet musicians, architects, painters, and dancers more than held their own in international competition. Yet the arts were subject to official Communist ideology. All liberal, bourgeois, or capitalistic literature (which was most

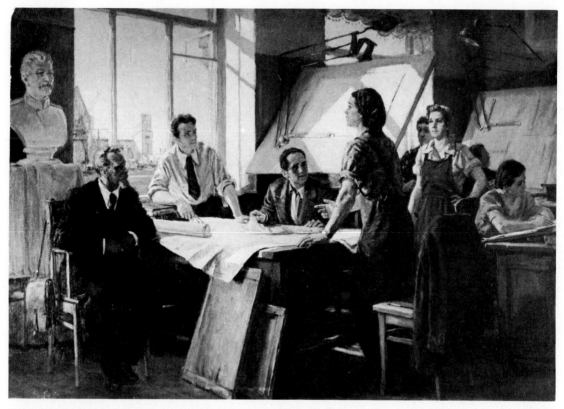

FIGURE 52.4 Women Workers and Architects Conferring The Soviet government promoted social realism to make art relevant to the working masses and carry explicit messages. Here the sun streams in on women workers and architects conferring over plans for a new factory. On the left a bust of Stalin looks on. (Tass from Sovfoto)

of it) was heavily censored. Such world-re-nowned composers as Prokofiev and Shostako-vich occasionally fell into official disfavor be-cause of their modern "bourgeois" music. When some powerful commissar decided that the Men-delian law of genetics, which is generally ac-cepted in the world of science, ran counter to the party line, Soviet geneticists were forced to dis-claim it.

Soviet society was made more egalitarian. Al-though the party, governmental, military, and cultural elite enjoyed some advantages, most class distinctions were eliminated. Women par-ticularly benefited, because all formal discrimi-nation against them was eliminated (see Figure 52.4). In the years just after the revolution, women gained the right to vote as well as legal

equality within marriage. Abortion was legalized and the right to divorce established. Thanks to the views of Bolshevik leaders and the demand for workers, Soviet women probably gained un-paralleled economic equality with men. They re-ceived equal pay and were offered equal edu-cational and professional opportunities. However, not all of these gains for women lasted. New policies in the 1930s made abortion illegal. Women rarely moved into the highest economic or political positions. Strong patterns of discrim-ination left Soviet women with the burdens of household management along with work outside of the home and some of the realities of inequal-ity that generally prevailed elsewhere in the West.

In many ways Soviet society displayed the

marks of totalitarian control. Most social organizations were saturated with official Communist ideology. The Communist party and the state took direct control when any social organization showed signs of gaining significant influence. Agents of the state, ranging from minor bureaucrats to members of the secret police, pervaded Soviet society. Terror, most evident during Stalin's Great Purges, was an ever-present weapon.

Religious Policy

The religious policy of the Bolsheviks upon gaining power in Russia was quite similar to that of the French revolutionists in 1789–1794. All church property was confiscated. The churches themselves were turned into museums or clubs of various kinds, although they were sometimes leased to religious congregations for purposes of worship. No religious instruction whatever was permitted in the schools, which were all public and secular. The churches were forbidden to give organized religious instruction and even to maintain seminaries for the training of their own clergy. At the same time, the schools were flooded with Communist propaganda.

The Communist leaders claimed that their harsh treatment of the churches was necessitated by the active opposition of the churches to the Communist government. They claimed that when they had first come to power, they had granted religious freedom for the first time in Russian history, but that the churches had immediately used this freedom to advocate the overthrow of the very government that had granted it. They further claimed that churches had always been the tools and agents of capitalistic governments and interests. Whatever truth there may be in these claims, it would appear that religion was perceived as a problem and danger to the Soviet regime.

6. THE SOVIET UNION AND THE WORLD

When the Bolsheviks first took over in 1917, they confidently expected some of the capitalistic governments in the war-weary world to collapse and follow Russia along the path to communism. To encourage them to do so and to avoid fulfillment of the harsh terms of the Treaty of Brest-Litovsk, the Communist leaders began an active campaign of revolutionary infiltration and subversion abroad, particularly in Germany. Although some headway was made in Germany, Bavaria falling under Communist control for a brief time, the only country to embrace communism was Hungary, where in 1919 Béla Kun set up a Communist dictatorship that lasted four months. To guide and aid the Communist parties in other countries in the common cause of world revolution, the Bolsheviks set up the Comintern (Communist International), with headquarters in Moscow.

The Western capitalistic powers were antagonistic to the Soviet Union. Thinking that the Bolshevik regime would soon collapse, France, Great Britain, Japan, and the United States landed troops on Russian soil in 1918 and aided the counterrevolutionary White forces. France helped the Poles to seize a large strip of Russian-speaking territory. Great Britain and France organized the anti-Soviet regimes in the countries of eastern Europe bordering the Soviet Union into a *cordon sanitaire* (health or quarantine belt). For several years, no Western power would recognize the Bolshevik regime. The Soviet Union was refused admission to the League of Nations until 1934, eight years after Germany had been admitted and one year after it had withdrawn under the guidance of Hitler. Even then the Western powers steadfastly refused to cooperate with the Soviet Union in any collective action against the rising Fascist menace.

Nonetheless, the failure of the Communist movements abroad and of the Bolsheviks' early efforts to communize Russia overnight caused the Soviet leaders to adopt a more conciliatory attitude toward the capitalist powers. The NEP needed foreign commerce and foreign capital in order to function. Eventually, the Soviet Union gained official recognition abroad. In 1922 Germany established official relations with the Soviet Union. Great Britain and France recognized the Soviet Union in 1924. The last capitalist state of the West to recognize the Soviet Union was the United States, which held off until 1933.

The five-year plans, which began in 1928, required much Western capital and technical assistance. Therefore, the next ten years represented the high tide of Soviet tractability toward the capitalist Western democracies. Stalin, unlike Trotsky, was more interested in "socialism in one country" than in world revolution, which he believed would come later. The Comintern was allowed to languish. Of course, the Soviet Union's fear of the growing Nazi German menace after 1933 was a significant factor in its conciliatory attitude toward the capitalistic democracies. This honeymoon ended in 1938 with the Munich crisis (see p. 686). From that time on, Stalin was apparently convinced that real cooperation with the Western democracies was impossible. The cooperation forced upon the Soviet Union and most of the capitalist world by the menace of the Axis during World War II lasted only until victory was assured. Meanwhile, after Hitler came to power in 1933, the greatest threat to both the Soviet Union and the capitalist democracies was Nazi Germany.

SUGGESTED READING

General

E. H. Carr, *A History of Soviet Russia,* 7 vols. (1951–1964). Scholarly and highly respected.

R. W. Clark, *Lenin* (1988). A good recent study.

I. Deutscher, *Stalin: A Political Biography* (1967). Not only a scholarly biography of Stalin but also a good history of the whole Communist movement in Russia.

The Russian Revolution and the Rise of the Bolsheviks

R. Daniels, *Red October* (1969). A well-written account of the Bolshevik revolution.

W. Lincoln, *Red Victory: A History of the Russian Civil War* (1989). Recent and comprehensive.

A. Ulam, *The Bolsheviks* (1968). A good introduction stressing Lenin's doctrines.

The Bolsheviks in Power, the Five-Year Plans, and the Purges

R. Conquest, *The Great Terror* (1968). An excellent study of Stalin's purges.

S. Fitzpatrick. *The Russian Revolution.* 1982. A brief, analytical treatment of the period.

G. Leggett, *The Cheka: Lenin's Secret Police* (1981). A good study of this topic.

J. P. Nettl, *The Soviet Achievement* (1967). A good analysis of economic development in the Soviet Union.

Totalitarian Control

S. Fitzpatrick, *Cultural Revolution in Russia, 1928–1931* (1978). A good analysis.

K. Geiger, *The Family in Soviet Russia* (1968). Well written.

R. Marshall, *Aspects of Religion in the Soviet Union, 1917–1967* (1971). A good book on this difficult subject.

R. Pipes, *The Formation of the Soviet Union* (1964). Stresses the problem of Soviet minorities.

The Soviet Union and the World

G. Kennan, *Russia and the West Under Lenin and Stalin.* By a former American ambassador to the Soviet Union; a harsh perspective.

A. Ulam, *Expansion and Coexistence: Soviet Foreign Policy* (1974). Scholarly, by a respected expert.

Historical Fiction

A. Koestler, *Darkness at Noon* (1956). A classic novel of bolshevism and the purges.

B. Pasternak, *Doctor Zhivago* (1974). Nobel Prize winner's novel depicting life in the Soviet Union by a man who experienced it.

A. Solzhenitsyn, *The Gulag Archipelago* (1974). A vivid account of terror.

CHAPTER 53
The Rise of Fascism and Authoritarianism

FIGURE 53.1 Mussolini Addresses the Masses
This photo of Mussolini addressing a huge crowd in Rome after a victory of the Italian forces in Ethiopia shows some of the typical traits of fascism and authoritarianism during the 1920s and 1930s: nationalism (the flag), militarism (the uniform), and mass politics (the cheering crowd). (UPI/Bettmann Newsphotos)

During World War I many hoped that victory against the Central Powers would be a blow to authoritarianism and a triumph for liberal democracy. By the time of the Paris Peace Conference in 1919, a shadow was already being cast on these hopes by the triumph of the Bolsheviks in Russia. Nevertheless, the arrangements made at Paris seemed to establish parliamentary democracy in the states of eastern Europe and affirm it in western Europe. But in only a few years these optimistic hopes were dashed by the rise of authoritarian governments in southern, eastern, and central Europe and by the growth of authoritarian political movements within several Western democracies.

1. TOTALITARIANISM, FASCISM, AND AUTHORITARIANISM

The 1920s and 1930s witnessed a great growth of totalitarianism, fascism, and right-wing authoritarianism. Of these political systems, totalitarianism was the most revolutionary and rigorous. In a totalitarian system, a single political party with a revolutionary ideology controls the government. It appeals for active support from the masses and is dominated by a dictatorial leader. No opposition is tolerated. Propaganda, force, and terror are openly used to ensure control and further the goals of the government. Modern communications, technology, and organization are used to control the economic, social, religious, and cultural life of the nation as much as possible. The liberal ideology of limited government and individual rights is formally rejected in a totalitarian system.

As we have already seen in Chapter 52, totalitarianism had its beginnings in the Soviet Union under Lenin and came to full flower under Stalin during the 1930s. Since this totalitarianism was based on Communist ideology, it is often called totalitarianism of the Left. Totalitarianism arose in a mild form in Italy during the 1920s and in a virulent form in Germany during the 1930s. Since this totalitarianism was based on Fascist ideology, it is often called totalitarianism of the Right.

Both fascism and communism were ideologies—sets of ideas and values—that were gaining strength in the West throughout the 1920s and 1930s, but fascism proved to be the greater immediate threat to liberal democracy. Generally, fascism was antiliberal, antidemocratic, anti-individualistic, and anti-Communist. It was ultranationalistic and militaristic. It was tied to somewhat mystical ideas of the all-powerful expansive state, of race, and of will. Fascism was initiated by Mussolini during the 1920s. During the 1920s and 1930s Fascist parties spread throughout Europe. The greatest triumph of fascism came with the rise to power of Hitler and nazism in Germany during the 1930s. Some other governments in southern, central, and eastern Europe were influenced by fascism and had some of its trappings, but for the most part they were right-wing authoritarian regimes.

Right-wing authoritarian regimes were less ideologically based than Fascist regimes, and they controlled life in their nations to a much lesser degree than totalitarian systems did. Usually they amounted to a dictatorship backed by the military and conservative forces of the nation. They tended to be most concerned with preserving order and protecting the established status quo against perceived threats from liberal democracy, socialism, or communism.

Together totalitarianism, fascism, and right-wing authoritarianism posed a serious threat to the advocates of liberal democracy in the West. Indeed, the hoped-for triumph of liberal democracy after World War I seemed to be turning into a triumph for its enemies—a triumph that would lead to growing conflict and a renewal of war in 1939. The story of the rise of fascism and authoritarianism begins with Italy, where Mussolini set up the first Fascist dictatorship (see Figure 53.1).

2. MUSSOLINI CREATES THE FIRST FASCIST STATE

Italy emerged from World War I battered and humiliated. Although it was one of the victorious Allies, Italy's armies had made a poor showing, and Italy had realized few of the grandiose ambitions for which it had entered the war. In the Paris peace settlements Italy had been awarded the adjacent Italian-speaking areas of Austria-Hungary but had been denied further acquisitions east of the Adriatic and in Asia and Africa, some of which it ardently desired. These frustrations were severe blows to Italian national pride.

Italy's weak economy emerged from the war acutely maladjusted. The national debt was huge and the treasury empty. The inflated currency, together with a shortage of goods, raised prices ruinously. Hundreds of thousands of demobilized veterans could find no jobs. In the summer of 1919, there was widespread disorder. Veterans began seizing and squatting on idle, and sometimes cultivated, lands. Sit-down strikes developed in the factories. During the winter of 1920–1921, several hundred factories were seized by the workers, and Marxism seemed to be gaining strength. The Italian government, torn by factions, seemed too weak to prevent the disorder and protect private property. Although the strife diminished and the Marxist threat waned before the end of 1921, landlords and factory owners were thoroughly frightened. Many of them, and indeed many small-business and professional people, longed for vigorous leadership and a strong government. The vigorous leader who stepped forward was Benito Mussolini. The strong government was his Fascist dictatorship.

Mussolini was a dynamic organizer and leader. The son of a blacksmith, he became first a teacher and later a radical journalist and agitator. Before World War I he was a pacifistic socialist, but during the war he became a violent nationalist. After the war he began organizing unemployed veterans into a political action group with a socialist and extremely nationalistic program. During the labor disturbances of 1919–1921, Mussolini stood aside until it became apparent that the radical workers' cause would lose; then he threw his support to the capitalists and the landlords. Crying that he was saving Italy from communism and waving the flag of nationalism, Mussolini organized his veterans into terror squads of blackshirted "Fascisti," who beat up the leaderless radical workers and their liberal supporters. He thereby gained the support of the frightened capitalists and landed aristocracy. By 1922 Mussolini's Fascist party was strong enough to "march on Rome" and seize control of the faction-paralyzed government. Appointed premier by the weak and distraught King Victor Emmanuel III, Mussolini acquired extraordinary powers. Between 1924 and 1926

Mussolini turned his premiership into a dictatorship. All opposition was silenced. Only the Fascist party could engage in organized political activity. The press and the schools were turned into propaganda agencies. The secret police were everywhere. Eventually, the Chamber of Deputies itself was replaced by Mussolini's hand-picked Fascist political and economic councils.

Italy's economic life was strictly regimented, but in such a way as to favor the capitalistic classes. Private property and profits were carefully protected. All labor unions were abolished except those controlled by the Fascist party. Strikes and lockouts were forbidden. Wages, working conditions, and labor-management disputes were settled by compulsory arbitration under party direction. An elaborate system of planned economy was set up to modernize, coordinate, and increase Italy's production of both industrial and agricultural goods. The complicated economic and political machinery that Mussolini created for these purposes was called the corporate state. On the whole there was probably a small decline in per capita income under Italian fascism despite some superficial gains. The budget was balanced and the currency stabilized. But Italy's taxes were the highest in the world, and labor's share of economic production was small.

Fascism, however, was primarily political, not economic, in character. The essence of its ideology was nationalism run wild. Although Italy never became such a full-blown, viciously anti-Semitic police state as Germany, Mussolini understood the dynamic, energizing quality of militant nationalism. His writings and speeches rang with such words as *will, discipline, sacrifice, decision,* and *conquest*. "The goal," he cried, "is always—Empire! To build a city, to found a colony, to establish an empire, these are the prodigies of the human spirit. . . . We must resolutely abandon the whole liberal phraseology and way of thinking. . . . Discipline. Discipline at home in order that we may present the granite block of a single national will. . . . War alone brings up the highest tension, all human energy, and puts the stamp of nobility upon the people who have the courage to meet it." This grandiose vision was reflected in Fascist trappings and symbols, which were adopted from ancient Rome.

Fascism clashed head-on with Christianity

FIGURE 53.2 Max Beckmann, *The Night,* **1918–1919** Beckmann, a German artist, reflects the sense of violence and disillusionment stemming from World War I in this scene of overwhelming, absurd torture. (Kunstsammlung Nordrhein-Westfalen, Düsseldorf)

both in spirit and in deeds. Nevertheless, Mussolini realized the advantage of coming to terms with the powerful Catholic church and made a treaty with Pope Pius XI—the Lateran Treaty of 1929. The pope recognized Mussolini's regime. (Since the pope had been despoiled of his territories [1860–1870], he had refused to recognize the Italian government.) In return, Mussolini paid him nearly $100 million in cash and government bonds from a hard-pressed national treasury and allowed the teaching of religion by Catholic clergy in the public schools. This seeming accord, however, was uneasy and quarrelsome from the start.

The building of a powerful army and navy and the recovery of Italy's national prestige were always uppermost in Mussolini's thoughts. Fascist Italy's militarism, self-assertiveness, and expansive ambitions played an important part in the breakdown of the peace settlement and the return to war. But before we examine these activities, we must examine the rise of fascism in Germany and authoritarianism elsewhere, which contributed to the outbreak of World War II.

3. THE WEIMAR REPUBLIC IN GERMANY

Germany emerged from World War I defeated, humiliated, and angry. As late as July 1918 the nation had seemed to be close to victory; four months later it had been forced to surrender, hopelessly beaten. Then it was compelled to sign a dictated peace treaty, the terms of which it considered unjust. The Weimar Republic (so called from the city famous for Goethe and Schiller, where its constitution was drawn up), which the Germans set up in 1919, was structured to be a model liberal democracy. Politically divided and inexperienced, it inherited the taint of defeat from World War I and had to face tremendous postwar problems (see Figure 53.2).

Almost as soon as the Social Democrats, led by Friedrich Ebert, came to power, they were challenged, first by an uprising of radical Marxists (Spartacists), then by right-wing nationalists (under Wolfgang Kapp). Both of these challenges were met, but then economic problems threatened the new government. In the early 1920s inflation grew at an alarming rate. In January 1923, after the German government chose to default on its first payment of the huge reparations bill, French and Belgian troops occupied the Ruhr Valley, Germany's richest industrial area. The Germans fought back sullenly with passive resistance. The French countered by trying to stir up a secession movement from Germany in the Rhineland. Bloodshed between the occupying troops and the civilian population was frequent. Although the occupying forces were unable to collect any reparations, Germany's economy was paralyzed and a wild inflation swept the country. Thus more seeds of bitterness were sown.

In August 1923 Gustav Stresemann became head of the German government and offered conciliation. An international commission headed by Charles G. Dawes of the United States drew up a plan for the withdrawal of the occupying forces, for an international loan to Germany, and for the orderly payment of Germany's reparations installments. The German economy quickly recovered. From 1924 to 1929 Germany was the most prosperous nation in Europe and made its reparations payments as scheduled, mostly with loans from the United States. Under Stresemann's leadership Germany sought a *rapprochement* with its former enemies. In 1925 it signed the Treaty of Locarno with France, Great Britain, Italy, and Belgium, guaranteeing Germany's existing frontiers with France and Belgium. In 1926 Germany was admitted to the League of Nations, and Stresemann was elected president of the League. However, at home power was slipping from the moderate political parties toward the extremes, reflecting Germany's underlying economic and social maladjustments. One of the growing extremes was National Socialism, organized and led by Adolf Hitler.

4. THE RISE OF HITLER AND NATIONAL SOCIALISM

Adolf Hitler was the son of a middle-aged Austrian customs official and a young, sensitive, unhappily married mother. Of an artistic temperament, he went off to Vienna at an early age to seek an artist's career. Denied admission to the art academies for lack of training and too proud

to work as a laborer, he lived for years in poverty and sometimes in squalor. He fed his ego with German master-race theories and filled his heart with hatred of the Jews. At the outbreak of World War I Hitler was in Munich, Germany, eking out a living at crude artwork such as making posters. The ardent young German nationalist threw himself eagerly into the war, which he considered to be a righteous crusade for the beloved fatherland. Attaining the rank of corporal, he got his first taste of command. The experience of war—the sense of mission and unified struggle—would stay with Hitler and prove to be a source of appeal to many in future years. When the war ended, he was in a hospital, a victim of poison gas.

After the war Hitler frequented beer cellars, haranguing demobilized and unemployed troops and organizing them into violent political action groups. He soon discovered his magnetic powers of oratory and leadership. The disgruntled and the disenchanted, particularly the frustrated university students and demobilized lesser army officers, began attaching themselves to Hitler in increasing numbers. He organized them into the National Socialist (Nazi) party. Among his most important early followers were Hermann Göring, who became second in command; Rudolf Hess, who became head of the political section of the party; and Paul Joseph Goebbels, who became the chief Nazi propagandist. As early as 1923 Hitler, in league with the popular war hero Field Marshal Ludendorff, made his first grab for power (the famous Beer Hall Putsch). It was premature, however, and Hitler was jailed for nearly a year. While in jail he wrote *Mein Kampf* (*My Struggle*), which became the Nazi bible.

National Socialism, as outlined in *Mein Kampf*, was the German brand of fascism. In fact, the Nazis were heavily indebted to Mussolini for both ideology and methodology. At the center of its basic philosophy is the German master-race concept. The old Nordic myth of Gobineau and Chamberlain was revived. The terms *German*, *Nordic*, and *Aryan* were used interchangeably without regard to scientific fact. It was held that the Germans, the only pure representatives of the tall, blond Nordic "race," are superior to and destined to conquer and rule all other peoples. Militarism, indomitable will, pride, aggressiveness, and brute strength were held to be virtues; gentleness, peacefulness, tolerance, pity, and modesty, vices.

As a specific program of action, National Socialism was primarily concerned with foreign affairs. It called for repudiation of the Treaty of Versailles; all-out rearmament; the recovery of all territories, including colonies, lost at the end of World War I; and the annexation of all neighboring German-speaking territories such as Austria, the Netherlands, and most of Switzerland. Then the master race must have *Lebensraum* (living space), which was to be obtained by driving to the east (*Drang nach Osten*), particularly by conquering and enslaving the Soviet Union. There is little doubt that in the Nazi mind world domination was the ultimate goal.

The domestic program was vague and contradictory. Trusts and department stores were to be nationalized. Unearned income was to be abolished. Communism was to be destroyed and labor unions rigidly controlled. Finally, persecution of the Jews was part of the Nazi program. Over time, persecution escalated from legal discrimination to economic exploitation to violence and, finally, to literal extermination. The capitalist classes never took the socialist aspects of Hitler's program seriously. As in Italy, they looked to the Fascists to provide strong government, protect property, and control the working classes.

Hitler copied many of Mussolini's techniques. The rank and file of Nazi party members, wearing brown shirts, were organized along military lines as storm troopers. They marched, sang, and intimidated and beat up the opposition. An elite corps of black-shirted "SS" troops supervised and policed the brown shirts. Pagan symbolism, such as the swastika, was adopted. All party members swore unquestioning and undying allegiance to Hitler.

5. THE TRIUMPH OF HITLER

At first National Socialism grew slowly but steadily. National Socialism appealed particularly to youth, displaced veterans, and people from many classes who felt insecure and threatened by change. It promised much, seemed to provide membership in a movement with a clear

cause and direction, and offered simple solutions to difficult problems. From 1925 to 1929, when Germany under Stresemann's leadership was the most prosperous nation in Europe and was being wooed by her former enemies, Nazi party membership grew from 27,000 to 178,000.

After the Great Depression of 1929, which struck Germany along with the rest of the capitalistic world, the Nazis gained rapidly. In the parliamentary elections of 1930 they obtained several million votes and increased their seats in the Reichstag from 12 to 107. They appealed to a broad spectrum of disaffected workers, members of the middle and lower middle classes, veterans, and particularly the young. They were now strong enough to disrupt the orderly functioning of parliamentary government, and President Paul von Hindenburg resorted to ruling by presidential decree. In the presidential election of 1932 Hitler ran as the Nazi candidate. The moderate and liberal parties, which in 1925 had feared and opposed Hindenburg, now persuaded him to run again as the only man who could stop Hitler (Hindenburg was now eighty-five years old). Hitler got enough votes to force a runoff election against the popular and venerable idol. In the runoff election Hindenburg was elected, but Hitler received more than 13 million votes. In parliamentary elections a few months later, the Nazis obtained 230 out of 608 seats in the Reichstag, the largest number ever held by any party under the Weimar Republic. Hindenburg now offered to make Hitler vice-chancellor, but Hitler, sensing complete dictatorship in the offing, refused.

Meanwhile, the Nazis, under Hitler's instructions, paralyzed Germany's political life with terror. When chaos threatened to play into the hands of the Communists, in January 1933, Hindenburg offered and Hitler accepted the chancellorship. Franz von Papen, head of the militaristic Nationalist party, was made vice-chancellor. It was the great industrialists who finally gave the Nazis the necessary support to come to power. Hitler, determined to have nothing less than complete dictatorship, immediately called for parliamentary elections. Now in official control of the state police and the agencies of information in addition to their own highly disciplined party machinery, the Nazis skillfully used every device of propaganda to frighten and con-

WHERE HISTORIANS DISAGREE

What Caused Nazism?

The rise of nazism in Germany was so dramatic and of such consequence that it demands explanation. Yet perhaps no other development has remained more difficult to explain.

Perhaps the simplest explanation for the rise of nazism focuses on the politics of Hitler's rise in the 1920s and 1930s—that the political parties of the Weimar Republic were disorganized, that political leaders were weak, that there was so much political struggle and intrigue going on that Hitler did not even need to seize power. This interpretation stresses the political failure of the Social Democrats and Communists to unify against the Nazi threat and the political blindness of those conservatives who offered him the chancellorship even though they opposed him, believing that they could gain power themselves while controlling Hitler.

The economic interpretation, favored by many Marxists, holds that nazism was a logical consequence of the last, monopoly stage of capitalism—that large landowners and industrialists resorted to nazism in a period of economic crisis in order to prevent the collapse of capitalism and the spread of socialism. This interpretation stresses the growing strength of the Communist party and the restlessness of the working class. Thus Germany's real power holders tried to use Hitler and his nazism to control the threatening masses and maintain the endangered economic system that served the Junkers and industrialists.

A third interpretation holds that nazism was a logical continuation of German history itself. It stresses that the German people had long displayed tendencies favoring the authoritarianism, militarism, and racism that came to characterize nazism. This interpretation argues that in retrospect it is no surprise that Prussia had always been militaristic, that the liberal revolutions of 1848 failed in Germany, that Bismarck united the nation by blood and iron, that the leading philosophers of racism were German, and that the democratic Weimar Republic was never very popular or effective.

More recently, psychosocial interpretations have been proposed to explain the rise of nazism in Germany. According to these interpretations, nazism both reflected and responded to the desires of certain large groups of Germans—people traumatized by the war such as the veterans and the young who suffered hunger and loss of their fathers, people disoriented by the political and economic upheavals immediately following the war, and people weakened and immobilized by the Great Depression. Nazism seemed to promise a sense of direction, action, purpose, power, and pride to these people.

An underlying controversy among historians is whether nazism should be viewed as an aberration of Western history. Many historians stress that nazism should be viewed as limited in time and place, that it was an unlikely product of circumstances. They stress the extraordinary character and role of Hitler, the peculiar circumstances of Germany after World War I, and the extreme qualities of nazism.

Others argue that there were many points of continuity between nazism and Western history. They stress the growth of fascism and totalitarianism in the West, the widespread nationalism and racism, and the general appeal of authoritarian practices in times of war or socioeconomic crises.

These and other interpretations are evolving as historians gain distance from the 1920s, 1930s, and 1940s. The topic remains controversial, and the debates over the causes of nazism are likely to continue for some time.

FIGURE 53.3 Adolf Hitler at Buckeberg Walking between two lines of Nazi banners, Adolf Hitler makes a carefully staged, dramatic entrance to a mass meeting at Buckeberg, Germany, in 1934. (Heinrich Hoffman, *Life* Magazine © 1945 Time, Inc.)

fuse the people. Like the Fascists in Italy, they exaggerated and exploited the Communist threat. Five days before the elections, they made use of the burning of the Reichstag building, blaming the Communists. The elections themselves, however, were by secret ballot and were relatively free. The Communists polled 4.8 million votes, the Center (Roman Catholic) party 5.5 million, the Social Democrats (workers and small-business and professional people's party) 7.2 million, the Nazis 17 million, and von Papen's Nationalists 3 million. The Nazi and Nationalist votes combined gave Hitler 52 percent of the seats in the Reichstag. A few days later Hitler, wearing his Nazi party uniform, appeared before the newly elected Reichstag, from which the

every device of propaganda to frighten and con-Communists were excluded, and demanded dictatorial powers for four years. They were granted with only 94 opposing (Social Democratic) votes. Long before the four years had expired, the moderate parties had been destroyed, and the Nazi dictatorship was complete (see Figure 53.3).

6. NAZI GERMANY

The Reichstag, having voted Hitler dictatorial powers, adjourned, to meet henceforth only on the call of the *Führer* (leader) for the purpose of voting approval of his acts. Hitler disbanded all political parties except the National Socialist party. Freedom of speech, press, and assembly was abolished. An elaborate and all-powerful secret police, the Gestapo, was established under the direction of Heinrich Himmler to spy out and destroy opposition. Political opponents, homosexuals, and gypsies, among others, were made objects of persecution. Hitler's most intense hatred was vented on the Jews, who were subjected to every conceivable humiliation. As fast as their services could be dispensed with, they were driven out of public and professional life. Eventually the Nazis embarked on a program to exterminate all the Jews under their control. It is estimated that by the end of World War II the Nazis had murdered 6 million Jews out of a world total of 15 million.

The control and molding of thought always held high priority in Nazi activities. Indeed, this control appears to be an absolute necessity for any totalitarian dictatorship. Under the direction of Goebbels, minister of propaganda, the German press and radio spewed forth a constant stream of false or distorted information. To read or listen to foreign newspapers or broadcasts was made a crime. An incessant hate campaign was waged against the liberal democratic world. The schools were, of course, nazified. Only Nazi party members could be school administrators. Unsympathetic teachers were dismissed and punished. Members of Nazi youth organizations were set to spy on their teachers and parents. Textbooks were rewritten to conform to German master-race theories. The burning of liberal books, sometimes even those of Germany's greatest literary figures, such as Goethe and Schiller, became a national fad. The Nazi minister of education admitted that the sole function of education was the creation of Nazis. Hitler wrote in *Mein Kampf* that the German youth's "entire education and development has to be directed at giving him the conviction of being absolutely superior to the others . . . the belief in the invincibility of his entire nationality." The arts were nazified, and only party members or sympathizers were permitted to publish, exhibit, or perform.

Since National Socialism was essentially an anti-Christian ideology, the Nazis realized the necessity of controlling the religious establishment. Much of the Lutheran church, which was the official state church and included more than half the German people in its membership, was brought under Nazi domination. Nazi officials attempted to turn it into a propaganda agency. The few Lutheran pastors who resisted, like Martin Niemöller, were thrown into concentration camps. The smaller Protestant denominations met the same fate. Hitler found it much more difficult to deal with the Catholic church, whose higher authority lay outside Germany. Although he soon signed a concordat with the pope, the terms proved to be unworkable. Catholic clergy, churches, and schools were subjected to constantly increasing pressures, indignities, and physical abuse.

The Nazis rejuvenated and regimented Germany's economic life. The property and the profits of the capitalist classes were given special consideration. Labor unions were brought under Nazi control, and a system of enforced arbitration of disputes between labor and management was set up along the lines that Mussolini had established in Italy. Strikes and lockouts were forbidden. The entire German economy was forced into the overall pattern and policies of the Nazi government. The vast rearmament program gave employment to millions. Superhighways, airfields, hospitals, and apartment houses were built all over Germany. The most intricate financial trickery was resorted to, but the Nazis expected eventually to finance their huge undertakings out of the spoils of victorious war.

Even family life came under Nazi control. Until they were needed for the war effort, women were encouraged to fulfill their primary duties as homemakers subordinate to their husbands and as producers of Aryan children. Children were encouraged to join Nazi youth organizations, which expanded rapidly to encompass the majority of boys and girls by the late 1930s.

All other activities were subordinated to the prime purpose of making a military comeback. Shortly after assuming power, Hitler took Germany out of the League of Nations and out of the disarmament conference that was in progress in Geneva. Rearmament was pushed as rapidly as possible, and in 1935 Hitler openly repudiated the disarmament clauses of the Treaty of Versailles. In 1936 Hitler remilitarized the Rhineland and sent decisive aid to General Franco's Fascist rebels in Spain (see Chapter 54). The following year he made an alliance with Italy and Japan. This Berlin-Rome-Tokyo Axis was aimed specifically at the Soviet Union. More broadly, it was an aggressive antiliberal alliance for military expansion. Meanwhile, other events taking place elsewhere in Europe also threw liberal democracy into retreat.

7. AUTHORITARIAN REGIMES IN EASTERN AND SOUTHERN EUROPE

Beginning in the 1920s, hopes for permanently establishing parliamentary regimes in eastern and southern Europe were dashed by the rise of right-wing authoritarian governments. Some of them had elements of Fascist ideology and policy, but most were dictatorships by royal or military figures and individuals backed by the military and conservative powers of the nation.

The rise of right-wing authoritarian regimes in eastern and southeastern Europe was initiated in Hungary under the regency of Admiral Miklós Horthy and the rules of Count Stephen Bethlen during the 1920s and General Julius Gömbös during the 1930s. In 1926 General Josef Pilsudaski set up a military dictatorship in Poland. In 1929 a royal dictatorship was established in Yugoslavia under King Alexander I; after his assassination in 1934 an authoritarian regime was set up under the regent, Prince Paul. During the 1930s royal dictatorships were established in Rumania and Bulgaria. After 1934 Austria succumbed to authoritarian rule under Engelbert Dollfuss and then Kurt von Schuschnigg until its annexation by Hitler in 1938. In 1936 Greece's shaky parliamentary regime fell to the dictatorship of General Ioannes Metaxas. Czechoslovakia was an exception. There parliamentary democracy survived until the nation fell to Hitler in 1938.

The Iberian peninsula, a scene of considerable turmoil, was an area where fascism became attractive to many. In Portugal authoritarianism and political instability were the rule rather than the exception during the 1920s and eventually led to the establishment of a strong dictatorship under Antonio de Oliveira Salazar in 1932. In Spain General Miguel Primo de Rivera ruled as de facto dictator between 1923 and 1930. After a democratic interlude between 1930 and 1936, the rise of the Fascist Falange and the revolt of Span-

ish generals led to a civil war and the triumph of General Francisco Franco as dictator in 1939.

Almost all these authoritarian regimes emphasized nationalism and militarism. They were bolstered by a fundamental fear of change, particularly the kind of change liberal democracy and socialism represented. Many regimes provided fertile ground for the growth of Fascist organizations and the enactment of Fascist policies, but with the possible exception of Franco's Spain, these governments were not Fascist in the same sense as Italy under Mussolini and Germany under Hitler. This description of Europe's authoritarian regimes also describes Japan's government during the 1930s, which would become one of the Axis powers in 1937.

8. THE TRIUMPH OF AUTHORITARIANISM IN JAPAN

Three divergent groups competed for the leadership of postwar Japan. The dominant group was made up of the great industrialists. Seventy-five percent of Japan's industry and capital was concentrated in the hands of five great families, called the *zaibatsu*. This handful of industrial giants had such a stranglehold on the Japanese economy that it was also able to control the highly restricted government. The *zaibatsu*, enjoying this economic and political monopoly, wished to see no fundamental change in Japan's undemocratic society; it advocated instead the peaceful economic penetration of Asia.

The liberals constituted the second group. This faction, with university professors and students providing much of the leadership, set out to broaden the suffrage, which was restricted to the well-to-do, to encourage the more effective unionization of labor, and to diminish the power of the military. Because of the political inexperience and the long tradition of passive submission to authority on the part of the Japanese masses, these were difficult undertakings. They were made more difficult by the activities of Marxists, who confused liberal reform movements and tainted them with the suspicion of treason. Nevertheless, Japan made encouraging progress toward liberal democracy. In 1925 the suffrage was broadened. Soon afterward, two liberal political

FIGURE 53.4 Japan Invades China Here Japanese soldiers are celebrating victory after a new assault on China in 1937. This photograph, showing armed Japanese troops on Chinese soil under the Japanese flag, symbolizes key elements of Japanese policy during the 1930s: nationalism, militarism, and expansionism. (Ullstein Bilderdienst, West Berlin)

parties appeared. The military budget was reduced. The prestige of the professional military declined to such an extent that many officers ceased wearing their uniforms in public.

The professional military, however, was determined to strengthen and exploit its own traditional power. In the late 1920s a group of restless, ambitious young army officers began to accuse their leaders of softness and plotted to seize control of both the armed forces and the government. When a coup planned for early 1931 was exposed and blocked, the conspirators decided on a bold move to throw the country into such hysteria and confusion that they could seize power. In October 1931 the Japanese army sta-

tioned in Manchuria made an unauthorized attack on the Chinese forces and began the conquest of all Manchuria. The next year Japanese forces attacked Shanghai, the chief port of China (see Figure 53.4). Once the fighting with huge and potentially dangerous China began, war fever and patriotic hysteria swept Japan, just as the army plotters had foreseen. They then assassinated the premier and numerous other government officials and civilian leaders and cowed the rest into submission. Once in control, the military turned to the destruction of the liberals. Liberal university professors were accused of disloyalty and silenced, dismissed, or imprisoned. The schools and the press and radio were made organs of propaganda. All democratic processes of government and civil rights were destroyed. The military and state police were given unlimited authority. The *zaibatsu* were corrupted and won over with lush military contracts.

Meanwhile, Japanese overran all Manchuria, which was made into a puppet state of Manchu-kuo. When the League of Nations declared Japan an aggressor and ordered its withdrawal from Manchuria, Japan defied the League and instead withdrew from the organization. In 1937 Japan joined the Berlin-Rome Axis. That same year, Japan began an all-out assault on China proper. The Axis powers were on the march.

SUGGESTED READING

Totalitarianism, Fascism, and Authoritarianism

H. Arendt, *The Origins of Totalitarianism* (1951). A brilliant but difficult analysis.

F. L. Carsten, *The Rise of Fascism* (1982). A good, scholarly analysis.

E. Nolte, *The Three Faces of Fascism* (1963). A respected but difficult intellectual history of fascism in Italy, Germany, and France.

S. Payne, *Fascism: Comparison and Definition* (1980). A respected general interpretation.

H. A. Turner, Jr., ed., *Reappraisals of Fascism* (1975). A good collection of articles.

Mussolini and Italian Fascism

A. Lyttleton, *The Seizure of Power: Fascism in Italy, 1919–1929* (1973). An excellent analysis of the rise of fascism in Italy.

D. M. Smith, *Mussolini* (1982). An excellent biography.

E. R. Tannenbaum, *The Fascist Experience: Italian Society and Culture, 1922–1945* (1972). A fine examination of life in Fascist Italy.

The Weimar Republic

P. Gay, *Weimar Culture: The Outsider as Insider* (1968). An excellent examination of Weimar Germany.

E. Kolb, *The Weimar Republic* (1988). A useful recent introduction with bibliography.

Hitler and Nazi Germany

J. Bendersky, *A History of Nazi Germany* (1985). A useful brief survey.

A. Bullock, *Hitler: A Study in Tyranny* (1971). A classic biography of Hitler.

I. Kershaw, *The Nazi Dictatorship* (1985). A broad interpretation of policy and ideology.

J. Stephenson, *The Nazi Organization of Women* (1980). A useful study of women in Nazi Germany.

Authoritarian Regimes in Eastern and Southern Europe

B. Jelavich, *History of the Balkans*, vol. 2 (1983). A good survey.

J. Rothschild, *East Central Europe Between the Two World Wars* (1973). A useful general account.

The Triumph of Authoritarianism in Japan

R. Benedict, *The Chrysanthemum and the Sword* (1967). Examines the role of the professional military in Japan.

E. O. Reischauer, *The Japanese* (1977). A highly respected survey.

CHAPTER 54
Paralysis of the Democratic West

FIGURE 54.1 The Great Depression in New York Jobless and homeless men wait in line for a free meal in New York in 1930. These Depression breadlines are part of the reason for the seeming impotence of the democratic nations in the face of the growing Fascist menace. The Great Depression, which began in 1929, did not end until 1942, when World War II pumped billions of dollars into the American economy. (UPI/Bettmann Newsphotos)

The Western democracies emerged from World War I victorious. In many ways, each hoped to return to the way things had been before the war, to quickly get back to "normal." But instead of the hoped-for smooth sailing, the Western democracies were faced with a series of challenges in the two decades following the war.

1. CHALLENGES OF THE 1920s AND 1930s

The first challenge was the immediate problem of postwar dislocation and recovery. The human, material, and economic losses were unprecedented and unequally borne—France and Belgium suffered most among the Western democracies. Soldiers had to be reintegrated into civilian life, economies had to be shifted from wartime production, and trade patterns had to be reestablished.

The second challenge was the roller-coaster ride of tension, optimism, and disillusionment that characterized international affairs in the 1920s and 1930s. The Treaty of Versailles left few happy and many resentful. The payment of reparations and wartime debts threatened the international order during the years immediately following the war. Then from 1925 to 1929, a period known as the Locarno Era, international tensions diminished and progress was made toward peace and disarmament. The Locarno Pact in 1925 (guaranteeing international boundaries in Europe), the admission of Germany to the League of Nations in 1926, the Kellogg-Briand Pact of 1928 (proclaiming a commitment to international friendship), and the earlier Washington Conference of 1921–1922 (limiting naval strength) seemed to establish a basis for optimism in international affairs. After 1930, however, this optimism gave way to disillusionment as discord, rearmament, and aggression marked international affairs.

The third challenge was the Great Depression. Economic depressions were not new to the West, but one of this magnitude and duration was unprecedented. In October 1929 the American stock market, bloated by speculation and borrowed money, crashed. Since the end of World War I, the international economic order had become dependent on the United States, particularly to keep up the flow of loans, debt payments, and trade. The U.S. financial crisis quickly spread to Europe. Stocks lost their value, banks failed, and confidence collapsed. This sudden financial crisis reflected the fragility of the postwar economic order, and between 1929 and 1933 economies almost everywhere were in a tailspin. World industrial production fell by more than 33 percent. Unemployment grew to massive proportions. Policies adopted to deal with the crisis probably made things worse—trade barriers rather than cooperation typified international economic policy, and cuts in spending instead of deficit spending marked domestic economic policy. Some countries started to recover after 1933, but in other cases the Great Depression extended until World War II.

The final challenge was the threat from the political extremes—communism on the left, fascism on the right. The most obvious threats were international, since communism was growing stronger in the Soviet Union and fascism was spreading in central and southern Europe. But the threats were internal as well, for both Communist and Fascist political organizations were growing within the Western democracies, particularly during the 1930s.

The political and social development of each of the Western democracies greatly depended on how they met these four challenges. In retrospect it is easy to be harsh on the leaders of these societies, for in the end the world was immersed in another war even more destructive than World War I. However, these challenges were extraordinary, and the leaders trying to deal with them often labored under overwhelming difficulties.

2. THE HARASSED BRITISH EMPIRE

At the end of World War I the British Empire still included one-fourth of all the land and people on the globe. Nevertheless, Britain's economy, empire, and world position were shaken beyond recovery. Britain's far-flung possessions in Asia and Africa were beginning to stir restlessly as the spirit of nationalism, which had long provided the European world with so much of its expansive energy, spread eastward. Great Britain found it advisable to grant freedom to its already self-governing dominions in the hope of retaining their loyalty. In 1931 the Statute of Westminster gave complete independence and equality with the mother country to Canada, Australia, New Zealand, the Union of South Africa, Newfoundland, and the Irish Free State (free since 1922). Great Britain could no longer count on their material support in world policies, nor could it count on its restless colonies. Furthermore, Britain was now clearly second to the United States as an industrial and financial power. (It would require many years, however, for the British to readjust their thinking to the reality of their country's reduced position.)

At home, postwar Britain was harassed by acute economic problems. The national debt had quintupled during the war. Britain owed the United States a heavy war debt. German submarines had taken a toll of 9 million tons of British ships with their cargoes. British exports met sharply increased competition in the world markets, particularly from the United States. Rising protective tariffs all over the world hindered its commerce. Mines and industrial plants were antiquated and in disrepair. Returning servicemen found few jobs. Unemployment hovered around 3 million, a figure that came to be accepted as normal. Government support for the unemployed, sick, aged, and destitute increased Britain's financial problems.

These chronic economic ills were reflected in Great Britain's troubled postwar policies. In 1922 the Conservatives broke up Lloyd George's wartime coalition government of Liberals and Conservatives and won the ensuing parliamentary elections. They sought to restore classical nineteenth-century capitalism by means of rigid entrenchment of government spending, particularly on social services. This policy was so hard on the distressed masses that in 1924 a Labour-Liberal coalition headed by the Labour party leader, Ramsay MacDonald, ousted the Conservatives. The Labour party was now stronger than the Liberal party, and as times grew harder and feelings more bitter, the once-great Liberal party was virtually crushed between the more extreme parties—Labour on the left and Conservative on the right.

But the majority of the British people were not yet ready to accept the mildly socialistic pro-gram the Labour party advocated. MacDonald's ministry lasted less than a year. Dependent on the Liberals for his majority, he was forced to follow a moderate course. When he recognized the Soviet Union and made a commercial treaty with it, the Conservatives were able to capitalize on public suspicion and drive him from power. From 1925 to 1929 the Conservatives wrestled with rising discontent, strikes, and the steady growth of the Labour party. In 1929 a Labour victory, supported by the much-dwindled Liberals, again brought Ramsay MacDonald to the head of the government. His moderation in the face of the deepening economic depression, however, caused the majority of his Labour followers to repudiate him two years later. But MacDonald was unwilling to give up the honors of office. In 1931 he therefore formed a national coalition of right-wing Labourites, Liberals, and Conservatives to deal with the mounting domestic and foreign crises. This national coalition was dominated by the Conservatives, and MacDonald was really a captive of the Conservatives until he resigned in 1935. The Conservative-dominated coalition ruled Great Britain until the end of World War II. Although Great Britain was recovering from the Great Depression, the government was on the whole ineffective in dealing with social maladjustment at home and Fascist aggression abroad. The Conservative prime ministers Stanley Baldwin and Neville Chamberlain, who followed Ramsay MacDonald as head of the national government, were unimaginative and unprepared for the challenges that would face them.

3. FRUSTRATED FRANCE

Although France enjoyed the advantage of being economically more self-sufficient than Great Britain, France had suffered greater wounds in World War I than had its island neighbor. Most of the fighting had taken place on French soil. A tenth—the most productive tenth—of its land area had been devastated. The retreating Germans had laid waste much of what had not been destroyed in battle. Orchards had been chopped down and mines wrecked, many beyond repair. Even more tragic was the loss of life. France, with the lowest birthrate of any major nation in the world, suffered by far the heaviest casualties per capita of any of the combatants. Out of a population of less than 40 million, it suffered almost 1.4 million battle deaths and 1.7 million wounded. The civilian death rate from direct and indirect causes had also been high. France had fewer people in 1918 than in 1914, even after the return of Alsace and Lorraine.

Postwar France was confronted with a staggering job of economic reconstruction and an equally staggering war debt. To meet these obligations and to finance the reconstruction, the French government counted on German reparations, but little was forthcoming. Inflation became a chronic headache. A more basic and long-range problem was French industry, which was rapidly falling behind that of its competitors. The highly individualistic French had not gone in for large-scale corporate industry to the same extent as the Americans, British, and Germans. The little French family industries had difficulty competing with mass production. A like situation prevailed in French agriculture, most of which took place on thousands of little family farms too tiny to use machinery profitably. Industrial and agricultural production per worker was lower in France than in most other major Western nations.

Considering the serious plight of France's postwar economy and the habitual disorderliness with which its multiparty democracy traditionally functioned, one is impressed by the remarkable stability of the French government during the decade of the 1920s. From 1919 to 1924, a bloc of conservative parties was in power. It followed an antilabor, probusiness policy. It also favored the Roman Catholic church and pressed hard for collection of German reparations. Meanwhile, discontent among the laboring classes was mounting. In 1924, the year of MacDonald's first Labour ministry in Great Britain, the parties of the Left under the leadership of Edouard Herriot were victorious. Like MacDonald, Herriot pursued a prolabor policy, advocating an increase in social services and soft money. He was also conciliatory toward Russia and Germany. But, also like MacDonald, he lasted less than a year.

From 1926 to 1929, a strong right-of-center national bloc under the leadership of Raymond Poincaré was in power. Poincaré checked the inflation by rigid retrenchment. Upon his retirement in 1929, however, the increasing pressure of discontent threw the country into political turmoil. No leader or political combination seemed to be capable of dealing with the economic crisis brought on by the world depression, the growing menace of fascism, or the unrest in the French colonies. Ministry followed ministry in rapid succession. Scandals and riots occurred, and Fascist groups appeared. In 1936 the Popular Front, consisting of left-wing parties under the leadership of the mild Socialist Léon Blum, came to power (see Figure 54.2). The Blum ministry obtained a forty-hour week and two weeks' annual vacation with pay for the workers. It also nationalized the Bank of France and the great munitions industries. This was too much for the powerful propertied interests, who drove Blum from office the following year. But the conservative parties that regained control were unable to agree upon firm policies, whether domestic or foreign.

Thus France, like Great Britain, in the face of resurgent Nazi Germany, swashbuckling Mussolini, and militaristic Japan, could summon little strength or unity. The propertied classes were unwilling to share their wealth or privileges or to change their nineteenth-century practices. They feared and hated Léon Blum. The Great Depression persisted and fueled political turmoil. The army was basking in past glory. Seeking to maintain the status quo, the French were defense-minded. They constructed the Maginot line fortifications along the German border and formed defensive alliances with Poland, Czechoslovakia, Yugoslavia, and Rumania. These alliances, however, were no stronger than the faith those small countries had in France's ability to defend them, which by the late 1930s was very little.

4. THE UNITED STATES AND THE GREAT DEPRESSION

The United States emerged from World War I the world's richest nation. Although its entry into the war at its most critical phase was probably decisive in determining the outcome, the United

FIGURE 54.2 The Popular Front In 1935 Socialists, Communists, and others on the French Left united for the first time as the Popular Front. In 1936 the Popular Front came to power under the leadership of the Socialist premier, Léon Blum. This photo shows Blum (on the left) and Maurice Thorez, secretary of the French Communist party, at a 1937 Bastille Day rally in Paris. (Photo Trends)

States suffered far less war damage than any of the other major participants. President Wilson assumed a leading role in the making of the peace settlements and in the creation of the League of Nations.

When President Wilson returned from Paris in the summer of 1919 and sought to persuade his country to join the League of Nations, he faced a strong challenge from his political enemies, led by Henry Cabot Lodge. Wilson's opponents refused to accept the treaty, and particularly the League of Nations, as proposed by Wilson. Wilson, seeing the treaty and the League as a matter of principle, refused to compromise. In his struggle to rally support, Wilson suffered a paralytic stroke. Since he was unable thereafter to lead the fight for the treaty and was unwilling to give the leadership to others, his opponents easily defeated ratification in the Senate.

The League was not an issue in the presidential election of 1920. However, the victor, Warren G. Harding, announced that the League was now

a dead issue. And during the cynical and disillusioned decade of the 1920s American public opinion became overwhelmingly isolationist. When, during the international crises of the 1930s, the League and the harassed British and French governments sought the support of the United States against the Fascist aggressors, they sought in vain.

The decade following World War I was a period of relative but uneven prosperity in the United States. The all-out war effort had brought about a great expansion of American industry and unleashed huge quantities of money and credit. In 1914 the United States had been a debtor nation. It emerged from the war a creditor to most of Europe to the amount of $10 billion, a figure that doubled during the next ten years. Its chief economic competitors came out of the war battered and shaken. Production, profits, and purchasing power reached new heights. However, it was an uneven and unsound prosperity. Agriculture was depressed by surplus commod-

FIGURE 54.3 Food-lines in Paris While the Great Depression was initiated in the United States, it soon spread to most of Europe. Some of the consequences were unemployment and long lines of people waiting for free food, as indicated by this 1931 photograph of Parisians near a food distribution center. (Harlingue/Roger-Viollet)

ities and low prices, which meant low purchasing power for the farm population of the South and the Middle West. Nor did wages climb as rapidly as profits and prices in the industrial Northeast. Production was growing faster than consumer demand, which meant growing unemployment and industrial surpluses. Foreign markets were diminished by a policy of higher and higher tariffs designed to protect American industry from foreign competition. The government's philosophy of noninterference with free enterprise (except for tariffs) permitted unlimited speculation in the soaring stock market, often with other people's money and with unrestrained use of credit.

The stock market crashed in October 1929. Stock values tumbled. Thousands of banks and businesses failed. The crisis soon spread to Europe, where nations were dependent on American credit and commerce that rapidly dried up. The economic depression extended over the entire capitalist world. Millions were thrown out of work in country after country (see Figure 54.1). In 1932 unemployment in the West rose to 22 percent, leaving some 30 million out of work. Some nations—the United States, Germany, and Britain—were hit early and hard. Others—France, Italy, and states in eastern Europe where the economies were more self-sufficient or agricultural—were hit later and more softly (see Figure 54.3). A few others—the Scandinavian democracies with their Social Democratic governments, their welfare policies, and their economic cooperatives—managed to get through the Great Depression with relative ease. Most often, governmental policies in the United States and other leading states, such as raising tariffs, increasing currency controls, and otherwise relying on laissez-faire economics, probably made matters worse. The depression deepened.

In the presidential election of 1932 the Democratic candidate, Franklin D. Roosevelt, defeated Hoover, ending twelve years of Republican rule. The Roosevelt administration immediately launched a series of sweeping economic and social reforms that came to be called the New Deal. The New Deal was not a radical, new departure but, rather, a further advance along the progressive lines established by Theodore Roosevelt and Woodrow Wilson and during World War I, when the government had engaged in economic planning and control. First, emergency measures were taken to relieve the suffering of the 12 million unemployed and their families. The chief of these was the setting up of the huge Works Progress Administration, which provided a large number of jobs. The Wagner Act strengthened the position of the labor unions by guaranteeing the right of collective bargaining. Old-age and unemployment insurance were inaugurated. For the desperate farmers, measures were passed that granted debt relief, commodity loans, price supports, and payments for acreage reduction. Deflation was checked by a devaluation of the dollar. Investments and deposits were protected by strict government supervision. Steps were taken to conserve the nation's natural resources against wasteful private exploitation. Gradually, some popular confidence was restored and the nation's economy began to recover. However, economic problems persisted and full recovery was not achieved until World War II, which forced the government to finance the war with greater deficit spending.

5. DISILLUSIONMENT AND UNCERTAINTY IN THOUGHT AND CULTURE

The war, the movements of international and domestic politics, and the Great Depression affected all aspects of life during the 1920s and 1930s. The growing sense of disillusionment, uncertainty, and turning inward that marked political and social life was reflected in some of the most important cultural trends of the period.

In philosophy there was a wave of attacks on nineteenth-century optimism and rationalism that expanded the ideas set forth earlier by philosophers such as Friedrich Nietzsche in Germany and Henri Bergson in France (see p. 598). The most widely read of these post–World War I philosophers was Oswald Spengler. In his *Decline of the West* (1918), Spengler argued that the West was in decline, that World War I was the beginning of the end. This sense of decay and crisis appeared in many other works, most notably in José Ortega y Gasset's *Revolt of the Masses* (1930), which lamented the decline of liberal civilization and the rise of "mass man" in the West.

Sigmund Freud's ideas (see pp. 589–590), which emphasized the irrational, unconscious, and instinctual aspects of human thought and behavior, also stemmed from the period just before World War I, but during the 1920s and 1930s they gained wide acceptance. The unconscious and the irrational were also present in the best literature of the period. The Irish writer James Joyce (1882–1914) and German authors Franz

Kafka (1883–1924) and Hermann Hesse (1877–1962) (see pp. 729–730) wrote disquieting, introspective fiction. These same themes can be seen in artistic styles, such as the Dada movement, which stressed the purposelessness of life, and surrealism, with its exploration of dreams and the unconscious (see p. 731 and Color Plate 39).

Certainly there was a variety of cultural trends during the period, many of them far more traditional than these (see pp. 729–732). But it was the books and paintings and thoughts that emphasized uncertainty, doubt, and turning inward that best reflected experience in the Western democracies after World War I and that anticipated the violence that was to come.

6. THE ROAD TO WAR

Early in the 1930s, international affairs started slipping out of control. The League of Nations was challenged, rearmament spread, and aggression became the order of the day. Efforts to appease the aggressors and prevent the dreaded return to total war failed. By the end of the decade a new world war had broken out.

Breakdown of the League of Nations

The only international agency that existed for the maintenance of the peace was the League of Nations, which after the defection of the United States was largely dependent on Great Britain and France for support. For twelve years the League supervised the implementation of the peace treaties, administered relief to tens of thousands of war victims, promoted international goodwill, and settled numerous international disputes. None of these settlements, however, involved the disciplining of a major power, and thoughtful observers dreaded the time when the League would be called on to do so.

When in 1931 Japan began the conquest of Manchuria, China appealed to the League for protection. The League appointed a commission headed by Britain's Earl of Lytton to make an on-the-spot investigation. The Lytton Commission reported that Japan was guilty of aggression, having violated its solemn obligations both as a League member and as a signatory of the Kellogg-Briand Pact of Paris (1928), which outlawed war as an instrument of national policy. Forceful League action, however, would be largely dependent on Great Britain and France, which were unwilling to act without American support. President Herbert Hoover, reflecting the isolationist sentiment of American public opinion, would not consent to the use of force, the threat of force, or even economic pressure by the United States. The British and French governments, harassed by their own domestic economic and political problems and the rising menace of fascism in Europe, could not bring themselves to act alone. The League, without their backing, did nothing. It had failed its first major test and was on the way out as a potent force for peace. Japan's successful defiance of the League of Nations helped convince Mussolini and Hitler that they could safely launch aggressions of their own.

The death blow was struck by Mussolini. Late in 1935 the Italian dictator invaded Ethiopia in East Africa. Ethiopia was a member of the League and appealed to it for protection. Great Britain, concerned for its numerous interests in the Near and Middle East and for its lifeline to the Far East, now became greatly agitated. Under the leadership of Great Britain and France, the League declared Mussolini to be the aggressor and invoked economic sanctions (Article XVI) against him. A list of commodities that League members were not to sell Mussolini was drawn up. However, the list did not include oil, and it soon became obvious that this was the commodity upon which the success of his aggression depended. But it quickly became apparent that, to be effective, an embargo on oil would require the cooperation of the United States. American exports of oil to Mussolini had trebled since the beginning of his campaign against Ethiopia. When the British and French governments requested the cooperation of the United States in withholding excess oil from Mussolini, Secretary of State Cordell Hull and President Roosevelt were sympathetic but were unable to get the oil companies to comply or to get Congress to force compliance. The press and public opinion were overwhelmingly isolationist, and Congress reflected that view. Mussolini got his oil. Britain and France, unwilling to resort to the only other means of stopping him, a shooting war, gave up

the League struggle. Mussolini conquered Ethiopia. The League of Nations, for all practical purposes, was dead.

Appeasement

Since the triumph of the Nazis in 1933 Germany had been preparing for a military comeback. In March 1936 Hitler ordered his armed forces into the Rhineland, which, according to the Treaty of Versailles, was to be permanently demilitarized. France, recognizing this move as the gravest threat and challenge to itself, called for Great Britain's support. The British offered none. The French fretted and fumed but in the end did nothing. Hitler had won his gamble.

Fascism's next triumph was in Spain. Until 1931, it was dominated by the landed aristocracy, a few rich capitalists, aristocratic army officers, and the Catholic church. Most people were poor, landless peasants. Since the turn of the century and particularly since 1918, the pressure of discontent had been rising. In 1931 the king yielded, restored the constitution, and granted elections. The liberal and radical groups won such a sweeping victory that the king fled the country. The reformers then proceeded to make over the Spanish nation. They drew up a democratic constitution, granted local autonomy to Catalonia (the northeasternmost section of Spain, including Barcelona), began a sweeping program of public education, started to modernize the army by placing promotions on a merit basis, granted religious freedom, seized the lands and schools of the Catholic church, and planned to break up the great estates into peasant-owned farms.

There was much violence—riots and attacks on priests, nuns, and private property. After two years the conservative propertied interests, with the vigorous support of the pope, won the elections by a narrow margin and began to undo the reforms. Early in 1936, however, the liberal and radical parties won again and resumed their drastic reform program. The privileged classes were now desperate. In July 1936 a group of generals led by General Francisco Franco launched an armed rebellion against the government. Although the rebels enjoyed the advantage of professional military leadership, the regular army, and most of the country's wealth, they were unable to make headway against the Loyalists, who enjoyed the support of the majority of the rank and file of the people.

The Spanish Civil War soon became a battlefield in the world struggle of fascism, liberalism, and communism. Hitler and Mussolini, seeing in it an opportunity to advance the cause of fascism, gain a like-minded ally and a strategic military position, and test their new weapons, sent abundant arms and troops to aid Franco. The Loyalists appealed to the democracies for aid but received none, although a few volunteers from the democracies fought as individuals in the Loyalist cause. The only nation that supported the Loyalists was the Soviet Union, but the amount of aid it could send was quite small and tainted the Loyalist cause with the suspicion of communism. After three years of slaughter, Franco and his German and Italian allies beat down the last organized Loyalist resistance. A dictatorship was established over Spain. Liberalism was shattered. The world prestige of Fascist Germany and Italy rose while that of the democracies declined further.

The year 1937 was the year of decision—the point of no return on the road to war. In that year the three great Fascist powers formed the Berlin-Rome-Tokyo Axis, which was aimed specifically at the Soviet Union but was in reality an alliance of these aggressor nations for expansion. In that year the military strength of the Axis powers—their war plants running day and night—forged ahead of that of the rest of the world. In that year the Nazis blueprinted their timetable of conquests, and Japan began its all-out assault on China.

Early in 1938 the Nazis' timetable began to function. In March they overran Austria without opposition, annexing the 6.5 million Austrians to the German Reich (Empire). Great Britain and France denounced this open aggression and violation of the Treaty of Versailles but did nothing.

Almost immediately Hitler turned his big propaganda guns on his next victim, Czechoslovakia. In constructing this little country out of Austro-Hungarian territory at the end of World War I, the Allied peacemakers had left 3.5 million German-speaking people on the Czech side of the border. Although these Sudeten Germans had never been a part of Germany and were separated from Germany by the Sudeten Mountain Wall, Hitler now claimed them. The Czech republic was allied with France and Russia, and in the coming war that Hitler was planning against those two countries, Czechoslovakia could be a threat to the German flank.

As early as May 1938 Hitler threatened Czechoslovakia. The Czechs, however, surprised him by rushing to their defenses. Hitler spent the next four months arousing his people to readiness for war and softening up the democracies by keeping them in a constant state of tension and alarm. This psychological warfare culminated in a giant Nazi rally at Nuremberg in mid-September. There Hitler screamed to his frenzied followers that if the Sudeten areas were not surrendered to him by October 1, he would march. With France and the Soviet Union standing firm in their alliance with Czechoslovakia, the world anxiously awaited the beginning of a major conflict that was likely to become World War II.

At this juncture, British Prime Minister Neville Chamberlain took it upon himself to fly to Hitler's retreat at Berchtesgaden and plead for a compromise. The upshot was a conference at Munich on September 29, 1938 (see Figure 54.4). The participants were Hitler, Mussolini, Chamberlain, and Premier Édouard Daladier of France. Chamberlain persuaded Daladier to yield to Hitler's demands for the Sudeten areas of Czechoslovakia. Czechoslovakia and its ally, the Soviet Union, were not consulted. This was one of Hitler's greatest triumphs.

The Outbreak of War

Although the four participating powers at Munich had agreed to become joint protectors of what remained of Czechoslovakia, in March 1939 Hitler overran the remainder of the stricken little republic without warning. This crass act of betrayal opened the eyes of even Neville Chamberlain to the fact that Hitler could not be appeased. When Hitler threatened Poland, Great Britain and France decided to draw a line. In April 1939 they made a guarantee to Poland that they would come to its aid if it were attacked and resisted the attack. Hitler, however, was not deterred. He was demanding, among other things, the return to Germany of the Polish Corridor, which separated East Prussia from the rest of Germany, and the city of Danzig, which was

FIGURE 54.4 The Munich Conference The chief participants at the Munich Conference pose for the photographer in September 1938. Left to right: Chamberlain, Daladier, Hitler, and Mussolini. The sellout of Czechoslovakia and the Soviet Union at Munich by Chamberlain and Daladier, in an attempt to appease Hitler, destroyed any hope of maintaining a unified front in Europe against Nazi Germany. (UPI/Bettmann Newsphotos)

governed by the League of Nations. But by now it was apparent to almost everybody that specific Nazi demands were tied to unlimited aggression. Throughout the summer of 1939 the Germans made feverish preparations for war and kept up a drumfire of vilification of Poland and the democracies. Meanwhile, both sides were bidding for the support of the Soviet Union. But after Munich, Stalin had no confidence in the integrity of the capitalistic democracies. He decided to try to make his own peace with Hitler.

On August 23, 1939, the world was stunned by the signing of a ten-year peace pact by Hitler and Stalin. In return for the Soviet Union's neu-

trality while Germany conquered Poland, Hitler gave Stalin a free hand to reannex the territories in eastern Europe, including eastern Poland, that Russia had lost at the end of World War I.

With the Soviet Union safely neutralized, Hitler readied the attack on Poland as quickly as possible. At the last moment the British government instructed its ambassador in Berlin to ask Hitler what concessions by Poland he would accept to refrain from war. Hitler informed the ambassador that he was not interested in concessions, that his army and his people were ready and eager for war, and that he could not disappoint them now. The wires between Warsaw and

Berlin were cut, lest the Poles make a last-minute peaceable surrender to Hitler's demands. At dawn on September 1 the Germans launched an all-out attack on Poland by land, sea, and air.

Two days later Great Britain and France declared war on Germany, Hitler having ignored their ultimatum to desist. World War II had begun.

SUGGESTED READING

General

D. Silverman, *Reconstructing Europe after the Great War* (1982). A good analysis.

R. J. Sontag, *A Broken World, 1919–1939* (1971). An excellent survey of the period.

R. Wohl, *The Generation of 1914* (1979). A creative interpretation of the impact of World War I in the postwar years.

The Harassed British Empire

N. Branson and M. Heinemann, *Britain in the Nineteen Thirties* (1971). A social and economic perspective.

R. Graves and A. Hodge, *The Long Weekend: A Social History of Great Britain, 1918–1939* (1963). A vivid and witty picture of the British ruling classes between the wars.

J. Stevenson, *British Society 1914–1945* (1984). An important new analysis.

D. Thomson, *England in the Twentieth Century, 1914–1963* (1965). A good survey.

Frustrated France

J. Colton, *Léon Blum, Humanist in Politics* (1966). An excellent biography of Blum.

N. Greene, *From Versailles to Vichy: The Third Republic, 1919–1940* (1970). A good survey of France during the period.

The United States and the Great Depression

D. Aldcroft, *From Versailles to Wall Street, 1919–1929* (1977). An excellent economic analysis of the period.

C. Kindleberger, *The World in Depression, 1929–1939* (1986). A good comparative analysis.

G. Perrett, *America in the Twenties* (1982). A good general account.

Disillusionment and Uncertainty in Thought and Culture

J. Willett, *Art and Politics in the Weimar Period: The New Sobriety, 1917–1933* (1978). A broad analysis, well illustrated.

The Road to War

H. Browne, *Spain's Civil War* (1983). A useful analysis.

G. A. Craig and F. Gilbert, eds., *The Diplomats, 1919–1939* (1965). A good collection of essays on international relations.

W. Neuman, *The Balance of Power in the Interwar Years, 1919–1939* (1968). A good study of international relations.

A. Rowse, *Appeasement* (1961). By a bitter eyewitness of British appeasement efforts.

CHAPTER 55
World War II, 1939–1945

FIGURE 55.1 A German Concentration Camp World War II was the most destructive war in history. Of particular brutality were the genocidal programs of Nazi Germany, which resulted in scenes like this one from the Landsberg concentration camp. (AP/Wide World Photos)

To much of the disillusioned and paralyzed democratic world, the outbreak of World War II seemed the beginning of the end of liberal Western civilization. For over two years these dire fears appeared to be justified. The seemingly invincible German and Japanese military machines swept on to victory after victory. Although liberal Western civilization would survive, World War II was by far the most destructive conflict in history. It served as a capstone to the period of unmatched death, loss, disruption, and terror begun by World War I.

1. TWO YEARS OF AXIS TRIUMPH

Striking without official warning at dawn on September 1, 1939, the German air force caught the Polish air force on its various airfields and destroyed it on the ground. Thereafter the German *Luftwaffe*, by ravaging Polish cities and communications centers and harassing troop movements, prevented the complete mobilization of the Polish army. Meanwhile, Nazi tanks and infantry poured into Poland from the north, west, and south. The Poles cried for help from France and Great Britain. The French and the British mobilized their armies along the German West Wall fortifications, and the British fleet blockaded Germany by sea. But that was all. The mechanized might of Nazi Germany overwhelmed Poland in a matter of days.

The Soviet Union, in accordance with its agreement with Hitler, proceeded to reannex territories in Poland and Eastern Europe that it had lost at the end of World War I. Estonia, Latvia, and Lithuania were absorbed politically into the Soviet Union. In October 1939 the Soviet Union demanded three strategic little strips of Finnish territory. When the Finnish government refused, the Soviet Union attacked Finland and took these territories by force. In June 1940, while Hitler was busy in Western Europe, the Soviet Union demanded and procured from Rumania the return of Bessarabia.

Early in April 1940 the Germans suddenly overran Denmark and Norway. The British fleet, attempting to intercept the invasion of Norway, was beaten off with heavy losses by the German air force. Denmark and Norway provided the Nazis with important food, timber, and mineral resources, sea and air bases, and a safe route for vital iron ore coming from Sweden.

On May 10, 1940, the German armies assaulted Luxembourg, the Netherlands, Belgium, and France. Luxembourg offered no resistance. The Netherlands fought heroically but was overwhelmed in six days. Trusting to the Maginot line to hold along the German border, the British army and a large part of the French army moved into Belgium to support the hard-pressed Belgian forces. In a surprise move through the Ardennes forest, powerful German mechanized forces on May 14 smashed through the French defenses at Sedan and drove quickly to the English Channel, cutting off the Belgian, British, and French armies in Belgium. Again the German "blitzkrieg"—a combination of highly coordinated air strikes and rapid deployment of tanks and motorized columns—proved overwhelming. Although some 300,000 British and a few French troops escaped by sea from Dunkirk, all the Belgian troops, the bulk of the French troops together with their weapons and supplies, and the British weapons and supplies were captured.

Only five more days of fighting, June 5–10, were required for the Germans to crush the remaining organized French resistance and turn the French retreat into a disorderly rout. On June 10 Paris was declared an open city (see Figure 55.2). And on that day Mussolini, thinking it safe, declared war on France and Great Britain. On June 16 Marshal Philippe Pétain became premier of France and the following day dispatched a surrender team to Hitler. On June 25 the "fighting" ceased. The collapse of the French military machine after five days of fighting was a colossal military debacle. Hitler forced a harsh treaty on the helpless French. The northern half of France and all the Atlantic coastal area were placed under German occupation. The unoccupied portion was compelled to disarm and cooperate with Germany. Some 2 million French prisoners were held as hostages to ensure French good behavior. In unoccupied France, Marshal Pétain and Pierre Laval set up a semi-Fascist regime, with headquarters at Vichy, and undertook to cooperate with Hitler.

Not all of the French accepted defeat. Many resisted the German army of occupation courageously throughout the war, suffering heavy casualties in doing so. General Charles de Gaulle,

FIGURE 55.2 Hitler at the Eiffel Tower, Paris, June 1940 The first year of World War II was marked by a series of stunning German victories. In June 1940 Hitler was in Paris. The Eiffel Tower, a symbol of French independence and power, is behind him. (Brown Brothers)

having unsuccessfully attempted to warn his superiors of the unreadiness of the French army, escaped to Great Britain and declared himself leader of the Free French. With energy and skill he strove to rally the French both inside and outside the homeland to resist the Germans and the Vichy collaborators and to restore the dignity and honor of France.

The collapse of France left Great Britain to face the German fury alone. Hitler now demanded that Britain surrender or suffer annihilation. The situation was desperate. Nearly all of Britain's land armaments had been lost at Dunkirk. Against the nearly one hundred fifty battle-tried Nazi divisions, Britain had only one fully equipped division. And although Great Britain did have the English Channel and the world's greatest navy, the fighting around Norway had demonstrated that navies could no longer control narrow waters dominated by a hostile air force. Britain's chief weapon of defense was its relatively small but efficient air force. Not the least of its assets was Winston Churchill, who, on May 10, 1940, had at last replaced Neville Chamberlain as prime minister. The dynamic and eloquent Churchill defied Hitler: "We shall fight on the beaches; we shall fight on the landing grounds; we shall fight in the fields and in the

streets; we shall fight in the hills; we shall never surrender."

Throughout the month of July 1940 Nazi invasion forces gathered along the French coast opposite Britain, twenty-four miles away. To make the crossing, however, absolute control of the air over the Channel was required. Early in August, therefore, swarms of German bombers and fighter escorts flew over the Channel, seeking to destroy the British air force and its landing fields. In the ensuing air battles, the British pilots in their swift Spitfires and heavily armed and manueverable Hurricanes knocked down German planes at the ratio of two or three to one. Nevertheless, by the end of August the British air forces were facing annihilation by sheer weight of numbers. At this critical juncture the Nazis suddenly shifted to massive daylight attacks on London, the world's largest city. The destruction and the suffering were immense, but the British defenses were improving, thanks to the use of radar, the total mobilization of the economy, the breaking of the German secret code (project Ultra), and the high morale of the people. The loss of German planes was so great that early in October the Nazis once more shifted their tactics to night attacks, which were more terrifying but less effective. Although the destructive air raids on Great Britain's cities, together with the even more menacing submarine attacks on British shipping, continued until the end of the war, the immediate threat of invasion had now passed (a winter crossing of the Channel would be too risky); the Battle of Britain had been won.

While the Battle of Britain was at its height, Mussolini set into operation his grandiose schemes for conquering an empire. Upon entering the war in June 1940 he had closed the Mediterranean to British shipping. In September his armies moved on Egypt and the Suez Canal from Libya to the west and from Ethiopia to the south. In October his armies attacked Greece from Albania. To meet this threat, Churchill made a daring and farsighted military move. Believing Suez to be the most strategic spot in the world in a global war, he sent half of Britain's scarce supply of tanks and artillery around Africa to Egypt while the Nazis stood poised across the Channel for the invasion of Great Britain. Mussolini's forces met disaster everywhere. The Greeks defeated them and drove them back into Albania. A squadron of British torpedo planes delivered a lethal blow to the Italian fleet at its base in southern Italy. During the winter of 1940–1941 the Fascist armies moving on Egypt were completely destroyed by light, mobile British forces; Mussolini's bubble had burst with a feeble pop; henceforth he was hardly more than a prisoner of the German forces that were sent to save him.

When in October 1940 it became evident that Great Britain could not be invaded that year, Hitler ordered his planners to complete blueprints for the earliest possible invasion of the Soviet Union. The conquest of the Soviet Union had always been uppermost in Hitler's thoughts, but he had hoped first to dispose of the French and British threat to his rear. The plans called for an assault date not later than May 15, 1941. But first the Balkan flank was to be secured. Hungary and Rumania yielded to Hitler's threats and joined the Axis alliance in November 1940; Bulgaria, in March 1941. Immediately Nazi forces poured into those countries. Yugoslavia and Greece, however, refused to yield, and the Germans attacked them in April 1941. Yugoslavia was overrun in eleven days, Greece in three weeks. The British forces that Churchill had dispatched to Greece were driven out of the peninsula and also off the island of Crete. Suez now appeared to be

doomed. It was open to attack from the north; to the west Germany's Afrika Korps, which had been sent to replace the defeated Italians, had driven the British back to the border of Egypt; pro-Nazi movements had broken out in Iraq, Iran, and French Syria. At this point, however, Hitler hurled his main forces against the Soviet Union, giving the British a breathing spell to recoup their strength in the Near and Middle East.

On June 22, 1941, the Germans launched, against the Soviet Union, the most massive assault in history. They were joined by the Hungarians, Rumanians, and Finns. Although Stalin was able to throw an equal number of divisions against the invaders, his troops were not so well trained, led, or equipped. Hitler expected to crush Soviet resistance in six weeks; the top British and American military leaders were of the same opinion. The Russians fought with determination, but the Nazi war machine crunched ever forward until by December 1 it was within sight of Moscow. Leningrad was surrounded, and Rostov, the gateway to the Caucasus oil fields, was captured. The richest and most productive part of the Soviet Union was in German hands. The Russians had suffered such staggering casualties that Hitler announced that the Soviet Union was destroyed and would never rise again. At this point the Japanese entered the war by attacking the United States on December 7, 1941. By that time, however, the Arctic winter, the lack of adequate supplies, and the Soviet counterattacks had forced the Germans to halt and in some places retreat. The Soviet Union was still alive, and the United States was now in the war.

2. THE NAZI EMPIRE

By 1942 Hitler ruled most of continental Europe from the English Channel to Moscow. He had initiated his "New Order"—basically a program of racial imperialism—in the lands he controlled. The conquered peoples were used according to their ranking in Hitler's racial hierarchy. Those most directly related to the Nazi conception of the "Aryan race," such as the Scandinavians, the Anglo-Saxons, and the Dutch, were treated well and would supposedly be absorbed into the Nazi Empire as partners with the Germans. The "Latin races," such as the French, were considered clearly inferior but tolerable as supportive cogs in the New Order. Slavs were toward the bottom of Hitler's ranking; they were to be isolated, shoved aside, and treated like slaves. Large numbers of Russians, Poles, and others were removed from their lands and turned into slave laborers, more often than not perishing under the harsh conditions of their new existence.

Lowest on Hitler's scale were the Jews and such other groups as socialists, gypsies, intellectuals, Jehovah's Witnesses, and the mentally ill. These people were systematically hunted, rounded up, transported to concentration camps, and exterminated. This process was the "Final Solution to the Jewish Problem," and the SS, under Heinrich Himmler, was given the special duty of carrying it out. The quantity and quality of programmed inhumanity, torture, and death were so unprecedented that they could not be believed or understood. While some resistance did take place, Jews were trapped in an extraordinarily powerful system that was thoroughly organized against them. Rebellions within the camps were almost always in vain. Those on the outside who might have done something—the British and Americans who knew and might have bombed gas chambers or railway lines to the camps—did nothing. In the end some 6 million Jews were killed in that systematic, bureaucratized horror along with perhaps another 6 million victims of other groups (see Figure 55.1).

This massive effort to racially reorganize Europe and perpetuate genocidal policies took priority over even the war effort—continuing until the last days of the war and using up needed troops and materials. Indeed, Nazi Germany itself was only partially organized for the military effort in the early years of the war, finally turning to full mobilization after 1942. Under the leadership of Albert Speer, German production multiplied in 1943 and 1944 despite Allied bombing.

The resources and treasures of conquered lands were taken or put under the control of the Nazis and used to further the Nazi war effort and implement the New Order. The Nazis attempted to gain the submission and cooperation of conquered peoples through the use of force and terror. While the Nazis always managed to find collaborators in occupied lands, they were never able to stamp out persistent resistance.

Such resistance movements grew in France, Poland, Denmark, Greece, Yugoslavia—indeed, in almost every occupied territory. They established underground networks, provided intelligence to the Allied forces, conducted guerrilla actions, aided escaping prisoners or Jews, sabotaged military installations, and generally tied down Nazi forces that might have been used on the war fronts.

3. THE UNITED STATES' ENTRY INTO THE WAR

The outbreak of the war in Europe caused hardly a ripple in the isolationist sentiment of the American public and Congress. Most isolationists believed that the French army and Maginot line, together with the British navy, were capable of containing the Nazis.

But suddenly, in May–June 1940, the picture drastically changed. The French army and Maginot line ceased to exist, and the British navy was in grave danger. Much of it would be used up in the defense of Britain in case of invasion. Roosevelt promptly came forward with a three-point program: (1) all-out rearmament, (2) bipartisanship in foreign affairs, (3) all aid short of war to those fighting the Axis (which at the moment meant Great Britain). There was little opposition to the first two points, and Roosevelt managed to overcome objections to aiding the British. American involvement grew from the supply of arms to the convoying of ships across the Atlantic by the American navy. Aid was extended to the Soviet Union, and in June 1941 Axis consulates were closed.

In August 1941 Roosevelt and Churchill met at sea and drawn up the Atlantic Charter, a joint statement of ideals and war purposes. In it appeared such pregnant phrases as "their countries seek no aggrandizement, territorial or other; . . . they respect the right of all peoples to choose the form of government under which they will live; . . . after the final destruction of the Nazi tyranny, . . . the establishment of a wider and permanent system of general security. . . ." The Soviet Union subscribed to the Atlantic Charter shortly afterward. Thus, by October 1941 the United States was engaged in a shooting—but not yet official—war with Germany and was in a virtual alliance

FIGURE 55.3 Pearl Harbor
On December 7, 1941, the Japanese attacked Pearl Harbor, Hawaii, and destroyed the Pacific fleet in the harbor and the air force on the ground. The attack brought the United States into the war. This photo shows the USS *California* as it went down. (UPI/Bettmann Newsphotos)

with Great Britain, one of the belligerents. The American people's eyes were on the Atlantic, where at any moment some new German act of aggression might make war official and total.

It was not in the Atlantic, however, but in the Pacific that the history-changing blow was struck; and not by Germany, but by Japan. Early in 1939 the Japanese, having conquered all the populous coastal areas of China and having driven Chiang Kai-shek's forces far into the Chinese interior, turned southward toward the territories of Southeast Asia and the southwest Pacific. These territories, rich in rubber, tin, rice, copra, and oil, belonged (with the exception of independent Thailand) to France, the Netherlands, Great Britain, and the United States. Since the French, Dutch, and British had their hands full in Europe with the growing Nazi menace, President Roosevelt transferred the American fleet from the Atlantic to Pearl Harbor in Hawaii as a deterrent to further Japanese aggression. He also gave the Japanese the required six months' notice of the termination of the commercial treaty

of 1911. These moves appear to have given the Japanese pause.

In 1940, however, after Hitler's conquest of France and the Netherlands and threatened conquest of Great Britain, the Japanese became much bolder. They took advantage of France's helplessness to occupy northern French Indochina and threatened the Dutch East Indies. But in the following year, 1941, when the Germans overran the Balkans and launched what promised to be a lethal attack on the Soviet Union, the Japanese leaders decided that the day of Axis world triumph was at hand.

Tensions rose between Japan and the United States. Finally, on December 7, 1941, a large squadron of Japanese bombers and torpedo planes took off from carriers in a position north of Hawaii and caught the American fleet anchored in Pearl Harbor by surprise (see Figure 55.3). With little loss to themselves, the Japanese planes crippled the American navy in the Pacific and destroyed the air force in Hawaii on the ground. In rapid succession Japan and the

United States declared war on each other, and within four days the United States was at war with the other Axis powers.

4. THE HOME FRONT

As in World War I, it became necessary to mobilize not only the armed forces of a nation but the society as a whole for the war effort. Governments took greater control over their economies than in peacetime. Civilians had to live with hardship so that supplies could be produced for the armed forces. As labor shortages arose, women were asked to assume jobs normally reserved for men. Political executives assumed more powers than they usually held, political dissent was discouraged, and propaganda was used to support the efforts on the home front as well as the battlefield.

Not all the nations involved mobilized their home fronts to the same degree. Great Britain and the Soviet Union did the most, reflecting the fact that these two nations were most threatened in the early years of the war. Germany was slower to mobilize its home front fully, in the early years relying on quick victories and spoils from conquered lands to support its needs. The United States, less threatened by the war, mobilized more slowly and unevenly.

The circumstances of World War II made the home front experience different than in World War I in some important, frightening ways. New military technologies and strategies made civilians targets as never before. This was demonstrated most clearly in the German bombing of British cities and the Allied bombing of German cities. In Dresden alone, three days of Allied bombing in 1945 resulted in some one hundred thousand deaths, most of them civilians. Even worse were the civilian deaths caused by the atomic bombs dropped on Hiroshima and Nagasaki (see Figure 55.4). Internally, certain groups of civilians were made to suffer far more than others. The Nazis followed a policy of racial imperialism and extermination in their lands (see pp. 692–693). In the United States, Japanese Americans on the West Coast were removed from their homes and businesses and placed into camps. In various occupied areas of Europe, resistance movements blurred the lines between the military and civilian spheres (see p. 693).

5. THE CLIMAX AND TURNING POINT OF THE WAR, JUNE–AUGUST 1942

The entry of the United States, with its enormous resources and industrial potential, changed the whole complexion of the war. Together with the totally mobilized British economy and the massive economic and military resources of the Soviet Union, the long-term advantage was now clearly on the side of the Allies. However, many months would be required to mobilize America's resources, and the Axis was determined to win decisively before that mobilization could be achieved (see Map 55.1). To bring about Allied solidarity, Churchill hastened to Washington, where, on January 1, 1942, he and Roosevelt launched the United Nations Alliance. Twenty-six nations, of which the United States, Great Britain, and the Soviet Union were the Big Three, promised to give their all to the common effort, to make no separate peace, and to abide by the principles of the Atlantic Charter. By the end of the war, the number of member nations had risen to forty-seven.

The now-global war was fought in three major theaters: (1) the Soviet Union, (2) the Mediterranean and western Europe, and (3) the Pacific. The Axis powers made their climactic bid for victory on all three fronts between June and August 1942. The biggest front in terms of numbers of troops, weapons, and casualties involved was that in the Soviet Union. Despite frightful losses, the Soviets had managed to keep their army intact and to relocate or rebuild their wartime factories. The Soviet people were unified against the foreign aggressors in what they called the "Great Patriotic War of the Fatherland." The Germans, after having been stopped in December 1941 by the Russian winter and the counterattacks, resumed their forward thrust in June 1942, this time in the southern sector. Refreshed and reequipped, they seemed irresistible. By August they had reached the outskirts of Stalingrad on the Volga. Here Stalin ordered a stand; the battle of Stalingrad raged for six months. In Feb-

FIGURE 55.4 **Hiroshima after A-Bomb** This photo of Hiroshima, taken shortly after the first atom bomb was dropped, shows the incredible destructive power of atomic weapons. (Sygma)

ruary 1943, the Russians, having closed a pincer behind the Germans in Stalingrad, captured all who had not been killed of an army of almost three hundred thousand men. This action was the turning point; the Germans began a slow but general retreat.

The crucial battle on the Mediterranean and Western European front was fought in Egypt. General Rommel's tough Afrika Korps in its first drive on Suez in 1941 had been stopped and pushed back into Libya by the British. In June 1942 Rommel's forces, greatly strengthened, struck the British desert forces a shattering blow and chased them in near rout to El Alamein, only sixty-five miles from Alexandria. Suez seemed doomed, and the British fleet prepared to evacuate the Mediterranean before it could be bottled up. Churchill rushed to the scene and put in a

team of winning commanders: Sir Harold Alexander in overall command and General Bernard Montgomery as field commander. In August Rommel's forces assaulted the British positions at El Alamein and were stopped. A race to build up men and supplies ensued; the British, with massive aid from the United States, won. Late in October 1942 Montgomery's superior Eighth Army attacked Rommel's forces and, after a desperate battle, drove them back across the desert in defeat. Suez and the Middle East were now saved from the Axis, and for the first time Great Britain and the United States were in a position to assume the offensive.

President Roosevelt had agreed with Churchill that the first priority should be defeating Germany, which represented the gravest threat. Therefore the United States concentrated most of

Map 55.1 EUROPE, 1942 This map shows the furthest extent of Axis power during World War II. By the end of the year German expansion had been stopped at Stalingrad in the east and Egypt in North Africa.

its efforts toward Europe, which made the war in the Pacific more difficult and predominantly naval in character.

Three days after Pearl Harbor, Japanese carrier-based torpedo planes struck the British Asiatic fleet a crippling blow in the Gulf of Siam. Now, with unchallenged mastery of the Pacific, the Japanese within the space of a few months were able to conquer a vast area in the Southwest Pacific and Southeast Asia with relative ease. The American islands of Wake, Guam, and the Philippines; British Hong Kong, Malaya, Singapore, and Burma; and the Dutch East Indies were overrun. In May 1942 Japanese naval forces were turned back by the Americans in the Battle of the Coral Sea, northeast of Australia. However, the main Japanese fleet was preparing a major thrust at Hawaii, which it could easily have made immediately after Pearl Harbor. The U.S. navy, which had broken the Japanese code, massed for an all-out battle. Early in June 1942, just as the Stalingrad and El Alamein campaigns were beginning, the two powerful naval forces came within carrier plane range of each other off Midway Island, a thousand miles west of Hawaii. The climactic Battle of Midway was fought at long range entirely by aircraft and submarines. American planes sank all four of the Japanese carriers, while the Japanese were able to destroy only one of three American carriers. Pounded from the air and without air cover, the Japanese commander ordered a retreat, never to become so bold again. In August 1942 the Americans assumed the offensive by attacking Guadalcanal in the Solomon Islands northeast of Australia. By that time, it was evident that the tide was beginning to turn on all three fronts.

6. VICTORY

Although the greatest crises had passed by the end of 1942, two and a half more years of bloody fighting were required to subdue the Axis. In fact, the defeat of the Axis could not have been achieved at all without a high degree of cooperation among the Big Three allies. President Roosevelt, with his winsome personality, played an important part in maintaining mutual confidence and cooperation among the Allied powers, which were so divergent in their ideologies and specific interests. The chief planners of the coordinated global strategy were Churchill for Great Britain, Stalin for the Soviet Union, and Army Chief of Staff George Marshall for the United States.

The Russian Front

The Battle of Russia was the greatest and most destructive battle in history. Some 9 million men (five hundred divisions) were engaged. For two and a half years after Stalingrad, the Germans were slowly beaten back, doggedly contesting every foot of ground. At last, in April 1945, the Russians entered Berlin. Along the fifteen hundred miles between Stalingrad and Berlin lay the wreckage of the greater part of Hitler's war machine. But the richest and most productive part of the Soviet Union lay devastated. At least 20 million Russians had been killed—possibly many more.

The Mediterranean and Western European Front

In November 1942, just as the Germans were beginning to retreat from El Alamein, a combined Anglo-American force under the command of General Dwight D. Eisenhower landed in French North Africa. Early in 1943, the converging forces of Eisenhower and Montgomery cornered the Afrika Korps in Tunisia, where it surrendered in May.

Meanwhile, most of the threats from German submarines and planes were being eliminated as the British and Americans gained in the air and on the seas. Massive bombing raids pounded Germany. The distinction between strategic military targets and civilian populations blurred as Germany's cities were leveled.

In July 1943 the Anglo-American forces conquered the island of Sicily, which they used as a base for the invasion of southern Italy. Mussolini was forced to resign on July 25, and Italy surrendered. However, the peninsula was held by strong German forces. By the end of 1943 the Allies had reached Cassino Pass, about seventy-five miles south of Rome. At this point, the major objectives in the Mediterranean area had been achieved, and Eisenhower, along with most of his forces, was transferred to Great Britain to

Map 55.2 THE PACIFIC WAR This map shows the furthest extent of Japanese expansion, attained in June 1942, and the course of the American counterattack across the Pacific islands toward the Japanese mainland between 1942 and 1945.

command the main Anglo-American thrust across the Channel.

This thrust came on June 6, 1944. Thanks in large measure to complete Allied mastery of the skies, successful landings were made on the Normandy coast. After a rapid buildup, the Anglo-American forces broke out of the beachhead and before the end of the year cleared practically all of France. Germany, meanwhile, was being pulverized from the air. Early in 1945, the American and British forces, now joined by French units, broke through the German West Wall, crossed the Rhine, and joined forces with the Russians on the Elbe. Germany surrendered on May 8, ending the war in Europe. Near the end, Hitler and several other top Nazis committed suicide, and Mussolini was shot by Italian partisans.

The Pacific Front

Early in 1943, American forces under the command of General Douglas MacArthur and with a strong naval escort began an island-hopping campaign northwestward from their base in Australia (see Map 55.2). At the same time, under the command of Admiral Chester Nimitz, the main American fleet, now definitely superior to the Japanese fleet, thrust westward from Hawaii toward Japan, capturing the numerous Japanese-held islands in its path. Although the islands, many of them covered by jungles, were bloodily defended, the American forces moved steadily toward Japan itself. In October 1944 the American forces made a bold landing on Leyte Island in the Philippines, which brought the Japanese fleet out for a last desperate effort. In the Battle of Leyte Gulf, the Japanese fleet was annihilated. Cut off, uncovered, and subjected to ceaseless air and sea attacks, Japan was doomed. After Germany surrendered in May 1945, American, Brit-

ish, and Russian troops that had been engaged in the European theater were rapidly deployed to the Far East. In mid-July the atomic bomb, which American and British scientists had been developing for several years, was successfully completed and tested. The United States wanted to avoid the heavy casualties that a direct assault on the Japanese home islands would cause. The United States thus decided to use the bomb to shock Japan into surrender, a decision that has remained controversial ever since. On August 6, 1945, the first atomic bomb to be used in warfare destroyed the Japanese city of Hiroshima (see Figure 55.4) and some eighty thousand of its inhabitants. Two days later, the Soviet Union declared war on Japan and began to overrun Manchuria and northern Korea. The next day, August 9, the second and last atomic bomb then in existence demolished the industrial city of Nagasaki. The Japanese surrendered five days later, on August 14, 1945.

World War II had ended. Estimates of soldiers and civilians killed range from 30 million to 50 million; even more had suffered injuries from the war. Western society now faced an overwhelming task of recovery and reorganization.

SUGGESTED READING

General

B. Liddell Hart, *History of the Second World War* (1980). A good military history.

J. Keegan, *The Second World War* (1990). A lively recent survey.

D. Watt, *How War Came: The Immediate Origins of the Second World War* (1989). A step-by-step account.

G. Wright, *The Ordeal of Total War, 1939–1945* (1968). A thoughtful analysis; goes far beyond the military aspects.

Two Years of Axis Triumph

W. Churchill, *Their Finest Hour* (1949). The second and best of Churchill's great six-volume history of the war. Covers the defeat of France and the Battle of Britain.

M. Dziewanowski, *War at Any Price: World War II in Europe, 1939–1945* (1987). Has good chapters on the period.

The Nazi Empire

A. Dallin, *German Rule in Russia, 1941–1945* (1957). A good analysis.

L. Dawidowicz, *The War Against the Jews, 1933–1945* (1976). A thorough study.

T. Des Pres, *The Survivors* (1976). A good analysis of life in Hitler's concentration camps.

J. Haestrup, *Europe Ablaze* (1978). A thorough study of the resistance movements.

R. Hilberg, *The Destruction of the European Jews*, 3 vols. (1985). An exhaustive account.

M. Marrus, *The Holocaust in History* (1987). Covers all aspects.

The Entry of the United States

A. R. Buchanan, *The United States and World War II*, 2 vols. (1964). A good survey.

J. Campbell, ed., *The Experience of World War II* (1989). Good sections on this topic.

A. Iriye, *The Origins of the Second World War in Asia and the Pacific* (1987). An in-depth analysis.

Allied Victory

M. Sherwin, *A World Destroyed: The Atomic Bomb and the Grand Alliance* (1975). Analyzes the final years of the war and the role of the atomic bomb.

J. Toland, *The Last Hundred Days* (1966). A fine account of the end.

CHAPTER 56

The Recovery of Europe and the Superpowers, 1945–1980s

FIGURE 56.1 The Division Between East and West The post–World War II division between East and West in Europe is symbolized by the Berlin Wall and the Brandenburg Gate in Berlin, blocked by barbed wire and troops in 1961. (AP/Wide World Photos)

In 1945 much of Europe was in ashes. Disorganization was the rule, and effective governments were often virtually nonexistent. The economic destruction was so great that the immediate problem was not so much how to rebuild factories and initiate economic growth but how to minimize the starvation that faced millions and create shelter for the dislocated. The European nations would revive with amazing speed and go on to establish new patterns of relative political stability and economic growth. However, before that could happen, Europeans had to deal with the immediate problems of the settlement of World War II and the beginnings of the Cold War.

1. THE SETTLEMENT AND THE COLD WAR

In 1945 the leaders of the victorious nations were confronted with the tasks of making a lasting peace and restoring a shattered world. From the beginning these tasks were hampered by hostility between the United States and the Soviet Union. This hostility, which came to be called the "Cold War," pervaded and poisoned every area of postwar international relations. To understand the nature of the peace settlement and the origins of the Cold War, one must go back to the conferences held by the Allies during the war and to the legacy of assumptions held by participants in those conferences.

Legacy of Assumptions

Although Great Britain, the United States, and the Soviet Union had been cooperating allies during most of World War II, they approached one another with differing perceptions and a history of distrust. Since the Communists had come to power in Russia in 1917, the leaders of the Soviet Union and the capitalist democracies had viewed each other as opponents. As ideologies, communism and capitalism had always been in direct opposition. As practiced in the Soviet Union under Lenin and Stalin, communism took a totalitarian form, in sharp contrast to the democracies of Great Britain and the United States. Specific developments between the Russian Rev-

olution of 1917 and World War II added to the hostility between the Soviet Union and the capitalist democracies. During the Russian civil war, the Western nations had supported anti-Bolshevik forces with materials and some troops. The United States had not recognized the Bolshevik government until 1933. The Soviet Union had not even been invited to the Munich Conference of 1938. In viewing the rise of Fascist and authoritarian governments during the 1920s and 1930s, many in the Western democracies found consolation in the opposition of these governments to communism. In the 1930s, the Western democracies failed to ally with the Soviet Union against the growing threat of Nazi Germany. In 1939 Stalin entered into an astonishing pact with Hitler, enabling Nazi forces to concentrate on western Europe during the first years of World War II.

Hitler's invasion of the Soviet Union and the entry of the United States into the war united Great Britain, the United States, and the Soviet Union as allies more in opposition to Nazi Germany than in agreement over principles or goals. When concrete negotiations for war aims and terms of a settlement took place, the history of hostility, distrust, and fear between the capitalist and Communist powers caused problems. These problems would increase after the war, when the threat of Nazi Germany would no longer hold the Allies together.

The Conferences and the Settlement

The decisions that led to the peace settlements, that helped shape Europe in the immediate postwar years, and that laid the groundwork for the Cold War were made in a series of conferences held by the leaders of Great Britain, the United States, and the Soviet Union. The first conference took place in December 1943 at Teheran. There, Churchill's plan to open a front in Eastern Europe, which would have given Great Britain and the United States more influence there, was rejected. Eastern Europe was open to the advancing Soviet troops.

The next meeting of the three heads of state was in February 1945 at Yalta. They agreed to divide Germany into four occupation zones and to occupy Germany for a long time. Concerning

FIGURE 56.2 Allied Leaders at Yalta With victory over the Axis in sight, the terms of the settlement were negotiated at the Yalta Conference, February 1945. Churchill, Roosevelt, and Stalin, representing the Big Three Allied powers, made a series of agreements concerning the major postwar problems. (UPI/Bettmann Newsphotos)

Eastern Europe, Stalin argued that the area was already behind Soviet lines and was vital to his nation's security: The Soviet Union had been invaded through these countries in both world wars, and many of them had been Hitler's allies. Therefore, he asserted, the Soviet Union should maintain a measure of control over these countries. Roosevelt and Churchill insisted that these countries must be given complete independence. These disagreements were not resolved at Yalta nor at the last meeting, held in July 1945 at Potsdam (see Figure 56.2).

While the war ended in 1945 with a complete victory for the Allies, the basis of postwar problems was already present. The legacy of distrust and hostility between Communist Russia and the capitalist West had not been eradicated by the temporary period of cooperation during the war years. Decisions and disagreements at the wartime conferences had resulted in resentments and accusations on both sides, particularly over Eastern Europe. Faced with the reality of Eastern Europe's being behind Soviet lines, Great Britain and the United States were at a disadvantage. Europe, though struggling to recover, was already politically divided. Political divisions

would merge into Cold War divisions in the years following 1945.

The Cold War

The Cold War was the struggle between the United States and the Soviet Union, each supported by its respective non-Communist and Communist allies, that colored international relations during the four decades following World War II (see Map 56.1). On the one side the Soviet Union strove to secure itself from external threats and to spread its version of communism to the border states and elsewhere in the world. On the other side the United States strove to contain Soviet influence and to counter Communist threats wherever they were perceived throughout the world. It was a war fought in almost all ways except open military conflict, and the threat of military force was always present. At times, the Cold War became violent, but the two superpowers never came together in direct armed combat.

For the most part, the fragile spirit of cooperation between the Western democracies and the Soviet Union was broken by developments

Map 56.1 EUROPE DURING THE COLD WAR This map indicates the Cold War divisions in Europe during the 1950s. With some exceptions, the nations of Western Europe joined NATO, a non-Communist military organization headed by the United States. Also with a few exceptions, nations in Eastern Europe joined the Warsaw Pact, a Communist military organization headed by the Soviet Union.

in Eastern Europe. The United States and its allies felt that wartime agreements and a sense of justice should compel the Soviet Union to allow free elections in Eastern European states, all of which should be independent of Soviet control. The Soviet Union felt that these same wartime agreements and a higher sense of justice recognized the overriding need for the Soviet Union to make sure the Eastern European states remained friendly and under Soviet influence. The United States became increasingly outraged when developments in Eastern Europe went Stalin's way. By 1950 all the states of Eastern Europe were controlled by Communists and, with the

exception of Yugoslavia under Josip Broz Tito, were dominated by the Soviet Union.

The struggles over Eastern Europe spread to Western Europe, where strong Communist parties in France and Italy pursued policies approved by Moscow. The United States and its allies feared that these parties would subvert non-Communist governments and help spread Soviet control further south and west.

The verbal denunciations and discord over events in Europe were accompanied by a breakdown of cooperation between the United States and the Soviet Union. President Truman, who succeeded Roosevelt on April 12, 1945, was in favor of a tougher policy toward the Soviet Union. In May he cut off aid to the Soviet Union. When the possibility of international control of atomic weapons arose, the Americans and Russians could not agree. This led to the nuclear weapons race, which has flourished ever since.

The breakdown of cooperation was most striking in Germany. In accordance with the Potsdam agreements, most of Germany was divided into four occupation zones: American, Russian, British, and French. Berlin, which was in the Russian zone, was divided into four sectors and made the headquarters of a four-power coordinating commission. Sharp cleavages soon developed among the occupying powers, particularly between the United States and the Soviet Union. The Soviet Union, having suffered more at the hands of Germany during World Wars I and II than any other major nation, was determined to keep Germany permanently weak and as much as possible under Soviet domination. The United States, on the other hand, having little fear of Germany and seeing it as a valuable potential ally against the Soviet Union, set out to restore and rearm the nation. Matters came to a head in 1948–1949. In March 1948 the United States, having succeeded in merging the three western zones and stepping up their economy to a level much higher than that agreed upon at Potsdam, announced plans for the creation of an independent West German state. To the Soviet leaders, this was the last straw. They attempted to dissuade the Western powers from going ahead with the project by blockading the three western zones of Berlin in the hope of starving them out. For eleven months, from June 1948 to May 1949, the Soviets stopped all land traffic across their zone from the West to Berlin. The Western powers defeated the blockade through a giant airlift. The United States proceeded to set up the German Federal Republic, which began to function in September 1949. One month later the Soviet Union set up the German Democratic Republic in its zone.

Meanwhile, new policies were raising the Cold War to a higher level. In 1947 President Truman initiated a policy of military containment called the Truman Doctrine, which meant that the United States would draw a military ring around the Soviet Union and its satellites. His secretary of state, George Marshall, supplemented the Truman Doctrine with the Marshall Plan, a package of economic aid to European nations designed to strengthen them and tie them to American influence. Two years later the United States organized the North Atlantic Treaty Organization (NATO), which was a military alliance among the United States, Canada, and most of the nations of Western Europe against the Soviet Union (see p. 717).

The Soviet Union responded by establishing the Council for Mutual Economic Assistance (COMECON), a Soviet "Marshall Plan" for Eastern Europe. In the following years the Soviet Union continued to strengthen its military ties with its allies, eventually countering NATO by establishing the Warsaw Pact organization.

By 1950 one stage of the Cold War was completed. Europe was clearly divided into a Communist camp in the east under the control of the Soviet Union and a non-Communist camp in the west under the leadership of the United States. The Cold War would continue in different ways and with varying intensity over the next four decades. Both sides were pitted against each other in a worldwide war of propaganda. Political struggles almost anywhere, whether purely internal matters or not, became potential fields for a victory or defeat in a Cold War competition. This competition expanded to the non-Western world and to a variety of fields not usually thought of as political, from the exploration of space to the Olympic games.

In 1950 the Korean War shifted the focus of the Cold War from Europe to the non-Western world. It also revealed how real the risk of military combat was in the struggle between Communist and non-Communist forces. In the mid-1950s there were some signs of a relaxation in the Cold War. Stalin died in 1953, and later that year an armistice was signed in Korea. The Soviet government made overtures to the United States to end the Cold War. In 1955 Soviet troops left Austria, which became an independent, neutral state. That same year a conference was held in Geneva among the leaders of Great Britain, France, the United States, and the Soviet Union. Little of substance was accomplished, but at least it symbolized an effort to solve problems peacefully. Talk of "peaceful coexistence" between the superpowers became popular and seemed confirmed when the two powers agreed to talks for a nuclear test ban treaty in 1958.

This apparent thaw in the Cold War was mitigated by some chilling developments. In the same year that Stalin died, John Foster Dulles became U.S. secretary of state in the new Eisenhower administration. It was his belief that all communism was a Moscow-directed conspiracy bent upon world conquest. The time had come, he proclaimed, to pass over from containment to liberation. The United States tried to apply the lessons learned in the struggles over Eastern Europe and Korea to Southeast Asia, where the French had lost to Communist-led insurgents in Vietnam. Efforts to hold a meeting between the American and Soviet heads of state in 1960 broke down amid Cold War accusations. In 1961 irritations over Germany were exacerbated by the construction of the Berlin Wall, which sealed off democratic West Berlin from East Berlin and the rest of Communist East Germany (see Figure 56.1). In 1962 the Cuban missile crisis, a Cold War confrontation over the placement of Russian missiles in Cuba, came close to erupting into a real war.

Nevertheless, the 1960s and most of the 1970s witnessed a general lessening of tensions in the Cold War. A nuclear test ban treaty between the two powers was signed in 1963, and strategic arms limitation talks were initiated in 1969. After 1969 relations between the United States and the Soviet Union were often described by the word *détente,* which emphasized cooperation rather than confrontation.

In the later 1970s and early 1980s events proved that the Cold War was not over. The increasing ties between Communist China and the United States were perceived as a threat by the Soviet Union. When Jimmy Carter became president in 1977, the Soviet leaders quickly took offense at his insistence on the granting of human rights throughout the world, including the Soviet Union, and they were uncomfortable with his more open style of diplomacy. A Soviet invasion of Afghanistan in 1979 led to an American boycott of the Olympic Games in 1980 and an embargo on grain shipments to the Soviet Union. The Reagan administration took a much tougher stand toward the Soviet Union and communism

in general, reviving Cold War rhetoric and dramatically increasing arms production. In the 1980s the Polish crisis, American attempts to limit exportation of certain technology and materials by Western nations to the Soviet Union, the deployment of new American missiles in Europe, the American Strategic Defense Initiative, and the rejection of the 1979 Strategic Arms Limitation Treaty heightened the tensions between the two powers.

2. REVIVAL OF A DIVIDED EUROPE AND THE WEST

Within the context of the Cold War struggle, Europe survived the difficult years immediately following World War II, recovered by the 1950s, and grew in new directions in the following decades. Yet there was a fundamental division between west and east in Europe, with Western Europe turning toward parliamentary democracy and support from the United States and Eastern Europe turning toward communism and support from the Soviet Union.

Western Europe

After World War II the nations of Western Europe returned to liberal democratic forms of government. The political parties of the center generally came to power. On the Continent the Christian Democratic parties were particularly strong in France, West Germany, and Italy. They had ties to traditional prewar conservative parties but became more progressive after World War II. They stood for democracy, economic growth, moderate social reform, antifascism, and anticommunism. Their main competitors were a variety of moderate, democratic Socialist parties with ties to traditional prewar Socialist parties. With the exception of Great Britain, where the Labour party came to power in 1945, these Socialist parties usually found themselves in opposition rather than in power. Initially, Communist parties were also strong, but after 1947, when the Cold War heated up, these parties were systematically excluded from participation in national governments.

While the United States emerged from World

War II economically strong, the postwar European governments were faced with the tremendous task of leading their countries to economic and social recovery. After the first few very difficult years, when hunger and dislocation were more a rule than an exception, Western Europe entered into a period of strong economic recovery lasting well into the 1960s. The economic recovery was fueled by money from the American Marshall Plan, pent-up demand since the beginning of the war for goods and services, cheap skilled labor, and a surprisingly high birthrate. Different mixtures of national planning and free enterprise were used to direct the recovery. International cooperation, such as the Organization of European Economic Cooperation (OEEC) and the European Coal and Steel Community, and the already high level of industrial and technological sophistication attained by Western Europeans, facilitated the recovery. Accompanying economic growth were government social policies providing for health care, unemployment relief, old-age benefits, and family support.

In the late 1960s and 1970s new problems appeared. The economic growth of the 1950s and early 1960s leveled off. Inflation became widespread, particularly after 1973, when oil prices started a dramatic rise. At the same time, growth rates started to decline and unemployment began to rise. This "stagflation"—economic stagnation coupled with sharp inflation—persisted into the 1980s. Partial recovery in the mid-1980s, led by the United States, was uneven and purchased at a high price. Governmental deficits and problems with trade balances became common in the West. Nevertheless, a huge amount and array of new goods and services were produced and consumed in the decades after World War II. Far greater access to and use of consumer debt, particularly charge cards, enabled consumers to buy quickly and try to pay for it later. Electric household appliances, home entertainment equipment, and, more recently, computer and home office machines spread into homes throughout the West. Far more tourists than ever vacationed in foreign lands.

Social dissatisfaction was evidenced in a variety of movements, from the student protests of the late 1960s to the radical separatist movements of the 1970s and 1980s. Most dramatic was the increase of terrorism, which was used as a political tactic by desperate groups such as the Provisional Wing of the Irish Republican Army (IRA), the West German Baader-Meinhof gang, the Italian Red Brigades, and the Palestine Liberation Organization (PLO). While the period cannot be called one of political instability, voters often turned out incumbent parties in hopes that the opposition parties could solve problems. Socialist parties that came to power seemed to have as much trouble dealing with apparently intractable problems as their conservative counterparts.

These general trends and variations of them can best be understood by examining developments in some individual countries between 1945 and the present.

Great Britain

In Great Britain the Labour party swept to victory in elections held in July 1945, just as the war was coming to an end. Clement Attlee succeeded Churchill as prime minister. The problems confronting Britain and the Labour government were indeed formidable. More than half of Great Britain's merchant marine had been sunk; a third of its buildings had been destroyed or damaged; its foreign investments had been liquidated and used up; Great Britain owed the United States a huge debt; and its empire was tottering. The Labour government strictly rationed the short supplies, raised taxes on the rich, and lowered taxes on the poor. It nationalized the Bank of England, the coal mines, the electrical and gas industries, inland transportation, and the steel industry. Altogether, some 20 percent of Britain's economy was socialized. A vast program of social security, public education, public housing, and national health insurance was launched. The dismantling of the British Empire was begun—India, the biggest of all of Britain's colonial prizes, was given its independence in 1947 (see Chapter 58). The six years of Labour rule were years of austerity for the middle and upper classes. However, the general morale of the people was high, and Britain recovered.

Unfortunately, Great Britain's economic condition was fundamentally unsound. The loss of its overseas investments and resources and of the income from most of its prewar shipping, together with the antiquated state of most of its mines and factories, left Britain far short of the funds needed for war repair, debt repayment, and social services. By 1949 the serious deficit in the balance of trade had become apparent, followed by a weakening of the pound and mounting inflation. Rising discontent enabled Churchill and the Conservatives to return to power in 1951. With the exception of denationalizing the steel and trucking industries, they tampered little with the Labour party's program, most of which the great majority of the British people now clearly favored.

But neither the Conservatives, who governed Britain from 1951 to 1964 and again from 1970 to 1974, nor the Labourites, who governed from 1964 to 1970 and again from 1974 to 1979, were able to strengthen Britain's deteriorating economy, which was not yet socialistic but was too restricted to allow free competitive capitalism to function as it had in the nineteenth century. Furthermore, it was difficult for many Britishers to adjust to their greatly diminished place in the world. Many could still remember the glamorous days when Britain ruled the seas and an empire over which the sun never set. But increasing numbers of the young and the poor knew and cared little about past glories. Lawlessness and violence escalated, reaching its peak of intensity in Ulster. There the Roman Catholic minority struggled fiercely to gain equality with the Protestant majority; many of the Roman Catholics demanded separation from Britain and union with Ireland. The Protestants fought equally fiercely to maintain their supremacy. Violence begat violence. Hundreds on both sides were killed, and hopes for a harmonious society were destroyed for the foreseeable future.

Widespread dissatisfaction with the inability of the Labour party to discipline its own trade unions and to lessen the rate of inflation resulted in a sweeping victory for the Conservatives in 1979. Margaret Thatcher became Britain's first female prime minister. The coming into production of the North Sea oil discoveries of several years earlier promised to strengthen Britain's economy, which had been in decline since World War I. Nevertheless, during the early 1980s Britain's economy remained troubled. With unemployment at more than 12 percent year after year and economic growth modest, Britain was burdened with one of the poorest-performing economies in Western Europe. Urban riots reflected growing dissatisfaction. Yet thanks to the nationalistic unity fostered by the brief Falklands War with Argentina in the spring of 1982, the divisions within the Labour party (which led to the creation of a new party, the Social Democrats), and a moderately improving economy, Thatcher's Conservatives managed to maintain control over the government.

France

France emerged from the war not only ravaged but also, unlike Britain, defeated and demoralized. General Charles de Gaulle returned to France in 1944 with the American and British liberators, who gave official recognition to the government he set up in Paris. However, the first postwar elections, held in October 1945, resulted in a sweeping victory for the parties of the Left, with which the authoritarian de Gaulle could not cooperate. Early in 1946 he went into temporary retirement. The leftist coalition, suspicious of authority, drew up a constitution very similar to that of the Third Republic, with its weak executive. The one noteworthy advance made by the new constitution was the granting, at long last, of female suffrage. The Fourth Republic, like the Third, was plagued by a multiplicity of parties and political instability.

Despite these difficulties the Fourth French Republic made some noteworthy changes in French economic and social life. Under the Monnet Plan, free enterprise was combined with economic planning. Major banking and insurance facilities, coal mines, and gas and electrical utilities were nationalized. Social services, somewhat less comprehensive than those of the British Labour government, were inaugurated. A strong if uneasy economic recovery was achieved. By 1958 the output of goods and services was far in excess of that before World War II. These accomplishments of the Fourth Republic, however, were offset by its unsuccessful effort to hold on to the French Empire. A costly attempt to put down a war for independence in Indochina, which had broken out in 1942, resulted in humiliating defeat for the French (see p. 741). In 1954 France was forced to grant independence to Indochina. An even costlier war to try to save Algeria, in 1954–1962, also ended in failure (see pp. 746–747). Inability to solve the Algerian prob-

FIGURE 56.3 Charles de Gaulle After the French army in Algeria revolted against the French government in 1958, de Gaulle was recalled by popular acclaim and given an overwhelming mandate to rewrite the constitution. With dispatch he set up the Fifth French Republic and was elected its first president. This photo shows de Gaulle on tour of the French provinces. (Henri Cartier-Bresson/Magnum)

lem led to the mutiny of the French army in Algeria in May 1958, which brought down the government. Charles de Gaulle was recalled from his twelve-year retirement. The problems confronting him were formidable—a mutinous army, a disintegrating empire, a seemingly endless war in Algeria, a disgruntled working class, an inflated currency, governmental weakness amounting to anarchy, widespread cynicism.

De Gaulle was probably the only person in France who could have reestablished civilian control over the mutinous army, which he deftly proceeded to do. He drew up a new constitution that greatly strengthened the executive branch of the government, and in December 1958 he was elected first president of the Fifth French Republic by an overwhelming majority (see Figure 56.3). He immediately granted independence to all of France's colonies except Algeria, which had a large French population. Algerian independence was granted four years later. He undertook to strengthen France's capitalistic economy by means of an austerity program. In spite of widespread strikes, France's economy was soon operating at its highest level in history, and the French masses were enjoying new prosperity.

In foreign affairs, de Gaulle set out to restore France's "greatness"—its prestige in world affairs and its hegemony in Western Europe. He also sought to make Western Europe a "third force" independent of both American and Soviet domination. To achieve these ends, he created at great cost an independent nuclear strike force, cultivated cordial relations with Germany, withdrew France's military forces from NATO because of its domination by the United States, and vetoed Great Britain's entry into the European Common Market because of its close ties to its Commonwealth associates and to the United States.

For eleven years these policies worked with remarkable success. France regained much of the stability and prestige it had lost in 1940. De Gaulle's strong role, of course, encountered much opposition, mostly from the extreme Right and extreme Left. His position and that of France's economy were weakened by massive student and labor union strikes and riots in 1968. When, in early 1969, de Gaulle asked for a vote of confidence from the French people and lost by a narrow margin, he resigned.

During the early 1970s Gaullists remained in power under the more moderate leadership of Georges Pompidou. In 1974 the elegant, urbane Valéry Giscard d'Estaing, a moderate conservative, defeated his Communist- and Socialist-backed opponent by the narrowest of margins. Giscard d'Estaing represented France's technocratic Right and pursued a policy of slow modernization and social conservatism. Stunning change came in the elections of 1981, which brought the Socialists, under the leadership of François Mitterrand, into power. Immediately, policies stressing nationalization of industries and banks, shorter hours and increased pay for workers, and progressive social programs were enacted. Yet several years of persistent economic problems, particularly inflation and high unemployment, dampened the reforming zeal of the Socialists and led them to reverse some of their policies.

West Germany

The German Federal Republic was formally established in September 1949. It had a liberal democratic government similar to that of the Weimar Republic. The Christian Democratic party, a slightly right-of-center party with Roman Catholic leanings, won the first election, and its leader, the elderly and pro-Western Dr. Konrad Adenauer, became the first chancellor. The Western powers replaced their military governors with civilian commissioners and relaxed their control over Germany.

West Germany's industrial economy recovered rapidly, in part thanks to American assistance in replacing wrecked industrial plants with the most modern equipment and to American military protection, which relieved West Germany of the enormous military costs that burdened the economies of the United States, Great Britain, and France. By 1957 West Germany had regained its former industrial supremacy in Western Europe.

In 1963 Adenauer finally stepped down (at eighty-seven) as chancellor. His Christian Democratic successors vigorously pursued his policies of strengthening West Germany's military ties with the United States, demanding the reunification of Germany and the recovery of lost territories in Eastern Europe, and establishing a place in the family of nuclear nations.

In 1969 Willy Brandt, a Social Democrat, became chancellor and launched Germany on a new course. His government quickly signed a nuclear nonproliferation treaty that had been long pending and entered into bilateral talks with East Germany and the Soviet Union. In August 1970 Chancellor Brandt and Soviet Premier Kosygin signed a treaty renouncing force or the threat of force in international relations and accepting the existing boundary lines of Eastern Europe, including the Oder-Neisse line between East Germany and Poland. An official accompanying letter specified that the treaty left open the possibility of the future reunion of the two Germanies. This possibly momentous treaty was accompanied by trade agreements that promised a greatly stepped-up commerce between West Germany and the Soviet Union. The Social Democrats instituted and implemented many social programs, such as a comprehensive system of national health insurance and government ownership of public utilities. In economic policy, the German Social Democrats, unlike the French and British Socialists, who advocated government ownership or control, followed a policy of codetermination between labor and management—*mitbestimmung.* West Germany's industrial economy had become the most prosperous in the Western world.

The economic problems plaguing other Western nations finally caught up with West Germany in the early 1980s. In 1982 Helmut Schmidt and his Social Democratic party fell from power and were replaced by the more conservative Christian Democratic party, led by the new chancellor Helmut Kohl. The rise to power of Kohl and the Christian Democrats was affirmed by elections in 1983, which also witnessed the first substantial entry into national politics of the environmentalist Green party.

Southern Europe

Italy After the end of World War II Italy abolished the monarchy and established itself as a republic. The Christian Democrats under the leadership of Alcide de Gasperi emerged as the dominant political party. The Italian Communist party also came out of World War II in a strong position, initially sharing power with the Christian Democrats in a coalition government. After 1947 the Communists, although continuing to command 25 to 35 percent of the vote and winning control of local elections throughout Italy, were excluded from national government. For the next three decades the Christian Democrats dominated the Italian government, although almost always in shaky alliances with other parties. Even though governments did not last long, the government bureaucracy was resistant to change and the same group of high governmental officials continued in office in succeeding governments.

Italy, and particularly northern Italy, enjoyed rapid economic growth and modernization in the 1950s and 1960s, for the first time becoming a leading industrial power in Europe. After the late 1960s Italy experienced greater economic, social, and political instability. Inflation became a perennial problem. Industrial growth slowed. The government, with its entrenched and sometimes corrupt bureaucracy, became less able to react to problems. In the mid-1970s voters turned increasingly to the Italian Communist party, which under Enrico Berlinguer was adopting more moderate policies. Radical groups, such as the Red Brigades, resorted to terrorism. By the 1980s the dominant Christian Democratic party was losing control of the government for the first time. In August 1983 Bettino Craxi was named the first Socialist premier of Italy, but his coalition government was only moderately different from preceding governments. A decade later massive dissatisfaction with Italian politics would undermine Italy's post-war political system.

Spain, Portugal, and Greece The three southern European nations of Spain, Portugal, and Greece did not enter the mainstream of European developments until the 1970s. Both Spain, under Francisco Franco, and Portugal, under Antonio Salazar, remained out of World War II and retained their prewar authoritarian governments. Compared with the economies of other nations of Western Europe, their economies were less modernized and their people had a lower standard of living. Major political change came for both in the mid-1970s. In Portugal in 1974 General Antonio de Spinola headed a revolt that removed Marcelo Caetano, Salazar's authoritarian successor, from power. A year later Portugal held its first elections, and the Socialists, led by Mario Soares, gained control of the government. Spain underwent similar changes after the death of Franco in 1975. With the support of King Juan Carlos, a democratic constitution was approved in 1976. In 1982 the Socialists, under the popular Felipe Gonzáles, were elected to power for the

first time. Both nations went on to enjoy relative political stability and, particularly in Spain, economic growth.

Greece, which suffered greatly during World War II, emerged from it in chaos and civil war. The Greek Royalists, with the help of first the British and then the Americans, were victorious. Greece became politically stable and remained so until the mid-1960s, when threats from both the Left and Right led to the fall of the monarchy and, in 1967, a coup by conservative army officers. Their strong, authoritarian grip on Greek life was broken in 1974, when a confrontation with Turkey over Cyprus proved too difficult to handle. After 1975 Greece was governed by democratic rule, culminating in the election of the Socialists under Andreas Papandreou in 1981.

All three countries have followed a similar pattern: They broke from authoritarian rule in the mid-1970s, established a democratic form of government, and eventually elected a Socialist government. All three governments have had to deal with economies less modern than those in Western Europe and with societies that have had a lower standard of living. Yet events have pulled these southern European countries into the mainstream of Western European affairs; in the 1980s all three gained membership in the Common Market.

The United States

Of the Western powers, only the United States emerged from World War II virtually unscathed materially. The war had forced billions of dollars into circulation, ended the long depression, and destroyed much of the nation's foreign competition. The end of the war found big business and a high-spending military machine in close alliance and firmly entrenched. For most of the three decades following 1945, the United States enjoyed great economic prosperity. The pinnacle of prosperity came in the early and mid-sixties. Under presidents Kennedy and Johnson, the government pursued liberal policies of social reform, which included attacks on poverty, new educational programs, low-income housing projects, and governmental support of medical services. These policies put the United States more into line with other Western nations that had already established these social and "welfare state" institutions. However, the expansion of new social programs and unquestioned prosperity would come to an end in the 1970s and 1980s. Indeed, underlying the prosperity and confidence of the decades after World War II was a series of problems, which often resulted in anxiety, unrest, fear, and violence.

The first was the Soviet Union and communism. From the very beginning of the postwar era, Americans feared the Soviet Union and communism. Many journalists, military leaders, politicians, and business and professional people exploited this fear. During the early 1950s Senator Joseph McCarthy of Wisconsin fanned this fear into hysteria. In the eyes of McCarthy and his millions of followers, the American government, defense industries, armed forces, and educational system were honeycombed with Communists and fellow travelers.

In 1957, just as McCarthyism was subsiding, the American people were shocked by the news that the Soviet Union had orbited a satellite—Sputnik. The implication was that the lean and eager Russians had forged ahead in nuclear weapons and delivery systems while the soft, contented Americans had slept. The United States had, of course, been working on a satellite of its own for some time and in 1958 successfully orbited one. In 1961 the Soviet Union and the United States sent men into space and began to race each other to the moon. This race was won by the United States in 1969 at a cost of some $40 billion.

Americans were greatly concerned over repeated Communist successes in Asia (see Chapter 58), and closer to home a Communist takeover in Cuba in 1959 caused grave anxiety. The Cuban rebel leader, Fidel Castro, overthrew an American-supported rightist dictatorship. In 1961 the American government encouraged and aided an unsuccessful attempt by Cuban refugees to overthrow the Castro regime and the following year, by heavy threats, forced the Soviet Union to dismantle the missile bases it had constructed in Cuba. This was the most frightening of all the confrontations between the two nuclear powers, both of which had the nuclear capacity to destroy all the people on the earth.

America's next problem was its long-festering failure to integrate its large African-American population. By 1945 African Americans numbered some 20 million—about a tenth of the total population—and although some advancement in material well-being and social equality had been made, the gains fell far short of the promises. African-American veterans returning from World War II were particularly frustrated. In 1954 the Supreme Court outlawed segregation in the public schools and later mandated forced busing as a means of implementing the decision. In the following years the civil rights movement was born, as African Americans struggled for greater equality within American society. White resistance flared up first in the Deep South and later in the large industrial cities of the North. Federal troops and marshals were used to overcome white resistance in the South. Millions of whites in the large northern industrial cities fled to the suburbs. In 1964 Congress passed civil rights acts that guaranteed voting rights and broadly outlawed racial discrimination. Nevertheless, this legislation did not end the turmoil that had been unleashed. Riots occurred in major cities during the 1960s, reaching a climax in 1968 following the murder of Dr. Martin Luther King, Jr., the most prominent of the African-American leaders. During the 1970s and 1980s, the position of blacks in American society evolved, but the record has been mixed. On the one hand, the elevation of many African Americans to positions of political leadership and the growing numbers of African Americans in middle-class jobs and residential areas indicate important change. On the other hand, African Americans remain overrepresented in the growing core of inner-city unemployed who live below the poverty line.

Several other problems created social unrest during the 1960s. College students staged protests over a variety of issues including racial inequality, poverty, destruction of natural resources, and American involvement in the Vietnam War (see pp. 741–743). Women organized and demanded equal rights. Radical organizations, particularly on the political Left, grew and were unusually active.

While some of these problems became less immediate in the 1970s, new problems arose. In 1974, confidence in the American political system was shaken by the Watergate scandal, which revealed widespread misconduct and crimes within the highest levels of President Nixon's administration. Numerous high officials in the Nixon administration were forced to resign and were convicted and imprisoned. In August 1974, after it had become obvious that the president would be impeached by the full House and convicted by the Senate, Nixon resigned. He was succeeded by Gerald Ford, the conservative Republican leader who granted Nixon full pardon for all crimes he "may have committed while in office."

At almost the same time, economic problems stemming from the cost of the Vietnam War, an unfavorable balance of trade, growing inflation, and the fourfold increase in oil prices between 1973 and 1974 started catching up with the United States. The country was entering a new period of declining growth rates, increasing unemployment, and rising prices. In the world marketplace, it was losing its dominance.

In 1976 Ford was narrowly defeated by Jimmy Carter. The Carter administration was confronted by spiraling inflation, a threatened fuel shortage, a high rate of unemployment (particularly among African Americans and youths), a sense of disillusionment over the Vietnam War and its end, and widespread distrust of government at all levels—difficult problems that were not solved. The Carter administration was further burdened with trying to free American hostages from a hostile Iran and a new rise in oil prices.

In 1980 Ronald Reagan and the Republican party were elected to power and initiated a series of conservative policies in an attempt to undo several of the liberal reforms of the previous decades. Defense spending increased; a harsher line was taken toward communism; American arms and forces were sent to several areas throughout the world; programs to protect the environment, the worker, and the unemployed were attacked; and tax reforms that benefited mainly the corporations, the wealthy, and the middle class were enacted. The recession that began in the late 1970s deepened, with unemployment figures higher than in any years since the Great Depression of the 1930s. After 1983 the economy was in recovery, but the relative prosperity had been purchased by a series of huge governmental deficits.

Eastern Europe and the Soviet Union

The Soviet Union and Eastern Europe participated in the general European recovery from World War II, but their recovery was slower and not nearly as spectacular as in Western Europe. Certainly the economies of Eastern Europe started from a lower base and had to overcome greater difficulties. During the 1950s and 1960s the Soviet and Eastern European economies modernized and people enjoyed a rising standard of living. Soviet and Eastern European citizens did not participate nearly as fully in the consumerism experienced in the West, but they were assured of steady employment, inexpensive housing, and access to health and educational facilities. The basic social services were extensive. With the exception of the elite of the Communist party and certain professionals, the gap between the rich and poor classes narrowed. The Soviet Union initially set the pattern of economic and political development, but over time the various nations within the Soviet sphere of dominance moved in their own directions.

The Soviet Union The Soviet Union emerged victorious from World War II, but the social and economic costs were high. Few changes from prewar policies were evident. Stalin continued to assert totalitarian rule with a tightly planned economy stressing heavy industrialization. Political dissent was not allowed, and purges removed those perceived as potential threats. Prisons and forced-labor camps remained a feature of Stalin's rule. Despite the heavy expenditures required to maintain the Red Army, the Soviet Union recovered.

The death of Stalin in 1953 led to a liberalization of policies within the Soviet Union. Initially, Georgi Malenkov and Nikita Khrushchev struggled for power, but by 1955 Khrushchev had emerged as Stalin's successor. The most dramatic indication of changes from the Stalin era came in a 1956 speech in which Khrushchev denounced the crimes of Stalin before startled Communist leaders in Moscow. Khrushchev removed many of the conservative Stalinists within the party hierarchy but avoided the use of harsh Stalinist purges. Controls over cultural life were slightly loosened, as evidenced by the publication of novels by Boris Pasternak. Economically, there was a new stress on consumer goods and an attempt was made to reform agricultural policy. Khrushchev also embarked on an ambitious foreign policy. But he may have tried to do too much at once, for domestic and international difficulties began to undermine his position. The gravest problems occurred in foreign affairs. The Soviet Union became involved in a growing ideological dispute with the Chinese Communists, who were younger and more evangelical in the Marxist faith than the Russians (see p. 738). The split between the Soviet Union and China was intensified by boundary disputes. Then, in 1962, Khrushchev blundered into a showdown with the United States by trying to set up Soviet nuclear missiles in Cuba and was forced to make a humiliating retreat.

In October 1964 Khrushchev was suddenly ousted from power by his colleagues in the party's Central Committee. Leonid Brezhnev replaced him as party secretary, eventually emerging as the actual head of government by the late 1960s. Brezhnev reversed some of the liberalization of the Khrushchev years but did not fully return to Stalinist policies or practices. The Brezhnev era was marked by relative stability within the Soviet Union. The Soviet economy has continued to expand, but unevenly and not as rapidly as expected—in part thanks to the drain of military and administrative expenditures. By the 1980s the Soviet Union was a world leader in the production of steel, oil, and coal. Soviet agriculture was less successful. Although mechanization constantly increased, periodic droughts, poor management, and lack of incentive forced the government to make repeated and expensive grain purchases from the United States and Canada. The standard of living rose, but it still trailed that of the West and even that of some of the satellite countries in Eastern Europe. Soviet citizens did, however, enjoy free education and medical services and relative job security. The Soviet Union continued to assert itself internationally as a world power, as indicated by its involvement and intervention in Czechoslovakia in 1968, Africa in the 1970s, Afghanistan in 1979, and Poland during the 1980s.

Eastern Europe The governments and economies of Eastern Europe were brought under Stalin's control and set up in imitation of the Soviet model during the late 1940s. Initially the Soviet Union drained off economic resources from these countries to strengthen its own economy. Soon single-party "people's democracies" were established in Poland, East Germany, Czechoslovakia, Hungary, Rumania, Yugoslavia, and Albania. Each of these governments was dominated by the head of its Communist party, who usually ruled in Stalinist fashion. Each country developed a planned economy stressing industrialization and collectivization of agriculture, and generally a high rate of economic growth was achieved. Each was required to cooperate politically, economically, and militarily with the Soviet Union. All major policies were tightly coordinated with the wishes of Moscow. Contact with the West was strictly limited. The one exception was Yugoslavia, where in 1948 Tito managed to break from the rest of the Communist bloc and take an independent course. Tito initiated a more decentralized form of communism stressing increased local control and worker participation in management.

Nevertheless, Eastern Europe was not a mere appendage to the Soviet Union, even during the Stalinist period. Each state had its own sense of nationalism, each had its own particular ethnic mix, and each had its own history. The Soviet Union did not find it easy to gain or maintain control.

The first stirrings of revolt against Soviet control followed Stalin's death. In 1953 East Berliners rose but were quickly crushed by force. Following Khrushchev's 1956 speech denouncing Stalin and some of his policies, Poland rose in revolt and asserted some independence from Moscow. A compromise left Poland within the Soviet sphere of control while avoiding the use of Soviet troops in Poland. Poland would enjoy a mild liberalization of its intellectual life and greater independence in determining its economic policies. Shortly thereafter, a more violent armed revolt took place in Hungary. This more challenging demand for independence was met by an invasion of troops and the ouster of the new government. Nevertheless, under the Moscow-approved but moderate János Kádár, Hungarians were allowed increased individual freedom and greater national self-determination.

These revolts revealed some of the discontent and hopes for greater independence within the Eastern European nations, but the Soviet response also indicated the allowable limits to any deviance from the Soviet line. National differences between the various Eastern European

FIGURE 56.4 Soviet Tanks in Prague Efforts by Czechoslovakia to reform its socialist system and gain greater independence from Moscow were brought to an end in August 1968 by a Soviet invasion. Here Soviet tanks overwhelm any potential resistance in the streets of Prague. (Josef Koudelka/Magnum)

states and the Soviet Union were recognized. Contact with the West would be allowed. Cultural activities might be less restricted than in the Soviet Union. But the fundamental political, economic, and military cooperation with Moscow was not to be violated.

After the late 1950s the various Eastern European nations pursued separate courses within the limits set by the Soviet Union. East Germany, Hungary, and Rumania remained relatively tranquil during the 1960s, 1970s, and early 1980s. East Germany has closely followed the Soviet line while developing its industrial capacity. Hungary managed to orient its economy toward consumer goods, due to a loosening of state control and the introduction of limited capitalistic practices at the local level. Rumania took a more politically independent and conservative course

under the leadership of president Nicolae Ceauşescu.

Albania, Czechoslovakia, and Poland were more of a problem to Moscow. In 1961 Albania, under Enver Hoxha, broke from Moscow and took the side of the Chinese in the Sino-Soviet split. Since Albania was surrounded by the already independent Yugoslavia and Greece, there was little the Soviet Union could do. In 1968 the Alexander Dubĉek government in Czechoslovakia went too far in allowing intellectual freedom and some democratization. The Soviet Union mobilized the troops of the Warsaw Pact nations and occupied Czechoslovakia (see Figure 56.4). Dubĉek and his supporters, along with their liberalizing policies, were removed from power. In 1980 the Polish government began to have difficulty maintaining its control over the nation.

Mainly protesting the continuing economic mismanagement and corruption within the government, Polish workers struck and organized a union, Solidarity, under the leadership of Lech Wałesa. Solidarity became increasingly powerful and was succeeding in forcing the government to grant concessions. When the union seemed to be going too far, pressure from Moscow and resistance from conservative elements in the Polish government stiffened. In December 1981 martial law was declared by the new leader of the Polish Communist party, General Wojciech Jaruzelski. After a series of governmental crackdowns, Solidarity was outlawed in October 1982.

In the mid-1980s, most of the Eastern European nations remained Communist and under the shadow of the Soviet Union. This, as we shall see in a later chapter, would soon change.

3. INTEGRATION AND INTERNATIONAL ORGANIZATIONS

In the years following World War II it became evident that there were advantages to dealing with problems cooperatively and through international organizations. The European nations had long suffered from competitive nationalistic rivalries. The world in 1945 was no longer a place where a country such as Great Britain or France was strong enough to get its own way. The developing Cold War was forcing countries to take sides whether or not they wanted to. After the destruction of World War II and particularly under the new threat of atomic weapons, the international pursuit of peace seemed even more pressing.

During the 1940s and 1950s a number of cooperative international organizations were formed. Some were military, such as NATO (an alliance of the United States, Canada, and the non-Communist nations of Europe) and its counterpart, the Warsaw Pact (an alliance of the Soviet Union and the Communist nations it dominated in Eastern Europe). Others were economic, such as the Organization for European Economic Cooperation (for coordination among the recipients of Marshall Plan funds) and the Council for Mutual Economic Assistance, or COMECON (the Soviet response to the Marshall Plan). The

most important of these organizations were the efforts toward the integration of Western Europe and the United Nations.

European Integration

In 1949 several nations in Western Europe took an initial step toward political integration by setting up the Council of Europe. Many hoped that this organization would develop into a parliament of Europe with real political power. However, the major European nations were unwilling to give the council significant power, and it remained an organization of potential.

Western Europe was more successful in taking steps toward economic integration. In 1950 France and Germany created the French-German Coal and Steel Authority. In 1952 it was expanded into the European Coal and Steel Community with the addition of Italy, Belgium, Luxembourg, and the Netherlands. In 1957 these same six nations signed the Treaty of Rome establishing the European Economic Community (the Common Market). Its purpose was to eliminate tariff barriers, cut restrictions on the flow of labor and capital, and generally integrate the economies of the member nations. The organization was a surprising success in the 1960s, eliminating tariff and immigration barriers ahead of schedule while its member nations enjoyed relative prosperity. During the 1970s and 1980s other nations joined the Common Market: Great Britain, Ireland, and Denmark in 1973; Greece in 1981; Portugal and Spain in 1986.

The United Nations

In 1945 the world's leaders set up the United Nations to provide for international cooperation and act as a watchdog over peace. It did an enormous amount of work in economic, cultural, and humanitarian fields, most of which did not make headlines. It assisted in arranging cease-fires in several conflicts between Israel and the Arab states and helped stop wars between India and Pakistan, and the Netherlands and Indonesia. Under the leadership of the United States, it fought in the Korean War, 1950–1953 (see pp. 739–740). In recent years the United Nations has won prestige for its effective role in areas of conflict such as the Middle East (particularly in facilitating the cease-fire between Iran and Iraq in 1988), southern Africa, and the western Sahara. Yet from the beginning the United Nations has been hampered by the unwillingness of the major powers to submit to its authority, embodied formally in the right of the permanent members of the Security Council to veto any action involv-

ing the use of force or the threat of force. Often it has proven unable to prevent wars or assert its will over defiant nations. The United Nations has reflected more than controlled the domestic and international problems of its member nations over the past forty years.

SUGGESTED READING

General

W. Laqueur, *Europe since Hitler* (1982). A scholarly, respected survey.

D. Urwin, *Western Europe since 1945: A Political History* (1989). A full political survey.

J. R. Wegs, *Europe since 1945* (1983). A concise survey.

The Settlement and the Cold War

W. Lafeber, *America, Russia, and the Cold War, 1945–1966* (1978). A revisionist interpretation.

B. Weisberger, *Cold War, Cold Peace: The United States and Russia since 1945* (1984). A good general account.

D. Yergin, *The Shattered Peace* (1977). A balanced, well-written study of the Cold War.

Revival of a Divided Europe and the West

R. Aron, *The Imperial Republic: The United States and the World, 1945–1973* (1974). A sophisticated analysis of American dominance.

T. Ash, *The Polish Revolution: Solidarity* (1984). A full account.

S. Cohen, *Rethinking the Soviet Experience: Politics and History Since 1917* (1985). Analyzes the debates in Soviet studies.

W. Connor, *Socialism, Politics and Equality: Hierarchy and Change in Eastern Europe and the USSR* (1979). A good account.

A. W. De Porte, *Europe Between the Superpowers: The Enduring Balance* (1979). A good analysis of Europe in the context of the superpowers.

A. H. Halsey, *Change in British Society* (1981). A solid study.

D. L. Hanley et al., eds., *France: Politics and Society Since 1945* (1979). A good collection of essays.

J. Hough and M. Fainsod, *How the Soviet Union Is Governed* (1978). A useful general study.

W. Leonhard, *Three Faces of Communism* (1974). Analyzes the ideological divisions of the Communist world.

A. Marwick, *British Society Since 1945* (1982). A good survey.

A. Milward, *The Reconstruction of Western Europe, 1945–1951* (1984). A fine study.

T. Rakowska-Harmstone and A. Gyorgy, eds., *Communism in Eastern Europe* (1984). Covers each country.

H. Turner, Jr., *The Two Germanies since 1945* (1987). A good political history.

Integration and International Organizations

R. Mowat, *Creating the European Community* (1973). A study of European integration.

C. Tugenhat, *Making Sense of Europe* (1986). An evaluation of the Common Market.

CHAPTER 57

Society and Culture in the Twentieth Century

FIGURE 57.1 Don Eddy, "New Shoes for H," 1973–1974 This painting of a shoe store display in Manhattan reveals several trends of contemporary society and culture. The environment is one of urbanism and commercialism. The effect of the windowpanes is to show things from different perspectives and to distort. The style, photorealism, combines technology and the newest painting techniques. (The Cleveland Museum of Art)

Social, intellectual, and cultural trends have followed two broad patterns since World War I. Until 1945, there was a widespread sense of anxiety, disillusionment, and uncertainty in the West. In part, these feelings were an extension of a trend already developing in the two or three decades prior to World War I, but after World War I they were no longer confined to elite intellectual and cultural circles. They were also a reflection of the social turmoil and sense of decay that spread and deepened in frightening ways after 1914. Much of the art, literature, philosophy, and even science of the 1920s and 1930s reflected this insecurity, this doubting of established values, this questioning of the future.

Since 1945 social, intellectual, and cultural trends have been marked by a complex mixture of continuity and change. There is still much of the disillusionment and anxiety that characterized the earlier decades of the twentieth century. At the same time, there has developed a new sense of experimentation and productivity, which reflects the lessening of social turmoil and a greater sense of stability compared with the difficult decades prior to World War II.

With these two broad patterns in mind, let us attempt to identify and explore some of the social, religious, intellectual, and cultural developments of Western civilization in the twentieth century.

1. WESTERN SOCIETY IN THE TWENTIETH CENTURY

Demographic and Social Changes

Population in the West has been growing since World War I, but at varying rates. The broad pattern shows a slowing down of population growth as societies became more fully modernized, a pattern that has been evident in some countries since the end of the nineteenth century. During the 1940s and 1950s birthrates in most Western countries were relatively high (the "baby boom"), leading to an increase in the population. During the 1960s birthrates started to decline and reverse, to the point in the 1970s, 1980s, and 1990s where several countries have birthrates that are sufficient only to maintain the population or that will result in a declining population. Some governments, such as that of France, have encouraged larger families with financial aid. This encouragement of larger families probably came more from cultural and racial concerns than economic need, for immigrants were available and used to expand the labor pool. Changes in the makeup of the population are also evident. As a result of improved life expectancy, populations in the West have been growing older on the average, giving elderly persons' groups more potential political power and making the social needs of the elderly more pressing.

Perhaps more important than population changes have been changes in where and how people live. Urbanization has increased in recent decades. Large cities have been swollen by migration from rural areas and immigration from southern areas. Northern European cities have absorbed large numbers of people from southern Italy, Greece, Turkey, and Africa, just as cities in North America have been expanded by people from Latin America and Asia. With the people have come the traditional urban problems: congestion, overburdened transportation systems, insufficient social services, pollution, crime, and inadequate housing. At times the inner core of great cities has deteriorated and even suffered a decline in population, but this has usually been more than matched by the growth of surrounding suburbs. New shopping and industrial centers have grown up in the periphery of the older cities and even on the fringes of older suburbs. In reference to cities such as Paris, London, New York, and Moscow, it has become more accurate to include the metropolitan areas around them rather than merely the city itself.

In recent decades the most modern societies in the West have been termed "postindustrial," to emphasize the declining importance of traditional manufacturing industries and the growing importance of providing services—often through the use of high technology. The key figures in this postindustrial society are financiers, technicians, managers, and professionals rather than industrial entrepreneurs.

There have also been some broad shifts in the social classes that make up Western society. Generally, the shift has been away from rural classes to urban classes, away from traditional industrial jobs to service and white-collar jobs, and away from small firms toward corporate and governmental organizations. Class distinctions remain but are less clear than before. Society has become generally more mobile, both geographically and socially. While birth into wealth and position remains a great advantage, education or technical skill has increasingly become a relatively democratic avenue for social mobility.

In Western Europe and the United States the very wealthy have generally managed to retain or even improve their position at the top of society despite the growth of social welfare programs and efforts in some countries to lessen the gap between rich and poor. Most of the remnants of the traditional aristocracy have disappeared or merged with the wealthy upper middle class. While this elite class retains some protective barriers against intrusion from below and maintains itself through the aid of inheritance, it is increasingly being joined by a newer elite of corporate and governmental managers, successful professionals, and those with high scientific or technological expertise. These people tend to be highly educated, pragmatic, with a stake in the status quo, and yet always threatened by their younger, more recently educated competitors in the corporate or bureaucratic hierarchy.

Just below these elites is the bulk of the middle class. Made up primarily of middle- and lower-level managers in corporate and governmental bureaucracies, those who hold salaried white-collar jobs in services, and professionals in a growing number of fields, this class has grown substantially. Entrance into this class is gained primarily through education, specialization, and technical expertise.

Since the end of World War II the industrial working class has generally seen an improvement in its standard of living and, at least until the 1960s, relative job security. Yet its ranks were thinning as the traditional industrial base eroded, forcing many to become service workers or enter the bottom level of white-collar employment. As economic problems became more acute in the 1970s, the early 1980s, and again in the 1990s, industrial workers faced unemployment matched only by pre–World War II statistics and declines in real income that had to be compensated for by more married women entering the paid work force. As they have grown more affluent, the distinction between them and the lower middle class has lessened: The incomes, diets, housing, leisure-time activities, and often even political affiliations of the two classes are becoming similar. Yet the working class has remained distinct in many ways; it has fewer opportunities for social mobility and greater frustrations at the workplace.

Some of the problems faced by workers has been brought into focus by the influx of immigrants. After the 1950s, many of Western Europe's laborers were immigrants drawn by the lure of jobs from southern Europe and other places such as Turkey, North Africa, and former colonies where economic circumstances were often desperate. They filled the lowest-paid and least desirable jobs. Women were particularly vulnerable to exploitation. Often immigrants were not encouraged to put down roots and become assimilated. Rising unemployment in the recessionary years of the 1970s, 1980s, and 1990s created new pressures on this pool of immigrant workers. Laws were passed to restrict further immigration. The millions who remained or managed to get in anyway increasingly suffered racial and anti-immigrant attacks and became the victims of right-wing political movements such as France's National Front.

In many countries there remained a core of inner-city slum dwellers. They were usually without regular jobs, often marked by race or ethnic origin, and subject to the worst problems of urban life. In recent years there have been disturbing signs that this core of often homeless urban poor is growing.

The decline of rural populations has continued, with variations in each country. Generally, agricultural productivity has been increasing, lessening the need for people on the farms. Many rural people have moved into the cities, leaving a small percentage of the population to grow food for the rest and for export. Those who have adjusted to the changing rural life—by mechanizing, enlarging their land holdings, joining cooperatives, and specializing—have enjoyed an uneven but generally rising standard of living. But there remains a core of rural poor who have not adjusted to the agricultural changes since World War II or who have fallen victim to economic forces beyond their control. Rural life has also become less isolated with the spread of highways, cars, telephones, radio, and television.

In Eastern Europe social changes followed the model established in Russia after the revolution in 1917. The traditional landed aristocracy disappeared rapidly as their lands were taken away and redistributed or nationalized. Large collectivized farms arose. The Eastern European states nationalized the factories, the banks, the commercial houses, and the large retail outlets of the middle class. The distinctions between urban classes were lessened as the state standardized basic housing, social services, consumption, and even leisure activities. Nevertheless, a new privileged order arose. High-level party and governmental leaders, certain professionals, and the cultural elite enjoyed more access to consumer goods, improved housing, better educational opportunities, and greater political influence than the rest of the population. This social inequality within these Eastern European socialist societies has been a source of discontent and turmoil in recent years.

The Family

Since World War I, and in particular over the past few decades, the family in the West has become smaller, more mobile, and less stable. Although people still tend to marry within their social, religious, and ethnic groups and with an eye toward economic considerations, emotional attraction continues to grow as the primary consideration in mate selection. In the past few decades sexual fulfillment has been added as an increasingly important condition for marriage and its continuation. The development of new methods of contraception, particularly the contraceptive pill in the 1960s, and the accompanying acceptance of the idea of contraception (and, to a lesser extent, abortion) have given women and men greater sexual freedom and choice over marriage and childbearing. Since the baby boom of the immediate post–World War II years, married couples have had fewer children on average. The nuclear family—the couple and its children—has become more geographically mobile, and ties to extended family members such as grandparents, uncles, aunts, and cousins have become more distant. Other institutions, such as the school, the university, peer groups, family courts, family therapists, child psychologists, and day care centers, have grown to take over

functions that the family used to perform more exclusively.

The increase in premarital sex, cohabitation, gay lifestyles, divorce, and nontraditional family arrangements, as well as a recent trend toward declining marriage rates and postponing marriage and childbearing have led many to question the viability of the modern family. The single-parent household and the childless household are gaining acceptance. The rate of divorce has risen sharply since World War II, particularly since the 1960s. Yet the family is not disappearing, as some critics have argued. Rather, its form and its functions are evolving, as are the roles its members, particularly women, are expected to play.

Women

Some of the most important social changes have involved the role of women within the family and in society as a whole. In both World War I and World War II women assumed jobs and responsibilities previously thought beyond their "legitimate sphere," but with the return of the soldiers they were pressured to return to their more traditional domestic roles. However, the long-run trend in the twentieth century, and particularly since the 1950s, has been for women to enter the paid work force in a greater variety of jobs. In particular, married women have been moving out of their middle-class roles as housekeepers, child rearers, and supporters of their income-producing husbands. The female wage-earning work force is no longer dominated by the young and single, as it was earlier in the twentieth century. With a growing life expectancy (now over seventy-five years in most Western countries), more women have been turning to "second careers" at middle age, often involving a return to school to acquire new skills. Well over 50 percent of all married women in the United States now work outside the home, a dramatic increase from pre–World War II levels and a pattern that has generally prevailed in the West. Women, both married and unmarried, are moving into jobs that were once the almost exclusive domain of men, from the legal and medical professions to all varieties of blue-collar work. However, discrimination based on gender is far from over. Women remain underrepre-

FIGURE 57.2 French Women's Movement The women's movement since the 1960s has been international. Here French women demonstrate for equal pay with men for equal work. (Martine Franck/Magnum)

sented in most higher-paying, higher-status occupations and still earn only between 60 and 80 percent of men's salaries. And more often than not, women who work outside the home still remain responsible for most of the domestic work at home.

The women's liberation movement, gaining force since the 1960s, has made many women more conscious of their common concerns (see Figure 57.2). Generally, this movement demands that women no longer be oppressed or considered second-class citizens, whether in their political rights, the wages they earn, the positions they hold, or the attitudes they or their society share. This movement has struggled not only to open political, economic, and social life to all, regardless of sex, but also to change stereotypical portrayals of femininity and common assumptions about differences between the sexes that contribute to barriers facing women. Feminists have led the struggles to liberalize divorce laws and to legalize contraception and abortion and have pushed for changes in scholarship to reflect women's concerns and perspectives.

In some ways women's circumstances differed in the Soviet Union and Eastern Europe, while in some ways they were the same. More Soviet women worked, sometimes in traditionally elite occupations such as medicine, and held

political positions than in the West. Nevertheless, they usually received lower pay than men and were expected to maintain their traditional roles at home. For the most part they were kept out of higher political positions. Feminism as a political or social movement scarcely touched them.

These changes are of great potential significance to women and, by necessity, to men. As with most fundamental historical changes, they will take a long time to have full effect. The changes women are initiating will require numerous subtle changes in the way we raise our children and the messages our culture transmits about gender and sex roles.

Youth and Education

One of the institutions most affected by social changes, and in particular changes in the family, has been education. Schools have been expected to adapt to social and economic changes and take up functions that were once handled by parents as part of child rearing. Schools are expected to assist children who have emotional, social, and family problems as well as purely academic problems.

With the growing demands for democratization of educational opportunities, universities have had to open their doors to more than the traditional elite. The number of students attending college and going on for advanced degrees has increased dramatically since World War II. Universities have had to change their curricula to fit the new demands of a mobile society and a modern economy. The strains on universities were particularly great in the 1960s, when students in many Western nations combined discontent with the university with attitudes critical of the values and behavior of their parents' generation. Students attacked the lack of humaneness, the restrictive behavior and values, the social inequities, and the competitive impersonality of the traditional adult world of their parents as represented by the large, bureaucratized, impersonal university. They criticized governmental policies and rallied around issues such as opposition to the Vietnam War and support for national liberation movements in the non-Western world. The numerous demonstrations and disruptions of university life often spread into the surrounding communities, involving clashes with police and other public authorities. The most dramatic confrontations took place in 1968 in France, where a student revolt threatened to overturn the government, particularly when students gained the sympathetic, if temporary, support of workers. The government eventually retained control, but numerous reforms of universities in France and elsewhere were instituted in the late 1960s and early 1970s. Since then student activism has diminished. Students have veered away from the traditional liberal arts curriculum and have become more concerned with preparing for careers in an increasingly competitive economic environment. Programs and majors in fields such as business administration, computer science, and the professions have proliferated.

Social Welfare

After World War I and particularly after World War II, trends toward increased governmental responsibility for social welfare accelerated. Most countries increased their traditional social security benefits for unemployment, retirement, sickness, and old age. Government expenditures for education expanded. In some countries, particularly Great Britain, steps were taken to ensure that medical services were available to all. New governmental programs were established to provide family allowances, maternity grants, and low-income housing.

In general, governments began to be held responsible for providing a floor of social and economic well-being below which their citizens should not be allowed to fall. The expanded role of the state in providing a large array of social services within an economic system that still remained substantially capitalistic has been termed the creation of the "welfare state." The degree of involvement varied in each country. The governments of the Communist nations in Eastern Europe assumed the most control over social and economic matters, but the services they could provide were limited by the economic well-being of the nation. Among the nations of Western Europe the Scandinavian countries generally went the furthest in providing social services for their citizens. The United States, with its own particular problems and aversion to programs that hint of socialism, lagged behind in governmental provision of social services.

Of course, these services came at a price. Taxes rose to pay for them. Governmental bureaucracies grew to administer them. Moreover, critics question the quality of some of the services provided, particularly medical services. Yet once established, such social programs were rarely reversed—although the Reagan administration in the United States during the 1980s made efforts to do just that.

However, efforts by governments to promote social welfare did not end the persistant social problems. In addition to poverty, the high rate of crime and the proliferation of drug abuse in recent decades attest to the sense of alienation and dissatisfaction in many Western societies. In the 1980s and 1990s the spread of AIDS has challenged the ability of government and science to solve difficult new problems.

2. RELIGION AND THEOLOGY IN THE TWENTIETH CENTURY

Christianity remained an important religious force in Western civilization despite the secularization that took place during the twentieth century. However, in the long run, Christian churches as institutions have continued to suffer

FIGURE 57.3 Areas such as Africa and Latin America have gained increasing attention within the Catholic church in recent decades. Here, in one of his many trips outside of Europe, John Paul II rides in a motorcade in Zaire. (UPI/Bettmann Newsphotos)

a decline in influence in the West, particularly since World War II. Strenuous efforts were made to restore some of the lost unity of Christendom to enable the Christian church to face its problems with a united front. In 1948 leaders of hundreds of Protestant and Orthodox denominations met in Geneva and set up the World Council of Churches. The most spectacular step in this direction was taken by Pope John XXIII (1958–1963), who called the Second Vatican Council (1962–1965) in the spirit of Christian tolerance and unity. Although John XXIII died during the first year of the council and was succeeded by Paul VI (1963–1978), who was a less vigorous innovator, the Second Vatican Council introduced an ecumenical spirit into the Catholic church and showed a willingness to modernize the ritual and discipline that had been formalized by the Council of Trent in the sixteenth century. When Paul VI died in 1978, the College of Cardinals elected John Paul I, a man of great personal charm, who lived less than a month. The new pope, John Paul II, a Pole, was the first non-Italian pope since the early sixteenth century. Relatively young, forceful, and knowledgeable, John Paul II has traveled extensively, particularly to politically controversial areas such as Africa,

Central America, and Poland (see Figure 57.3). He has managed to convey an image of renewed dynamism and activism in the Catholic church. Nevertheless, he has been conservative in matters of faith and morals, refusing to liberalize Church policy toward theological doctrines, the priesthood, the family, and sex.

Theology in the Western world during the twentieth century for the most part reflected the materialism of the age and the influence of existentialist philosophy. Strong efforts were made to update Christian theology by making it a more secular philosophy. Paul Tillich (1886–1965), a German Protestant who spent his later years in the United States, conceived of God as "ultimate truth" and "inner reality." Such traditional terms as *original sin, salvation, forgiveness, immortality,* and *atonement* were useful symbols under his pen, actually referring to personal and social ethics. Harvey Cox (1929–) of Harvard University, in his widely read *The Secular City* (1965), defined Christianity as a continuing social revolution. During the 1960s numerous religious cults, some of them quite wealthy and some violent, sprang up to offer companionship and certainty in this materialistic, competitive, perplexing world.

On the other hand, a few powerful voices

FIGURE 57.4 Moon Walk In July 1969 human beings walked on the moon. The United States' Apollo 11 moon mission is an example of the powerful combination of government and science. (NASA)

called for a return to an enlightened orthodox Christianity, notably the neo-Calvinists Karl Barth (1886–1968) in Switzerland and Reinhold Niebuhr (1892–1971) in the United States. God, they said, created the universe and runs it for his holy purpose, but selfish pride separates human beings from God. Only the Christian religion can remove that pride and bring men and women into God's purpose. Jacques Maritain (1882–1973) in France called for a return to the teachings of St. Thomas Aquinas. These learned theologians contributed dignity to the continuing claims of traditional Christianity.

3. TWENTIETH-CENTURY SCIENCE

After World War I most scientific research was still carried out by individuals or small groups of scientists in a university setting. There was a sense of separation between the theoretical and applied sciences, between the research carried out by the best scientific minds and the later application of their discoveries by engineers or technicians. After World War II, that pattern would be modified by closer ties between science and technology and by a new infusion of funds for scientific research by government and big business (see Figure 57.4). Scientists tended to work in organized teams, in larger research laboratories with extremely expensive and sophisticated equipment, and with specific goals in mind. These trends are most clear in the physical sciences, particularly physics.

In the two decades after World War I, the main thrust in physics was to continue the probing of the atom, which was begun in the nineteenth century, to discover the truths concerning the nature of matter. The results tended to be disillusioning. Albert Einstein had undermined the Newtonian world of physical stability with his relativity theory (see p. 587). A more shattering blow was delivered by Max Planck (1858–1947). Although he published his quantum theory in 1900, its full impact was not realized until the decades following World War I. According to this theory, energy is transmitted not in a steady, measurable stream, as had long been supposed, but in little leaps or packets (quanta), and the behavior of subatomic particles is so irregular and complex that the ultimate secrets of nature can never be fathomed by objective observation. In 1919 Ernest Rutherford (1871–1937) opened the world of subatomic particles and the possibility of changing the structure of atoms by bombarding them with subatomic particles. The sense of relativity and uncertainty in physics was furthered by Werner Heisenberg (1901–1976), who in 1927 formulated the "principle of uncertainty." He argued that any model or measurement of atoms was inherently approximate and relative.

Since World War II, teams of physicists have used huge, powerful, expensive accelerators to explore the subatomic world to a far greater degree than was possible before the war. Astrophysicists combined computer and radio telescope technology to expand our understanding of the universe. At the same time, many of these scientists were employed by government and industry to create new, more destructive weapons of war or products, such as computer chips and superconductors, that are of economic importance to our consumer society.

The most exciting discoveries in the biological sciences were in the field of genetics. In 1953 the nature of the complicated DNA molecule, which controls the pattern of all living things, was discovered. It is assumed that by tampering with this molecule new forms of life may be created, and that given characteristics in all living things, including humans, can be controlled. Recent research into gene splitting and genetic engineering gives truth to this assumption.

The most beneficial discoveries in the field of biological science during the twentieth century have been those that prevent and cure human ailments. Viruses were isolated, and their role in causing many diseases, including infantile paralysis, influenza, and the common cold, was recognized. Vaccines were developed to combat the infantile paralysis virus and a number of others

successfully—but the common cold still plagues most of humanity. During the late 1920s and the 1930s penicillin and sulfa drugs were discovered. These "miracle drugs" kill or control the bacteria causing many human infections. Since World War II drugs have been found useful in treating mental illness, and artificial and transplanted kidneys and hearts have saved or lengthened many lives.

The chief drawback in the application of these wonderful discoveries has been their high and continually soaring cost and the shortage of trained personnel to administer them. Many nations, Great Britain and Sweden among the first, recognized the enormous importance of public health by developing comprehensive programs of national health insurance. Communist regimes, of course, always made the practice of medicine a public rather than a private matter.

The social sciences have continued to emphasize the application of the methods being used so successfully in the natural sciences—rigorous empirical research, inductive and deductive reasoning, conclusions couched in the value-free language of relativism and probabilities. In recent decades, three new approaches have been used in several of the social sciences. The first is an extension of previous methods—quantitative research aided by computers and newly developed statistical tools. Computers have enabled researchers to work with massive quantities of materials and factors. Statistical tools have sharpened the probability or predictability of their conclusions. The second is structuralism, which stresses the rules or the forms of behavior rather than the specific content. The third is relativism, which rejects universal values and assumes that societies and cultures should be viewed within their own time, place, and context.

Of all the social scientists, the sociologists and anthropologists have been the most optimistic and energetic. Like other social scientists, they attempted to apply the scientific method to the study of human behavior. Max Weber (1864–1920) of Germany set up ideal types or models as a method of scientifically analyzing various sociological problems—a method that has been widely used ever since. Émile Durkheim (1858–1917) established a sociological tradition emphasizing the use of statistics for analyzing social behavior. Karl Mannheim (1893–1947), a refugee from Nazi Germany to Great Britain, developed a sociology of knowledge. He argued that ideas are related to and influenced by social forces to a much greater degree than had been suspected. Anthropologists tended to move from their earlier measurements of skulls and other physical features to the concept that differing cultures are based essentially on differing ways of interpreting experience and adapting to the environment. Claude Lévi-Strauss, perhaps the most influential anthropologist of recent decades, used a structuralist perspective to analyze the forms and rules of culture.

Between World War I and the 1950s psychology continued to be strongly influenced by Freudian theory and practice, which emphasized the irrational, unconscious, sexual, and aggressive elements in human thought and behavior. Behaviorism was also growing, and by the 1960s it overshadowed Freudianism. In the past two decades so many theories, approaches, therapies, and subdisciplines have proliferated within psychology that no single trend can be identified as dominant. Perhaps the most promising discoveries in recent years have been in physiological psychology. With so many people turning inward for answers and with secular explanations for human behavior deemed so important, psychology remains a field of growing influence.

Of all the social sciences, economics has taken most advantage of computer-aided quantitative research and sophisticated statistical tools. It is also the social science that most directly influences policy. Both governmental and private institutions rely on economists for the decisions they make. Underlying the quantitative research and statistical tools used by economists are more fundamental economic theories. Since the 1930s Keynesian economic thought has been most influential in countries with capitalistic or mixed economies. In 1936, in the midst of the Great Depression, John Maynard Keynes (1883–1946) published *The General Theory of Employment, Interest and Money*, advocating government regulation of the capitalistic system. He claimed that in times of recession the government should increase the supply of money in circulation by lowering interest rates and by deficit spending on public works. In times of inflationary boom it

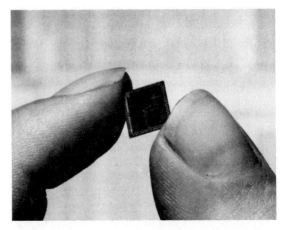

FIGURE 57.5 The Computer The development of tiny computer chips such as this has resulted in vast changes in science, business, and industry. (Charles Feil/Stock, Boston)

should restrict the money supply by raising interest rates and by other means. Liberals, not only in Keynes' native Britain but throughout the capitalistic world, accepted his theories, as indeed did many conservatives. But by the late 1970s and early 1980s it appeared that Keynesian theory could not account for many economic problems, particularly the combination of inflation and economic stagnation (with accompanying unemployment) that many termed "stagflation." Some theorists have called for greater governmental controls over wages and prices as well as general economic planning; others have attacked governmental involvement in the economy as doing more harm than good.

Probably the most important new tool for both the natural and social sciences is the computer (see Figure 57.5). The computer first became a tool of significance in the 1940s. By the 1950s and 1960s it was becoming linked with modern technology in a variety of ways, with a strong impact on the sciences and in the economy. With the new developments in computer technology, particularly miniaturization, the use of computers proliferated in almost all fields of science during the 1970s, 1980s, and 1990s. Its ability to store and manipulate information has made the computer a necessity rather than a luxury for most scientists. Yet it is still no more than a tool. The scientist must feed the computer the right information, ask useful questions, and interpret the answers.

4. TWENTIETH-CENTURY CULTURE

Philosophy

Philosophical thought in the twentieth century has been dominated by three trends, all of which can be traced back to the period just before World War I (see pp. 597–598 and 684). The first trend, which has clearly prevailed in Great Britain and the United States, is a combination of analytical philosophy and logical positivism. Analytical philosophy was first developed by Alfred North Whitehead (1861–1947) and Bertrand Russell (1872–1970) of Great Britain on the eve of World War I. The outstanding philosopher of logical positivism (or logical empiricism) was Ludwig Wittgenstein (1889–1951). Both analytical philosophy and logical positivism spurned any concept that could not be rationally and mathematically expressed. Under the influence of these doctrines, philosophy became highly technical, focusing on the exact meaning of words and logical relationships rather than the broad and ethical questions that traditionally concerned philosophers.

The second trend, which became more dominant on the European continent, is existentialism. Existentialism has its roots in the disenchantment of the late nineteenth century and the environment of anxiety resulting from the two world wars, the Great Depression, and the tensions of the Cold War. Existentialism drew heavily from Friedrich Nietzsche, who argued that there were no absolutes when he said "God is dead." Existential philosophy was also influenced by the mid–nineteenth-century Danish theologian Søren Kierkegaard, who rejected systematized and institutionalized Christianity in favor of personal inspiration and individual commitment. In Germany during the 1920s Martin Heidegger and Karl Jaspers developed aspects of existentialist philosophy. Thereafter, the center of existentialist thought shifted to France.

The most influential existentialist philosopher has been Jean-Paul Sartre (1905–1980). He argued that ultimately there is no meaning to existence and no final rights or wrongs. Individuals are born and simply exist. Individuals are free and responsible for the decisions and actions they take in life. Individuals must establish their own standards and their own rules, and each must take responsibility for living up to them. In the end, one simply dies.

The third trend, which has been a school of philosophy of varying strength, is Marxism (see pp. 527–528). Marxism emphasized historical determinism, ethical relativism, and social meaning behind philosophical concepts. During the 1920s and 1930s, it grew in influence in several academic circles and disciplines. Since World War II its influence has waxed and waned, and its doctrines have been modified in several ways. But on the whole, it has remained influential as a philosophical and historical perspective in a variety of disciplines.

Literature

The literature of the twentieth century, like the philosophy, is essentially an outgrowth and continuation of the literature of the late nineteenth century. A number of the great realistic writers of the early twentieth century lived and wrote until the middle of the century. The realism that had shocked many Victorians was succeeded by the more starkly naked naturalism. The focus tended to shift to a more subjective point of view and to the feelings, uncertainties, and unconscious motives of individuals.

In English-speaking Europe, James Joyce (1882–1941), an Irish expatriate in Paris, Virginia Woolf (1882–1941), an English novelist and critic, and T. S. Eliot (1888–1965), an American expatriate in London, developed the stream-of-consciousness technique. They placed words and thoughts out of sequence, providing new insights into the psyche with dramatic effect. This method clearly reflected the introspection of Freudian psychology.

In Germany, Franz Kafka (1883–1924) depicted the alienation and frustrations of an intellectual in the World War I era. The haunting, ambiguous quality of his fiction symbolizes the uncertainties and fears of his age. Most of his work was published after his death, and he enjoyed wide popularity only after World War II. Hermann Hesse (1877–1962) also reflected the uncertainty and sense of alienation in Germany during the World War I era in his novels. His writings, particularly those stressing a youthful and psychologically insightful search for meaning in a life always threatened by despair, became particularly popular after World War II. Perhaps the towering figure of twentieth-century German literature was Thomas Mann (1875–1955). His style and content were more traditional than that of Kafka or Hesse, always stressing a reverence for human beings in the often distressing environment of Mann's lifetime.

In France, Marcel Proust (1871–1922) developed introspective writing to new depths in his influential *Remembrance of Things Past.* In seven volumes of exquisitely polished prose he subjects to withering psychological analysis the remnants of French noble society and the vulgar social-climbing *nouveau riche* bourgeoisie who were trying to imitate the nobility. During the 1940s and 1950s, Albert Camus (1913–1960) popularized existentialism in his novels and plays, stressing the plight of the individual seeking understanding and identity in an amoral and purposeless universe. One of the leading playwrites of the era, the Irishman Samuel Beckett (1906–1990), also lived in France. He helped develop perhaps the most important trend in plays written since World War II—the "Theater of the Absurd." In works such as *Waiting for Godot* (1952), Beckett used unconventional staging and writing to break from traditionally realistic action. Audiences were forced to focus on what might be happening and how it might relate to human feelings and problems of existence. In this sense, the "Theater of the Absurd" reflected similar concerns expressed by existentialists. During the 1960s writers such as Alain Robbe-Grillet and film directors such as François Truffaut and Jean-Luc Godard made France the center of the *nouvelle vague* (new wave) in literature and film, stressing experimentation and imaginative techniques.

In the Soviet Union, Boris Pasternak (1890–1960) wrote in the grand manner of Tolstoy and Dostoyevski. His most well-known novel is *Doctor Zhivago*, which traces life in Russia before, during, and after the Bolshevik Revolution in 1917. More recently, Alexander Solzhenitsyn (1919–), who has lived in the United States since his expulsion from the Soviet Union in 1974, has written novels critically depicting life in the Soviet Union during the Stalinist era.

In the United States Sinclair Lewis (1885–1951), much like Theodore Dreiser, ridiculed both the hypocritical and "puritanical" bourgeoisie and the stupid, vulgar masses. Babbitt, Elmer Gantry, and Arrowsmith, the deflated heroes of Sinclair Lewis' novels by those titles, became stereotypes of typical Americans in the minds of thousands of atypical American readers of books. Eugene O'Neill (1888–1953) wrote plays in which the dramatic tension was maintained by psychological conflict (like those of Anton Chekhov—see p. 600) rather than development of plot and action. Ernest Hemingway (1898–1961) was an existentialist, entertaining his readers with his crisp, sophisticated prose. William Faulkner (1897–1962), with great depth and artistry, tore away the veil woven by civilization to conceal the violent and animallike nature of ordinary people. He extended the complex stream-of-consciousness technique.

The Fine Arts

The fine arts of the Western world in the twentieth century, like the philosophy and the literature, have generally proceeded along the guidelines laid down by the artists and writers of the late nineteenth century—disenchantment, rejection of tradition, a search for new values, and experimentation. These characteristics have become intensified by the materialism and the uncertainties of the twentieth century.

Without a doubt, the most gifted and influential painter of the twentieth century was Pablo Picasso (1881–1973) (see Figure 57.6). A Spaniard, he emigrated to Paris as a young man. There he was influenced by the French postimpressionists (see pp. 600–601). In order to penetrate the surface and reveal the inner reality of things, Picasso would take his subjects apart—arms, heads, violin parts—and rearrange and distort them for maximum effect. Early in the century,

FIGURE 57.6 Picasso's *Guernica* This large mural in black and white by one of the greatest artists of the twentieth century captures some of the worst features of the century—war, terror, brutality, disjointedness, lack of direction, and despair. Guernica was a small Spanish town destroyed by the German air force during the Spanish Civil War. (Museo Nacional del Prado)

at about the same time that young Whitehead and Russell were proclaiming their analytic philosophy based on mathematics, Picasso introduced cubism into the world of painting (see Figure 52.1). This technique was an effort, suggested by Cézanne, to demonstrate the solidity of the material universe by portraying the geometric composition of objects—spheres, cones, and cylinders. Cubism suggests the twentieth century's obsession with science.

Another prominent style of twentieth-century painting came to be called surrealism, whose chief proponents were Max Ernst (1891–1976) (see Color Plate 29), a German who later moved to the United States, and Salvador Dali (1904–1989) (see Color Plate 30), a Spaniard who lived many years in the United States. The surrealists, under the influence of Freud and his psychoanalytical techniques, attempted to express their imagination uncontrolled by reason and to suggest the activities of the subconscious mind, whether dreaming or awake. Picasso and Matisse, who were really laws unto themselves, painted many canvases in the surrealist style.

A third popular twentieth-century style of painting was expressionism, which had its origin in northern Europe, particularly Germany (see Figure 53.2). Its chief proponent was Vasili Kandinsky (1866–1944), a Russian who came to live in Germany. The expressionists, motivated by inner necessity, attempted to express freely their emotional reactions rather than the representation of the natural appearance of objects, resorting to abstraction and to violent distortion of color and form.

In recent decades, artistic styles such as pop art, op art, photo-realism (see Figure 57.1), and postmodernism have proliferated, often crossing boundaries between commercial and high art, between representational and abstract art (see Color Plate 31), and between traditional and non-traditional mediums (see Color Plate 32). All these styles reflect the artistic and the speculative mind of the Western world in the twentieth century—disenchantment, rejection of tradition, search for new values, and a turning inward for inspiration.

Twentieth-century architecture has been

FIGURE 57.7 Pompidou Center of Art and Culture, Paris
The controversial Pompidou Center of Art and Culture, built in the center of Paris during the 1970s, carries the idea of functionalism in architecture to an aesthetic extreme. Structural and functional elements of the building show prominently on the outside, creating a vast open space on the inside. (B. Annebicque/Sygma)

dominated by the functional style (see Figure 57.7), developed in Germany by Walter Gropius' Bauhaus school, in France by architects such as Le Corbusier, and in the United States by Louis Henry Sullivan (see pp. 602–603). Sullivan's most illustrious student, and perhaps the best-known architect of the twentieth century, was Frank Lloyd Wright (1869–1959). Like his teacher, Wright believed that function is the sole purpose of architecture. He further insisted that form should conform to the materials used and to the setting. He made brilliant use of the cantilever (a projecting member supported at only one end) to achieve striking horizontal lines and an unobstructed spaciousness. These effects were made possible by the tensile strength of steel. Wright combined artistic skill with a Shavian scorn for traditional values and institutions. The most spectacular monuments of functional architecture are, of course, the great bridges and skyscrapers, most of them in the United States.

Twentieth-century music, too, is for the most part a continuation and development of styles formulated during the period 1871–1914. Richard Strauss (1864–1949) and Igor Stravinsky (1882–1971), two of the originators of modern music, lived far into the twentieth century. During the course of the century, Western music became increasingly dissonant, atonal, and experimental. These qualities probably found their ultimate composer in the Viennese Arnold Schoenberg (1874–1951), who abolished key, revolutionized the conception of melody, and replaced the seven-tone scale with one of twelve tones. Recent decades have witnessed the introduction of a universe of everyday and electronically produced sounds into music.

Popular Culture

The twentieth century has witnessed an explosion of popular culture. Several developments account for the huge variety and availability of popular literature, art, and music. There has been a tremendous expansion of communications—from cheap newspapers and paperback novels to radio, cinema, and television. Numerous large public facilities—from museums and concert halls to stadiums—have been built. The rising level of education has stimulated greater interest in cultural activities. Increasing affluence and leisure time among the urban classes have enabled more people to take advantage of cultural offerings.

FIGURE 57.8 Fritz Lang's *Metropolis* This eerie, futuristic scene from Fritz Lang's film *Metropolis* (1925) illustrates the overwhelming power of urban architecture and technology as well as the potential of the cinema as an artistic medium. (National Film Archive, London)

The products of popular culture are usually distinct from those of elite culture, but there has been some blurring of the lines between the two in recent decades. In cinema, an almost endless stream of what critics consider undistinguished but popular films are produced year after year. Yet cinema is perhaps the most original art form produced during the twentieth century (see Figure 57.8). The works of filmmakers such as Ingmar Bergman in Sweden and Federico Fellini in Italy reveal the potential of cinema as a sophisticated, creative, artistic medium. In music there

is much that distinguishes the dissonant, atonal music of Arnold Schoenberg from rock and roll performed by groups such as the Beatles, but the distinction blurs with jazz, a development of America's black culture emphasizing sophisticated improvisation and rhythm. In art, most of the abstract or expressionistic paintings of the twentieth century remain outside popular taste, but what was once elite art, such as the romantic or realistic paintings of the nineteenth century, or even avant-garde, such as impressionism, is now extremely popular.

SUGGESTED READING

General

M. Crouzet, *The European Renaissance since 1945* (1971). A balanced account emphasizing society and culture.

S. Hoffmann and P. Kitromilides, *Culture and Society in Contemporary Europe* (1981). A good collection of essays.

Western Society in the Twentieth Century

S. de Beauvoir, *The Second Sex* (1962). A classic, crucial analysis of women.

C. Bouchier, *The Feminist Challenge: The Movement for Women's Liberation in Britain and the United States* (1983). A useful study.

D. Caute, *The Year of the Barricades: A Journey Through 1968* (1988). A study of youth culture since World War II.

A. Cherlin, *Marriage, Divorce, Remarriage* (1981). An interpretive analysis of the American family.

J. Lovenduski, *Women and European Politics: Contemporary Feminism and Public Policy* (1986). A good recent analysis.

R. Rubinstein, *Alchemists of Revolution: Terrorism in the Modern World* (1987). A comparative study.

E. Shorter, *The Making of the Modern Family* (1978). Well written, controversial.

Religion and Theology in the Twentieth Century

S. P. Schilling, *Contemporary Continental Theologians* (1966). A good survey of modern theology.

Twentieth-Century Science

J. Galbraith, *Age of Uncertainty* (1978). Writing lucidly for the nonspecialist, Galbraith argues for tight economic controls.

J. Ziman, *The Force of Knowledge: The Scientific Dimension of Society* (1976). An excellent analysis and bibliography.

Twentieth-Century Culture

W. Barrett, *Irrational Man* (1962). A good treatment of existentialism.

M. Biddiss, *Age of the Masses: Ideas and Society since 1870* (1977). A fine intellectual history.

R. Maltby, ed., *Passing Parade: A History of Popular Culture in the Twentieth Century* (1989). An excellent survey.

M. Marrus, ed., *Emergence of Leisure* (1974). An important collection.

A. Neumeyer, *The Search for Meaning in Modern Art*. A useful guide for the nonspecialist.

J. Passmore, *A Hundred Years of Philosophy* (1968). A good, concise survey.

H. Read, *A Concise History of Modern Painting* (1974). An excellent brief survey.

E. Salzman, *Twentieth Century Music: An Introduction*. A good survey.

R. Stromberg, *European Intellectual History since 1789* (1986). Chapters survey the period.

R. Williams, *Communications* (1976). Analyzes the media.

CHAPTER 58

Decolonization and the Non-Western World, 1945–Present

FIGURE 58.1 Victory Parade in China, 1970 An imposing ninety-foot statue of Chairman Mao Tse-tung towers over marchers celebrating the twenty-first anniversary of the Communist victory in China. The rise of China as a world power in recent decades exemplifies the growing importance of connections between the Western and non-Western worlds. (Sipahioglu/Sipa/Special Features)

The devastation of two world wars and the rising movements for independence within their colonies were too much for the European imperial powers to handle. Sometimes gracefully and sometimes only after protracted violence, Europe lost almost all its colonies in the two decades following World War II. As the formerly colonized peoples acquired their independence, they began to assert their power in many areas of the non-Western world. It soon became clear that neither Europe nor the superpowers could act without taking into account the concerns, power, and problems of the non-Western world.

1. JAPAN BETWEEN EAST AND WEST

Japan emerged from World War II defeated on sea and land, the shocked victim of history's first two atomic bombs used for military purposes. Since the United States had played by far the major role in the defeat of Japan, the United States refused to share the occupation and governing of the Japanese islands with its former allies. President Truman appointed General Douglas MacArthur supreme commander of the Allied powers in Japan and gave him absolute authority.

During the first year and a half of MacArthur's command a democratic constitution similar to that of Great Britain was drawn up and put into effect. In the first elections under the new constitution, which gave women the right to vote and guaranteed civil liberties, the Social Democrats, who were somewhat similar to the British Labourites, won the largest number of seats in the national legislature. The activities of Japanese labor unions were encouraged, and they became effective for the first time. The five great families (the *zaibatsu*) who had monopolized Japan's industry and finance disbanded their great business combinations under pressure from the occupation authorities. Demilitarization was carried out, and a number of top Japanese war leaders were tried and executed or imprisoned.

Of greatest significance was MacArthur's land-reform program. The great mass of Japanese farmers were poverty-stricken, landless sharecroppers, giving up from 50 to 70 percent of their yield to absentee landlords. Laws sponsored by MacArthur forced the landlords to sell the government all land in excess of seven and a half acres (more in less fertile areas). The government, in turn, sold the land in plots of seven and a half acres to the tenant farmers, who were given thirty years to pay for them. By the end of 1946 Japan appeared to be on the way to becoming a liberal democracy.

Early in 1947, when the Cold War was being stepped up in intensity, General MacArthur suddenly reversed his liberal policy. He first cracked down on the newly formed labor unions. Industrial decentralization ceased, and land redistribution slowed down. Obviously, the United States was now interested in making Japan, like Germany, a link in the containment chain that it was forging around the Soviet Union. By 1949 the more conservative Liberal party, which later became the Liberal Democratic party, gained power and would hold it in elections through the following four decades.

During the 1950s and 1960s Japan made an astounding economic recovery that surpassed even that of West Germany. Like West Germany, Japan received massive American aid. In rebuilding its ruined industries, Japan adopted the most modern and scientific labor-saving devices (see Figure 58.2). It benefited from the rapid expansion of higher education and readily available, high-quality labor. By the mid-1960s Japan was the third greatest industrial power in the world, outranked only by the United States and the Soviet Union, and the Japanese people were enjoying a standard of living and social peace such as they had never known before. The Japanese, like the Germans, benefited greatly from American military protection, which relieved them of the enormous cost of maintaining a big military establishment. They also sold large quantities of industrial products, particularly electronics and automobiles, to the United States and bought relatively few American goods in return. Furthermore, the Japanese labor unions, like the German unions, but unlike the American, British, and French unions, have followed a policy of cooperation—codetermination—with their corporate managers.

Political stability and economic prosperity continued through the 1970s. In 1978 Japan signed a treaty of friendship and commerce with

FIGURE 58.2 Matsushita Electrical Industrial Company By the 1970s Japan was a leading industrial power, particularly in electronics. Plants such as this Matsushita Electrical Industrial Company (producing VCRs) used technology and disciplined labor to manufacture products for the home and foreign markets. (Courtesy Matsushita)

the People's Republic of China. During the 1980s Japan managed to maintain a striking degree of economic health with a comparatively high growth rate and lower rates of unemployment and inflation than any industrial power of the West.

2. THE RISE OF COMMUNIST CHINA

Across the Sea of Japan a very different and even more exciting drama was being enacted in China. Here, a massive upheaval involving one-fourth of the world's population took place. Sun Yat-sen, after launching his revolution against both China's foreign exploiters and its own reactionary and conniving government (see p. 630), died in 1925, in the midst of the struggle. His place at the head of the revolutionary Chinese government was taken by his young, vigorous supporter, General Chiang Kai-shek, who soon gained control of all China. Chiang, a professional soldier, was much more interested in making China a powerful and independent nation than in liberalizing its government and society. Under him, the revolutionary Kuomintang party, then dominant in China, swung definitely to the right. When the Chinese Nationalist armies were

defeated by the Japanese in 1937–1938 and driven deep into the interior, Chiang and the Kuomintang were cut off from the chief bases of their liberal support, which were the great coastal cities. Heavily dependent then on the warlords and landlords of the interior, they moved still further to the right.

Meanwhile, as China's Confucian civilization was crumbling faster than Sun's Western liberalism could replace it, another Western influence moved into the vacuum: Marxism. The hostility that the Western democracies showed to Sun's revolutionary liberal movement encouraged the Chinese Communists. In 1927 the Communists found an able leader in the scholarly and shrewd Mao Tse-tung (see Figure 58.3). This dedicated revolutionary from well-to-do peasant stock had risen to leadership by sheer force of intellect, personality, and energy. Chiang exerted every effort to crush the Chinese Communists—much more, in fact, than he spent to drive out the Japanese invaders. During the years 1939–1945, when the Kuomintang forces were getting further and further out of touch with the Chinese masses, Mao's Communists were waging incessant guerrilla warfare against the Japanese and gaining a greater following among the Chinese people.

Following the surrender of Japan in August 1945, a bitter struggle for the control of China

FIGURE 58.3 Mao Tse-tung and Ho Chi Minh These men were two of East Asia's most dynamic leaders since World War II. The North Vietnamese, though eager to get aid from China, were always suspicious and fearful of their big neighbor to the north. (Brian Brake/Rapho/Photo Researchers)

ensued between Chiang's Kuomintang forces, now known as the Chinese Nationalists, and the Chinese Communists. In this struggle the United States supported the Nationalists. However, the Communists won the support of ever-increasing numbers of the Chinese people. Morale in the long inactive and graft-ridden Nationalist armies was low, while that in the Communist armies, toughened by the continuous fighting against the Japanese, was high. During 1949 the victorious Communists swept over the entire Chinese mainland. Chiang, with a remnant of his Nationalist forces, mostly officers, fled to the island of Formosa (Taiwan), where after June 1950 they were protected by the U.S. navy.

In 1949 Mao proclaimed the People's Republic of China, and the following year he formed an alliance with the Soviet Union. With Soviet aid, he began the enormous task of industrializing and communizing the world's most populous nation. In 1953, after a delay caused by China's involvement in the Korean War (see the following section), Mao launched his First Five-Year Plan, which was similar to Stalin's First Five-Year Plan of twenty-five years earlier. The Chinese Communists, however, were starting from a much lower base than the Russians. Industry and agriculture were both collectivized, and the emphasis was on building heavy industry. In 1957 the government announced that the First Five-Year Plan had been a great success.

The following year it launched its Second Five-Year Plan. The vast new goals in industry and agriculture were to be achieved by communizing Chinese society more completely than had ever been attempted in the Soviet Union. The entire population was organized into strictly regimented communes. China's huge and rapidly growing population was set to building irrigation dams and ditches, steel mills, factories, railroads, schools, and hospitals in a frenzied hurry. This plan was called the "Great Leap Forward." But the plan was too ambitious. In 1959 a series of droughts and floods produced near-famine conditions in many areas. Overzealous local party officials provoked resentment and resistance among the harried populace. The realistic Red leaders slackened the pace and eased the regimentation.

The failure of the Great Leap Forward gave rise to ideological differences and set off a power struggle within the Communist party hierarchy. A moderate group led by Liu Shao-chi, president of the republic and second in command to Party Chairman Mao, wished to slow down the pace of communization, produce more consumer goods, and encourage, at least temporarily, individual initiative. Mao took a different line. He believed that many dangerous remnants of prerevolutionary capitalistic China and the newly bloated bureaucracy had to be destroyed. In 1966 he unleashed tens of thousands of Red Guards—fanatical Communist youths—upon the moderate element in what he called a "cultural revolution" and with the support of the regular army succeeded, after three years of turmoil, in crushing the moderates.

Meanwhile, China and the Soviet Union were drifting apart. In 1956 an ideological dispute had begun when Khrushchev denounced Stalin. Peking accused Moscow of becoming soft toward the capitalistic, imperialist West. In 1960 the Soviet Union began to withhold promised economic and technological aid from China. In 1964 Red China exploded its first nuclear device. The Soviets moved many of their best mechanized divisions to the Far East, where in 1968 they clashed with Chinese units along their disputed border—the longest international border in the world. Both Red giants, fearful of each other, sought a détente with the United States. In 1971 the United States ceased to block the admission of Red China to the United Nations, making it possible for the United Nations to admit the People's Republic of China (1971) and expel the Republic of China on Taiwan. Emissaries were exchanged between Peking and Washington.

In a power struggle following Mao's death in 1976, more moderate officials led by Deng Xiaoping came to power. In 1978 they initiated the policy of the "Four Modernizations." The policy was a dramatic departure from many elements of Mao's economic policies in favor of more pragmatic methods. To foster rapid economic development and greater productivity, there was a new emphasis on economic decentralization. A more market-oriented economy was introduced into the countryside and, later, some urban areas. By the mid-1980s these policies were resulting in new relations with Japan and the United States, more foreign loans, the opening of China to tourism and foreign investment, new economic growth, and greater economic freedom (see p. 762).

3. THE KOREAN WAR

The bitter Left-Right conflict among the Asiatic peoples and the global Cold War struggle between the United States and the Soviet Union merged in Korea to produce a shooting war of major proportions. In August 1945, in accordance with the Yalta Agreements, the forces of the Soviet Union overran Japanese-held Korea north of the thirty-eighth parallel, and the forces of the United States began to occupy Korea south of the thirty-eighth parallel. These moves were supposed to be for the purpose of setting up a free and united Korean nation. However, the Soviet

Union immediately proceeded to set up a Communist dictatorship in North Korea under Kim Il-sung. The land was distributed to the peasants, and industry was nationalized. In South Korea the United States authorities sponsored a right-wing government under the leadership of the aged and reactionary Korean patriot Syngman Rhee. Late in 1948 the Soviet forces withdrew from North Korea, leaving behind an energetic Communist regime well armed with the latest Soviet weapons. Six months later the American forces withdrew from South Korea, leaving behind the Syngman Rhee landlord regime armed mostly with the weapons that had been captured from the Japanese. Both the North and South Korean governments talked loudly of conquering each other.

On June 25, 1950, North Korea suddenly attacked South Korea. The high-spirited, well-armed North Korean Communists easily defeated the South Koreans. The United States persuaded the United Nations to take drastic action. Taking advantage of the absence of the Soviet Union's representative, the Security Council called upon all the members of the United Nations to furnish military forces to repel the North Korean aggression and asked President Truman to name the commander of the U.N. forces. Truman named General MacArthur to command them. Truman also announced that he had already ordered American forces into the Korean War, that the American navy would protect Chiang's Chinese Nationalists on Taiwan against the Chinese Communists, and that American aid to the French fighting the native Communists in Indochina would be greatly increased.

The forces of the United Nations, mostly Americans, quickly defeated the North Koreans. By late November 1950 MacArthur's forces were approaching the Yalu River, which forms the Korean-Chinese border. At this point Red China entered the war and severely defeated MacArthur's forces, driving them in headlong retreat back down the peninsula. Eventually the battle line became stabilized roughly along the thirty-eighth parallel. Two years of negotiations brought an armistice in 1953. Total casualties—dead, wounded, and missing—are estimated to have been approximately a million and a half on each side. The war ended just about where it had started. However, Communist military aggression had been checked with severe punishment. The United Nations had functioned effectively and increased its prestige. Probably of equal significance is the fact that a revolutionary new Asiatic power, Red China, had fought the greatest Western power, the United States, to a standstill.

Since the end of the war, North and South Korea have gone their separate ways. North Korea has remained a tightly controlled Communist state under the long rule of Kim Il-sung. South Korea has remained under the control of right-wing authoritarian leaders, but its society is more open and more economically dynamic than that of the North. During the 1970s and 1980s it became one of the most rapidly growing and industrializing economies in the world, and recently it has shown signs of broadening political participation.

4. THE REVOLT OF SOUTHERN ASIA

The end of World War II found the huge British, Dutch, and French empires in southern Asia aflame with the spirit of nationalism and revolt. Of the Western imperial powers, only the United States escaped direct embroilment in this revolt by granting independence to the Philippines in 1946.

In India, the world's second most populous country, the leader of the independence movement was Mohandas K. Gandhi (1869–1948), one of the most dynamic personalities of the twentieth century. This middle-class Hindu, educated in Great Britain, was a master of the psychology of the Indian masses. His chief tactics were passive resistance and civil disobedience. The British were unable to cope with him.

Indian nationalism reached its peak during World War II, but Churchill would not hear of Indian independence. "I did not become the king's first minister," said the doughty warrior, "in order to preside over the liquidation of the British Empire." The British Labour party, however, upon coming to power in 1945 immediately announced its determination to grant India independence. In 1947 independence was granted to India, containing some 350 million people, and Pakistan, with more than 70 million people.

Religious and national strife soon broke out between Hindu India and Moslem Pakistan. Gandhi tried to quell the strife, but he was assassinated in 1948 by a fanatical Hindu nationalist. Open war between the two states began in 1948 over possession of the disputed state of Kashmir. The United Nations was able to end the shooting but not the dispute.

One of Gandhi's most devoted followers, Jawaharlal Nehru, a charming, wealthy British-educated Hindu of the highest (Brahmin) caste, became the first prime minister of India (see Figure 58.4). The problems confronting him were staggering. Most of India's millions were poverty-stricken and illiterate. They spoke more than eight hundred languages and dialects (fewer than 50 percent spoke the official Hindi). Some 100 million Indians were of the untouchable class. Nehru inaugurated a liberal and mildly socialistic program somewhat similar to that of the British Labour government. Border clashes with Pakistan and Red China pushed India into accepting military aid from both the United States and the Soviet Union.

When Nehru died in 1964, his successors were confronted by rising discontent. In 1966 Nehru's daughter, Indira Gandhi, became prime minister. Many Indians felt that the economic and social reform program of the Nehrus was not drastic enough. In spite of sizable loans and much technical assistance from the United States, Great Britain, and the Soviet Union, India's standard of living was not keeping abreast of its ever-mounting population. In 1974, while millions of its people stood on the brink of starvation, India exploded its first nuclear device. In 1975 the opposition to Prime Minister Gandhi's administration became so disruptive that she invoked constitutional emergency decrees that amounted to dictatorship. But the opposition only increased. In 1977 Mrs. Gandhi granted national elections and was driven from power. However, her successors had little success in dealing with the overwhelming problems facing India. Indira Gandhi returned to power as prime minister in 1980, but she was assassinated by Sikh extremists in 1984. She was succeeded by her son, Rajiv Gandhi, who held office until 1989 and who was assassinated during the 1991 elections. India still struggles with the problems of religious differences (particularly with the Sikhs of Punjab) and linguistic differences (as with the Tamils in the

FIGURE 58.4 Nehru and Gandhi Two great charismatic leaders of Asian independence, India's Jawaharlal Nehru and Mahatma Gandhi, are shown during a meeting of the All India Congress in Bombay in 1946. (UPI/Bettmann Newsphotos)

south) in a difficult environment of uneven economic development, overpopulation, and poverty.

Pakistan, divided into two states more than a thousand miles apart (see Map 58.1) and with a fragile constitutional government, soon became a military dictatorship closely aligned with the United States. In 1971 East Pakistan rebelled against the less populous but dominant West Pakistan and, with the help of India, gained its independence as the Republic of Bangladesh—but not before some 3 million of its helpless citizens had been slaughtered by the West Pakistani army. From 1977 to his death in 1988, Muhammad Zia ul-Haq held power and remained an important if difficult ally of the United States.

The British Labour government also granted independence to Ceylon, Burma, and Malaya. This left only Hong Kong as a reminder of British imperialism in Asia.

The rich and populous Dutch East Indies declared independence at the end of World War II. The Dutch resisted fiercely for four years but yielded to pressure from the United Nations. In 1949 the Republic of Indonesia was recognized as an independent nation—a nation of approximately 125 million people, mostly Moslems, living on several thousand tropical islands rich in tin, rubber, oil, and many other valuable products.

Of all the European colonial regimes in Asia, that of the French in Indochina was probably the most predatory and the most hated. Immediately after the surrender of Japan in August 1945, the Indochinese nationalists, under the leadership of Ho Chi Minh, a Russian-trained Communist, proclaimed the independent "democratic" Republic of Vietnam. The returning French imperialists were fiercely resisted by the native Communist nationalists. Heavy fighting ensued, in which the French were aided by American Marshall Plan money. The majority of the Vietnamese people apparently preferred the Communists to the French, and the forces of Ho Chi Minh won victory after victory despite American aid to the French.

In 1954 the French government admitted defeat and ceded the northern half of Vietnam to the Communists. Although South Vietnam technically remained a part of the French Union, French influence quickly vanished. The United States, in accordance with its policy of military containment of communism—both Russian and Chinese—undertook to establish its power not only in South Vietnam but also in Laos and Cambodia, which the French had also freed. Vigorous military and financial aid was given to the conservative Ngo Dinh Diem regime in South Vietnam. Fearful of a Communist victory at the polls, American authorities refused to permit the hold-

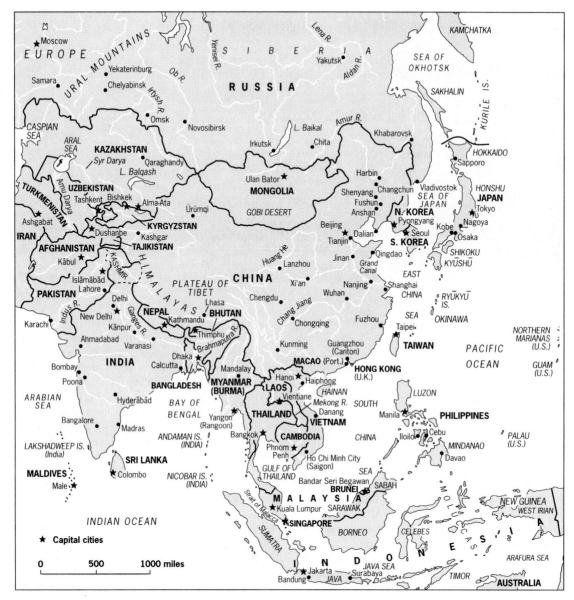

Map 58.1 ASIA, 1993 Containing more than one-half of the world's population, Asia has been of growing concern to the Western nations since 1945. Two wars (the Korean and Vietnamese) have directly involved Western nations, while the economic might of Japan and the potential power of China are seen as threatening to many Western interests.

FIGURE 58.5 Vietnam, 1969
The intervention of the United States in Vietnam for the purpose of containing communism (Russian and Chinese, it was believed) resulted in greater bombing and destruction than in World War II. Millions of Vietnamese were killed, maimed, and made homeless. (Philip Jones Griffiths/Magnum)

ing of national elections, which had been promised by an international commission when the French withdrew. Diem became increasingly unpopular. Almost immediately, he was faced with a rebellion of his own people supported and soon led by the Communists in both South and North Vietnam. In 1963 Diem, having lost the confidence and support of his American protectors, was overthrown and assassinated by a group of his own officers, who set up a harsh military dictatorship of their own. Early in 1965 the Vietnamese Communists, with significant material aid from both the Soviet Union and Red China, greatly stepped up their war against the American-supported but weakening South Vietnamese forces. The United States retaliated with heavy bombing of North Vietnam and increased its armed forces to over 500,000 troops. Vietnam was rapidly being devastated (see Figure 58.5).

Meanwhile, public opinion all over the world, including the United States, was becoming incensed at the wanton destruction. In 1968 a massive North Vietnamese surprise offensive convinced the American government that victory could not be won, and the United States began long, dreary peace talks with the North Vietnamese in Paris. In 1969 Ho Chi Minh died, but the war and new massive bombings (the United States dropped more explosives on Vietnam than were used by all combatants during World War

II) dragged on until 1973, when peace agreements were finally signed and the United States withdrew its armed forces, leaving behind huge stores of war matériel for the South Vietnamese.

The civil war in Vietnam, however, continued as both sides refused to abide by the terms of the peace agreements. As in China and Korea, the graft-ridden armed forces of a corrupt government trying to maintain the old aristocratic society of a bygone era were no match for the high-spirited Communist forces. In 1975 the Communists swept to victory over all Vietnam and shortly thereafter over the rest of Indochina—Cambodia and Laos. Even then the violence did not end. In Cambodia the Communist Pol Pot regime devastated that society, resulting in the death of over a million people and ending in an invasion and occupation of Cambodia by Vietnam. Relations between Vietnam and China remain shaky, with violence having broken out along their border more than once in recent years.

5. THE EMBATTLED MIDDLE EAST

One of the most explosive areas in the world of the latter half of the twentieth century was the Middle East—that area between and including Egypt and Iran, where East meets West (see Map

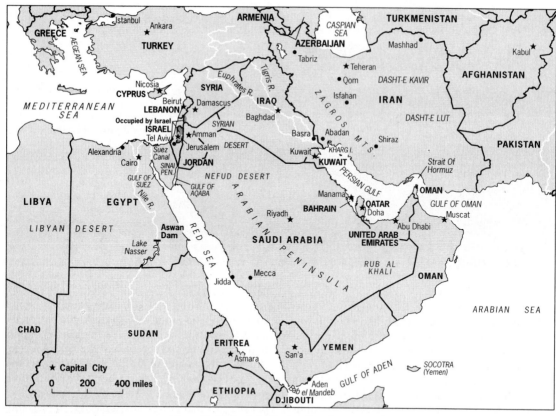

Map 58.2 THE MIDDLE EAST, 1993 Since 1945 the Middle East has been wracked by several outbreaks of war involving Israel and its neighbors. Cold War involvements, the growing strength of Arab nationalism, and OPEC control over oil production have made this part of the world of crucial concern to the West.

58.2). It is probably the most strategic area in the world. It forms the bridge between the world's two greatest land masses, Eurasia and Africa, and through it pass the chief communication lines between the East and the West. The Middle East is the heart of the Islamic world, which stretches from Morocco to Indonesia and contains over 500 million followers of the Prophet. It is also the heart of the tumultuous Arab world. Moreover, the area contains more than half the world's known oil reserves.

During the early part of the century, while the great European powers competed for control of the Middle East, Arab nationalism was rising. This nationalism was vented first against the British, who were the dominant power in that

area. As anti-British hostility mounted in the years between the two world wars, Great Britain began to relax its control. By the end of World War II only Cyprus, Palestine, and the Suez Canal remained in Britain's possession, and the British were bidding strongly for Arab friendship. But continued British possession of the Suez Canal and the admission of tens of thousands of Jews into Palestine under the Balfour Declaration of 1917 proved to be effective barriers to Anglo-Arab accord.

Palestine was the ancient home of the Jews. However, in A.D. 70 they were dispersed by the government of the Roman Empire. In the seventh century the Islamic Arabs conquered Palestine and lived there until the twentieth century—thirteen hundred years. In the late nineteenth century, the Zionist movement began—a movement to restore Palestine as a national home for the Jews. During the anti-Semitic persecutions of the Hitler era, thousands of European Jewish refugees, many of them wealthy, poured into Palestine, buying up the land and dispossessing the Arabs. The whole Arab and Islamic world became incensed.

In 1948 the British Labour government turned Palestine over to the United Nations. The Jews immediately proclaimed the State of Israel and accepted the boundary lines the United Nations had drawn to divide Palestine between the Jews and the Arabs. The Arab League refused to accept this arrangement and began hostilities with a view to eliminating the Jewish state. Tiny Israel, however, well armed and well financed, was more than a match for the Arabs. After a year of fighting, the United Nations succeeded in bringing about a truce. Israel had somewhat expanded its original borders, and it had expelled nearly half a million Arabs who had fought to destroy the State of Israel. Arab nationalism was thoroughly aroused, and border raids recurred as the Arabs armed for a renewal of the struggle. Israel, in the meantime, receiving financial aid from Jews abroad, prospered, built modern cities, introduced irrigation and scientific agriculture, and became a vigorous, democratic, cooperative Western society.

The Arabs found a vigorous leader when in 1952 a military coup in Egypt brought Gamel Abdul Nasser to power. Nasser set out to unite the Arab world and inflame it against the West. When he threatened Israel, seized the Suez Canal, and aided France's rebellious subjects in North Africa, he was attacked by Israel, Great Britain, and France in 1956. He was saved only by the threatened intervention of the Soviet Union, which caused the United States to exert sufficient pressure on the three invading powers to force them to give up their assault. But nothing had been settled. Nasser continued to arouse Arab nationalism against Israel, and the Arab states received a swelling stream of arms from the Soviet Union.

In 1967 Nasser again brought on a showdown. He had prohibited the use of the Suez Canal by the Israelis since the 1956 war. When he blockaded Israel's only port on the Red Sea

and Egyptian, Syrian, and Jordanian armies massed along the Israeli borders, the Israelis suddenly attacked them and crushed them in six days' time. The Israelis then occupied Egyptian territory east of the Suez Canal, Syria's Golan Heights, and Jordanian territory west of the Jordan—territories the Israelis claimed were necessary for their security.

The six-day 1967 war humiliated not only the Arab world but also the Soviet Union, which rushed billions of dollars' worth of arms, including deadly surface-to-air missiles (SAMs), together with thousands of military "advisers," to Egypt and Syria. Nasser died in 1970 and was succeeded as president of Egypt by Anwar Sadat.

As the Israelis were celebrating their Yom Kippur holidays in October 1973, Egypt and Syria, supported by the rest of the Arab states (except Morocco), suddenly attacked them. This time the Arabs, much better armed and trained than before, inflicted serious casualties on the Israelis and pushed them back on all fronts. Several weeks were required for the heavily outnumbered Israelis to recover from their initial shock, receive massive fresh supplies from the United States, and mount offensives of their own. They then crossed the Suez Canal, surrounded an entire Egyptian army, and began advancing on Cairo to the west and Damascus, the Syrian capital, to the east. At this juncture the Soviet Union threatened to intervene. The United States alerted its armed forces and forced the Israelis to halt their advance. The United Nations helped to arrange a cease-fire.

The Arabs now made full use of their oil weapon; they quadrupled the price of their oil, curtailed production, and placed a complete embargo on its shipment to the United States and the Netherlands. These measures added greatly to the strain of inflation that had long gripped the capitalistic world. The poorer nations of Asia and Africa were particularly distressed.

In November 1977 Egyptian President Sadat surprised the world by going to Jerusalem and beginning negotiations with Israeli Premier Menachem Begin for a peace settlement. Sadat was denounced by all his Arab neighbors for breaking the solid Arab front against Israel. Negotiations soon broke down, but in 1978 U.S. President Carter persuaded Sadat and Begin to sign the first draft to a peace treaty, which was finalized in 1979 and led to an Israeli withdrawal from the Sinai and open borders between the two nations.

The Palestinian refugees were one of the most tumultuous elements in the whole Middle Eastern complex. Fleeing Palestine after the 1948 war, they first attempted to overthrow the government of Jordan. Failing there, they took refuge in Lebanon, which was too weak to expel them. Their numbers grew constantly until by 1975 there were between 2 million and 3 million of them. In that year they joined the Islamic Lebanese majority in attempting to overthrow the Christian-dominated government. In the civil war that followed, Beirut, the capital city and one of the most prosperous banking and commercial centers in the Middle East, was wrecked. Syria took advantage of the turmoil to move in and gain military control over most of the country. In 1982 Israel invaded Lebanon and occupied the southern half of the country. In vain, troops from Western nations, including Italy, France, Great Britain, and the United States, were stationed in Beirut by 1983, only to be withdrawn in 1984. Lebanon would continue to be wracked by civil war and international animosities, and the Palestinian's struggles with Israel seem far from over. Under the leadership of the Palestine Liberation Organization and other radical groups, Palestinians continued to resist Israeli troops from within Israeli-occupied territories and resort to guerrilla and terrorist tactics almost everywhere. Israel responded with intransigence. Recently, however, the Palestine Liberation Organization, under the leadership of Yasir Arafat, gained increased international stature. By admitting Israel's right to exist and rejecting terrorism, the Palestine Liberation Organization convinced the United States to open negotiations with it for the first time. In 1991, 1992, and 1993 new Middle East talks and the election of the more flexible Labour party to power in Israel brought more hope for peace between Israel and its neighbors, culminating in September 1993 with a treaty of mutual recognition between Israel and the Palestine Liberation Organization and the promise of new agreements in the Middle East.

The enormous oil wealth pouring into the Middle East accelerated the demands for change. Countries such as Saudi Arabia and Kuwait suddenly became wealthy, commanding strategic oil reserves and great financial muscle. But in other countries, problems arose. In 1978 Iran, second only to Saudi Arabia in the production of oil and precariously situated between the Soviet Union and the Persian Gulf, was the scene of massive uprisings. The shah's government was strongly supported by the United States as a military strong point on the border of the Soviet Union. Though modernizing the country, the shah's government was a military dictatorship. Now it was beset on the one hand by young liberals who wanted to democratize and further modernize Iran and on the other by the masses led by Islamic fundamentalists who rejected the West and secularism in favor of old Islamic values. Early in 1979 the shah was forced to flee, and the reins of government were seized by the seventy-nine-year-old popular Islamic mystic Ayatollah Khomeini, who set up an Islamic republic (see Figure 58.6). The nationalistic Khomeini was strongly anti-American, anti-Soviet, and anti-Israeli. The violence and instability continued and indeed was increased in 1980 by the outbreak of a costly war between Iran and Iraq that lasted until 1988. More violence was to come. In 1979 the Soviet Union invaded Afghanistan, sparking strong Islamic resistance that continued after the Soviet withdrawal in 1989. In 1990 Iraq invaded and overwhelmed Kuwait. The next year an American-led and United Nations-sanctioned coalition massively bombed Iraq and threw Iraqi troops out of Kuwait. These events indicate that the turmoil that has marked the Middle East has few boundaries.

6. THE EMANCIPATION OF AFRICA

Africa was the last of the continents to rise against European imperialism (see Map 58.3). France and Great Britain, which held the most territory in Africa, were the first to begin to dismantle their vast empires there.

The end of World War II found France's huge North African empire seething with unrest. Its population, largely Islamic, was agitated by the rampaging Arab nationalism in the Middle East. In 1956, France granted independence to Morocco and Tunisia. The problem of independence or autonomy for Algeria was much more complex because of the presence there of more than

FIGURE 58.6 Khomeini In 1979 the Shiites' leader, Ayatollah Khomeini, gained power in Iran. As spiritual head of an Islamic fundamentalist movement, Khomeini commanded the passionate allegiance of masses of followers. (UPI/Bettmann Newsphotos)

Africa, and invited them to form a voluntary union with France. All but one, French Guinea, did so.

Great Britain's experiences in Africa following World War II were quite similar to those of France. All the native populations caught the spirit of nationalism and turned in resentment against their white masters. Native terror bands, notably the Mau Mau in Kenya, made British life and property increasingly unsafe. In 1957 Great Britain granted independence to its Gold Coast colony, which became the Republic of Ghana. This proved to be the first step in the eventual freeing of Britain's remaining African colonies. During the next few years one after another of Britain's African territories was freed. By 1965 all of Britain's African empire had been dismantled.

In two of the former British African colonies sizable white minorities attempted to continue their domination over the black majorities and in so doing created tensions that became global in scope. In Rhodesia approximately a quarter million whites ruled 6 million blacks. When in 1965 the British government pressed the all-white government of Rhodesia to grant suffrage to blacks, that government declared its independence from Great Britain. Almost immediately the black majority demanded suffrage and civil equality; when it was refused, many of them resorted to guerrilla warfare, aided by neighboring black nations and by the Soviet Union. In 1980 freedom was gained. Zimbabwe acquired full independence from Great Britain, and Robert Mugabe, one of the principal black guerrilla leaders, was named prime minister.

South Africa was the scene of a bigger and potentially even more dangerous racial conflict. The Dominion of South Africa had since 1931 (by the Statute of Westminster) been completely free. There the prosperous white minority of 4 million whites clung desperately to its superiority over 18 million blacks and other nonwhites. In 1948 and thereafter, the white minority took severe measures to suppress the increasingly restless black majority and to enforce *apartheid* (racial segregation). When in 1961 several fellow members of the British Commonwealth censured South Africa because of its racial policies, South Africa withdrew from the Commonwealth, taking its large mandate, South-West Africa (Namibia), with it. Under pressure from the angry

a million French settlers who feared reprisals from the 8 million Islamic Algerians. Efforts to hold back independence resulted in open revolt by Algerians that France could not handle and that helped bring de Gaulle back to power in France. In 1962, bowing to the force of Arab nationalism, he granted Algeria independence. Meanwhile, he had granted independence to all the other French colonies, most of which were in

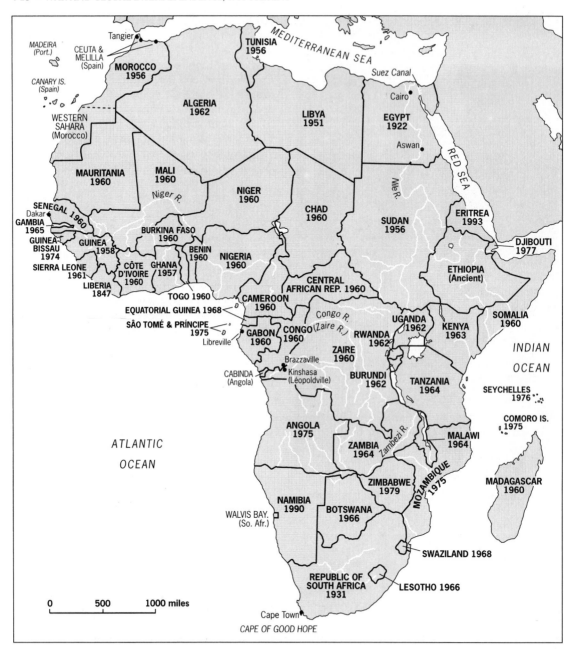

Map 58.3 AFRICA, 1993 As this map indicates, the vast majority of African nations gained their independence during the 1950s and 1960s. Instability, often stemming from the legacy of Western colonialism, has plagued much of the continent.

black majority and from the Organization of African Unity (set up in 1963 by the completely freed African nations), the United Nations, and world opinion, the all-white government of the Republic of South Africa from time to time made token concessions to apartheid but steadfastly refused to grant majority rule. During the 1970s and 1980s the situation became increasingly polarized and explosive. White South Africa remained almost completely isolated in the world, censured because of its racism, a place where massive violence was expected to break out as peaceful alternatives for change were rejected. In 1989 F. W. de Klerk was elected prime minister, and he initiated policies that promised real change for South Africa. Over the next few years relations were established with the African National Congress, much of apartheid was abolished, negotiations to share political power with South African blacks were initiated, and South Africa withdrew from Namibia.

The decision of the World War II Allies to free oil-rich Libya from Italian control was consummated in 1951. In 1960 Italy granted independence to Somalia in East Africa, and Belgium gave up the Congo. Finally, Portugal freed her large African colonies in 1975, bringing to an end (with the exception of a few bits of territory here and there) the era of European domination of Africa that had begun in the fifteenth century.

The granting of independence, of course, did not bring peace and prosperity to the African people. The boundaries of the African states had been drawn in many cases quite arbitrarily by nineteenth-century European imperialists sitting around plush green-topped tables in London or Brussels dividing up the spoils. In the Congo, for instance, tribal warfare flamed up immediately after independence. Russian and Chinese Communist agents moved in to exploit the chaos. U.N. Secretary-General Dag Hammarskjöld lost his life there in a plane accident while trying to mediate the differences. In Nigeria, the Ibos in the eastern region attempted to secede and set up the independent Republic of Biafra. Thousands died in the futile struggle, and tens of thousands died by starvation. Since the newly freed African people were left without political experience and with few, if any, self-generated political institutions, instability, bloodshed, and rule by military strongmen were often the result. Charismatic liberation leaders such as Kwame Nkrumah in Ghana and Jomo Kenyatta in Kenya (where a relatively stable parliamentary system was established) were more the exception than the rule.

Economically the European colonial powers did not leave African countries with a firm basis for balanced prosperity or self-sufficiency. In the early 1990s Africa's economy was still primarily agricultural, despite a large development of oil and gas production in Libya, Algeria, and Nigeria and a beginning of industrialization (mostly foreign) in certain areas such as the Ivory Coast. Of course, gold and diamond mining in South Africa was still a source of great wealth. Africa's rapidly growing population, dependent for the most part on agriculture, was faced with an increasing threat of hunger and starvation. An unprecedented drought in the huge sub-Saharan region of northern Africa during the 1970s, 1980s, and 1990s brought death by starvation to tens of thousands (see Figure 58.7).

7. LATIN AMERICA

Finally, there remains to be examined a large and populous area of the world which is, in a sense, neither East nor West—Latin America (see Map 58.4). Just as Japan is a highly industrialized nation located in the East, Latin America is *in* but, in many respects, not *of* the West. Its religion and languages are, of course, Western. But the poverty and illiteracy of the masses, the underdeveloped economies, and the unstable political institutions more closely resemble those of southern Asia and Africa than Western Europe and the United States.

At the end of World War II the governments of the twenty independent Latin American states were all republics in name. In reality, however, most of them were rightist dictatorships, representing the interests of the well-to-do bourgeoisie, the landowning classes, and the professional military. The Roman Catholic church, which during the nineteenth century had been one of the most powerful rightist forces, had during the twentieth century tended to become much more liberal. In some of the Latin American republics,

FIGURE 58.7 Ethiopian Refugee In recent decades, large areas of Africa have suffered from war, drought, and overpopulation. The results have been malnutrition, disease, starvation, and death. This photo of a starving child at a refugee camp in Ethiopia is all too common. (Michel Philippot/Sygma)

notably Chile, the Church was now actively engaged in liberal social and economic reform movements. Costa Rica was the most democratic of the republics. In Mexico a stable (though primarily one-party) democratic regime had since 1934 been pursuing a liberal program of economic, social, and educational reforms.

Throughout most of Latin America the poor, illiterate, and ever more numerous masses became increasingly restive after World War II. Many of them turned to communism and were encouraged and supported by the Soviet Union. The United States, on the other hand, supported the rightist governments. In 1954 a military force armed by the United States invaded and overthrew the leftist government of Guatemala. Ten years later a rightist military takeover in Brazil was encouraged and applauded by the United States. In 1948 the twenty Latin American "republics" were persuaded to join the United States in an Organization of American States

(OAS) for the purpose of resisting outside (Communist) interference. The Latin Americans were primarily interested in economic aid from the United States and were generally disappointed.

In Cuba the policy of the United States backfired. In 1959 the rightist dictator, Fulgencio Batista, long supported by the United States, was overthrown by the leftist revolutionary Fidel Castro. Castro began a sweeping program of social and economic reforms including the seizure of property owned by citizens and corporations of the United States. The fumbling efforts of the United States to overthrow the Castro regime drove it into the arms of the Soviet Union. Cuba became a Communist beachhead in the Western Hemisphere.

In 1970 Chile became the first nation in the world to vote a Marxist regime into power. As a result of a split between the conservatives and the moderate liberals, Salvador Allende was elected president (with 36 percent of the vote) and immediately launched a Marxist program. All industrial properties, the biggest of which were owned by U.S. corporations, were nationalized. The U.S. government determined to destroy the Allende regime. In 1974 the Central Intelligence Agency admitted that it had spent $11 million bribing Chilean legislators, stirring up labor strife, and supporting right-wing elements. In 1973 the Allende regime was overthrown by the professional military, which set up a rightist military dictatorship. Allende and thousands of his followers were executed.

In 1979 the Sandinistas, a leftist revolutionary force, overthrew the Somoza dictatorship in Nicaragua. During the 1980s, the new government pursued policies of radical social and economic reform, but it was weakened by pressure from the United States and the American-backed contra guerrillas.

In the 1990s Latin America, like much of the non-Western world, remains an area of sharp and dangerous contrasts. Its rich natural resources are not being developed and used for the benefit of the rapidly increasing population, which for the most part is poor and illiterate. Increases in productivity seem more than matched by a rapid inflation of prices for goods and services. Great modern cities such as Mexico City and São Paulo, which rival New York and Chicago in size and modernity, stand sur-

Map 58.4 LATIN AMERICA, 1993 With one of the world's highest population growth rates and seemingly un-bridgeable gaps between the rich few and the poor masses, Latin America has become an area of great political, economic, and social instability. This instability has drawn the Western powers, particularly the United States, into Latin American affairs.

rounded by wretched hovels and an economically depressed countryside. Wealth is enjoyed by a small class of large landowners, industrialists, financiers, and governmental officials. The U.S. government supplies financial and technical assistance, but as in other parts of the world, it often supports conservative regimes that are more interested in retaining their power than in aiding their people. Moreover, a massive and mounting debt burden threatens relations with the United States and international financial stability. Even countries bolstered by income from oil production, such as Venezuela and Mexico, seem unable to keep their debts from growing to alarming proportions. Latin America thus remains an area of political instability and potential revolutionary activity, as revealed by the continuing guerrilla activity, coups d'état, mass demonstrations, and revolutions of recent years.

SUGGESTED READING

General

R. von Albertini, *Decolonization* (1971). A good survey.

C. E. Black, *The Dynamics of Modernization: A Study in Comparative History* (1966). Spans the Western and non-Western worlds.

R. Critchfield, *Villages* (1980). Focuses on rural life in non-Western nations.

T. Von Laue, *The World Revolution of Modernization: The Twentieth Century in Global Perspective* (1987). Good on the impact of modernization.

Asia and Africa

F. Ansprenger, *The Dissolution of the Colonial Empires* (1989). A full historical analysis.

W. Brown, *The United States and India, Pakistan, and Bangladesh* (1972). An excellent brief survey.

F. Butterfield, *China, Alive in the Bitter Sea* (1982). Well-written observations by a journalist.

P. Caputo, *A Rumor of War* (1977). Fine book on the Vietnam War, by a Marine officer who served in Vietnam.

C. Fitzgerald, *The Birth of Communist China*. By a leading expert.

I. K. Y. Hsu, *China Without Mao: The Search for a New Order* (1982). A highly respected work.

A. Mazrui and M. Tidy, *Nationalism and New States in Africa* (1984). A good survey.

E. Reischauer, *The Japanese* (1977). A brilliant and highly readable analysis.

The Middle East

A. Goldschmidt, Jr., *A Concise History of the Middle East* (1987). A useful overview.

W. Polk, *The Elusive Peace: The Middle East in the Twentieth Century* (1980). A fine survey.

J. Voll, *Islam: Continuity and Change in the Modern World* (1982). A brief survey.

Latin America

D. Collier, ed., *The New Authoritarianism in Latin America* (1979). Points to political problems in Latin America.

W. La Faber, *Inevitable Revolutions: The United States in Central America* (1984). A good background to this tension-filled area.

R. J. Shafer, *A History of Latin America* (1978). A useful survey.

CHAPTER 59

The Collapse of Communism and New Realities

FIGURE 59.1 The Berlin Wall symbolized the Cold War division between East and West in Europe. In November 1989, as revolutions swept Eastern Europe and brought an end to the Cold War, Germans from east and west climbed over the wall near the Brandenburg Gate. (Regis Bossu/Sygma)

Historians rely on time to gain a historical perspective on events. Therefore, it is difficult to evaluate the importance of very recent events. Nevertheless, it appears that three developments over the past few years mark an end of an era stretching back to World War II or even World War I and the beginning of a new period. The first of these is the collapse of communism in the Soviet Union and Eastern Europe. The second is a series of steps that have changed international relations and the positions of the principal powers in the West, most notably the movement toward economic integration in Western Europe, the growing power of the newly unified Germany, and the changing position of the United States. The third is the increasing economic strength of areas rimming the Pacific Ocean, particularly in East Asia.

All of these developments have roots going back into the 1970s if not earlier, but it was after the mid-1980s that these developments appeared or acquired new significance. As a beginning date, 1985 might be chosen, for it marked the coming to power of reformers led by Mikhail Gorbachev in the Soviet Union; or 1989, when the nations of Eastern Europe broke from their Soviet ties and communism; or 1991, when the Soviet Union itself fell apart.

1. THE COLLAPSE OF COMMUNISM

Certainly the collapse of communism in the years between 1985 and 1991 is the most dramatic and far-reaching development of recent years, for it marks an end to the Cold War era, which began just after World War II, and to Soviet communism, which stretches back to World War I. In this sense, the collapse of communism may signal the end of the twentieth century as a historical period and the beginning of the twenty-first century.

Origins

Long-term economic problems underlay the collapse of communism in the Soviet Union and Eastern Europe. The Soviet Union and Eastern Europe experienced economic growth in the years after World War II and enjoyed relative prosperity during the 1960s. But it may be that the Soviet brand of state socialism was effective only for initial industrialization, such as the creation of large textile and steel factories, and for certain focused projects, such as the construction of large dams, military hardware, or manned rockets. It was not well adapted to the more complex, rapidly changing, technologically sophisticated economy of the 1970s and 1980s.

During the 1970s, central planning and collectivization, the hallmarks of the Soviet economic system, caused growing problems. Central planning created a large bureaucracy that discouraged economic efficiency and reduced productivity. Planners ordered factories to produce goods that did not meet more rapidly changing producers' or consumers' demands. Plant managers were often unable to get needed materials or labor without long delays while distant officials made decisions. Workers had guaranteed employment and few incentives, which encouraged poor work, low productivity, and absenteeism. Similar problems arose in agriculture, where collectivization discouraged effective decision making, hard work, and productivity. The rates of economic growth were declining, the Soviet Union had to import grain from the capitalist West (in part due to unusually poor weather conditions), and there was a growing sense that the Soviet economy would not catch up with the more rapidly moving economies of the West.

By the 1980s, the Soviet economy was characterized by more and more inefficiency, the decline of old industries and factories built decades earlier, an inability to incorporate new technological innovations into production rapidly, labor imbalances, the production of low-quality goods, and shortages of food, raw materials, and consumer goods. Workers had money but not the selection or quality of goods they wanted and knew were available in the West. Well-educated urban professionals, managers, and technicians—wealthier and by then constituting some 20 to 25 percent of the population—were experiencing similar frustrations with the economy. Commonly, the only way to get many desired goods was through the expensive and illegal black market—which was of growing importance—or through corruption. It was increasingly apparent that only a small elite, mostly made up of Communist party and government officials, had real access to desired goods and services. It was this elite, which clung to its power and privilege, that enjoyed the higher standard of living available to the middle and upper classes in the West.

Three developments occurring during the decade between 1975 and 1985 exacerbated these fundamental economic problems undermining Soviet communism. The first was the decline of the Soviet leadership. After 1975 Brezhnev weakened noticeably and was probably often ill in the seven years before his death in 1982. Most of the Soviet leadership was made up of old men in long-established offices; the immediate successors to Brezhnev, Yuri Andropov (1982–1984) and Konstantin Chernenko (1984–1985), died shortly after assuming office. These leaders were reluctant to alter course or make way for a new generation of leaders who might try out new ideas to meet the problems that were undermining the Communist economy.

The second was the spread of modern communications and the growing dissident movement within the Soviet Union. Everything from television to tourism was making censorship more difficult and allowing images of life in the wealthier West to spread in Soviet society. Computers and photocopiers further facilitated the spread of uncontrolled information in the Soviet Union and aided the growing dissident movement, whose most notable leader was the Nobel Prize–winning physicist Andrei Sakharov (1921–1989). It was becoming more difficult to hide the economic as well as the political and human rights problems of the Soviet Union.

The third was the Soviet invasion of Afghanistan in 1979, which turned into a costly military quagmire. The Soviet economy was already burdened by large annual expenditures for the military, in part asociated with the Cold War arms race (which the United States under Reagan in the 1980s vigorously pursued) and with the Brezhnev doctrine of willingness to intervene when nations threatened to drop out of the Communist fold. The conflict in Afghanistan stretched on for years, putting new strains on the Soviet economy and increasing the unpopularity of the Soviet leadership, which was unable or unwilling to extract itself from this widely condemned war.

Gorbachev and New Leadership: *Perestroika, Glasnost,* and Disarmament

From a peasant background, Mikhail Gorbachev (1931–) received a strong university education and rose rapidly through the Communist party ranks. In 1985, Gorbachev, at the relatively young age of 54, was appointed leader of the Soviet Union. He reflected the views of reformers within and outside the party who had recognized the fundamental economic problems plaguing the Soviet Union and who were willing to initiate change. Over the next few years he embarked on a three-pronged policy of reform in hopes of transforming the Soviet economy and bringing it up to the standard of Western capitalist economies: *perestroika, glasnost,* and disarmament.

Perestroika constituted Gorbachev's policy for fundamental economic reform. The goal of *perestroika* was to decentralize planning, to allow prices to be influenced by market forces rather than be set by the government, and to remove some of the control over land and agricultural practices exercised by large state farms and place it into the hands of families and cooperatives. In short, *perestroika* constituted a transition to a mixed socialist-capitalist economy, with both socialist planning and a capitalist free market. The process would take time and would be painful, for in the short run it would cause further shortages of consumer goods, inflation of prices, and unemployment. In part to get the strength and resources to carry out *perestroika,* Gorbachev embarked on the policies of *glasnost* and arms reduction.

Glasnost curtailed censorship, encouraged more open discussion of everything from culture to politics, and opened the doors to democratization of the Communist party and the Soviet political system. Dissidents such as Andrei Sakharov were freed. Governmental proceedings were made more public, even televised. In the spring of 1989 the first open elections since 1917 were held, resulting in the defeat of numerous Communist dignitaries. As a logical extension of *glasnost*, Gorbachev indicated that the Brezhnev doctrine of intervention in Eastern Europe, where there were renewed demands for change, had ended. Gorbachev hoped the policies of *glasnost* would elevate his prestige internationally, win foreign political and financial support, and provide cultural and political acceptance at home for his bold restructuring of the Soviet economy.

In 1985 Gorbachev initiated a series of steps to limit and reduce the Soviet military forces. He recognized that the arms race with the United States and the war in Afghanistan were great burdens on the already strained Soviet economy. In meetings with U.S. presidents almost every year between 1985 and 1991, Gorbachev pushed for more and more dramatic arms reductions. These meetings resulted in agreements for important reductions in nuclear weapons and conventional forces in the Soviet Union, the United States, and Europe. At the same time, Gorbachev pursued policies to extract Soviet forces from the war in Afghanistan. These efforts were completed in 1989, when the Soviet Union withdrew its last troops. These dramatic acts elevated Gorbachev's stature both abroad and at home and promised to lighten the burden of military expenditures.

By 1989 the policies of *glasnost* and arms reduction were well under way. However, *perestroika* was proving more difficult and creating much resistance. Only halting steps were made toward fundamental restructuring of the Soviet economy. At this point, events in Eastern Europe took a dramatic turn.

Revolution in Eastern Europe

In 1989 the Communist regimes of Eastern Europe fell one after another. In a series of mostly "velvet," or nonviolent, revolutions, the Eastern European nations cut the ties binding them to the Soviet Union, enacted democratic political reforms, and introduced capitalism into their economies (see Map 59.1). These revolutions had roots in the past but in the short run were made possible by the example of the reforms being instituted by Gorbachev in the USSR and his stated willingness to let events in Eastern Europe unfold without fear of Soviet intervention.

Poland led the movement early in 1989 when negotiations between Communist leader Wojciech Jaruzelski and the outlawed opposition union Solidarity resulted in the legalization of Solidarity and, in June, elections. Solidarity's stunning victory caused Jaruzelski to ask Solidarity to form a new government. By the end of the year Jaruzelski had stepped down, and new elections were called for. Communist rule in Poland was over.

Hungary and Czechoslovakia quickly followed. In the summer and fall of 1989 Hungary, which already had a more mixed economy than the Soviet Union and had experienced some hints of reform in 1988, called for elections, established a multiparty political system, and initiated economic reforms to open the country to private enterprise. By the end of 1989 Hungary's Communist party had reorganized itself into the Hungarian Socialist party. Czechoslovakia was hit with nationwide demonstrations for political reform in the fall of 1989. These soon resulted in the resignation of the hard-line Communist government and the rise to power of Vaclav Havel, a playwright who had recently been imprisoned for his views, and Alexander Dubček, the leader who had tried to liberalize Czechoslovakia in 1968.

The Communist regime in East Germany was the most powerful in Eastern Europe. In the fall of 1989 antigovernment demonstrations spread in East Germany. The hard-line Communist leader Erich Honecker was soon ousted from office. East Germans were increasingly able to cross borders to the West. Finally, in November 1989, the Berlin Wall, erected in 1948 and the most powerful symbol of the Cold War, was torn down and the border to West Germany was opened (see Figure 59.1). In a few months the Communists were ousted from power, and within a year East and West Germany were reunified.

The old Communist regimes in the rest of Eastern Europe were also soon toppled. In Bulgaria an internal coup deposed the Stalinist ruler, Todor Zivkov. In Rumania, the relatively independent but dictatorial Communist leader Nicolae Ceauşescu was overthrown in the most violent of the Eastern Europe revolutions. The follwing year witnessed the collapse of Albania's independent but highly Stalinist regime.

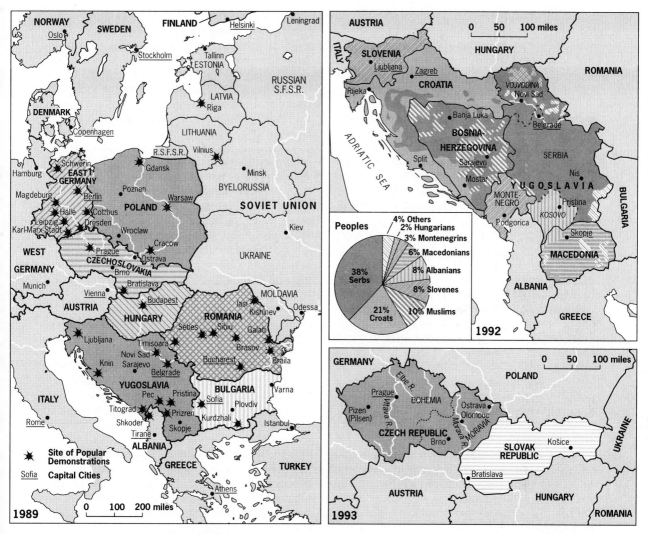

Map 59.1 UPHEAVAL IN EASTERN EUROPE SINCE 1989 These maps indicate the upheavals in Eastern Europe since 1989. The first shows the sites of popular demonstrations during 1989, which led to the fall of communist regimes there. The next two reveal continuing problems with ethnic and religious divisions in the region causing Yugoslavia to disintegrate and Czechoslovakia to divide.

Finally Yugoslavia, long independent from the Soviet Union, was falling apart. In 1991 and 1992, Slovenia, Croatia, Bosnia-Herzegovina, and Macedonia declared their independence as what was once Yugoslavia sank into the chaos of ethnic and religious civil war (see Map 59.1).

In less than a year the old Communist regimes had been removed from power in Eastern Europe, generally being replaced by new governments supporting independence, democratic institutions, and fundamental economic reforms. These events had repercussions in the Soviet Union, where developments were moving beyond the control of Gorbachev and the reformers.

The Collapse and Disintegration of the Soviet Union

In a logical extension of his policy of *glasnost*, Gorbachev pushed through political reforms that called for elections. In 1990 Gorbachev got the Communist party's Central Committee to eliminate the party's constitutional monopoly on political power. He also instituted new political reforms calling for more elections and creating a new, strong presidency—an office separate from the Communist party hierarchy. These policies had the effect of democratizing Soviet politics and undermining the political power of the Communist party. They also had the effect of weakening support for Gorbachev within the party. Moreover, these same policies were facilitating the rise of his chief rival in the opposition, Boris Yeltsin, the newly elected president of the Russian Republic.

Meanwhile, Gorbachev was making only halting steps in his effort to restructure the Soviet economy—*perestroika*. Plans were announced to move the economy away from central planning and then delayed or withdrawn, perhaps in anticipation of the difficulties (unemployment, inflation, and dislocation) the transition would cause. Some steps were taken, but these steps were often theoretical and difficult to put into practice. Uncertainty grew as economic decision makers and the populace did not know what to expect. The reformers, who wanted to move faster, grew frustrated, and the old Communist guard grew more and more alienated. As the economic pain grew, Gorbachev's popularity declined, and resistance—both from Communists who thought he was moving too fast and from reformers who thought he was moving too slowly—grew.

At the same time movements for independence and ethnic tensions were growing within the Soviet Union. Estonia, Lithuania, and Latvia pressed Moscow for independence. In 1991 the Ukraine also voiced a desire for independence. Ethnic conflict and nationalistic demands were spreading in Armenia, Azerbaijan, Moldavia, Georgia, and elsewhere. Gorbachev resisted the demands for independence and tried to quell the ethnic conflicts, but he was losing control of the situation. As a compromise solution, in the spring of 1991 he proposed a "treaty of union," which would have granted independence to the republics while holding them together as a confederation.

In August 1991, as the treaty of union was about to take effect, Communist hard-liners from inside the government and the KGB seized power from Gorbachev. Within three days this coup failed, thanks to the hard-liners' ineptitude and the opposition marshaled by Russian President Boris Yeltsin and his supporters (see Figure 59.2). Gorbachev and Yeltsin then stripped the Communist party of much of its power. By the end of the year, Gorbachev resigned, much of the former Soviet Union was reorganized into a loose confederation called the Commonwealth of Independent States, and several chunks of the former Soviet Union had acquired complete or partial independence (see Map 59.2).

Summary: Collapse and Conflict

In 1985, Mikhail Gorbachev came to power in the Soviet Union. Attempting to deal with growing problems that his predecessors refused to acknowledge, he and the reformers who supported him pursued the risky policies of *perestroika, glasnost,* and arms reductions. The course of history in the Soviet Union, Eastern Europe, and the West changed. In 1989 most of the Communist regimes of Eastern Europe fell, ties to the Soviet Union were severed, and political and economic reforms were initiated. Soviet support for Marxist regimes in the rest of the world was also end-

FIGURE 59.2 Mikhail S. Gorbachev and Boris Yeltsin were the two central figures in the collapse of Communism in the Soviet Union. Here Gorbachev is interrupted by Yeltsin while speaking before the Russian parliament just after the failed August 1991 coup. (Agence France-Presse)

ing. In 1991 the Communist party fell from power in the Soviet Union and the union itself fell apart.

The years after 1991 indicate that this period remains one of transition, with the results still unclear. In the former Soviet Union, Boris Yeltsin retains a very precarious hold on power as President of Russia, but his efforts at reform have been met with resistance and few positive results. Nationalistic, ethnic, religious, and cultural conflict rage in several republics of the former Soviet Union. Disappointment and pessimism probably outweigh relief and optimism for most people. There are signs that things are likely to get even worse before they get better. In Eastern Europe, the economic transition is going at varying rates—more quickly in Poland and Hungary, more slowly in Bulgaria, Rumania, and Albania—but almost everywhere painfully and with still-disappointed expectations. In some areas nationalistic, ethnic, and religious rivalries have created divisions, most dramatically in Yugoslavia, where civil wars have marked the collapse of that country, more peacefully in Czechoslovakia, which reluctantly agreed to divide itself into the Czech Republic and Slovakia.

Finally, it should be stressed that a few nations in the world remain Communist, though they are now more isolated and their commitment to communism seems more fragile. Moreover, while the collapse of communism has weakened Communist beliefs and movements in Europe and elsewhere, the Soviet model of communism should not be confused with the socialist policies adopted quite successfully in the Scandinavian nations in particular and many Western nations in general. While many analysts herald events in this period as the triumph of capitalism, others argue that in the long run the collapse of Soviet communism could facilitate the adoption of moderate policies associated with democratic socialism.

2. INTEGRATION, THE RISE OF GERMANY, AND CONSERVATISM IN EUROPE

During the late 1980s and early 1990s, Europe's international system was being restructured by new impulses toward integration. European integration took root in the late 1950s, when six

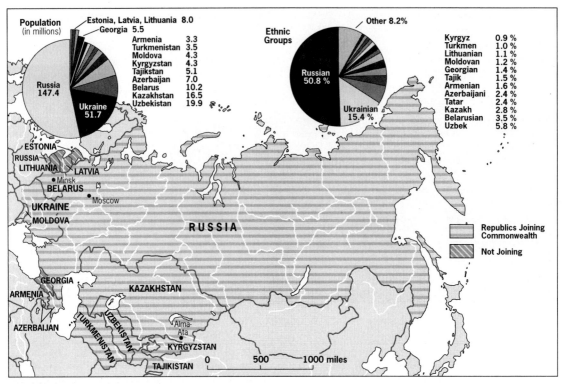

Map 59.2 THE NEW COMMONWEALTH In 1991 the Soviet Union dissolved. Most of the republics within that union joined the new Commonwealth of Independent States, a loose confederation, while some republics, such as Lithuania, Latvia, and Estonia, broke away.

Western European nations established the European Economic Community (Common Market). In slow, uneven steps, the European Community grew during the 1960s and 1970s (see pp. 717–718).

During the 1980s and early 1990s, new steps were taken to broaden and deepen its importance. In 1981 a European Parliament at Strasbourg was elected; while not yet politically strong, it was a significant step that signaled the possibility of greater political and military integration. In 1986 Portugal and Spain joined the European Community. In 1990 the former East Germany, thanks to its unification with West Germany, became part of the community. In 1992 the twelve members of the European Community eliminated all major internal barriers to trade, the flow of capital, and the movement of people. That same year the European Commu-

nity agreed with the seven-member European Free Trade Association to form the European Economic Area, creating the world's largest trading bloc and paving the way for several new countries to seek full membership. A number of Eastern European nations are also anxious to join. Also in 1992, France and Germany agreed to form a joint army corps, the European Corps, open to other members of the Western European Union. With the Maastricht Treaty, the European Community made plans to establish a common currency and a central bank by 1999. However, growing opposition to the Maastricht Treaty casts doubt on whether those plans will be carried out.

The potential of the European Community is tremendous. The present twelve members have more than 340 million inhabitants and a combined gross national product approximately equal to that of the United States. Its people are relatively wealthy and enjoy free access to an immense single market. Despite some strong resistance to further integration and disagreement on common policies such as what to do about the conflicts in Yugoslavia, there are signs that a more collective European identity is forming and that the European Community may be willing to start acting in common both politically and militarily.

Two other trends of considerable importance arose in Europe during the late 1980s and early 1990s. The first was the new importance of Germany. During the decades after World War II West Germany successfully rebuilt its economy to the point where it enjoyed even greater prosperity than the other large states of Europe such as France, Great Britain, and Italy. With communism collapsing in the late 1980s and early 1990s, Germany acted early, sending far more aid and investing far more extensively in Eastern Europe and the former Soviet Union than any other nation did. These costly efforts may bear the fruits of new economic and political influence in the future. Meanwhile, German unification in 1990 gave Germany new recognition as a European power and confirmed Germany as a world economic leader—first in exports, second in favorable balance of trade, and third in gross domestic product. West German Chancellor Helmut Kohl and his conservative Christian Democrats emerged victorious from reunified Germany's first national elections.

This victory of the conservative Christian Democrats in Germany was part of the second trend sweeping most of Europe since the mid-1980s: a general political shift toward the right. The traditional strength of Communist parties in Western Europe was waning, and socialists were being converted, at least in part, to capitalism. In general, political parties of the Left, whether in power as they were in France under François Mitterrand and Spain under Felipe González Marquez or not, were moderating their policies. Nationalized industries were being privatized—sold to private investors—under the conservatives in Great Britain and the socialists in France. Economic planning and state regulation of economic affairs were broadly under attack. The cost of social programs was being questioned. Even the Scandinavian nations, long the bastions of social democracy, were taking steps toward the right.

It is too early to tell if this trend toward the right will be fundamental and lasting or whether it is part of a cycle of swings between Left and Right that has been going on since World War II. However, when coupled with the fall of communism and the political conservatism of the United States, this trend seems to take on an added significance for the future.

3. THE UNITED STATES: MILITARY ASCENDANCY AND ECONOMIC PROBLEMS

The collapse of communism and disturbing economic trends left the United States in a mixed and unfamiliar position in the late 1980s and early 1990s.

With the former Soviet forces in decline and the dissolution of the Warsaw Pact in 1991, the United States emerged as the world's only military superpower. Some of that military dominance was demonstrated when, in 1991, the United States led a United Nations–authorized coalition to repel Iraq's invasion of Kuwait. In a six-week war the U.S.-dominated coalition was easily victorious.

At almost the same time, there were more indications that the United States, while still wealthy and with the world's largest gross domestic product, was a declining economic power. By the mid-1980s, years of budget deficits, in part fueled by high military spending and tax cuts, created a massive, growing national debt. In 1985 the United States, long a creditor nation, became the world's largest debtor nation, and almost every year since 1985 the debt has grown at an increasing rate. Meanwhile, the United States has been suffering in the economic competition with its Asian and European rivals. Large trade imbalances and major losses in manufacturing to overseas competitors have become common. One response to this economic competition, particularly in light of the European Community's moves to create a single European market, has been the effort to create a free trade zone among Mexico, the United States, and Canada—the North American Free Trade Agreement.

Debate has grown in the United States over

the significance of the convergence of military dominance and relative economic decline. Some argue that there is no longer a need for such costly military expenditures and that money saved from military expenditures should be used for domestic programs or to lower the public debt. Others worry that the United States will be more tempted to use military might to disguise economic problems or pursue economic goals; they point to the role that U.S. interests in Middle East oil played in the U.S.-led war with Iraq.

4. THE PACIFIC RIM, JAPAN, AND CHINA

The recent steps toward economic integration in Europe and the economic problems experienced by the United States are related to economic developments in the lands along the rim of the Pacific Ocean, particularly in East Asia.

Countries enjoying relative political stability, offering cheap and disciplined labor, and open to capitalism—such as Hong Kong, Taiwan, South Korea, and Singapore—have attracted investment (particularly from large multinational corporations) and experienced strong economic growth. Over the last decade these countries have competed successfully with the United States and Europe, particularly in electronics, textiles, plastics, and heavy manufacturing.

Japan has enjoyed economic leadership in Asia for decades (see pp. 736–737) and has become more of a world economic power. Year after year this relatively small country has led the world in enjoying a large favorable balance of trade and now has the world's second largest gross domestic product. By the mid-1980s Japan was a world leader in automobile production and electronics. The country has made numerous foreign investments and become a major worldwide creditor, in recent years acquiring a dominant position in international banking. It has a growing opportunity to translate that economic position into political power.

China has had a great economic potential for a long time. By the mid-1980s the new economic policies initiated by Deng Xiaoping in 1978 (see p. 739) that relaxed state controls over the economy were bearing fruit. Trade agreements with Japan and the United States increased foreign investment in China and rapidly expanded trade. By the mid-1980s Chinese farmers were producing a surplus of food for export. In certain areas of the country, particularly the "New Economic Zones" in the southeast, new capitalistic investments and manufacturing created large growth rates. As opposed to the Soviet Union, China's economic reforms were made without corresponding political reforms. China attempted to embrace capitalism while retaining its Communist political structure. Whether that can continue was called into question in 1989, when massive demonstrations, organized by students and intellectuals and calling for political reform, were held in Beijing. Supported by China's rural population and most of the army, the government used violence to end the demonstrations. Nevertheless, many analysts expect change in the upcoming years as China's leadership ages and new pressures for political reform increase.

These developments in East Asia challenge some of the economic dominance enjoyed by the West for so long. They are another sign that the West has become deeply tied to other areas of the world and that we need to view recent history from a global as well as a Western perspective.

5. PROBLEMS OF THE PRESENT AND FUTURE

Along with the hopes engendered by the collapse of communism, the promises of integration in Europe, and the realities of economic growth in East Asia, there are several growing and persisting problems in Western civilization.

In the wake of communism's collapse, division and ethnic conflict have arisen in several areas of Eastern Europe and the former Soviet Union. The most costly armed conflict in Europe since World War II broke out in Yugoslavia in the early 1990s. Continued conflict in the Middle East, where Europeans and Americans have important interests, again drew Western forces into combat. Though the threat that the Cold War would turn into a world war has diminished, the large-scale arms trade continues and the worldwide spread of nuclear weapons remains out of control.

Experience in the 1970s, 1980s, and again in the 1990s shows us that economic growth cannot be taken for granted. Unemployment, inflation,

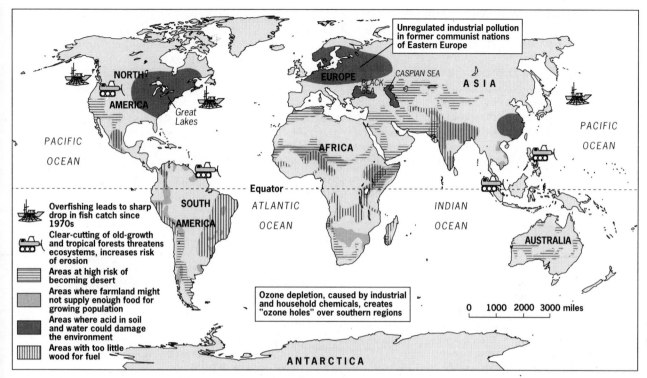

Map 59.3 GLOBAL ENVIRONMENTAL PROBLEMS This map indicates some widespread environmental problems, most of which stem from population increases, industrial production, and exploitation of natural resources. Other problems could be added to this list, such as the emissions of "greenhouse gases" by industry believed to be causing a rise in global temperature, with uncertain consequences for coastal areas, agriculture, and wildlife, and the depletion of species as thousands of plant and animal species become extinct each year. While this map reveals how some areas of the world are affected more than others, it also shows how global and interconnected these environmental problems are.

and declining personal incomes have created social discontent that governments seem impotent to master. Moreover, the price we pay for economic growth and modernization seems to have been rising in recent years. Industrialization, urbanization, and affluence have strained our natural resources (see Map 59.3). Our air, our fresh water, even our seas are becoming more polluted. Depletion of the protective ozone layer and a heating up of the atmosphere, hastened by deforestation, threaten us. Our land is becoming blighted by concrete, tasteless commercial development, and poisonous wastes. Our cities have become sources of poverty, crime, and drug addiction as much as wealth and hope. The relent-

less march of technology, with its accompanying urbanization, has brought many creature comforts to the masses, but it has robbed millions of their manual skills, social contacts, and sense of community. Government has expanded the social services it provides, but that has not created a greater sense of inclusion in modern society; rather, a sense of alienation seems to persist and new conflicts arise as immigrants, minorities, and women assert themselves. Science and government, so successful in creating new military weapons and certain large projects such as space exploration, have been unable to halt the deadly worldwide AIDS epidemic.

There is a growing awareness that the relatively affluent West cannot ignore the non-Western areas of the world—some in East Asia with a new competitive edge, far more with crushing debts, pressing needs, and unmet demands. Indeed, the gap between the affluent, industrialized nations of the north and the poor, developing nations of the south has been growing rather than narrowing. Worse, it is in the south that the burden of population growth is by far the heaviest.

All these problems now weigh upon the West and are not likely to go away in the foreseeable future. In some ways Western civilization and its institutions, which have been so long in developing—the family, governments, courts of law, churches, traditions of social and moral behavior—are being severely tested. While problems of the present usually seem more difficult than those of the past, the consequences of not dealing with today's problems are likely to be catastrophic. Whether and how Western civilization handles these challenges remains to be seen.

SUGGESTED READING

The Collapse of Communism

T. G. Ash, *The Magic Lantern: The Revolution of '89 Witnessed in Warsaw, Budapest, Berlin and Prague* (1990). A fine account of events by a knowledgeable observer.

J. F. Brown, *Surge to Freedom: The End of Communist Rule in Eastern Europe* (1991). A useful summary.

R. Dahrendorf, *Reflections on the Revolution in Europe* (1991). A careful analysis of political and economic prospects in Eastern Europe.

G. Hosking, *The Awakening of the Soviet Union* (1990). Focuses on the social changes underlying reform in the Soviet Union.

R. J. Kaiser, *Why Gorbachev Happened: His Triumphs and His Failures* (1991). Stresses the difficulties facing Gorbachev.

B. Nahaylo and V. Swoboda, *Soviet Disunion: A History of the Nationalities Problem in the USSR* (1990). Reveals the problems facing Gorbachev and the republics of the former Soviet Union.

Integration, Germany, and European Politics

N. Colchester and D. Buchan, *Europower: The Essential Guide to Europe's Economic Transformation in 1992* (1990). Historical analysis of and speculations on the future of the European Community.

J. W. Friend, *Seven Years in France: François Mitterrand and the Unintended Revolution, 1981–1988* (1989). Emphasizes how adaptable Mitterrand and the French Socialists have been.

P. Jenkins, *Mrs. Thatcher's Revolution: The Ending of a Socialist Era* (1988). A study of Europe's leading conservative politician.

D. Marsh, *The Germans: Rich, Bothered and Divided* (1990). A good recent analysis prior to unification.

The United States

David Halberstam, *The Next Century* (1991). A well-written analysis and speculations.

P. Kennedy, *The Rise and Fall of the Great Powers: Economic Change and Military Conflict from 1500 to 2000* (1987). Sections focus on connections between economic and military power in the United States.

J. R. Schlesinger, *America at Century's End* (1989). A good recent analysis.

The Pacific Rim, Japan, and China

D. Aikman, *Pacific Rim: Area of Change, Area of Opportunity* (1986). Emphasizes the significance of economic changes.

D. W. W. Chang, *China under Deng Xiaoping: Political and Economic Reform* (1991). An optimistic analysis.

M. Fathers and A. Higgins, *Tiananmen: The Rape of Peking* (1990). A study of the Democracy Movement and demonstrations in Beijing in 1989.

C. V. Prestowitz, Jr., *Trading Places: How We Allowed Japan to Take the Lead* (1988). Analyzes Japan's economic challenge to the United States.

Problems of the Present and Future

D. B. King, *The Crisis of Our Time: Reflections on the Course of Western Civilization, Past, Present, and Future* (1988). An interesting, speculative account.

State of the World. A Worldwatch Institute Report on Progress Toward a Sustainable Society (1984 to present). An annual report emphasizing environmental conditions.

RETROSPECT

A long period of relative peace, growing prosperity, and sense of progress ended in August 1914. World War I initiated a three-decade period in which Europe would be shattered politically, economically, and socially by war, revolution, and depression.

The European nations were plunged into World War I by an entangling alliance system that enhanced economic and nationalistic rivalries and by persistent domestic tensions that encouraged national governments searching for unity to adopt belligerent policies. The hoped-for short war turned into a nightmarish struggle between the Central Powers and the Allies. The destruction went beyond the massive human and material toll to the political entities themselves. The German, Austro-Hungarian, Russian, and Ottoman empires did not survive the war. The British and French empires were both weakened, as indeed were Britain and France themselves. Efforts to make a durable peace and to set up an international organization, the League of Nations, to keep the peace foundered on the rocks of national self-interest. Instead, the peace settlements left a legacy of resentment that would haunt the West during the following two decades.

The victors in World War I were the liberal democratic nations, and it was hoped that this victory would be turned into a permanent gain for liberal democracy. The trend toward totalitarianism, fascism, and authoritarianism during the 1920s and 1930s dashed these hopes. The first blow to liberalism and capitalism came during the final stages of World War I, when revolution brought a Communist regime to power in Russia. Lenin led the revolutionary Bolsheviks to victory in November 1917 and over the next few years extracted the Soviet Union from World War I, defeated rivals in a bloody civil war, and established the foundations of a totalitarian state. By the end of the 1920s Lenin's successor, Stalin, had initiated the five-year plans that would collectivize Soviet agriculture and industrialize the nation. His Great Purges in the 1930s eliminated all resistance, completing the transformation of the Soviet Union into a totalitarian state.

The next blow to liberalism came with the rise of fascism in Italy under Mussolini during the early 1920s. Over the next few years Mussolini took steps to turn his Fascist regime into a totalitarian state, but these steps were always incomplete. Full-blown totalitarian fascism was established during the 1930s in Nazi Germany under Hitler. Much more than the Italian variety, German fascism was tinged with violence and racism. Both regimes denounced liberal democracy and, indeed, most of the developments since the French Revolution that Western liberals had pointed to with pride. With their emphasis on nationalism, militarism, and expansion, these Fascist regimes represented a direct threat to peace and the democratic West.

Two more blows to liberalism seriously undermined the position of the democratic West. The first was the rise of authoritarian regimes in southern Europe, eastern Europe, and Japan— almost all replacing governments that had more liberal leanings. The second was the Great Depression, which encouraged authoritarian movements everywhere and caused the Western democracies to turn inward. Thus, during the 1930s, when the threat from Fascist and authoritarian nations was growing, the Western democracies were increasingly paralyzed by their own domestic problems.

Neither the foundering League of Nations nor a policy of appeasement could restrain Germany, Italy, and Japan from pursuing their policies of expansion. In 1939 World War II broke out. For over two years the Axis powers seemed unstoppable, gaining victory after victory. By the end of 1942, however, overexpansion by the Axis forces, the stiff resistance by Soviet troops, the heroic struggle by the British, and the entrance of the United States into the war had started to turn the tide. Almost three years of struggle on a world-wide basis were necessary to end the war in 1945. By that time the Nazis had carried out a policy of genocide and enslavement as part of Hitler's racist "New Order," and war had claimed some 40 million lives.

At the end of World War II devastation and disorganization were the rule rather than the exception. Most nations of Europe were so weakened that they had to rely on one of the two new superpowers that had emerged from World War II: the United States and the Soviet Union. Soon, even the unity of the victorious allies, which included the United States and the Soviet Union, proved too fragile to last. Deep-seated discord between these respective leaders of the non-Communist and Communist worlds broke out into the Cold War. Europe became divided into two camps—one of democratic capitalism (though often with elements of socialism mixed in) led by the United States, the other of communism modeled and led by the Soviet Union. This division of Europe and the broader Cold War struggle would dominate international policies for decades to come. Yet, despite the destruction of World War II, the emergence of the dominating superpowers, and the disunity brought about by the Cold War, European nations recovered, expanded their economies, and enjoyed relative political stability during the following decades. Problems in the 1970s and 1980s did not diminish from that record; rather, they indicated that Western civilization had to face and deal with new and previoulsy ignored difficulties. One way that nations attempted to solve common problems was through regional integration and internationalism, but the results were mixed.

The most significant social, intellectual, and cultural changes in Western civilization during the twentieth century are more difficult to pinpoint than the concrete political and economic developments. For the most part, the social, intellectual, and cultural developments have been a continuation of trends already under way by the end of the nineteenth century. Western society became more urbanized as it adjusted to the demands of continuing economic modernization. Women changed their roles and their perception of themselves, a reflection of some of the changes occurring within the basic unit of Western society: the family. The Christian churches continued to have difficulty adjusting to a changing, secularizing, scientific world. Intellectual and cultural trends reflected the richness of Western life as well as the often discouraging problems encountered by the West since the end of the ninetenth century.

In the decades following World War II, France, England, Belgium, the Netherlands, and other Western nations lost most of their colonial empires. The new and old nations of the non-Western world struggled to get onto their feet and assert themselves in an environment marked by Cold War rivalries, deep-rooted internal discord, and the disruption caused by the incomplete spread of Western values and institutions to their lands. In different ways, Japan and China emerged as leading economic and political powers in the Far East. The struggle between Hindus and Moslems in India, Pakistan, and Bangladesh and the wars in Southeast Asia made the British and French (and, later, American) withdrawals from southern Asia problematic. The Middle East has been marked by a series of wars and disruptions as well as the emergence of a new power bloc based on wealth from oil production. The long-lasting lack of peace between Israel and most of its neighbors, violence in divided Lebanon, and the war between Iran and Iraq suggest that this area of the world will remain explosive for the foreseeable future. Africans face tremendous difficulties in creating unity in nations artificially created by colonial powers and burdened by harsh economic conditions. The political instability of most African nations attests to these difficulties. Most Latin American nations have for decades been dominated by a wealthy elite and often right-wing authoritarian governments (supported, and usually staffed, by the military). As the area's population grows, so does the contrast between the few haves and the mass of have-nots. Revolutions, guerrilla activities, and political upheavals indicate that stability may be the exception rather than the rule in Latin America.

In recent years, new developments have marked the end of a period that stretches back to World War II or even World War I and the beginning of what may be a new historical era. The most dramatic and significant change is the collapse of communism in the Soviet Union and Eastern Europe. The roots of the collapse stretch back to economic and political problems that were growing in the 1970s and 1980s. Trying to deal with these problems, Gorbachev initiated policies of *perestroika, glasnost,* and disarmament in the Soviet Union and gave the Eastern European nations more of a free hand in determining their own destinies. In 1989 revolutions toppled Communist regimes through Eastern Europe. By 1991 the Communists were also out of power in the Soviet Union, which itself disintegrated.

Less dramatic but important developments were occurring elsewhere. Europe was taking new, if halting, steps toward full economic integration and even some political and social integration. Germany, newly unified, was gaining strength and stature. The United States found itself in the position of being an uncontested mil-

itary superpower but facing more and increasingly successful economic competition. Much of that economic competition came from the East Asian nations along the Pacific Rim, to which economic development was shifting the world's economic balance of power.

At the same time, new and persistent social and environmental problems are facing the West and the world. These problems promise to test both our spirit and our abilities in disturbing ways.

INDEX

Note: Page numbers followed by the letter *f* or *m* indicate figures or maps, respectively.

Bourgeoisie: Dutch, 441–443; and French Revolution, 493, 495–498, 500; Marxian view on, 528
Boxer Rebellion, 629
Boyle, Robert, 463, 464
Brahe, Tycho, 459, 461
Brahmins, 451
Brahms, Johannes, 603
Brandenburg, 426
Brandt, Willy, 711
Brazil, 512, 750, 751m; independence, 513; in Napoleonic era, 508–509
Brest-Litovsk, Treaty of, 647, 659, 664
Brezhnev, Leonid, 715, 755, 756
Briand, Aristide, 609
Britain, Battle of, 691–692
British East India Company, 635
Brothers Karamazov, The (Dostoyevski), 600
Browning, Robert, 599
Brueghel, Pieter, the Younger, 418f
Brusilov, General Aleksei, 647
Bukharin, Nikolai, 658
Bulgaria and Bulgarians, 614m, 615, 645, 649, 675, 756
Bundesrat, 571
Burke, Edmund, 531, 540
Burma (Myanmar), 629, 741, 742m
Burns, Robert, 414, 532–533
Burschenschaften, 545
Byron, George Gordon, Lord, 531, 533, 535, 536, 544
Byzantine Empire, 427

Cabinet system (Great Britain), 440–441
Caetano, Marcelo, 712
Cahiers, 495
Calculus, 461, 463
Calcutta, 449
Calhoun, John C., 618
California, 619
Calvin, John, 476
Calvinism, 435, 482
Cambodia, 742m, 743
Camp David Agreements, 745
Camus, Albert, 730
Canada, 446, 455, 485, 576, 596; dominion status, 635
Canal building, 518
Canning, George, 543, 547
Cape Colony (Dutch), 448, 632, 633m, 634
Cape-to-Cairo railroad, 634
Capitalism: destruction of (Marxian view), 528; and Nazi threat, 671; opposition to communism, 664; in Pacific rim, 762; Russian, 658; United States, 623–624
Carbonari, 558
Caribbean Sea, 446
Carlsbad Decrees, 545
Carlyle, Thomas, 597
Carmen (Bizet), 537
Carnegie, Andrew, 623
Carnot, Lazare, 503
Carnot, Sadi, 579
Carson-Pirie-Scott Department Store, Chicago, 603f
Cart, The (le Nain), 407f
Cartels, 578
Carter, Jimmy, 707, 714, 745
Cartesian dualism, 463
Cartwright, Edmund, 517
Casino Pass, battle of, 698
Caste system, 451
Castlereagh, Robert Stewart, Lord, 540, 541f
Castro, Fidel, 713, 750
Catalonia, 685
Catherine II, the Great, Tsarina, 411, 430, 431, 474, 477
Cavaliers, 436

Cavendish, Margaret, 464
Cavour, Camillo Canso, Count of, 565–566, 639
Ceaușescu, Nicolae, 716, 756
Celebes, 447
Central America: independence, 512–513; precolumbian, 450
Central Intelligence Agency, 750
Central Powers (WWI), 643–651, 646m
Cézanne, Paul, 600, 601, 731
Chamberlain, Houston Stewart, 598, 670
Chamberlain, Neville, 680, 686, 687f, 691
Chamber of Deputies (Paris), 607–608
Champlain, Samuel de, 446
Chancellor Sequier (Lebrun), 424f
Change: concept of, 467
Charity institutions, 523
Charles I, king of England, 435–437
Charles II, king of England, 438–439, 440, 459
Charles V, Holy Roman emperor, 463
Charles X, king of France, 544–545, 555
Charles XII, king of Sweden, 430, 431
Chartism, 522, 553–554, 554f
Chateaubriand, François-René de, 534
Checks and balances, 473, 488
Chekhov, Anton, 600, 730
Chemistry, 576
Chernenko, Konstantin, 755
Chiang Kai-shek, 694, 737
Chiaroscuro, 416
Child labor, 410, 520, 523, 553
Chile, 750, 751m
China: European impact on, 448, 451; Japanese aggression against, 677, 684, 686; Western imperialism and, 628m, 629–630
China, People's Republic of, 707, 715, 735, 737–739, 740, 766; contemporary, 762; economy, 762; and Korean War, 739–740; and Vietnam War, 743
Chopin, Frédéric, 536–537
Christ at Gethsemane (El Greco), 415
Christian Democratic parties, 707; German, 711, 761; Italian, 711–712
Christianity. *See also* Religion: and anti-Semitism, 591, 615; in colonial America, 482–483; contemporary, 724–726; Enlightenment and, 472–473; growth of pietism (17th–18th c.), 412; and imperialism, 627; modernists, 593; 19th c. scientific challenge to, 590–594
Christian Socialist party (Austria), 615
Christian Social Workers' party (Germany), 615
Christina, queen of Sweden, 411
Churchill, John, duke of Marlborough, 441
Churchill, Winston, 691, 692, 693, 695, 696, 698, 703–704, 704f, 708, 709, 740
Cinema, 597, 730, 733
City-states: Swahili, 452
Civil Constitution of the Clergy, 499
Civil rights movement (American), 713
Civil War (England), 436–438
Civil War (U.S.), 564, 565, 620–622, 639
Clarendon, Earl of, 438
Clarendon Code, 438
Clarissa Harlowe (Richardson), 414
Classical era (modern), 413–418, 477, 532
Clay, Henry, 618
Clayton Antitrust Act, 624
Clemenceau, Georges, 651, 652f
Clergy: and French Revolution, 493, 499, 501; and liberal secularism, 591–592; Napoleon and, 507
Clive, Robert, 455
Clock, pendulum, 464
Cobden Treaty, 565
Cockfighting, 418

Deffaud, Madame du, 472
de Gaulle, Charles, 690–691, 709–710, 710f, 747
Deism, 532
de Klerk, F. W., 749
Delacroix, Eugène, 535
Democracy: modern European, 606–609
Democratic party (U.S.), 622, 624
Demoiselles d'Avignon, Les (Picasso), 595f
Deng Xiao-ping, 739, 762
Denmark, 509, 578, 609, 690, 693; border dispute with Germany, 569m, 569–570, 610; in Common Market, 717
de Sade, Marquis, 471
Descartes, René, 442, 462–463, 464, 532
Descent of Man (Darwin), 588, 591
Despotism, "enlightened," 474–475
Détente policy, 707
Dialectical system, 532
Dialogue on the Two Chief Systems of the World (Galileo), 460–461
Dickens, Charles, 599
Diderot, Denis, 469, 470, 471, 532
Diesel, Rudolf, 576
Diesel engine, 576
Diets: German Confederation, 545; Polish, 430, 431
Directory (France), 504, 506
Discourse of Methodology (Descartes), 462
Disraeli, Benjamin, 505, 553
Divorce: contemporary, 721; in early modern times (17th–18th c.), 411
DNA research, 727
Dnepropetrovsk dam, 661
Doctor Zhivago (Pasternak), 730
Dogfighting, 418
Dollfus, Engelbert, 675
Doll's House, A (Ibsen), 600
Domesticity: cult of, 584
Dominion status (Canada), 635
Don Giovanni (Mozart), 418
Doré, Gustave, 522f
Dostoyevski, Fyodor, 600, 730
Drama: modern, 730; realist, 600
Drang nach Osten, 671
Dreiser, Theodore, 599–600, 730
Dresden, 695
Dreyfus, Alfred, 599, 608
Dreyfus case, 591, 599, 608
Dryden, John, 414
Dual Monarchy (Austria-Hungary), 613–615, 614m, 652; and World War I, 643–645
Dubček, Alexander, 716, 756
Dulles, John Foster, 707
Du Marais, Cèsar, 470
Duma (Russia), 613, 656
Dumas, Alexander, 535, 537f
Dunkirk, battle of, 690, 691, 697m
Duquesne, Fort, 455
Durkheim, Émile, 727
Dutch East India Company, 442, 447
Dutch War, 425
Dutch West India Company, 447
Dvorak, Antonín, 603
Dynamo, 575

Eakins, Thomas, 586f
Eastern Europe: absolutism and, 425–431; authoritarianism in, 675; collapse of communism in, 756–758, 757m, 767; contemporary social changes, 721; nationalism, conservatism, and militarism in, 609–615; nationalist feelings under Hapsburgs, 546; post-WWII, 715–717; Soviet hegemony over, 704, 705, 715–717

Eastern Orthodox church, 594 (*See also* Greek Orthodox church)
East Germany, 707, 711, 715, 716; dissolution, 756, 757m
East Indies: European trade, 442
Ebert, Friedrich, 669
Economy: collapse of communism, 754–755; commercial revolution, 406; contemporary problems, 762–764; early Soviet problems, 658–662; Enlightenment and, 473–474; and French absolutism, 423, 425; and French Revolution, 499; Great Depression, 671, 678f, 679, 681–684; history and (Marxian view), 528; household, 410; Japanese postwar and contemporary, 736, 762; in Latin America, 750, 752; liberalism and, 525–526; mercantilism, 473; in Nazi Germany, 674; post-WWI, 680, 681, 683–684; theories of, 471, 473–474; 20th c. theory, 728
Eddy, Don, 719f
Edict of Nantes, 421, 422, 424
Edison, Thomas A., 575
Education: contemporary, 723–724; early modern (18th c.), 418; industrialization and, 523; and popular culture, 732; public modern, 596; secularization of, 591; Soviet, 662
Egalitarianism: American, 487; Soviet, 663–664
Egypt, modern: Napoleon in, 506; nationalism, 744, 744m, 745–746; wars and treaty with Israel, 745–746; and Western imperialism, 630–631; World War II in, 692, 696, 697m, 698
Einstein, Albert, 588, 589f, 598, 726
Eisenhower, Dwight D., 698, 707
El Alamein, battle of, 696, 697m, 698
Electricity, 575–576, 587
Electrons, 588
Elements of the Philosophy of Newton (Voltaire), 469
Eliot, George (Mary Ann Evans), 599
Eliot, T. S., 729
Elizabeth I, queen of England, 434, 476
Elizabeth, Tsarina, 427
Emerson, Ralph Waldo, 534
Emigration, 580, 581f, 611–612
Emigrés (France), 497, 501
Émile (Rousseau), 533
Empiricism, 467, 468
Ems dispatch, 571
Enclosures, 408
Encyclopedia, 469, 469f, 470, 471
Enemy of the People, An (Ibsen), 600
Engels, Friedrich, 528, 578
England: agricultural revolution in, 408; challenge to absolutism, 434–441, 476; Civil War, 436–438, 476; Far East colonies and trade, 448–449, 451; Glorious Revolution, 414, 439–441; mercantile wars, 454; North American colonies, 446–447, 448m, 454–456; pietism in, 412; Protectorate, 437–438; Restoration, 438–439; 17th and 18th c. literature, 413–414; Stuart, 414, 434–437, 438–439; war with Holland (17th c.), 438–439
English East India Company, 448–449, 455
English Poor Laws, 410
Enlightenment, 413, 466–475, 476, 485, 512, 527, 532, 540, 656; concepts, 467–468; despots and, 474–475; *philosophes*, 468–471, 474; political and economic aspects of, 473–474; and religion, 472–473; salons, 466f, 472; women and, 466f, 472
Entrepreneurship, 577
Environmental problems, global, 763m, 763–764, 767
Epidemics: industrial age, 523
Equality (French concept of), 513
Erie Canal, 518
Ernst, Max, 731
Eroica (Beethoven), 535
Essay Concerning Human Understanding (Locke), 468
Essay on Population (Malthus), 525, 588

Genoa, 540
Geocentrism, 459
Geoffrein, Madame, 466f, 472
George I, king of England, 417, 440, 441
George II, king of England, 440
George III, king of England, 485
Georgia, 446, 758
German Communist party, 579
German Confederation, 541, 542m, 545–546, 557–558, 567, 569m, 570–571
German Democratic Republic (East Germany), 707, 711, 715, 716; dissolution, 756, 757m
German Federal Republic (West Germany), 706, 711, 736, 761
German National party, 615
Germany: in Africa, 633, 633m; anti-Semitism, 615; Bismarck's militarism, 611; conservatism (1815–1830), 545–546; educational advances, 596; emigration, 580, 611–612, 619; empire, 569m, 570–572, 610–612, 765; industrialization, 516, 575, 576, 611, 612; in Napoleonic era, 508; nationalism, 545, 567, 569–572, 597, 598; Nazi, 667, 670–675 (see also Nazi Germany); and Ottoman Empire, 611, 631–632; pietism in, 412; post-WWII partition, 706, 711; reunification, 759–760, 761, 767; Revolution of 1848, 558; romantic era, 534, 535, 536, 537; unification of modern, 566–567, 569m, 569–572; union movement, 578; Weimar, 669–670, 671, 672, 673; West, 706, 711, 736, 761; and World War I, 643–653, 646m, 650m, 658; and World War II, 661, 686–688, 690–693, 695–700, 697m
Gestapo, 674
Ghana, 452, 747, 748m, 749
Ghosts (Ibsen), 485
Gibraltar, 454
Giolitti, Giovanni, 609
Girondins, 501, 503
Giscard d'Estaing, Valéry, 710–711
Gladstone, William E., 553, 606
Glasnost, 755, 756, 758, 766
Gleaners, The (Millet), 535
Glorious Revolution, 414, 439–441
Gobineau, Comte de, 598, 670
Godard, Jean-Luc, 730
Goebbels, Paul Joseph, 670, 674
Göring, Hermann, 670
Goethe, Johann Wolfgang von, 414, 490, 534, 674
Gogh, Vincent van, 601
Golan Heights, 745
Gold Coast, 747
Golden Bough, The (Frazer), 592
Gömbös, Julius, 675
Gompers, Samuel, 623
Gonzáles, Felipe, 712, 761
Gorbachev, Mikhail, 754, 755–756, 758, 759f, 766
Gorky, Maxim, 600
Gothic art and architecture, 602
Götterdämmerung (Wagner), 537
Gounod, Charles-François, 537
Government: age of absolutism, 420–432; American colonial, 483; American republicanism, 487–490; challenge to absolutism in England, 433–441; Enlightenment and, 473–474; French Revolution and, 499–500; under Louis XIV, 423; and 19th c. liberalism, 551, 553
Grand Cyrus (Scudéry), 413
Grand National Union, 522
Gravitation, laws of (Newton), 461
Great Awakening, 483
Great Britain, 440; Act of Union, 440; in Africa, 632, 633, 633m, 634; American colonies, 481–483; and American Revolution, 483–486; and appeasement, 685, 686; Bismarck's Germany and, 610, 611; and China, 629; in Common Market, 717; and Congress of Vienna, 540;

conservatism (1815–1830), 546–547; contemporary, 709; Crimean War, 564; democratic reforms, 606–607; educational advances, 596; in Egypt, 631; emigration, 580; empire, 607, 628m (see also Colonies; India), 633m, 634–636, 708; and French Revolution, 501; independence for African colonies, 747–749, 748m; Industrial Revolution, 516–519, 521–523, 525–526, 575; liberalism and reform, 550f, 551, 553–554; and Mideast, 744–745; and Napoleonic wars, 506, 507, 508, 509; nationalism, 597; post-WWI, 679–680, 684, 685; post-WWII, 707, 708–709, 710; Quadruple Alliance, 543; romantic era, 532–533, 535; socialism, 579; union movement, 578; Victorian and realist literature, 599; War of 1812, 618, 622; welfare state, 724; and World War I, 643–647, 646m, 648, 649, 650–652, 653; and World War II, 686–688, 690, 691–692, 693, 695, 696, 698
Great Depression, 671, 678f, 679, 681–684, 683f, 765
Great Fear, 497
Great Leap Forward (China), 738
Great Purges (Soviet), 661–662, 765
Greco, El (Domenikos Theotokopoulos), 414–415, 600
Greece, ancient: and Italian Renaissance, 458; and neoclassicism, 413, 414
Greece, modern, 693; in Common Market, 717; contemporary, 712; independence, 531, 543–544, 615
Green party, 711
Grenouillère, La (Monet), 601f
Grenville acts, 484
Grey, Earl, 553
Grieg, Edvard, 603
Gropius, Walter, 732
Gross Clinic, The (Eakins), 586f
Grotius, Hugo, 442
Guadalcanal, battle of, 698, 699m
Guadeloupe, 446, 455
Guam, 629
Guarneri family, 417
Guatemala, 750, 751m
Guernica (Picasso), 731f
Guilds, 407, 519
Guizot, François, 555
Gulliver's Travels (Swift), 414
Gustavus Adolphus, king of Sweden, 431

Haeckel, Ernst, 591–592
Hals, Franz, 416, 442
Hamilton, Alexander, 489
Hammarskjöld, Dag, 749
Handel, George Frederick, 417
Hanover, 569m, 570
Hanover dynasty, 440
Hapsburg dynasty: and absolutism, 425, 426–427; after Congress of Vienna, 545–546; Austrian and Spanish branches, 421; Dual Monarchy, 613–615, 614m; and Enlightenment, 474; and Revolution of 1848, 557–558; and World War I, 643–645
Harding, Warren G., 624, 682
Hardy, Thomas, 599
Hargreaves, James, 517
Harmsworth, Alfred, 597
Harvey, William, 463, 464, 589
Hausaland, kingdom of, 452
Haussman, Georges, 563
Havel, Vaclav, 756
Haydn, Franz Joseph, 417
Hearst, William Randolph, 597
Hegel, Georg Wilhelm, 528, 532, 597
Heidegger, Martin, 729
Heine, Heinrich, 531, 534
Heisenberg, Werner, 727
Heliocentrism, 459–460

Progressive party (Germany), 612
Prokofiev, Sergei, 663
Propaganda: Cold War, 706; Nazi, 674; and World War I, 648
Protectorate (England), 437–438
Protestant Reformation, 458; in England, 412, 434–435, 438 (*see also* Anglicanism; Puritans); and Scientific Revolution, 458–459
Protestants: in northern Ireland, 709
Proudhon, Pierre-Joseph, 578
Proust, Marcel, 730
Provincial Letters (Pascal), 413
Provisional Wing of the Irish Republican Army (IRA), 708
Prussia, 425, 427, 428, 429*m*, 431, 431*m*, 474, 610, 639; border dispute with Denmark, 569*m*, 569–570; and Congress of Vienna, 540–541, 542, 542*m;* and French Revolution, 500–501; Holy Alliance, 542–543; and Napoleonic wars, 508, 509, 510*m;* Quadruple Alliance, 543; relations with Austria, 566–567, 570; Revolution of 1848, 558; war against France, 565, 571, 572*f*, 607, 645
Psychoanalysis, 589–590, 728
Psychology, 589, 590, 592, 728
Ptolemy, 457, 459, 460, 461
Public education, 596
Public health, 727
Public Safety, Committee of, 503
Pugachev (Don Cossack), 430
Pulitzer, Joseph, 596, 597
Purcell, Henry, 417
Puritans, 439–440; and Civil War, 414, 434, 436–438, 476; in colonial America, 482
Pushkin, Alexander, 535
Putting-out system, 519
Pythagoras, 459

Quadruple Alliance, 543
Quakers (Society of Friends), 412
Quantum theory, 727
Quebec, 445*f*, 446, 455
Quebec Act, 484
Queen Anne's War, 454
Quesnay, François, 473

Racine, Jean, 413, 414, 533
Racism: origins of modern, 597–598
Radium, 588
Railroads, 517, 518, 518*f*, 577, 612; Berlin-to-Baghdad, 611, 632; Cape-to-Cairo, 634
Ranke, Leopold von, 590
Rasputin, Grigori Efimovich, 656
Razin, Stenka, 428
Reagan, Ronald, 707, 714, 724, 755
Realism: in literature, 598–600, 729
Reason, 467, 468
Red Army, 714
Red Brigade (Italy), 708, 712
Red Guards, 738
Red Sunday, 613
Reform Bill (British): of 1832, 550*f*, 551, 553; of 1867, 606; of 1884, 606
Reichstag, 571, 610, 611, 673
Reign of Terror, 503, 638
Relativism, 727
Relativity, theory of, 587, 588
Religion: American state-church separation, 487; in colonial America, 482–483; contemporary, 724–726; Enlightenment and, 469, 472; French absolutism and, 423–424; French Revolution and, 499; fundamentalism vs. modernism, 593; growth of pietism (17th–18th c.), 412; Napoleon and, 507; Puritan conflict in England,

434–438; scientific challenge to, 590–594; in Soviet Union, 664
Religious wars (16th–17th c.), 412
Rembrandt van Rijn, 416, 442, 443*f*
Remembrance of Things Past (Proust), 730
Renaissance: and Scientific Revolution, 458
Renan, Ernest, 592
Renoir, Auguste, 600
Republicanism: American, 487–490
Republican party (U.S.), 622
Rerum Novarum (Leo XIII), 593–594
Return of the Native (Hardy), 599
Revolt of the Masses (Ortega y Gasset), 684
Revolutionary era: American, 483–488; French (1789–1799), 492–504; industrial, 515–529; liberal (1830–1850), 550–559; scientific, 457–465
Revolution of 1848, 553*m*, 556–559, 562; in central Europe, 557*f*, 557–558; in France, 556–557; in Italy, 558–559, 565
Reynolds, Joshua, 415
Rhee, Syngman, 739
Rheingold, Das (Wagner), 537
Rhineland, 541
Rhodes, Cecil, 634
Rhodesia, 747
Ricardo, David, 525–526, 528
Richardson, Samuel, 414
Richelieu, Armand-Jean du Plessis, Cardinal, 422, 477
Rights of Man and the Citizen, Declaration of, 497, 638
Rigoletto (Verdi), 537
Rimsky-Korsakov, Nikolai, 603
Risorgimento, Il, 565
Robbe-Grillet, Alain, 730
Robespierre, Maximilien de, 500, 501, 503, 540
Rockefeller, John D., 623
Rococo style, 413
Rodin, Auguste, 602, 602*f*
Roentgen, Wilhelm von, 588
Romagna, 566
Roman Catholic church: in Bismarck's Germany, 610; conflicts in England, 439–440; contemporary, 725; Counter-Reformation, 414; Enlightenment and, 469, 472; and fascists, 674; and French liberalism, 608, 609; and French Revolution, 493, 499, 500; in Latin America, 749–750; and modernists, 593; Napoleon and, 507; scientific challenge to, 591, 592, 593–594; and Spanish Civil War, 685
Roman culture: and neo-classicism, 413, 414
Romanov, Michael, Tsar, 428
Romanov dynasty, 427–430, 429*m;* end of, 656
Roman Republic (19th c.), 565
Romanticism, 530–537, 596; art and architecture, 535; idealist philosophy and, 531–532; literature, 532–535, 599; music, 535–537; nature of, 530
Rome, Treaty of, 717
Rommel, General Erwin, 696
Romney, George, 415
Roosevelt, Franklin D., 683, 685, 693, 696, 698, 704, 704*f*, 705
Roosevelt, Theodore, 624, 683
Rossini, Gioacchino, 537*f*
Rothschild, Baron de, 615
Roundheads, 436–438
Rousseau, Jean-Jacques, 413, 414, 471, 473, 531–532, 533, 535
Royal Society (England), 459
Rubens, Peter Paul, 414, 415*f*
Ruhr Valley, 670
Rumania and Rumanians, 544, 564, 652, 675, 681, 690, 716, 756, 757*m*, 759; under Hapsburgs, 546, 614*m*, 615, 643